MIDWEST GETAWAY GUIDE

Contents

Photo Credits:
©RJ and Linda Miller – p. 4; ©Getty Images/Tim Bieber – p. 64; ©Galena/Jo Daviess County Convention & Visitors Bureau – p.66, p.67 (T); ©Andre Jenny/Alamy – p.67 (B), p.79 (T), p.82, P.115, p.127 (T) & (B), p.131 (R), p.171 (B), p.190 (R); ©Don Smetzer/Alamy – p.69, p.74; ©Alton Convention & Visitors Bureau/Keith Wedoe – p.70; ©Alton Convention & Visitors Bureau/Tim Parker – p.71 (T); ©Alton Convention & Visitors Bureau – p.71 (M); ©Illinois Historic Preservation Agency – p.71 (B); ©dk/Alamy – p.75; ©Wm. Baker/GhostWorx Images/Alamy – p.78; ©Wanda Hertz, Madison Area CVB – p.79 (B), p.80; ©Lake County Convention & Visitors Bureau – p.86, p.87 (T) & (B), p.88; ©Michael Vaughn Photography – p.83 (T); ©Mike Michaelson – p.83 (B); ©Iowa Tourism Office – p.90, p.92, p.93, p.95 (B), p.98, p.99 (T) & (B); ©Mason City Convention & Visitors Bureau – p.91; ©Peter Arnold, Inc./Alamy – p.94; ©Winneshiek County CVB – p.95 (T), p.96; ©Melissa Farlow/Aurora Photos – p.102; ©Kentucky Department of Travel – p.103 (T-R), p.110; ©Buffalo Trace Distillery, Inc. – p.103 (T-L); ©Harrison Shull/Aurora Photos – p.103 (B); ©Land Between The Lakes – p.106; ©Ilene MacDonald/Alamy – p.107; ©Lee Thomas – p.111 (T); ©Daniel Dempster Photography/Alamy – p.111 (B); ©Danita Delimont/Alamy – p.114; ©Tom Buchkoe – p. 115 (T); ©Vito Palmisano – p.118; ©Frederik Meijer Gardens & Sculpture Park – p.119; ©Raymond J. Malace – p.122; ©Media Matters Detroit – p.123 (T); ©Travel Michigan – p.123 (B); ©Visit Grand Rapids – p.126; ©Saint Paul Convention and Visitors Bureau – p.130; ©Ordway Center for the Performing Arts – p.131 (L); ©Tom Tracy Photography/Alamy – p.134; ©Brainerd Lakes Area Conservation Collaborative – p.135; ©Ilene MacDonald/Alamy – p.138; ©Missouri Tourism Bureau – p.139 (T) & (B), p.140, p.142, p.147, ©Cliff Keeler/Alamy – p.143 (T) & (B); ©Ohad Shahar/Alamy – p.146 ©Warren County CVB – p.150, p.151 (B); ©Vicky Boring – p. 151 (T); ©The Workshops of David T. Smith – p. 153; ©travelcleveland.com – p. 154, p.155 (T) & (B); ©terry vacha/Alamy – p.158; ©Jeff Greenberg/Alamy – p.159, p.162, p.180; ©Chocolate Café and Museum – p.160; ©USDA Fish and Wildlife Service – p.163 (L); ©Glacial Lake Cranberries Inc. – p.163; ©Racine County CVB – p.166, P.168; ©Arcaid/Alamy – p.167; ©Noreen Rueckert – p.170; ©Bill Wyss – p.171 (T); ©Green County Tourism – p.172; ©Rand McNally – p.181, p.182, p.184 (B), p.188 (T) & (B), p.191; ©Jon Arnold Images/Alamy – p.183; ©Lyroky/Alamy – p.184 (T); ©Science Museum of Minnesota – p.185; ©Steve Skjold/Alamy – [illegible]
Briner/Alamy – p.190 (L); ©V

Every effort has been made to provide accurate information. Changes can and do occur, however, and we cannot be legally responsible for any errors, changes, omissions, or any loss, injury, or inconvenience sustained by any person or entity as a result of information or advice contained in this book.

Library of Congress Catalog
For licensing and copyright
If you have questions, conc
website at **go.randmcnally.**
or write to:
Rand McNally Consumer Af
P.O. Box 7600
Chicago, Illinois 60680-9915

Made in the U.S.A. Printed in the U.S.A.
1 2 3 4 5 6 **WC** 10 09 08 07

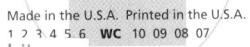

USING YOUR GETAWAY GUIDE

How do I find a great place to explore that's just a couple of hours away?

1. Turn to the **PageFinder™** map on the inside front cover. Find your general location, then see which regional map corresponds to your location.

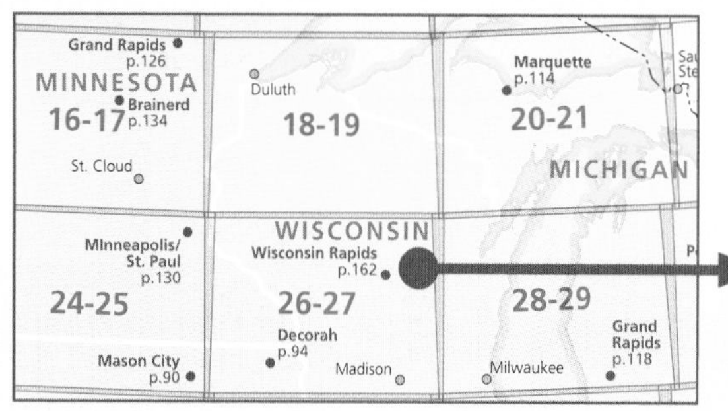

2. See that page number? Now you know where to turn for the correct regional map.

3. Once you get to the regional map, you'll see yellow boxes with page numbers attached. That's where fun stuff happens, and this book describes that area in detail starting on that page number. There are 27 destinations in the book—one is sure to be close by.

How do I get to that fun place (the one in the yellow box)?

You can use the regional maps—a terrific "big picture"—to see what major roads will get you there. You can also go to randmcnally.com for directions.

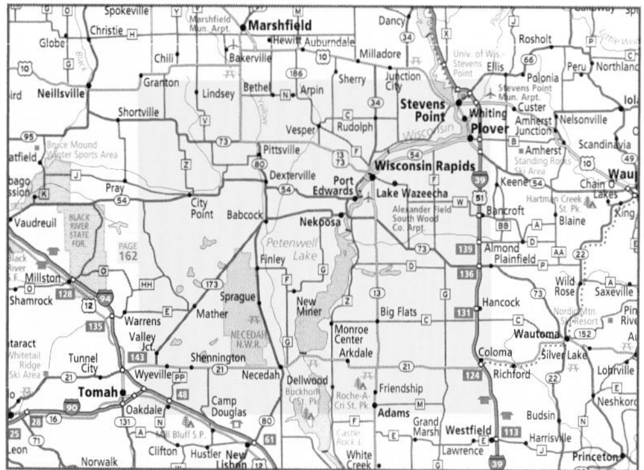

What's happening there?

Read all about what there is to see and do, what the shopping scene's like, where you can stay overnight, the best food to try and where you can find it, and even if there's a festival happening during your visit. These destination sections also offer specially designed maps to help figure out where attractions and restaurants are in relation to each other (and how to drive between them).

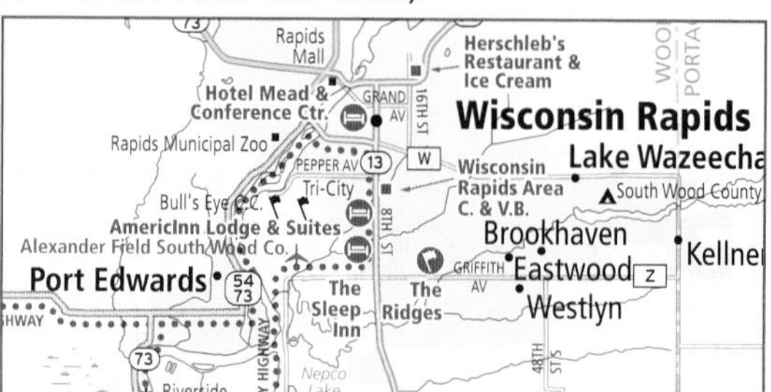

Why are some names on the map and in the article red?

If something's red, it means it's discussed in the article and also shown on the map. When the important name is on a colored background within the article, however, it's in thicker type—and the name is still red on the map.

What are those pictures on the map?

Those pictures (a.k.a. icons) show you at a glance whether something is a restaurant, shopping opportunity, or place to stay.

Dining · Shopping · Lodging · Museum · Park · Golfing · Information

How do I find out more about the festivals?

We've included descriptions of the festivals on pages 174-178.

USING YOUR GETAWAY GUIDE

How do I find something that isn't included in one of the destination articles?

The Point of Interest (POI) Index lists items that appear on the regional maps. Turn to page 194. Items are listed alphabetically in four categories, with a page and grid reference (map location) to help find them on the map. This list is also great for browsing things to do in the entire Midwest region.

How far is it to where I want to go?

This book offers three ways to figure out how far and how long you'll drive. At the back of the book, on pages 220-221, you'll find a mileage and driving times map. On the next two pages, there's a mileage chart listing distances between 60 cities in the Midwest. And on each regional map, there's a scale bar (for those of you who like to calculate things yourselves).

? What do all those symbols on the maps mean?

Those symbols, such as the ovals with numbers in them, are explained in the legend.

This book's legend is on the inside back cover.

Find the symbol and learn what it means. In the margins of the regional maps, several commonly used symbols are explained in detail.

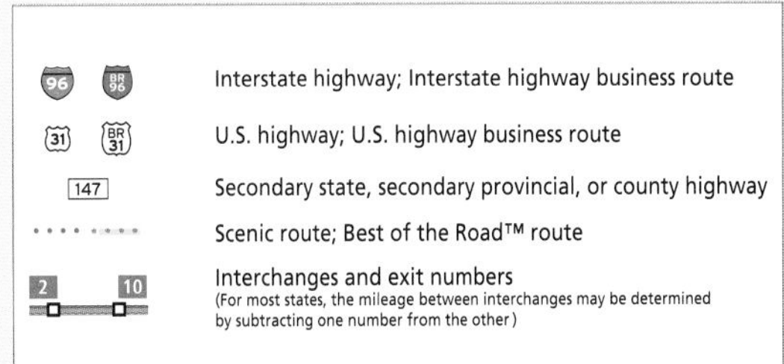

How do I find a city or town on the regional maps?

Near the back of the book, starting on page 200, an index lists many of the cities and towns located in the Midwest region. The index includes page numbers and grid references.

Am I going to run into road construction on my trip?

You can find out using the list of road construction and conditions hotlines and websites provided on page 224. You can also get up-to-date construction info at randmcnally.com.

Are there any other ways to find great things to see and do?

This book includes four of Rand McNally's Best of the Road™ drives. They start on page 180. Each drive provides details on the best shopping, attractions, activities, and dining along a route researched in person by Rand McNally editors. (More Best of the Road™ trips are at go.randmcnally.com/BR.) You'll find places and faces that make a trip unforgettable.

Fall colors in Marinette County, Wisconsin

Road Maps

Minnesota **Missouri** Michigan **Wisconsin** Illinois **Indiana** Iowa **Kentucky** Ohio **Minnesota** Missouri **Michigan** Wisconsin **Illinois** Indiana **Iowa**

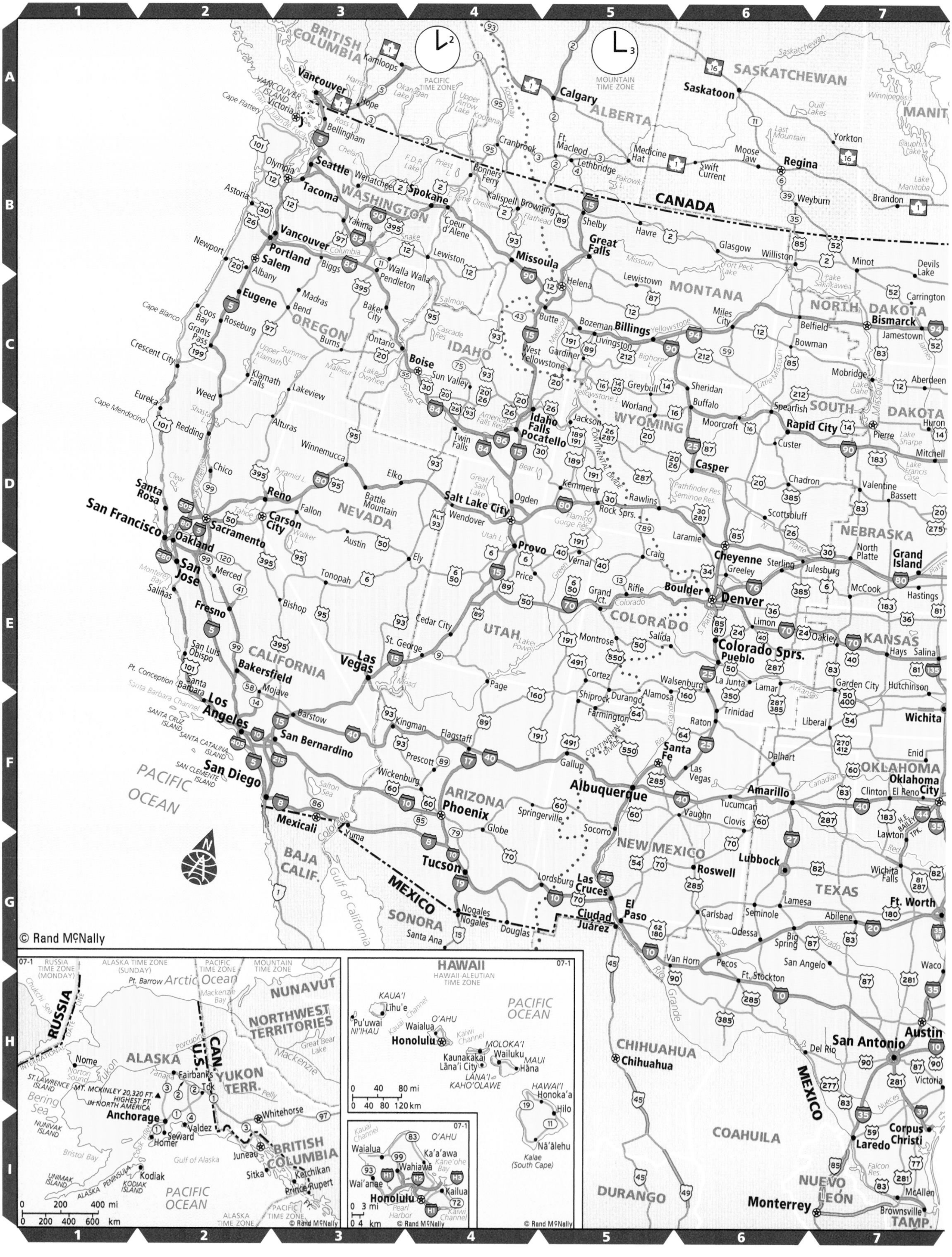
1
2
3
4
5
6
7
A
B
C
D
E
F
G
H
I
BRITISH COLUMBIA
PACIFIC TIME ZONE
MOUNTAIN TIME ZONE
SASKATCHEWAN
ALBERTA
MANITOBA
CANADA
Kamloops
Vancouver
VANCOUVER ISLAND
Victoria
Cape Flattery
Hope
Calgary
Saskatoon
Yorkton
Regina
Moose Jaw
Swift Current
Medicine Hat
Lethbridge
Ft. Macleod
Cranbrook
Weyburn
Brandon
Bellingham
Seattle
Olympia
Tacoma
Astoria
WASHINGTON
Wenatchee
Spokane
Yakima
Coeur d'Alene
Bonners Ferry
Kalispell
Browning
Shelby
Havre
Glasgow
Williston
Minot
Devils Lake
Vancouver
Portland
Salem
Newport
Albany
Eugene
Biggs
Walla Walla
Pendleton
Lewiston
Missoula
Great Falls
Helena
Lewistown
MONTANA
Carrington
NORTH DAKOTA
Bismarck
Cape Blanco
Coos Bay
Roseburg
Grants Pass
Madras
Bend
OREGON
Baker City
Burns
Ontario
Boise
IDAHO
Sun Valley
Butte
Bozeman
Billings
Livingston
West Yellowstone
Gardiner
Miles City
Belfield
Jamestown
Bowman
Crescent City
Klamath Falls
Lakeview
Eureka
Cape Mendocino
Weed
Redding
Alturas
Winnemucca
Twin Falls
Idaho Falls
Pocatello
Jackson
WYOMING
Worland
Greybull
Sheridan
Buffalo
Moorcroft
Spearfish
Rapid City
SOUTH DAKOTA
Pierre
Huron
Mobridge
Aberdeen
Mitchell
Custer
Chico
Santa Rosa
Reno
Carson City
Battle Mountain
Elko
NEVADA
Salt Lake City
Ogden
Wendover
Kemmerer
Rawlins
Casper
Chadron
Valentine
Bassett
San Francisco
Sacramento
Oakland
San Jose
Fallon
Austin
Ely
Provo
Vernal
Rock Sprs.
Laramie
Cheyenne
Scottsbluff
NEBRASKA
North Platte
Grand Island
Monterey
Salinas
Merced
Fresno
Tonopah
Bishop
Price
Craig
Grand Jct.
Rifle
Boulder
Denver
Sterling
Greeley
Julesburg
McCook
Hastings
Cedar City
UTAH
COLORADO
Montrose
Salida
Limon
Colorado Sprs.
Pueblo
Oakley
KANSAS
Hays
Salina
San Luis Obispo
CALIFORNIA
Bakersfield
Santa Barbara
Pt. Conception
Los Angeles
Mojave
Las Vegas
St. George
Page
Cortez
Durango
Alamosa
Walsenburg
La Junta
Lamar
Garden City
Hutchinson
Wichita
SANTA CRUZ ISLAND
SANTA CATALINA ISLAND
SAN CLEMENTE ISLAND
Barstow
San Bernardino
Kingman
Flagstaff
Prescott
Shiprock
Farmington
Trinidad
Raton
Santa Fe
Liberal
Enid
OKLAHOMA
Oklahoma City
PACIFIC OCEAN
San Diego
Wickenburg
ARIZONA
Phoenix
Gallup
Albuquerque
Las Vegas
Amarillo
Clinton
El Reno
Mexicali
Yuma
Globe
Springerville
Socorro
Tucumcari
Vaughn
Clovis
Lawton
BAJA CALIF.
Tucson
NEW MEXICO
Roswell
Lubbock
Wichita Falls
TEXAS
MEXICO
Nogales
Douglas
Lordsburg
Las Cruces
El Paso
Ciudad Juárez
Carlsbad
Seminole
Lamesa
Abilene
Ft. Worth
SONORA
Santa Ana
Gulf of California
Odessa
Big Spring
San Angelo
Waco
Van Horn
Pecos
Ft. Stockton
Rio Grande
CHIHUAHUA
Chihuahua
Del Rio
San Antonio
Austin
Victoria
COAHUILA
Laredo
Corpus Christi
DURANGO
NUEVO LEÓN
Monterrey
McAllen
Brownsville
TAMP.
© Rand McNally
RUSSIA TIME ZONE (MONDAY)
ALASKA TIME ZONE (SUNDAY)
PACIFIC TIME ZONE
MOUNTAIN TIME ZONE
Pt. Barrow
Arctic Ocean
NUNAVUT
NORTHWEST TERRITORIES
RUSSIA
ALASKA
CAN. U.S.
YUKON TERR.
Nome
Norton Sound
ST. LAWRENCE ISLAND
MT. MCKINLEY 20,320 FT. HIGHEST PT. IN NORTH AMERICA
Fairbanks
Tok
Bering Sea
Anchorage
Valdez
Seward
Homer
Whitehorse
NUNIVAK ISLAND
Bristol Bay
Gulf of Alaska
Juneau
BRITISH COLUMBIA
Kodiak
KODIAK ISLAND
Sitka
Ketchikan
Prince Rupert
UNIMAK ISLAND
ALASKA PENINSULA
PACIFIC OCEAN
0 200 400 mi
0 200 400 600 km
ALASKA TIME ZONE
PACIFIC TIME ZONE
© Rand McNally
HAWAII
HAWAII-ALEUTIAN TIME ZONE
KAUA'I
Līhu'e
Pu'uwai
NI'IHAU
O'AHU
Waialua
Honolulu
MOLOKA'I
Kaunakakai
Lāna'i City
LĀNA'I
KAHO'OLAWE
Wailuku
MAUI
Hāna
PACIFIC OCEAN
HAWAI'I
Honoka'a
Hilo
Nā'ālehu
Kalae (South Cape)
0 40 80 mi
0 40 80 120 km
O'AHU
Waialua
Ka'a'awa
Wahiawā
Wai'anae
Kailua
Honolulu
Pearl Harbor
0 3 mi
0 4 km
© Rand McNally
© Rand McNally

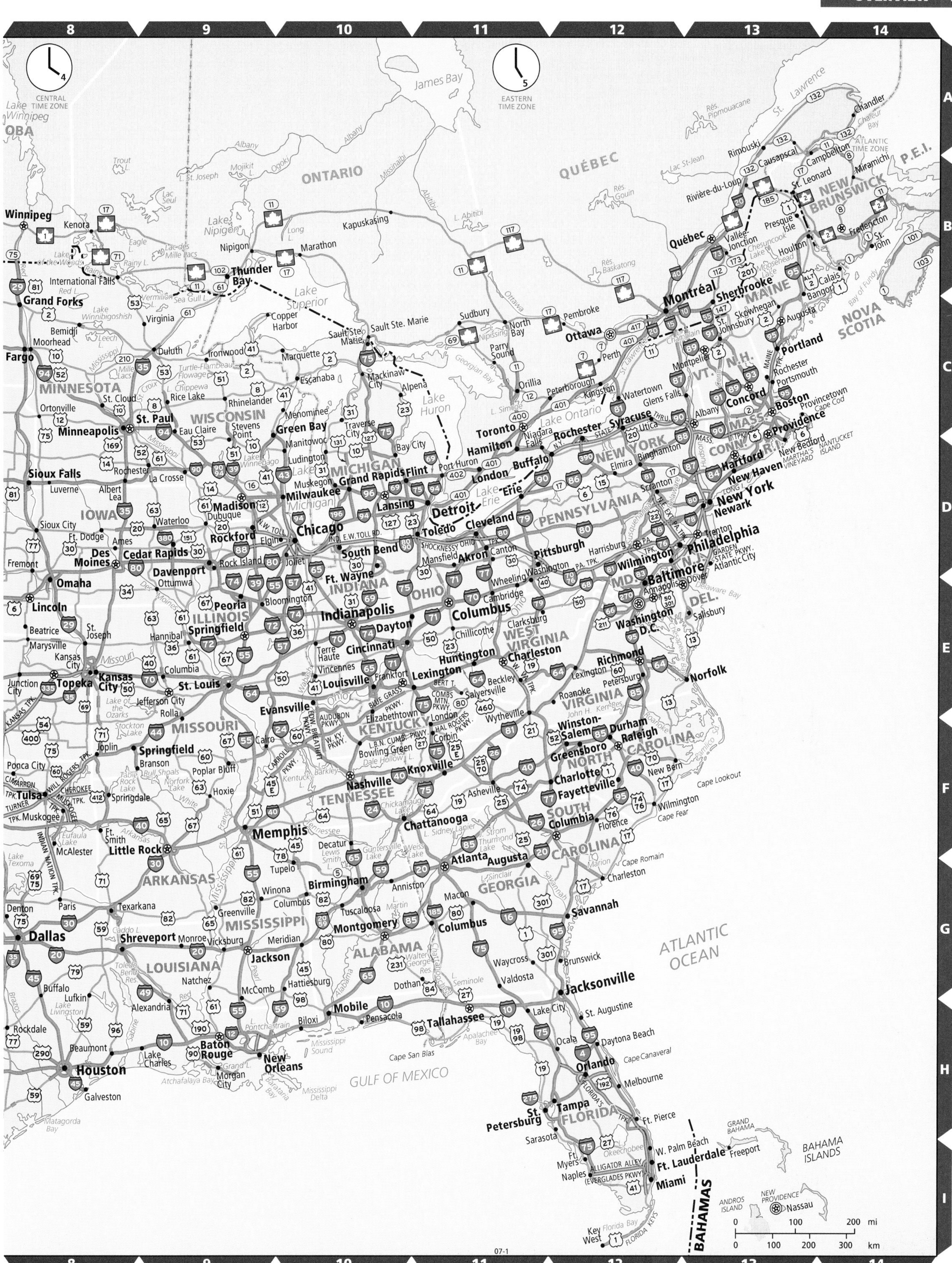
8
9
10
11
12
13
14
A
B
C
D
E
F
G
H
I
CENTRAL TIME ZONE
EASTERN TIME ZONE
ATLANTIC TIME ZONE
James Bay
ONTARIO
QUÉBEC
NEW BRUNSWICK
NOVA SCOTIA
P.E.I.
MINNESOTA
WISCONSIN
MICHIGAN
IOWA
ILLINOIS
INDIANA
OHIO
PENNSYLVANIA
NEW YORK
VT.
N.H.
MAINE
MASS.
CONN.
R.I.
N.J.
MD.
DEL.
WEST VIRGINIA
VIRGINIA
KENTUCKY
TENNESSEE
NORTH CAROLINA
SOUTH CAROLINA
GEORGIA
FLORIDA
ALABAMA
MISSISSIPPI
LOUISIANA
ARKANSAS
MISSOURI
BAHAMAS
BAHAMA ISLANDS
ATLANTIC OCEAN
GULF OF MEXICO
Lake Superior
Lake Michigan
Lake Huron
Lake Erie
Lake Ontario
Winnipeg
Kenora
International Falls
Thunder Bay
Nipigon
Marathon
Kapuskasing
Sudbury
North Bay
Pembroke
Ottawa
Montréal
Québec
Sherbrooke
Rimouski
Rivière-du-Loup
Fredericton
St. John
Toronto
Hamilton
London
Grand Forks
Fargo
Duluth
St. Cloud
St. Paul
Minneapolis
Sioux Falls
Sioux City
Des Moines
Cedar Rapids
Davenport
Omaha
Lincoln
Topeka
Kansas City
Madison
Milwaukee
Green Bay
Chicago
Rockford
Peoria
Springfield
St. Louis
Indianapolis
Ft. Wayne
South Bend
Grand Rapids
Lansing
Flint
Detroit
Toledo
Cleveland
Akron
Columbus
Dayton
Cincinnati
Louisville
Lexington
Pittsburgh
Buffalo
Rochester
Syracuse
Albany
Boston
Providence
Hartford
New Haven
New York
Newark
Philadelphia
Wilmington
Baltimore
Washington D.C.
Richmond
Norfolk
Charleston
Huntington
Roanoke
Winston-Salem
Greensboro
Durham
Raleigh
Charlotte
Fayetteville
Columbia
Savannah
Augusta
Atlanta
Chattanooga
Knoxville
Nashville
Memphis
Little Rock
Tulsa
Springfield
Birmingham
Montgomery
Jackson
Shreveport
Dallas
Houston
Baton Rouge
New Orleans
Mobile
Tallahassee
Jacksonville
Orlando
Tampa
St. Petersburg
Ft. Lauderdale
Miami
Key West
Nassau
Portland
Concord
Cape Cod
Cape Lookout
Cape Fear
Cape San Blas
0 100 200 mi
0 100 200 300 km

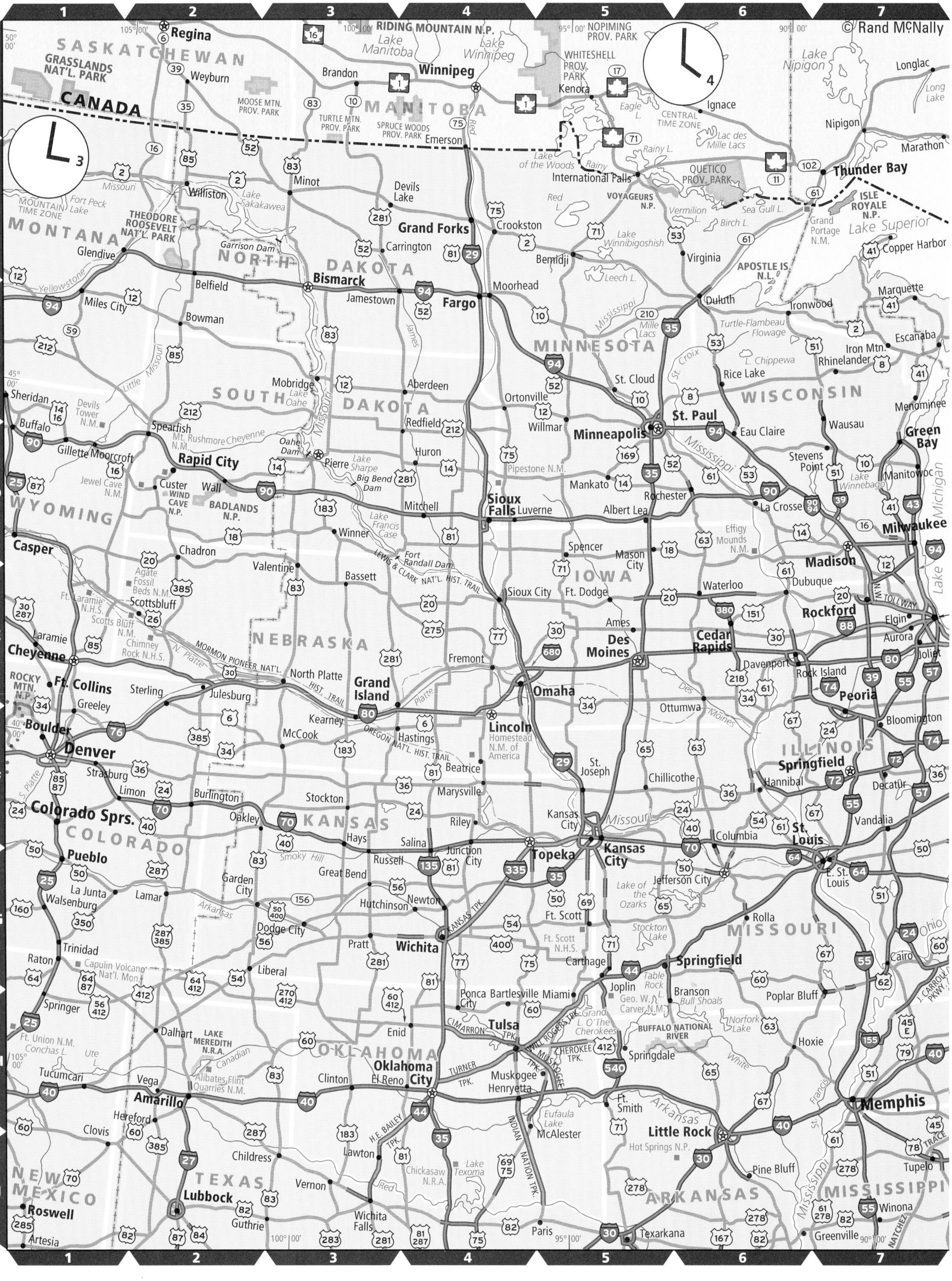

1 2 3 4 5 6 7

© Rand McNally

A B C D E F G H I

SASKATCHEWAN
Regina
GRASSLANDS NAT'L. PARK
Weyburn
CANADA
RIDING MOUNTAIN N.P.
Lake Manitoba
Lake Winnipeg
Brandon
Winnipeg
MOOSE MTN. PROV. PARK
TURTLE MTN. PROV. PARK
SPRUCE WOODS PROV. PARK
MANITOBA
Emerson
Red
NOPIMING PROV. PARK
WHITESHELL PROV. PARK
Kenora
Eagle L.
CENTRAL TIME ZONE
Ignace
Lake Nipigon
Longlac
Long Lake
Nipigon
Marathon
Lac des Mille Lacs
Rainy L.
Lake of the Woods
International Falls
QUETICO PROV. PARK
Thunder Bay
Minot
Williston
Missouri
Lake Sakakawea
MOUNTAIN TIME ZONE
Fort Peck Lake
MONTANA
THEODORE ROOSEVELT NAT'L. PARK
Devils Lake
Grand Forks
Crookston
Red L.
VOYAGEURS N.P.
Vermilion L.
Sea Gull L.
Birch L.
Grand Portage N.M.
ISLE ROYALE N.P.
Lake Superior
Copper Harbor
Glendive
Garrison Dam
NORTH DAKOTA
Carrington
Bemidji
Lake Winnibigoshish
Virginia
APOSTLE IS. N.L.
Yellowstone
Belfield
Bismarck
Jamestown
Fargo
Moorhead
Leech L.
Duluth
Miles City
Bowman
James
Mississippi
Mille Lacs
Turtle-Flambeau Flowage
Ironwood
Marquette
Escanaba
MINNESOTA
L. Chippewa
Rhinelander
Iron Mtn.
Sheridan
Little Missouri
Mobridge
Lake Oahe
Aberdeen
St. Cloud
Rice Lake
WISCONSIN
SOUTH DAKOTA
Devils Tower N.M.
Buffalo
Spearfish
Mt. Rushmore N.M.
Cheyenne
Oahe Dam
Redfield
Ortonville
Willmar
Minneapolis
St. Paul
Eau Claire
Wausau
Menominee
Green Bay
Gillette
Moorcroft
Rapid City
Pierre
Lake Sharpe
Big Bend Dam
Huron
Pipestone N.M.
Stevens Point
Manitowoc
Lake Winnebago
Jewel Cave N.M.
Custer
Wall
WIND CAVE N.P.
BADLANDS N.P.
Mankato
Rochester
La Crosse
Lake Michigan
WYOMING
Mitchell
Lake Francis Case
Sioux Falls
Luverne
Albert Lea
Milwaukee
Casper
Winner
Chadron
Valentine
Fort Randall Dam
LEWIS & CLARK NAT'L. HIST. TRAIL
Bassett
Spencer
Mason City
Effigy Mounds N.M.
Madison
Dubuque
IOWA
Agate Fossil Beds N.M.
Scottsbluff
Ft. Laramie N.H.S.
Scotts Bluff N.M.
Chimney Rock N.H.S.
Sioux City
Ft. Dodge
Waterloo
Rockford
N.W. TOLLWAY
Elgin
Laramie
Cheyenne
N. Platte
MORMON PIONEER NAT'L. HIST. TRAIL
NEBRASKA
Ames
Des Moines
Cedar Rapids
Aurora
Joliet
ROCKY MTN. N.P.
Ft. Collins
Sterling
Julesburg
North Platte
Grand Island
Fremont
Omaha
Davenport
Rock Island
Peoria
Greeley
Platte
Kearney
Lincoln
Ottumwa
Des Moines
Bloomington
Boulder
Denver
McCook
OREGON NAT'L. HIST. TRAIL
Hastings
Homestead N.M. of America
ILLINOIS
Springfield
Strasburg
Limon
Burlington
Beatrice
St. Joseph
Chillicothe
Hannibal
Decatur
Colorado Sprs.
Stockton
Marysville
COLORADO
Oakley
KANSAS
Riley
Kansas City
Missouri
Columbia
St. Louis
Vandalia
Pueblo
Hays
Salina
Junction City
Topeka
Kansas City
Smoky Hill
Russell
Great Bend
E. St. Louis
La Junta
Lamar
Garden City
Newton
Jefferson City
Lake of the Ozarks
Walsenburg
Arkansas
Hutchinson
KANSAS TPK.
Ft. Scott
Rolla
Dodge City
Pratt
Wichita
Ft. Scott N.H.S.
Stockton Lake
MISSOURI
Ohio
Trinidad
Raton
Capulin Volcano Nat'l. Mon.
Liberal
Carthage
Springfield
Cairo
Springer
Ponca City
Bartlesville
Miami
Joplin
Table Rock L.
Geo. W. Carver N.M.
Branson
Bull Shoals L.
Poplar Bluff
J. CARROLL PKWY.
Dalhart
LAKE MEREDITH N.R.A.
Enid
CIMARRON TPK.
Tulsa
WILL ROGERS TPK.
Grand L. O' The Cherokees
BUFFALO NATIONAL RIVER
Norfork Lake
Ft. Union N.M.
Conchas L.
Ute L.
Canadian
OKLAHOMA
MUSKOGEE TPK.
CHEROKEE TPK.
Springdale
Hoxie
White
Tucumcari
Vega
Alibates Flint Quarries N.M.
Clinton
El Reno
Oklahoma City
TURNER TPK.
Muskogee
Henryetta
Ft. Smith
Arkansas
Francis
Amarillo
Memphis
Hereford
Clovis
H.E. BAILEY TPK.
Eufaula Lake
McAlester
INDIAN NATION TPK.
Little Rock
Hot Springs N.P.
Tupelo
Childress
Lawton
Chickasaw N.R.A.
Lake Texoma
Pine Bluff
NEW MEXICO
TEXAS
Vernon
Red
ARKANSAS
Mississippi
MISSISSIPPI
Lubbock
Roswell
Guthrie
Wichita Falls
Paris
Texarkana
Winona
NATCHEZ
Greenville
Artesia

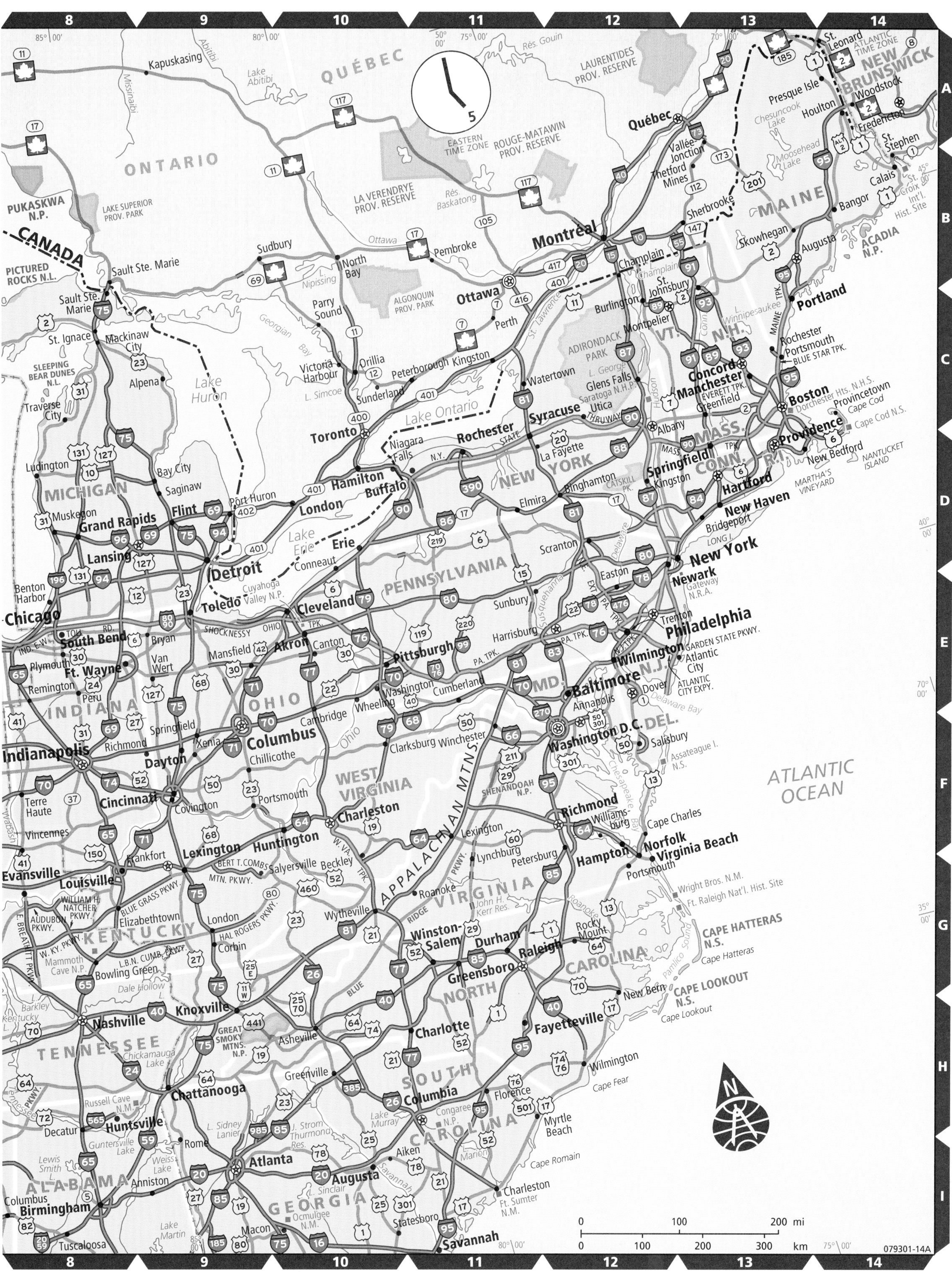
QUÉBEC
ONTARIO
MAINE
NEW BRUNSWICK
MICHIGAN
NEW YORK
PENNSYLVANIA
OHIO
INDIANA
WEST VIRGINIA
VIRGINIA
KENTUCKY
TENNESSEE
NORTH CAROLINA
SOUTH CAROLINA
GEORGIA
ALABAMA
CANADA
EASTERN TIME ZONE
ATLANTIC TIME ZONE
ATLANTIC OCEAN
Lake Huron
Lake Ontario
Lake Erie
APPALACHIAN MTNS.
Montréal
Ottawa
Toronto
Québec
Detroit
Chicago
Cleveland
Pittsburgh
Buffalo
New York
Philadelphia
Baltimore
Washington D.C.
Boston
Providence
Hartford
Richmond
Norfolk
Virginia Beach
Raleigh
Charlotte
Columbia
Atlanta
Nashville
Knoxville
Chattanooga
Birmingham
Savannah
Charleston
Indianapolis
Columbus
Cincinnati
Louisville
Lexington
Charleston
0 100 200 mi
0 100 200 300 km
079301-14A

For a complete listing of symbols, see inside back cover; for an index of cities, see page 200.

DISTANCE SCALE

One inch represents 16 miles

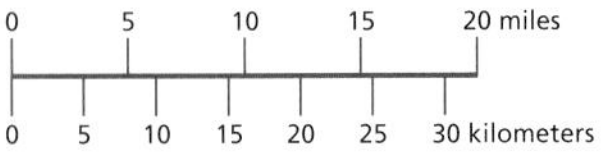

LOCATOR MAP

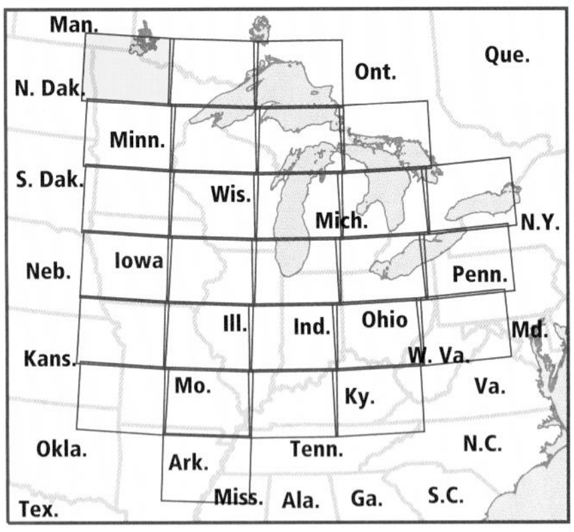

See the Pagefinder™ map on the inside of the front cover for map page numbers.

What are all those short blue lines, some with tufts on them?

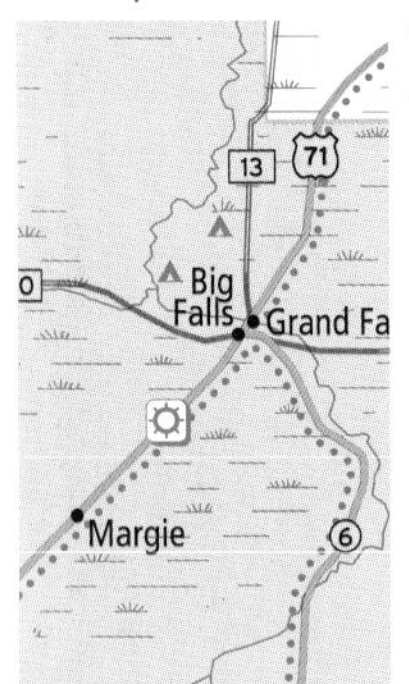

When you see this pattern, you are in an area that has marshes, swamps or mangrove swamps. The terrain is damp, boggy and sometimes even underwater for part of the year. Be sure to stay on the roadways in these areas.

What are those yellow boxes (with little numbers) on the maps?

That's where fun stuff happens, PAGE 52 and this book describes that area in detail starting on the page number you see. Read all about what there is to see and do, what the shopping scene's like, where you can stay overnight, what the best food to try is and where you can find it, and even if there's a festival happening during your visit. These destination sections also offer specially designed maps to help figure out where attractions and restaurants are in relation to each other (and how to drive between them).

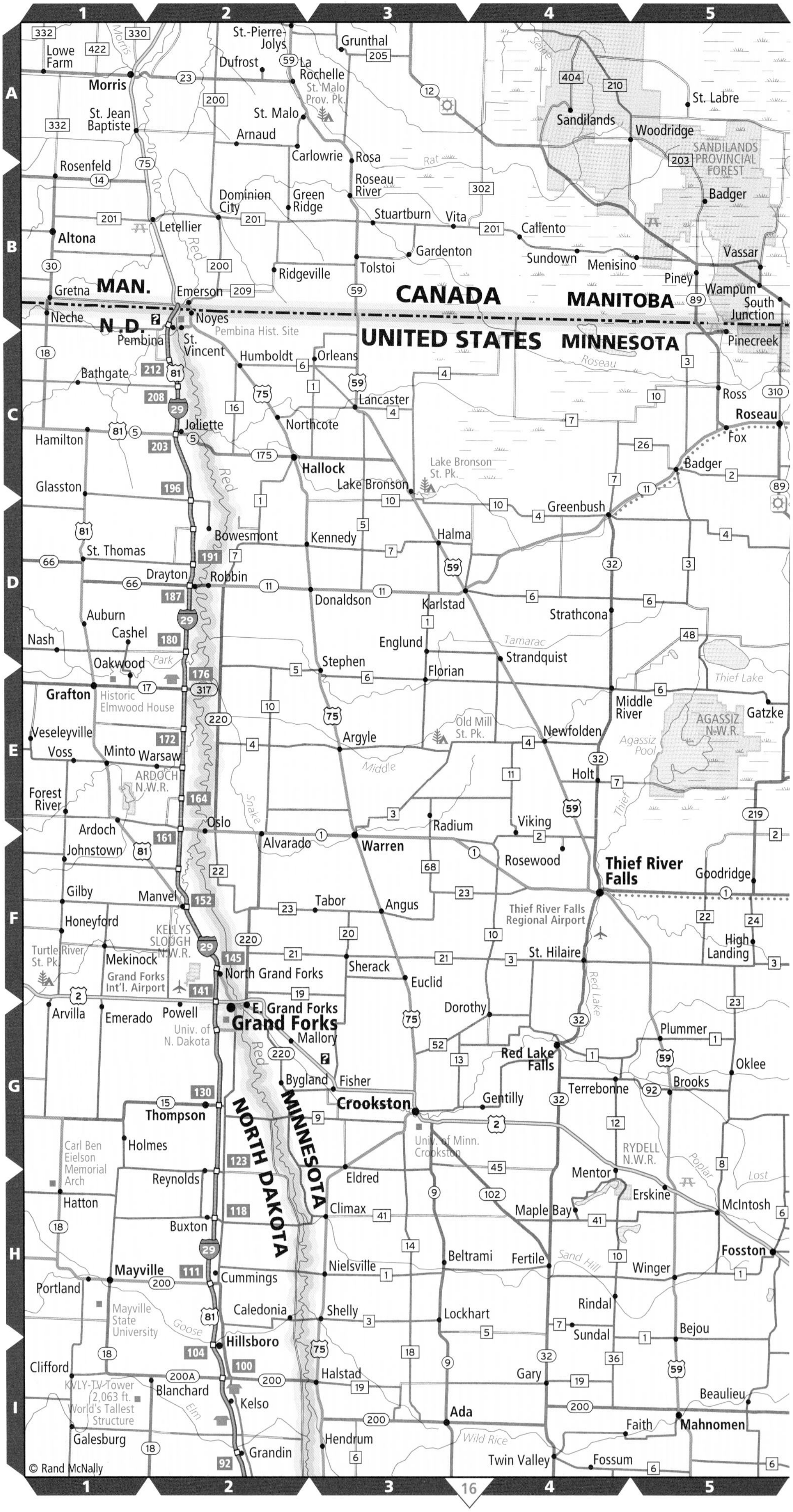

16

When you see this sign , the map continues on the page number indicated.

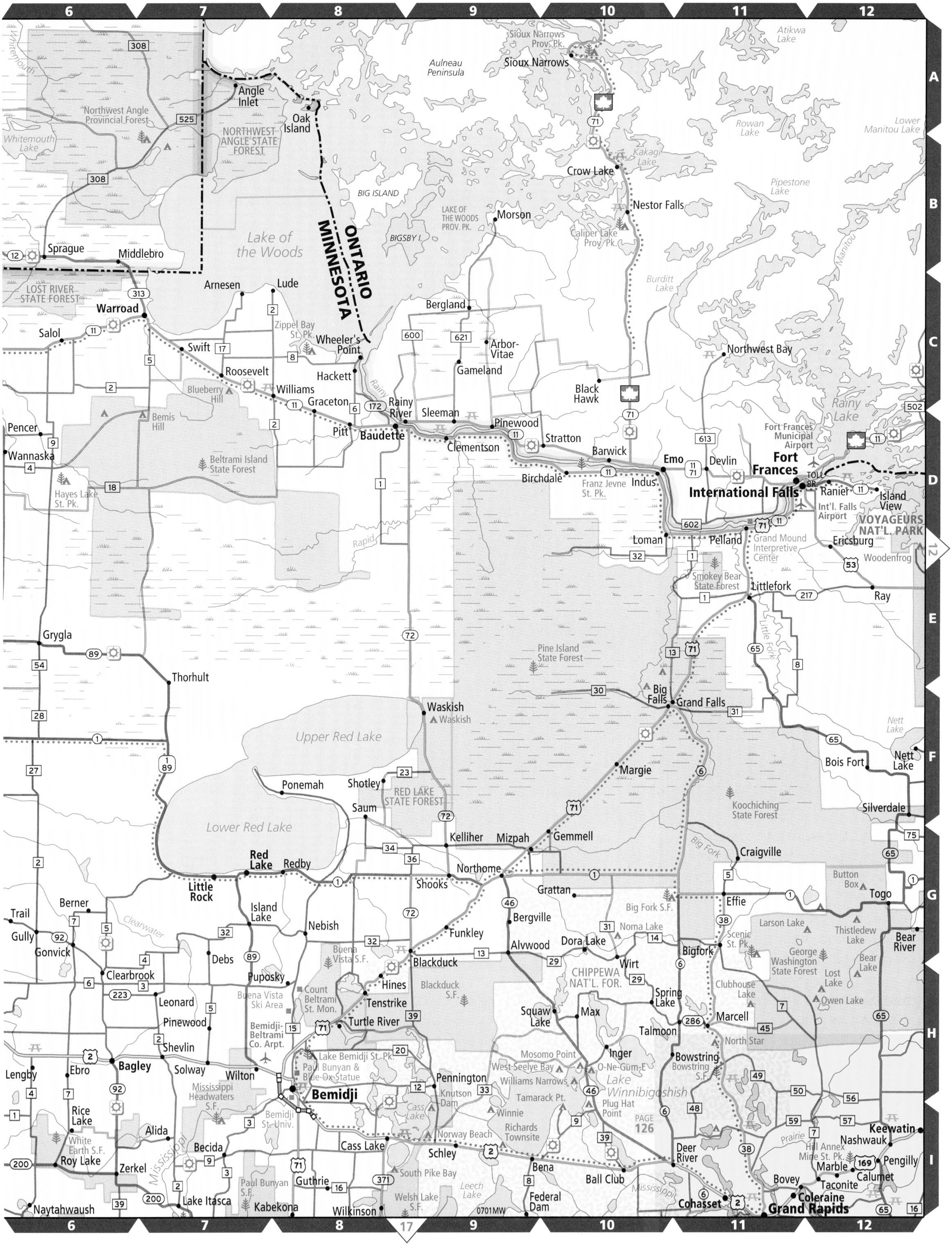

6 7 8 9 10 11 12

Whitemouth
308
Northwest Angle Provincial Forest
525
Whitemouth Lake
308
Angle Inlet
Oak Island
NORTHWEST ANGLE STATE FOREST
Sioux Narrows Prov. Pk.
Sioux Narrows
Aulneau Peninsula
Atikwa Lake
71
Rowan Lake
Lower Manitou Lake
Kakagi Lake
Crow Lake
Pipestone Lake
BIG ISLAND
LAKE OF THE WOODS PROV. PK.
Morson
Nestor Falls
Caliper Lake Prov. Pk.
BIGSBY I.
Lake of the Woods
ONTARIO
MINNESOTA
12
Sprague
Middlebro
LOST RIVER STATE FOREST
313
Arnesen
Lude
Warroad
Burditt Lake
Manitou
Salol
11
Zippel Bay St. Pk.
Wheeler's Point
Bergland
600
621
Arbor-Vitae
Swift
17
5
8
Roosevelt
Hackett
Gameland
Northwest Bay
2
Blueberry Hill
Williams
Rainy
Black Hawk
Bemis Hill
11
Graceton
172
Rainy River
Sleeman
71
502
Rainy Lake
2
6
Pinewood
Pencer
9
Pitt
Baudette
Clementson
11
Stratton
613
Fort Frances Municipal Airport
11
Wannaska
Beltrami Island State Forest
Barwick
Emo
11 71
Devlin
Fort Frances
4
18
Birchdale
11
Franz Jevne St. Pk.
Indus
International Falls
TOLL BR.
Ranier
11
Island View
Hayes Lake St. Pk.
1
602
71
11
Int'l. Falls Airport
VOYAGEURS NAT'L. PARK
Rapid
Loman
Pelland
Grand Mound Interpretive Center
Ericsburg
12
32
1
Woodenfrog
53
Smokey Bear State Forest
1
Littlefork
217
Ray
72
Grygla
89
Pine Island State Forest
13
71
65
Little Fork
8
54
Thorhult
30
Big Falls
Grand Falls
31
28
Waskish
Waskish
Nett Lake
1
Upper Red Lake
65
Nett Lake
1
89
27
Margie
6
Bois Fort
Ponemah
Shotley
23
RED LAKE STATE FOREST
Koochiching State Forest
Silverdale
Saum
71
Lower Red Lake
72
Big Fork
Kelliher
Mizpah
Gemmell
75
Craigville
65
Red Lake
Redby
34
36
Northome
2
Little Rock
1
1
5
Button Box
Shooks
Grattan
Togo
1
Berner
Island Lake
46
Big Fork S.F.
Effie
1
Trail
7
Clearwater
72
Bergville
31
Noma Lake
Gully
92
5
32
Nebish
Funkley
38
Larson Lake
Scenic St. Pk.
Thistledew Lake
Bear River
Gonvick
4
Debs
89
32
Buena Vista S.F.
Blackduck
13
Alvwood
Dora Lake
14
Bigfork
George Washington State Forest
Bear Lake
Clearbrook
6
3
Puposky
Hines
Blackduck S.F.
29
CHIPPEWA NAT'L. FOR.
Wirt
29
6
Lost Lake
223
Leonard
5
Buena Vista Ski Area
Count Beltrami St. Mon.
Tenstrike
Spring Lake
Clubhouse Lake
Owen Lake
7
Pinewood
Bemidji-Beltrami Co. Arpt.
15
71
Turtle River
39
Squaw Lake
Max
286
Marcell
45
65
2
Shevlin
Talmoon
North Star
2
Bagley
Solvay
20
Lake Bemidji St. Pk.
Paul Bunyan & Blue Ox Statue
Mosomo Point
Inger
Bowstring
Bowstring S.F.
Lengby
Ebro
Wilton
West Seelye Bay
O-Ne-Gum-E
49
4
92
Mississippi Headwaters S.F.
Bemidji
12
Pennington
33
Williams Narrows
Lake Winnibigoshish
50
7
Knutson Dam
46
56
Rice Lake
Cass Lake
Tamarack Pt.
Plug Hat Point
1
3
Bemidji St. Univ.
Winnie
9
PAGE 126
48
59
57
Keewatin
White Earth S.F.
Alida
Richards Townsite
6
Prairie
7
Nashwauk
200
Roy Lake
Zerkel
Becida
9
Cass Lake
Norway Beach
2
39
38
Hill Annex Mine St. Pk.
169
Pengilly
Mississippi
3
71
Schley
Deer River
Marble
Calumet
South Pike Bay
Bena
Ball Club
Bovey
Taconite
Paul Bunyan S.F.
Guthrie
16
371
Leech Lake
Mississippi
6
Coleraine
200
2
Lake Itasca
Welsh Lake S.F.
8
Federal Dam
Cohasset
2
Grand Rapids
65
16
Naytahwaush
39
Kabekona
Wilkinson
0701MW

A B C D E F G H I

17

6 7 8 9 10 11 12

For a complete listing of symbols, see inside back cover; for an index of cities, see page 200.

DISTANCE SCALE

One inch represents 16 miles

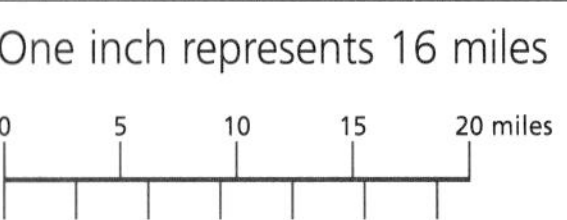

LOCATOR MAP

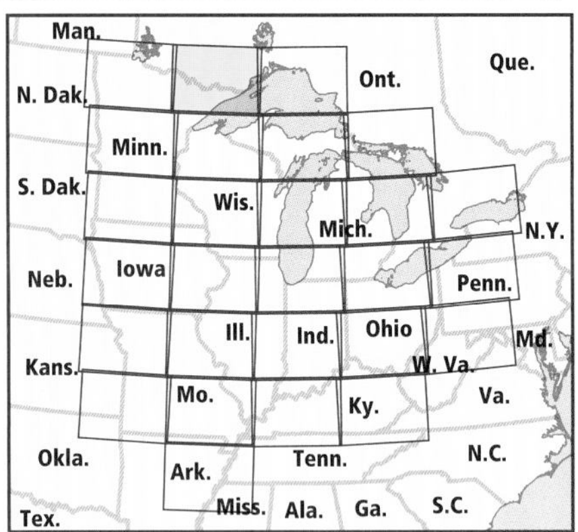

See the Pagefinder™ map on the inside of the front cover for map page numbers.

Looking for something to do along the way?

Keep an eye out for this symbol: ■

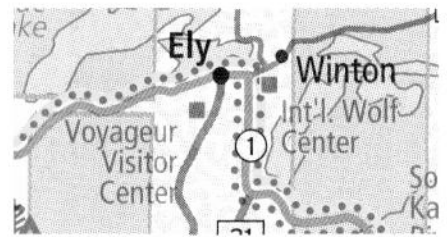

This is a point of interest—a place with something unique to see or do. See pages 194-199 for a listing of featured points of interest in this book.

What are those yellow boxes (with little numbers) on the maps?

That's where fun stuff happens, PAGE 52 and this book describes that area in detail starting on the page number you see. Read all about what there is to see and do, what the shopping scene's like, where you can stay overnight, what the best food to try is and where you can find it, and even if there's a festival happening during your visit. These destination sections also offer specially designed maps to help figure out where attractions and restaurants are in relation to each other (and how to drive between them).

Why is there a red ribbon on this map?

The red award ribbon marks a Rand McNally Best of the Road™ trip route. Our editors have chosen scenic drives peppered with tasty dining, unique shopping, and memory-making things to do. Read more about four of these drives on pages 180-191. For more trip routes, visit go.randmcnally.com/BR.

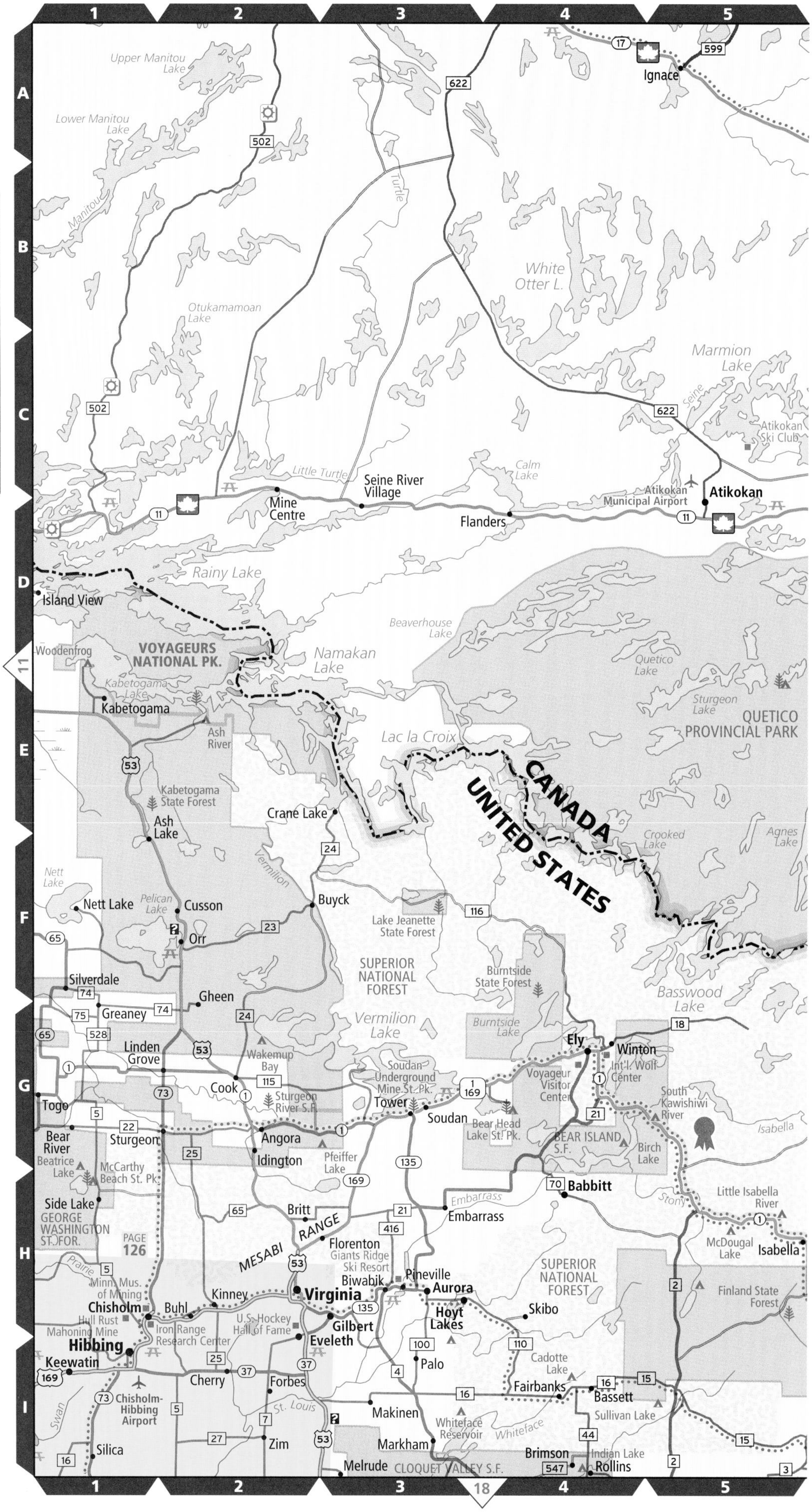

When you see this sign 14, the map continues on the page number indicated.

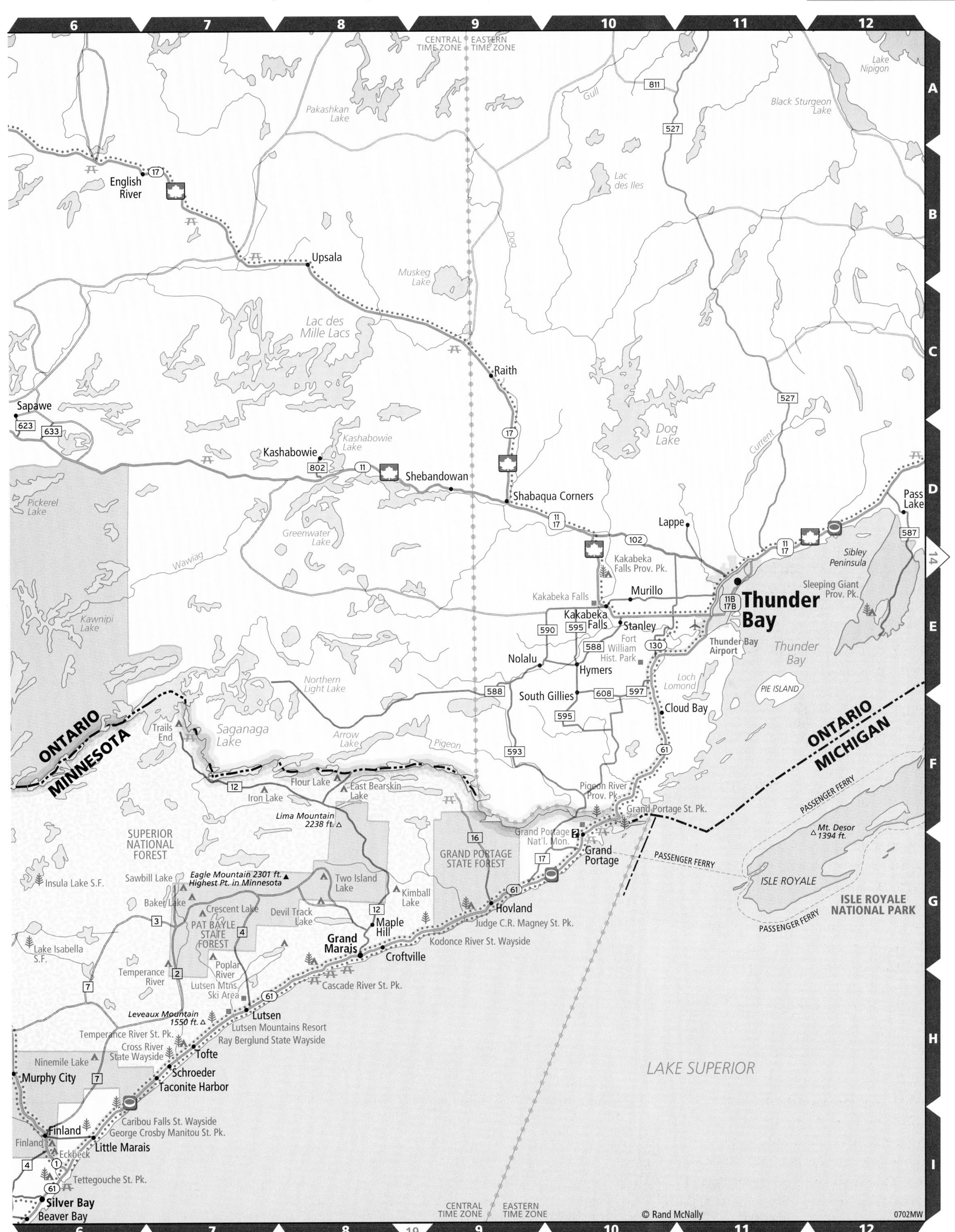
CENTRAL TIME ZONE
EASTERN TIME ZONE
Lake Nipigon
Black Sturgeon Lake
Pakashkan Lake
Gull
Lac des Iles
English River
Upsala
Dog
Muskeg Lake
Lac des Mille Lacs
Raith
Sapawe
Kashabowie
Kashabowie Lake
Shebandowan
Shabaqua Corners
Dog Lake
Current
Pickerel Lake
Greenwater Lake
Wawiag
Lappe
Pass Lake
Kakabeka Falls Prov. Pk.
Sibley Peninsula
Sleeping Giant Prov. Pk.
Murillo
Kakabeka Falls
Thunder Bay
Kawnipi Lake
Stanley
Fort William Hist. Park
Thunder Bay Airport
Thunder Bay
Nolalu
Hymers
Loch Lomond
Northern Light Lake
South Gillies
PIE ISLAND
Cloud Bay
ONTARIO
MINNESOTA
Trails End
Saganaga Lake
Arrow Lake
Pigeon
ONTARIO
MICHIGAN
Flour Lake
East Bearskin Lake
Iron Lake
Pigeon River Prov. Pk.
Grand Portage St. Pk.
PASSENGER FERRY
Lima Mountain 2238 ft.
SUPERIOR NATIONAL FOREST
Grand Portage Nat'l. Mon.
Grand Portage
GRAND PORTAGE STATE FOREST
PASSENGER FERRY
Mt. Desor 1394 ft.
Sawbill Lake
Eagle Mountain 2301 ft. Highest Pt. in Minnesota
Two Island Lake
Insula Lake S.F.
ISLE ROYALE
Kimball Lake
ISLE ROYALE NATIONAL PARK
Baker Lake
Crescent Lake
Devil Track Lake
Hovland
PASSENGER FERRY
PAT BAYLE STATE FOREST
Maple Hill
Judge C.R. Magney St. Pk.
Lake Isabella S.F.
Grand Marais
Kodonce River St. Wayside
Croftville
Temperance River
Poplar River
Lutsen Mtns. Ski Area
Cascade River St. Pk.
Leveaux Mountain 1550 ft.
Lutsen
Lutsen Mountains Resort
Temperance River St. Pk.
Ray Berglund State Wayside
Cross River State Wayside
Tofte
Ninemile Lake
Schroeder
Murphy City
Taconite Harbor
LAKE SUPERIOR
Caribou Falls St. Wayside
Finland
George Crosby Manitou St. Pk.
Finland
Little Marais
Eckbeck
Tettegouche St. Pk.
Silver Bay
Beaver Bay
© Rand McNally
0702MW
6 7 8 9 10 11 12
A B C D E F G H I

14

19

For a complete listing of symbols, see inside back cover; for an index of cities, see page 200.

DISTANCE SCALE

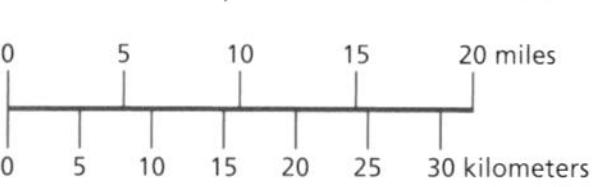

LOCATOR MAP

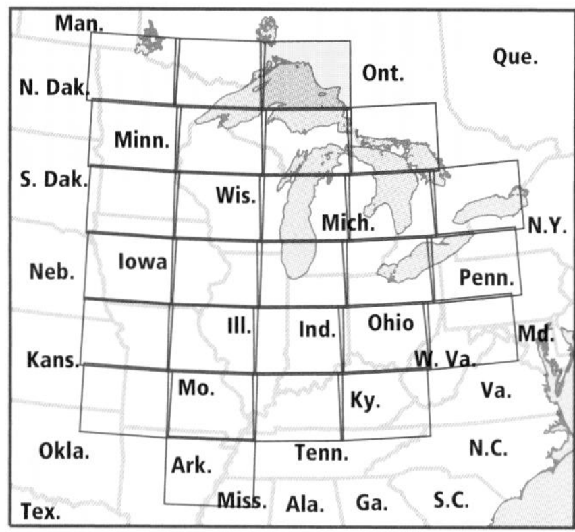

See the Pagefinder™ map on the inside of the front cover for map page numbers.

Where on these maps can I find public camping facilities?

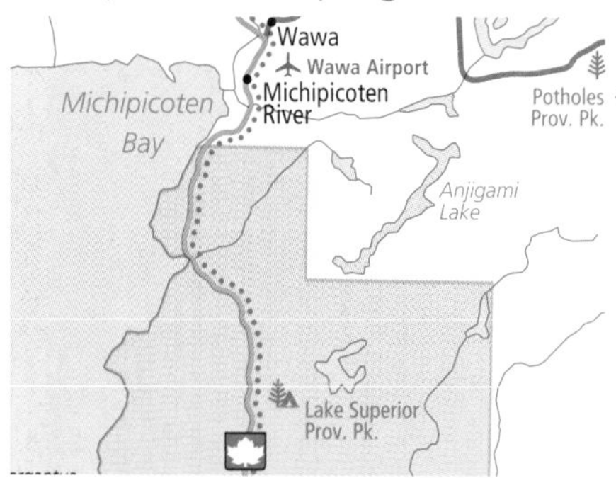

Look for the fir tree symbols. These symbols indicate a state- or provincial-run park, forest, historic site, or recreation area.

A tent next to the fir tree means there are modern public camping facilities (running water, flush toilets and electricity available); no tent means no camping.

A tent all by itself indicates public camping facilities within a federally run park, monument, forest, or recreation area.

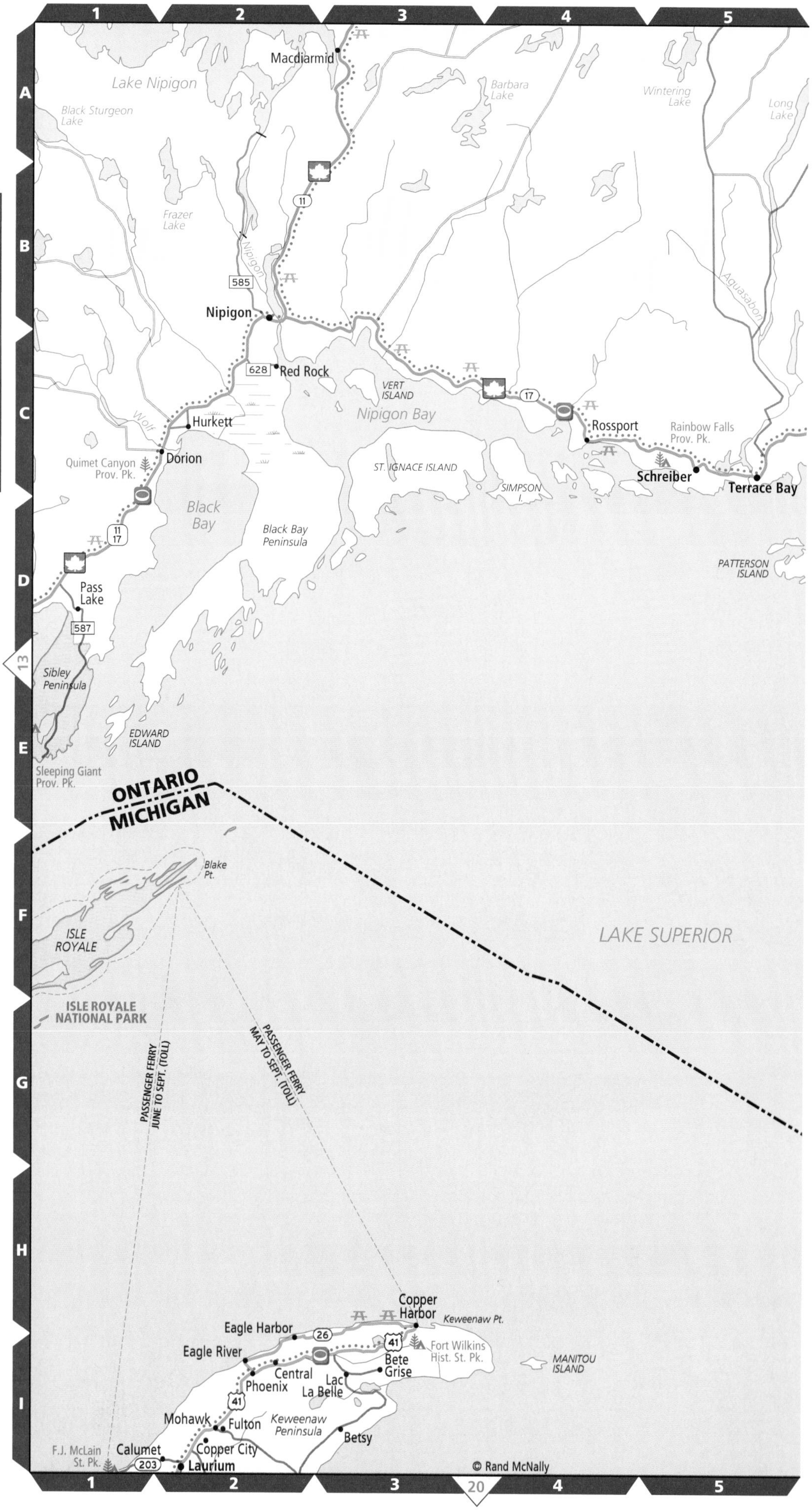

1 2 3 4 5

A B C D E F G H I

Lake Nipigon
Macdiarmid
Black Sturgeon Lake
Barbara Lake
Wintering Lake
Long Lake
Frazer Lake
Nipigon
Aguasabon
11
585
Nipigon
628
Red Rock
Vert Island
Nipigon Bay
17
Rossport
Rainbow Falls Prov. Pk.
Wolf
Hurkett
Dorion
Ouimet Canyon Prov. Pk.
St. Ignace Island
Simpson I.
Schreiber
Terrace Bay
Black Bay
Black Bay Peninsula
11 17
Patterson Island
Pass Lake
587
Sibley Peninsula
Edward Island
Sleeping Giant Prov. Pk.
ONTARIO
MICHIGAN
Blake Pt.
Isle Royale
LAKE SUPERIOR
ISLE ROYALE NATIONAL PARK
PASSENGER FERRY JUNE TO SEPT. (TOLL)
PASSENGER FERRY MAY TO SEPT. (TOLL)
Copper Harbor
Keweenaw Pt.
Eagle Harbor
26
41
Fort Wilkins Hist. St. Pk.
Eagle River
Bete Grise
Manitou Island
Central
Phoenix
Lac La Belle
41
Mohawk
Fulton
Keweenaw Peninsula
Betsy
F.J. McLain St. Pk.
Calumet
203
Copper City
Laurium

13
20

When you see this sign 14, the map continues on the page number indicated.

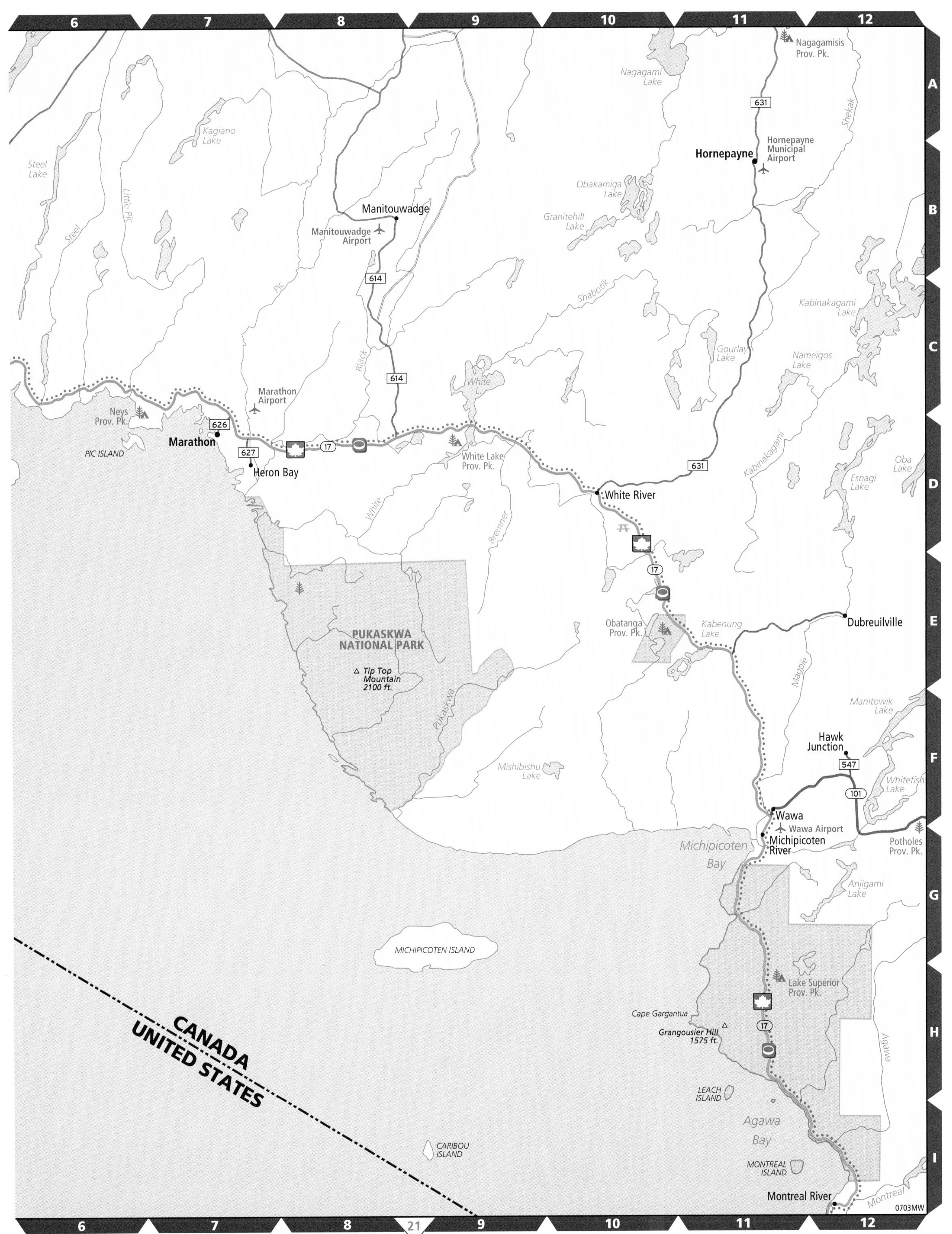

21

For a complete listing of symbols, see inside back cover; for an index of cities, see page 200.

DISTANCE SCALE

One inch represents 16 miles

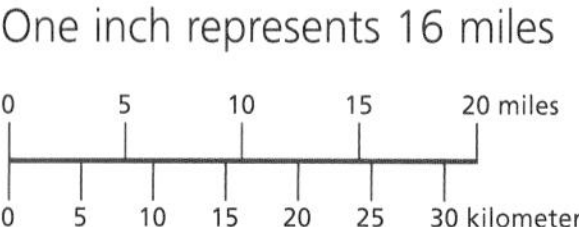

LOCATOR MAP

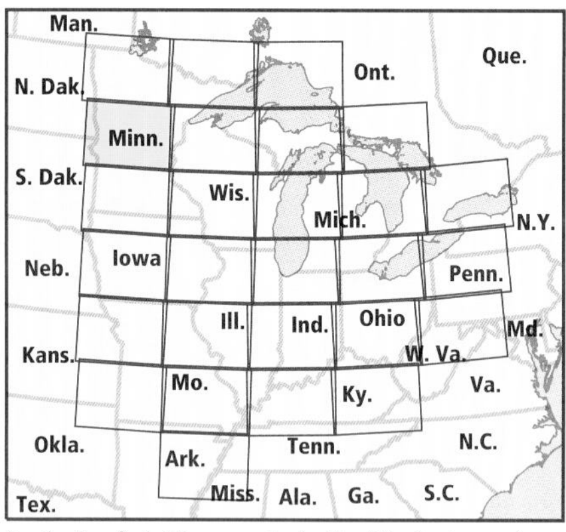

See the Pagefinder™ map on the inside of the front cover for map page numbers.

Why are some city names bigger than others?

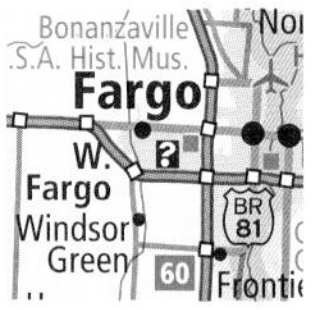

The difference in the size of the type helps quickly show which cities are more populous than others. The bigger the type, the more people live in that city. More people means more amenities—food, lodging, gas and shopping. In the example above, Fargo is a more populous city than West Fargo, and both are larger than Windsor Green.

What are those yellow boxes (with little numbers) on the maps?

PAGE 52

That's where fun stuff happens, and this book describes that area in detail starting on the page number you see. Read all about what there is to see and do, what the shopping scene's like, where you can stay overnight, what the best food to try is and where you can find it, and even if there's a festival happening during your visit. These destination sections also offer specially designed maps to help figure out where attractions and restaurants are in relation to each other (and how to drive between them).

Why is there a red ribbon on this map?

The red award ribbon marks a Rand McNally Best of the Road™ trip route. Our editors have chosen scenic drives peppered with tasty dining, unique shopping, and memory-making things to do. Read more about four of these drives on pages 180-191. For more trip routes, visit go.randmcnally.com/BR.

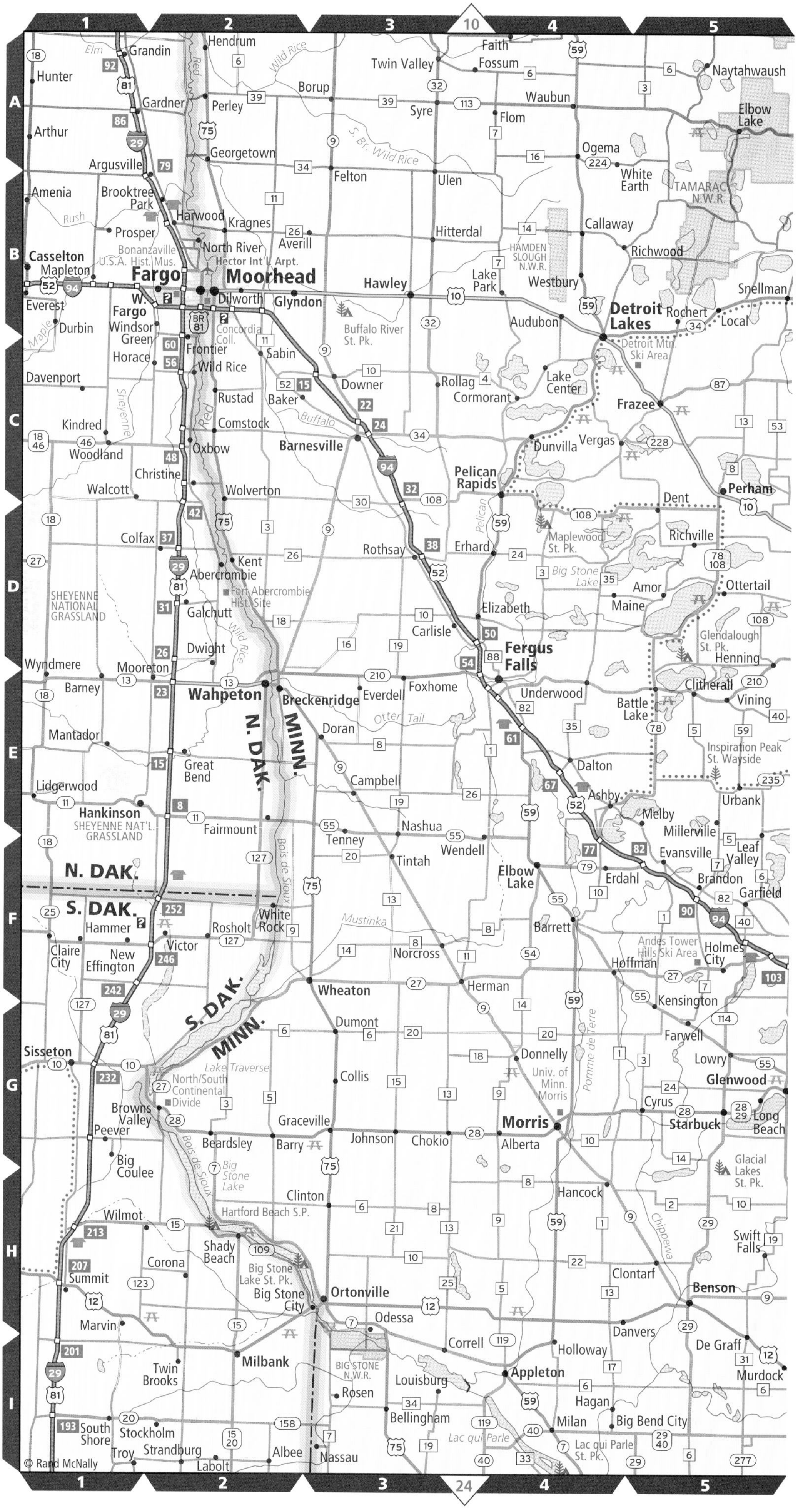

When you see this sign 14, the map continues on the page number indicated.

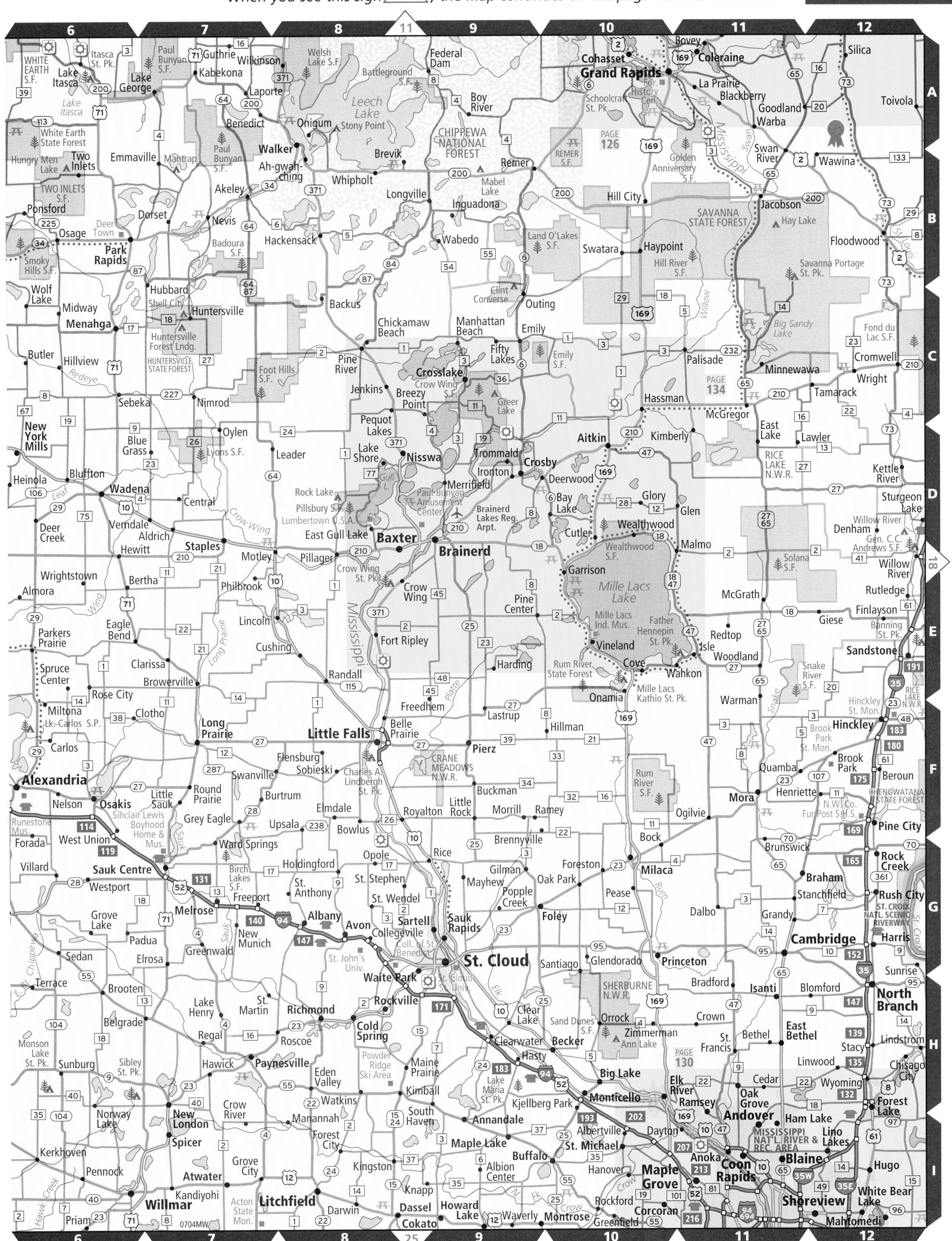

For a complete listing of symbols, see inside back cover; for an index of cities, see page 200.

DISTANCE SCALE

One inch represents 16 miles

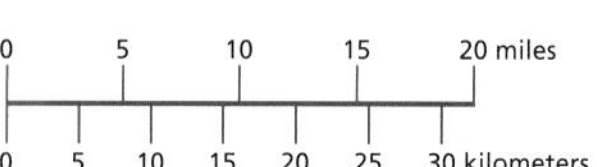

LOCATOR MAP

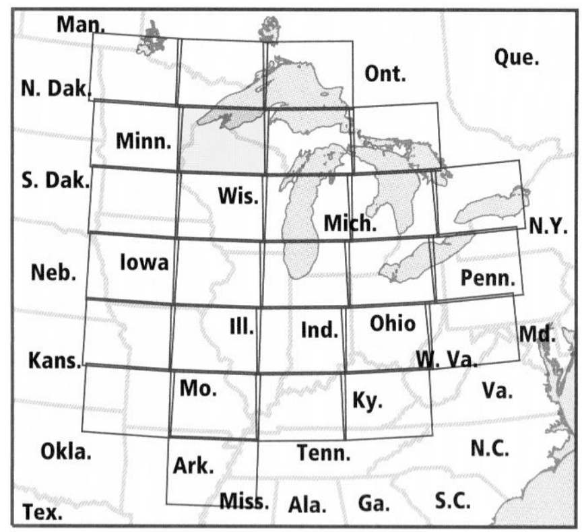

See the Pagefinder™ map on the inside of the front cover for map page numbers.

What are those little green dots alongside the road?

These green dots •••• mean the road is a specially chosen scenic route. You're almost guaranteed great views while driving.

If the dots have a ribbon of color beneath them • • • •, the route is one of Rand McNally's Best of the Road™ drives. These drives have plenty to see and do along them. (See pages 180-191 for full descriptions.)

What are those yellow boxes (with little numbers) on the maps?

PAGE 52 That's where fun stuff happens, and this book describes that area in detail starting on the page number you see. Read all about what there is to see and do, what the shopping scene's like, where you can stay overnight, what the best food to try is and where you can find it, and even if there's a festival happening during your visit. These destination sections also offer specially designed maps to help figure out where attractions and restaurants are in relation to each other (and how to drive between them).

Why is there a red ribbon on this map?

The red award ribbon marks a Rand McNally Best of the Road™ trip route. Our editors have chosen scenic drives peppered with tasty dining, unique shopping, and memory-making things to do. Read more about four of these drives on pages 180-191. For more trip routes, visit go.randmcnally.com/BR.

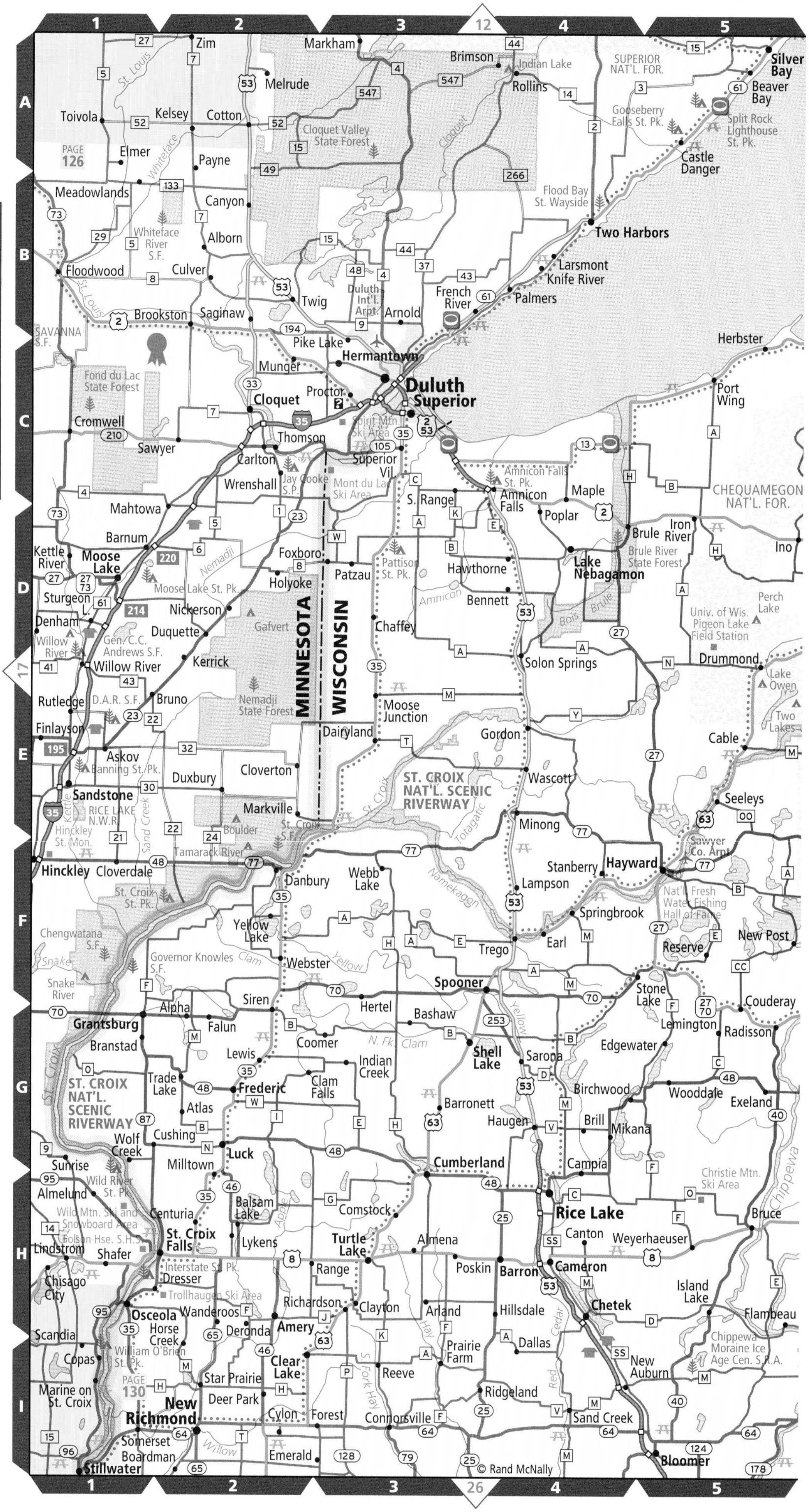

MINNESOTA

WISCONSIN

© Rand McNally

When you see this sign 14, the map continues on the page number indicated.

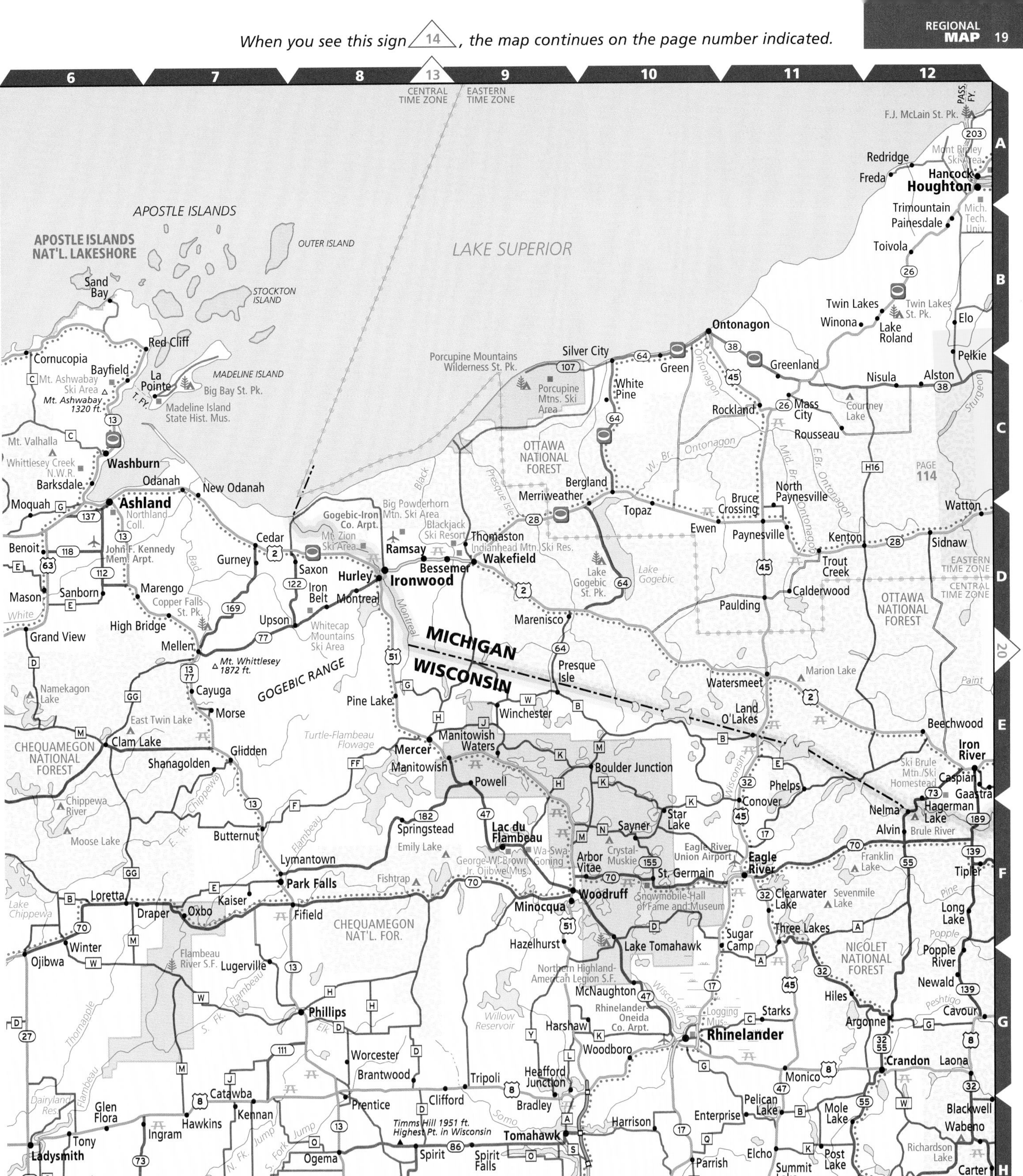

For a complete listing of symbols, see inside back cover; for an index of cities, see page 200.

DISTANCE SCALE

One inch represents 16 miles

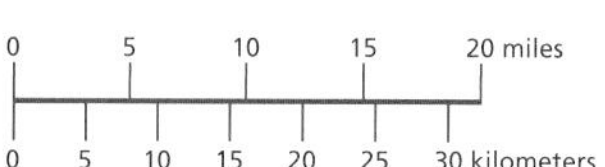

LOCATOR MAP

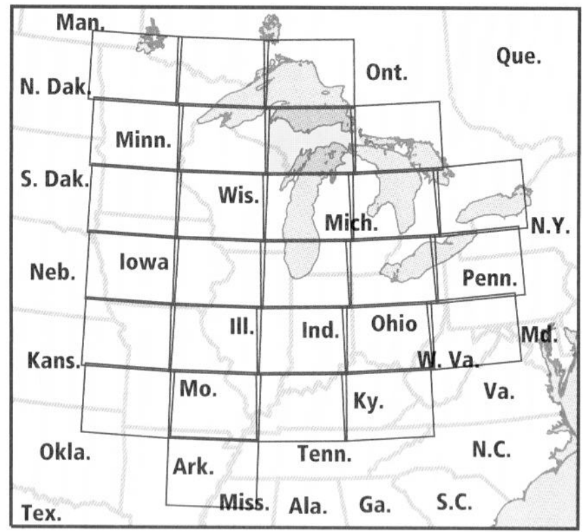

See the Pagefinder™ map on the inside of the front cover for map page numbers.

What are those thick pink lines?

The double pink line represents a political boundary, either between states or nations. A national boundary has a black center line with a dash followed by two dots. A state or provincial boundary has a dash followed by a single dot.

When the boundary runs along a river, the center black line is removed.

On the other hand, when the boundary runs through a lake or ocean, the pink line is removed, and the black line remains.

What are those yellow boxes (with little numbers) on the maps?

PAGE 52 That's where fun stuff happens, and this book describes that area in detail starting on the page number you see. Read all about what there is to see and do, what the shopping scene's like, where you can stay overnight, what the best food to try is and where you can find it, and even if there's a festival happening during your visit. These destination sections also offer specially designed maps to help figure out where attractions and restaurants are in relation to each other (and how to drive between them).

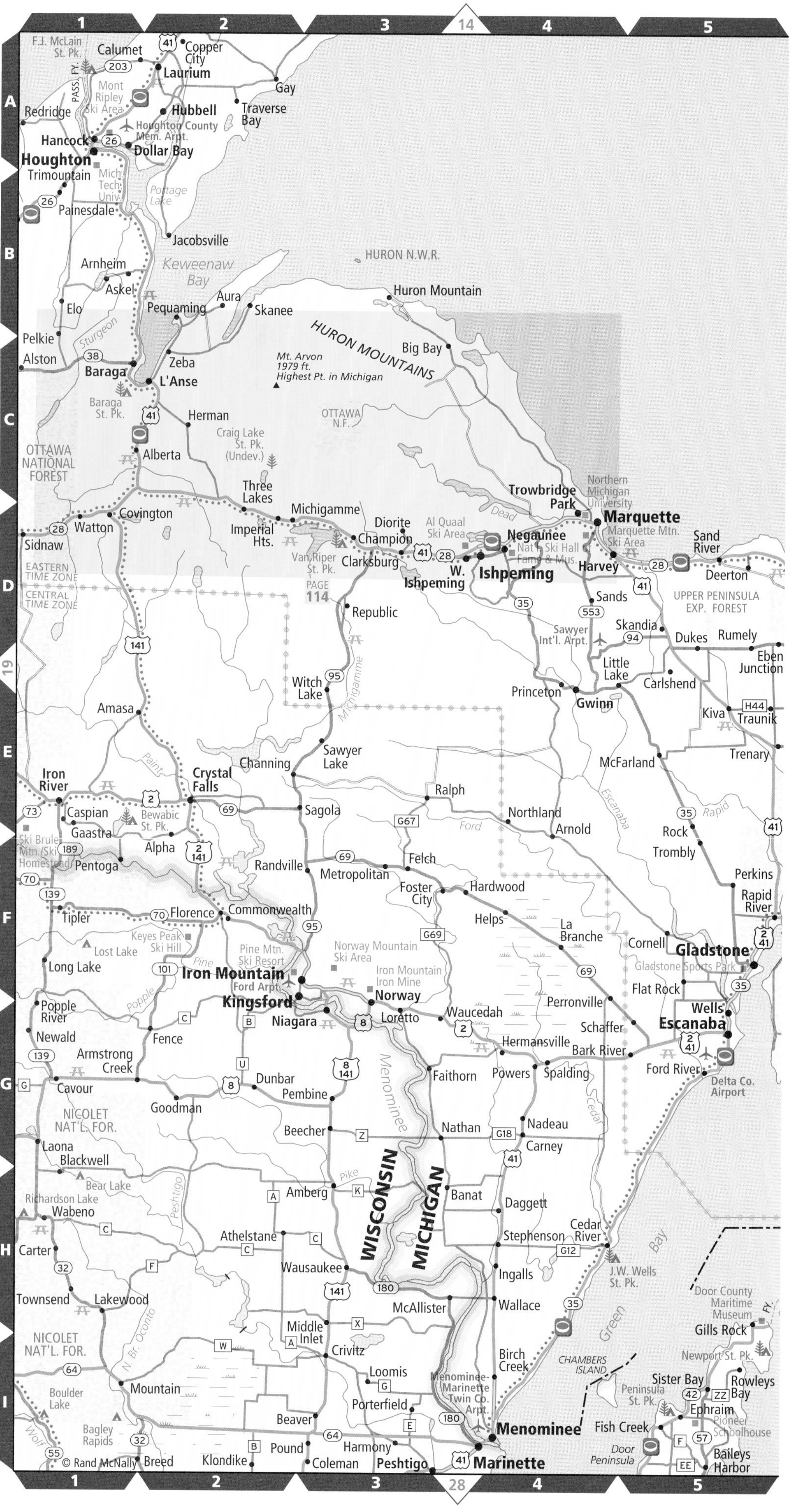

When you see this sign 14, the map continues on the page number indicated.

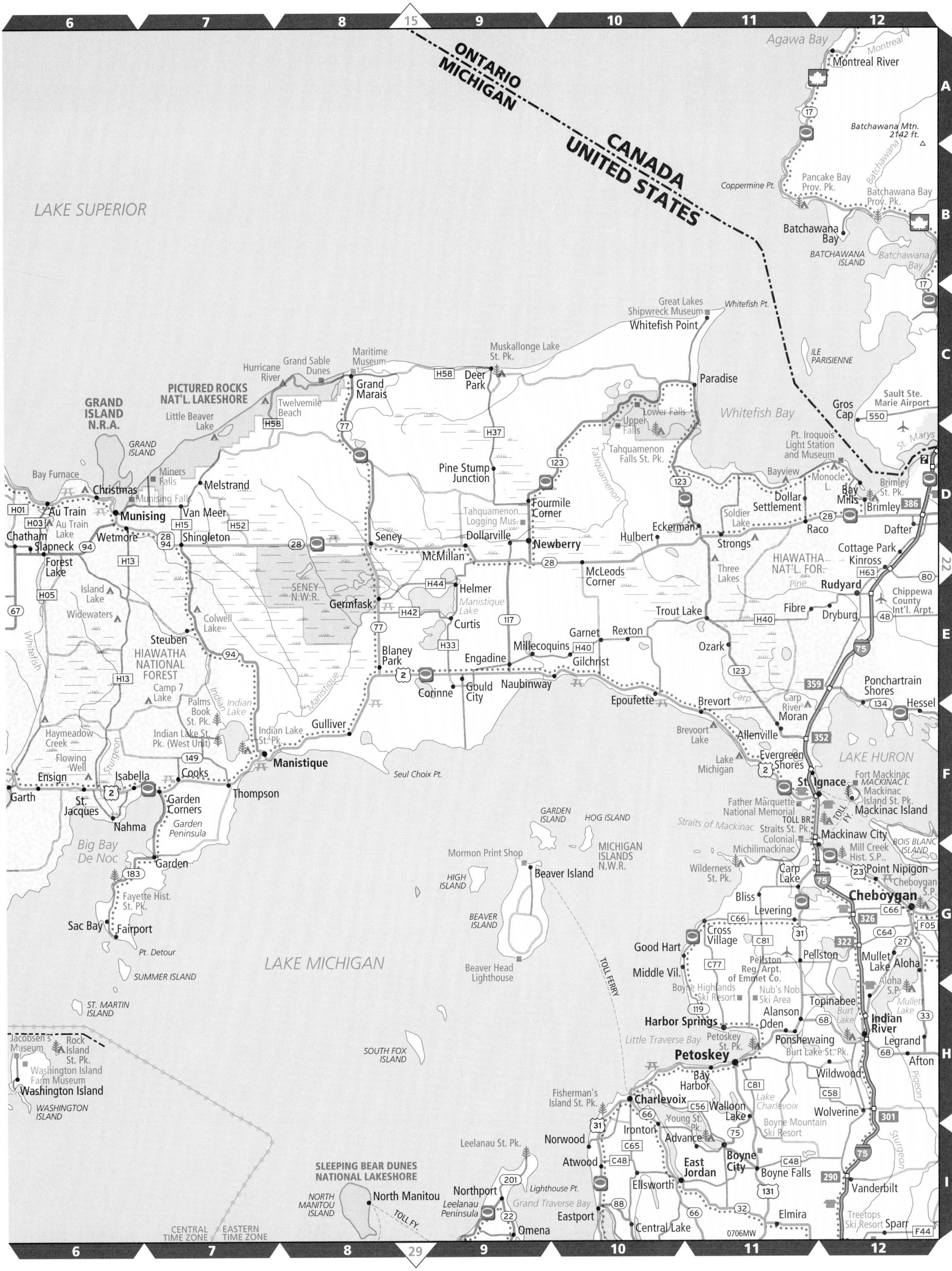

6 7 8 15 9 10 11 12

A B C D E F G H I

ONTARIO
MICHIGAN
CANADA
UNITED STATES

LAKE SUPERIOR

Agawa Bay
Montreal River
Batchawana Mtn. 2142 ft.
Pancake Bay Prov. Pk.
Coppermine Pt.
Batchawana Bay Prov. Pk.
Batchawana Bay
BATCHAWANA ISLAND
Great Lakes Shipwreck Museum
Whitefish Pt.
Whitefish Point
ILE PARISIENNE
Paradise
Whitefish Bay
Gros Cap
Sault Ste. Marie Airport
Pt. Iroquois Light Station and Museum
Bayview
Monocle L.
Bay Mills
Brimley St. Pk.
Brimley
Dollar Settlement
Soldier Lake
Raco
Dafter
Cottage Park
Kinross
HIAWATHA NAT'L. FOR.
Rudyard
Chippewa County Int'l. Arpt.
Fibre
Dryburg
Trout Lake
Ozark
Ponchartrain Shores
Hessel
Carp River
Moran
Brevort
Brevoort Lake
Allenville
Evergreen Shores
Lake Michigan
LAKE HURON
St. Ignace
Fort Mackinac
MACKINAC I.
Mackinac Island St. Pk.
Mackinac Island
Father Marquette National Memorial
TOLL BR.
TOLL FY.
Straits of Mackinac
Straits St. Pk.
Colonial Michilimackinac
Mackinaw City
BOIS BLANC ISLAND
Mill Creek Hist. S.P.
Point Nipigon
Cheboygan S.P.
Cheboygan
Wilderness St. Pk.
Carp Lake
Bliss
Levering
Cross Village
Good Hart
Pellston
Pellston Reg. Arpt. of Emmet Co.
Mullet Lake
Aloha
Aloha S.P.
Middle Vil.
Boyne Highlands Ski Resort
Nub's Nob Ski Area
Topinabee
Burt Lake
Mullett Lake
Indian River
Harbor Springs
Alanson
Oden
Ponshewaing
Little Traverse Bay
Petoskey St. Pk.
Burt Lake St. Pk.
Legrand
Afton
Petoskey
Bay Harbor
Wildwood
Pigeon
Fisherman's Island St. Pk.
Charlevoix
Walloon Lake
Lake Charlevoix
Young St. Pk.
Boyne Mountain Ski Resort
Wolverine
Norwood
Ironton
Advance
Atwood
East Jordan
Boyne City
Boyne Falls
Sturgeon
Ellsworth
Vanderbilt
Eastport
Elmira
Central Lake
Treetops Ski Resort
Sparr
Muskallonge Lake St. Pk.
Deer Park
Grand Marais
Maritime Museum
Grand Sable Dunes
Hurricane River
PICTURED ROCKS NAT'L. LAKESHORE
Twelvemile Beach
Little Beaver Lake
GRAND ISLAND N.R.A.
GRAND ISLAND
Lower Falls
Upper Falls
Tahquamenon
Tahquamenon Falls St. Pk.
Pine Stump Junction
Fourmile Corner
Tahquamenon Logging Mus.
Newberry
Eckerman
Hulbert
Strongs
Three Lakes
McLeods Corner
Pine
Bay Furnace
Christmas
Miners Falls
Munising Falls
Melstrand
Au Train
Au Train Lake
Munising
Van Meer
Chatham
Slapneck
Wetmore
Shingleton
Seney
Dollarville
McMillan
Forest Lake
SENEY N.W.R.
Germfask
Helmer
Manistique Lake
Curtis
Island Lake
Widewaters
Colwell Lake
Whitefish
Steuben
HIAWATHA NATIONAL FOREST
Garnet
Rexton
Millecoquins
Gilchrist
Engadine
Blaney Park
Gould City
Corinne
Naubinway
Epoufette
Camp 7 Lake
Indian
Indian Lake
Palms Book St. Pk.
Manistique
Gulliver
Haymeadow Creek
Indian Lake St. Pk. (West Unit)
Indian Lake St. Pk.
Flowing Well
Sturgeon
Ensign
Isabella
Cooks
Manistique
Thompson
Seul Choix Pt.
Garth
St. Jacques
Garden Corners
Nahma
Garden Peninsula
Big Bay De Noc
Garden
Fayette Hist. St. Pk.
Sac Bay
Fairport
Pt. Detour
SUMMER ISLAND
ST. MARTIN ISLAND
GARDEN ISLAND
HOG ISLAND
MICHIGAN ISLANDS N.W.R.
Mormon Print Shop
Beaver Island
HIGH ISLAND
BEAVER ISLAND
LAKE MICHIGAN
Beaver Head Lighthouse
TOLL FERRY
Jacobsen's Museum
Rock Island St. Pk.
Washington Island Farm Museum
Washington Island
WASHINGTON ISLAND
SOUTH FOX ISLAND
Leelanau St. Pk.
SLEEPING BEAR DUNES NATIONAL LAKESHORE
NORTH MANITOU ISLAND
North Manitou
TOLL FY.
Northport
Lighthouse Pt.
Grand Traverse Bay
Leelanau Peninsula
Omena
CENTRAL TIME ZONE
EASTERN TIME ZONE

22
29

0706MW

6 7 8 9 10 11 12

For a complete listing of symbols, see inside back cover; for an index of cities, see page 200.

DISTANCE SCALE

One inch represents 16 miles

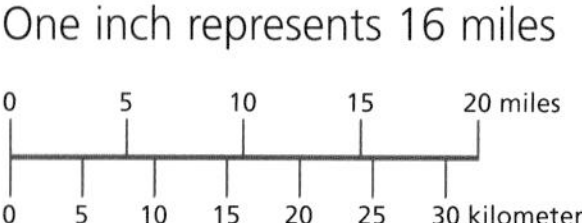

LOCATOR MAP

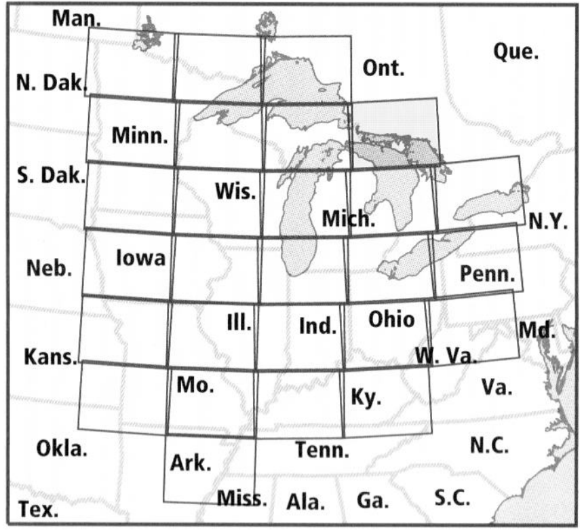

See the Pagefinder™ map on the inside of the front cover for map page numbers.

What are those different shapes on the roads with letters or numbers in them?

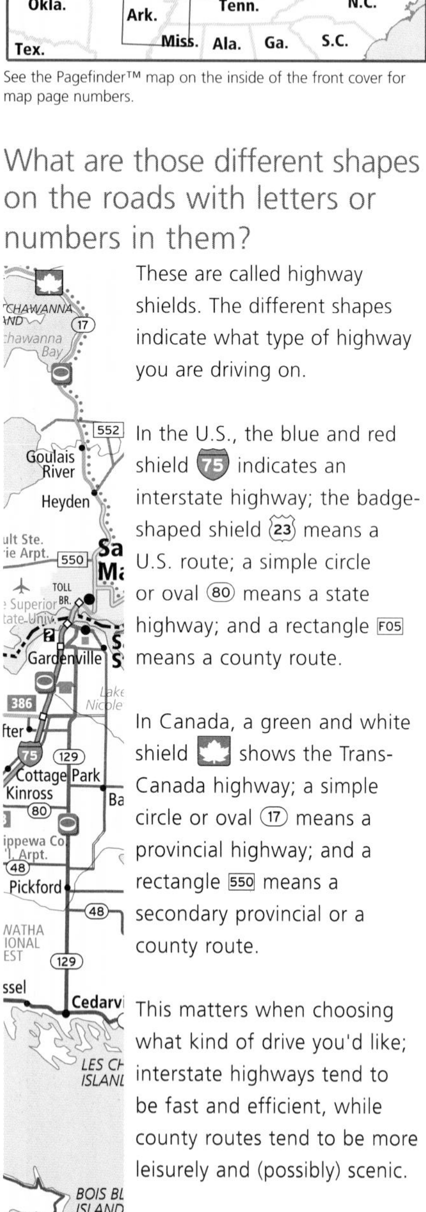

These are called highway shields. The different shapes indicate what type of highway you are driving on.

In the U.S., the blue and red shield 75 indicates an interstate highway; the badge-shaped shield 23 means a U.S. route; a simple circle or oval 80 means a state highway; and a rectangle F05 means a county route.

In Canada, a green and white shield shows the Trans-Canada highway; a simple circle or oval 17 means a provincial highway; and a rectangle 550 means a secondary provincial or a county route.

This matters when choosing what kind of drive you'd like; interstate highways tend to be fast and efficient, while county routes tend to be more leisurely and (possibly) scenic.

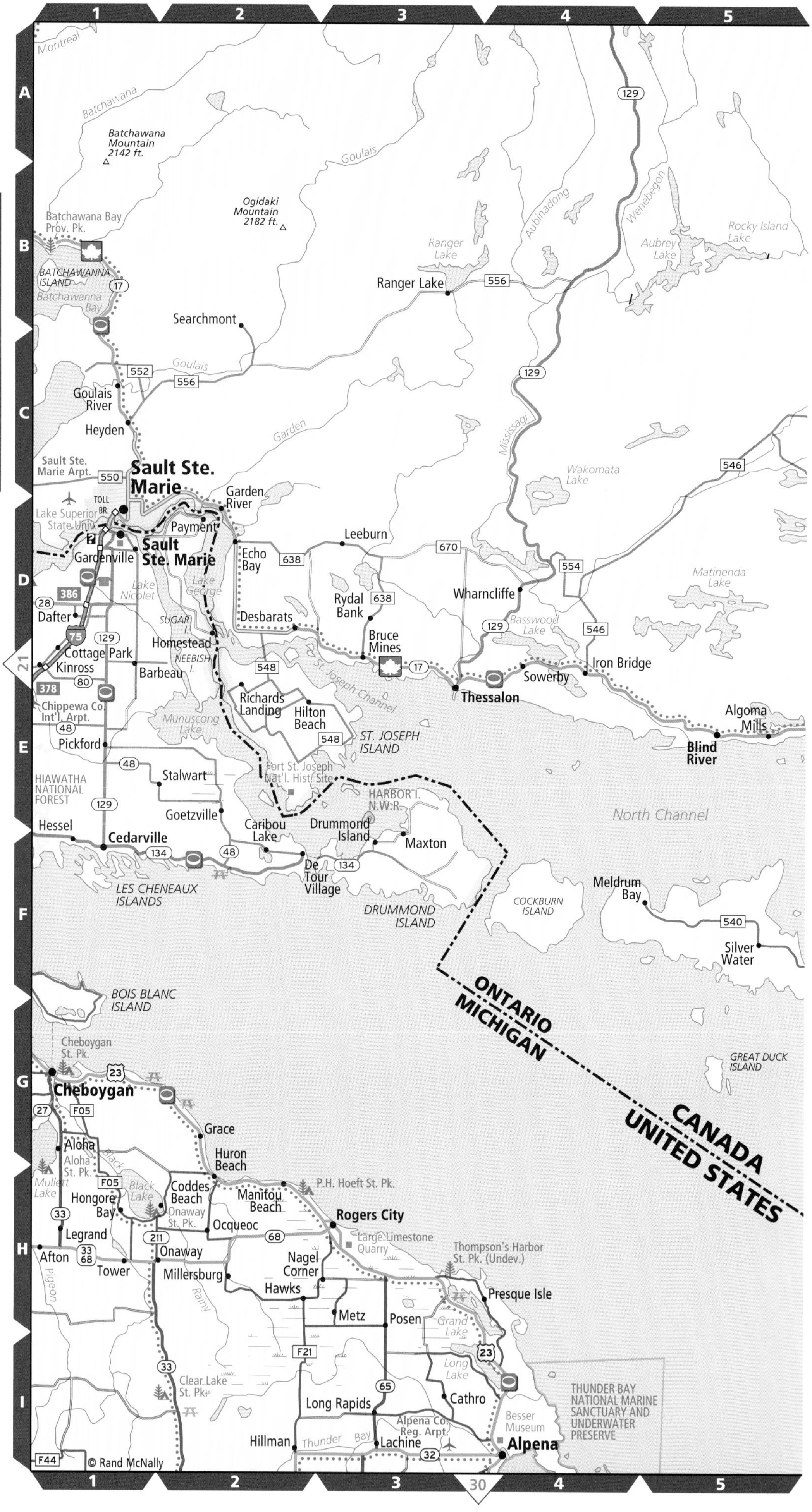

When you see this sign 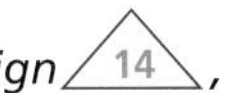 *, the map continues on the page number indicated.*

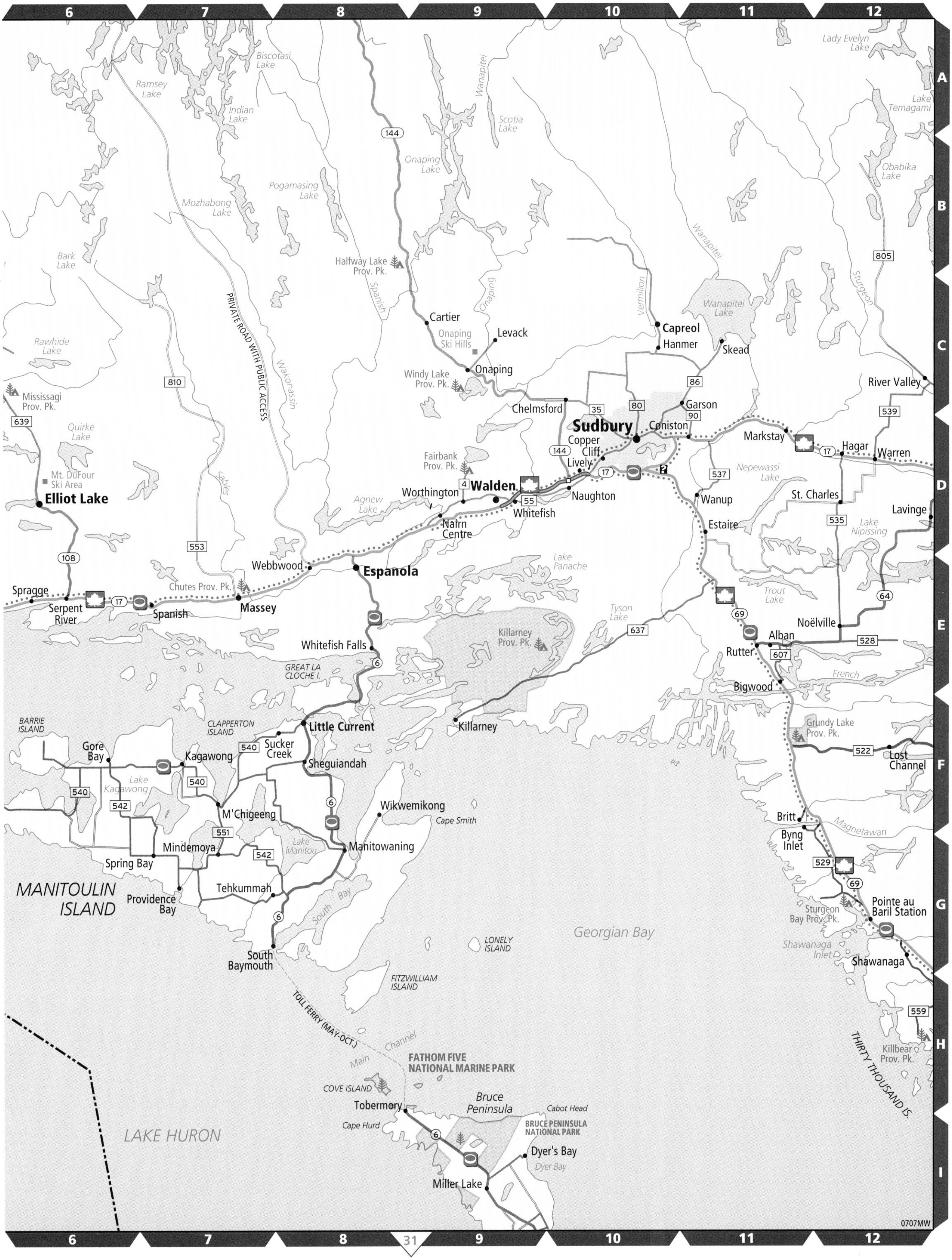

6 7 8 9 10 11 12

A B C D E F G H I

Lady Evelyn Lake
Biscotasi Lake
Ramsey Lake
Indian Lake
Wanapitei
Scotia Lake
Lake Temagami
144
Onaping Lake
Obabika Lake
Pogamasing Lake
Mozhabong Lake
Wanapitei
Bark Lake
Halfway Lake Prov. Pk.
805
Spanish
Onaping
Vermilion
Sturgeon
PRIVATE ROAD WITH PUBLIC ACCESS
Wanapitei Lake
Cartier
Onaping Ski Hills
Levack
Capreol
Rawhide Lake
Hanmer
Skead
Wakonassin
Onaping
Windy Lake Prov. Pk.
86
River Valley
810
Mississagi Prov. Pk.
Chelmsford
35
80
Garson
90
539
639
Quirke Lake
Sudbury
Coniston
Markstay
Copper Cliff
144
17
Hagar
Warren
Fairbank Prov. Pk.
Lively
Mt. DuFour Ski Area
Sables
17
537
Nepewassi Lake
4
Walden
Naughton
Worthington
Elliot Lake
Agnew Lake
55
Whitefish
Wanup
St. Charles
Lavinge
Nairn Centre
Estaire
535
Lake Nipissing
553
108
Webbwood
Espanola
Lake Panache
Spragge
Chutes Prov. Pk.
Trout Lake
64
Serpent River
17
Spanish
Massey
Tyson Lake
69
Noëlville
Killarney Prov. Pk.
637
Whitefish Falls
Alban
528
Rutter
607
6
GREAT LA CLOCHE I.
French
Bigwood
BARRIE ISLAND
CLAPPERTON ISLAND
Little Current
Killarney
Grundy Lake Prov. Pk.
Gore Bay
540
Sucker Creek
Kagawong
522
Lost Channel
Sheguiandah
540
Lake Kagawong
540
542
6
Wikwemikong
M'Chigeeng
Cape Smith
Britt
551
Magnetawan
Mindemoya
542
Lake Manitou
Manitowaning
Byng Inlet
Spring Bay
529
69
MANITOULIN ISLAND
Tehkummah
Providence Bay
South Bay
Pointe au Baril Station
Sturgeon Bay Prov. Pk.
6
Georgian Bay
LONELY ISLAND
South Baymouth
Shawanaga Inlet
Shawanaga
FITZWILLIAM ISLAND
559
TOLL FERRY (MAY-OCT.)
Main Channel
THIRTY THOUSAND IS.
Killbear Prov. Pk.
FATHOM FIVE NATIONAL MARINE PARK
COVE ISLAND
Tobermory
Bruce Peninsula
Cabot Head
Cape Hurd
BRUCE PENINSULA NATIONAL PARK
LAKE HURON
6
Dyer's Bay
Dyer Bay
Miller Lake

0707MW

6 7 8 9 10 11 12

31

For a complete listing of symbols, see inside back cover; for an index of cities, see page 200.

DISTANCE SCALE

One inch represents 16 miles

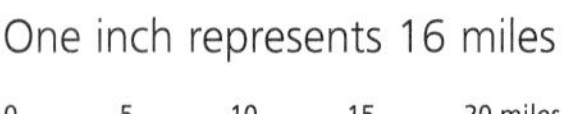

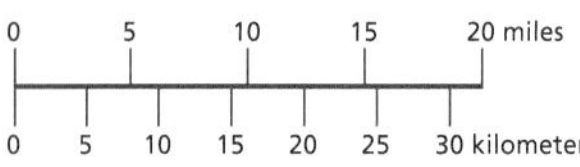

LOCATOR MAP

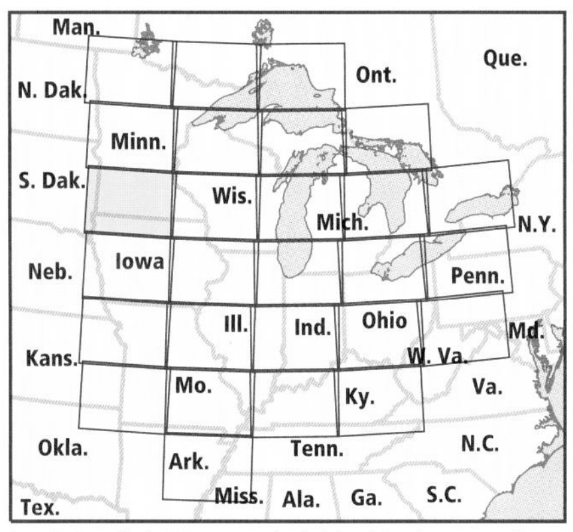

See the Pagefinder™ map on the inside of the front cover for map page numbers.

Why are some of the city dots stars?

Stars indicate the capital city for either the state/provincial government ★ or for the national government ★. This is where the executive, legislative and judicial branches of the state, provincial or national government work.

What are those yellow boxes (with little numbers) on the maps?

That's where fun stuff happens, and this book describes that area in detail starting on the page number you see. Read all about what there is to see and do, what the shopping scene's like, where you can stay overnight, what the best food to try is and where you can find it, and even if there's a festival happening during your visit. These destination sections also offer specially designed maps to help figure out where attractions and restaurants are in relation to each other (and how to drive between them).

Why is there a red ribbon on this map?

The red award ribbon marks a Rand McNally Best of the Road™ trip route. Our editors have chosen scenic drives peppered with tasty dining, unique shopping, and memory-making things to do. Read more about four of these drives on pages 180-191. For more trip routes, visit go.randmcnally.com/BR.

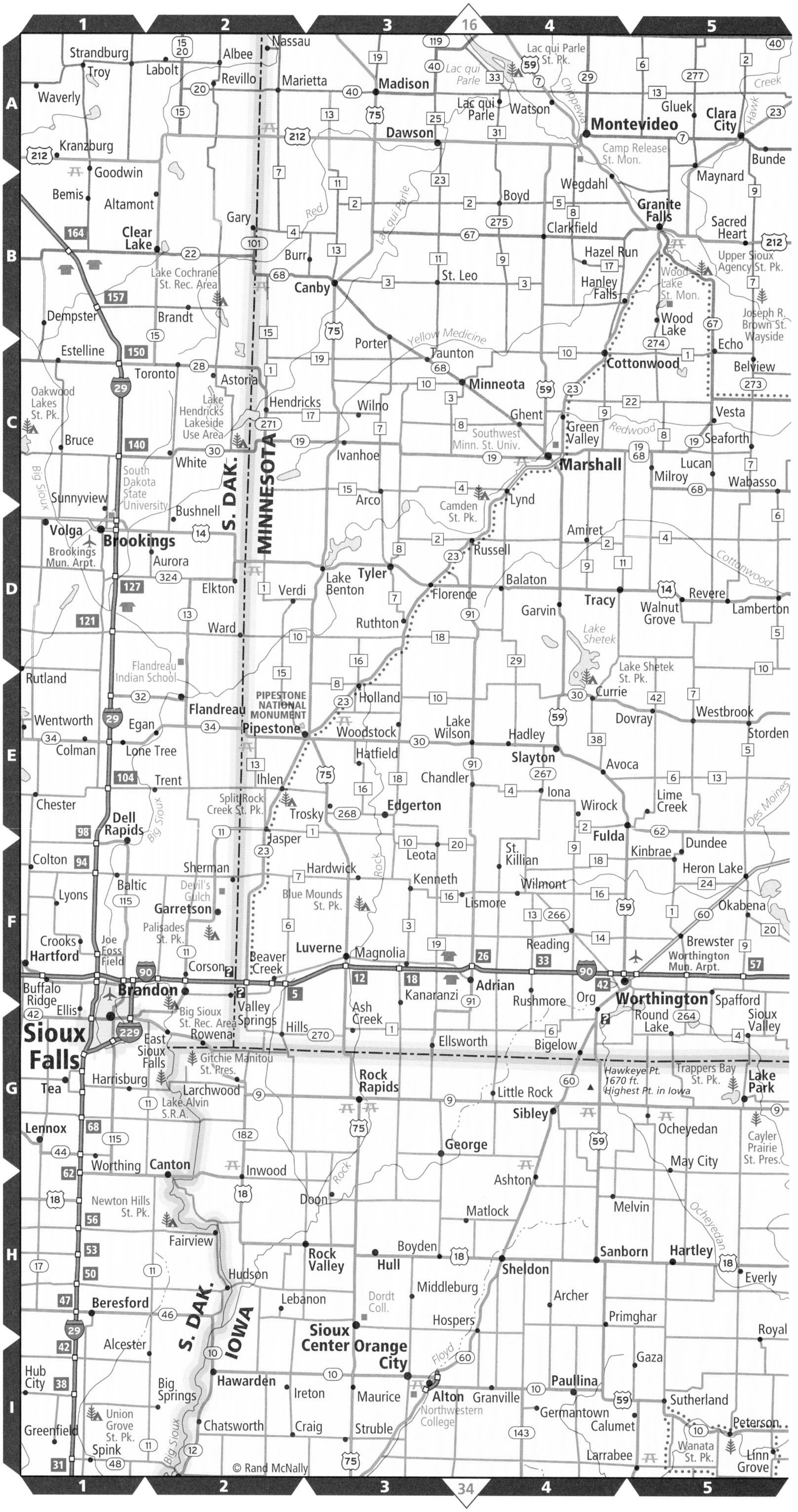

When you see this sign 14, the map continues on the page number indicated.

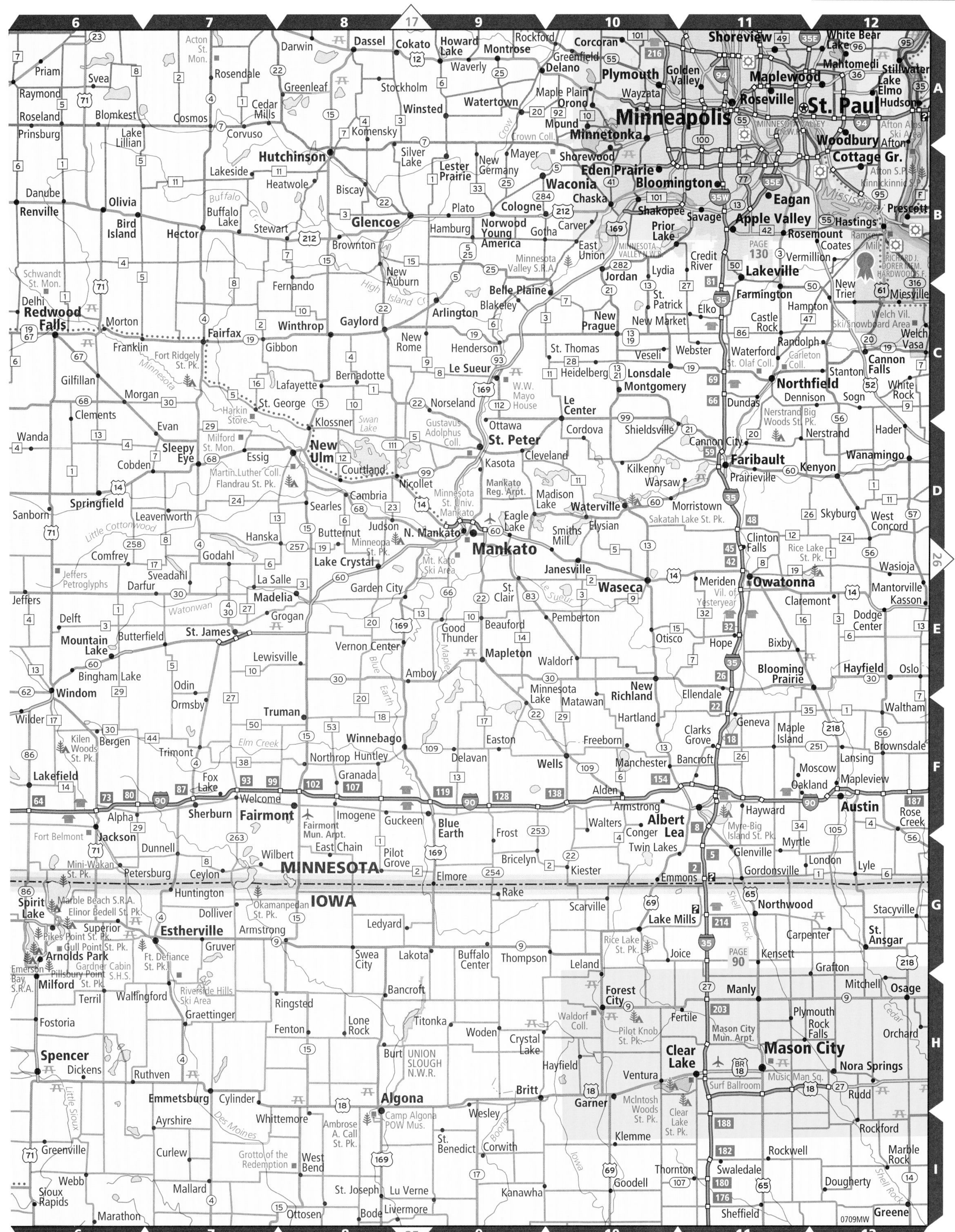

For a complete listing of symbols, see inside back cover; for an index of cities, see page 200.

DISTANCE SCALE

One inch represents 16 miles

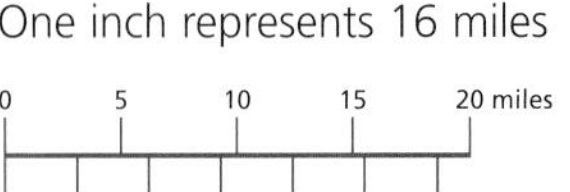

LOCATOR MAP

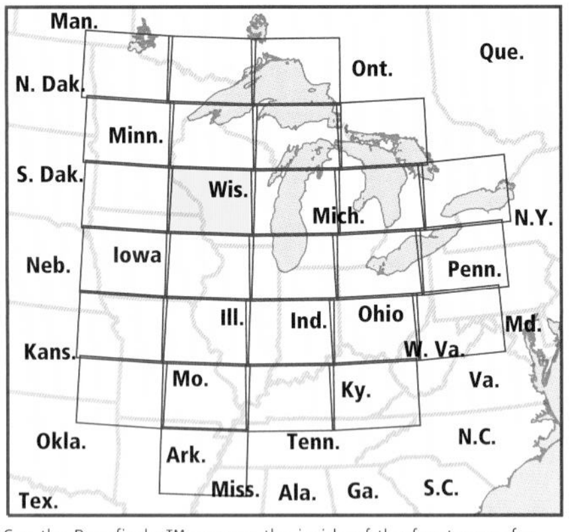

See the Pagefinder™ map on the inside of the front cover for map page numbers.

Why are there question marks on the map?

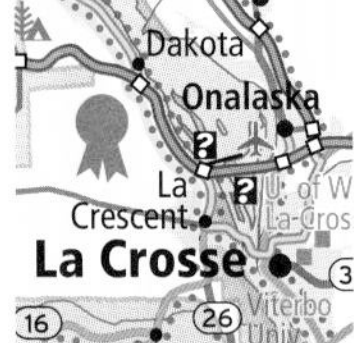

Those question marks indicate locations of tourist information centers. You might want to stop there for local and state attraction information.

What are those yellow boxes (with little numbers) on the maps?

That's where fun stuff happens, and this book describes that area in detail starting on the page number you see. Read all about what there is to see and do, what the shopping scene's like, where you can stay overnight, what the best food to try is and where you can find it, and even if there's a festival happening during your visit. These destination sections also offer specially designed maps to help figure out where attractions and restaurants are in relation to each other (and how to drive between them).

Why is there a red ribbon on this map?

The red award ribbon marks a Rand McNally Best of the Road™ trip route. Our editors have chosen scenic drives peppered with tasty dining, unique shopping, and memory-making things to do. Read more about four of these drives on pages 180-191. For more trip routes, visit go.randmcnally.com/BR.

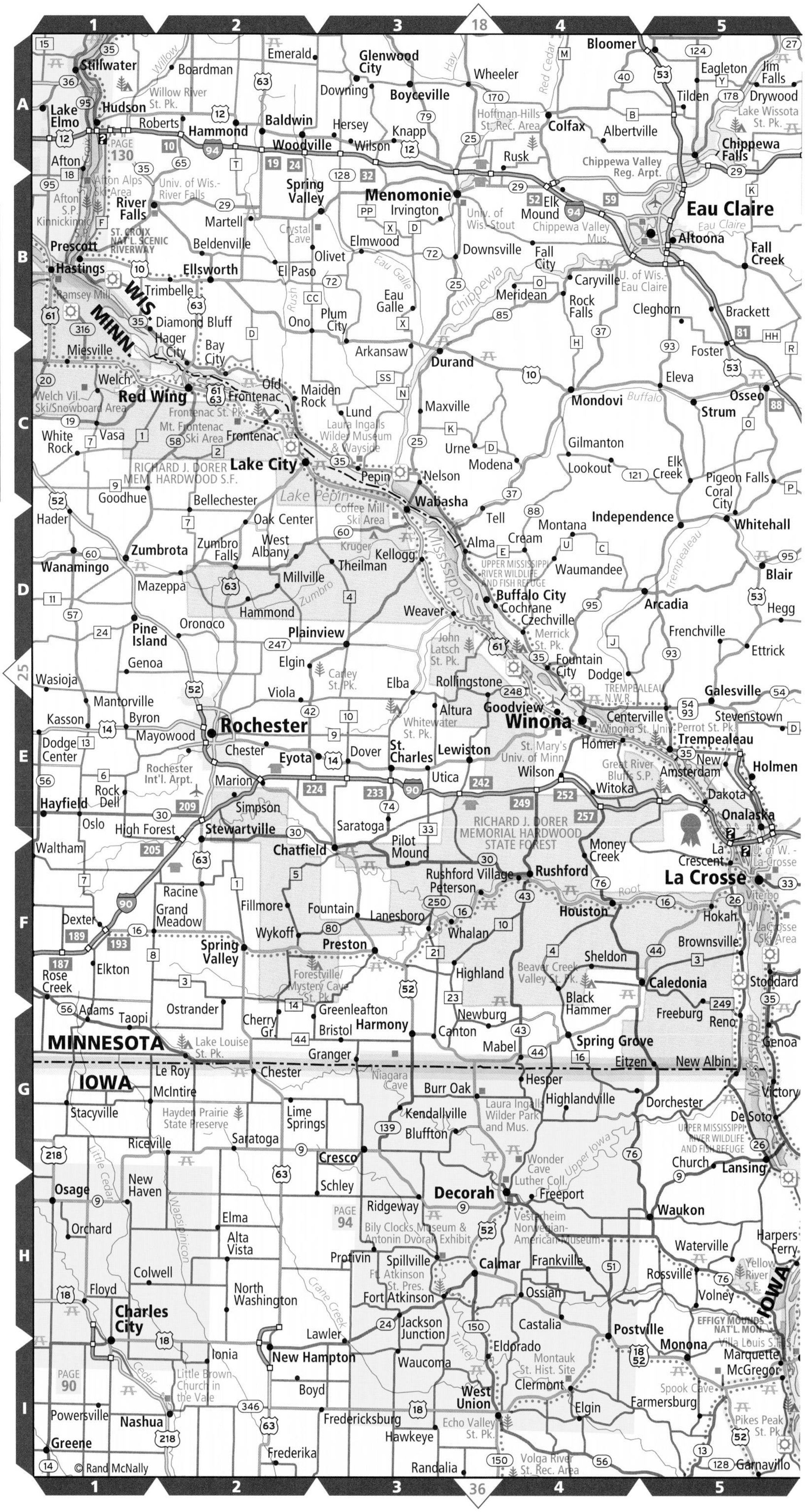

When you see this sign 14, the map continues on the page number indicated.

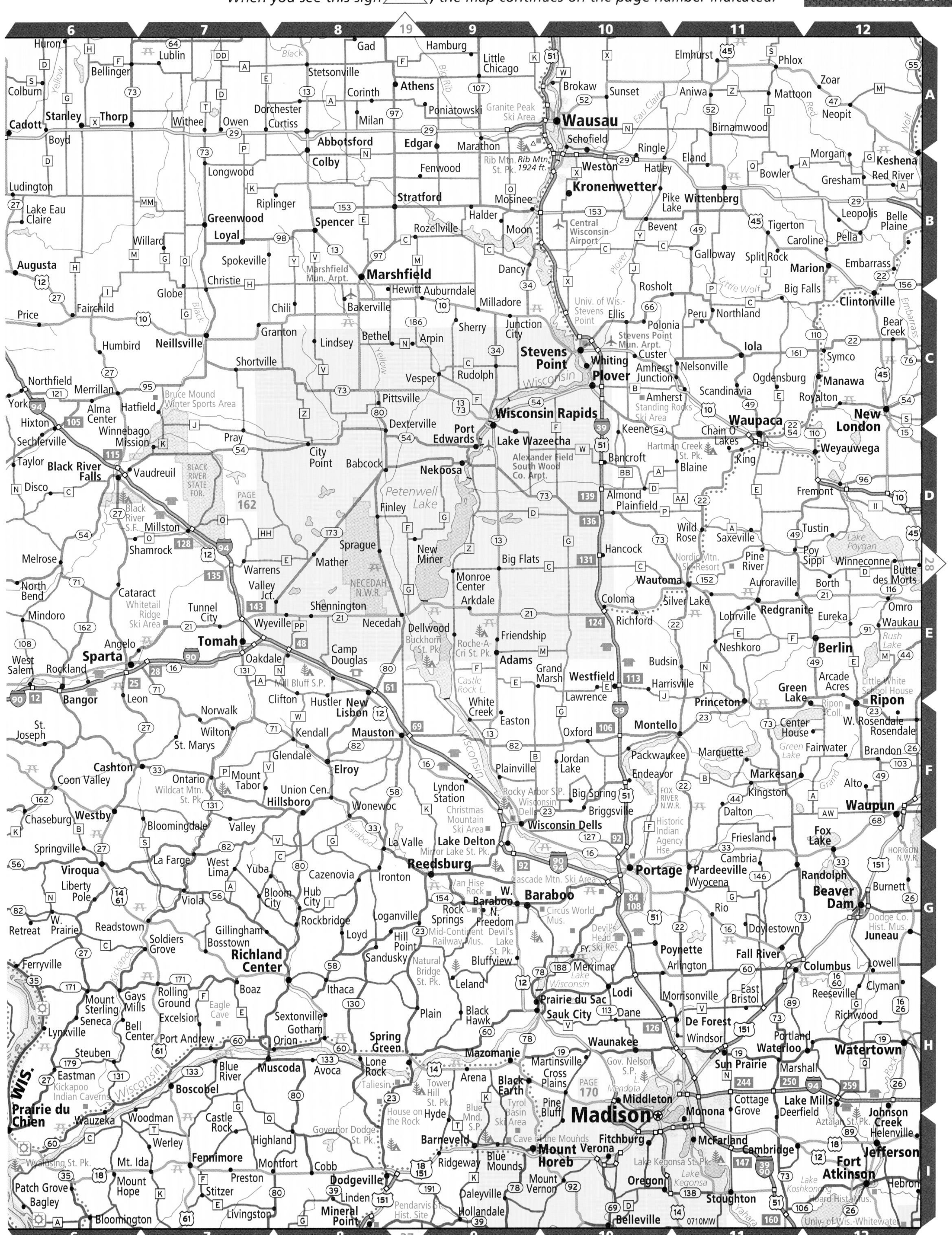

For a complete listing of symbols, see inside back cover; for an index of cities, see page 200.

DISTANCE SCALE

One inch represents 16 miles

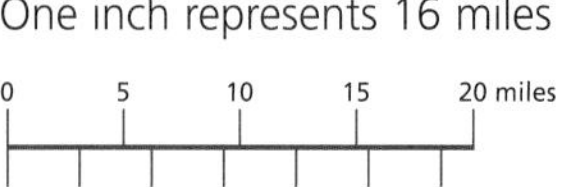

LOCATOR MAP

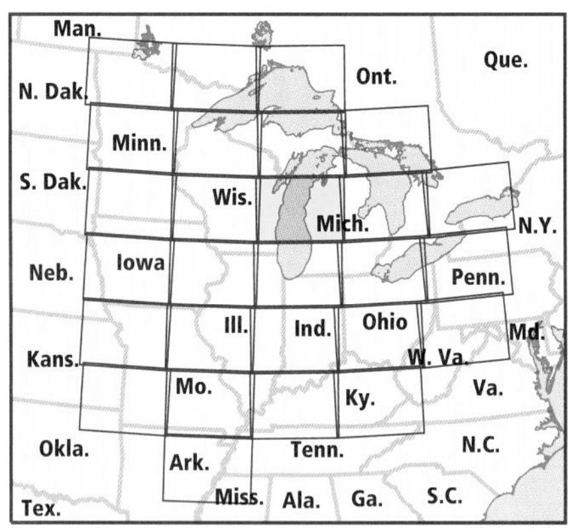

See the Pagefinder™ map on the inside of the front cover for map page numbers.

These square symbols don't look like highway shields (part 1).

These maps show five different square symbols: Each represents a specially designated historic or scenic route.

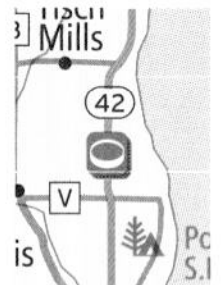

For more than 6,500 miles, the **Great Lakes Circle Tour** follows the shoreline of the "Fresh Coast," the 5 Great Lakes and the St. Lawrence Seaway.

Read more about the others on pp. 34 and 46.

What are those yellow boxes (with little numbers) on the maps?

PAGE 52

That's where fun stuff happens, and this book describes that area in detail starting on the page number you see. Read all about what there is to see and do, what the shopping scene's like, where you can stay overnight, what the best food to try is and where you can find it, and even if there's a festival happening during your visit. These destination sections also offer specially designed maps to help figure out where attractions and restaurants are in relation to each other (and how to drive between them).

When you see this sign 14, the map continues on the page number indicated.

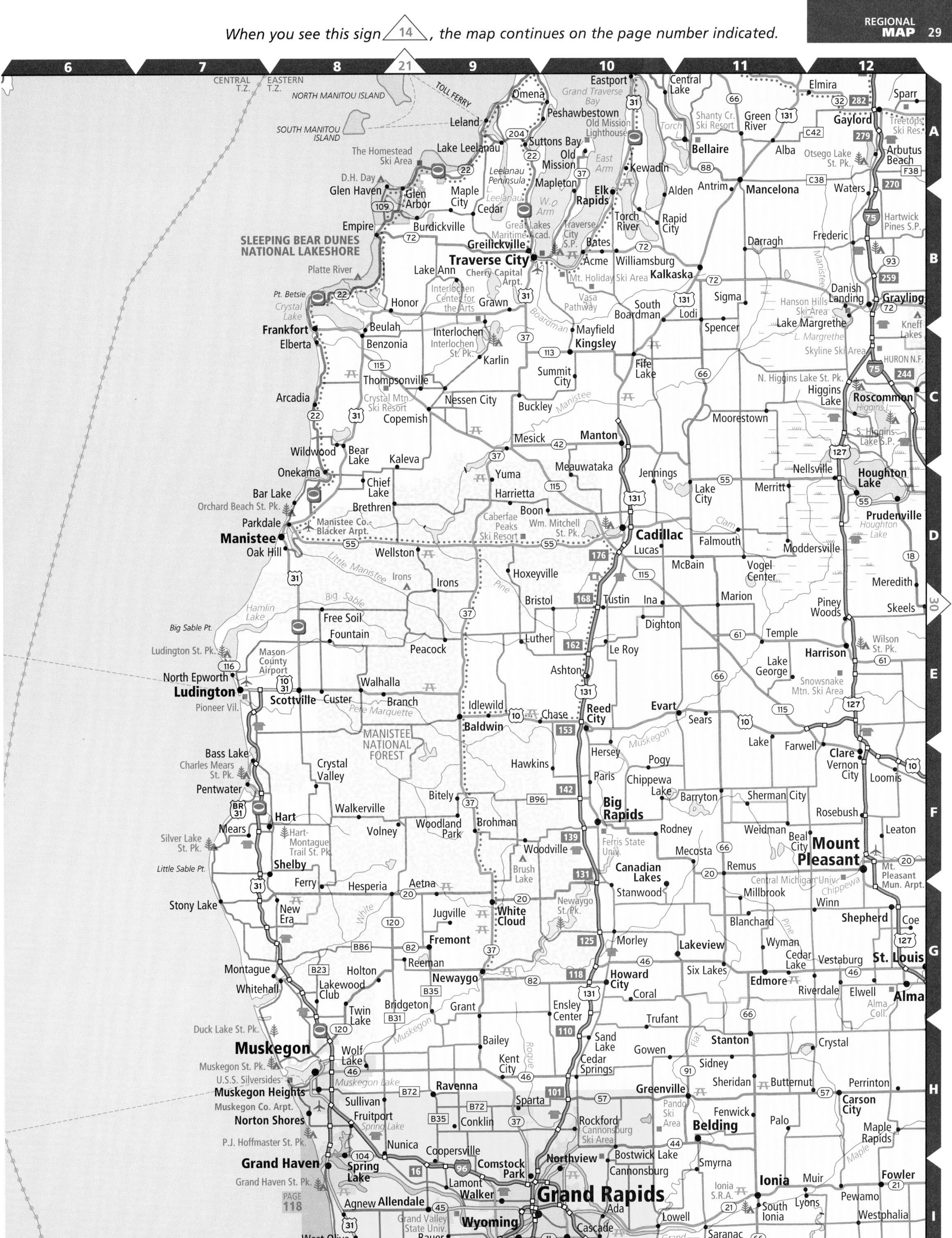

For a complete listing of symbols, see inside back cover; for an index of cities, see page 200.

DISTANCE SCALE

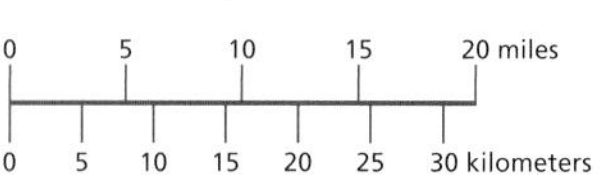

LOCATOR MAP

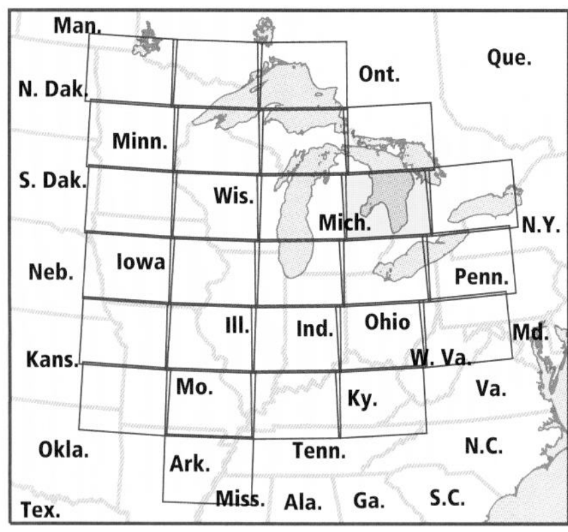

See the Pagefinder™ map on the inside of the front cover for map page numbers.

I need to find a rest stop. Does the map show where one is located?

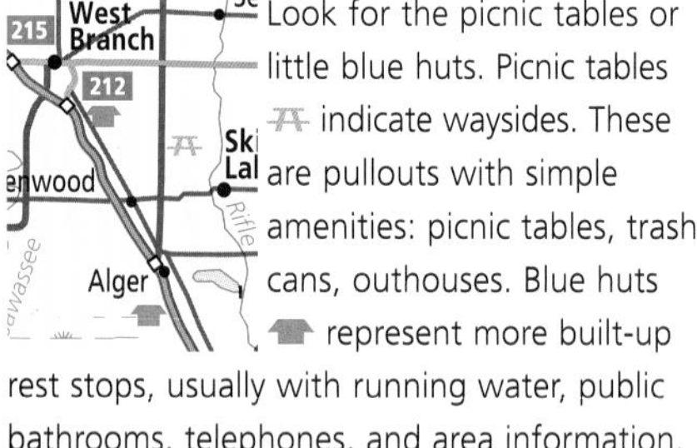

Look for the picnic tables or little blue huts. Picnic tables indicate waysides. These are pullouts with simple amenities: picnic tables, trash cans, outhouses. Blue huts represent more built-up rest stops, usually with running water, public bathrooms, telephones, and area information. (If the hut has a white spot in it, there are no bathrooms and very few amenities.)

What are those yellow boxes (with little numbers) on the maps?

That's where fun stuff happens, and this book describes that area in detail starting on the page number you see. Read all about what there is to see and do, what the shopping scene's like, where you can stay overnight, what the best food to try is and where you can find it, and even if there's a festival happening during your visit. These destination sections also offer specially designed maps to help figure out where attractions and restaurants are in relation to each other (and how to drive between them).

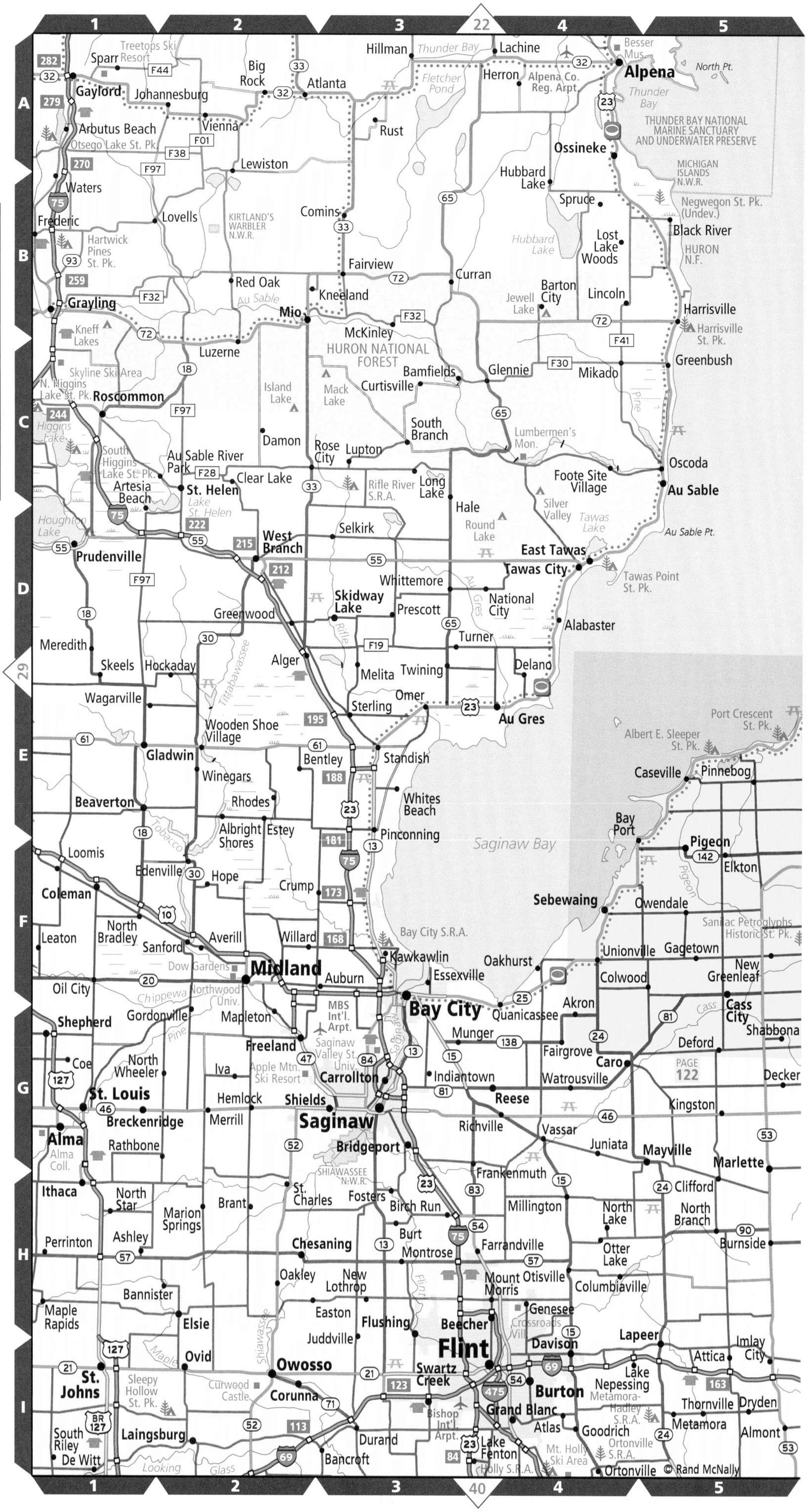

When you see this sign 14, the map continues on the page number indicated.

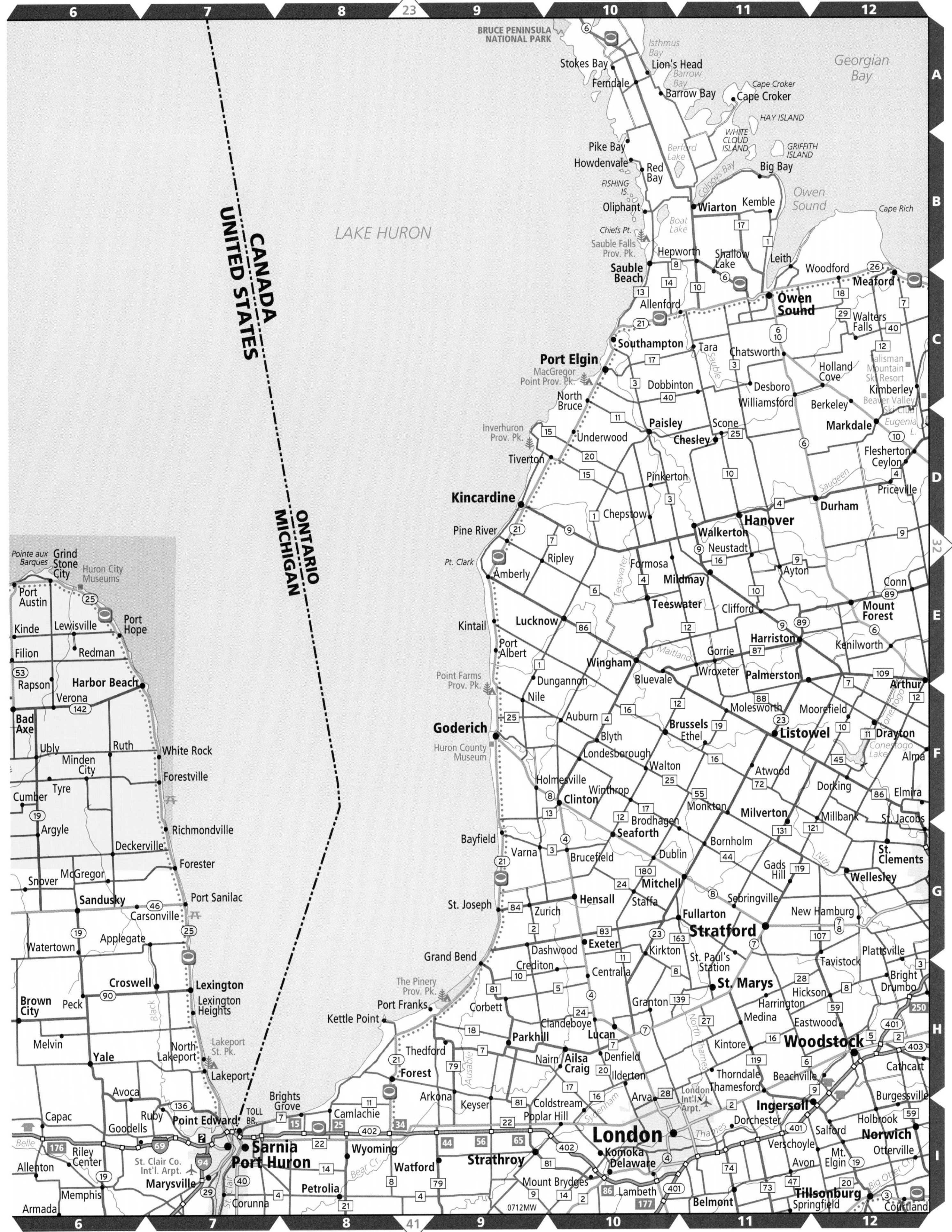

For a complete listing of symbols, see inside back cover; for an index of cities, see page 200.

DISTANCE SCALE

One inch represents 16 miles

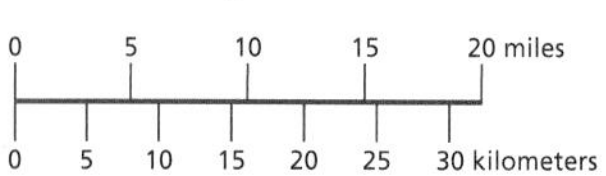

LOCATOR MAP

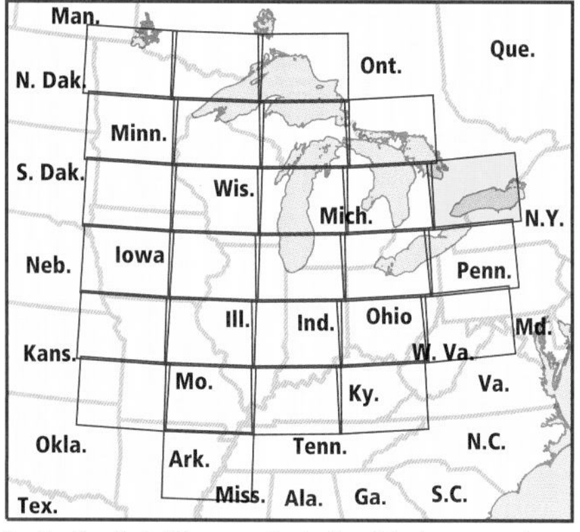

See the Pagefinder™ map on the inside of the front cover for map page numbers.

I wonder why some roads are blue, some green, some red, and some gray.

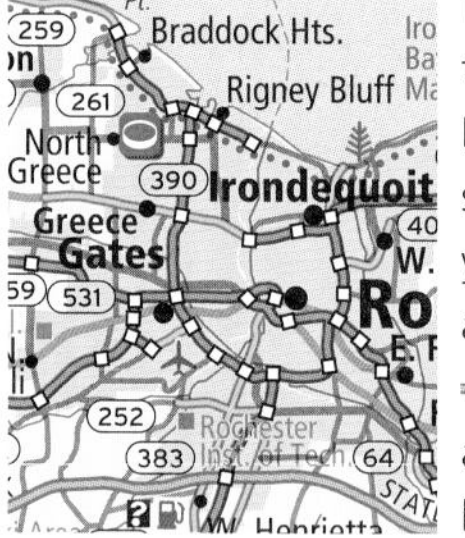

The colors refer to the class of road. If you want to get somewhere quickly, you should drive on a blue ═ or green ═ road. These are "limited-access" highways, meaning the only way on or off is by ramps, which are shown by this symbol. No pesky stoplights there. The green roads are toll roads, which means you will have to pay to get onto or while driving these roads. The toll payment areas are indicated on the map as well.

The yellow roads ═ are multi-lane, but are not limited access. Red roads — are important through-ways, but do not have multiple lanes.

If you want a more leisurely drive, however, choose a gray road. The thicker gray roads — are more heavily used than the thin —.

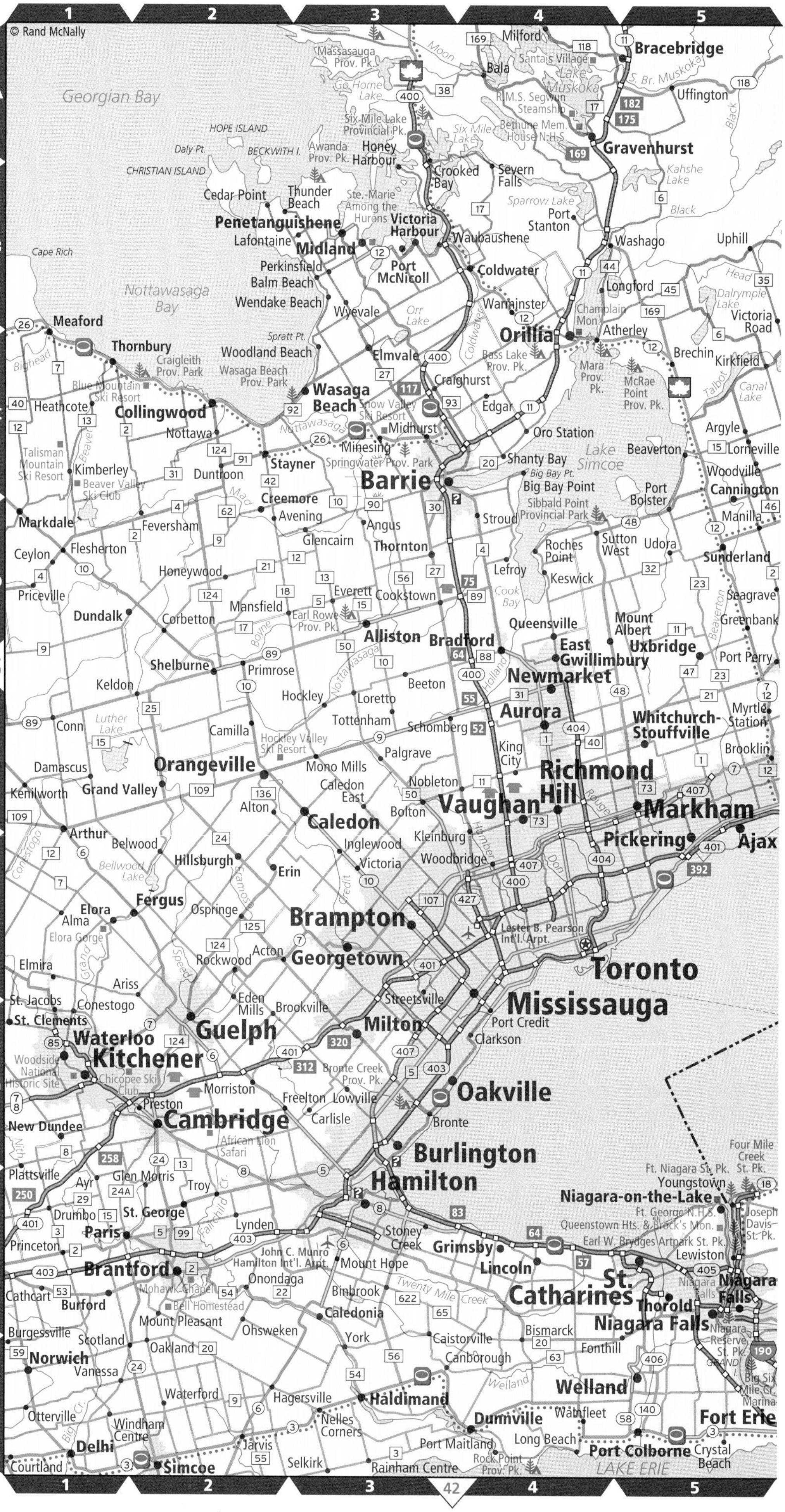

When you see this sign 14, the map continues on the page number indicated.

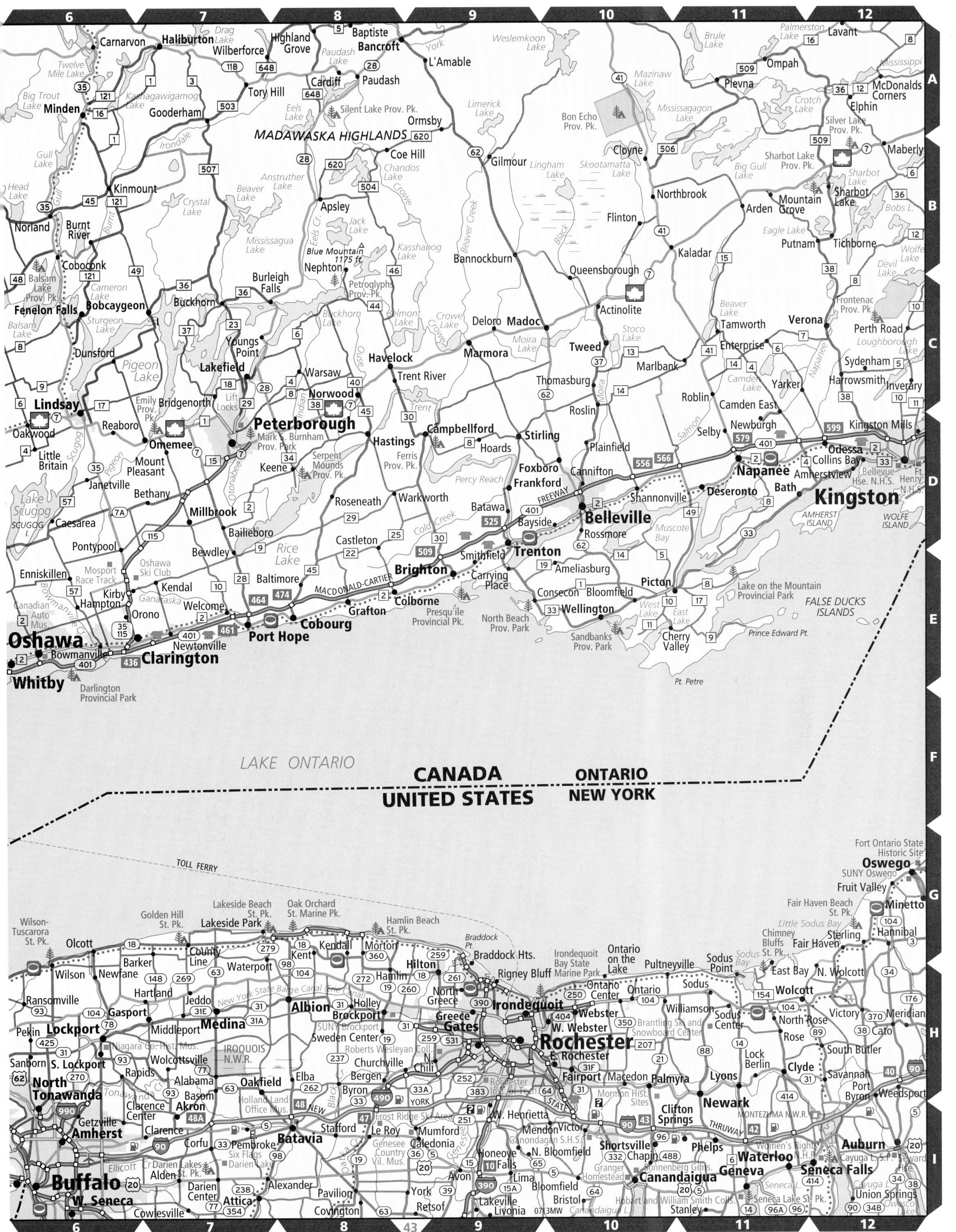

For a complete listing of symbols, see inside back cover; for an index of cities, see page 200.

DISTANCE SCALE

One inch represents 16 miles

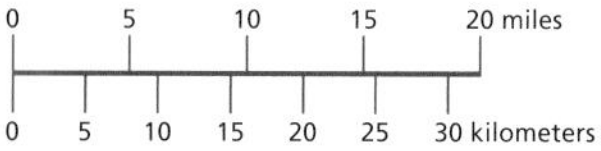

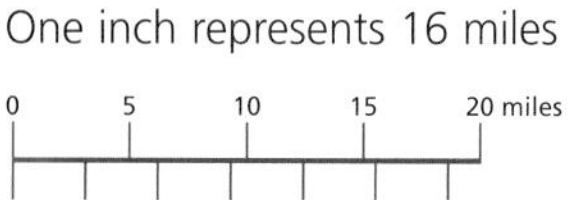

LOCATOR MAP

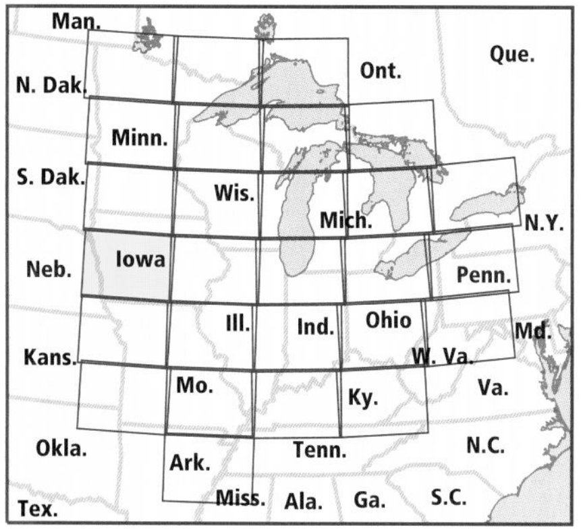

See the Pagefinder™ map on the inside of the front cover for map page numbers.

These square symbols don't look like highway shields (part 2).

These maps show five different square symbols: Each represents a specially designated historic or scenic route.

Spanning the United States from New York to San Francisco, the **Lincoln Highway** was the country's first paved transcontinental highway.

Follow the route of the Corps of Discovery on the **Lewis and Clark Trail Highway**.

Read more about the others on pp. 28 and 46.

What are those yellow boxes (with little numbers) on the maps?

PAGE 52 That's where fun stuff happens, and this book describes that area in detail starting on the page number you see. Read all about what there is to see and do, what the shopping scene's like, where you can stay overnight, what the best food to try is and where you can find it, and even if there's a festival happening during your visit. These destination sections also offer specially designed maps to help figure out where attractions and restaurants are in relation to each other (and how to drive between them).

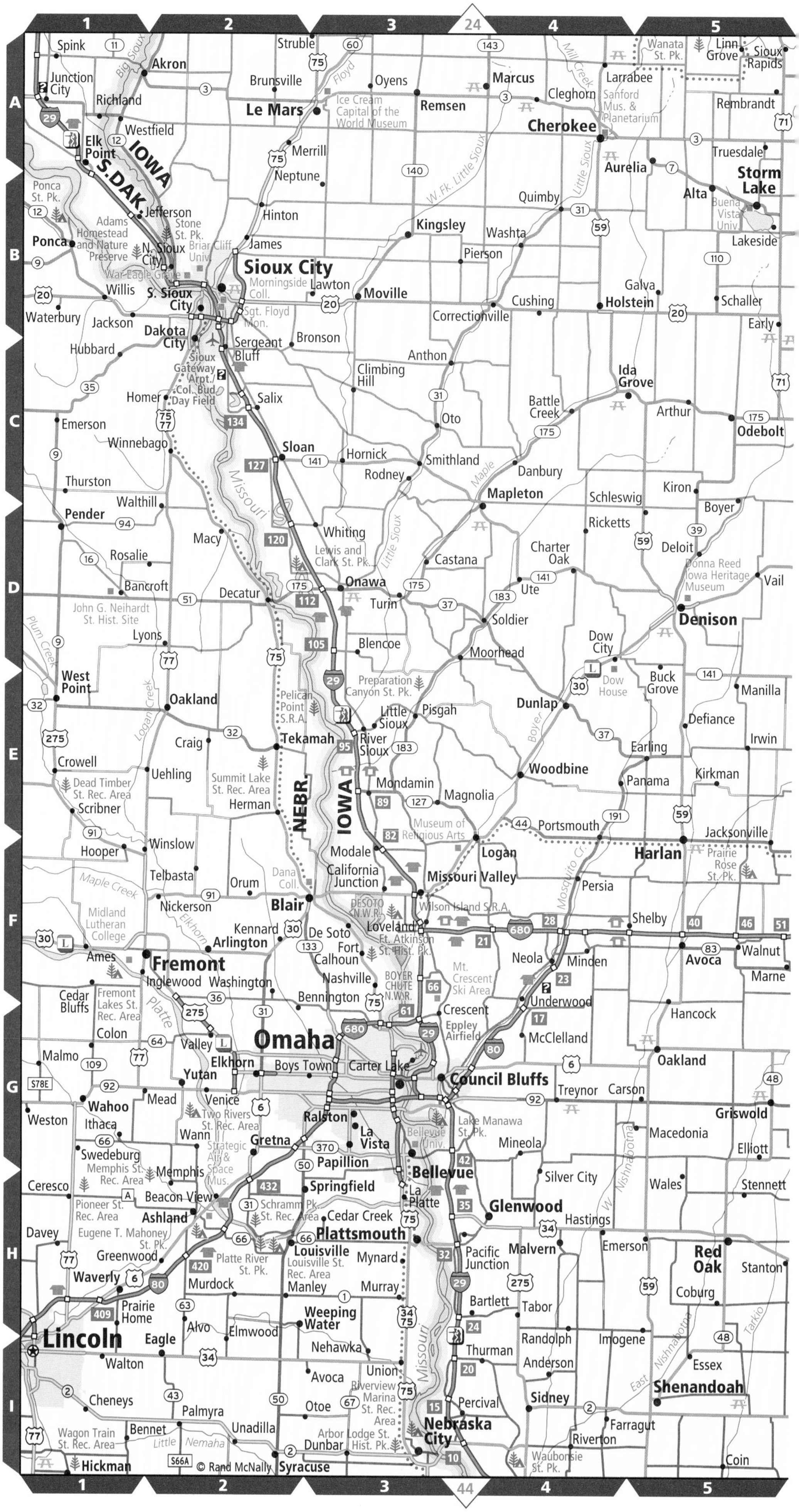

When you see this sign 14, the map continues on the page number indicated.

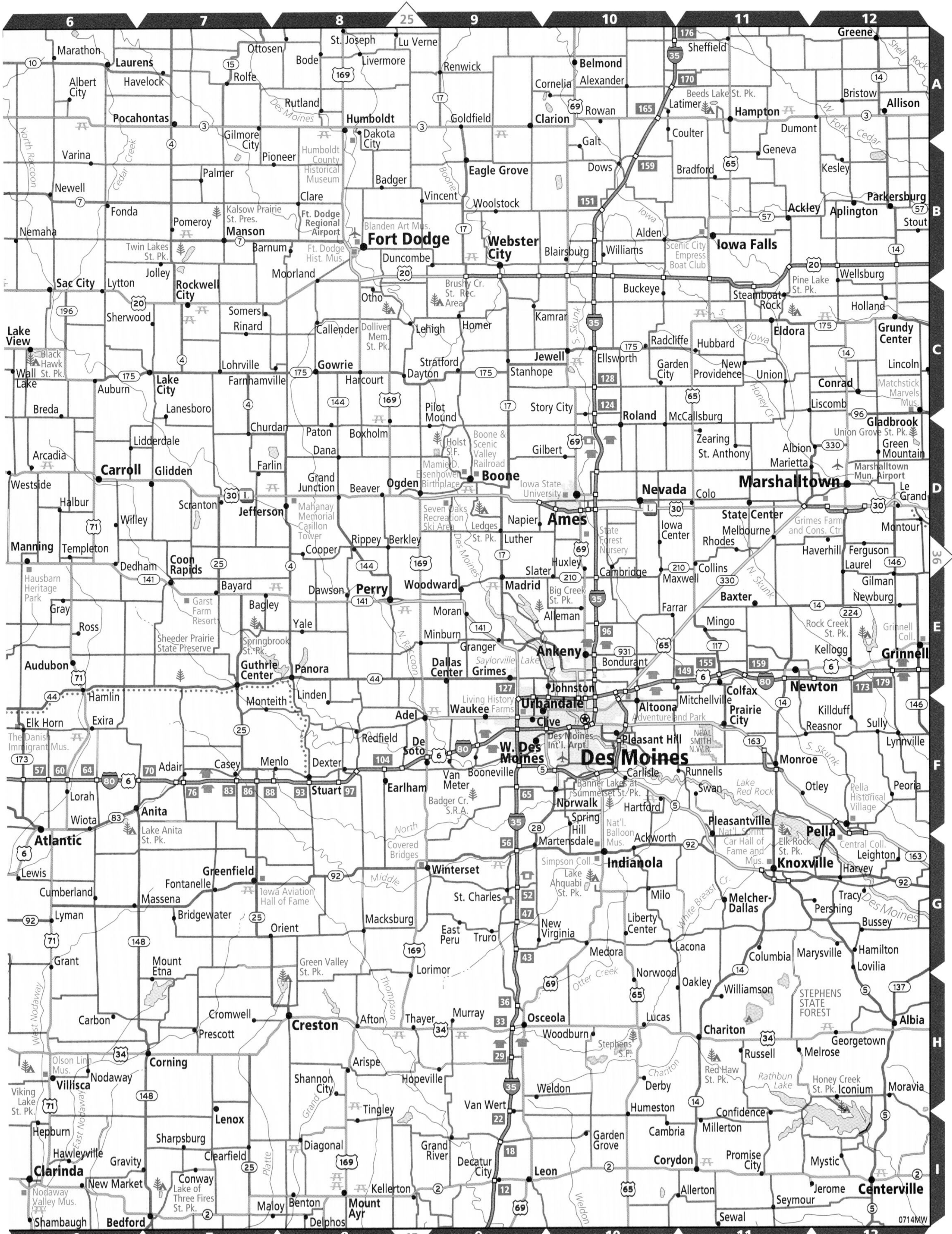

For a complete listing of symbols, see inside back cover; for an index of cities, see page 200.

DISTANCE SCALE

One inch represents 16 miles

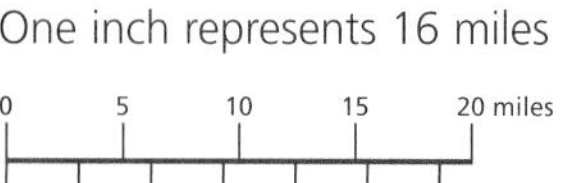

LOCATOR MAP

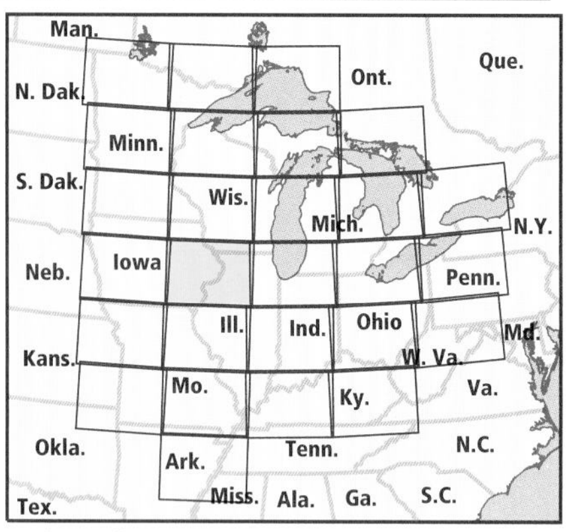

See the Pagefinder™ map on the inside of the front cover for map page numbers.

Are there any roads on the map I should watch out for?

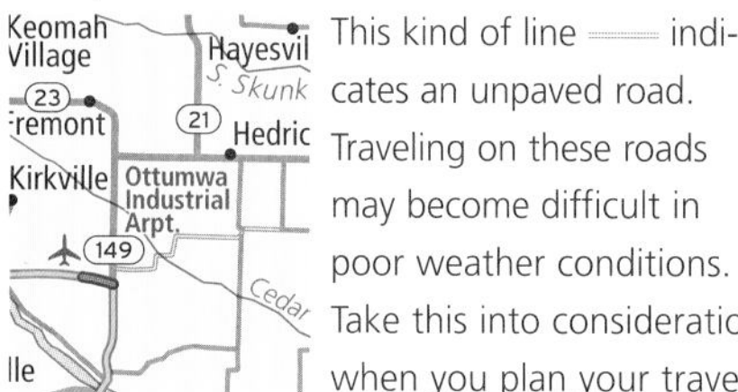

This kind of line ══ indicates an unpaved road. Traveling on these roads may become difficult in poor weather conditions. Take this into consideration when you plan your travel.

What are those yellow boxes (with little numbers) on the maps?

That's where fun stuff happens, PAGE 52 and this book describes that area in detail starting on the page number you see. Read all about what there is to see and do, what the shopping scene's like, where you can stay overnight, what the best food to try is and where you can find it, and even if there's a festival happening during your visit. These destination sections also offer specially designed maps to help figure out where attractions and restaurants are in relation to each other (and how to drive between them).

Why is there a red ribbon on this map?

The red award ribbon marks a Rand McNally Best of the Road™ trip route. Our editors have chosen scenic drives peppered with tasty dining, unique shopping, and memory-making things to do. Read more about four of these drives on pages 180-191. For more trip routes, visit go.randmcnally.com/BR.

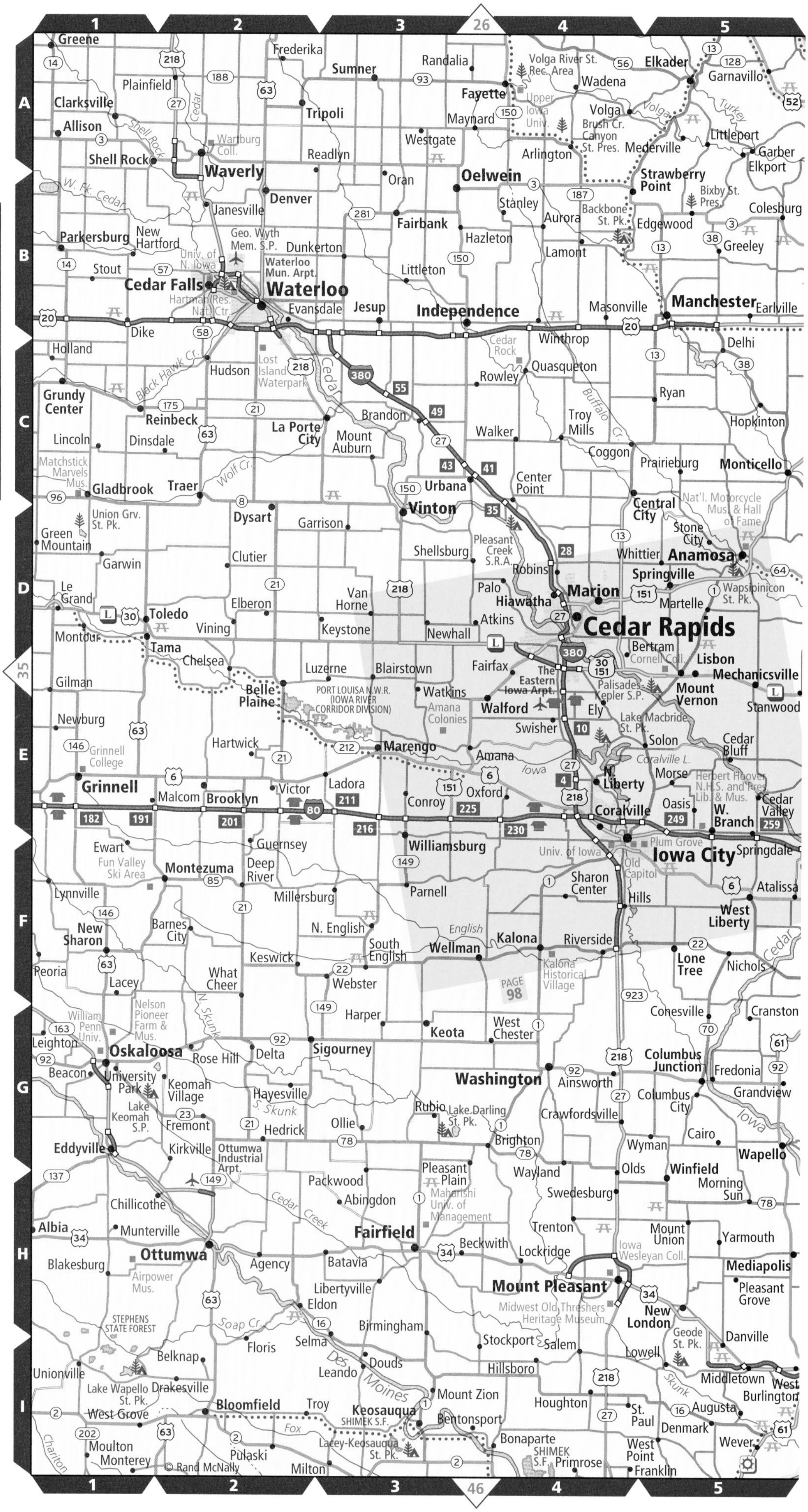

When you see this sign 14, the map continues on the page number indicated.

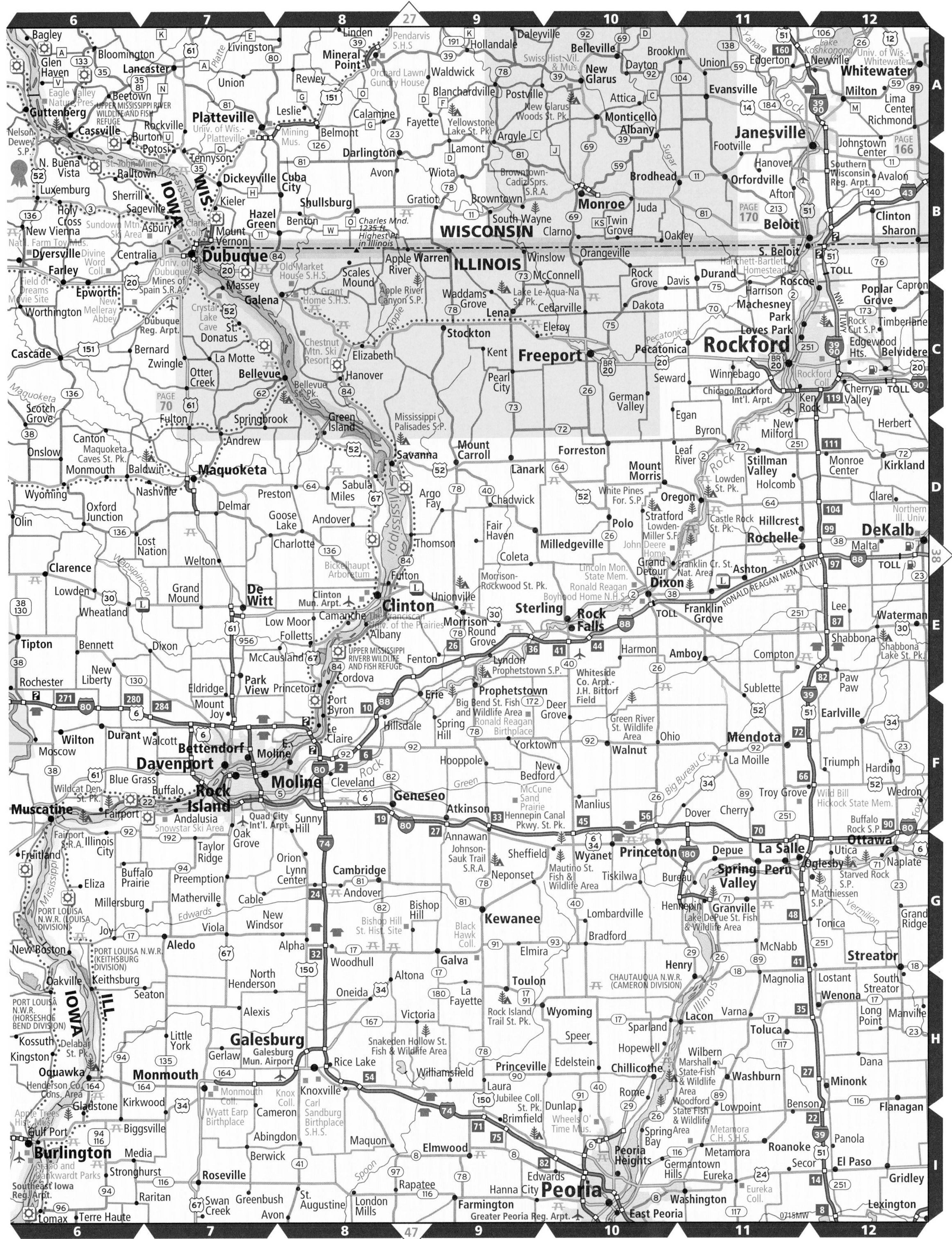

For a complete listing of symbols, see inside back cover; for an index of cities, see page 200.

DISTANCE SCALE

One inch represents 16 miles

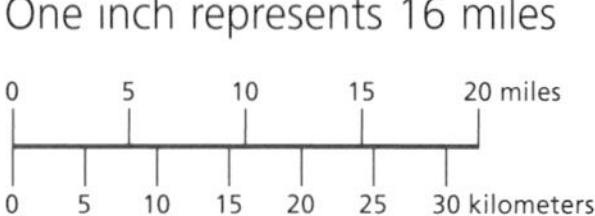

LOCATOR MAP

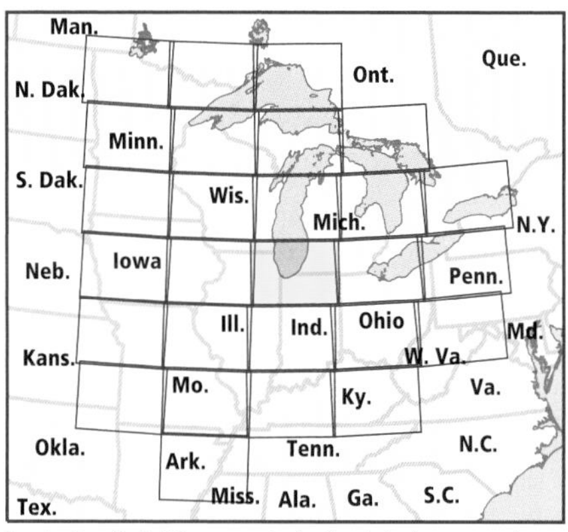

See the Pagefinder™ map on the inside of the front cover for map page numbers.

Making sense of the interstate highway numbering system (part 1).

The one- and two-digit signs indicate the main interstate routes. Even numbers are on routes that run west-east. The lowest even numbers are in the southern part of the U.S.; the higher the number, the farther north the route. The major east-west cross-country routes end in a zero. Odd numbers are on north-south routes. The lowest odd-numbered routes are in the western part of the U.S.; the higher the number, the farther east the route. The major north-south cross-country routes end in a five.

What are those yellow boxes (with little numbers) on the maps?

That's where fun stuff happens, and this book describes that area in detail starting on the page number you see. Read all about what there is to see and do, what the shopping scene's like, where you can stay overnight, what the best food to try is and where you can find it, and even if there's a festival happening during your visit. These destination sections also offer specially designed maps to help figure out where attractions and restaurants are in relation to each other (and how to drive between them).

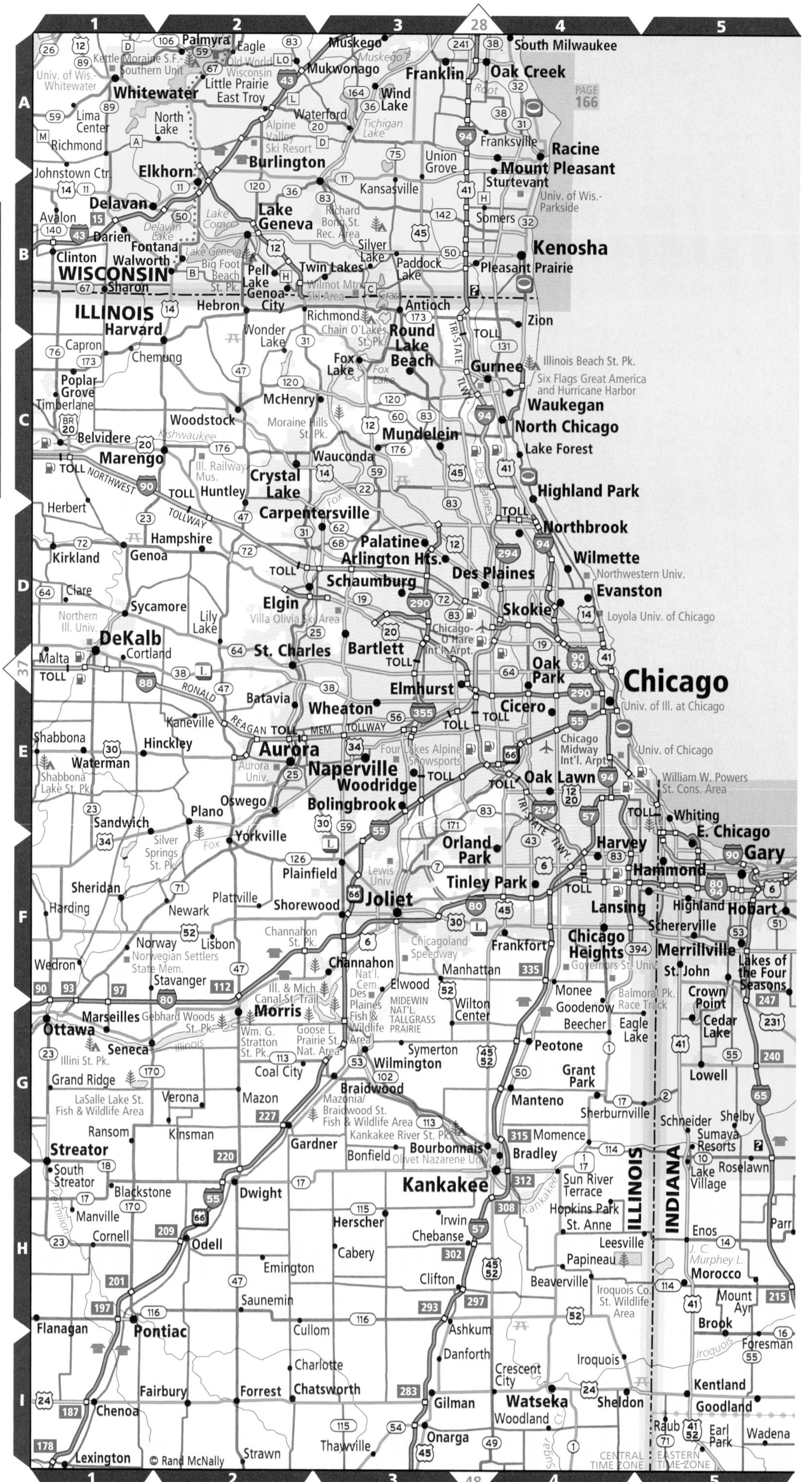

When you see this sign 14, the map continues on the page number indicated.

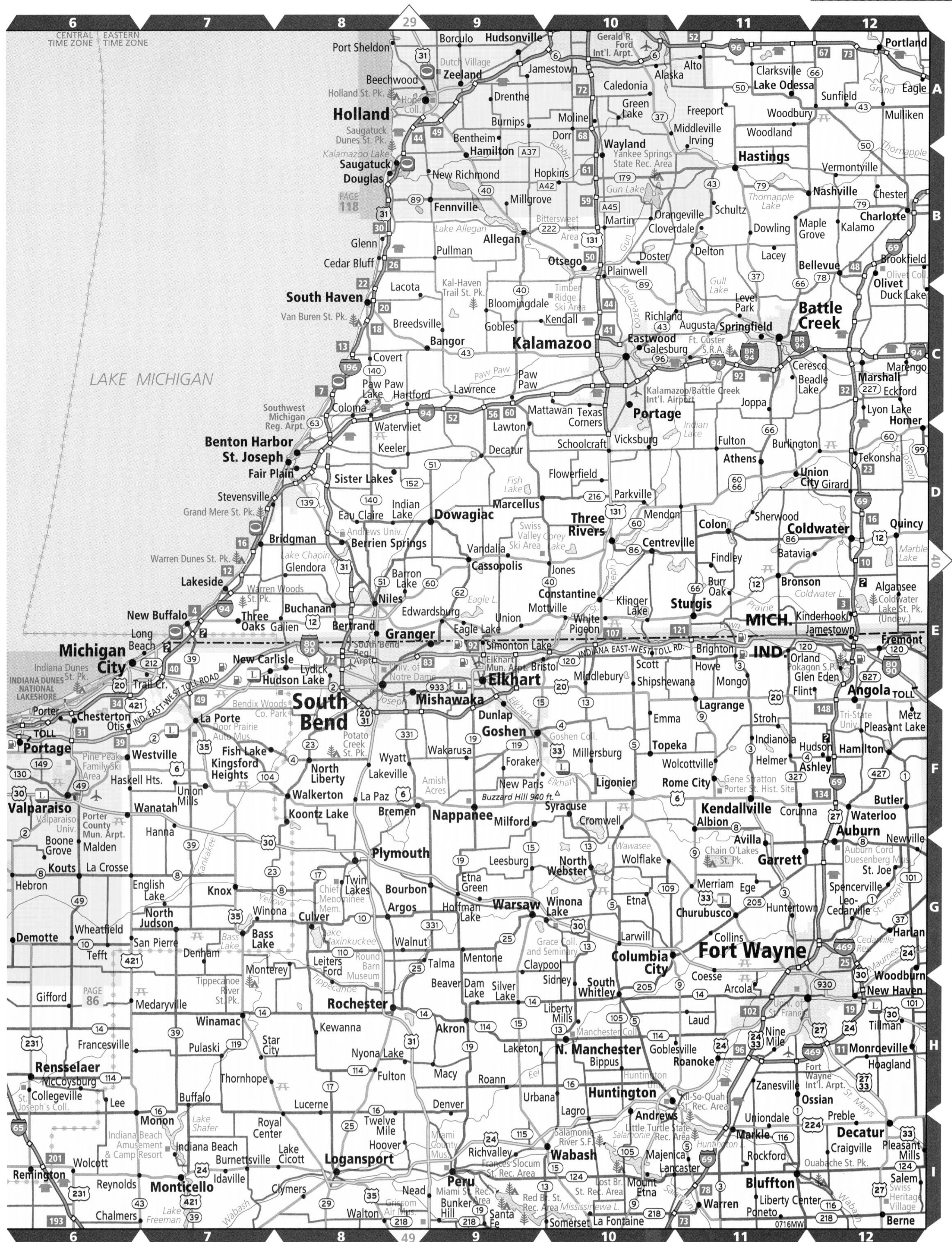

For a complete listing of symbols, see inside back cover; for an index of cities, see page 200.

DISTANCE SCALE

One inch represents 16 miles

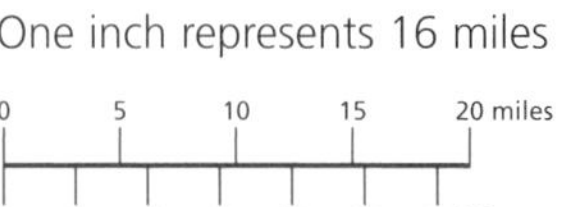

LOCATOR MAP

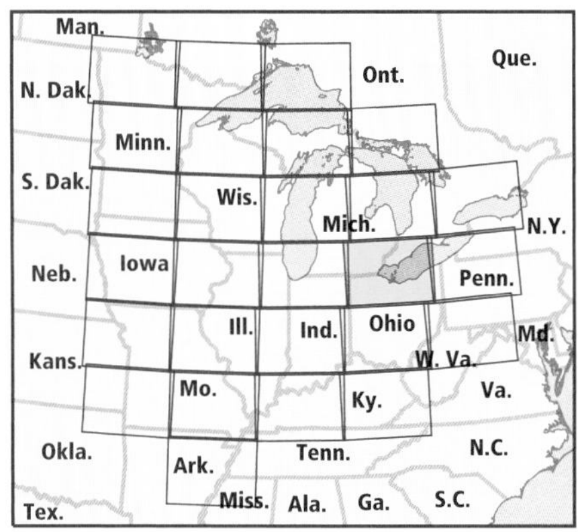

See the Pagefinder™ map on the inside of the front cover for map page numbers.

Making sense of the interstate highway numbering system (part 2).

Three-digit signs indicate spur or bypass routes, replacing the abbreviations "SPUR" and "BYP" in the signs. An even first digit 290 indicates a bypass route around a city or its downtown area. These routes eventually reconnect with the main interstate route to provide a quick way around congested urban areas. An odd first digit 595 indicates a spur into a city that does not reconnect to the main route. Three-digit interstate routes are always associated with a one- or two-digit interstate route. In the example on the left, I-475 is a bypass around Toledo that reconnects to I-75.

What are those yellow boxes (with little numbers) on the maps?

PAGE 52 That's where fun stuff happens, and this book describes that area in detail starting on the page number you see. Read all about what there is to see and do, what the shopping scene's like, where you can stay overnight, what the best food to try is and where you can find it, and even if there's a festival happening during your visit. These destination sections also offer specially designed maps to help figure out where attractions and restaurants are in relation to each other (and how to drive between them).

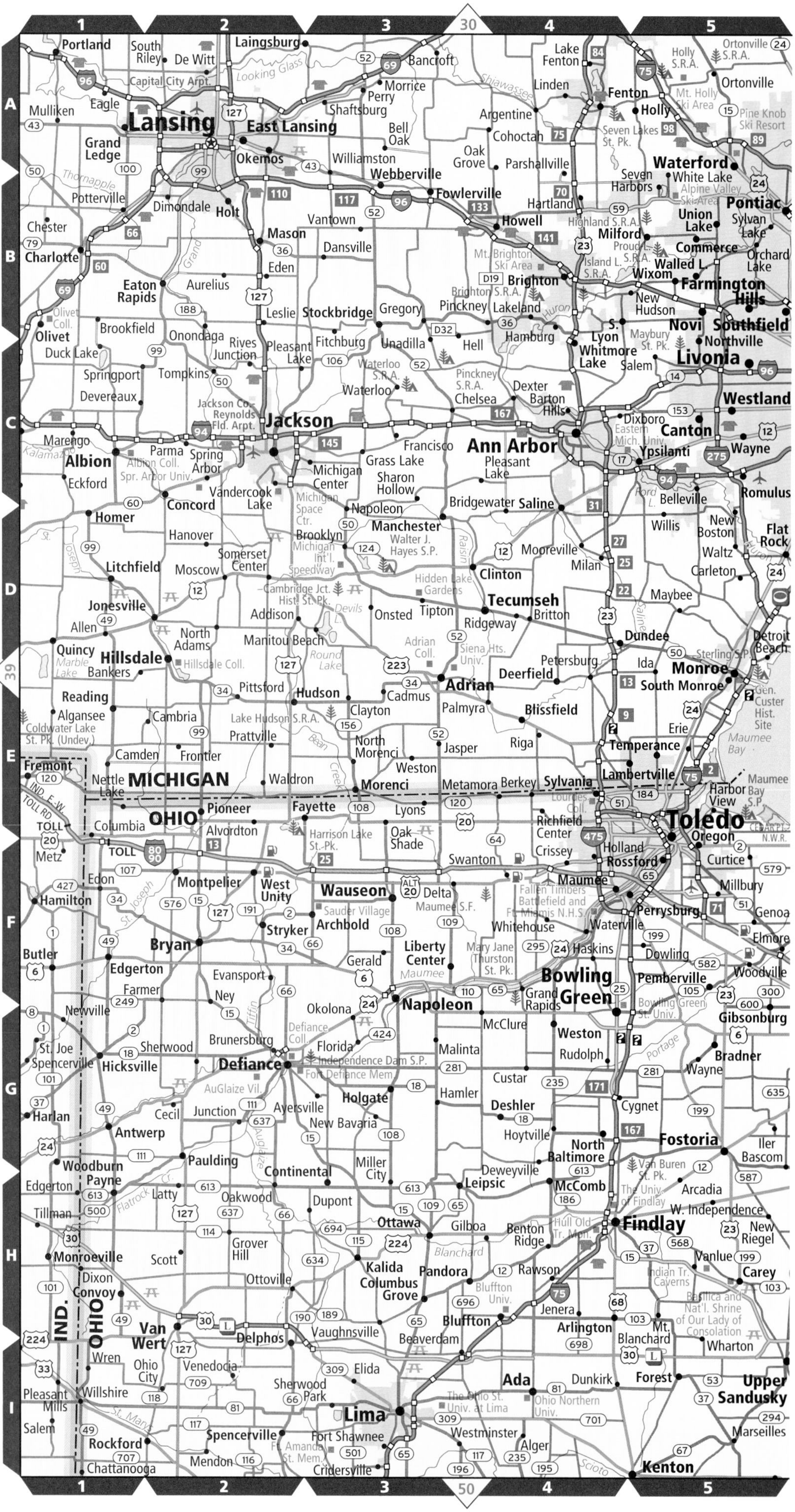

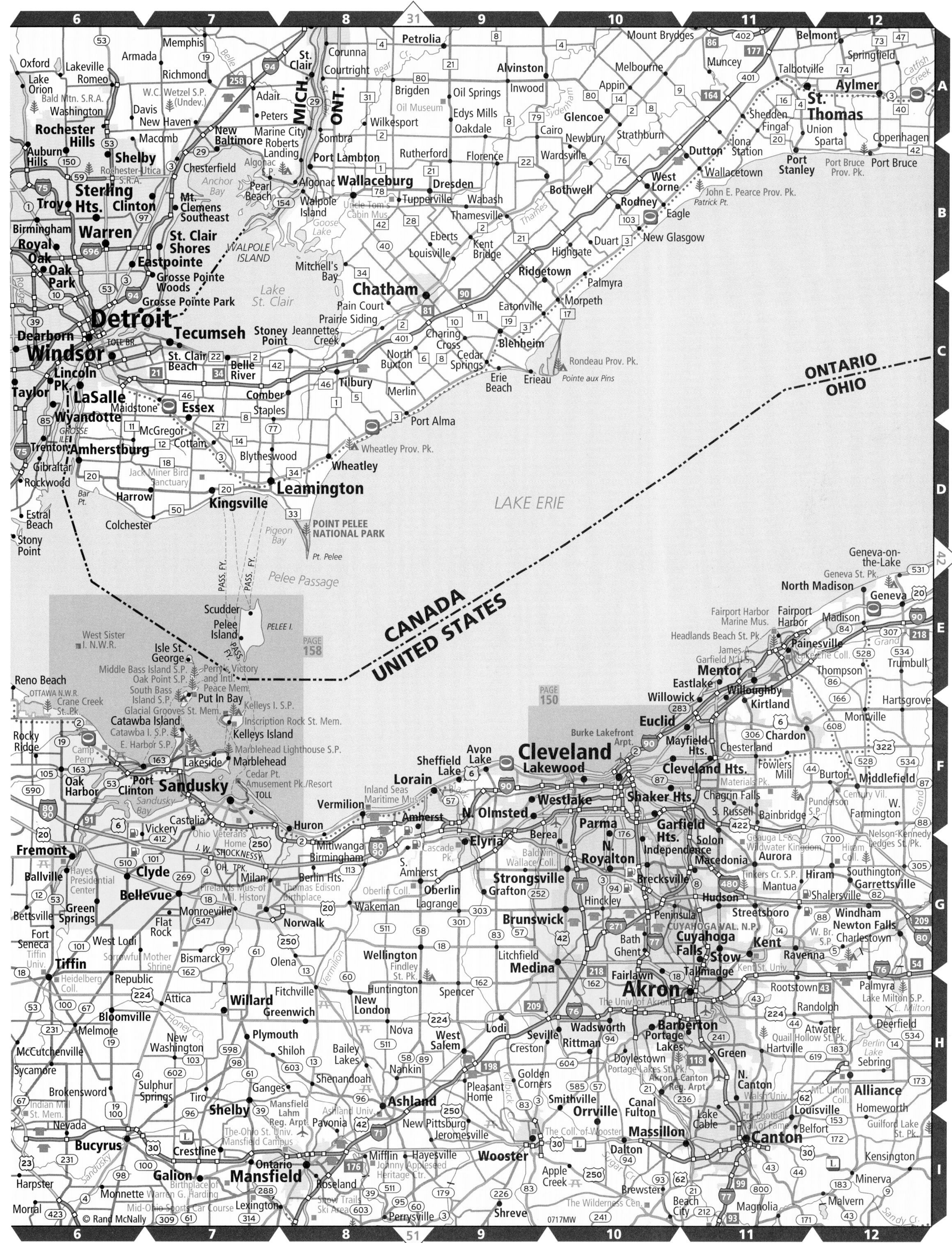
6
7
8
31
9
10
11
12
A
B
C
D
E
F
G
H
I
42
51
Memphis
Armada
Oxford
Lakeville
Romeo
Lake Orion
Bald Mtn. S.R.A.
Washington
Richmond
W.C. Wetzel S.P. (Undev.)
Davis
New Haven
Rochester Hills
Macomb
Auburn Hills
Shelby
Rochester-Utica S.R.A.
Chesterfield
New Baltimore
Sterling Hts.
Troy
Clinton
Mt. Clemens
Southeast
Birmingham
Warren
St. Clair Shores
Royal Oak
Eastpointe
Oak Park
Grosse Pointe Woods
Grosse Pointe Park
Detroit
Dearborn
Windsor
Tecumseh
Lincoln Pk.
Taylor
LaSalle
Wyandotte
Grosse Ile
Trenton
Amherstburg
Gibraltar
Rockwood
Estral Beach
Stony Point
Bar Pt.
Harrow
Colchester
Jack Miner Bird Sanctuary
Kingsville
Leamington
Maidstone
Essex
McGregor
Cottam
Blytheswood
Comber
Staples
St. Clair Beach
Belle River
Stoney Point
Jeannettes Creek
Lake St. Clair
Walpole Island
Mitchell's Bay
Anchor Bay
Pearl Beach
Algonac
Algonac S.P.
Marine City
Roberts Landing
St. Clair
Corunna
Courtright
Sombra
Port Lambton
Wallaceburg
Adair
Peters
MICH.
ONT.
Petrolia
Brigden
Oil Museum
Oil Springs
Edys Mills
Oakdale
Wilkesport
Rutherford
Florence
Dresden
Tupperville
Uncle Tom's Cabin Mus.
Goose Lake
Wabash
Thamesville
Eberts
Louisville
Kent Bridge
Chatham
Pain Court
Prairie Siding
Charing Cross
North Buxton
Cedar Springs
Tilbury
Merlin
Erie Beach
Erieau
Port Alma
Wheatley
Wheatley Prov. Pk.
Blenheim
Eatonville
Morpeth
Palmyra
Ridgetown
Highgate
Duart
Rondeau Prov. Pk.
Pointe aux Pins
Alvinston
Inwood
Glencoe
Newbury
Cairo
Wardsville
Bothwell
Thames
Mount Brydges
Melbourne
Appin
Strathburn
Muncey
Dutton
Iona Station
Wallacetown
West Lorne
Rodney
Eagle
New Glasgow
John E. Pearce Prov. Pk.
Patrick Pt.
Belmont
Springfield
Talbotville
Aylmer
St. Thomas
Shedden
Fingal
Union
Sparta
Copenhagen
Port Stanley
Port Bruce Prov. Pk.
Port Bruce
ONTARIO
OHIO
LAKE ERIE
POINT PELEE NATIONAL PARK
Pigeon Bay
Pt. Pelee
Pelee Passage
PASS. FY.
Scudder
Pelee Island
PELEE I.
CANADA
UNITED STATES
PAGE 158
West Sister I. N.W.R.
Isle St. George
Middle Bass Island S.P.
Oak Point S.P.
Perry's Victory and Int'l Peace Mem.
South Bass Island S.P.
Put In Bay
Glacial Grooves St. Mem.
Kelleys I. S.P.
Inscription Rock St. Mem.
Kelleys Island
Catawba Island
Catawba I. S.P.
E. Harbor S.P.
Marblehead Lighthouse S.P.
Lakeside
Marblehead
Cedar Pt. Amusement Pk./Resort
Reno Beach
Ottawa N.W.R.
Crane Creek St. Pk.
Rocky Ridge
Camp Perry
Oak Harbor
Port Clinton
Sandusky
Sandusky Bay
Castalia
Vickery
Ohio Veterans Home
J.W. Shocknessy Oh. Tpk.
Fremont
Ballville
Hayes Presidential Center
Clyde
Bellevue
Milan
Firelands Mus. of Mil. History
Berlin Hts.
Thomas Edison Birthplace
Huron
Mitiwanga
Birmingham
Vermilion
Inland Seas Maritime Mus.
Lorain
Sheffield Lake
Avon Lake
Amherst
S. Amherst
Oberlin
Oberlin Coll.
Elyria
Cascade Pk.
N. Olmsted
Westlake
Cleveland
Lakewood
Burke Lakefront Arpt.
PAGE 150
Euclid
Willowick
Eastlake
Mentor
Willoughby
Kirtland
Painesville
Lake Erie Coll.
Fairport Harbor
Fairport Harbor Marine Mus.
Headlands Beach St. Pk.
James A. Garfield N.H.S.
Madison
North Madison
Geneva
Geneva St. Pk.
Geneva-on-the-Lake
Thompson
Trumbull
Hartsgrove
Montville
Chardon
Chesterland
Mayfield Hts.
Cleveland Hts.
Shaker Hts.
Materials Pk.
Chagrin Falls
S. Russell
Bainbridge
Fowlers Mill
Burton
Middlefield
Century Vil.
Punderson S.P.
W. Farmington
Nelson-Kennedy Ledges St. Pk.
Geauga L. & Wildwater Kingdom
Hiram Coll.
Parma
Berea
Baldwin-Wallace Coll.
N. Royalton
Garfield Hts.
Solon
Independence
Macedonia
Aurora
Strongsville
Grafton
Brecksville
Tinkers Cr. S.P.
Hiram
Southington
Garrettsville
Mantua
Shalersville
Hudson
Hinckley
Peninsula
Cuyahoga Val. N.P.
Streetsboro
Windham
Newton Falls
Charleston
W. Br. S.P.
Ravenna
Kent
Stow
Cuyahoga Falls
Bath
Ghent
Brunswick
Litchfield
Medina
Fairlawn
Akron
The Univ. of Akron
Tallmadge
Kent St. Univ.
Rootstown
Palmyra
Lake Milton S.P.
L. Milton
Randolph
Atwater
Deerfield
Quail Hollow St. Pk.
Hartville
Berlin Lake
Sebring
Alliance
Mt. Union Coll.
Homeworth
Guilford Lake St. Pk.
Louisville
Belfort
Kensington
Minerva
Malvern
Sandy Cr.
Canton
N. Canton
Walsh Univ.
Pro Football Hall of Fame
Lake Cable
Green
Barberton
Portage Lakes
Doylestown
Portage Lakes St. Pk.
Akron-Canton Reg. Arpt.
Wadsworth
Rittman
Seville
Creston
Lodi
Golden Corners
Smithville
Orrville
Canal Fulton
Massillon
Dalton
Brewster
Beach City
Magnolia
The Wilderness Cen.
Wooster
The Coll. of Wooster
Apple Creek
Shreve
Sugar Cr.
Killbuck Cr.
Wakeman
Lagrange
Norwalk
Monroeville
Flat Rock
Green Springs
Bettsville
Fort Seneca
Tiffin
Tiffin Univ.
Heidelberg Coll.
West Lodi
Sorrowful Mother Shrine
Bismarck
Olena
Republic
Attica
Willard
Greenwich
Fitchville
Wellington
Findley St. Pk.
Huntington
New London
Spencer
Vermilion
Bloomville
Melmore
Honey Cr.
New Washington
Plymouth
Shiloh
Nova
West Salem
Bailey Lakes
Nankin
Shenandoah
Ganges
McCutchenville
Sycamore
Brokensword
Sulphur Springs
Tiro
Shelby
Mansfield Lahm Reg. Arpt.
Ashland Univ.
Ashland
Pavonia
New Pittsburg
Jeromesville
Pleasant Home
Indian Mill St. Mem.
Nevada
Bucyrus
Crestline
The Ohio St. Univ. Mansfield Campus
Ontario
Mansfield
Mifflin
Hayesville
Johnny Appleseed Heritage Ctr.
Galion
Birthplace of Warren G. Harding
Monnette
Harpster
Morral
Mid-Ohio Sports Car Course
Lexington
Roseland
Snow Trails Ski Area
Perrysville
Sandusky
© Rand McNally
0717MW

For a complete listing of symbols, see inside back cover; for an index of cities, see page 200.

DISTANCE SCALE

One inch represents 16 miles

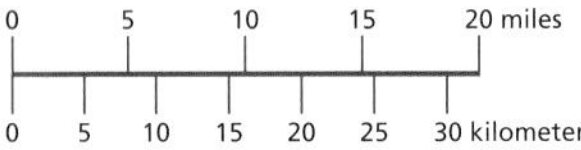

LOCATOR MAP

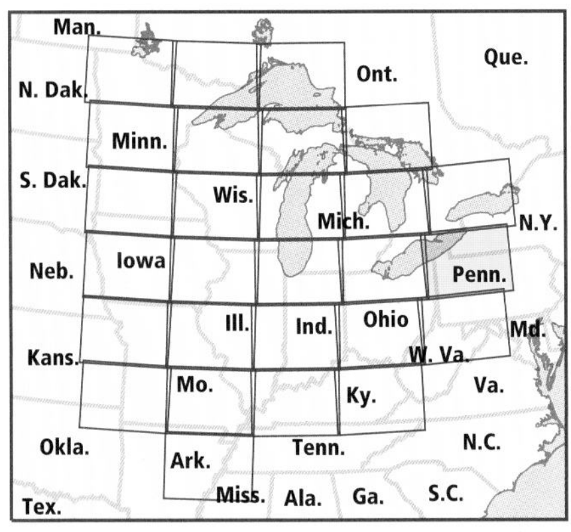

See the Pagefinder™ map on the inside of the front cover for map page numbers.

Why are some roads shown as dotted lines?

Dotted lines, or, indicate a major road that is being built. This route tends to be near completion, but is not yet ready for use when the map is published. Don't confuse these routes with tunnels, which have the entrances marked.

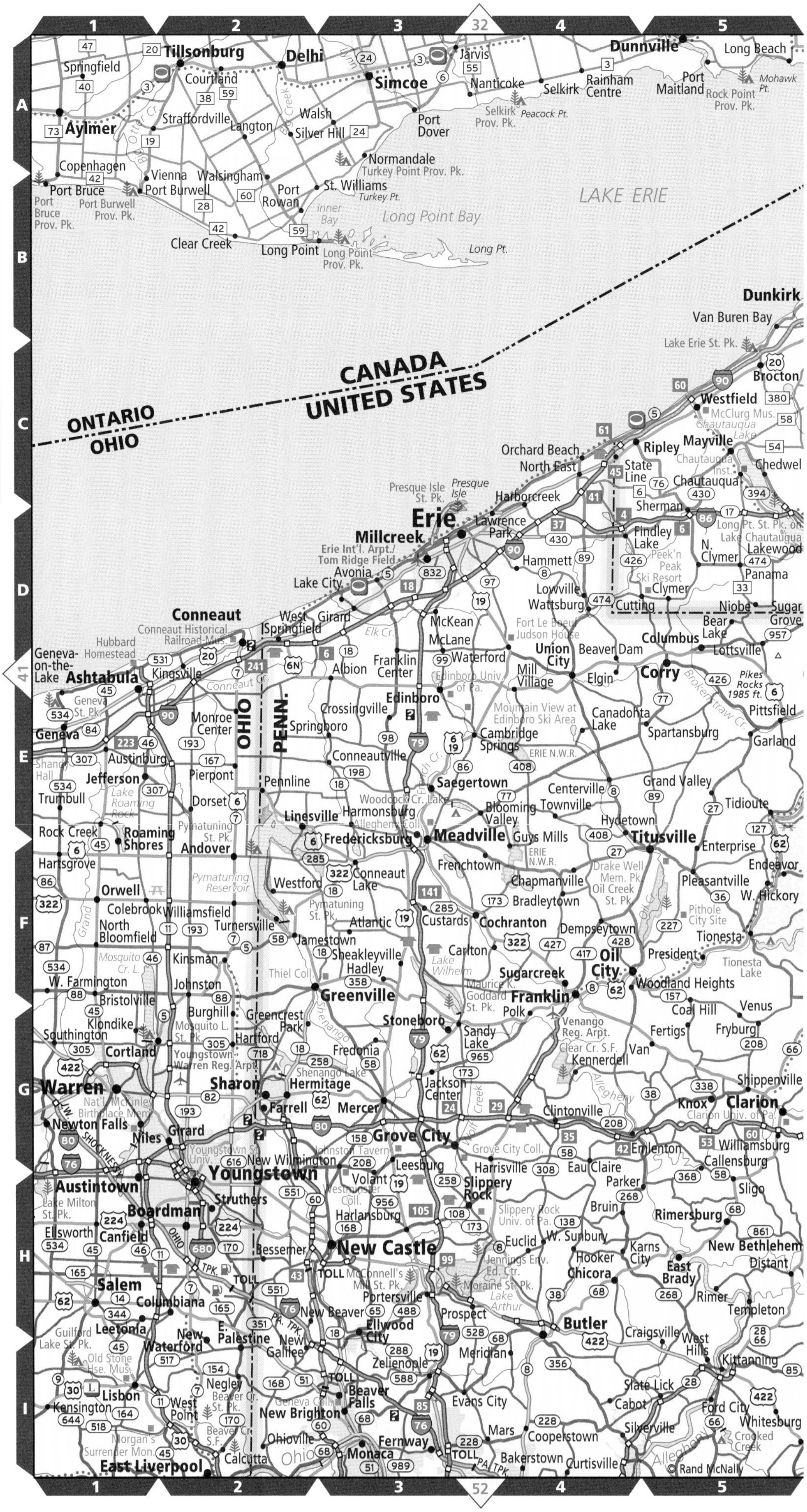

CANADA
UNITED STATES
ONTARIO
OHIO
LAKE ERIE
PENN.

© Rand McNally

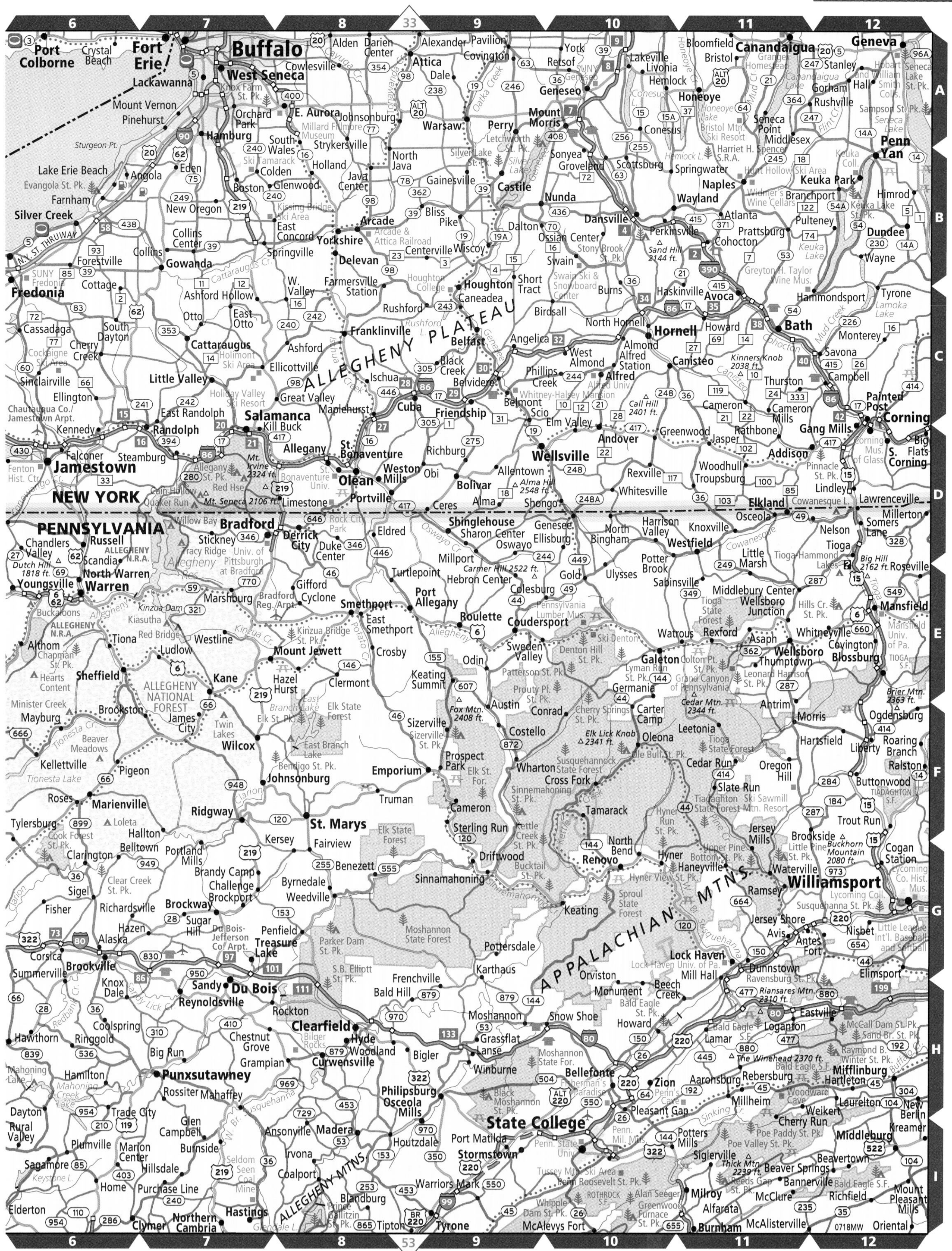
6
7
8
33
9
10
11
12
A
B
C
D
E
F
G
H
I
Port Colborne
Crystal Beach
Fort Erie
Buffalo
West Seneca
Lackawanna
Cowlesville
Alden
Darien Center
Alexander
Pavilion
Covington
Attica
Dale
York
Retsof
Geneseo
Lakeville
Livonia
Hemlock
Honeoye
Bloomfield
Bristol
Canandaigua
Geneva
Stanley
Gorham
Rushville
Hall
Mount Vernon
Pinehurst
Orchard Park
E. Aurora
Johnsonburg
Warsaw
Perry
Mount Morris
Conesus
Seneca Point
Middlesex
Penn Yan
Sturgeon Pt.
Hamburg
South Wales
Strykersville
North Java
Silver Lake
Letchworth St. Pk.
Sonyea
Groveland
Scottsburg
Springwater
Naples
Keuka Park
Lake Erie Beach
Angola
Eden
Colden
Holland
Java Center
Gainesville
Castile
Nunda
Dansville
Wayland
Atlanta
Branchport
Himrod
Evangola St. Pk.
Farnham
Boston
Glenwood
Silver Creek
New Oregon
Bliss
Pike
Arcade
Dalton
Ossian Center
Perkinsville
Cohocton
Prattsburg
Pulteney
Dundee
Wayne
Collins Center
East Concord
Yorkshire
Delevan
Centerville
Wiscoy
Swain
Sand Hill 2144 ft.
N.Y. ST. THRUWAY
Forestville
Collins
Gowanda
Springville
Fredonia
Cottage
Ashford Hollow
W. Valley
Farmersville Station
Houghton
Caneadea
Short Tract
Burns
Haskinville
Avoca
Hammondsport
Tyrone
Otto
East Otto
Rushford
Birdsall
North Hornell
Hornell
Howard
Bath
Cassadaga
South Dayton
Cherry Creek
Cattaraugus
Ashford
Franklinville
ALLEGHENY PLATEAU
Belfast
Angelica
West Almond
Alfred Station
Alfred
Almond
Canisteo
Kinners Knob 2038 ft.
Savona
Monterey
Sinclairville
Ellington
Little Valley
Ellicottville
Ischua
Black Creek
Belvidere
Phillips Creek
Thurston
Campbell
Chautauqua Co./Jamestown Arpt.
East Randolph
Great Valley
Maplehurst
Cuba
Friendship
Belmont
Scio
Call Hill 2401 ft.
Cameron
Cameron Mills
Painted Post
Corning
Kennedy
Randolph
Salamanca
Kill Buck
Elm Valley
Andover
Greenwood
Jasper
Rathbone
Gang Mills
Falconer
Steamburg
Allegany
St. Bonaventure
Richburg
Wellsville
Addison
S. Corning
Big Flats
Jamestown
Mt. Irvine 2324 ft.
Olean
Weston Mills
Obi
Bolivar
Allentown
Alma Hill 2548 ft.
Rexville
Whitesville
Woodhull
Troupsburg
Lindley
Pinnacle St. Pk.
NEW YORK
Mt. Seneca 2106 ft.
Limestone
Portville
Ceres
Alma
Shongo
Elkland
Cowanesque L.
Lawrenceville
PENNSYLVANIA
Willow Bay
Bradford
Derrick City
Rock City Park
Eldred
Shinglehouse
Sharon Center
Oswayo
Genesee
Ellisburg
North Bingham
Harrison Valley
Knoxville
Westfield
Osceola
Millerton
Somers Lane
Nelson
Tioga
Chandlers Valley
Russell
Stickney
Tracy Ridge
Duke Center
Allegheny N.R.A.
Scandia
North Warren
Univ. of Pittsburgh at Bradford
Dutch Hill 1818 ft.
Youngsville
Warren
Turtlepoint
Millport
Carmer Hill 2522 ft.
Hebron Center
Gold
Ulysses
Potter Brook
Sabinsville
Little Marsh
Tioga-Hammond Lakes
Big Hill 2162 ft.
Roseville
Gifford
Cyclone
Marshburg
Port Allegany
Coudersport
Colesburg
Middlebury Center
Wellsboro Junction
Mansfield
Kinzua Dam
Kiasutha
Smethport
East Smethport
Roulette
Pennsylvania Lumber Mus.
Ski Denton
Hills Cr. St. Pk.
Buckaloons
Tiona
Red Bridge
Westline
Kinzua Bridge St. Pk.
Watrous
Rexford
Whitneyville
Covington
Blossburg
Althom
Chapman St. Pk.
Ludlow
Mount Jewett
Crosby
Odin
Sweden Valley
Denton Hill St. Pk.
Galeton
Asaph
Wellsboro
Thumptown
Sheffield
Hearts Content
ALLEGHENY NATIONAL FOREST
Kane
Hazel Hurst
Clermont
Keating Summit
Patterson St. Pk.
Lyman Run St. Pk.
Germania
Leonard Harrison St. Pk.
Antrim
Brier Mtn. 2363 ft.
Minister Creek
Mayburg
Brookston
James City
East Branch Lake
Elk State Forest
Elk St. Pk.
Fox Mtn. 2408 ft.
Austin
Prouty Pl. St. Pk.
Conrad
Cherry Springs St. Pk.
Carter Camp
Cedar Mtn. 2344 ft.
Morris
Ogdensburg
Beaver Meadows
Twin Lakes
Wilcox
Sizerville
Costello
Elk Lick Knob 2341 ft.
Oleona
Leetonia
Tioga State Forest
Hartsfield
Roaring Branch
Liberty
Kellettville
Pigeon
Bendigo St. Pk.
Emporium
Prospect Park
Wharton
Susquehannock State Forest
Ole Bull St. Pk.
Cedar Run
Oregon Hill
Ralston
Tionesta Lake
Johnsonburg
Cross Fork
Slate Run
Buttonwood
Roses
Marienville
Ridgway
Truman
Cameron
Sinnemahoning St. Pk.
Tamarack
Tiadaghton State Forest
Ski Sawmill Mtn. Resort
Trout Run
Tylersburg
Loleta
Hallton
Cook Forest St. Pk.
St. Marys
Kersey
Elk State Forest
Sterling Run
Kettle Creek St. Pk.
Hyner Run St. Pk.
Jersey Mills
Brookside
Buckhorn Mountain 2080 ft.
Cogan Station
Clarington
Belltown
Portland Mills
Fairview
Driftwood
North Bend
Renovo
Hyner
Upper Pine Bottom St. Pk.
Little Pine St. Pk.
Waterville
Haneyville
Williamsport
Sigel
Clear Creek St. Pk.
Brandy Camp
Challenge
Brockport
Benezette
Sinnamahoning
Byrnedale
Weedville
Hyner View St. Pk.
Sproul State Forest
Ramsey
Lycoming Coll.
Susquehanna St. Pk.
Fisher
Richardsville
Brockway
Sugar Hill
Keating
APPALACHIAN MTNS
Jersey Shore
Avis
Nisbet
Little League Int'l. Baseball and Softball
Hazen
Du Bois-Jefferson Co. Arpt.
Penfield
Treasure Lake
Parker Dam St. Pk.
Moshannon State Forest
Pottersdale
Lock Haven
Lock Haven Univ. of Pa.
Antes Fort
Corsica
Summerville
Brookville
Alaska
S.B. Elliott St. Pk.
Karthaus
Orviston
Mill Hall
Dunnstown
Ravensburg St. Pk.
Elimsport
Knox Dale
Sandy
Du Bois
Reynoldsville
Frenchville
Bald Hill
Monument
Beech Creek
Bald Eagle St. Pk.
Rians are Mtn. 2310 ft.
Rockton
Clearfield
Hyde
Moshannon
Show Shoe
Howard
Eastville
Loganton
Coolspring
Ringgold
Hawthorn
Chestnut Grove
Bilger Rocks
Woodland
Curwensville
Bigler
Grassflat
Lanse
Winburne
Moshannon State For.
Lamar
McCall Dam St. Pk.
Sand Br. St. Pk.
Big Run
Grampian
Bellefonte
Zion
Aaronsburg
Rebersburg
Raymond B. Winter St. Pk.
Mifflinburg
Hartleton
Mahoning Lake
Hamilton
Punxsutawney
Rossiter
Mahaffey
Philipsburg
Osceola Mills
Black Moshannon St. Pk.
Fisherman's Paradise
Penn's Cave
Millheim
Woodward Cave
Laurelton
New Berlin
Dayton
Rural Valley
Trade City
Glen Campbell
Burnside
Madera
Ansonville
Houtzdale
State College
Pleasant Gap
Weikert
Cherry Run
Poe Paddy St. Pk.
Kreamer
Middleburg
Plumville
Marion Center
Irvona
Port Matilda
Stormstown
Penn State Univ.
Potters Mills
Poe Valley St. Pk.
Sagamore
Hillsdale
Seldom Seen Coal Mine
Coalport
ALLEGHENY MTNS
Siglerville
Thick Mtn. 2239 ft.
Beaver Springs
Beavertown
Keystone L.
Home
Purchase Line
Blandburg
Warriors Mark
Tussey Mtn. Ski Area
Penn Roosevelt St. Pk.
Reeds Gap St. Pk.
Bannerville
Bald Eagle S.F.
Richfield
Mount Pleasant Mills
Elderton
Northern Cambria
Hastings
Prince Gallitzin St. Pk.
Tipton
Tyrone
Whipple Dam St. Pk.
Rothrock S.F.
Alan Seeger
Greenwood Furnace St. Pk.
Milroy
McClure
Alfarata
McAlisterville
Clymer
Glendale L.
McAlevys Fort
Burnham
Oriental
0718MW
53

For a complete listing of symbols, see inside back cover; for an index of cities, see page 200.

DISTANCE SCALE

One inch represents 16 miles

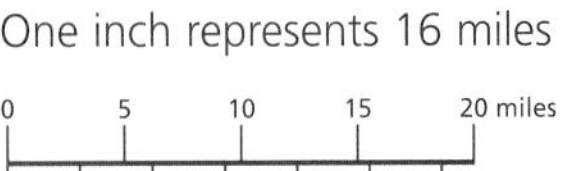

LOCATOR MAP

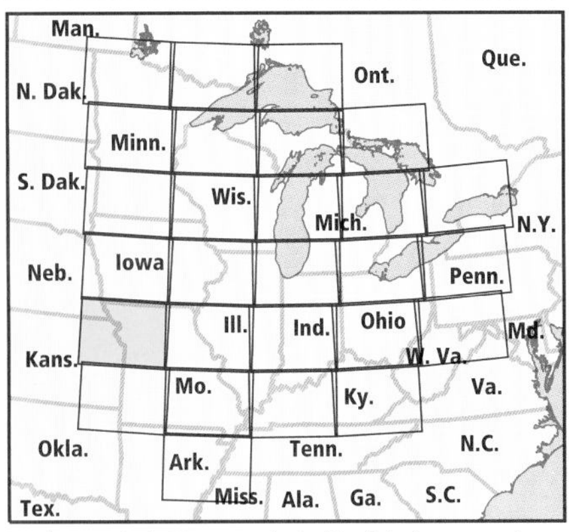

See the Pagefinder™ map on the inside of the front cover for map page numbers.

What do the little blue gas tanks represent?

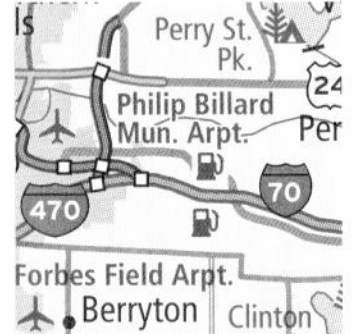

These symbols will only be seen along toll roads. They represent places where you can stop to fuel up without having to leave the tollway. Here you will find gas for your car as well as food for yourself.

What are those yellow boxes (with little numbers) on the maps?

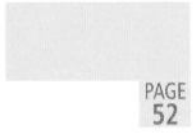

PAGE 52 That's where fun stuff happens, and this book describes that area in detail starting on the page number you see. Read all about what there is to see and do, what the shopping scene's like, where you can stay overnight, what the best food to try is and where you can find it, and even if there's a festival happening during your visit. These destination sections also offer specially designed maps to help figure out where attractions and restaurants are in relation to each other (and how to drive between them).

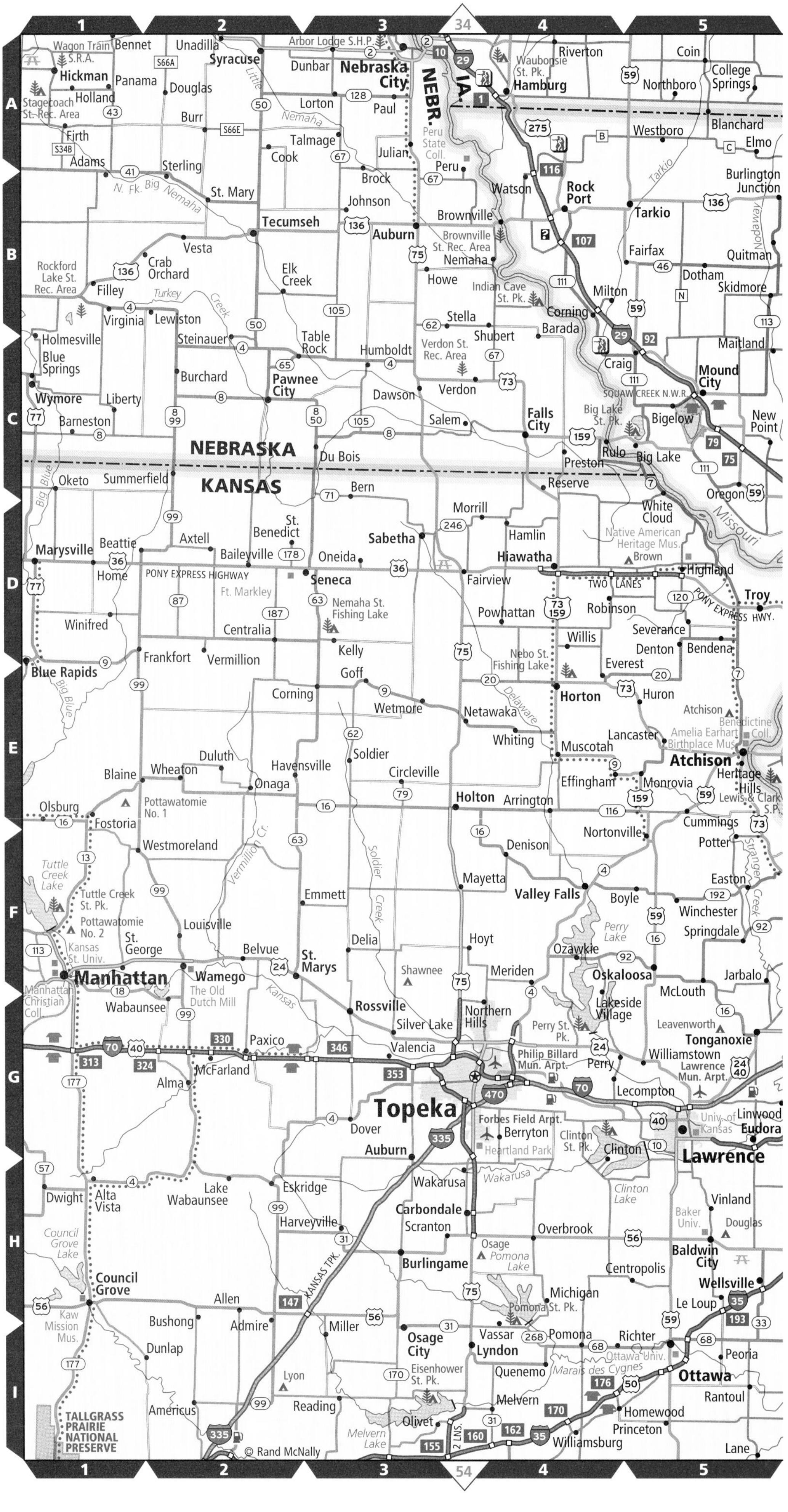

When you see this sign 14, the map continues on the page number indicated.

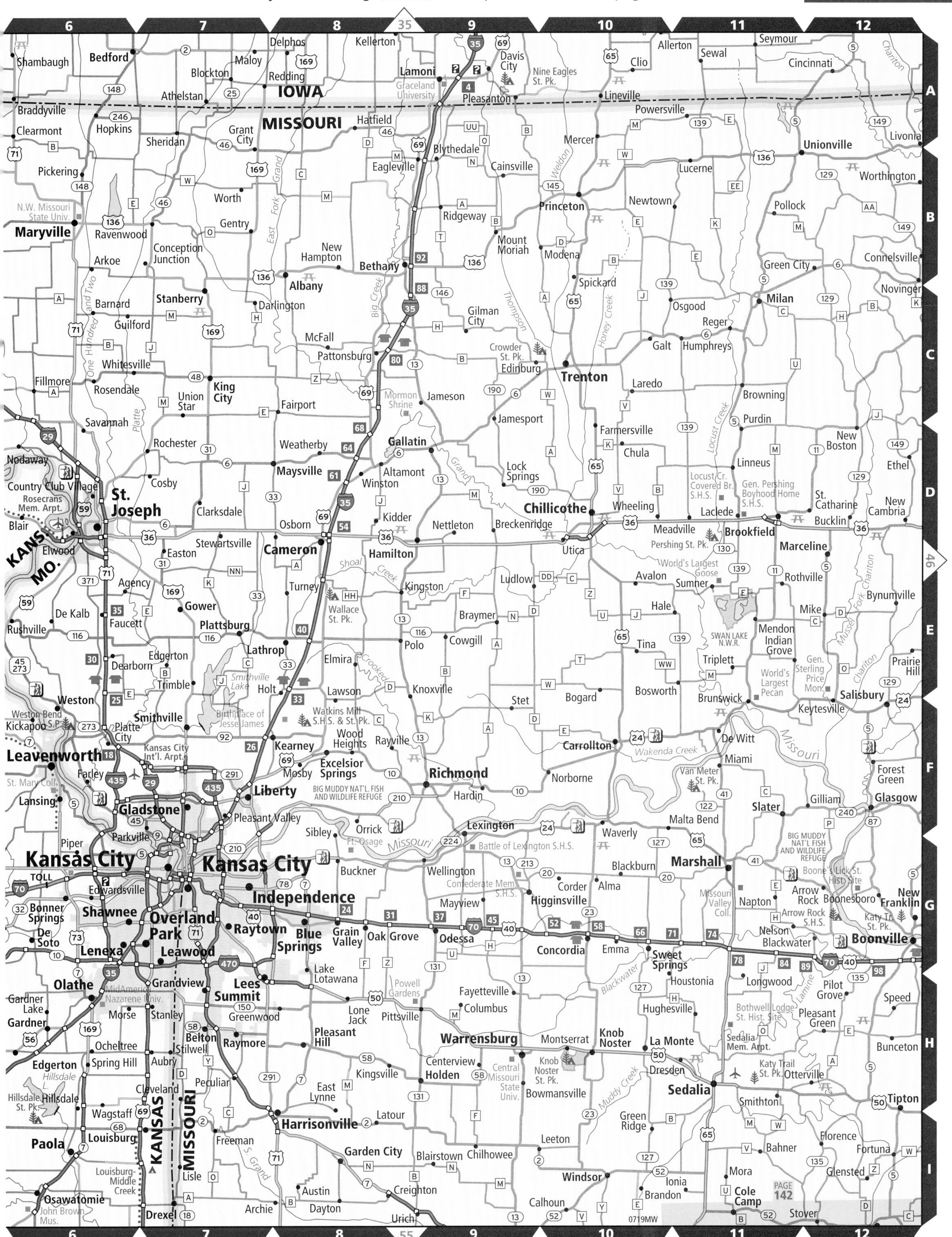

For a complete listing of symbols, see inside back cover; for an index of cities, see page 200.

DISTANCE SCALE

One inch represents 16 miles

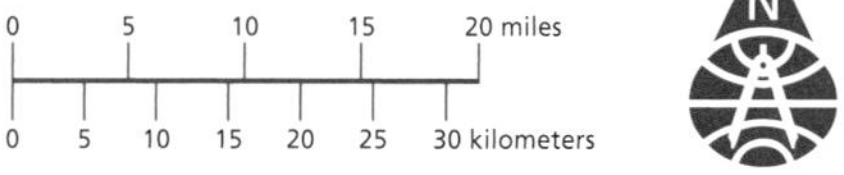

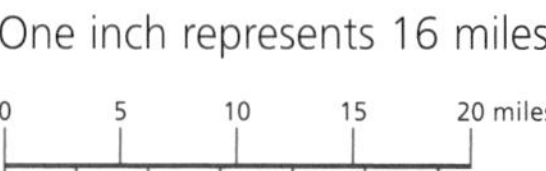

LOCATOR MAP

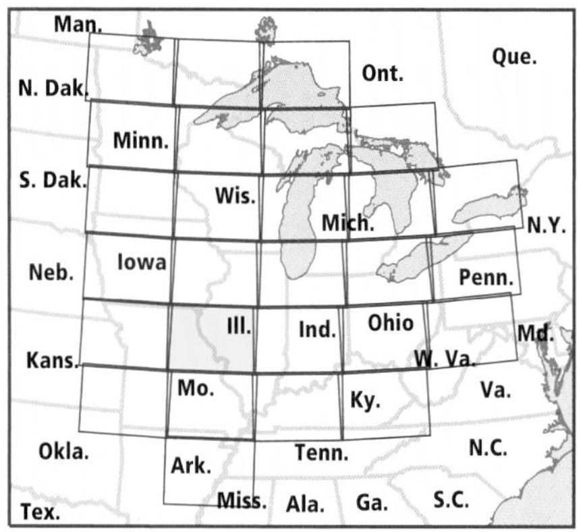

See the Pagefinder™ map on the inside of the front cover for map page numbers.

These square symbols don't look like highway shields (part 3).

These maps show five different square symbols: Each represents a specially designated historic or scenic route.

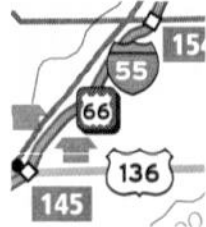

Stretching from Chicago to Los Angeles, **Historic Route 66** — the Mother Road — offers glimpses of lesser-known American landscapes.

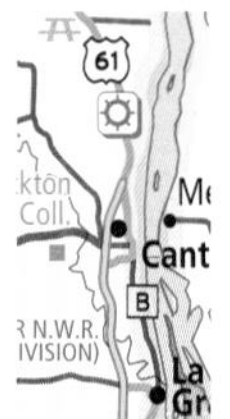

Following the captain's wheel takes you along the **Great River Road**. One of the oldest and longest scenic highways in the U.S., it runs through 10 states for 3,000 some miles along both sides of the Mississippi River.

Read more about the others on pp. 28 and 34.

What are those yellow boxes (with little numbers) on the maps?

That's where fun stuff happens, and this book describes that area in detail starting on the page number you see. Read all about what there is to see and do, what the shopping scene's like, where you can stay overnight, what the best food to try is and where you can find it, and even if there's a festival happening during your visit. These destination sections also offer specially designed maps to help figure out where attractions and restaurants are in relation to each other (and how to drive between them).

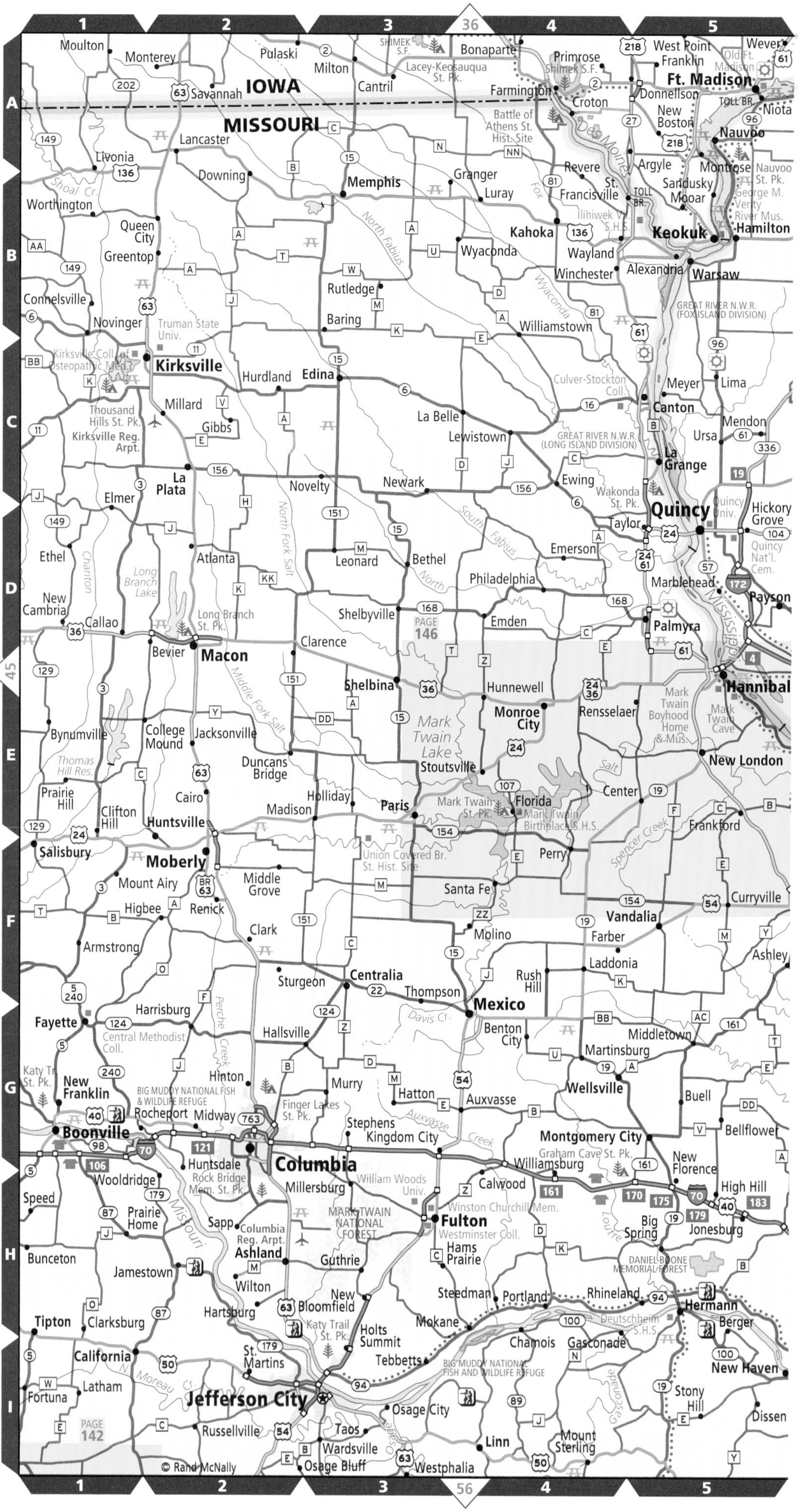

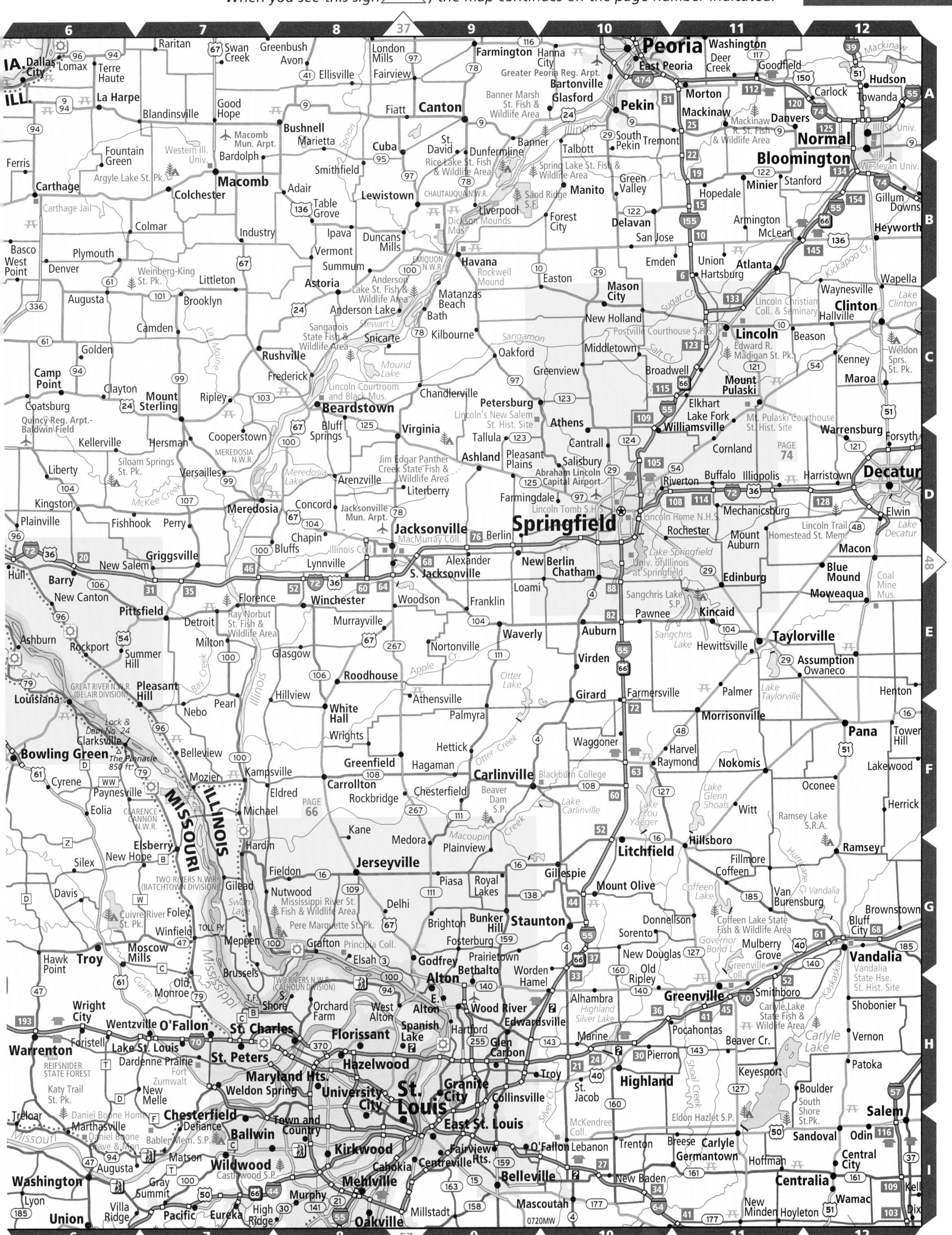
6
7
8
37
9
10
11
12
A
B
C
D
E
F
G
H
I
48
57
Peoria
East Peoria
Washington
Deer Creek
Goodfield
Hudson
Carlock
Towanda
Farmington
Hanna City
Greater Peoria Reg. Arpt.
Bartonville
Glasford
Canton
Pekin
Morton
Mackinaw
Danvers
Normal
Bloomington
Wesleyan Univ.
Ill. St. Univ.
Stanford
Minier
Hopedale
Gillum Downs
Heyworth
Armington
McLean
Atlanta
Delavan
Manito
Green Valley
South Pekin
Tremont
Talbott
San Jose
Emden
Union
Hartsburg
Havana
Forest City
Liverpool
Dickson Mounds Mus.
Lewistown
Cuba
Fairview
Ellisville
London Mills
Avon
Greenbush
Swan Creek
Raritan
Dallas City
Lomax
Terre Haute
La Harpe
Blandinsville
Good Hope
Bushnell
Marietta
Macomb
Macomb Mun. Arpt.
Western Ill. Univ.
Bardolph
Colchester
Fountain Green
Argyle Lake St. Pk.
Carthage
Carthage Jail
Ferris
Colmar
Industry
Adair
Table Grove
Smithfield
Ipava
Vermont
Duncans Mills
Summum
Astoria
Plymouth
Basco
West Point
Denver
Augusta
Weinberg-King St. Pk.
Littleton
Brooklyn
Camden
Golden
Camp Point
Clayton
Mount Sterling
Ripley
Rushville
Frederick
Beardstown
Coatsburg
Quincy Reg. Arpt.-Baldwin Field
Kellerville
Hersman
Cooperstown
Versailles
Siloam Springs St. Pk.
Liberty
Kingston
Plainville
Fishhook
Perry
Meredosia
Concord
Chapin
Bluffs
Griggsville
New Salem
Barry
Hull
New Canton
Pittsfield
Detroit
Milton
Ashburn
Rockport
Summer Hill
Pleasant Hill
Louisiana
Nebo
Pearl
Clarksville
Bowling Green
Belleview
Mozier
Kampsville
Cyrene
Paynesville
Eolia
Michael
Hardin
Elsberry
New Hope
Silex
Davis
Gilead
Foley
Winfield
Moscow Mills
Troy
Hawk Point
Old Monroe
Wright City
Wentzville
O'Fallon
St. Charles
Warrenton
Foristell
Lake St. Louis
Dardenne Prairie
St. Peters
New Melle
Treloar
Marthasville
Augusta
Washington
Chesterfield
Defiance
Ballwin
Wildwood
Gray Summit
Villa Ridge
Union
Lyon
Pacific
Eureka
High Ridge
Murphy
Oakville
Mehlville
Kirkwood
St. Louis
University City
Maryland Hts.
Hazelwood
Florissant
Spanish Lake
Granite City
East St. Louis
Collinsville
Fairview Hts.
O'Fallon
Belleville
Cahokia
Centreville
Millstadt
Mascoutah
Lebanon
Troy
St. Jacob
Highland
Marine
Pierron
Edwardsville
Glen Carbon
Hartford
Wood River
Alton
East Alton
West Alton
Godfrey
Elsah
Grafton
Brussels
Meppen
Orchard Farm
Bethalto
Worden
Hamel
Prairietown
Fosterburg
Brighton
Bunker Hill
Staunton
Delhi
Nutwood
Fieldon
Jerseyville
Piasa
Royal Lakes
Medora
Plainview
Kane
Eldred
Carrollton
Rockbridge
Greenfield
Hagaman
Chesterfield
Carlinville
Hettick
Palmyra
Wrights
White Hall
Athensville
Hillview
Roodhouse
Glasgow
Murrayville
Winchester
Florence
Woodson
Franklin
Waverly
Nortonville
Virden
Girard
Auburn
Loami
New Berlin
Chatham
Springfield
Berlin
Alexander
S. Jacksonville
Jacksonville
Lynnville
Arenzville
Literberry
Bluff Springs
Virginia
Chandlerville
Ashland
Pleasant Plains
Tallula
Petersburg
Athens
Cantrall
Salisbury
Farmingdale
Greenview
Oakford
Kilbourne
Bath
Matanzas Beach
Snicarte
Easton
Mason City
New Holland
Middletown
Broadwell
Lincoln
Elkhart
Lake Fork
Williamsville
Cornland
Riverton
Buffalo
Illiopolis
Harristown
Decatur
Mechanicsburg
Rochester
Mount Auburn
Edinburg
Elwin
Macon
Blue Mound
Moweaqua
Kincaid
Pawnee
Taylorville
Hewittsville
Assumption
Owaneco
Palmer
Morrisonville
Pana
Tower Hill
Farmersville
Waggoner
Harvel
Raymond
Nokomis
Lakewood
Oconee
Herrick
Witt
Hillsboro
Ramsey
Litchfield
Gillespie
Mount Olive
Fillmore
Coffeen
Van Burensburg
Brownstown
Donnellson
Sorento
New Douglas
Old Ripley
Mulberry Grove
Bluff City
Vandalia
Greenville
Smithboro
Shobonier
Pocahontas
Beaver Cr.
Vernon
Patoka
Keyesport
Boulder
Salem
Sandoval
Odin
Central City
Centralia
Hoffman
Carlyle
Breese
Germantown
Trenton
New Baden
Wamac
New Minden
Hoyleton
Mount Pulaski
Beason
Clinton
Waynesville
Wapella
Kenney
Maroa
Warrensburg
Forsyth
Hallville
Lincoln Home N.H.S.
Abraham Lincoln Capital Airport
Lake Springfield
Henton
0720MW

For a complete listing of symbols, see inside back cover; for an index of cities, see page 200.

DISTANCE SCALE

One inch represents 16 miles

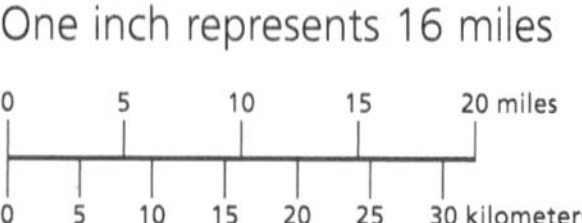

LOCATOR MAP

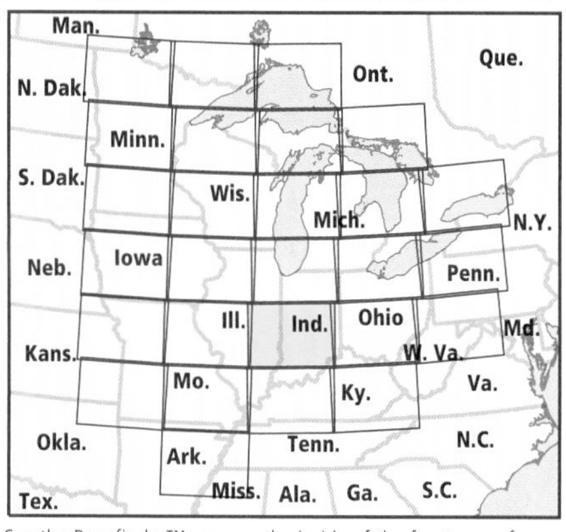

See the Pagefinder™ map on the inside of the front cover for map page numbers.

Does that string of pink dots represent a road?

No — this line ----- represents the boundary between time zones. Don't forget to adjust your watch when you cross it.

What are those yellow boxes (with little numbers) on the maps?

That's where fun stuff happens, and this book describes that area in detail starting on the page number you see. Read all about what there is to see and do, what the shopping scene's like, where you can stay overnight, what the best food to try is and where you can find it, and even if there's a festival happening during your visit. These destination sections also offer specially designed maps to help figure out where attractions and restaurants are in relation to each other (and how to drive between them).

Why is there a red ribbon on this map?

The red award ribbon marks a Rand McNally Best of the Road™ trip route. Our editors have chosen scenic drives peppered with tasty dining, unique shopping, and memory-making things to do. Read more about four of these drives on pages 180-191. For more trip routes, visit go.randmcnally.com/BR.

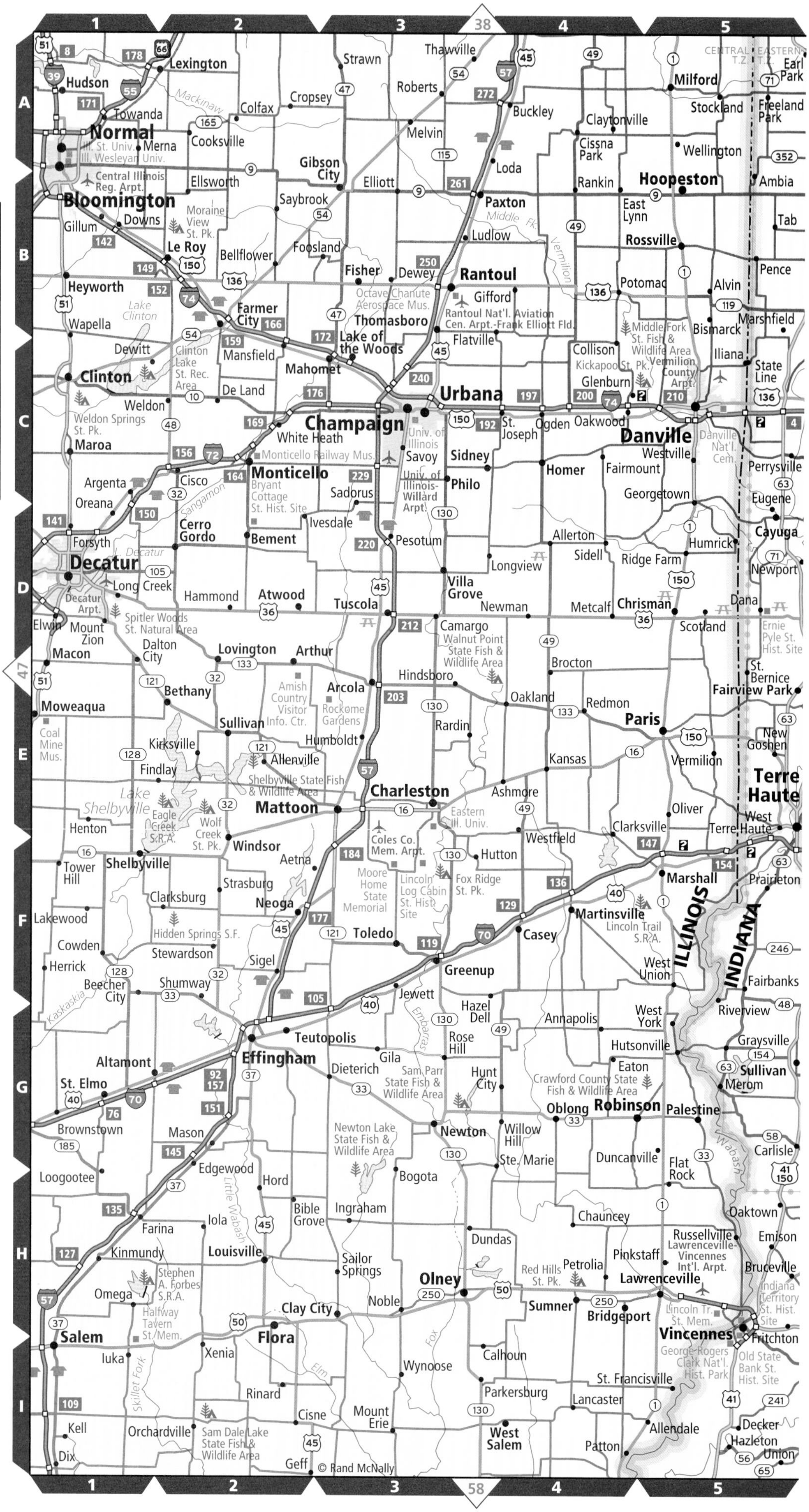

When you see this sign 14, the map continues on the page number indicated.

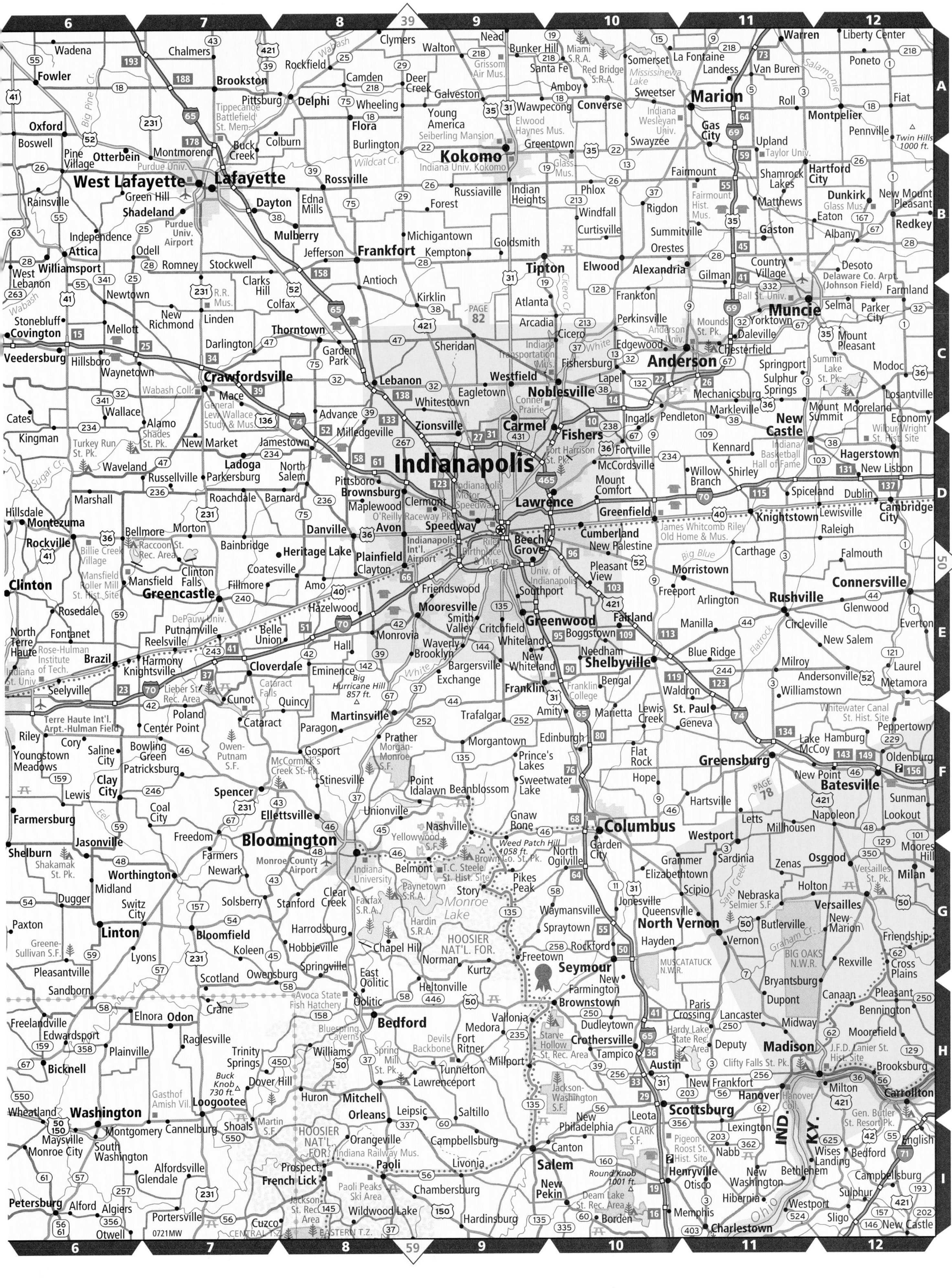

For a complete listing of symbols, see inside back cover; for an index of cities, see page 200.

DISTANCE SCALE

One inch represents 16 miles

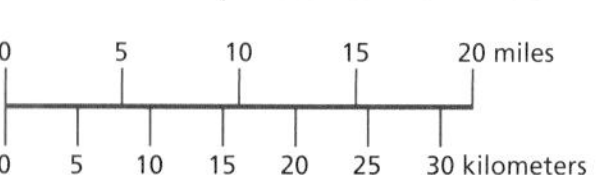

LOCATOR MAP

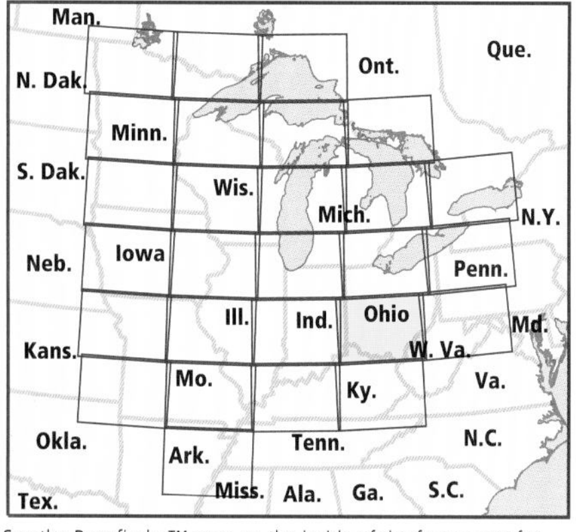

See the Pagefinder™ map on the inside of the front cover for map page numbers.

Why do some cities have orange colored areas around them?

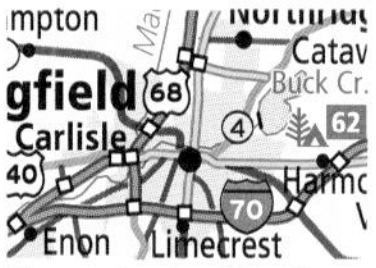

Basically, this color shows where the people are. It does not indicate the city limits. Rather, it shows the extent of built-up urban areas around cities. You'll be certain to find stores, gas stations, hotels, and restaurants in these areas.

What are those yellow boxes (with little numbers) on the maps?

PAGE 52 That's where fun stuff happens, and this book describes that area in detail starting on the page number you see. Read all about what there is to see and do, what the shopping scene's like, where you can stay overnight, what the best food to try is and where you can find it, and even if there's a festival happening during your visit. These destination sections also offer specially designed maps to help figure out where attractions and restaurants are in relation to each other (and how to drive between them).

Why is there a red ribbon on this map?

The red award ribbon marks a Rand McNally Best of the Road™ trip route. Our editors have chosen scenic drives peppered with tasty dining, unique shopping, and memory-making things to do. Read more about four of these drives on pages 180-191. For more trip routes, visit go.randmcnally.com/BR.

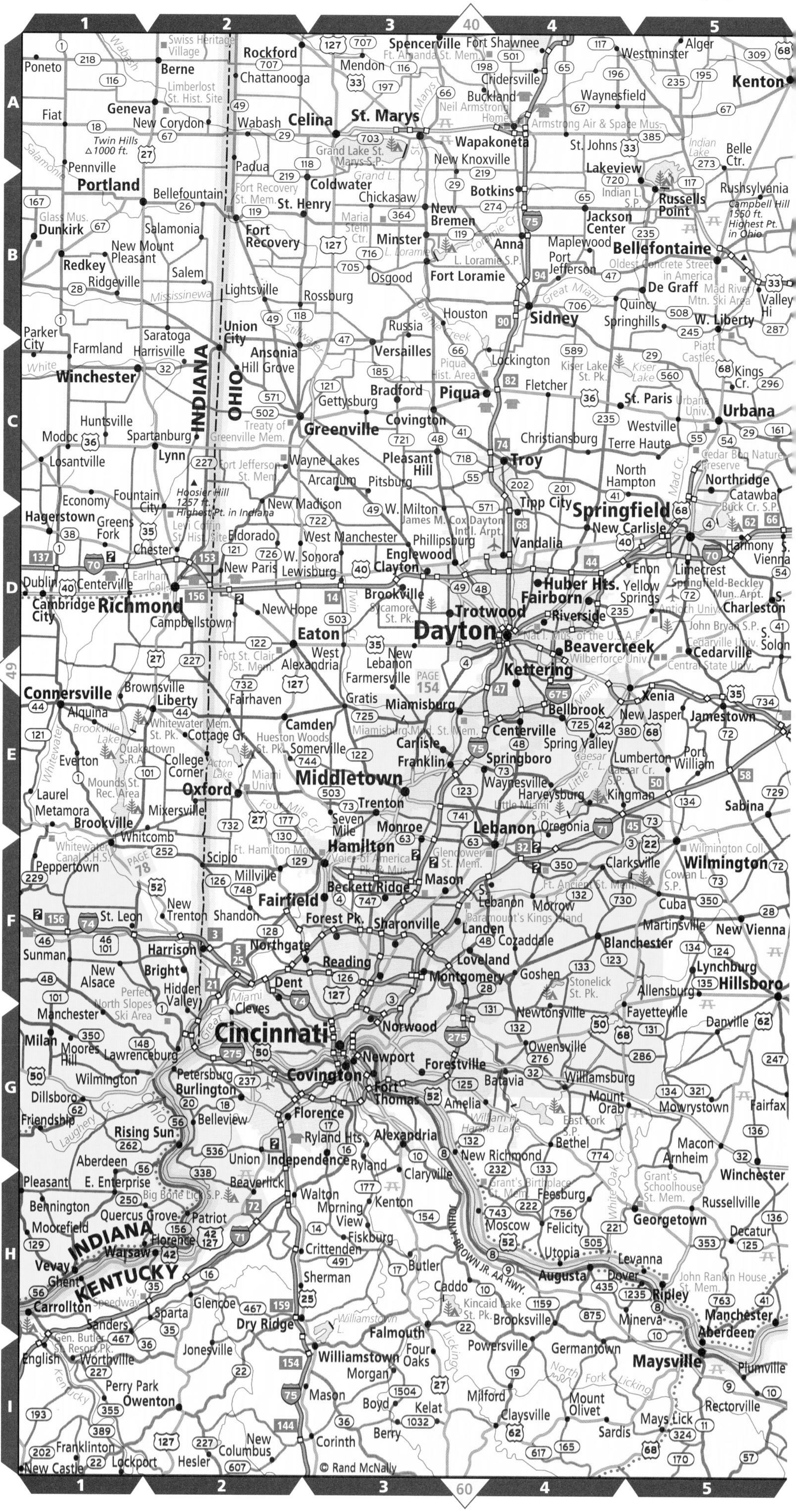

When you see this sign 14, the map continues on the page number indicated.

For a complete listing of symbols, see inside back cover; for an index of cities, see page 200.

DISTANCE SCALE

One inch represents 16 miles

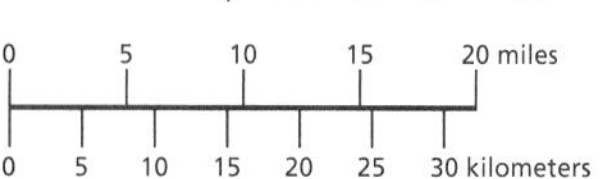

LOCATOR MAP

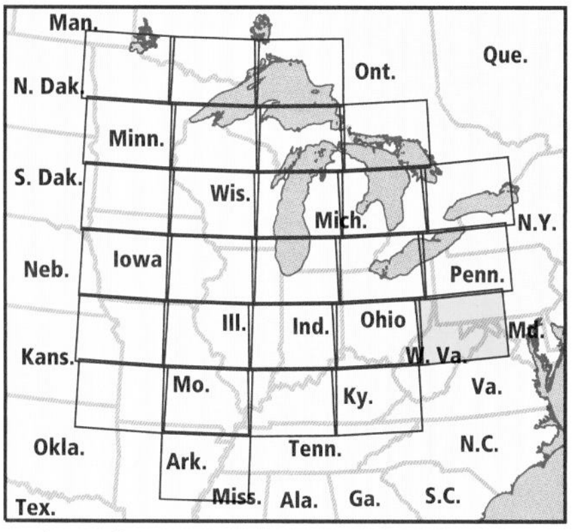

See the Pagefinder™ map on the inside of the front cover for map page numbers.

What are those numbers in the green boxes?

Those represent exit numbers 8. You'll see those same numbers in the big green signs over or alongside the highway that say "Exit." In most states, the exits are numbered according to how many miles from the southern or western border the exit is located.

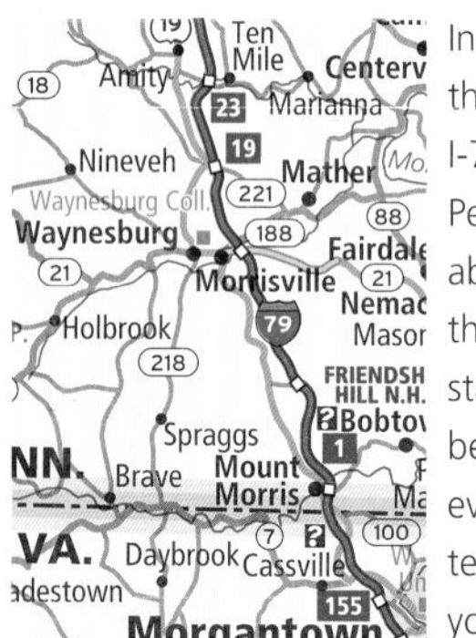

In the example on the left, exit 23 on I-79 near Ten Mile, Pennsylvania, is about 23 miles from the West Virginia state line. This can be helpful in the event you need to tell someone where you are along the interstate, or in determining how much farther you need to go.

Why is there a red ribbon on this map?

The red award ribbon marks a Rand McNally Best of the Road™ trip route. Our editors have chosen scenic drives peppered with tasty dining, unique shopping, and memory-making things to do. Read more about four of these drives on pages 180-191. For more trip routes, visit go.randmcnally.com/BR.

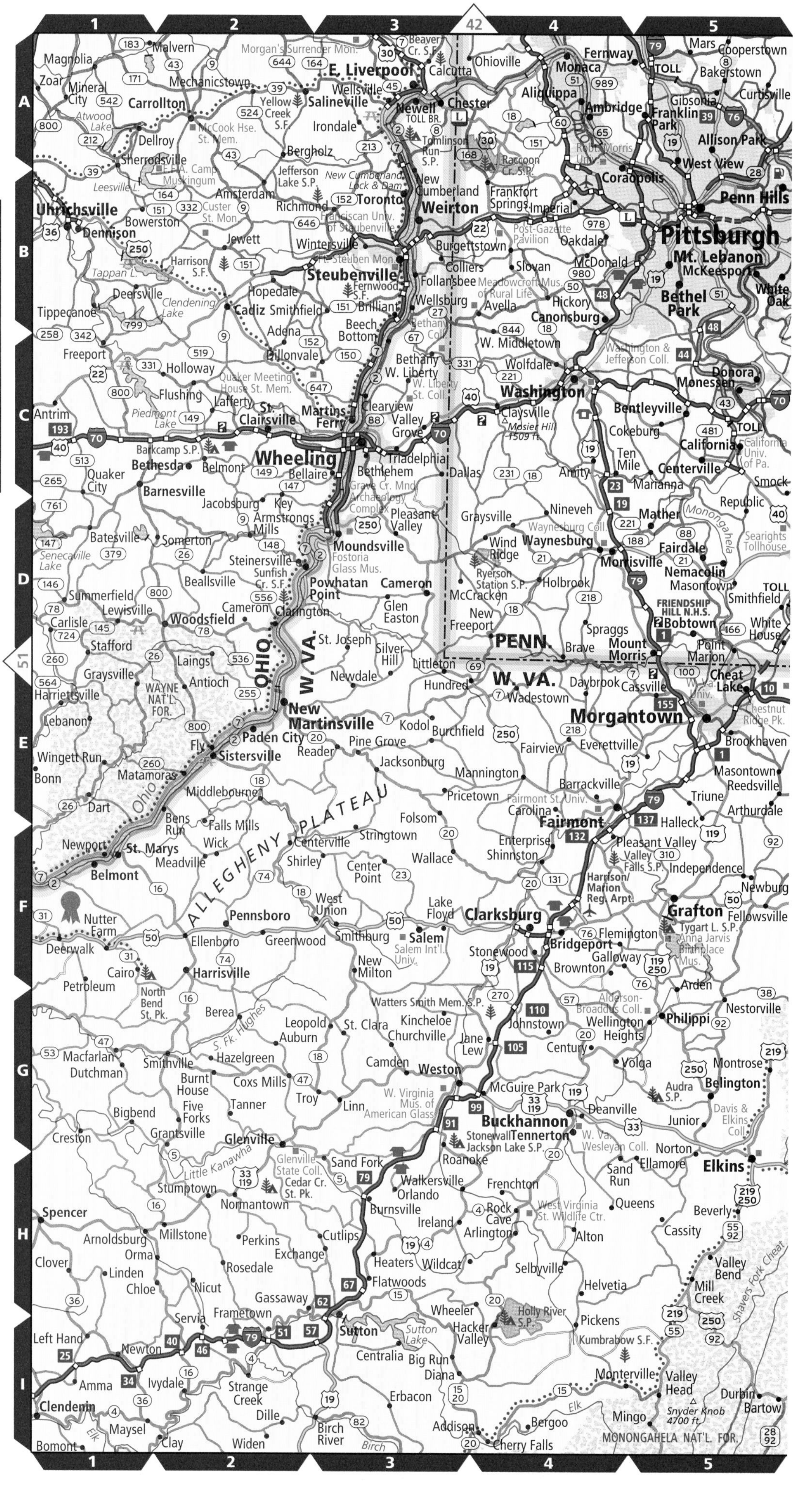

When you see this sign  , the map continues on the page number indicated.

6 7 8 9 10 11 12

43

A B C D E F G H I

Silverville, Crooked Creek, Elderton, Clymer, Hastings, Seldom Seen Coal Mine, Glendale Lake, Prince Gallitzin S.P., Blandburg, Tyrone, Warriors Mark, Neffs Mills, Whipple Dam S.P., Alan Seeger, Milroy, Burnham, Highland Park, Lewistown, Natrona Hts., Leechburg, Chevy Chase Hts., Indiana, Northern Cambria, Penn Run, Yellow Cr. S.P., Heilwood, Patton, Beaver Valley, Tipton, Rothrock S.F., McAlevys Fort, Greenwood Furnace S.P., McCoy House, Belleville, Lower Burrell, Vandergrift, Clune, Strongstown, Bellwood, Ft. Roberdeau, Indian Caverns, Petersburg, Allensville, New Kensington, Iselin, Kent, Homer City, Colver, Ebensburg, Loretto, Altoona, Greenwood, Canoe Cr. S.P., Etna Furnace, Lincoln Caverns, Strodes Mills, Tuscarora Academy, Plum, Monroeville, Murrysville, Saltsburg, Conemaugh River Lake, Slickville, Nanty Glo, St. Francis Univ., Horseshoe Curve, Smithfield, Huntingdon, Juniata Coll., Swigart Antique Auto Mus., McVeytown, Loyalhanna Lake, Blairsville, Bolivar, Five Points, Robinson, Vinco, John Murtha Johnstown-Cambria Co. Arpt., Cresson, Allegheny Portage R.R. N.H.S., Portage, Hollidaysburg, Canoe Creek, Williamsburg, Mount Union, Tuscarora S.F., Honey Grove, Jeannette, Keystone S.P., New Florence, Johnstown, Johnstown Flood Nat'l. Mem., Blue Knob, Roaring Spring, Raystown Lake, Mapleton Depot, East Waterford, Blain, Irwin, Greensburg, Latrobe, Derry, Westmont, Blue Knob 3130 ft., Blue Knob Ski Resort, Martinsburg, Trough Cr. S.P., Allenport, Richvale, Blairs Mills, Bowers Mtn. 2104 ft., New Stanton, St. Vincent Coll., Seton Hill Univ., Arnold Palmer Reg. Arpt., Ft. Ligonier, Ligonier, Idlewild & Soak Zone, Geistown, Salix, Dunlo, Univ. of Pittsburgh at Johnstown, Blue Knob S.P., Altoona-Blair Co. Arpt., Saxton, Cassville, E. Broad Top R.R. (Narrow Gauge), Orbisonia, Big Spr. S.P., Fowlers Hollow S.P., W. Newton, Yukon, Welty, The Springs at Laurel Mtn. Ski Area, Jerome, Gallitzin S.F., Woodbury, Raystown Lake, Saltillo, Tuscarora S.F., Blue Mtn., Penn Tpk., Linn Run S.P., Boswell, Hooversville, Osterburg, Fishertown, Loysburg, Warriors Path S.P., Broad Top, Three Springs, Dry Run, Spring Run, Newburg, Scottdale, Frick Birthplace, Mt. Pleasant, Donegal, Laurel Mtn. S.P., Forbes S.F., Kooser S.P., Somerset Hist. Ctr., Cairnbrook, Central City, Riddlesburg, Roxbury, Shippensburg Univ., Star Junction, White, Hidden Valley Ski Resort, Bakersville, Friedens, Schellsburg, Shawnee S.P., Graceville, Buchanan S.F., King Knob 2107 ft., Fort Littleton, Upperstrasburg, Connellsville, Seven Sprs., Seven Sprs. Mtn. Ski Resort, New Baltimore, Everett, Hustontown, Fannettsburg, Bear Valley, Shippensburg, Normalville, Laurel Ridge S.P., Somerset, Manns Choice, Bedford, Ft. Bedford & Bedford Vil., Earlston, Breezewood, Cowans Gap S.P., Buchanan S.F., Mainsville, Oliver, S. Connellsville, Mill Run, Fallingwater, Rockwood, Bard, Crystal Spring, Clearville, McConnellsburg, Edenville, Wilson Coll., Chambersburg, Michaux S.F., Caledonia S.P., Uniontown, Metzler, Kingwood, Berlin, Glen Savage, Rainsburg, Fort Loudon, St. Thomas, Old Brown's Mill School, Fayetteville, Chalkhill, Ohiopyle, Ohiopyle S.P., Casselman, Garrett, Needmore, Cito, Buchanan's Birthplace St. Pk., Mont Alto S.P., Laurel Caverns, Haydentown, Farmington, Mt. Davis 3213 ft. Highest Pt. in Pennsylvania, Ursina, Confluence, Meyersdale, Fairhope, Hyndman, Centerville, Buchanan State Forest, Chaneysville, Amaranth, Dott, Big Cove Tannery, Williamson, Mercersburg, Mont Alto, Snowy Mtn. 2062 ft., Forbes S.F., Fort Necessity Nat'l. Bfld., Markleysburg, Wittenberg, Purcell, Shimpstown, Greencastle, Waynesboro, Addison, Forbes S.F., Grantsville, Salisbury, Rocky Gap S.P., Sideling Hill Exhibit Ctr., Whitetail Ski Resort, Penn., State Line, Wayne Hts., Appalachian Tr., Coopers Rock S.F., Brandonville, National Frwy., Savage River S.F., New Germany, New Germany S.P., Frostburg, Cumberland, La Vale, Flintstone, Gilpin, Little Orleans, Berkeley Sprs. S.P., Hancock, Md., Clear Spring, Fairview, Catoctin Mtn. Pk., Smithsburg, Pisgah, Hazelton, Friendsville, Accident, Frostburg St. Univ., Cresaptown, Greater Cumberland Reg. Arpt., Warrior Mtn. 2185 ft., Green Ridge S.F., Great Cacapon, Bath, W. Va., Ernstville, Big Pool, Williamsport, Ft. Frederick, Halfway, Hagerstown, Cunningham Falls St. Pk., Valley Point, Cranesville Pine Swamp, Savage River State Forest, Deep Cr. Lake S.P., Lonaconing, Oldtown, Paw Paw, Pinkerton Knob 1800 ft., Tomahawk, Marlowe, Greenbrier St. Pk., Gambrill St. Pk., Cheat, Albright, White Oak Springs, McHenry, Swallow Falls S.P., Big Run S.P., High Rock 2991 ft., Westernport, Fort Ashby, Green Spring, Levels, Potomac, Cacapon Resort S.P., Jones Springs, Martinsburg, Forest Hill Estates, Boonsboro, Myersville, Kingwood, Terra Alta, Swanton, Piedmont, McCoole, Keyser, Springfield, St. Fish Hatchery, Unger, Shanghai, Sharpsburg, Crystal Grottoes, Antietam Nat'l. Bfld., Middletown, Tunnelton, Herrington Manor S.P., Garrett, Oakland, Shallmar, Kitzmiller, Reeses Mill, Forks of Cacapon, Glengary, Shepherdstown, Shepherd Univ., Rowlesburg, Cathedral S.P., Mountain Lake Park, Elk Garden, Burlington, Romney, Slanesville, Bloomery, Siler, Bunker Hill, Inwood, Harpers Ferry, Harpers Ferry N.H.P., Brunswick, Aurora, Potomac S.F., Appalachian Mtns., Gainesboro, Charles Town, Ranson, Bolivar, Potomac, Eglon, Laurel Dale, Antioch, Junction, Shanks, Augusta, Capon Bridge, Summit Point, Lovettsville, Point of Rocks, Md., Backbone Mtn. 3360 ft. Highest Pt. in Maryland, Gormania, Silver Lake, Mount Storm, Nancy Hanks Mem., Golden Acres, Gore, Sunnyside, Clear Brook, Shenandoah Univ., Va., Hannahsville, Bayard, Bismarck, Purgitsville, Patterson Cr., Cacapon, Yellow Spring, Frederick Hts., Berryville, Waterford, Paeonian Sprs., Lead Mine, Fairfax Stone Hist. Mon. St. Pk., Williamsport, Stonewall Jackson's Headquarters Mus., Winchester, Purcellville, Horseshoe, Thomas, Davis, Blackwater Outdoor Ctr., Scherr, Medley, Rio, Capon Springs, Pinnacle 2844 ft., Boyce, Pine Grove, Leesburg, Parsons, Blackwater Falls S.P., Canaan Valley N.W.R., Maysville, Hawk, Stephens City, Millwood, Bluemont, George Washington Univ.-Va. Campus, Hendricks, Canaan Valley Ski Resort, Canaan Valley, Timberline Four Seasons Ski Resort, Moorefield, Arkansas, Wardensville, Middletown, White Post, Appalachian Trail, Ashburn, Oatlands, Canaan Valley Resort S.P., Rig, Baker, Belle Grv. Plantation, Fishers Hill, St. Arboretum of Va., Upperville, Waxpool, Aldie, Arcola, Toll, Red Creek, Smoke Hole Caverns, Cabins, Petersburg, Bass, George Washington Nat'l. For., W. Va., Virginia, Strasburg, Cedarville, Paris, Sky Meadows St. Pk., Middleburg, Monongahela Nat'l. For., Mt. Porte Crayon 4770 ft., Hopeville, Lost City, Front Royal, Rectortown, Pleasant Valley, Stuart, Alpena, Harman, Spruce Knob-Seneca Rocks Nat'l. Rec. Area, Big Bend, Perry, Liberty Furnace, Lost River St. Pk., Skyline Caverns, Manassas Gap 887 ft., Markham, Marshall, The Plains, Manassas Nat'l. Bfld. Pk., Bowden, Onego, Mathias, Columbia Furnace, Woodstock, Limeton, N. Fk. Shenandoah, Hume, Bemis, Whitmer, Seneca Rocks, Milam, Bryce Ski Resort, Bentonville, Shenandoah R. "Andy Guest" S.P., Huntly, Glady, Seneca Shadows, Seneca Rocks, Upper Tract, Mozer, Basye, Orkney Springs, Mount Jackson, Edinburg, George Washington Nat'l. For., Browntown, Flint Hill, Rappahannock, Warrenton, New Baltimore, Bull Run, Manassas, Spruce Knob L., Spruce Knob 4863 ft. Highest Pt. in W. Virginia, Seneca Caverns, Kline, Bergton, Riverton, Shenandoah Caverns, South Jackson, Mathews Arm, Mt. Marshall 3368 ft., Washington, Shenandoah Nat'l. Pk., Nokesville, Sinks of Gandy, New Market Bfld. S.H.P., Luray Caverns, Luray, Sperryville, Amissville, Cedar Run, Catlett, Aden, Circleville, Franklin, Oak Flat, George Washington Nat'l. For., Fulks Run, Timberville, New Market, Morning Star, Skyland, Thornton Gap 2307 ft., Castleton, Jeffersonton, Calverton, Cherry Grove, Brandywine, Broadway, Woodville, Rixeyville, Remington, Marsh Run, Flying Circus Aerodrome, W. Va., Va., Sugar Grove, Brandywine Lake, Singers Glen, Endless Caverns, Stanley, Skyline Dr., Nethers, Morrisville, Harper, Rawley Springs, Lacey Spring, Big Meadows, Syria, Etlan, Hazel, Salem, Brandy Station, Roseville, Blue Grass, Reddish Knob 4397 ft., Park View, Eastern Mennonite Univ., Shenandoah, Culpeper, Goldvein

 0723MW

6 7 8 9 10 11 12

For a complete listing of symbols, see inside back cover; for an index of cities, see page 200.

DISTANCE SCALE

One inch represents 16 miles

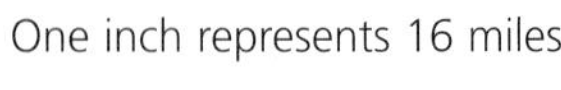

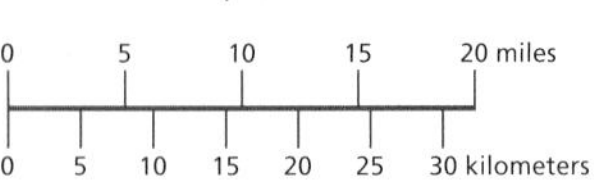

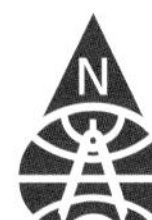

LOCATOR MAP

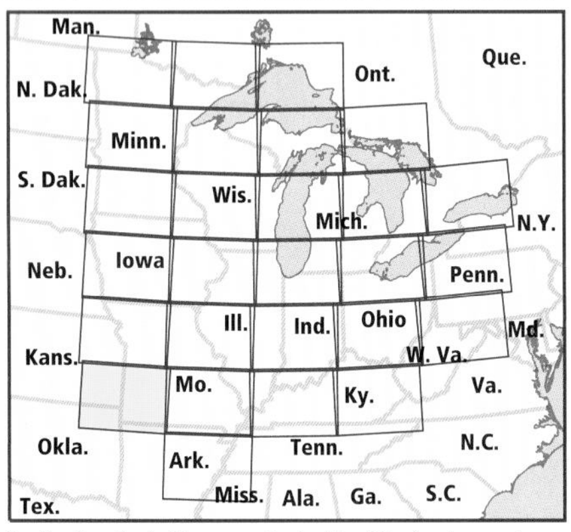

See the Pagefinder™ map on the inside of the front cover for map page numbers.

Why do some highway shields have letters or words inside them?

These letters or words indicate particular types of highways.

"ALT" stands for alternate route, which provides an optional path to take while going in the same general direction as the original highway.

"BR" stands for business route, which runs through the business district of a city. You will find places to shop, eat and get gas along this route.

"BYP" stands for bypass, which is a route around a major city that avoids traffic snarls.

"SPUR" indicates a way to get directly into the center of a town from a nearby highway fast.

For interstate highways, the shield is also colored green, instead of the normal red, white, and blue.

What are those yellow boxes (with little numbers) on the maps?

PAGE 52 That's where fun stuff happens, and this book describes that area in detail starting on the page number you see. Read all about what there is to see and do, what the shopping scene's like, where you can stay overnight, what the best food to try is and where you can find it, and even if there's a festival happening during your visit. These destination sections also offer specially designed maps to help figure out where attractions and restaurants are in relation to each other (and how to drive between them).

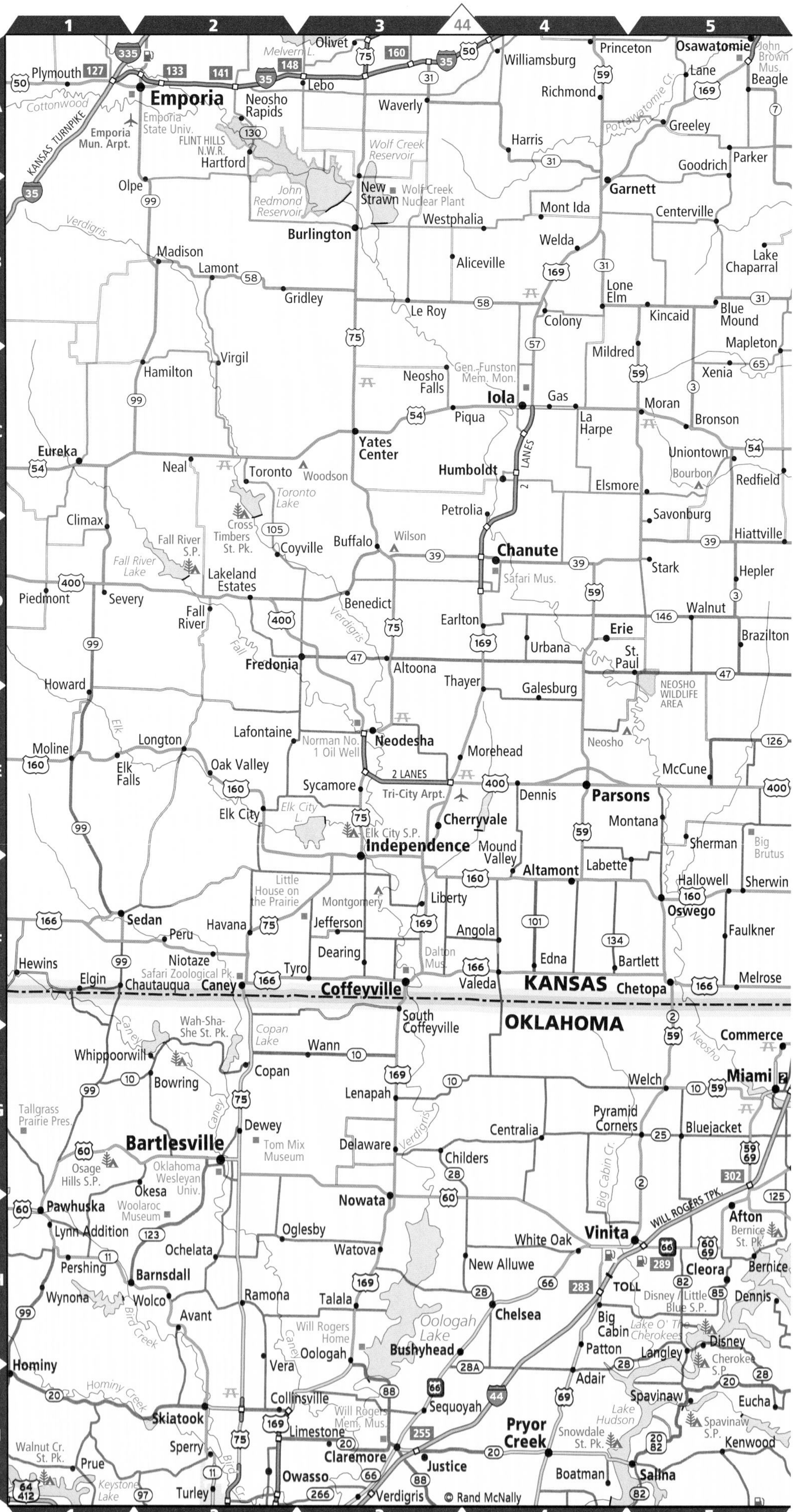

When you see this sign 14, the map continues on the page number indicated.

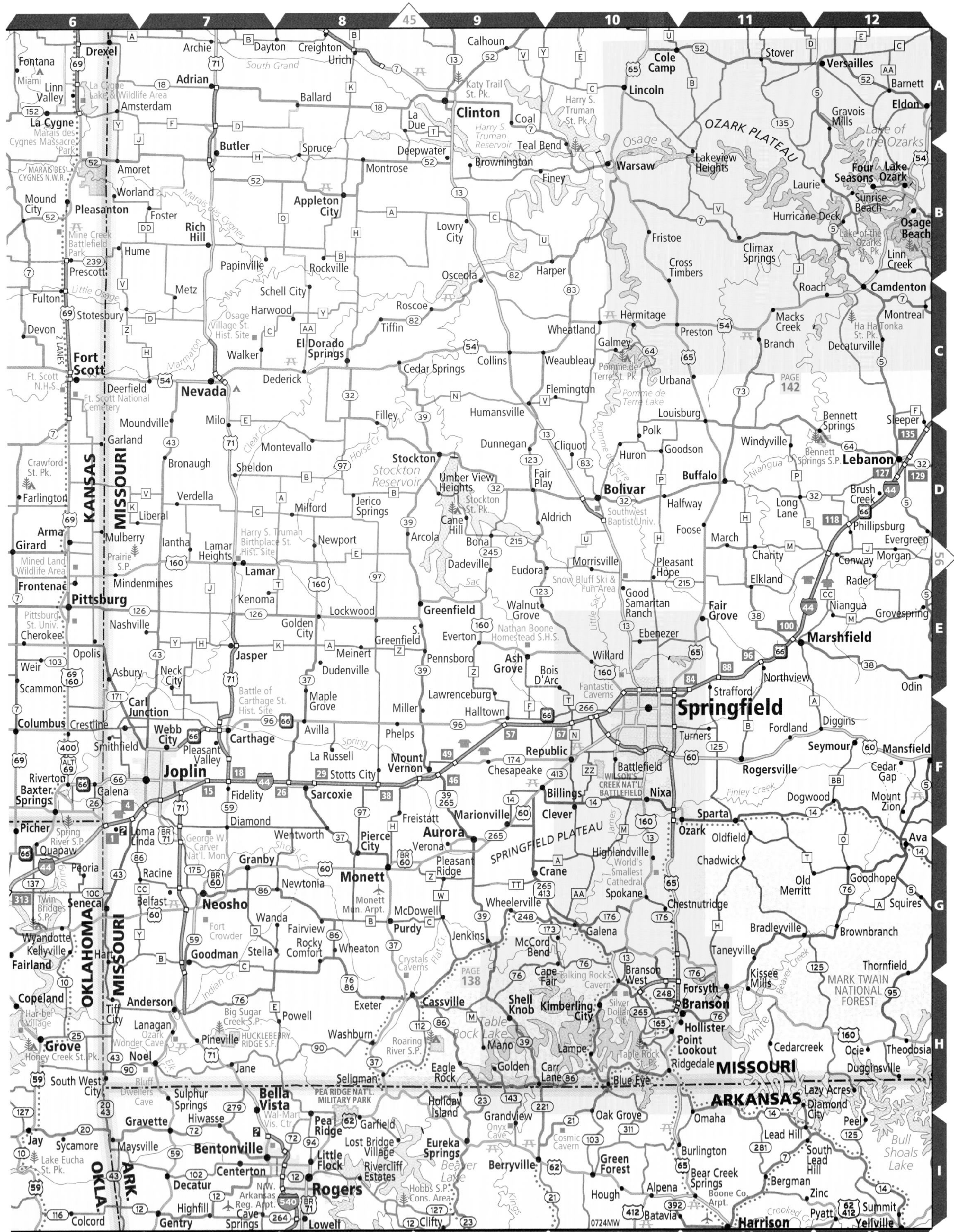

For a complete listing of symbols, see inside back cover; for an index of cities, see page 200.

DISTANCE SCALE

One inch represents 16 miles

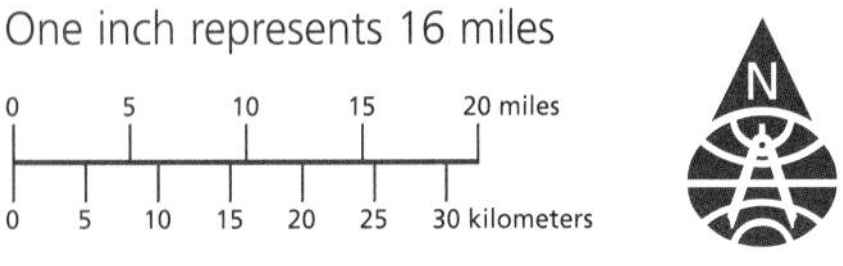

0 5 10 15 20 miles

0 5 10 15 20 25 30 kilometers

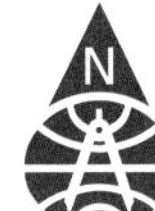

LOCATOR MAP

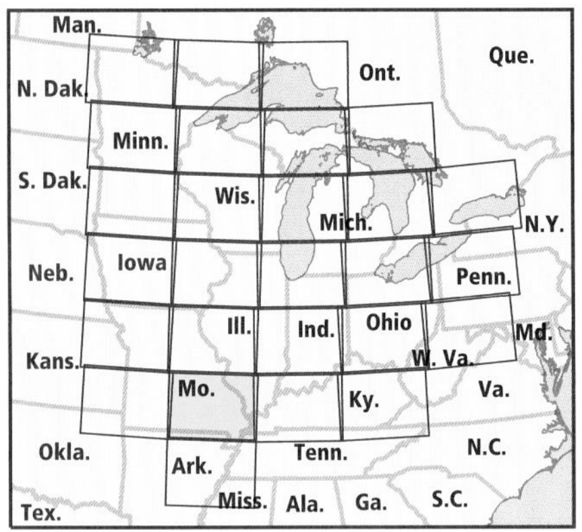

See the Pagefinder™ map on the inside of the front cover for map page numbers.

Why do some shields have more than one number in them?

You won't see these alongside the road, as this is a space-saving trick cartographers use on maps.

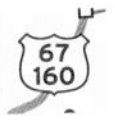

67 160 In this example, this route is both U.S. Highway 67 *and* U.S. Highway 160.

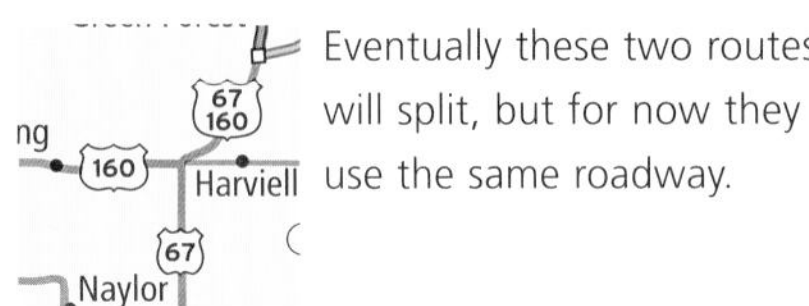

Eventually these two routes will split, but for now they use the same roadway.

What are those yellow boxes (with little numbers) on the maps?

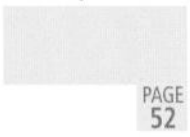

PAGE 52 That's where fun stuff happens, and this book describes that area in detail starting on the page number you see. Read all about what there is to see and do, what the shopping scene's like, where you can stay overnight, what the best food to try is and where you can find it, and even if there's a festival happening during your visit. These destination sections also offer specially designed maps to help figure out where attractions and restaurants are in relation to each other (and how to drive between them).

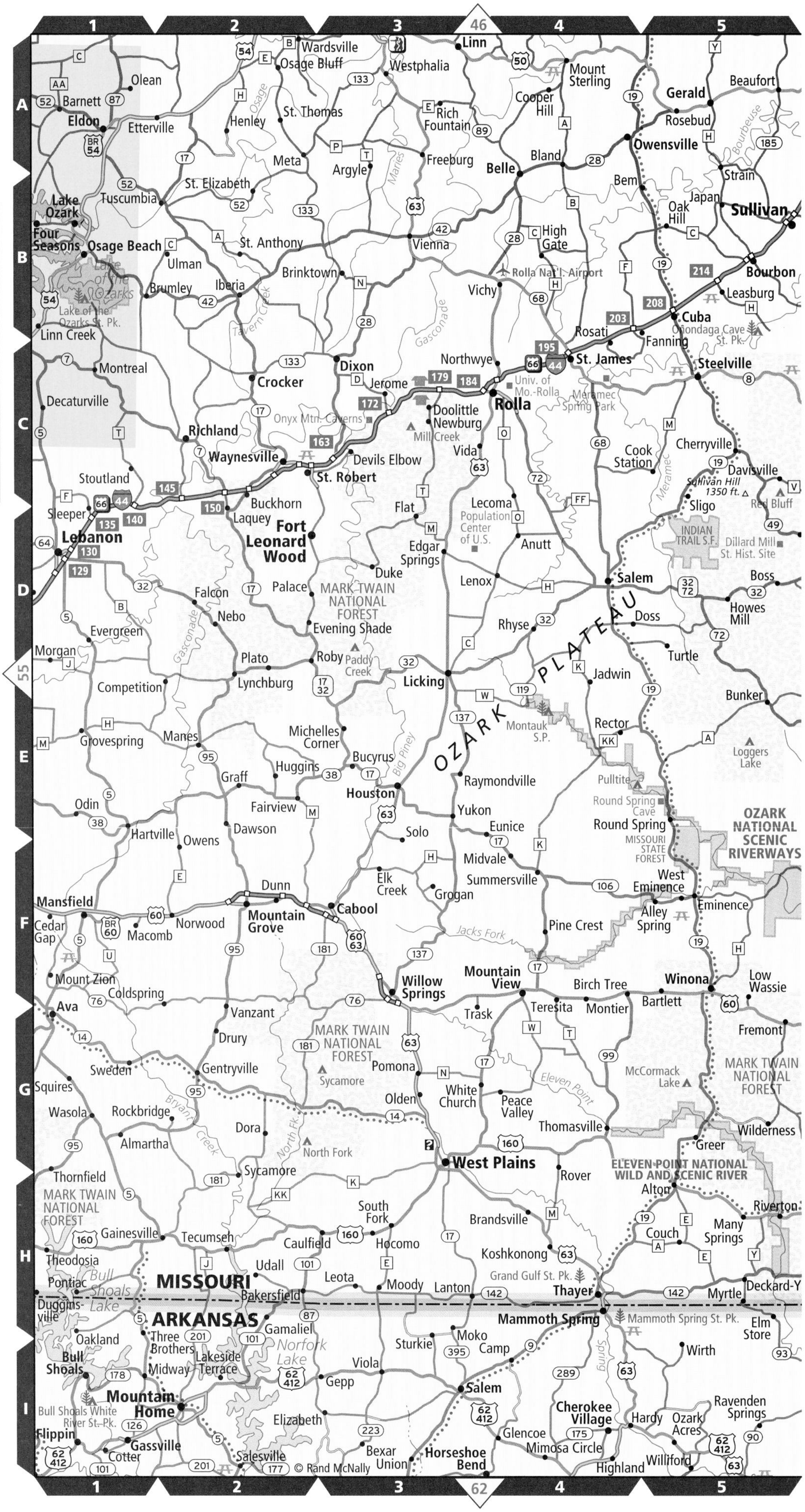

When you see this sign 14, the map continues on the page number indicated.

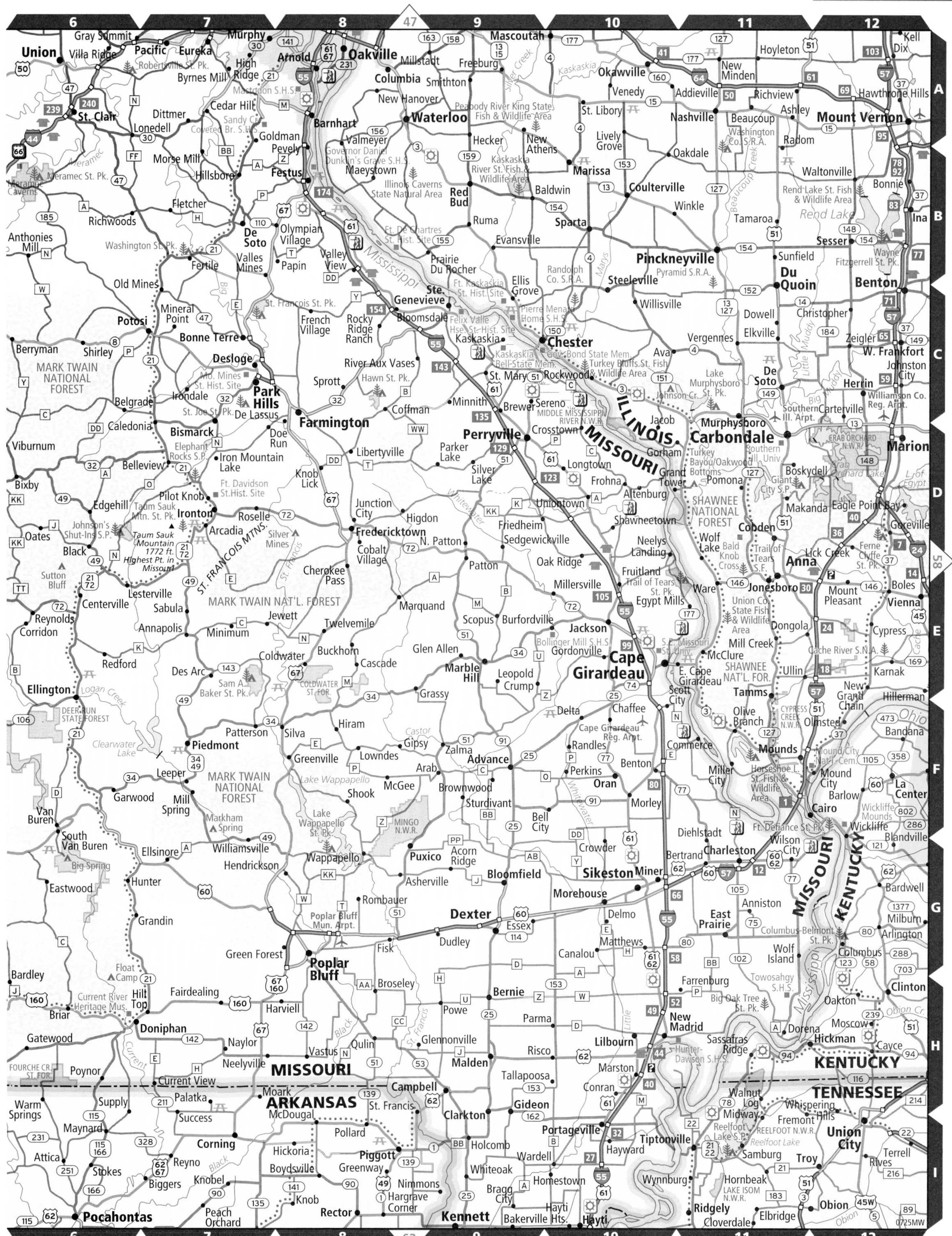

For a complete listing of symbols, see inside back cover; for an index of cities, see page 200.

DISTANCE SCALE

One inch represents 16 miles

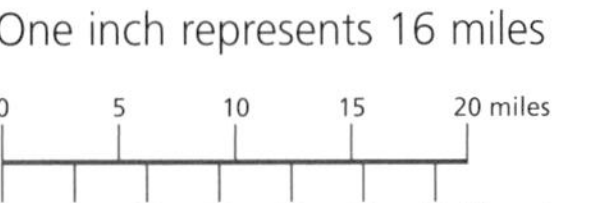

LOCATOR MAP

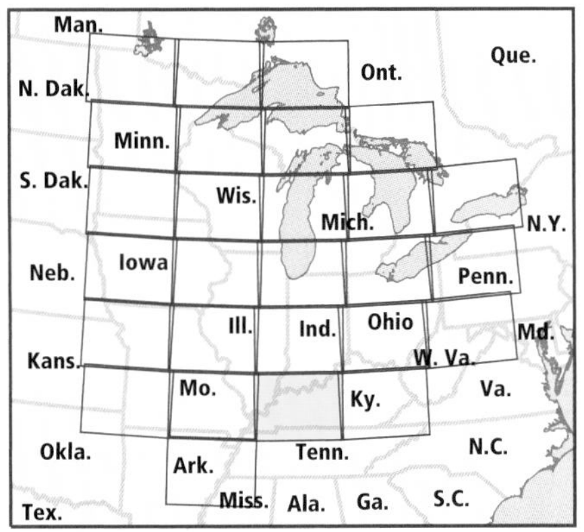

See the Pagefinder™ map on the inside of the front cover for map page numbers.

What can the map tell me about airports?

Airports represented by this symbol, ✈, are commercial, have paved runways 5,000 feet or longer, and have regularly scheduled passenger service–though some airports have many more flights than others.

What are those yellow boxes (with little numbers) on the maps?

That's where fun stuff happens, and this book describes that area in detail starting on the page number you see. Read all about what there is to see and do, what the shopping scene's like, where you can stay overnight, what the best food to try is and where you can find it, and even if there's a festival happening during your visit. These destination sections also offer specially designed maps to help figure out where attractions and restaurants are in relation to each other (and how to drive between them).

Why is there a red ribbon on this map?

The red award ribbon marks a Rand McNally Best of the Road™ trip route. Our editors have chosen scenic drives peppered with tasty dining, unique shopping, and memory-making things to do. Read more about four of these drives on pages 180-191. For more trip routes, visit go.randmcnally.com/BR.

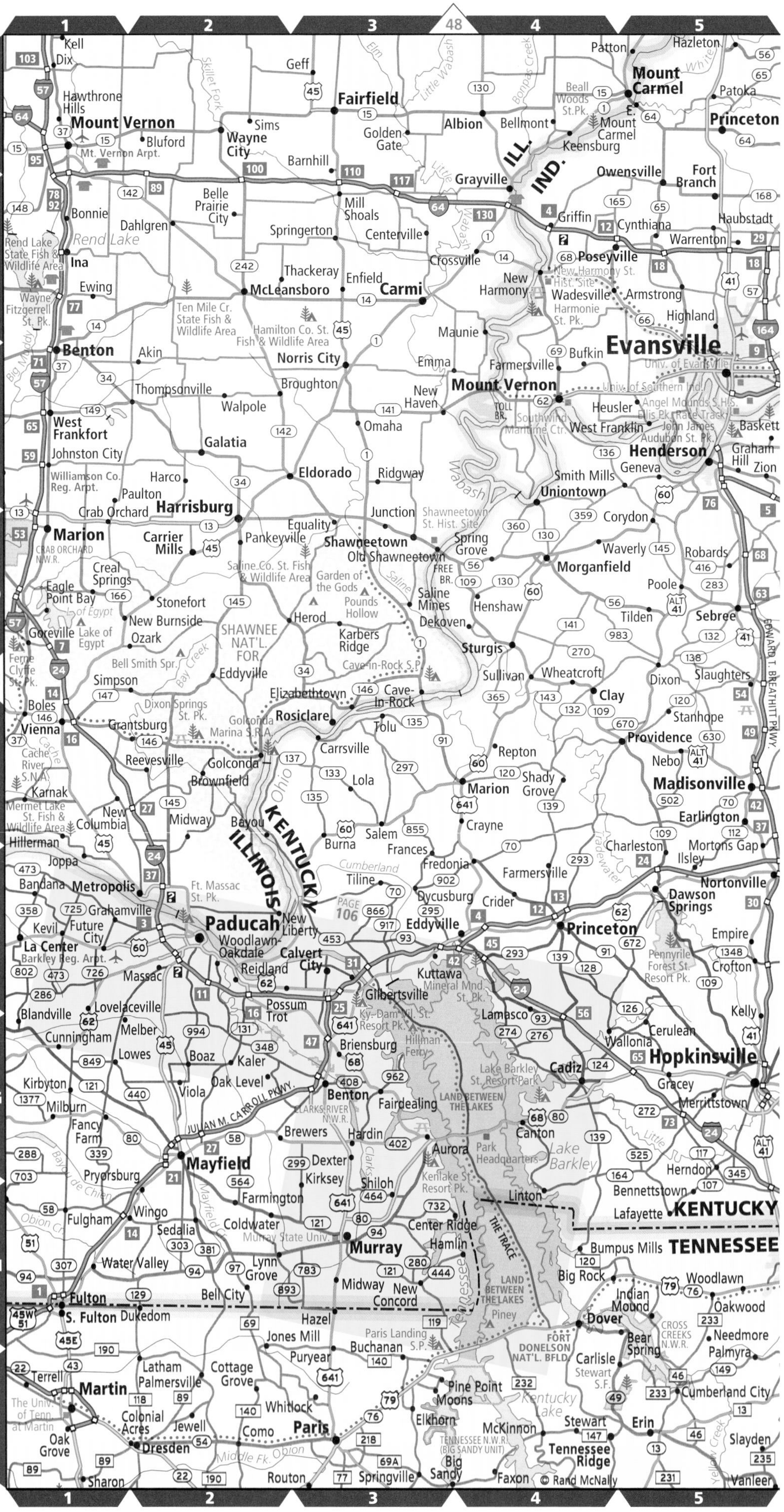

When you see this sign 14, the map continues on the page number indicated.

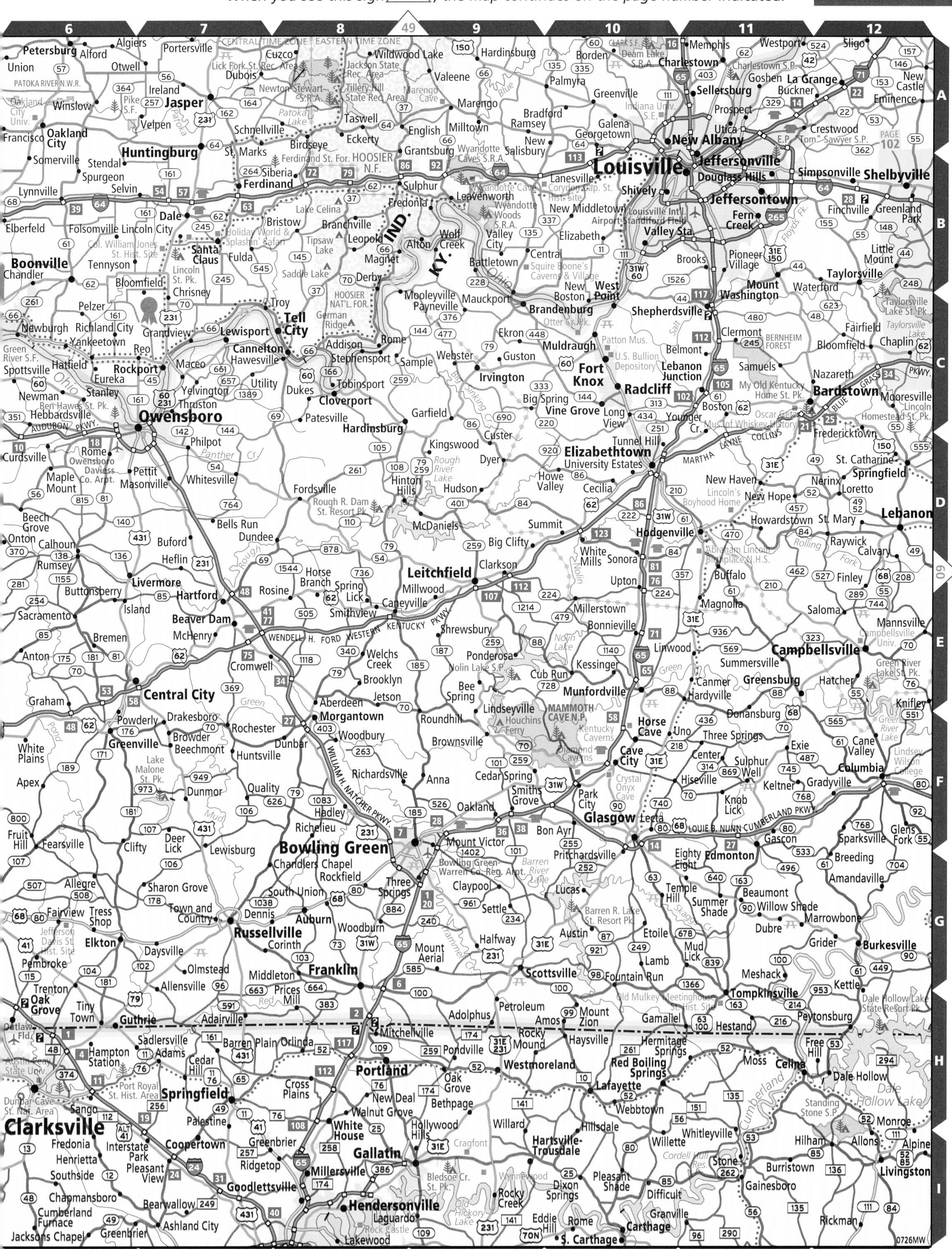

For a complete listing of symbols, see inside back cover; for an index of cities, see page 200.

DISTANCE SCALE

One inch represents 16 miles

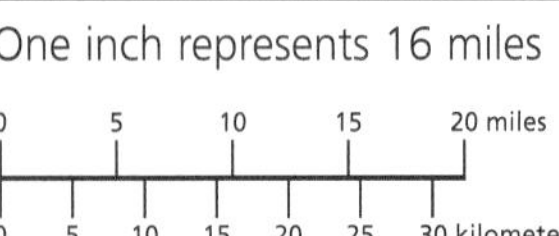

LOCATOR MAP

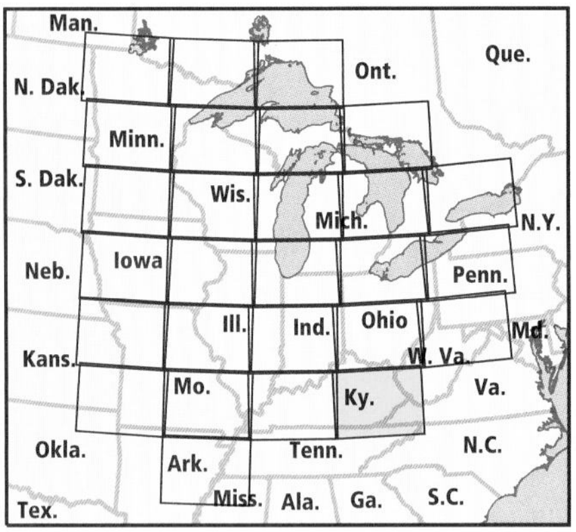

See the Pagefinder™ map on the inside of the front cover for map page numbers.

What are these little triangles on the map?

These indicate the peaks of mountains or hills. A filled-in triangle ▲ indicates the highest point in that state. A clear triangle △ indicates a landmark peak, which can help orientate you on your travels.

What are those yellow boxes (with little numbers) on the maps?

That's where fun stuff happens, and this book describes that area in detail starting on the page number you see. Read all about what there is to see and do, what the shopping scene's like, where you can stay overnight, what the best food to try is and where you can find it, and even if there's a festival happening during your visit. These destination sections also offer specially designed maps to help figure out where attractions and restaurants are in relation to each other (and how to drive between them).

Why is there a red ribbon on this map?

The red award ribbon marks a Rand McNally Best of the Road™ trip route. Our editors have chosen scenic drives peppered with tasty dining, unique shopping, and memory-making things to do. Read more about four of these drives on pages 180-191. For more trip routes, visit go.randmcnally.com/BR.

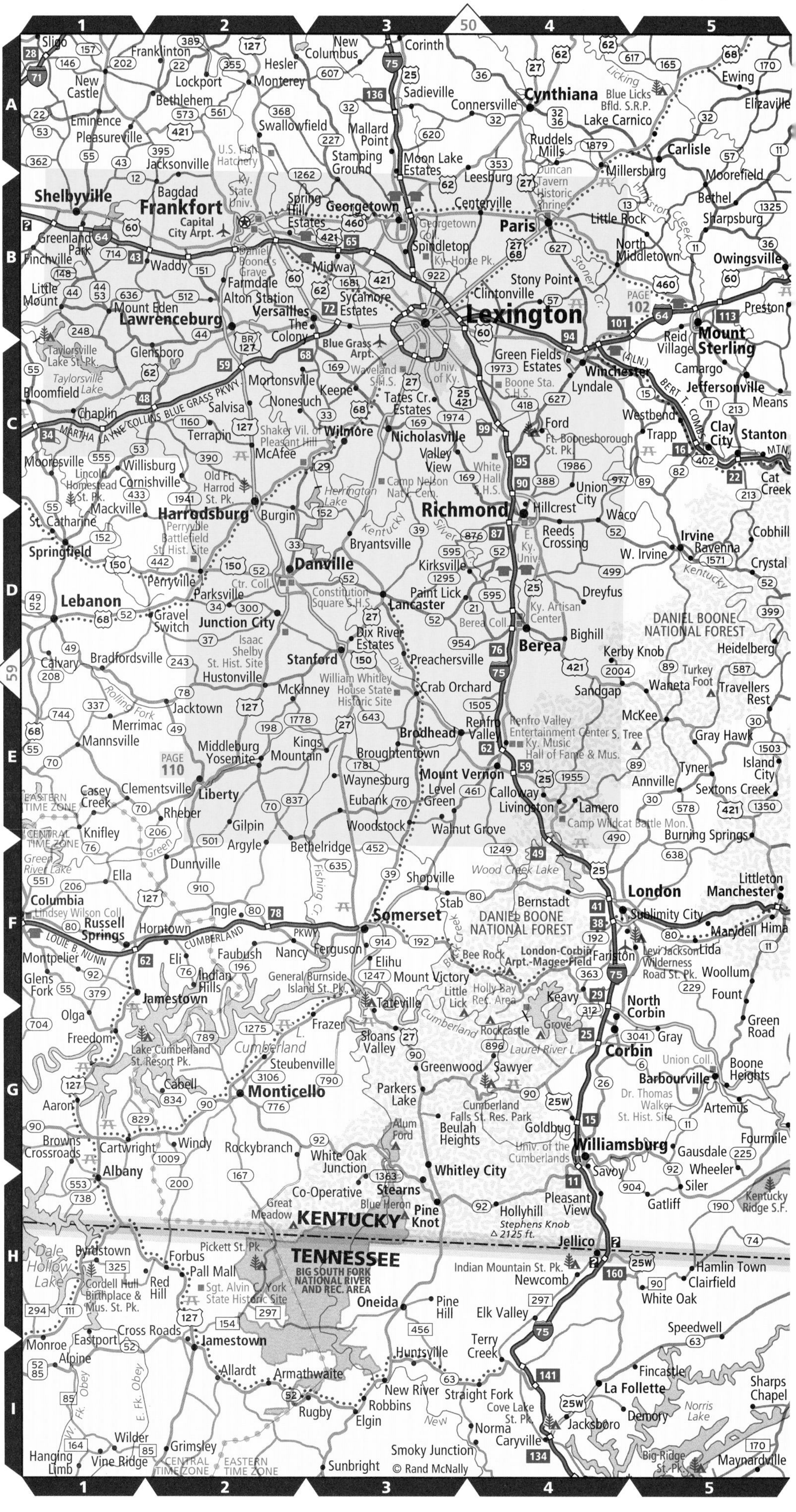

When you see this sign 14, the map continues on the page number indicated.

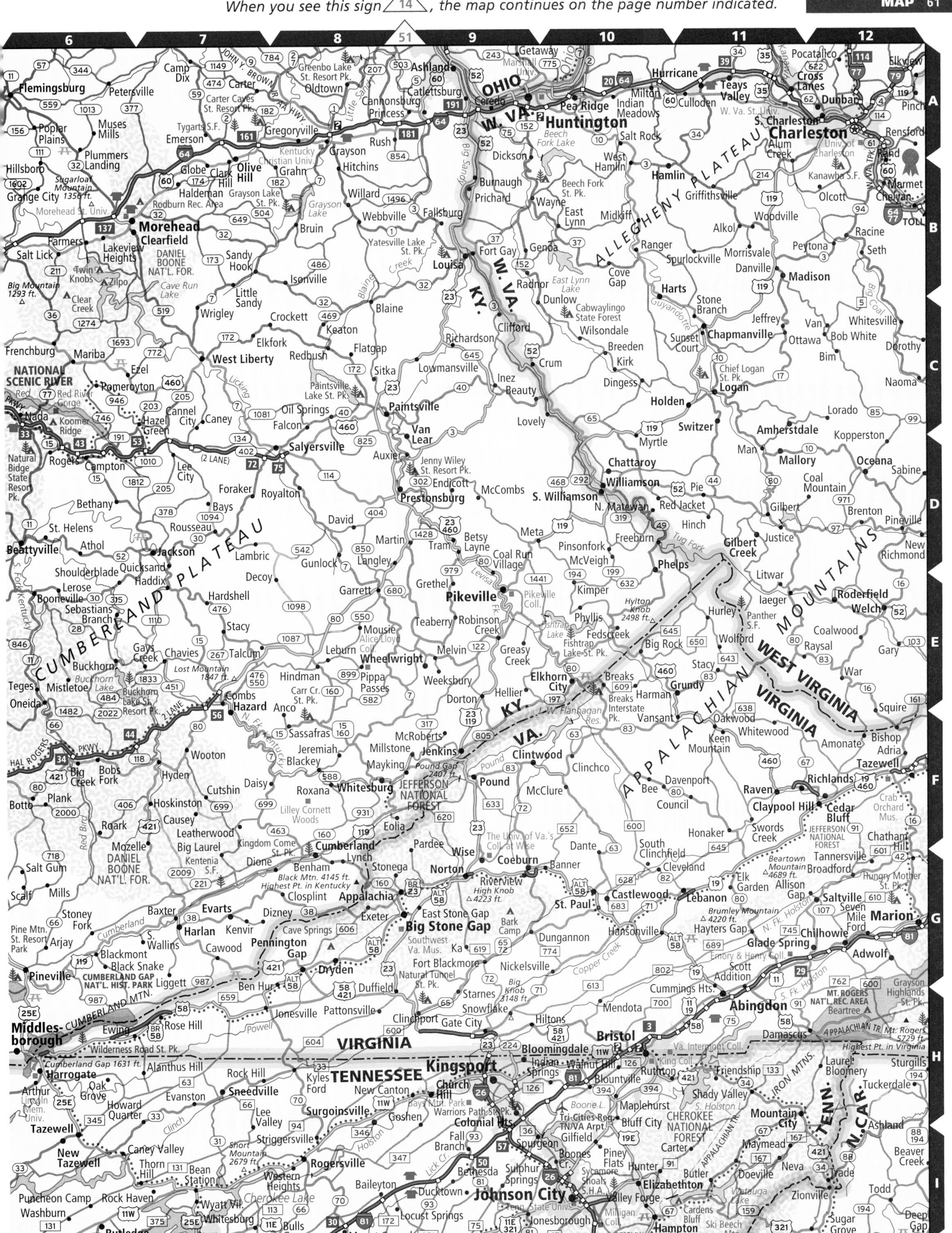

For a complete listing of symbols, see inside back cover; for an index of cities, see page 200.

DISTANCE SCALE

One inch represents 16 miles

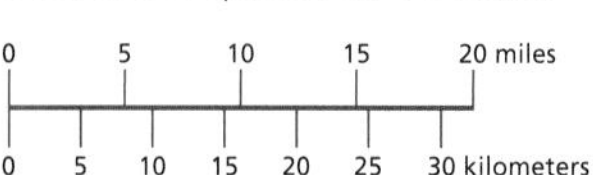

LOCATOR MAP

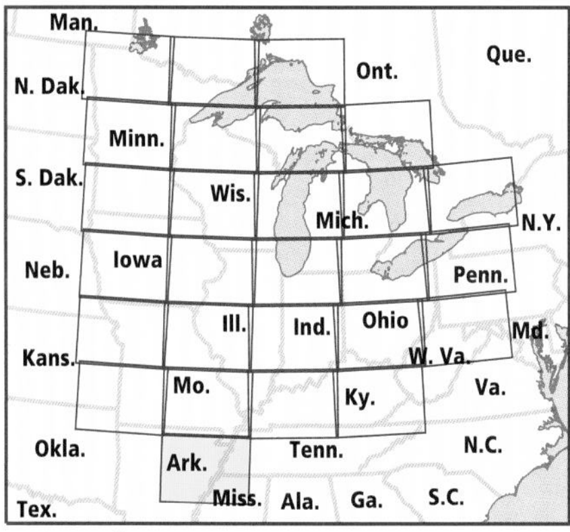

See the Pagefinder™ map on the inside of the front cover for map page numbers.

Why do some routes have more than one highway shield on them?

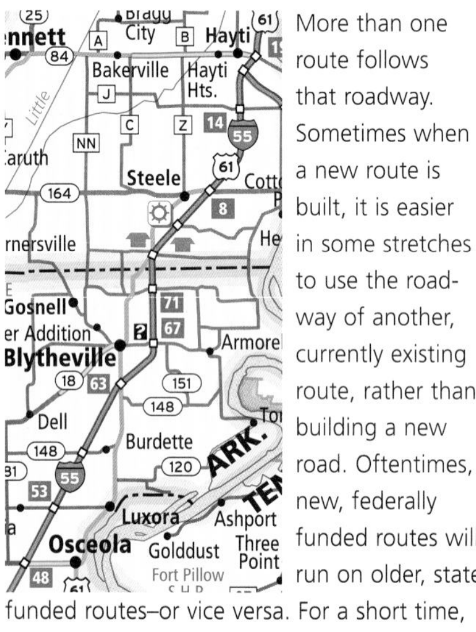

More than one route follows that roadway. Sometimes when a new route is built, it is easier in some stretches to use the roadway of another, currently existing route, rather than building a new road. Oftentimes, new, federally funded routes will run on older, state funded routes–or vice versa. For a short time, both routes will run along the same road. Or, as in the example above, an interstate (I-55) will run along the route of an older U.S. highway route (U.S. 61). Eventually though, they will split apart and go their separate ways.

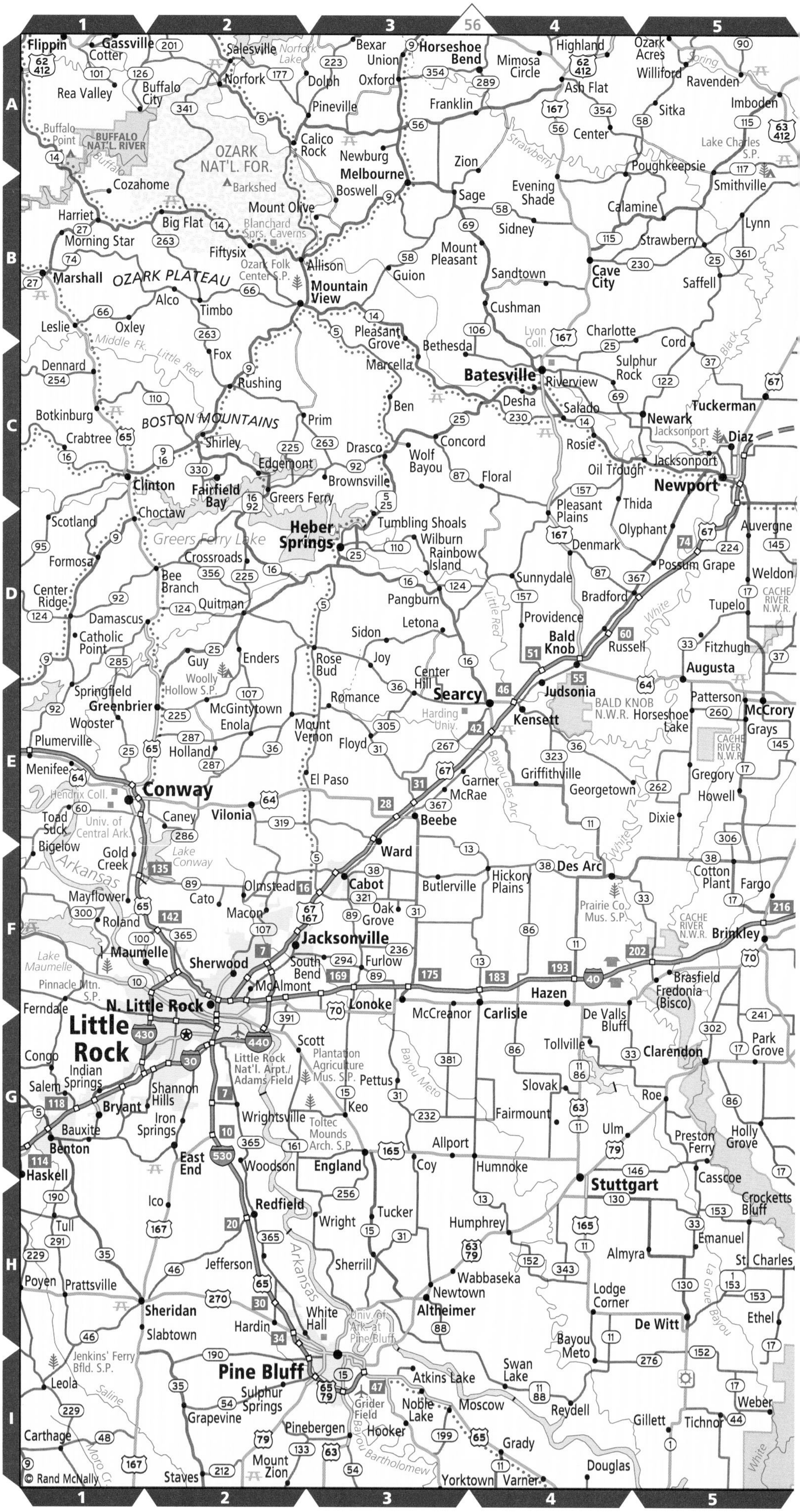

When you see this sign 14, the map continues on the page number indicated.

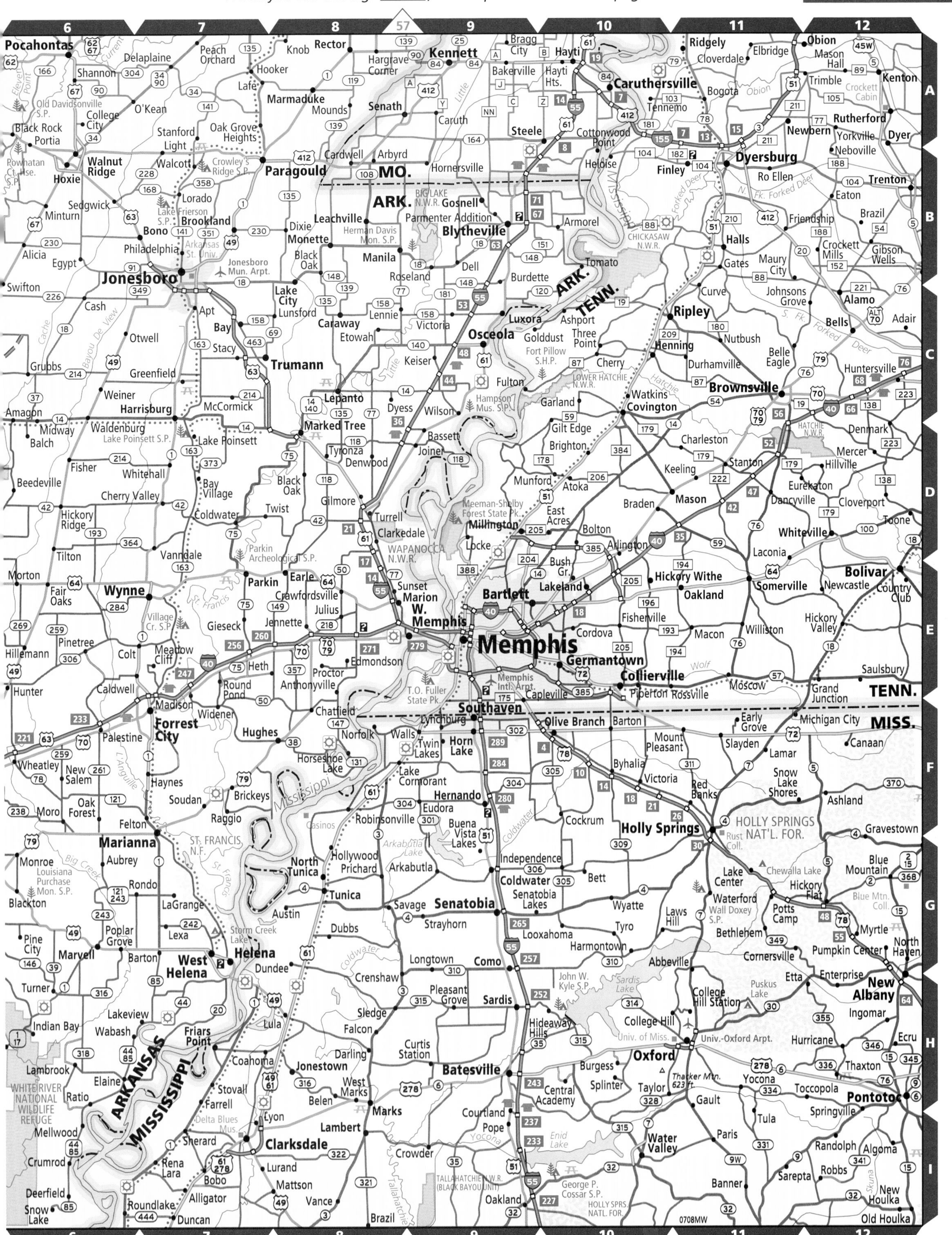

Illinois State Capitol Building, Springfield

Destination Guide

a Marquette **Racine** Cleveland **Lexington** Branson **Iowa City** Saint Paul **Grafton** Brainerd **Lowell** Mason City **Port Austin** Lebanon **Hannibal** Gra

Choosing the High Ground

Galena, a 19th-century lead mining boomtown, was a major river port attracting more than 350 steamboats a year. By the 1850s, Galena's population numbered around 16,000—at a time when Chicago was still a military outpost on a swampy lakeshore. Then the lead ore played out, the river silted over, and growing railroads bypassed Galena. The town went bust and languished for decades.

Now the boom is back. The mother lode: Tourism, fueled by flourishing arts and crafts and historic streets packed with boutiques, antique shops, interesting restaurants, and about 40 bed-and-breakfasts. More than 85 percent of Galena is on the National Register of Historic Places. Galena makes a good walking town, with challenging bluffs that flank Main Street. Perhaps because there's so much to see on foot, many visitors overlook the trolley tours that provide a good introduction to the town (often from atop the bluffs). Riverboat mining fortunes built several grand mansions. Several remain as private homes and bed-and-breakfast inns.

One not-to-be-missed historic site, the **Ulysses S. Grant Home** (500 Bouthillier St.), was built in 1860 in the Italianate style and presented as a gift in 1865 to the returning Civil War hero from the people of Galena. Restoration continues, as the home returns to the way it appeared in the November 14, 1868 issue of *Frank Leslie's Illustrated Newspaper*. The house contains much of the Grant family's original furniture.

Grant Park, Galena

Ulysses S. Grant Home, Galena

Send a bit of history to friends via a postcard hand-canceled at the nation's second-oldest continuously operating post office (Commerce and Green Sts.). Built from 1857 to 1859, it was selected by the Smithsonian as the "First Great American Post Office." This Renaissance Revival limestone building features mahogany counters beautified by arched lead-lined windows.

Visitors enjoy the surrounding hilly countryside, which includes the highest point in prairie-flat Illinois—**Charles Mound**, 1,235 feet. To enjoy spectacular vistas, follow the "Stagecoach Trail" from Galena to Lena. In the mid-19th century, this trail led stagecoaches through the rugged northwestern corner of Illinois. Stop to visit the vineyards of **Galena Cellars Winery** (which also has a retail outlet in downtown Galena, housed in a restored 1840s granary).

Carved into these gently rolling hills on 6,800 acres six miles east of Galena, **Eagle Ridge Resort & Spa** (444 Eagle Ridge Dr.) offers a wide range of outdoor activities to everyone, even non-guests. A trail system known for its flora and fauna (including native prairie plants, wild ginger, muskrat, and wild turkey) winds around Lake Galena and into hills and woodland. (Trail maps are available in the inn's lobby.) Boats may be rented at the marina; for a fee, equestrians may ride on more than 40 miles of trails. In winter, find cross-country skiing and sledding. With 63 holes at four separate courses, Eagle Ridge frequently makes "best" golf lists. Two-time U.S. Open champion Andy North helped design one of its courses, **The General**—one of the best in the Midwest.

Lincoln lore and old-fashioned sodas await in **Freeport**, Ill., site of the second of the famous seven debates between Abraham Lincoln and Stephen A. Douglas as they vied for a U.S. Senate seat in 1858. A life-size statue of the two politicians, the work of local sculptor Lily Tolpo, marks the spot. Stop at adjacent **Alber Ice Cream Parlor** (126 E. Douglas St.) for a creamy shake, cherry Coke, or Green River (a classic soda first developed in 1919). With chrome stools and a vintage soda fountain, this 1950s-style diner also offers good burgers.

Find two other foodie stops in nearby **Lena**. The late food maven James Beard raved about the brie at **Kolb-Lena Cheese Company** (3990 N. Sunnyside Rd., off US 20). **Lena Maid Meats** (500 W. Main St.), a butcher's shop started half a century ago by a Geman immigrant, produces excellent bratwurst.

Main Street, Galena

South of Galena, on the banks of the Mississippi, **Fulton** is as Dutch as the Delftware and fine lace in its shops. About 35 to 40 percent of its population is of Dutch heritage (as all the last names starting with "van" attest). **"De Immigrant"** (10th Ave. & 1st St.), a 90-foot-tall working windmill, was prefabricated in the Netherlands, disassembled, and transported to its Fulton home. Inside, volunteers trained by a Dutch miller wear authentic garb, down to their wooden shoes, to mill wheat, rye, buckwheat, and corn. Outside, wind turns the giant sails and flutters the flags of the 12 Dutch provinces. The gift shop sells stone-ground flour (along with "Life's a Grind" T-shirts).

What to eat

The name says it all: **Fried Green Tomatoes** (213 N. Main St.), a perennially popular eatery in downtown Galena, occupies an historic building that has housed an iron stove shop, a theater, a tombstone carver, and the Jo Daviess County Courthouse. Sample its eponymous appetizer—lightly breaded sliced green tomatoes, sautéed in olive oil and sprinkled with mozzarella and Parmesan, on a bed of tomato sauce.

What to buy

A brief walk from touristy Main Street (albeit via steep bluffs) takes visitors to the short stretch of Spring St./US 20 known as **"Artists Row."** Its destination shops encourage the curious to linger. You'll find artists such as Jane McNeely, who creates hand-wrought gold and silver jewelry at her **Milagro Studios** (402 Spring St.), housed in a small brick building dating from the 1850s. Pick up coffee beans to take home at **Isabella Imports** (230 N. Main St.), a wholesale/retail coffee roaster in Galena. Its unique décor includes chipped turquoise paint on the doors, a tin ceiling, bare-brick walls, sacks of beans, a couple of scarred wooden chairs, and a gleaming hand-built roaster. For a cup of the coffee, check out **Kaladi's** (309 S. Main St.) or the **Railway Café** (100 Bouthillier St.).

What to do

Stephenson County Barn Tour, mid-October.
Nouveau Wine Festival, Galena, weekend before Thanksgiving.
For more details about these festivals, please see page 174.

Information

Galena/Jo Daviess County Convention & Visitors Bureau, (877) 464-2536, www.galena.org.

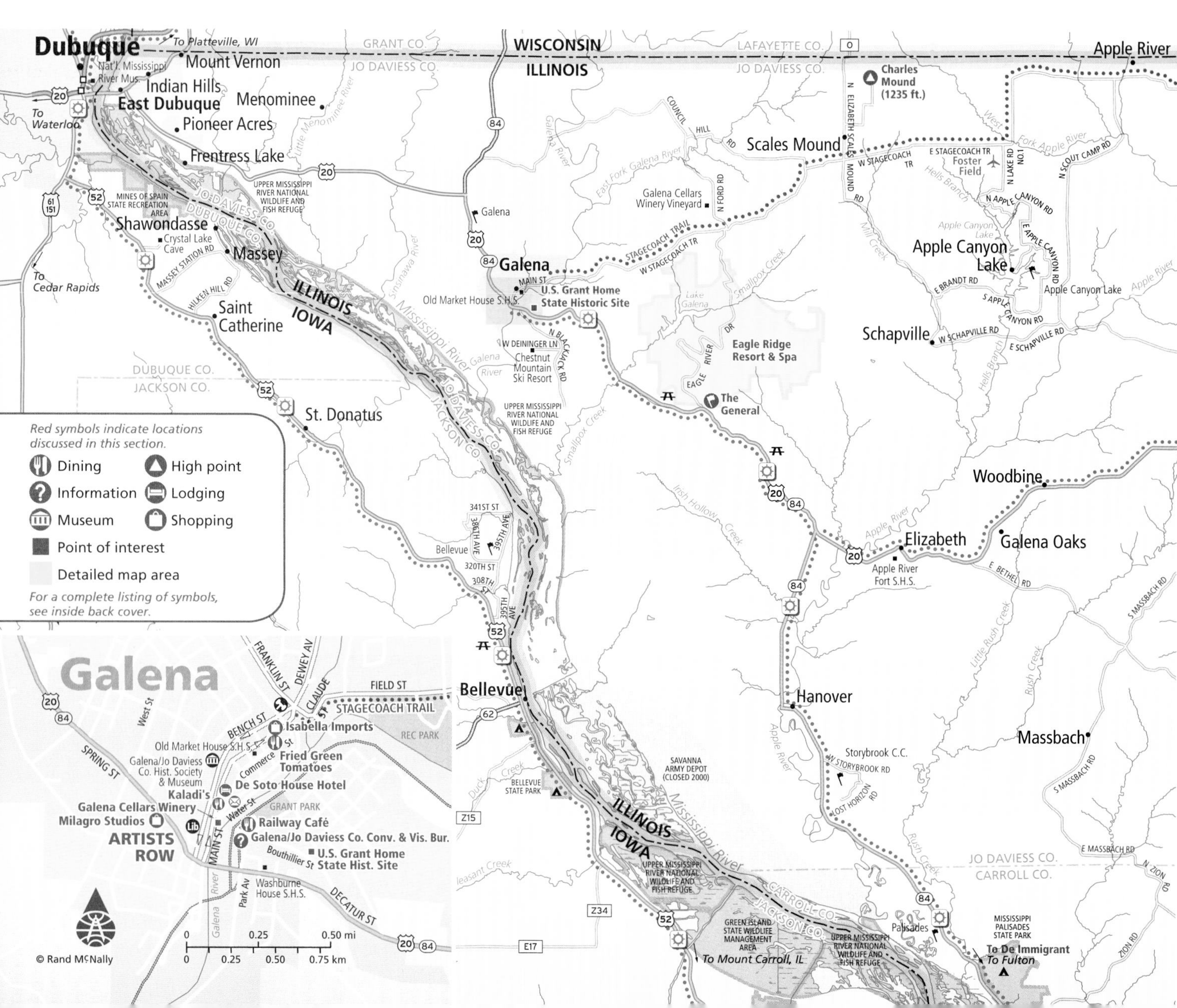

THE DE SOTO
HOUSE
OPENED IN APRIL, 1855, THE
FIVE-STORY 240 ROOM DE SOTO
HOUSE WAS THE LARGEST AND
MOST LUXURIOUS HOTEL IN THE
WEST. ABRAHAM LINCOLN SPOKE
FROM ITS BALCONY IN 1856 AND
STEPHEN A. DOUGLAS IN 1858.
ULYSSES S. GRANT MAINTAINED
HIS 1868 PRESIDENTIAL CAMPAI-
GN HEADQUARTERS HERE. BY 1880
GALENA'S PROSPERITY HAD FAD-
ED AND THE HOTEL'S TWO UPPER
STORIES WERE REMOVED.
ERECTED BY THE ILLINOIS STATE
HISTORICAL SOCIETY

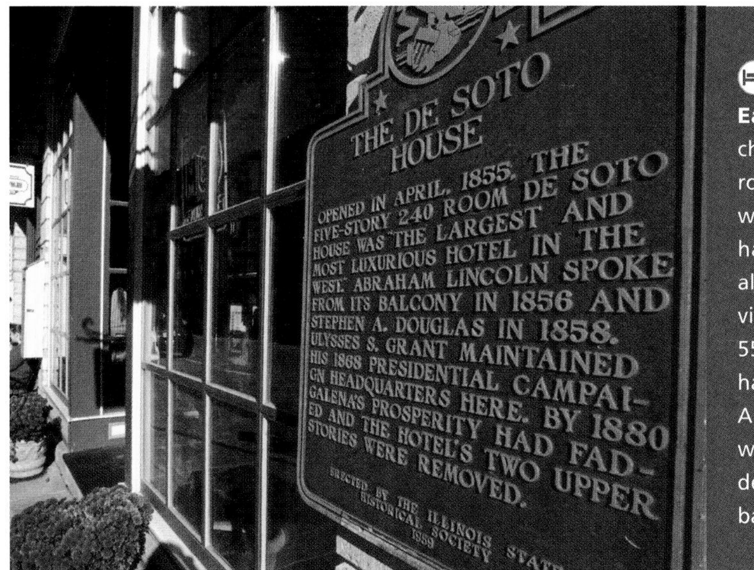

De Soto House Hotel, Galena

Lodging tips

Eagle Ridge Resort & Spa is a flexible lodging choice and includes an 80-room inn where guestrooms decorated in the Arts-and-Crafts style feature walkout patios with lake or woodland views. Some have whirlpool tubs and/or fireplaces. The resort also offers for rent more than 400 privately owned villas, condos, and spacious homes. Downtown, the 55-room **De Soto House Hotel** (230 S. Main St.) has hosted such notables as Mark Twain, Susan B. Anthony, Theodore Roosevelt, and Ulysses S. Grant, who used the hotel as headquarters for his presidential campaign. Abraham Lincoln spoke from a balcony here on July 23, 1856.

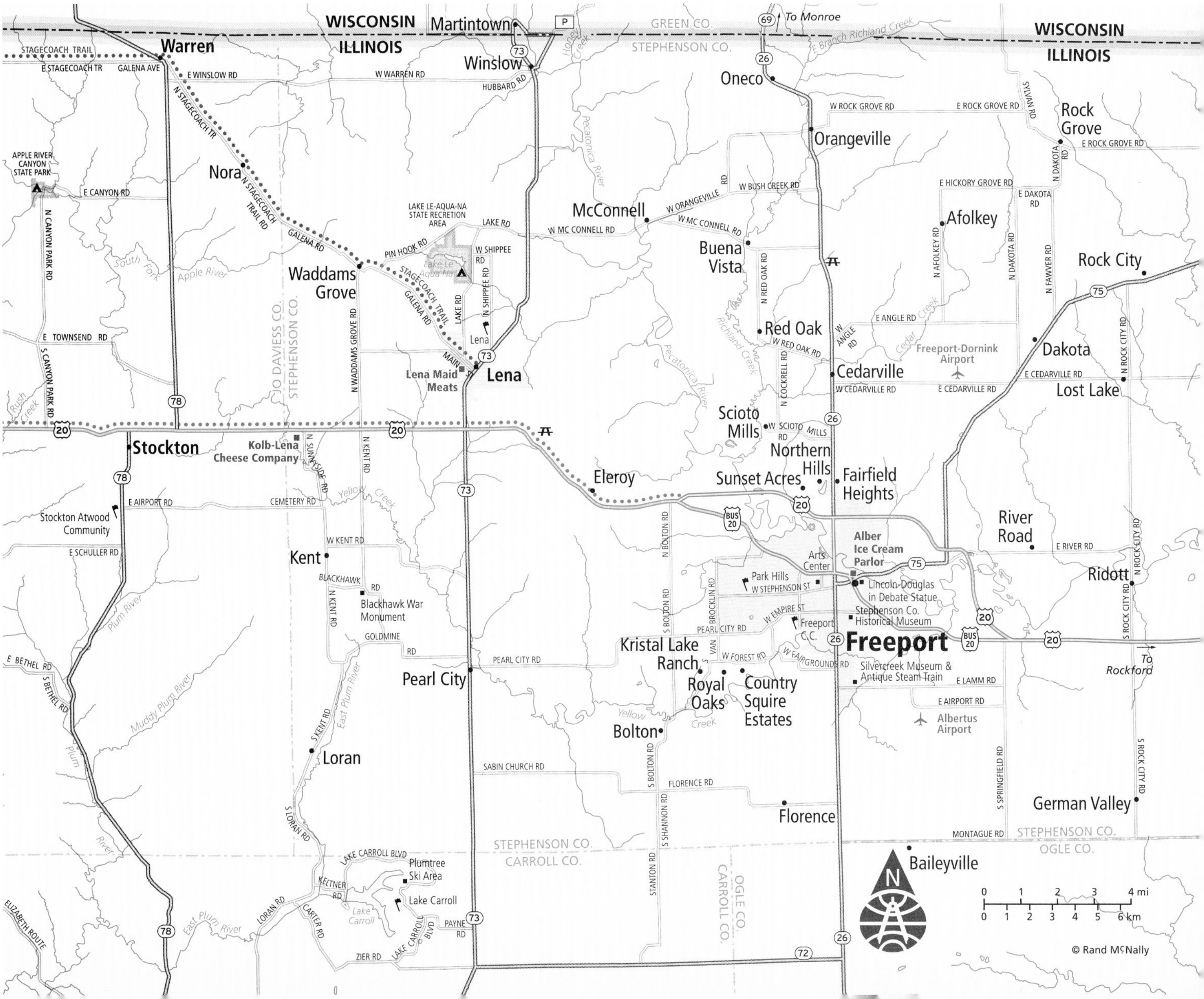

WISCONSIN
ILLINOIS
Martintown
Warren
Winslow
To Monroe
GREEN CO.
STEPHENSON CO.
Oneco
Orangeville
Rock Grove
Nora
APPLE RIVER CANYON STATE PARK
LAKE LE-AQUA-NA STATE RECREATION AREA
McConnell
Afolkey
Buena Vista
Rock City
Waddams Grove
Red Oak
Dakota
Lena
Lena Maid Meats
Cedarville
Freeport-Dornink Airport
Lost Lake
JO DAVIESS CO.
STEPHENSON CO.
Scioto Mills
Northern Hills
Stockton
Kolb-Lena Cheese Company
Eleroy
Sunset Acres
Fairfield Heights
Stockton Atwood Community
River Road
Alber Ice Cream Parlor
Arts Center
Park Hills
Lincoln-Douglas in Debate Statue
Stephenson Co. Historical Museum
Ridott
Kent
Blackhawk War Monument
Freeport C.C.
Freeport
Kristal Lake Ranch
Silvercreek Museum & Antique Steam Train
To Rockford
Pearl City
Royal Oaks
Country Squire Estates
Albertus Airport
Bolton
Loran
Florence
German Valley
STEPHENSON CO.
CARROLL CO.
OGLE CO.
Plumtree Ski Area
Lake Carroll
Baileyville
0 1 2 3 4 mi
0 1 2 3 4 5 6 km
© Rand McNally

Down by the **Riverside**

At **Hartford**, Ill., Meriwether Lewis and William Clark camped with their Corps of Discovery during the winter of 1803-1804. The expedition, begun on May 14, 1804, would carve a route from the Mississippi to the Pacific Ocean. Lewis and Clark's legacy now draws visitors to a clutch of small towns on the meandering Mississippi riverbank, where they discover ancient Americans, migrating birds, and lifeways carved by the Big Muddy.

At Camp River Dubois, Lewis and Clark recruited and trained a group of about 45 men, selecting leaders and weeding out troublemakers, dullards, and the lazy. The Corps practiced marksmanship and stowed their keelboat with food, weapons, tools, personal effects, and gifts for Native Americans. A cutaway full-scale replica of that keelboat—the primary vessel of the Corps (which also used two canoe-like pirogues)—is a major exhibit at the **Lewis & Clark Interpretive Center** (1 Lewis & Clark Trail, Hartford). A 32-foot mast, its square sail unfurled, sprouts from the deck of the 55-foot boat. A 12-minute film, "At Journey's Edge," examines the anticipation—and fears—of the Corps. Displays include "Across the Continent," which introduces visitors to the United States of 1803, with the Mississippi as its western border. Maps show how little was known at that time about the west; journal excerpts chronicle the expedition. At an adjacent replica of the fortified encampment, re-enactors and interpreters explain what life was like at Camp River Dubois.

Grafton, with its expansive river views, boasts antique shops, interesting down-home eateries, and cozy bed-and-breakfasts. It is home to the 19th-century **Ruebel Hotel** (217 E. Main St.), a weekend flea market with plenty of "junque," and two wineries. **Grafton Canoe and Kayak** (on the bike trail in front of the public boat launching ramp) offers bike rentals and float trips by canoe and kayak.

Bluffs along the Mississippi River

Re-enactors at Camp Dubois

Keelboat at the Lewis & Clark Interpretive Center, Hartford

Neighboring **Elsah**, a tiny river town, nestles amid soaring limestone bluffs. Postcard-pretty, quaint 19th-century stone cottages dot its winding, flower-lined streets. It has a pottery studio and, tucked among green hills, a lovely Methodist church. The entire community appears on the National Register of Historic Places. Nearby diversions include visiting apple and peach orchards.

Alton, the quintessential rivertown, throbs with the rhythms of the Mississippi, ever ready to show visitors the high water mark of the devastating 1993 flood. This town of red brick homes on cobbled streets was once considered the industrial "Pittsburgh of the Mississippi," known particularly for its glass. It's a great place to bicycle on a levee bike path, shop for colorful antique bottles and jars, sample local cafés and tearooms, and watch birds—especially eagles and pelicans. During winter, bald eagles fish the open waters at the lock and dam at Alton. In spring and fall, migrating American white pelicans travel the Mississippi Flyway between northern breeding grounds and their winter retreat on the Gulf of Mexico.

Opened in 2003, the **National Great Rivers Museum** (#2 Lock & Dam Way in East Alton) explains how the river has shaped the region's culture, history, economy, and ecology as it tells the story of the Mississippi and the people who live beside it and work on it. Built adjacent to the Melvin Price Locks & Dam, the newest and largest on the Mississippi, this state-of-the-art museum examines the development of the lock and dam system. You'll navigate a towboat through the locks and dam via a simulator—one of more than 20 interactive displays—and learn about river inhabitants such as the spotted gar and giant paddlefish, which can grow up to six feet long and weigh more than 125 pounds. Public tours are available seven days a week; admission is free.

Collinsville is to condiments what Colby is to cheese. Its most prominent landmark is a bright red, 170-foot-tall catsup bottle—actually a 100,000-gallon water tower. Collinsville's signature festival: the International Horseradish Festival (mid-June). Sixty-two percent of the world's horseradish supply grows in this region, where the soil is rich in potash. Believe it or not, it's acceptable to speak of Collinsville in the same breath as the Taj Mahal and Great Pyramids.

Cahokia Mounds State Historic Site

Like those wonders of the world, Collinsville's **Cahokia Mounds State Historic Site**—site of a prehistoric city dating back to AD 1100—is a UNESCO World Heritage Site. An interpretive center includes a re-created village and the screening of "City of the Sun," a 15-minute film about Cahokia.

What to eat

Legend has it that Upper Alton got its nickname "Pietown" from the local women's custom of baking pies with locally grown cherries for soldiers encamped nearby during the Mexican War of 1846 and the Civil War and, later, for soldiers traveling through Alton on trains. **My Just Desserts** (31 E. Broadway, Alton & 18 Lasalle St., Elsah) serves about a dozen different pies daily, handmade early in the morning, with "Mrs. Ledbetter's chocolate pie" a favorite (ask for a recipe card). Other varieties include apple praline, Amish walnut, peach, lemon truffle, pumpkin pecan, cherry almond crunch, and Ozark berry pie.

What to buy

At the Lewis & Clark Interpretive Center, the Store of Discovery (a gift shop operated by the Lewis & Clark Society of America) specializes in books and memorabilia commemorating the five months that Lewis and Clark and the Corps of Discovery spent at Camp River Dubois. Find books by local authors, hand-dipped candles, and homemade soaps from local artisans. In Alton, **History & Hauntings Book Co.** (515 E. 3rd St.) specializes exclusively in ghost-related books (Alton is said to be one of the most haunted small towns in America). Owner Troy Taylor, a local author, leads tours to haunted venues in the region (including walking tours of downtown Alton).

What to do

Bald Eagle Days, Grafton,
late December through February.
Great Rivers Towboat Festival, Grafton,
last weekend of June.
For more details about these festivals, please see page 174.

Information

Alton Regional Convention & Visitors Bureau,
(800) 258-6645, www.visitalton.com

Lodging tips

In the 1930s, the Civilian Conservation Corps (CCC) built lodges and cabins in many Illinois state parks. These historic structures have since been refurbished and modernized. The **Pere Marquette Lodge and Conference Center** (13653 Lodge Blvd., Grafton) lies in pretty Pere Marquette State Park. Accommodations include 50 rooms in the lodge plus 22 cabins built of natural stone. A rustic Great Room features a beamed ceiling, a 700-ton stone fireplace, and a human-size chessboard. There is a cocktail lounge and a 150-seat restaurant that specializes in catfish and prime rib dinners. Find more than a dozen bed-and-breakfasts in Alton, Elsah, and Grafton, as well as a wide selection of hotels and motels.

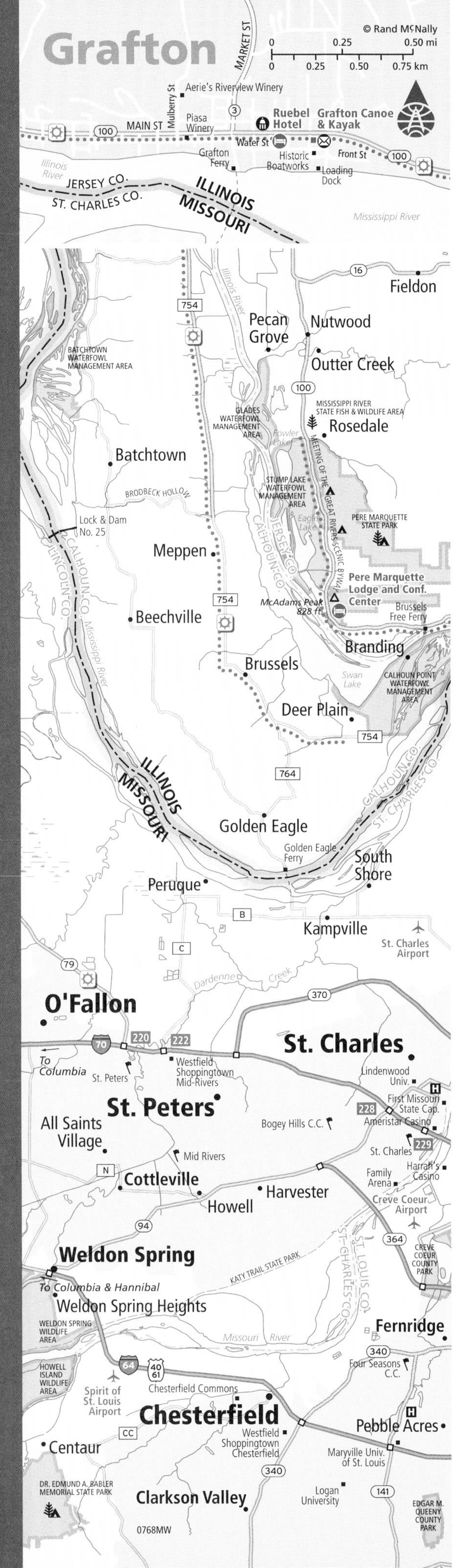

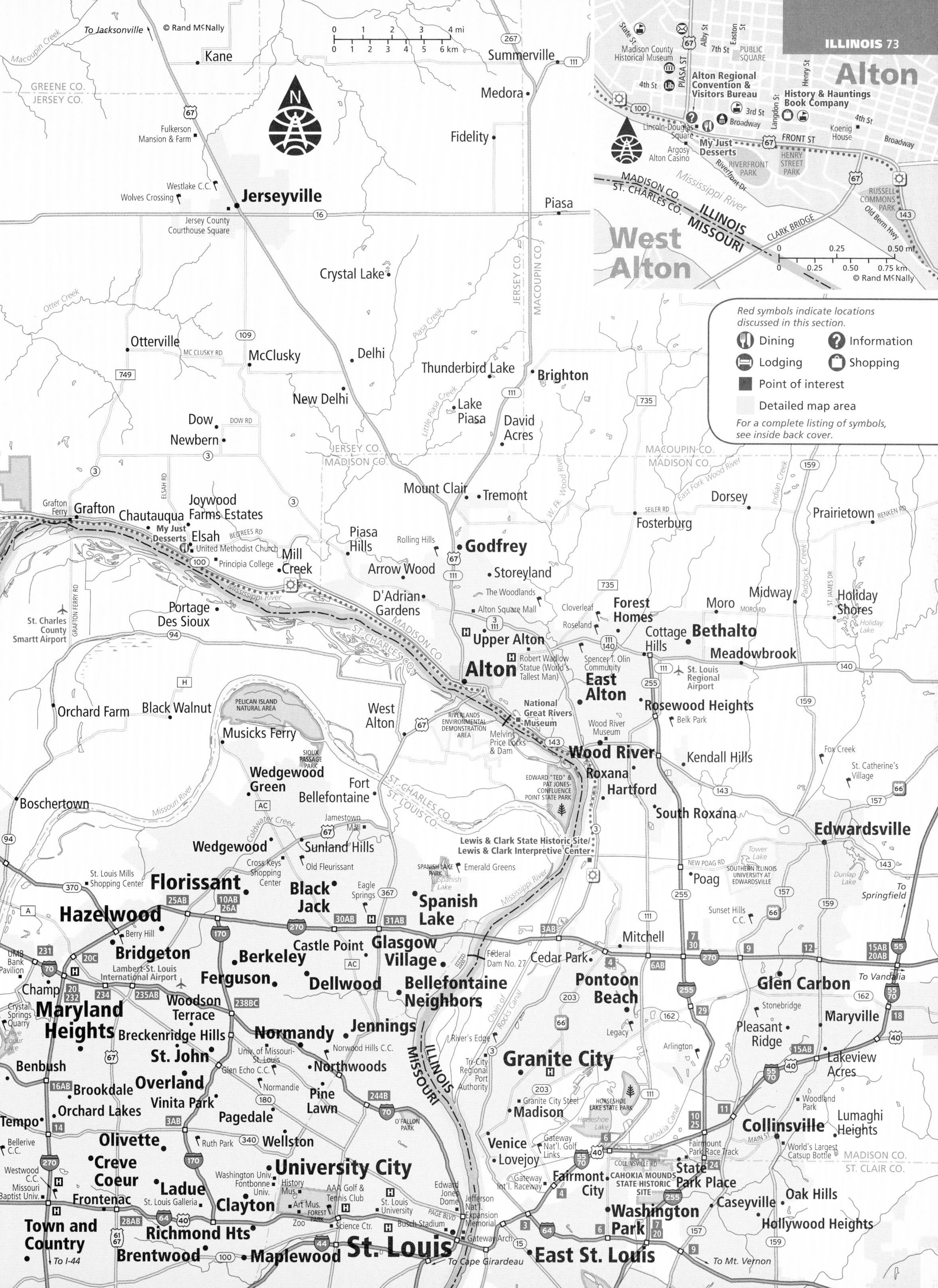
Alton
West Alton
Red symbols indicate locations discussed in this section.
Dining
Information
Lodging
Shopping
Point of interest
Detailed map area
For a complete listing of symbols, see inside back cover.
© Rand McNally
Jerseyville
Godfrey
Alton
East Alton
Wood River
Bethalto
Edwardsville
Glen Carbon
Collinsville
Granite City
East St. Louis
St. Louis
Florissant
Hazelwood
Maryland Heights
University City
Clayton
Madison
Washington Park
Fairmont City
Pontoon Beach
Alton Regional Convention & Visitors Bureau
History & Hauntings Book Company
My Just Desserts
National Great Rivers Museum
Lewis & Clark State Historic Site/ Lewis & Clark Interpretive Center
Cahokia Mounds State Historic Site
Grafton
Elsah
Brighton
Piasa
Summerville
Medora
Fidelity
Kane
Crystal Lake
Delhi
Otterville
McClusky
New Delhi
Dow
Newbern
Mount Clair
Tremont
Dorsey
Fosterburg
Prairietown
Forest Homes
Moro
Midway
Holiday Shores
Cottage Hills
Meadowbrook
Rosewood Heights
Roxana
Hartford
South Roxana
Kendall Hills
Mitchell
Cedar Park
Maryville
Pleasant Ridge
Lakeview Acres
Lumaghi Heights
State Park Place
Caseyville
Oak Hills
Hollywood Heights
Venice
Lovejoy
Black Jack
Spanish Lake
Bridgeton
Berkeley
Glasgow Village
Ferguson
Dellwood
Bellefontaine Neighbors
Jennings
Normandy
Northwoods
Overland
St. John
Pine Lawn
Pagedale
Wellston
Olivette
Creve Coeur
Ladue
Richmond Hts
Brentwood
Maplewood
Town and Country
Frontenac
Benbush
Brookdale
Orchard Lakes
Tempo
Vinita Park
Woodson Terrace
Breckenridge Hills
Wedgewood Green
Wedgewood
Sunland Hills
Fort Bellefontaine
Musicks Ferry
Black Walnut
Orchard Farm
Boschertown
Portage Des Sioux
Piasa Hills
Arrow Wood
Storeyland
D'Adrian Gardens
Upper Alton
Thunderbird Lake
Lake Piasa
David Acres
Chautauqua
Joywood Farms Estates
Mill Creek
Poag
To Springfield
To Vandalia
To Mt. Vernon
To Cape Girardeau
To Jacksonville
ILLINOIS
MISSOURI

Mr. Lincoln's Hometown

Wander around **Springfield**, Ill., tracing the footsteps of the 16th president, and it seems as though you have just missed running into him. A black, stovepipe hat hangs in the hall of Abraham Lincoln's former home; documents and deeds are scattered in disarray on the desk of the law offices from which he practiced—as if "Big Abe" had just stepped out for lunch. So much is the Illinois state capital imbued with his spirit and presence that it truly lives up to its appellation, "Mr. Lincoln's Hometown."

His presence also pervades the only home he ever owned, a modest, two-story frame house (426 S. 7th St.), purchased for $1,200. With neat green shutters and a brown picket fence, the **Lincoln Home National Historic Site** has been restored and furnished to look as it did in the Lincoln era. It even houses a few belongings of the Lincoln family. You'll visit the parlor where Lincoln was asked to run for president—and where he spread papers out on the floor to read, unable to find a comfortable chair to fit his long legs. In the **Lincoln-Herndon Law Offices** (6th & Adams), his lanky six-foot-four-inch frame once stretched on the floor as the future president monitored hearings in the federal court below through a convenient crack in the floorboards.

It was from Springfield's red brick railroad depot (10th & Monroe), now called the **Lincoln Depot,** that he departed to assume the burdens of the presidency. On the rainswept morning of February 11, 1861, he said: "Here I have lived a quarter of a century and have passed from a young to an old man ... I now leave, not

Lincoln tomb, Oak Ridge Cemetery

Cozy Dog Drive In, Springfield

knowing when or whether ever I may return, with a task before me greater than that which rested upon Washington." Other popular Lincoln sites include the **Old State Capitol** where he delivered his famous "house divided" speech, and the **Oak Ridge Cemetery** where, in the tomb area, are carved the poignant words "Now He Belongs to the Ages."

Schedule at least a half-day to explore the 100,000-square-foot **Abraham Lincoln Presidential Library and Museum** (212 N. 6th St.). Twice the size of any other presidential museum, it sprawls over an entire city block. Twenty-first century technology leads the tour through Lincoln's heroic life. You'll encounter ghostly holographic images and startling sound effects, such as the rumbling Civil War cannon fire that shakes your seat as smoke erupts into the museum's 250-seat Holavision® theater during the "Ghosts of the Library" presentation. You'll also confront life-size figures from Lincoln's time—such as the sinister John Wilkes Booth—realistically created from silicon-latex, with hair added one strand at a time. The "Ask Mr. Lincoln" exhibit lets visitors solicit the president's opinion on topics such as marriage, while the Treasures Gallery provides close-up views of everything from Lincoln's spectacles to his wife's jewelry.

About 20 miles northwest of Springfield lies **Lincoln's New Salem State Historic Site**, a reconstructed village with timber houses and shops. Lincoln spent six of his formative years in New Salem (1831-1837), working as postmaster and in the general store, and studying his law books in the cooper's shop by the light of a fire made from wood shavings.

Of course, Springfield offers visitors more than the Lincoln legacy, such as the restored birthplace and home of poet **Vachel Lindsay** (603 S. 5th St.). The first American poet invited to recite at Oxford University and the author of poems such as "The Congo," Lindsay was known as a young man to recite his poems in exchange for room and board.

Many Frank Lloyd Wright admirers regard the **Dana-Thomas House** (301 E. Lawrence) as one of the best-preserved and most complete of his early Prairie School houses. When the rising young architect was commissioned to design a house for socialite and women's activist Susan Lawrence Dana, he took the opportunity to experiment freely with new design ideas and techniques. Completed in 1904, the house is one of Wright's largest and most elaborate, with more than 100 pieces of original Wright-designed white oak furniture as well as 250 art glass doors, windows, and light panels. Two hundred original light fixtures and skylights illuminate its interior.

A segment of famed Route 66 runs through Springfield, offering hot dog fans the chance to visit the classic **Cozy Dog Drive In** (2935 S. 6th St.), a landmark since 1949. Try its eponymous Cozy Dog (a hot dog deep-fried in a secret bread batter). And at **Shea's Gas Station Museum** (2075 Peoria Rd.), you'll find an original Texaco station with an extensive museum of Route 66 memorabilia.

What to eat

Visiting celeb foodies from Al Roker to Burt Wolf have sampled the "horseshoe sandwich," created in 1928 by the head chef of the Red Lion Inn, a popular upscale restaurant in the Leland Hotel. This gooey cheese mountain comprises two slices of bread layered with meat, fish, or poultry, smothered with a rich, tangy cheese sauce, and finished off with mounds of crispy fries. While the Leland Hotel is long gone, the horseshoe lives on at several local pubs and restaurants.

What to buy

Stop at Salisbury to visit the studio of self-taught folk artist **George Colin**, who retired from his job as a flour-mill laborer to create a huge body of work as colorful as he is. Large-scale florals and whimsical takes on the outdoors, cast in bold colors, make the work stand out. The **Abraham Lincoln Presidential Library and Museum** sells a huge selection of Lincoln memorabilia, including stovepipe hats for kids. Find quirky items—such as a Lincoln bobble head—at **Mr. Lincoln's Souvenirs** (603 S. 7th St.). Also in demand: a "Cozy Couple" pair of plush-toy wieners from **Cozy Dog Drive In.**

What to do

International Route 66 Mother Road Festival, Springfield, September.
Candlelight New Salem Tour, New Salem State Historic Site, early October.
For more details about these festivals, please see page 174.

Information

Springfield Illinois Convention & Visitors Bureau, (800) 545-7300, www.springfield.il.us/visit.

Lodging tips

Accommodations range from the deluxe 288-room **Crowne Plaza Hotel** (3000 S. Dirksen Pkwy.), well endowed with such amenities as concierge floors, an indoor pool, a fitness center, and a rooftop garden, to a stylish bed-and-breakfast, **The Inn at 835** (835 S. Second St.). Built in 1909 as Springfield's first modern apartment house, the inn appears on the National Register of Historic Places. It offers 10 luxurious guest rooms.

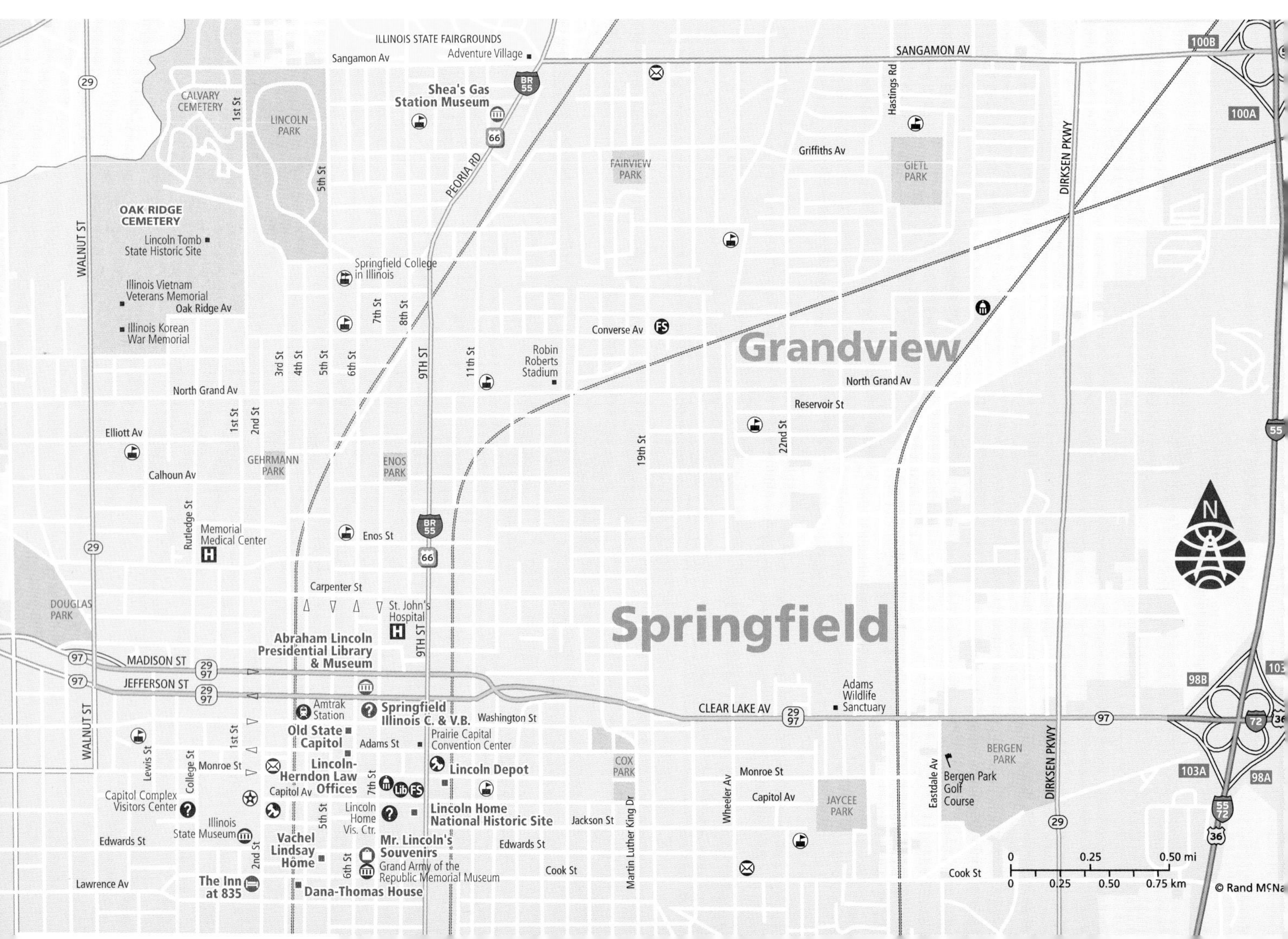

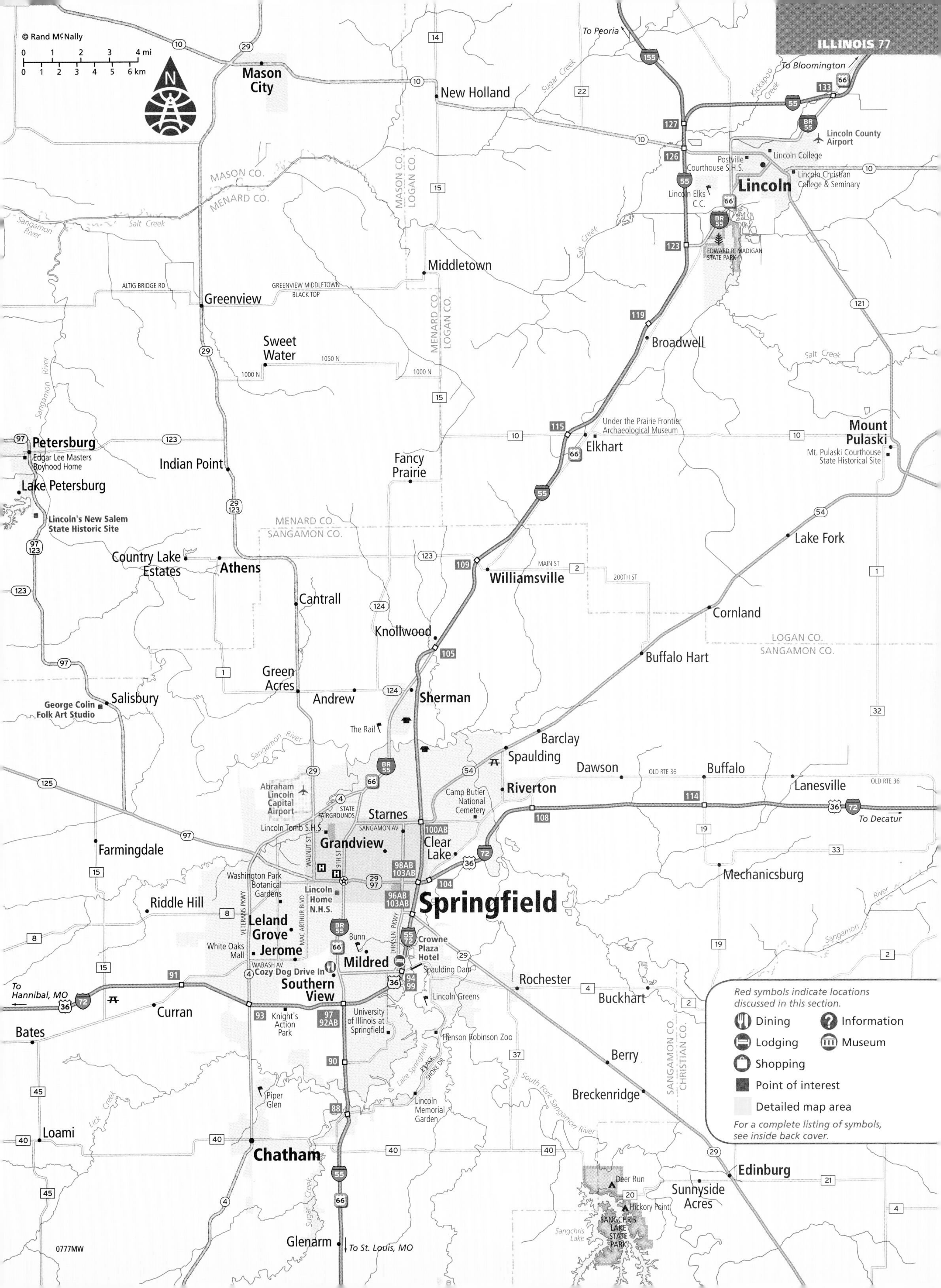
© Rand McNally
0 1 2 3 4 mi
0 1 2 3 4 5 6 km
N
Mason City
New Holland
To Peoria
To Bloomington
Sugar Creek
Kickapoo Creek
Lincoln County Airport
Lincoln College
Postville Courthouse S.H.S.
Lincoln Christian College & Seminary
Lincoln
Lincoln Elks C.C.
EDWARD R. MADIGAN STATE PARK
MASON CO.
MENARD CO.
LOGAN CO.
Sangamon River
Salt Creek
Middletown
ALTIG BRIDGE RD
Greenview
GREENVIEW MIDDLETOWN BLACK TOP
Sweet Water
1050 N
1000 N
Broadwell
Petersburg
Edgar Lee Masters Boyhood Home
Indian Point
Lake Petersburg
Lincoln's New Salem State Historic Site
Under the Prairie Frontier Archaeological Museum
Elkhart
Fancy Prairie
Mount Pulaski
Mt. Pulaski Courthouse State Historical Site
SANGAMON CO.
Lake Fork
Country Lake Estates
Athens
MAIN ST
200TH ST
Williamsville
Cantrall
Cornland
Knollwood
Buffalo Hart
Green Acres
Andrew
Sherman
Salisbury
George Colin Folk Art Studio
The Rail
Barclay
Spaulding
Dawson
OLD RTE 36
Buffalo
Lanesville
Abraham Lincoln Capital Airport
STATE FAIRGROUNDS
Camp Butler National Cemetery
Riverton
Starnes
To Decatur
Lincoln Tomb S.H.S.
SANGAMON AV
Grandview
Clear Lake
Farmingdale
WALNUT ST
9TH ST
Washington Park Botanical Gardens
Lincoln Home N.H.S.
Mechanicsburg
Springfield
Riddle Hill
VETERANS PKWY
Leland Grove
MAC ARTHUR BLVD
Jerome
White Oaks Mall
DIRKSEN PKWY
Bunn
Crowne Plaza Hotel
Mildred
WABASH AV
Cozy Dog Drive In
Spaulding Dam
Southern View
Rochester
Buckhart
To Hannibal, MO
Lincoln Greens
Curran
Knight's Action Park
University of Illinois at Springfield
Bates
Henson Robinson Zoo
Berry
Lake Springfield
E LAKE SHORE DR
South Fork Sangamon River
Breckenridge
Piper Glen
Lick Creek
Lincoln Memorial Garden
CHRISTIAN CO.
Loami
Chatham
Edinburg
Deer Run
Hickory Point
Sunnyside Acres
Sugar Creek
SANGCHRIS LAKE STATE PARK
Sangchris Lake
Glenarm
To St. Louis, MO
0777MW
Red symbols indicate locations discussed in this section.
Dining
Information
Lodging
Museum
Shopping
Point of interest
Detailed map area
For a complete listing of symbols, see inside back cover.

Down a **Lazy River**

The late Charles Kuralt, television's intrepid chronicler of Americana, called **Madison**, Ind., "the most beautiful river town in America." Tucked into rolling hills along a scenic, meandering stretch of the Ohio River Valley, Madison showcases the largest historic district in the state—the National Register of Historic Places includes 133 of its blocks. Its leafy streets welcome tourists with an appealing mix of quaint bed-and-breakfasts, shops, galleries, wineries, and more. Winter often descends gently on agreeable slow-paced, sleepy Madison, making this a year-round getaway destination.

Settled in 1809, Madison was a major river port and supply town that outfitted pioneers moving into the Northwest Territory. Steamboat traffic and the construction of roads and railroads brought wealth and influence—but they also helped shape other business and industrial hubs that drew commerce away from Madison. The boom went bust, and Madison slipped into a century of slumber.

You'll soak up much of this history at local museums and homes offering guided tours—such as **Lanier Mansion** (601 W. First St.), a Greek Revival residence completed in 1844. It was the home of James Lanier, whose loans allowed Indiana to equip Union troops during the Civil War. Its expansive grounds include a restored 1850s garden and antique varieties of flowers, vegetables, and dwarf trees.

In 1802, a group of Swiss immigrants established what was said to be the nation's first commercial winery at **Vevay**, Ind., about 20 miles east of Madison. By the middle of the 19th century, viticulture so flourished in the region that the stretch of the Ohio River between Cincinnati and Louisville became known as the "Rhineland of America."

Clifty Falls State Park

Lanier Mansion, Madison

Continuing this heritage: wineries such as the **Thomas Family Winery** (208 E. Second St., Madison), which occupies a rehabbed 1850s stable and carriage house. It's a spot for tasting wine and imported cheeses, with (on most Saturday nights) live music, ranging from jazz and blues to bluegrass and Celtic. The family-owned vineyard also produces strong, Welsh-style dry cider made from craggy old cider apples.

Known for events such as hog roasts and music festivals, **Madison Vineyards Estate Winery** (1456 E. 400 North) offers vineyard and winery tours and serves cheese, fruit, and meat trays on a deck overlooking a 37-acre vineyard planted on south-facing hillsides of the river valley. It produces several dry, off-dry, and sparkling wines.

Madison Vineyards wine tasting

Just west of town lies 1,416-acre **Clifty Falls State Park** (2221 Clifty Dr.), Indiana's prettiest. With its deeply cut limestone gorges, sheer rock walls, and plunging waterfalls, the park offers popular hiking trails and a nature center with interpretive programs.

Because of its many steeples, some call photogenic **Oldenburg** the "Village of Spires." The region's rolling hills looked like home to the German immigrants who settled it in the early 1800s. Begun as a tiny hamlet, Oldenburg—affectionately dubbed "Neu Oldenburg" by arriving Germans—was platted as a town in 1837.

Oldenburg was added to the National Register of Historic Places in 1983. Today, it exudes Old World charm with old stone and brick structures, tin façades and cornices, and bilingual street signs. View the town's most ornate tinwork, fashioned by Prussian-born master tinsmith Casper Gaupel at **Hackman's General Store** (Main & Pearl Sts.). Find the work of local artisans at the **Schwestern Gallery of Art** (22169 Main St.), including paintings, photography, hand-blown glass, pottery, and jewelry. There's handcrafted furniture and cabinetry at **The Village Workshop** (3047 Washington St.) and German food and potables at **The Brau Haus** (22170 Water St.).

German heritage is equally strong in **Batesville**, which offers German food and lodgings at the **Sherman House Inn** (35 S. Main St.), established in 1852 as a "stage stop" tavern—a place for stagecoaches to stop along their route. Surrounding Ripley County offers wine tastings at the **Villa Milan Winery**, picturesque covered bridges, a handsome 1860s courthouse (in **Versailles**), and numerous Underground Railroad sites on driving tours. The **Ripley County Tourism Bureau** offers CD and DVD audio narrations of the tours for $5 and $10, respectively, at their office (102 N. Main St., Versailles).

In the river town of **Rising Sun**, William Rees fashions Celtic harps at his shop **Harps on Main** (222 Main St.). Users include All-Ireland harp champions and musicians who have recorded Grammy-winning CDs and movie soundtracks. Take a self-guided tour of the workshop where William and sons Bryant and Garen create harps known for their large voice and stature.

What to eat

At the **Sherman House Inn** in Batesville, Bavarian favorites include bacon-wrapped pork loin, wiener schnitzel (veal), and chicken schnitzel, as well as assorted plump sausages served with sauerkraut, potato pancakes, and mustard sauce.

What to buy

At Rising Sun, check out William Rees, master harp maker of **Harps on Main**. Although concert lever harps are priced around $6,000, there are less expensive options. The company produces a $295 well-crafted lap harp ideal for beginners. At only 4 1/2 pounds, it's light enough to be comfortably played while standing or moving around. Many harp teachers across the country favor it.

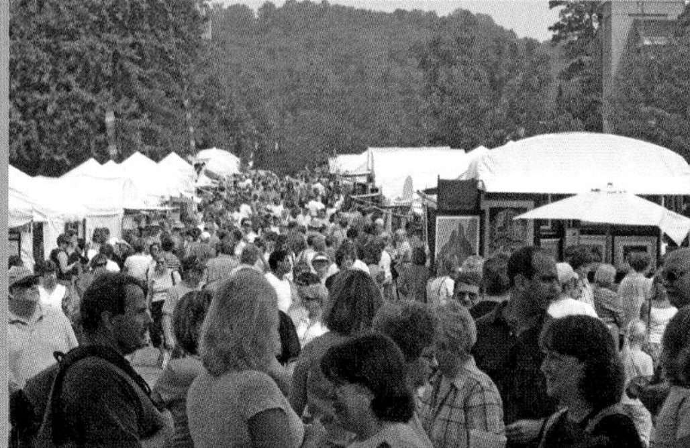

Chautauqua Festival of Art

What to do

Madison in Bloom, Madison, mid-May.
Madison Chautauqua Festival of Art, Madison, late September.

For more details about these festivals, please see page 174.

Information

Down the Lazy River (regional group representing Dearborn, Jefferson, Ohio, Ripley and Switzerland counties), (800) 322-8198, www.downthelazyriver.org.

Lodging tips

Find lodgings at **Clifty Inn**, which sits high atop a bluff overlooking the Ohio River at Clifty Falls State Park. Dating from 1924, the renovated inn has 64 rooms and seven suites, many with balconies overlooking the river and the historic town. Amenities include an indoor swimming pool and hot tub, lighted tennis courts, a gift shop, and a restaurant. A new lodging choice: **Madison Vineyards Bed & Breakfast**, which began welcoming guests in 2005. It offers four large guestrooms overlooking its 37-acre vineyard. Each features a private bathroom, satellite TV, and Restonic® pillow mattress with luxurious bedding. Guests enjoy the daily full breakfast, as well as periodic tastings in the private wine cellar.

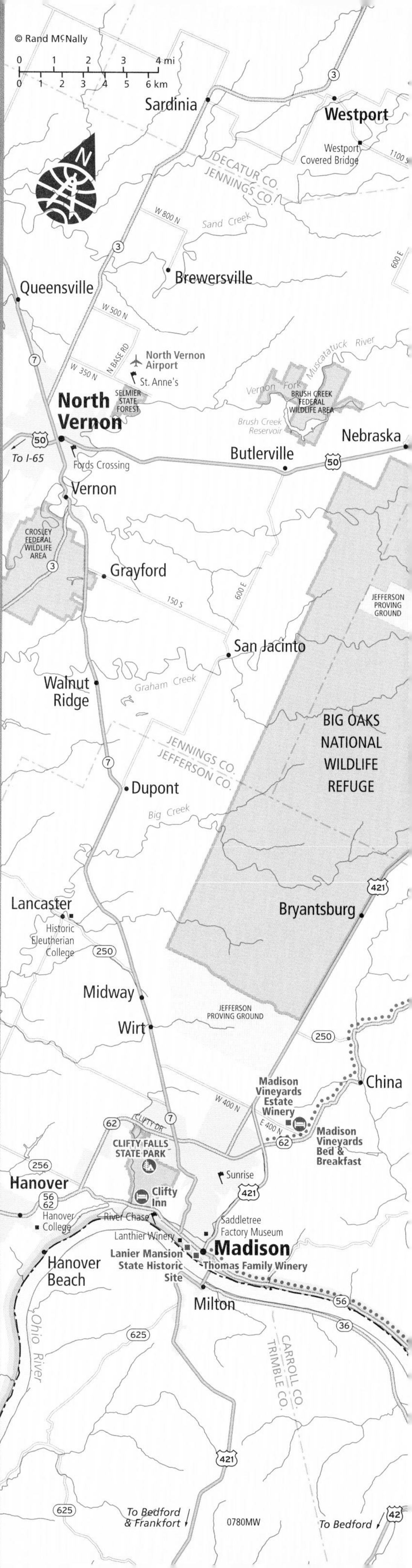

© Rand McNally
0 1 2 3 4 mi
0 1 2 3 4 5 6 km
Sardinia
Westport
Westport Covered Bridge
DECATUR CO.
JENNINGS CO.
Sand Creek
Queensville
Brewersville
North Vernon Airport
St. Anne's
SELMIER STATE FOREST
North Vernon
Vernon Fork Muscatatuck River
BRUSH CREEK FEDERAL WILDLIFE AREA
Brush Creek Reservoir
Nebraska
To I-65
Fords Crossing
Butlerville
Vernon
CROSLEY FEDERAL WILDLIFE AREA
Grayford
JEFFERSON PROVING GROUND
San Jacinto
Walnut Ridge
Graham Creek
BIG OAKS NATIONAL WILDLIFE REFUGE
JENNINGS CO.
JEFFERSON CO.
Dupont
Big Creek
Lancaster
Historic Eleutherian College
Bryantsburg
Midway
Wirt
JEFFERSON PROVING GROUND
China
Madison Vineyards Estate Winery
Madison Vineyards Bed & Breakfast
CLIFTY FALLS STATE PARK
Clifty Inn
Sunrise
Hanover
Hanover College
River Chase
Lanthier Winery
Saddletree Factory Museum
Lanier Mansion State Historic Site
Madison
Thomas Family Winery
Hanover Beach
Milton
Ohio River
CARROLL CO.
TRIMBLE CO.
To Bedford & Frankfort
To Bedford
0780MW

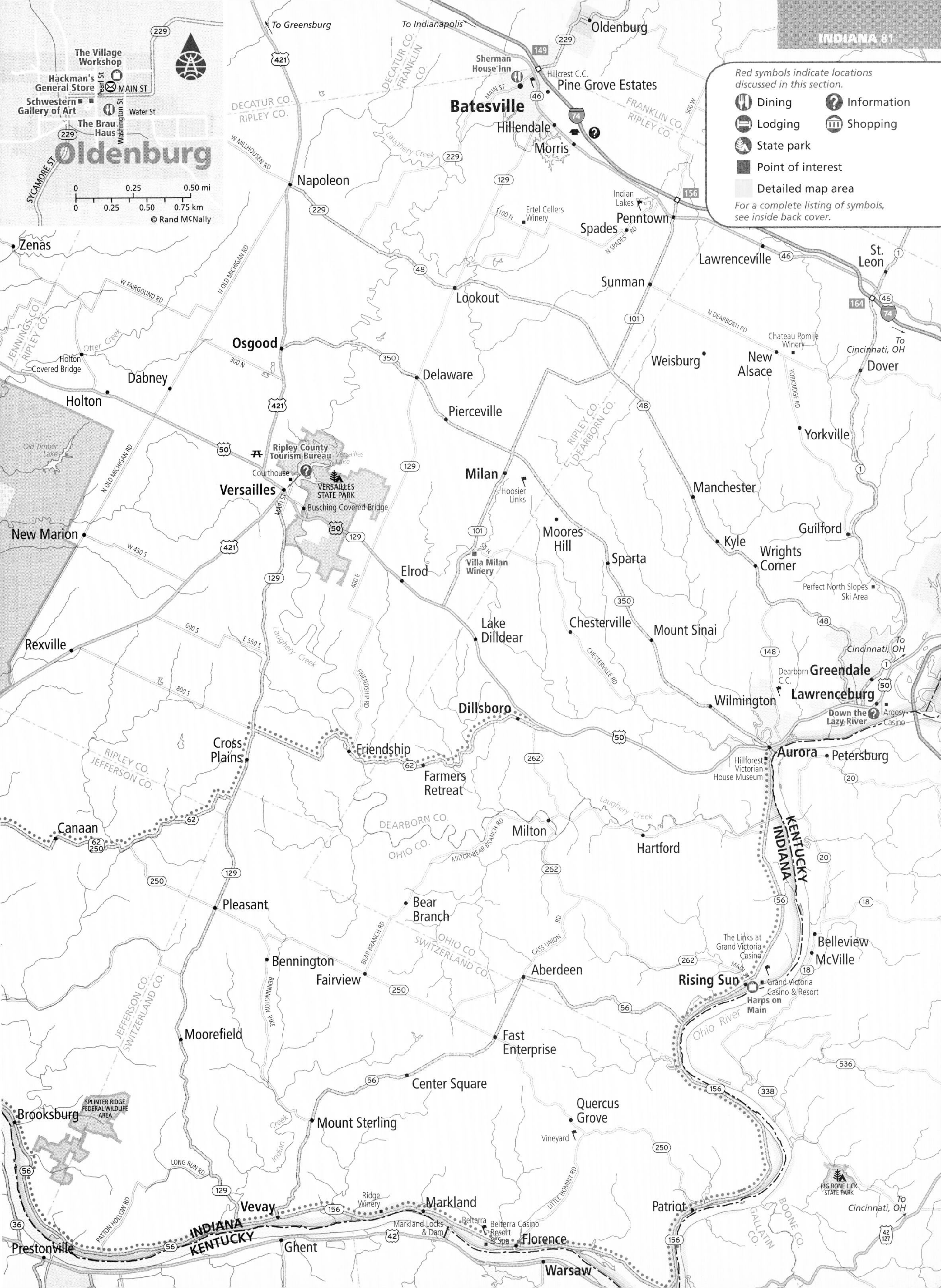

Red symbols indicate locations discussed in this section.
Dining
Information
Lodging
Shopping
State park
Point of interest
Detailed map area
For a complete listing of symbols, see inside back cover.
The Village Workshop
Hackman's General Store
MAIN ST
Pearl St
Schwestern Gallery of Art
Water St
The Brau Haus
Washington St
SYCAMORE ST
Oldenburg
0 0.25 0.50 mi
0 0.25 0.50 0.75 km
© Rand McNally
To Greensburg
To Indianapolis
Oldenburg
Sherman House Inn
Hillcrest C.C.
Pine Grove Estates
Batesville
Hillendale
Morris
DECATUR CO.
RIPLEY CO.
DECATUR CO.
FRANKLIN CO.
FRANKLIN CO.
RIPLEY CO.
Laughery Creek
W MILLHOUSEN RD
Napoleon
Ertel Cellers Winery
Indian Lakes
Penntown
Spades
N SPADES RD
Zenas
Lawrenceville
St. Leon
Sunman
Lookout
W FAIRGOUND RD
N OLD MICHIGAN RD
N DEARBORN RD
JENNINGS CO.
RIPLEY CO.
Otter Creek
Osgood
Holton Covered Bridge
300 N
Dabney
Delaware
Chateau Pomije Winery
Weisburg
New Alsace
To Cincinnati, OH
Dover
Holton
Pierceville
RIPLEY CO.
DEARBORN CO.
YORKRIDGE RD
Yorkville
Old Timber Lake
Ripley County Tourism Bureau
Versailles Lake
Courthouse
VERSAILLES STATE PARK
Versailles
MAIN ST
Busching Covered Bridge
Milan
Hoosier Links
Manchester
New Marion
W 450 S
Moores Hill
Guilford
Kyle
Wrights Corner
Villa Milan Winery
Elrod
Sparta
400 E
Perfect North Slopes Ski Area
Lake Dilldear
Chesterville
Mount Sinai
Rexville
600 S
E 550 S
Laughery Creek
CHESTERVILLE RD
FRIENDSHIP RD
To Cincinnati, OH
Dearborn C.C.
Greendale
800 S
Lawrenceburg
Wilmington
Dillsboro
Down the Lazy River
Argosy Casino
Cross Plains
Friendship
Aurora
Petersburg
RIPLEY CO.
JEFFERSON CO.
Farmers Retreat
Hillforest Victorian House Museum
DEARBORN CO.
Laughery Creek
Canaan
Milton
MILTON-BEAR BRANCH RD
Hartford
OHIO CO.
KENTUCKY
INDIANA
Pleasant
Bear Branch
The Links at Grand Victoria Casino
Belleview
McVille
CASS UNION RD
BEAR BRANCH RD
OHIO CO.
SWITZERLAND CO.
Bennington
Aberdeen
MAIN ST
Rising Sun
Grand Victoria Casino & Resort
Harps on Main
Fairview
BENNINGTON PIKE
JEFFERSON CO.
SWITZERLAND CO.
Ohio River
Moorefield
Fast Enterprise
Center Square
Quercus Grove
SPLINTER RIDGE FEDERAL WILDLIFE AREA
Brooksburg
Mount Sterling
Indian Creek
Vineyard
LONG RUN RD
LITTLE HOMINY RD
BIG BONE LICK STATE PARK
To Cincinnati, OH
Ridge Winery
Markland
Vevay
Patriot
Markland Locks & Dam
Belterra
Belterra Casino Resort & Spa
BOONE CO.
GALLATIN CO.
PATTON HOLLOW RD
INDIANA
KENTUCKY
Florence
Prestonville
Ghent
Warsaw

Indy Rides the Cultural Fast Track

While the word "Hoosiers" still calls to mind feverish basketball games in cramped high school gyms, **Indianapolis** is no bench warmer. Besides hosting professional sports franchises such as the Colts and Pacers, and along with the Indianapolis 500, Indiana's capital city is on a cultural fast track, too. Its vibrant arts, performing arts, dining, and nightlife scenes have made America's 12th-largest city one of its most entertaining.

Case in point: the splendid **Eiteljorg Museum of American Indians and Western Art** (500 W. Washington St.), which has earned plaudits since opening in 1989 as one of only two museums east of the Mississippi with both Native American objects and Western paintings and bronzes. With a 45,000-square-foot addition opened in 2005 that includes galleries, gardens, and a café, it has even more to offer. The museum houses the work of such icons as Remington, Russell, and O'Keeffe. Even its honey-colored stone exterior evokes the Southwest. Trunks of large cedars from the Pacific Northwest support its main canopy.

Another massive arts project: the Indianapolis Museum of Art's recent $220-million expansion (4000 Michigan Rd.). Occupying 152 acres of gardens and grounds just 15 minutes from downtown, the complex offers three distinct art experiences: the enhanced **Indianapolis Museum of Art,** featuring new acquisitions and major special exhibitions; the new 100-acre Virginia Fairbanks Arts and Nature Park; and Oldfields, the restored former J.K. Lilly, Jr. estate. It ranks among the nation's largest general art museums, with a collection of more than 50,000 works that spans the range of art history, both in terms of eras and kinds of art. Highlights include paintings and prints by Paul Gauguin, the works of Georges Seurat, and the largest J.M.W. Turner collection outside of Great Britain.

Richard and Billie Lou Deer Fountain, Eiteljorg Museum, Indianapolis

The contemporary **Indiana State Museum** (650 W. Washington St.), located in White River State Park in the heart of Indianapolis, catches the eye, too. It celebrates Indiana and its people as it traces their history. Here you'll learn about Indiana's music legends Cole Porter, Hoagy Carmichael, and John Mellencamp as you browse a marvelous collection of Americana encompassing nearly 10,000 objects such as military uniforms, weaponry, and communications artifacts (including Indiana-made television sets, radios, and broadcast equipment and the personal memorabilia of significant Indiana broadcasters). The museum itself is a work of art, with an exterior that serves as a canvas for sculptures representing each of the state's 92 counties.

Plan lunch at the museum and you'll find yourself in what may seem like a time warp. You'll dine in the sedate tearoom of the L.S. Ayres department store—which actually closed its doors and fell to the wrecking ball in 1990. Opened in 1905 in downtown Indianapolis, the original tearoom was the place to go for special occasions. Now patrons can "return" for chicken pot pie and large helpings of nostalgia. They meet friends for lunch, order the famous chicken velvet soup, and enjoy old-time views of downtown Indianapolis outside its windows. The views may be painted on, but the food is real and the furnishings are authentic.

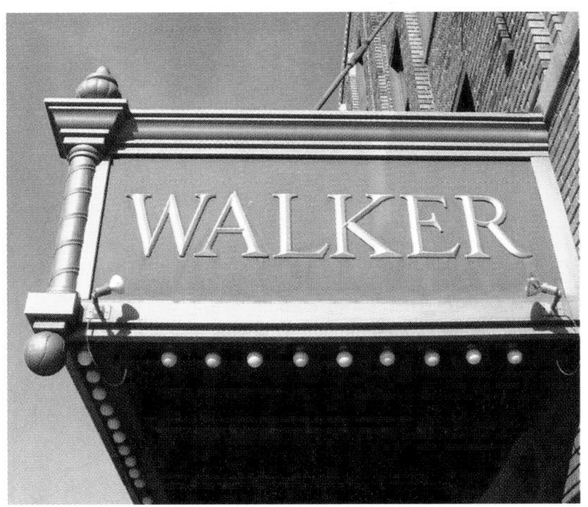

Madame Walker Theatre Center

On the fourth Friday of the month, jazz aficionados head for the Indiana Avenue Cultural District for "Jazz on the Avenue" at the **Madame Walker Theatre Center** (617 Indiana Ave.). Held in the fourth-floor Casino Ballroom, it is one of a variety of programs dedicated to the nurturing and celebration of the arts and culture from an African American perspective. Entertainment ranges from performances by

White River State Park canal

operatic diva Paula Dione Ingram to "Christmas with the Boys Choir of Harlem." Completed in 1927, this National Historic Landmark is named for its benefactor, entrepreneur, philanthropist, and activist Madam C.J. Walker (she wrote her name without the "e"). Walker, who came from the cotton fields of the south, established a hair products manufacturing business. It propelled her from washerwoman to America's first self-made female millionaire. Her inspirational story unfolds during tours of the center.

Central Canal Towpath (a 5.23-mile landscaped waterway just north of downtown) and the 10.5-block downtown Canal Walk make great outdoor exercise spots, with walkways, jogging paths, gardens, decorative bridges, and antique-style street lamps. Along Canal Walk, the **USS *Indianapolis* Memorial** honors sailors aboard the last American ship sunk during World War II—a scant two weeks before the war ended.

Travel to Fishers to immerse yourself in one of America's premier living-history museums. **Conner Prairie** (13400 Allisonville Rd.) comprises five historic areas, peopled by costumed interpreters (who remain strictly in character, no matter how intensely 21st-century visitors coerce them). At Conner Prairie, you can witness the joyful festivity of an 1836 wedding —as well as the dark uncertainty of a trip on the Underground Railroad. Here you can celebrate Independence Day as they might have in mid-19th-century Indiana, with a reading of the Declaration of Independence, an old-time baseball game, and homemade ice cream.

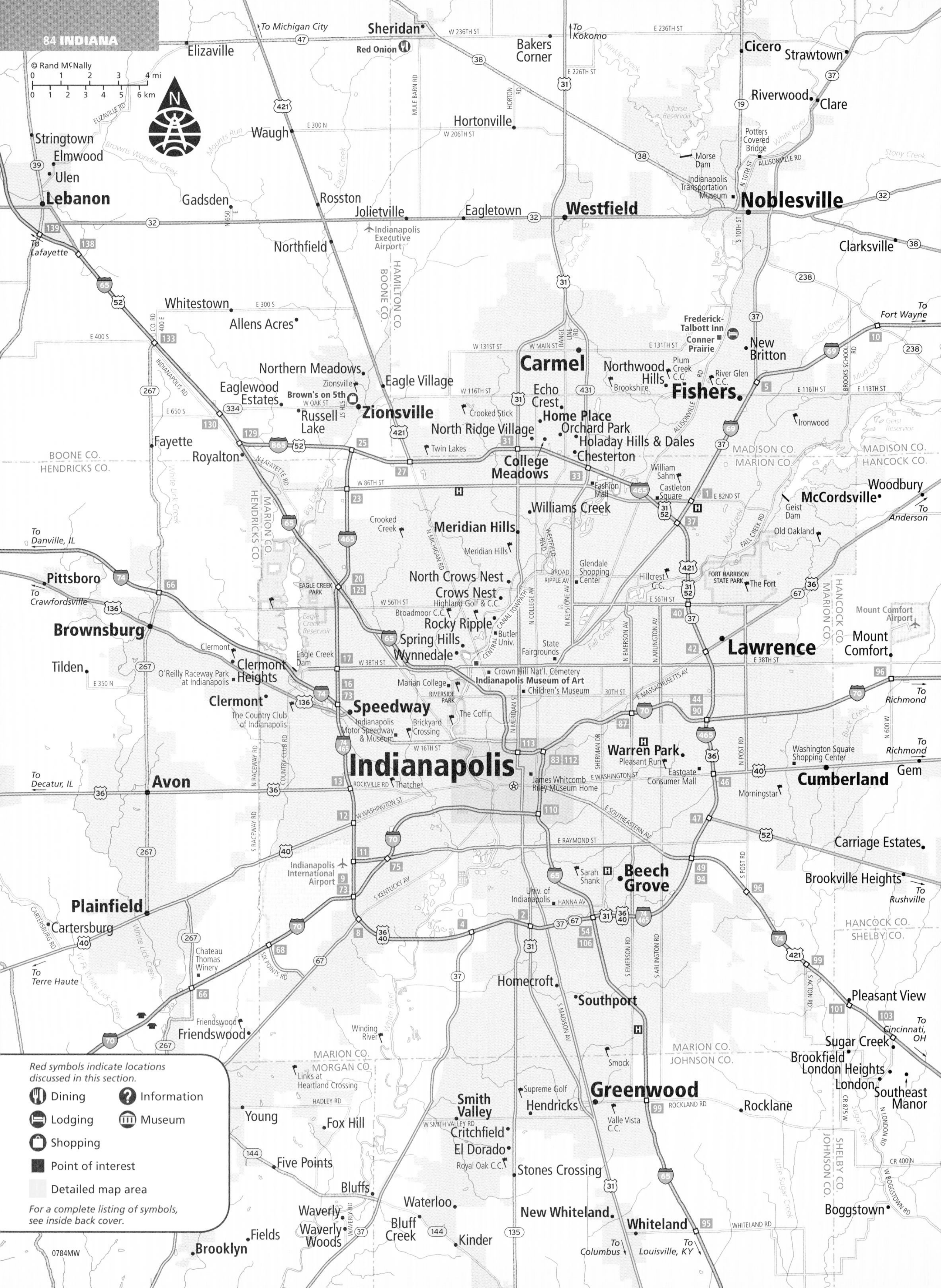

© Rand McNally
0 1 2 3 4 mi
0 1 2 3 4 5 6 km
N
Sheridan
Red Onion
To Michigan City
To Kokomo
Bakers Corner
Elizaville
Cicero
Strawtown
Riverwood
Clare
Hortonville
Waugh
Stringtown
Elmwood
Ulen
Lebanon
Gadsden
Rosston
Jolietville
Eagletown
Westfield
Noblesville
Morse Dam
Potters Covered Bridge
Indianapolis Transportation Museum
To Lafayette
Indianapolis Executive Airport
Northfield
Clarksville
Whitestown
Allens Acres
Frederick-Talbott Inn
Conner Prairie
New Britton
To Fort Wayne
Carmel
Northwood Hills
Fishers
Northern Meadows
Eagle Village
Eaglewood Estates
Brown's on 5th
Zionsville
Russell Lake
Echo Crest
Home Place
Orchard Park
North Ridge Village
Holaday Hills & Dales
Chesterton
Fayette
Royalton
College Meadows
BOONE CO.
HENDRICKS CO.
HAMILTON CO.
BOONE CO.
MADISON CO.
MARION CO.
HANCOCK CO.
Williams Creek
Woodbury
McCordsville
To Anderson
Meridian Hills
To Danville, IL
North Crows Nest
Crows Nest
Glendale Shopping Center
Pittsboro
To Crawfordsville
Rocky Ripple
Brownsburg
Spring Hills
Wynnedale
Lawrence
Mount Comfort
Mount Comfort Airport
Tilden
Clermont Heights
Clermont
Crown Hill Nat'l. Cemetery
Indianapolis Museum of Art
Children's Museum
To Richmond
Speedway
Indianapolis Motor Speedway & Museum
Warren Park
Indianapolis
James Whitcomb Riley Museum Home
Eastgate Consumer Mall
Cumberland
Gem
To Decatur, IL
Avon
Carriage Estates
Indianapolis International Airport
Beech Grove
Brookville Heights
To Rushville
Plainfield
Cartersburg
To Terre Haute
Chateau Thomas Winery
Homecroft
Southport
Pleasant View
To Cincinnati, OH
Friendswood
Sugar Creek
Brookfield
London Heights
London
Southeast Manor
MARION CO.
MORGAN CO.
MARION CO.
JOHNSON CO.
HANCOCK CO.
SHELBY CO.
Greenwood
Smith Valley
Hendricks
Young
Fox Hill
Rocklane
Critchfield
El Dorado
Five Points
Stones Crossing
Bluffs
Waterloo
Waverly
Waverly Woods
Bluff Creek
New Whiteland
Whiteland
Boggstown
Fields
Kinder
Brooklyn
To Columbus
To Louisville, KY
Red symbols indicate locations discussed in this section.
Dining
Information
Lodging
Museum
Shopping
Point of interest
Detailed map area
For a complete listing of symbols, see inside back cover.
0784MW

What to eat

Plate-sized, two-fisted breaded pork tenderloin sandwiches, a staple throughout Indiana, totally dwarf the bun on which they arrive. They're a specialty at the **Red Onion** (3901 IN 47) in the tiny town of Sheridan, due north of Indy.

What to buy

In the heart of the Midwest, shop for items from the Southwest. That may not seem like such odd advice after viewing the mind-boggling stock at the White River Trader, the **Eiteljorg Museum's** handsome gift shop. Its items range from Native American jewelry (including turquoise) to folk art, weavings, basketry, pottery, and dolls. A large line of Western clothing runs to vests, shirts, and skirts, as well as shoes, boots, and handbags. Fans of Vera Bradley bags and accessories might want to check out **Brown's on 5th** (315 N. 5th St.) in Zionsville. It claims one of the largest collections available. With distinctive red brick main street and leafy streets lined with renovated 19th-century storefronts, this quaint village (less than 30 minutes from downtown Indianapolis) has more than 50 shops and plenty of diversions in the form of fine restaurants and cafés.

What to do

Indy Jazz Fest, Indianapolis, June.

Indian Market, Indianapolis, late June.

For more details about these festivals, please see page 174.

Information

Indianapolis Convention & Visitors Association, (800) 323-4639 (INDY), www.indy.org.

Lodging tips

For a splurge in downtown Indy, check into the **Conrad Indianapolis** (50 W. Washington St.). The 23-story hotel offers 241 luxury guestrooms, along with upscale dining in a 200-seat French restaurant, a sophisticated spa, and fitness facilities. For something comfortable and rustic, check out the **Frederick-Talbott Inn** in Fishers (13805 Allisonville Rd.), just across the street from Conner Prairie and looking as though it, too, might be part of the historical village. The largest bed-and-breakfast in the area, it offers 10 guestrooms as well as a parlor, meeting room, dining area, and kitchen. Filled with vintage furniture rescued from Indy landmarks such as the L.S. Ayers department store and Union Station, the inn incorporates an 1870s Gothic-style farmhouse and a cottage circa 1906.

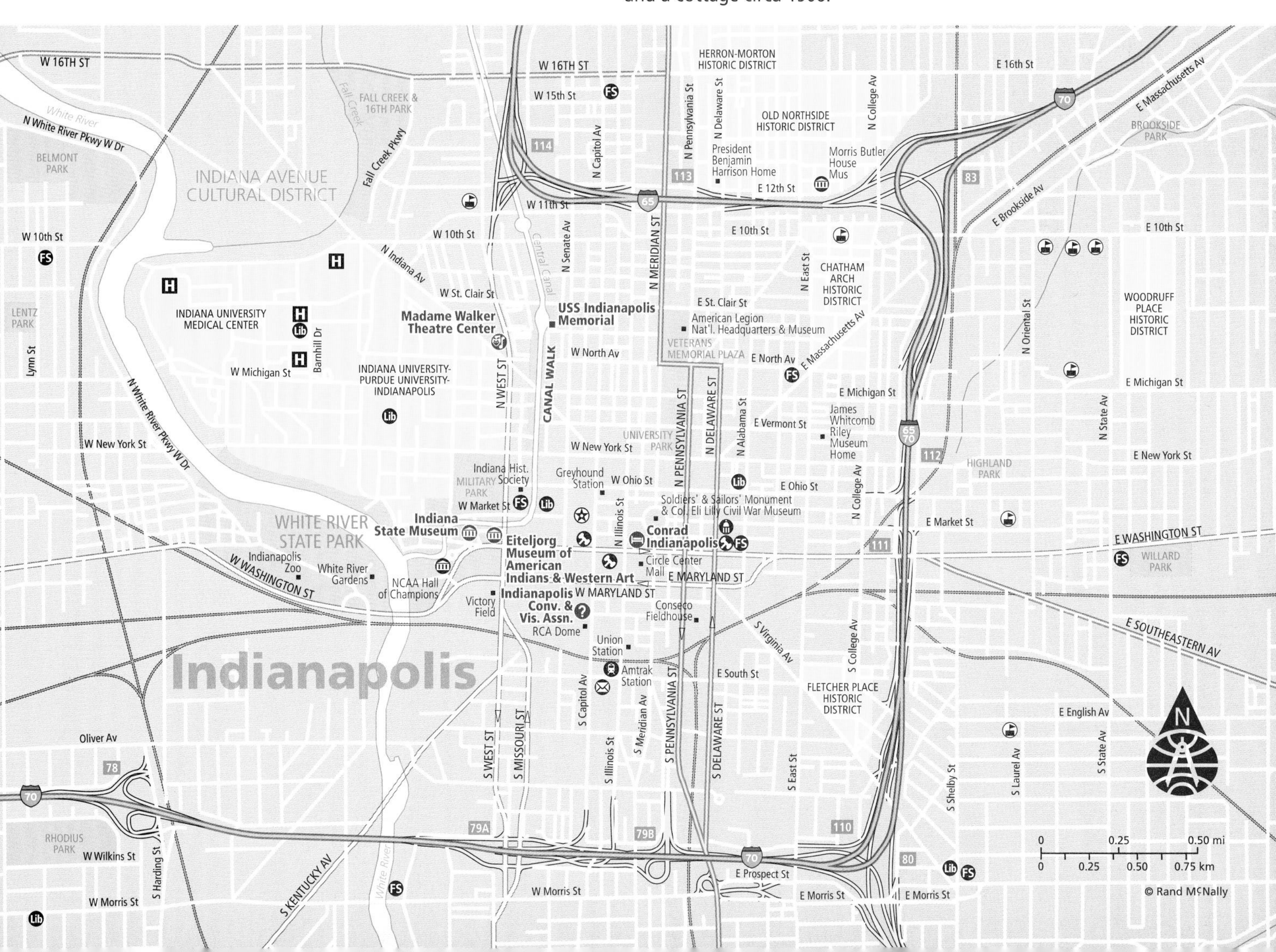

A Norman Rockwell
Kind of Place

Less than an hour's drive southeast of the steel-and-glass canyons of Chicago, quiet, restful scenes cluster: a working gristmill so pretty that newlyweds choose it as a photo backdrop, a living-history farm where time stands still, and a town that looks straight out of a Norman Rockwell drawing. There's also the Midwest's premier beach playground and baseball games played politely by 1858 rules.

Clean-cut **Lowell**, Ind., is as small-town American as the apple pie its restaurants serve. Founded in 1852, it draws day-tripping Chicagoans with a main street lined with one-of-a-kind boutiques, antique stores, and cafés. Its seasonal European market features artisanal foods, crafts, and entertainment.

East of town at **Buckley Homestead** (3606 Belshaw Rd.), visitors to this circa-1849 historical farm hear cocks crow, photograph horses grazing in the pasture, and meet a small herd of sheep and, if the time is right, their wobbly-legged newborn lambs. You'll ride in a cart pulled by a pair of sturdy Belgians, then tiptoe into a one-room schoolhouse as kids settle down with primers and wrestle with arithmetic. The orchard boasts heirloom fruit trees, a mix of apple, pear, cherry, and quince. Visit with costumed interpreters as they use wood-burning cooking stoves in the primitive outbuildings and the kitchen of the main house to prepare cookies, hearty beef barley soup, and cornbread from an oft-requested 150-year-old recipe (unfortunately for the casual visitor, the food is prepared only for large groups or special events attendees).

Buckley Homestead, Lowell

Gristmill at Deep River County Park

Gentrification has a firm grip on **Miller Beach**, a lakeshore artists' community annexed by Gary in the early 1920s. This historic area lies near the sand dunes where pioneer aviator Octave Chanute tested gliders in 1896 and 1897. Miller Beach is again becoming a tourist destination, sporting brick sidewalks and vintage street lighting. Chicago foodies zip across the Skyway toll bridge to visit the stylish **Miller Bakery Café** (555 S. Lake St.). It offers food and ambience as chic as those in Chicago's trendiest eateries and live jazz—at Indiana prices. Neighboring **Lake Street Gallery** (613 S. Lake St.) showcases local artists and craftspeople from across North America, mounting a half dozen shows annually.

Just a few miles from the commercialism of Merrillville and located in pretty **Deep River County Park** near Hobart lies a working **gristmill** built in 1838 and rebuilt in 1876 (9410 Old Lincoln Hwy.). A miller uses 4,000-pound stones to grind corn, wheat, and rye (cornmeal is available by the sack for purchase). Nestled against a still pond, this handsome brick mill provides a setting so picturesque that on virtually every weekend during warm-weather months, weddings are celebrated there. The best photo ops occur in early May, peak bloom time for about 5,000 tulips planted alongside a gazebo close by the mill.

In a nearby meadow, the Deep River Grinders, a vintage "base ball" team playing according to 1858 rules, takes on visiting teams from around the Midwest. It's a genteel affair, with an umpire attired in top hat and tails who imposes fines for swearing and spitting. Fans cheer good plays with "Well struck, sir!" Calling an opposing player "milk boy" or "puddin'" is as close as players get to talking trash.

The region's most famous attraction: sloping white expanses of the **Indiana Dunes**, stretching across the tops of Lake and Porter and touching La Porte counties. They encompass a state park and national lakeshore and flank Lake Michigan, which can be as unpredictable as any ocean. Go camping, biking, and swimming, or strike out on an interpretive hike or field trip to follow trails leading to flora unexpected in the Midwest, including southern dogwoods, orchids, and prickly-pear cacti. This magnificent beach playground, with lofty dunes and sugar-fine sand, offers secluded spots for romantic picnics amid tall clumps of grass. A popular and exhilarating activity is slogging up the steep slopes of 100-foot-tall dunes and tumbling down helter-skelter. Enjoy fresh lake breezes, vast views of Lake Michigan, and, on a clear day, the Chicago skyline, shimmering on the horizon.

Indiana Dunes National Lakeshore's Chellberg Farm, an 1885 farmstead, tells the story of the hardworking Swedish immigrant family that farmed this land for three generations. Rangers lead tours through the farmhouse's main rooms, which have been restored to their 1890-1910 appearance: dining room, parlor, downstairs bedroom, and kitchen (the busiest room in the house when it was occupied by the Chellbergs). A popular event, held every Saturday and Sunday year-round, is "Feeding Time at Chellberg Farm," when visitors help feed the farm animals.

Miller Beach, Gary

What to eat

Thousands of diners travel to Phil Smidt's of Hammond (1205 N. Calumet Ave.) for the house specialties, pan-fried perch and gooseberry pie. Phil and Marie Smidt opened this small bar and seafood grill serving fresh perch in 1910. It remains the best place around for heaping platters of perch, either deep-fried or lightly sautéed. Traditionally, patrons end their meal with a slab of sweet-tart gooseberry pie à la mode.

What to buy

Lowell is a prime spot for antique hunters. Try Tish's Antiques (201 E. Commercial Ave.) for flapper-era hats and dresses, Art Deco furnishings, and collectibles such as costume jewelry. Also in Lowell is The Davis Store (402 E. Commercial Ave.), founded in 1884, which offers value-priced fashions that attract shoppers all the way from Chicago. Customers line up waiting for the store to open during major sales in January and July.

What to do

Maple Syrup Time, Deep River County Park, early March.

For more details about this festival, please see page 174.

Information

Lake County CVB,
(800) 255-5253 (ALL-LAKE), www.alllake.org.

Porter County Convention, Recreation & Visitor Commission,
(800) 283-8687, www.indianadunes.com.

Lodging tips

In Lowell, the Inn Town Bed and Breakfast at the Spencer House (1651 E. Commercial Ave.) is a bright and airy bed-and-breakfast inn, with Asian décor and a white-and-maroon color scheme. Homemade breakfasts include the likes of fruit kabobs, stuffed French toast, and scrambled eggs. Another bed-and-breakfast choice: The Inn at Aberdeen in Valparaiso (3158 South IN 2), a stylish 11-suite hostelry dating back to 1857 that once was a working farm with horses and dairy cattle.

Maple Syrup Time, Deep River County Park

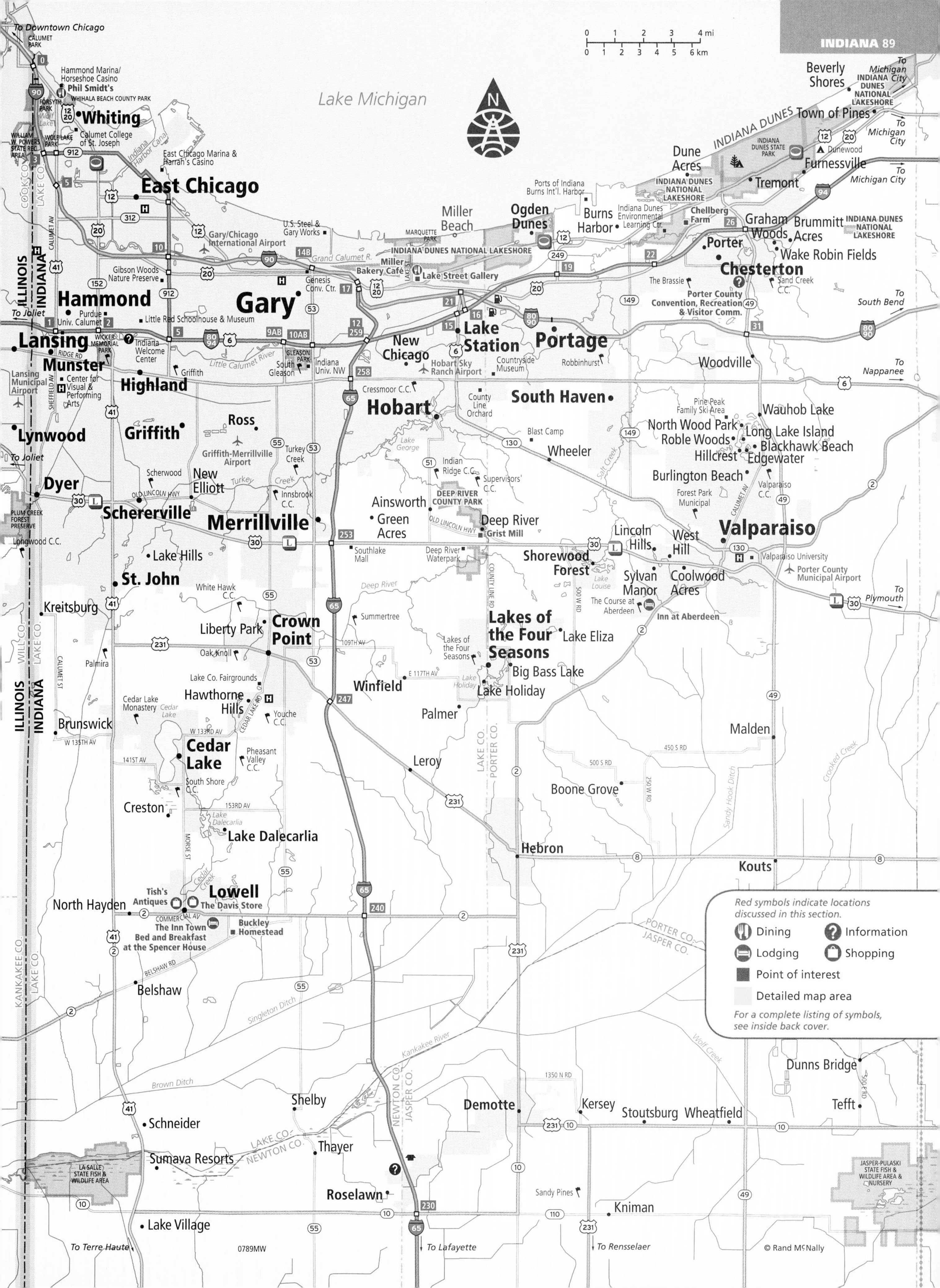

To Downtown Chicago
Calumet Park
0 1 2 3 4 mi
0 1 2 3 4 5 6 km
Lake Michigan
N
Hammond Marina/
Horseshoe Casino
Phil Smidt's
Whihala Beach County Park
Forsyth Park
Wolf Lake
Whiting
William W. Powers State Rec. Area
Wolf Lake Park
Calumet College of St. Joseph
Indiana Harbor Canal
East Chicago Marina &
Harrah's Casino
East Chicago
Cook Co.
Lake Co.
Calumet Av
U.S. Steel &
Gary Works
Gary/Chicago International Airport
Gibson Woods Nature Preserve
Illinois
Indiana
Hammond
Purdue Univ. Calumet
Little Red Schoolhouse & Museum
Gary
Genesis Conv. Ctr.
To Joliet
Lansing
Wicker Memorial Park
Indiana Welcome Center
Ridge Rd
Munster
Center for Visual & Performing Arts
Lansing Municipal Airport
Sheffield Av
Griffith
Little Calumet River
South Gleason
Gleason Park
Indiana Univ. NW
Highland
Lynwood
Griffith
Ross
Griffith-Merrillville Airport
To Joliet
Dyer
Scherwood
New Elliott
Old Lincoln Hwy
Turkey Creek
Turkey Creek
Innsbrook C.C.
Schererville
Plum Creek Forest Preserve
Longwood C.C.
Merrillville
Lake Hills
St. John
White Hawk C.C.
Kreitsburg
Liberty Park
Crown Point
Oak Knoll
Palmira
Will Co.
Lake Co.
Calumet St
Illinois
Indiana
Lake Co. Fairgrounds
Cedar Lake Monastery
Cedar Lake
Hawthorne Hills
Cedar Lake Rd
Youche C.C.
Brunswick
W 133rd Av
W 135th Av
141st Av
Cedar Lake
Pheasant Valley C.C.
South Shore C.C.
Creston
153rd Av
Lake Dalecarlia
Lake Dalecarlia
Morse St
Cedar Creek
Lowell
Tish's Antiques
The Davis Store
North Hayden
Commercial Av
The Inn Town Bed and Breakfast at the Spencer House
Buckley Homestead
Belshaw Rd
Belshaw
Kankakee Co.
Lake Co.
Singleton Ditch
Brown Ditch
Schneider
Lake Co.
Newton Co.
Sumava Resorts
La Salle State Fish & Wildlife Area
Lake Village
To Terre Haute
0789MW
Miller Beach
Marquette Park
Grand Calumet R.
Indiana Dunes National Lakeshore
Miller Bakery Café
Lake St
Lake Street Gallery
Ogden Dunes
Ports of Indiana Burns Int'l. Harbor
Burns Harbor
Indiana Dunes Environmental Learning Ctr.
Chellberg Farm
New Chicago
Hobart Sky Ranch Airport
Lake Station
Portage
Countryside Museum
Robbinhurst
Cressmoor C.C.
County Line Orchard
South Haven
Hobart
Lake George
Blast Camp
Wheeler
Indian Ridge C.C.
Supervisors' C.C.
Deep River County Park
Ainsworth
Green Acres
Old Lincoln Hwy
Deep River Grist Mill
Southlake Mall
Deep River Waterpark
Deep River
County Line Rd
Summertree
109th Av
Lakes of the Four Seasons
Lakes of the Four Seasons
Lake Eliza
E 117th Av
Winfield
Lake Holiday
Big Bass Lake
Lake Holiday
Palmer
Leroy
Lake Co.
Porter Co.
Boone Grove
Hebron
Shelby
Newton Co.
Jasper Co.
Thayer
Demotte
Roselawn
To Lafayette
Beverly Shores
To Michigan City
Indiana Dunes National Lakeshore
Town of Pines
Indiana Dunes
To Michigan City
Dune Acres
Indiana Dunes State Park
Dunewood
Furnessville
To Michigan City
Indiana Dunes National Lakeshore
Tremont
Graham Woods
Brummitt Acres
Indiana Dunes National Lakeshore
Porter
Wake Robin Fields
Chesterton
The Brassie
Sand Creek C.C.
Porter County Convention, Recreation & Visitor Comm.
To South Bend
Woodville
To Nappanee
Pine Peak Family Ski Area
Wauhob Lake
North Wood Park
Long Lake Island
Roble Woods
Blackhawk Beach
Hillcrest
Edgewater
Salt Creek
Burlington Beach
Calumet Av
Valparaiso C.C.
Forest Park Municipal
Valparaiso
Lincoln Hills
West Hill
Shorewood Forest
Valparaiso University
Porter County Municipal Airport
Lake Louise
Sylvan Manor
Coolwood Acres
To Plymouth
500 W Rd
The Course at Aberdeen
Inn at Aberdeen
Malden
450 S Rd
500 S Rd
250 W Rd
Sandy Hook Ditch
Crooked Creek
Kouts
Porter Co.
Jasper Co.
Kankakee River
Wolf Creek
Dunns Bridge
500 E Rd
1350 N Rd
Kersey
Stoutsburg
Wheatfield
Tefft
Sandy Pines
Kniman
To Rensselaer
Jasper-Pulaski State Fish & Wildlife Area & Nursery
© Rand McNally
Red symbols indicate locations discussed in this section.
Dining
Information
Lodging
Shopping
Point of interest
Detailed map area
For a complete listing of symbols, see inside back cover.

Right Here **in River City**

Walk around **Mason City**, Iowa, and, before long, you'll likely find yourself whistling or humming "Seventy-Six Trombones." This was the hometown of Meredith Willson, composer of the blockbuster Broadway musical *The Music Man*, whose setting Willson modeled on Mason City.

In contrast, neighboring **Clear Lake**, with its iconic Surf Ballroom, most likely brings to mind such songs as "That'll Be the Day," "Peggy Sue," and "Chantilly Lace." Near here, on a cold, snowy night more than 40 years ago, rock-and-roll legends Buddy Holly, Ritchie Valens, and J.P. "The Big Bopper" Richardson died when their single-engine plane crashed in a soybean field. February 3, 1959, will be forever known as "the day the music died," a phrase taken from the lyrics of Don McLean's hit Buddy Holly tribute "American Pie."

A simple **"Day the Music Died" Monument** marks the crash site: a stainless steel guitar inscribed with each performer's name and three stainless steel records bearing the names of their hits. Fans make an annual pilgrimage to attend an informal memorial service at the crash site. They also visit the **Surf Ballroom** (460 North Shore Dr.) along the shore of Clear Lake. The ballroom, with its Miami-style architecture and machines that make "clouds" drift across the ceiling, fascinates fans. They linger by the "hall of fame," which overflows with posters, handbills, memorabilia, and photographs of the legendary performers who played there, including Duke Ellington, Louis Armstrong, and Benny Goodman. These days, the performers are less well known, with the exception of occasional headliners such as Cheap Trick.

North Iowa Band Festival

You can ride a trolley between Clear Lake and Mason City—just as folks did when trolleys traveled the route on electric tracks. Meredith Willson might have traveled this route too, perhaps with haunting melodies playing in his head. Willson was born on May 18, 1902, and lived in his parents' new home in Mason City. Today, the **Meredith Willson Home** (314 S. Pennsylvania Ave.) is open for tours, while the house next door—home of Willson's childhood friend Marjorie—now is a charming shop.

Music Man Square (308 S. Pennsylvania Ave.), an entertainment complex, resembles a 1912 streetscape, with brick sidewalks, vintage lampposts, and shop façades. It includes an ice cream parlor/soda fountain, candy store, gift shop, and barbershop and incorporates set designs from the Warner Brothers

American artists and a famous puppeteer are celebrated at Mason City's **Charles H. MacNider Art Museum** (303 2nd St. SE). It is housed in a handsome English Tudor Revival-style building that sits atop a limestone cliff overlooking a deep ravine.

Its collection of the works of some of America's best known artists—such as Thomas Hart Benton and Arthur Dove—are the stuff of unhurried, relaxed visits. However, many visitors go to view Snarky Parker, Birdie, and other whimsical creations of another local celebrity, world-famous puppet master Bil Baird.

In a long career in television, theater, and movies, Baird created close to 3,000 puppets. He worked with Orson Welles and Walter Cronkite, and his

River City Streetscape at Music Man Square

1962 motion picture based on the musical. You'll find the porch of the Paroo home—where Professor Hill went to win the affections of Marian the librarian—and the infamous pool hall, corrupter of the young, against which Hill railed. Think Disneyland meets *Field of Dreams*. A museum displays Willson memorabilia and music-related exhibits, while an "exploratorium" offers hands-on activities. If, right there in River City, you can't resist those well-known lyrics, you can sing along in an interactive radio booth.

Another notable showman—architect Frank Lloyd Wright—also had a lasting impact on Mason City. The community has an outstanding collection of Prairie School architecture, including a house designed by Wright himself, the 1908 **Stockman House** (530 1st St. NE), which is open for tours. Mason City also features the world's only remaining Wright-designed hotel, currently under restoration.

puppets appeared in the movie *The Sound of Music* (for which he created the "Goat Herd" marionette). Baird was nominated for an Emmy Award for "Art Carney Meets Peter and the Wolf" and pioneered the use of puppetry on television, illustrating the Apollo moon landings.

Providing a close-up look at a 21st-century energy solution—and an unusual photo op—is the **Cerro Gordo Wind Farm** (10586 Balsam Ave., Ventura), home to 55 "Gentle Giants." These wind energy turbines stand tall and stark on the empty prairie, with propellers mounted on slim towers, resembling a modernistic steel sculpture. Each blade, though, is 80 feet long and the towers are 187 feet tall. They harness winds that blow through at an average of 17 mph as a free, renewable source of clean energy that produces enough electricity to service approximately 20,000 homes and businesses.

What to eat

Next door to Meredith Willson's boyhood home stands the house where his friend Marjorie lived. Today, it's occupied by **Marjorie's Tea House** (320 S. Pennsylvania Ave.), a good luncheon stop with homemade soups, signature beef stew, and spinach-and-mushroom frittata. On selected days (and by appointment), the tearoom offers afternoon tea—with finger sandwiches and classic scones with clotted cream, lemon curd, and blackberry jam.

What to buy

The MacNider Art Museum shop sells Bil Baird posters from a 1988 show for $5, and a booklet by Richard Leet, former director of the museum, entitled "Bil Baird, He Pulled a Lot of Strings," for $15. The museum also carries locally crafted sculpture, jewelry, ceramics, and glass works.

What to do

North Iowa Band Festival, Mason City, late May.

Lakefest, Clear Lake, late July.

For more details about these festivals, please see page 174.

Information

Mason City Convention & Visitors Bureau, (800) 423-5724, www.masoncitytourism.com.

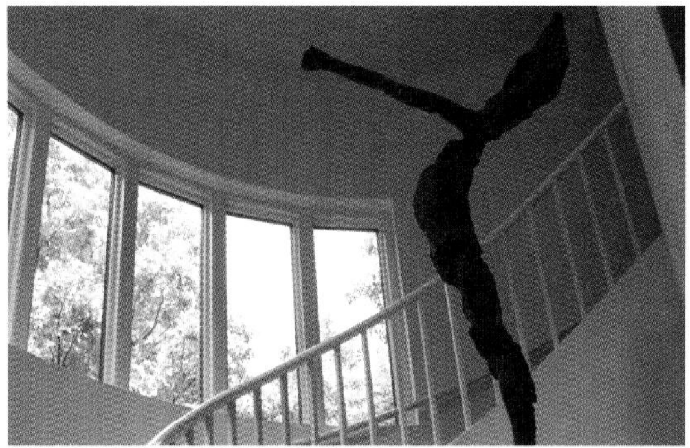

The Charles H. MacNider Art Museum

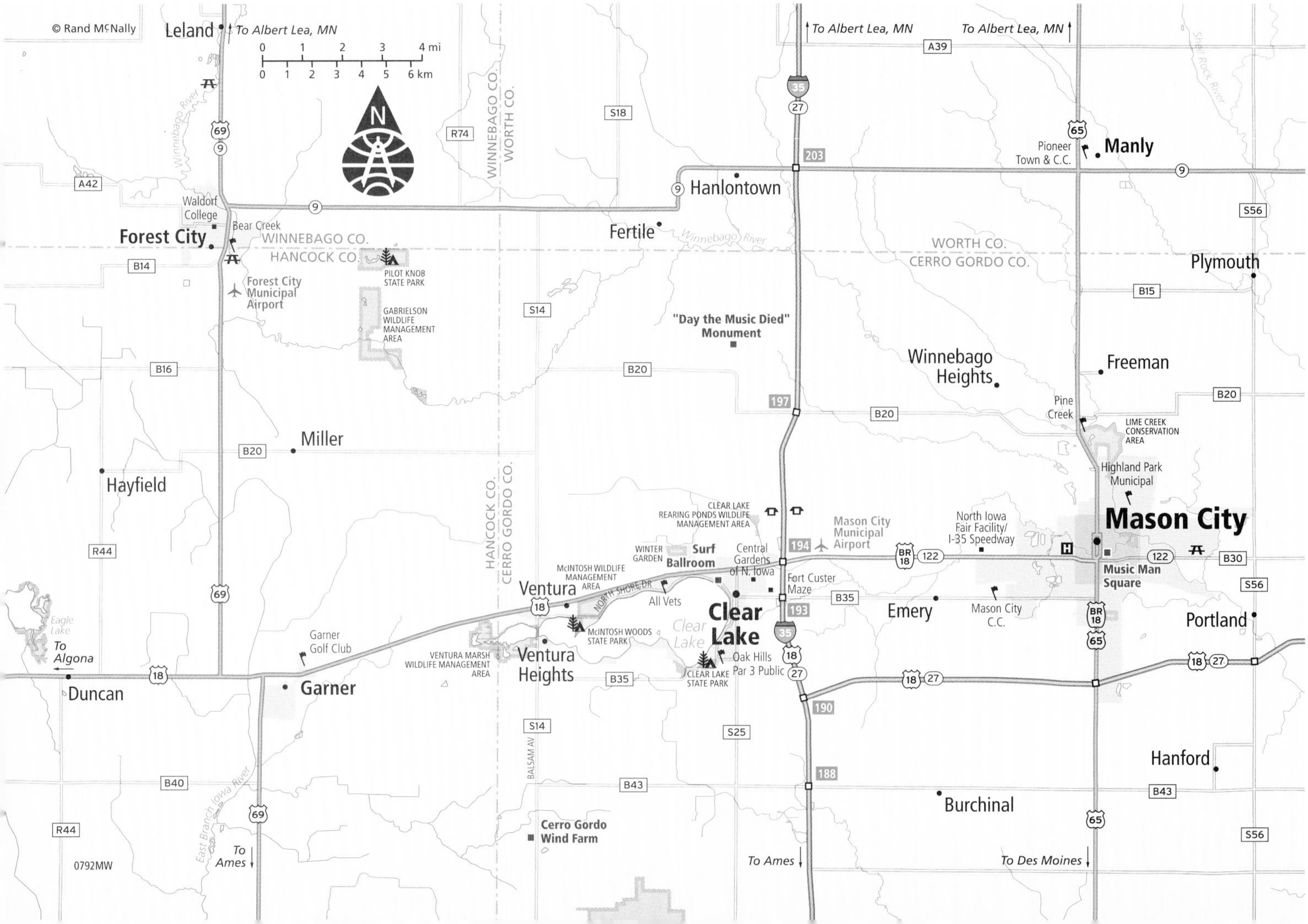

© Rand McNally
Leland
To Albert Lea, MN
To Albert Lea, MN
To Albert Lea, MN
0 1 2 3 4 mi
0 1 2 3 4 5 6 km
A39
S18
R74
WINNEBAGO CO.
WORTH CO.
Pioneer Town & C.C.
Manly
A42
Hanlontown
Waldorf College
Bear Creek
Forest City
WINNEBAGO CO.
HANCOCK CO.
Fertile
Winnebago River
WORTH CO.
CERRO GORDO CO.
S56
Plymouth
B14
PILOT KNOB STATE PARK
Forest City Municipal Airport
GABRIELSON WILDLIFE MANAGEMENT AREA
S14
B15
"Day the Music Died" Monument
Winnebago Heights
Freeman
B16
B20
B20
B20
Pine Creek
LIME CREEK CONSERVATION AREA
B20
Miller
Hayfield
Highland Park Municipal
HANCOCK CO.
CERRO GORDO CO.
CLEAR LAKE REARING PONDS WILDLIFE MANAGEMENT AREA
Mason City Municipal Airport
North Iowa Fair Facility/ I-35 Speedway
Mason City
R44
WINTER GARDEN
Surf Ballroom
Central Gardens of N. Iowa
B30
Music Man Square
MCINTOSH WILDLIFE MANAGEMENT AREA
Ventura
NORTH SHORE DR
Fort Custer Maze
B35
S56
All Vets
Clear Lake
Emery
Mason City C.C.
Portland
Eagle Lake
To Algona
Garner Golf Club
MCINTOSH WOODS STATE PARK
VENTURA MARSH WILDLIFE MANAGEMENT AREA
Ventura Heights
B35
Oak Hills Par 3 Public
CLEAR LAKE STATE PARK
Duncan
Garner
S14
S25
BALSAM AV
Hanford
B40
East Branch Iowa River
B43
Burchinal
B43
R44
Cerro Gordo Wind Farm
S56
0792MW
To Ames
To Ames
To Des Moines

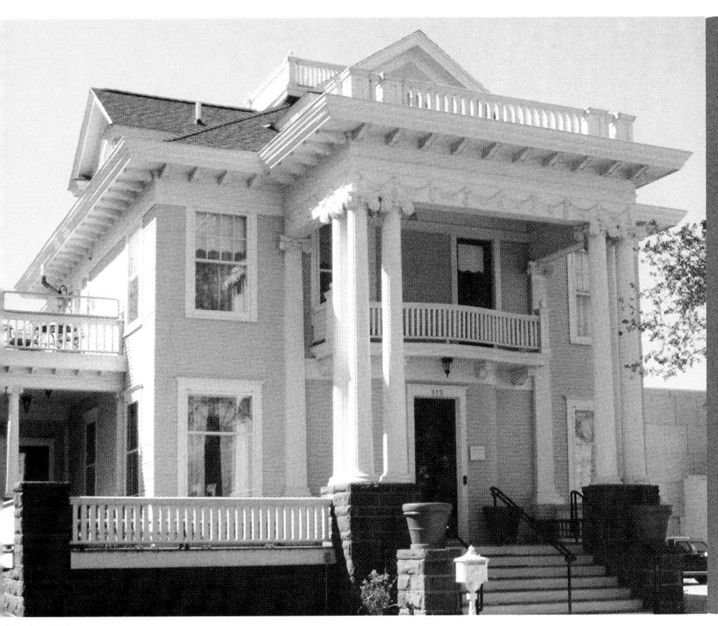

Decker House

Lodging tips

Find extraordinary accommodations and good food at the **Decker House** bed-and-breakfast and the adjoining **Sour Grapes Bistro**. This 1890s neoclassical mansion once belonged to one of Mason City's leading families. It offers four rooms and a large Jacuzzi suite. Breakfasts are served in a sunny dining area; a full-service kitchen provides meals for both the inn and bistro. Alternatively, a number of national hotel/motel chains are represented, including Holiday Inn, Days Inn, Super 8, and Country Inns & Suites.

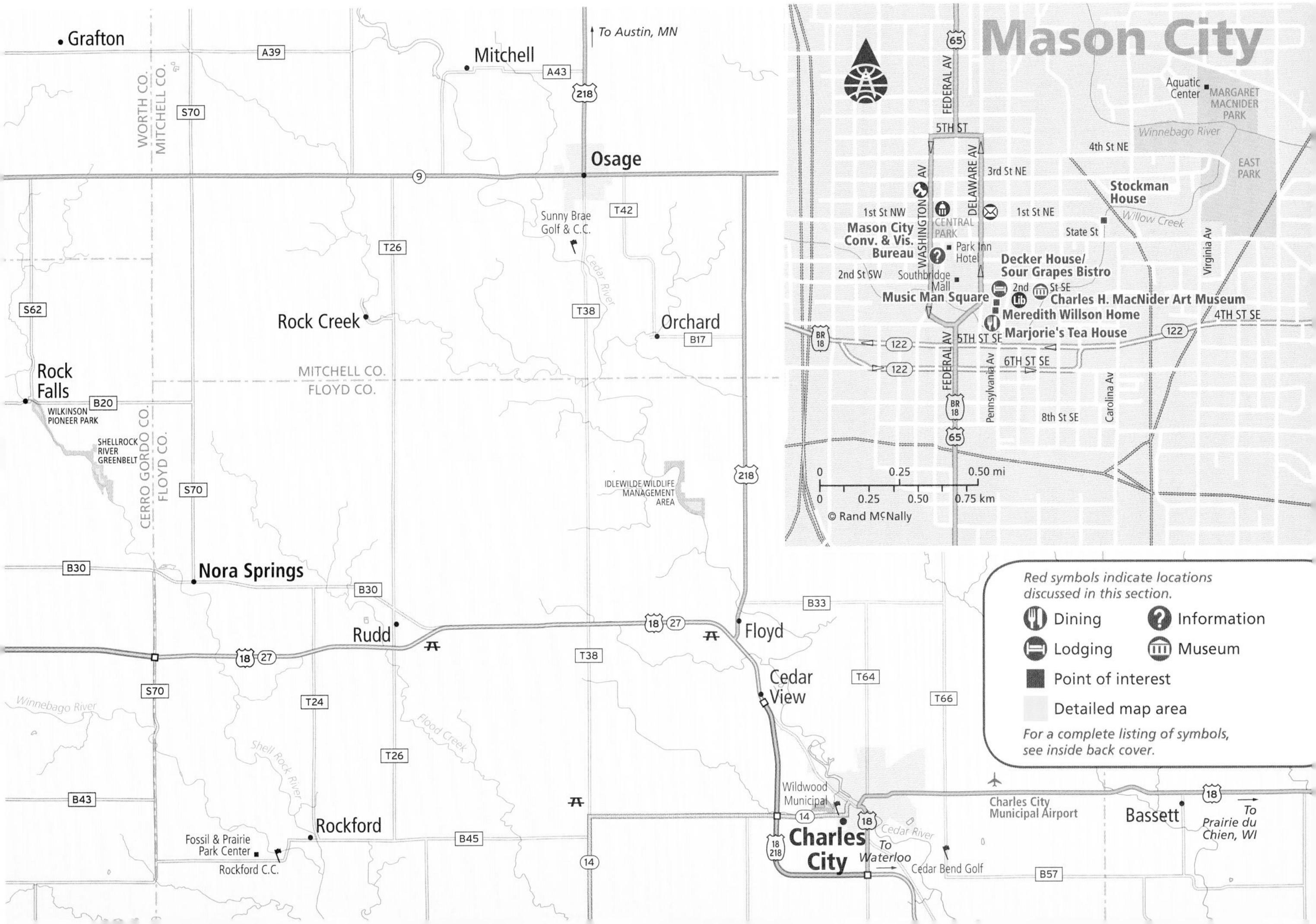

Grafton
Mitchell
To Austin, MN
Osage
Sunny Brae Golf & C.C.
Rock Creek
Orchard
Rock Falls
WILKINSON PIONEER PARK
SHELLROCK RIVER GREENBELT
WORTH CO.
MITCHELL CO.
FLOYD CO.
CERRO GORDO CO.
IDLEWILDE WILDLIFE MANAGEMENT AREA
Nora Springs
Rudd
Floyd
Cedar View
Winnebago River
Shell Rock River
Flood Creek
Cedar River
Rockford
Fossil & Prairie Park Center
Rockford C.C.
Wildwood Municipal
Charles City
To Waterloo
Cedar Bend Golf
Charles City Municipal Airport
Bassett
To Prairie du Chien, WI
Mason City
Aquatic Center
MARGARET MACNIDER PARK
EAST PARK
Winnebago River
Willow Creek
Stockman House
Mason City Conv. & Vis. Bureau
CENTRAL PARK
Park Inn Hotel
Southbridge Mall
Decker House/ Sour Grapes Bistro
Music Man Square
Charles H. MacNider Art Museum
Meredith Willson Home
Marjorie's Tea House
FEDERAL AV
WASHINGTON AV
DELAWARE AV
Pennsylvania Av
Carolina Av
Virginia Av
5TH ST
3rd St NE
4th St NE
1st St NW
1st St NE
State St
2nd St SW
4TH ST SE
5TH ST SE
6TH ST SE
8th St SE
0 0.25 0.50 mi
0 0.25 0.50 0.75 km
© Rand McNally
Red symbols indicate locations discussed in this section.
Dining
Information
Lodging
Museum
Point of interest
Detailed map area
For a complete listing of symbols, see inside back cover.

Sampling **Iowa**

Iowa, the quintessential Midwestern state, is as American as its famous state fair, its endless acres of cornfields, and native son Grant Wood's iconic painting, *American Gothic*. But Iowa also reflects America's ethnic diversity.

No where is that more evident than in northeastern Iowa—especially at **Postville** (pop. 2,300). More than a score of ethnic groups have converged on the formerly homogeneous farming community, creating a cauldron of cultures. The prospect of work in food processing plants attracted this influx of work-seeking immigrants, including El Salvadorans, Nigerians, and people from the Ukraine, Kazakhstan, and other countries of the former Soviet Union. About 200 Hasidic Jews also reside in this corner of Iowa, having reopened a shuttered meat-packing plant, where a small army of rabbis (more per capita that any other community in America) oversees its strict Kosher operation. Another component of Postville's population is 500 Hispanics drawn by jobs at a turkey-processing plant.

A stroll through town reveals why Postville has been dubbed "Hometown to the World." Along its tiny main street, **Jacob's Table Jewish Deli & Grocery** (121 W. Greene St.) offers glatt pastries in a dining room decorated with a mural of Jerusalem's Wailing Wall. Across the street sits a Mexican food market with a taco stand in back. Filipinos and Scandinavians share the sidewalks and park benches alongside Guatemalans wearing hand-tooled leather boots and wide-brimmed white hats, and rabbis in hats and long black coats.

White Embden geese and winter squash in Decorah

There's no question about the identity of the ethnic group that settled at **Decorah**, less than 35 miles northwest of Postville. Decorah is as Norwegian as the colorful rosemaling (decorative painting) you'll find throughout town and the nisse—mischievous elves said to bring good luck—that hang in windows. In the second half of the 19th century, Decorah welcomed a surge of Norwegian immigrants to this charming valley of the Upper Iowa River, where bluffs fall away from town like the steps of a Roman amphitheater.

Nordic dancing, Decorah

It should come as no surprise, then, to find that Decorah hosts the **Vesterheim Norwegian-American Museum** (523 W. Water St.), founded in 1877. It chronicles Norwegian immigration to America—and the impact of America on families who sought new beginnings here. One of its most evocative paintings shows a family seated somberly at a table set with the empty chair of the father who has gone to America hoping to carve out a better life for them all. Exhibits at the sprawling museum trace the roots of Norwegians who sought a "vesterheim" (western home), reliving the saga of perilous Atlantic crossings and portraying the harshness of pioneer life in America. The museum and 16 historic buildings cover a square block in downtown Decorah, with a farmstead and country church seven miles outside the city.

Although a young winery— it opened in October 2005—the **Winneshiek Wildberry Winery** (1966 337th St.) has established itself as fun to visit, with lively events and a definite affinity for fruit wines, such as blackberry and cherry (and also apparently for alliteration). Step up to a handcrafted oak bar to sample red raspberry wine or try a glass of Chambourcin, the winery's first dry red wine. Pick a nice day to follow walking trails around three acres of vineyards and two acres of rhubarb.

A tour of the Midwest reveals not a few communities that claim *Little House on the Prairie* author Laura Ingalls Wilder as their own. Travel about a dozen miles north of Decorah to **Burr Oak** to visit the only childhood home of Wilder that remains on its original site. She moved there with her family in 1876 when her father took a position as manager of the Burr Oak Masters Hotel. The hotel, restored to its 1876 appearance, is now the **Laura Ingalls Wilder Park and Museum** (3603 236th Ave.) and is listed on the National Register of Historic Places, along with the 1910 bank building that houses a visitor center. Dolls, clothing, and of course books by Wilder fill the gift shop.

Another ethnic group with a strong presence in the area is Czechoslovakians. Just 19 miles southwest of Decorah lies **Spillville**, where diversions include a visit to St. Wenceslaus Church, completed in 1860. Famed Czech composer Antonin Dvorak played the organ at mass there when he and his family spent the summer of 1893 at a house in Spillville (323 S. Main St.). Upstairs in that house is the Antonin Dvorak Exhibit devoted to him.

Clocks in the Bily Clocks Museum, Spillville

Downstairs: another remarkable collection well worth visiting. The **Bily Clocks Museum** displays exquisite clocks carved by brothers Frank and Joseph Bily. As farmers and carpenters, they created these clocks purely as a hobby-clocks so unique and artistic that in the 1920s Henry Ford offered them $1 million for one of the masterpieces. They turned him down.

What to eat

While visiting Decorah, don't miss the opportunity to sample lefse (thin pancakes), fruit soup and pastries such as krasnkakke (Norwegian wedding cake) and krumkakke (a flat, crispy cookie rolled into a cone shape). For Norwegian specialties try the **Dayton House Café** (516 W. Water St.), which offers a Norwegian lunch menu, and the café that adjoins the Vesterheim museum. Another "don't miss" foodie stop: Albert's Lounge in the **Hotel Winneshiek** (104 E. Water St.), known for smoky, fall-off-the-bone ribs that are marinated for hours in spices, then grilled.

What to buy

In Decorah, shop for rosemaling and exquisite woodcarvings (the gift shop of the Vesterheim Museum carries a good selection). The **Winneshiek Wildberry Winery** gift shop offers ornate hand-painted glasses and log furniture and—for the chocoholic in you—hand-dipped truffles.

What to do

Nordic Fest, Decorah, late July.

For more details about this festival, please see page 174.

Information

Postville Visitor Center, (563) 864-3440.

Winneshiek County Convention & Visitors Bureau, (800) 463-4692, www.decoraharea.com.

Lodging tips

Where to stay? Look no further than Decorah to find lodgings fit for a king—and a queen. The deluxe **Hotel Winneshiek**, built in 1904-05 (with a massive restoration completed in 2000) hosted Norway's Crown Prince Olav and Crown Princess Martha in 1939. It offers 24 rooms, six junior suites, and a presidential suite that provide luxurious amenities and service. The handsome hostelry features original marble wainscoting and an octagonal three-story lobby that opens onto a nine-panel stained glass skylight. An alternative is the **Old World Inn** (331 S. Main St.) in Spillville, where a $1 million restoration has created a charming spot for lodging and fine or casual dining. Its signature restaurant is named for Antonin Dvorak, who sent the manuscript for his "New World Symphony" from Spillville (the score had been written in New York City).

Hotel Winneshiek

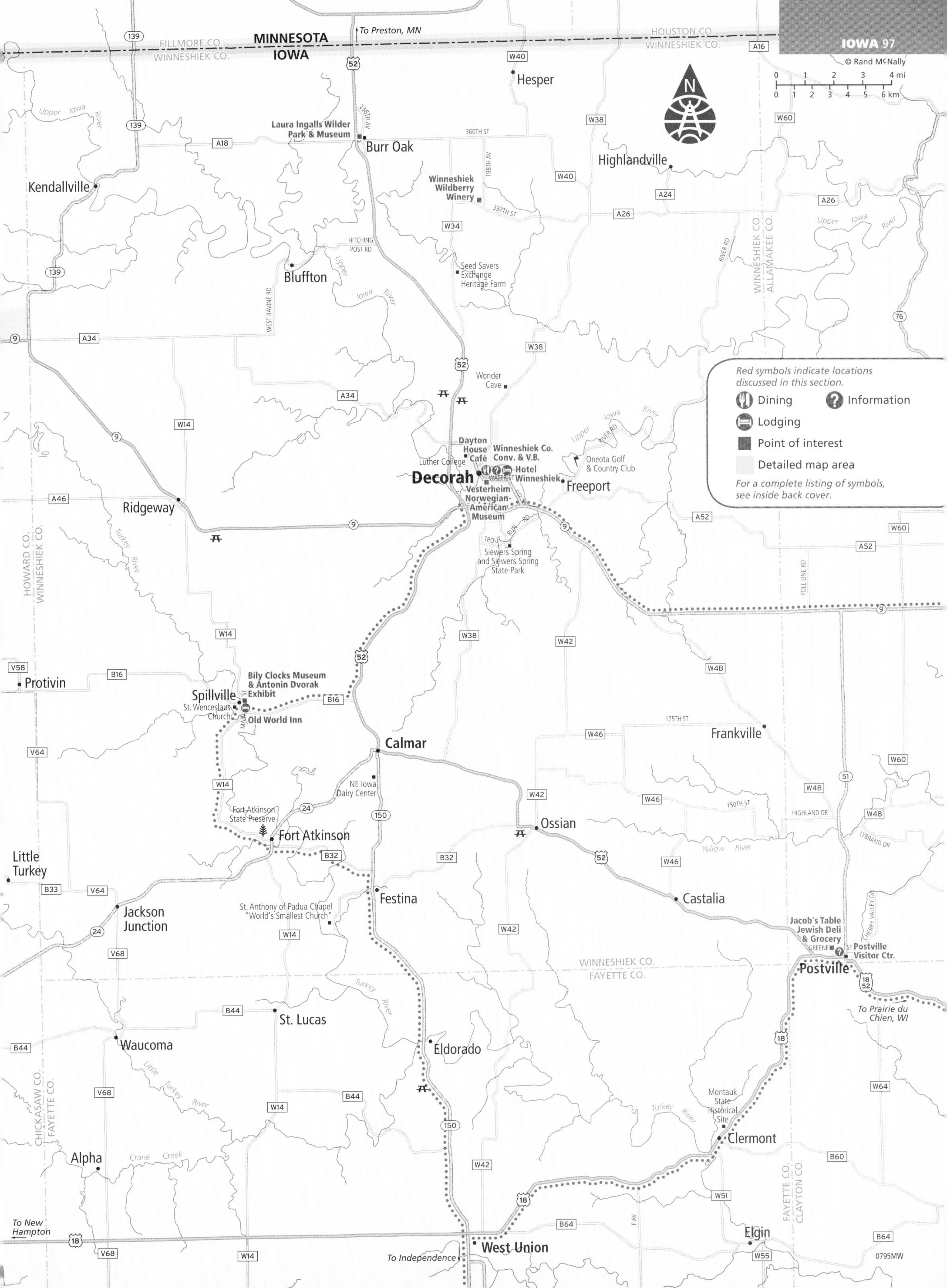
© Rand McNally
MINNESOTA
IOWA
FILLMORE CO.
WINNESHIEK CO.
HOUSTON CO.
WINNESHIEK CO.
To Preston, MN
Hesper
Burr Oak
Laura Ingalls Wilder Park & Museum
Highlandville
Kendallville
Winneshiek Wildberry Winery
Bluffton
Seed Savers Exchange Heritage Farm
Upper Iowa River
WINNESHIEK CO.
ALLAMAKEE CO.
Wonder Cave
Red symbols indicate locations discussed in this section.
Dining
Information
Lodging
Point of interest
Detailed map area
For a complete listing of symbols, see inside back cover.
Dayton House Café
Winneshiek Co. Conv. & V.B.
Luther College
Hotel Winneshiek
Decorah
Oneota Golf & Country Club
Freeport
Vesterheim Norwegian-American Museum
Ridgeway
Siewers Spring and Siewers Spring State Park
HOWARD CO.
WINNESHIEK CO.
Turkey River
Protivin
Bily Clocks Museum & Antonin Dvorak Exhibit
Spillville
St. Wenceslaus Church
Old World Inn
Calmar
Frankville
NE Iowa Dairy Center
Fort Atkinson State Preserve
Fort Atkinson
Ossian
Little Turkey
Festina
Castalia
Yellow River
Jackson Junction
St. Anthony of Padua Chapel "World's Smallest Church"
Jacob's Table Jewish Deli & Grocery
Postville Visitor Ctr.
Postville
WINNESHIEK CO.
FAYETTE CO.
To Prairie du Chien, WI
St. Lucas
Waucoma
Eldorado
Little Turkey River
CHICKASAW CO.
FAYETTE CO.
Montauk State Historical Site
Clermont
Alpha
Crane Creek
FAYETTE CO.
CLAYTON CO.
To New Hampton
Elgin
West Union
To Independence
0795MW

Wandering
Grant Wood Country

Even if you don't recognize the name Grant Wood, you probably know the grim-faced, pitchfork-toting couple from his most famous and most spoofed work, *American Gothic*. The original painting hangs in the Art Institute of Chicago. But to enjoy the landscape that inspired it, travel the hills and valleys along Iowa's Wapsipinicon River to **Cedar Rapids, Stone City,** and **Anamosa**—popularly known as "Grant Wood Country."

Here stand many of the handsome buildings of locally quarried limestone that Wood captured with his brush. You'll also discover the site he chose for his art colony, where students bunked down in retired horse-drawn wagons donated by an ice company. At the **Cedar Rapids Museum of Art** (410 Third Ave. SE), view the world's largest collection of Wood paintings (sans *American Gothic*, of course) and other important American artists (including Wood's long-time painter friend, Marvin Cone). Its permanent collection includes more than 500 works by these two seminal Midwestern artists.

Although he lived and studied in Europe, Grant Wood himself was the image of rural America. He preferred to wear overalls while working in his studio and teaching high school. "I had to go to France to appreciate Iowa," Wood observed. He also claimed: "All the really good ideas I'd ever had came to me while I was milking

Tree of Five Seasons, downtown Cedar Rapids

a cow. So I went back to Iowa." Visit the **studio** (5 Turner Alley) of this quintessential folk artist. Opened to public tours in 2004, it occupies the loft of a 19th-century carriage house (later a two-car garage) next to a funeral home. Wood lived and worked here between 1924 and 1934, creating some of his most famous paintings, including *American Gothic*. The lower floor now houses a visitor center that features exhibitions, a video presentation on Wood, and a gift shop.

Cedar Rapids Museum of Art

To strike an *American Gothic* pose as a fun souvenir, head to **Ushers Ferry Historic Village** (5925 Seminole Valley Tr. NE) in northeast Cedar Rapids, which portrays a small Iowa town stuck in a time warp at the turn of the last century. Visitors are invited to pose for pictures in front of a replica of the *American Gothic* house.

The area's Czech heritage attracts visitors, too. Soak some up at **Czech Village** (76 16th Ave. SW), site of ethnic restaurants, a bakery, gift shops, and a large ethnic museum. With one in five of its residents of Czech descent, Cedar Rapids celebrates this culture at the **National Czech & Slovak Museum & Library** (30 16th Ave. SW). It features exceptional examples of hand-crafted folk art, glass, and ceramics, as well as prints, rare maps, military objects—and even a classic 1935 Jawa motorcycle. The museum also showcases an internationally recognized collection of Bohemian, Moravian, and Slovak folk costumes. Typical designs feature brilliant colors, flourishes of gold thread, and intricate lace work.

An excellent side trip from Cedar Rapids: the seven German villages that make up the **Amana Colonies** (622 46th Ave., Amana). Located just 19 miles southwest, they offer tours of museums, furniture and clock-making shops, wineries, bakeries, and a woolen mill. Craftspeople make fine furniture from walnut, oak, and cherry at individual workbenches rather than on production lines and personally sign every piece.

Drive south to **Kalona**, where you'll find yourself sharing the road with the squat black buggies of the Old Order Amish. Join a "Countryside Tour" and spend the day traveling scenic backroads past Amish homes, farms, and schools. You'll inspect beautiful hand-stitched quilts, painstakingly wrought over long winters' nights, and see demonstrations of noodle making and traditional crafts such as woodworking. Later in the evening, a family-style dinner is served in a Mennonite home, where you'll enjoy perhaps roast beef, pork, chicken, or ham, with home-baked bread, tapioca pudding, and homemade pies.

A presidential stop awaits at **West Branch**, birthplace of Herbert C. Hoover, 31st president of the United States from 1929 to 1933. The **Herbert Hoover Presidential Library and Museum** (210 Parkside Dr.) is a National Historic Site where you can tour Hoover's birthplace cottage and visit the gravesite of Mr. and Mrs. Hoover. Also on site is a 76-acre reconstructed prairie, a blacksmith shop, and a Quaker meeting house (Hoover was born into a Quaker family).

Czech Village, Cedar Rapids

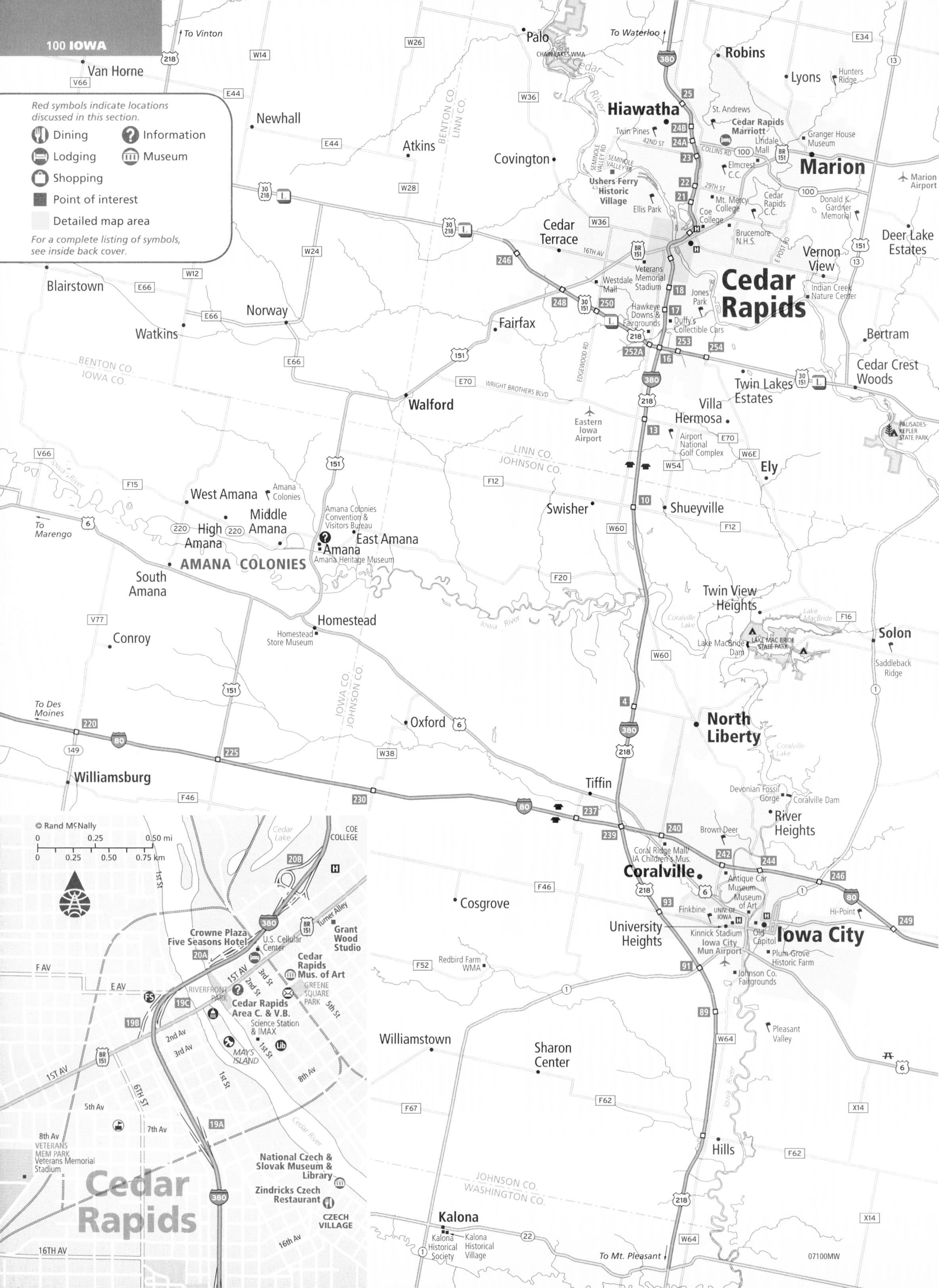

Red symbols indicate locations discussed in this section.
Dining
Information
Lodging
Museum
Shopping
Point of interest
Detailed map area
For a complete listing of symbols, see inside back cover.
Cedar Rapids
Marion
Hiawatha
Robins
Lyons
Iowa City
Coralville
North Liberty
Amana Colonies
Amana
East Amana
West Amana
Middle Amana
High Amana
South Amana
Homestead
Walford
Fairfax
Norway
Watkins
Blairstown
Newhall
Atkins
Van Horne
Palo
Covington
Cedar Terrace
Swisher
Shueyville
Ely
Solon
Tiffin
Oxford
Williamsburg
Conroy
Cosgrove
University Heights
Williamstown
Sharon Center
Hills
Kalona
Kalona Historical Society
Kalona Historical Village
To Vinton
To Waterloo
To Marengo
To Des Moines
To Mt. Pleasant
© Rand McNally
07100MW

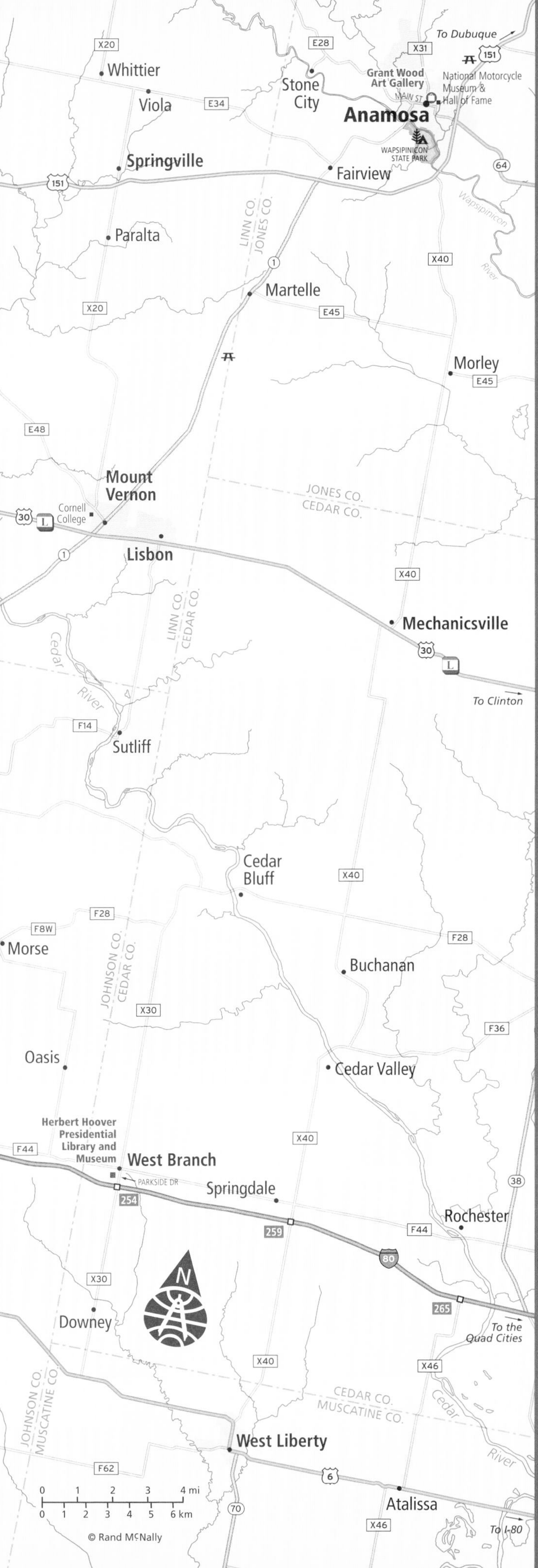

What to eat

Zindricks Czech Restaurant (86 16th Ave. SW), in the heart of **Czech Village**, is decorated with antiques, paintings, and prints from the old country as well as collections of Czech pottery and crystal. It offers authentic Czech food as well as a good selection of imported beers and wines. Starters include cabbage rolls, pierogis, and liver dumpling soup; entrées feature roast pork loin, goulash with a rich gravy, and chicken paprika, roast duck, and liver sausage served with grilled onions.

What to buy

In Anamosa, the **Grant Wood Art Gallery** (124 E Main St.) carries prints, posters, lithographs, notecards, and other Grant Wood items, as well as the opportunity to snap the obligatory photograph of your subjects as the stern-faced duo of *American Gothic*. You'll also learn the extent to which the iconic couple has penetrated pop culture. Find them in TV commercials and cereal ads, on billboards and neckties. Wood's dour-faced duo has been spoofed in a beer ad, in a Dick Tracy strip, as Hawaii vacationers, and in weed-control advertising.

In Cedar Rapids, the store at the **National Czech & Slovak Museum & Library** sells books, glassware, ceramics, and jewelry. Look especially for garnet pieces, this gem being a specialty of the Czech and Slovak Republics.

What to do

Grant Wood Art Festival, Stone City and Anamosa, early June.
Grand Celebration of Brass Bands, Cedar Rapids, mid-June.
For more details about these festivals, please see page 174.

Information

Cedar Rapids Area Convention & Visitors Bureau, (800) 735-5557, www.cedar-rapids.com.

Lodging tips

Most of the budget and moderately priced hotel/motel chains are represented at Cedar Rapids, such as Hampton Inn, Red Roof Inn, and Super 8, along with Holiday Inn Express and Residence Inn by Marriott. Higher-end properties include the 275-room **Crowne Plaza Five Seasons Hotel**, located downtown, which includes a business-class floor and business center, and the 221-room **Cedar Rapids Marriott**, featuring a seven-story atrium.

Bluegrass and Bourbon

Kentucky's Bluegrass Country presents a palette of colors. In spring, bluish-purple buds give the fields a blue cast. Thoroughbred horses with glistening coats of chestnut, black, and roan live like royalty in elaborate ash-gray limestone "barns" and graze on pastures enclosed by immaculate white fences. Deep limestone shelves beneath the bluegrass help provide nutritious, potassium-rich grazing. Limestone also purifies water used to make bourbon. The art of making fine whiskey and the mystique surrounding Thoroughbred racehorses provide visitors with much to see, do, and taste.

Many of the region's 450 horse farms welcome guests. Visit them with a guided tour group or on a private customized tour. Or call ahead to visit on your own. You'll quickly discover that Thoroughbreds are royalty, their "barns"—some with crystal chandeliers—as grand as mansions. On these farms champions are bred, foaled, trained, bought, sold, raced, and retired, and earn their owners millions in stud fees. Tour guides explain how horses have their upper lips tattooed for identification, and that a Thoroughbred can gallop up to 50 miles per hour. Guides may also point out that while most racehorses are past their prime by age six or seven, the legendary John Henry was still competing at age nine.

Consider a visit to **Three Chimneys Farm**, home of Smarty Jones, winner of the 2004 Kentucky Derby and Preakness. It's on Old Frankfort Pike, west of Lexington. Or stop at **Normandy Farm** (4701 Paris Pike), which takes its name from the French barn in which then-owner Joseph Widener hid after his plane crashed in World War I. Widener commissioned a replication of the L-shaped barn. The **Kentucky Horse Park** (4089 Iron Works Pkwy., Lexington) is part working horse farm, part educational theme park, and the region's number-one attraction. Museums (including one that traces the history of the horse through the ages), galleries, theaters, and more than 50 breeds of horses chronicle and demonstrate how people and horses have interacted for centuries. You can watch action on a racetrack and on steeplechase and cross-country courses, as well as in show rings and on the polo field; observe the arts of saddle- and harness-making and horseshoeing; and visit the draft-horse barn, home of the "gentle giants."

Kentucky horse farm

Keeneland Race Course, Lexington

Buffalo Trace Distillery, Frankfort

Ivy covers the stone buildings of the gracefully landscaped **Keeneland Race Course** (4201 Versailles Rd., Lexington). Beyond the track, green swaths of sweet pastureland nestle between rolling, wooded hills. On race days, as parasols bloom like lilies, Keeneland attracts racing's elite. Owner and enthusiast Queen Elizabeth II visited in 1984, while in 1998 Princess Anne attended Keeneland's inaugural steeplechase. Best-selling novelist Dick Francis has spent countless hours doing research in Keeneland's renowned library, where the collection includes a volume dating to 1611. Head for Keeneland in early morning for the daily workouts. Plan a breakfast stop at the **Track Kitchen**, open to the public and patronized by owners, trainers, and jockeys talking shop.

Buffalo Trace Distillery (1001 Wilkinson Blvd., Franklin County) sits on the banks of the Kentucky River near the site of an ancient buffalo crossing. There has been a working distillery at this site since 1787. Bourbon ages in century-old brick warehouses in virgin, white oak barrels that have been charred on the inside. For each year of aging, about three percent of the bourbon evaporates or leaches into the wood of the barrel itself. The bourbon that disappears is known as the "angel's share."

Another historic distillery: **Woodford Reserve**, formerly known as Labrot & Graham (7855 McCracken Pike, Versailles). Dating from 1812, it occupies pretty stone buildings on 42 acres of undulating grassland in the heart of horse country. Tours are available, after which visitors may enjoy complimentary peach-flavored iced tea or bourbon-flavored coffee, depending on the season. For those of age, a distillery tour may conclude with a ½-ounce taste of bourbon served in a commemorative plastic shot glass. Bourbon balls are enjoyed year-round by all. The well-stocked gift shop offers the coffee and bourbon balls in addition to local crafts. Several rocking chairs on the wrap-around porch beckon visitors to sit awhile. From April through October, picnic-style lunches featuring sandwiches, salads, bourbon chocolate cake, and freshly squeezed lemonade may be purchased at the lunch stand.

A town of antebellum mansions, **Paris**, the Bourbon County seat, was named in appreciation of French support for the American Revolution. Bringing more colors to Bluegrass Country are purple and green classic wine grapes such as riesling, chardonnay, vidal blanc, and cabernet sauvignon, all of which thrive in trellised rows at nearby 35-acre **Equus Run Vineyards** (1280 Moores Mill Rd., Midway). Opened in 1999 on a former tobacco farm, the winery already has won medals for wine produced by co-owner and winemaker Cynthia Bohn.

Woodford Reserve distillery, Versailles

What to eat

Fried green tomatoes, country ham with redeye gravy, and spoon bread are local favorites. Find them at **Campbell's** in Paris (519 Main St.), a restaurant dating back to the 1880s with original tin ceilings. This also is the spot to try (or buy to-go) beer cheese, a popular savory cheese spread made with beer, and to sample a Hot Brown—an open-faced turkey sandwich with cheese, bacon, and sliced turkey on toast with Mornay sauce and a tomato slice. Invented in 1923 at Louisville's Brown Hotel, it's a Kentucky original.

What to buy

Take home a taste of Kentucky with a bottle of premium aged bourbon, or perhaps a box of chocolates made with Kentucky's favorite whiskey. **Keeneland's** elegant gift shop offers polos, fleecy wear, glassware, clocks, videos, figurines, furniture, books, and such specialty items as an English-style shooting stick (a stylish portable seat). Most items are, as you'd expect, horse-themed.

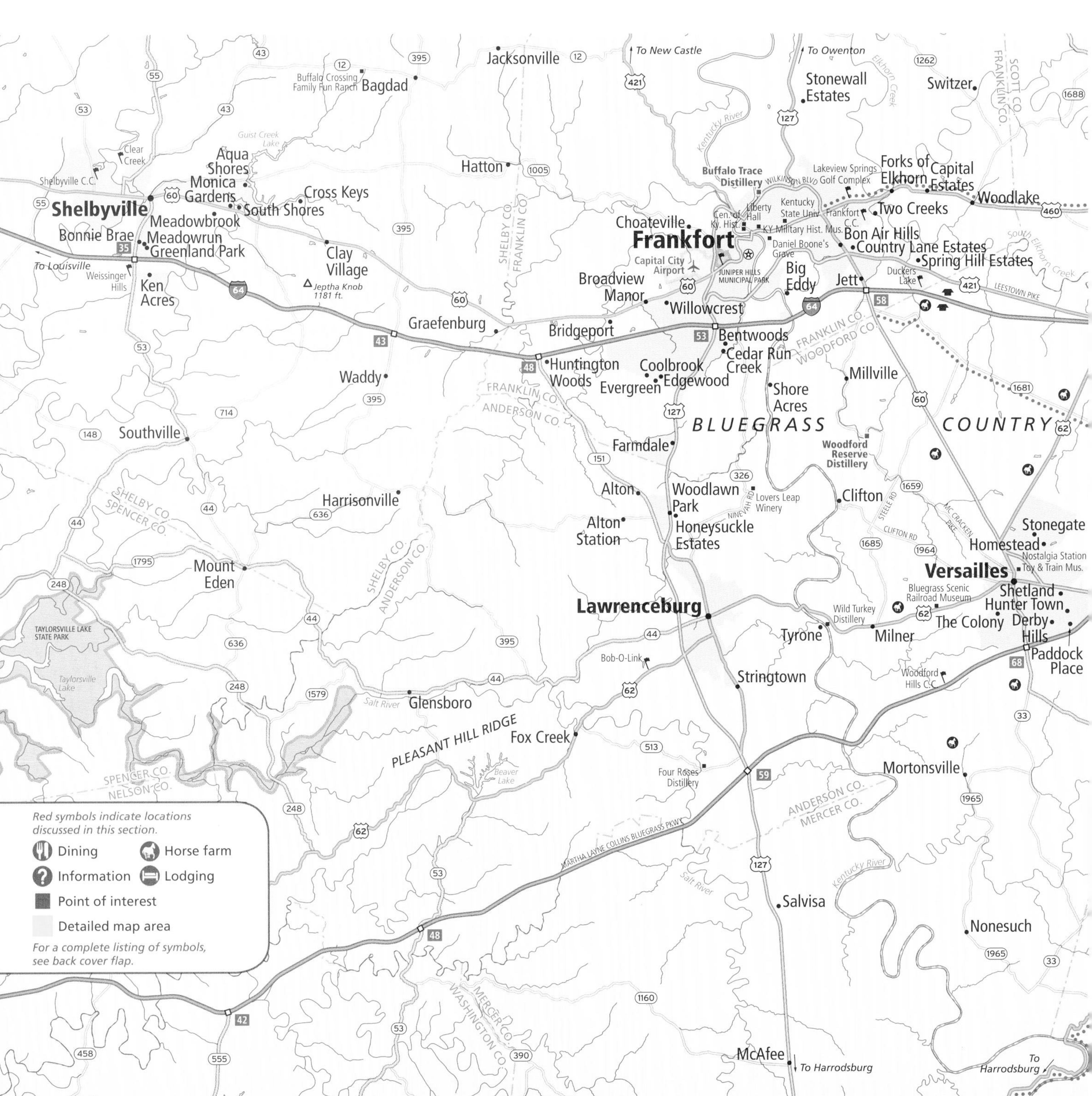

What to do

Woodland Art Fair, Lexington, third weekend in August.

Festival Latino de Lexington, Lexington, September.

For more details about these festivals, please see page 174.

Information

Lexington Convention and Visitors Bureau, (800) 845-3959, www.visitlex.com.

Lodging tips

Get into the spirit of Bluegrass Country with lodgings at a prominent horse farm near Keeneland Race Course. Accommodations at **Swann's Nest at Cygnet Farm** (3463 Rosalie Ln., Lexington) include two spacious suites overlooking the broodmare paddocks. Another option is **Bed & Breakfast at Silver Springs Farm** (3710 Leestown Pike, Lexington), a Federal-style house that originally was part of a distillery. Other choices in Lexington include a range of chain properties, including all-suites hotels such as the Hilton and Country Inns & Suites.

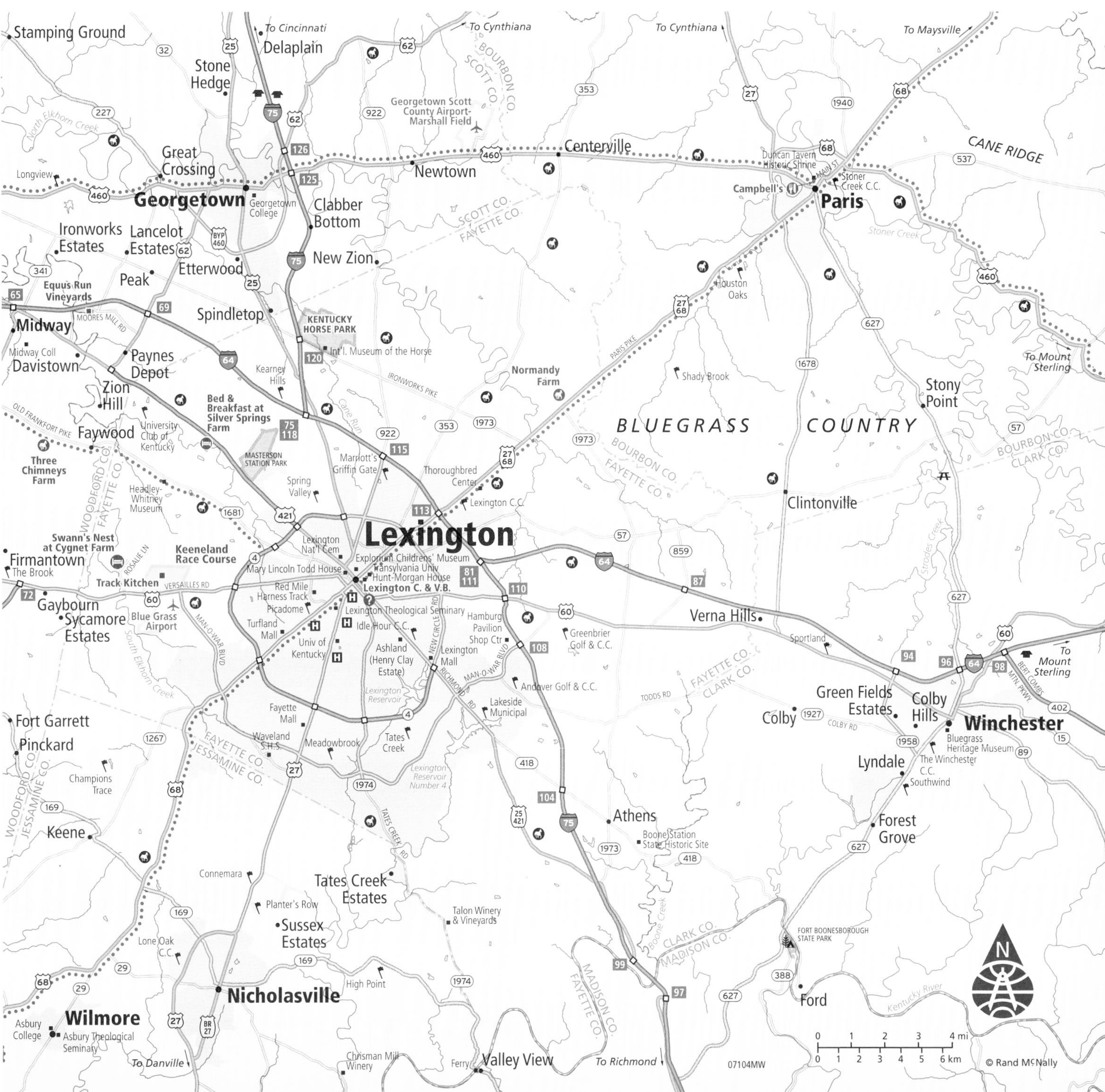

Exploring the Land Between The Lakes

In the western reaches of Kentucky, two massive lakes and a vast tract of land beckon nearly two million visitors annually. They come to view wildlife and to visit a nature center, living history farm, planetarium and observatory, and to ride horses and mountain bikes.

In the 1930s President Roosevelt's New Deal policies chartered the Tennessee Valley Authority. The TVA dammed the Tennessee River to form Kentucky Lake. Later, the U.S. Army Corps of Engineers dammed the Cumberland River to create Lake Barkley. Together, these lakes comprise one of the world's largest manmade bodies of water. These remarkable engineering projects also created the peninsula known as **Land Between The Lakes** (LBL), a 170,000-acre national recreation area.

Throughout LBL, more than 100 miles of horse and wagon trails and 200 miles of hiking and biking trails wind their way through rolling woodlands and along isolated shorelines. The rich and varied habitats support more than 1,300 plant species, 240 kinds of birds, and 53 different species of mammals. The main north-south road is known as **"The Trace,"** named for ancient buffalo trails.

US 68 cuts across this long finger of land and intersects the Trace. At this juncture sits the **Golden Pond Visitor Center**, inside which resides a state-of-the-art planetarium with an 81-seat theater with shows several times daily. It's home to the Western Kentucky Amateur Astronomers, who hold monthly meetings and star-gazing sessions (to which the public is invited without charge).

Land Between The Lakes

Bison herd at Land Between The Lakes

When buckskin-clad Daniel Boone first traveled this region in the late 18th century, vast herds of American bison—perhaps as many as 60 million—darkened the prairies, often extending as far as the eye could see. Then came buffalo hunters with powerful rifles. In a few short years, the bison was on the brink of extinction. Captive breeding and re-introduction to the wild have helped save the species. In 1996, Land Between The Lakes opened its Elk & Bison Prairie, a 700-acre restoration of the native tallgrass prairie habitat that thrived in Western Kentucky more than 200 years ago. Waving stands of chest-high grasses sprinkled with wildflowers hum with the sound of busy insects. Seasonal wildflowers include red-blooming Indian paintbrush and brilliant orange butterfly weed. Bobcats stalk small game as hawks and bald eagles glide gracefully on the thermals. On a quiet afternoon you can listen to the chirp of an indigo bunting. Take a self-guided driving tour along a three-and-a-half-mile road with three interpretive stops, or hike a trail at the South Buffalo Range to view a herd of up to 50 bison.

Mountain bikes are ideal for exploring LBL, providing access to remote areas. A wealth of old logging roads, fire access lanes, and other little-used roads supplement the three trails developed expressly for mountain bikes. Rent bikes at the Hillman Ferry and Piney campgrounds (adult mountain bikes $15/day, child bikes $9/day).

Three LBL sites are listed on the National Register of Historic Places: Fort Henry, site of a major Civil War battle; the Center Furnace; and the Great Western Iron Furnace. The region was primarily an iron production center during the mid-19th century, when an iron-ore boom brought charcoal-fed blast furnaces. Seventeen iron furnaces operated within what now is LBL. The ruins of two of these are accessible to visitors. Sharp-eyed hikers sometimes uncover the pretty turquoise and deep blue rocks that are smelting slag.

Tucked into a hollow in the southern portion of this vast reserve is The Homeplace, a mid-19th-century living history farm. In addition to re-creating such daily activities as cultivating and harvesting tobacco, The Homeplace spotlights social events of the period, such as an 1850s wedding and a fall Agricultural Heritage Fair. The farm grows heirloom varieties of vegetables and raises rare breeds of livestock—many considered to be endangered. These include Cotswold sheep (of which there are fewer than 2,000 worldwide), a species dating back to the Roman occupation of England. Other historic breeds include shorthorn dairy cattle and a species of chicken developed in the 18th century.

The nearest large urban area to LBL is **Paducah**, where the Museum of the American Quilter's Society (215 Jefferson St.) chronicles the vigorous rebirth of quiltmaking. Three galleries display heirloom and contemporary quilts. Admire sunlit stained glass windows based on quilt patterns and shop at a well-stocked museum store. In Paducah, galleries and studios populate a fast-developing Lower Town Arts District. Overlooking the confluence of the Ohio and Tennessee Rivers, murals on the town's floodwall portray Paducah's history.

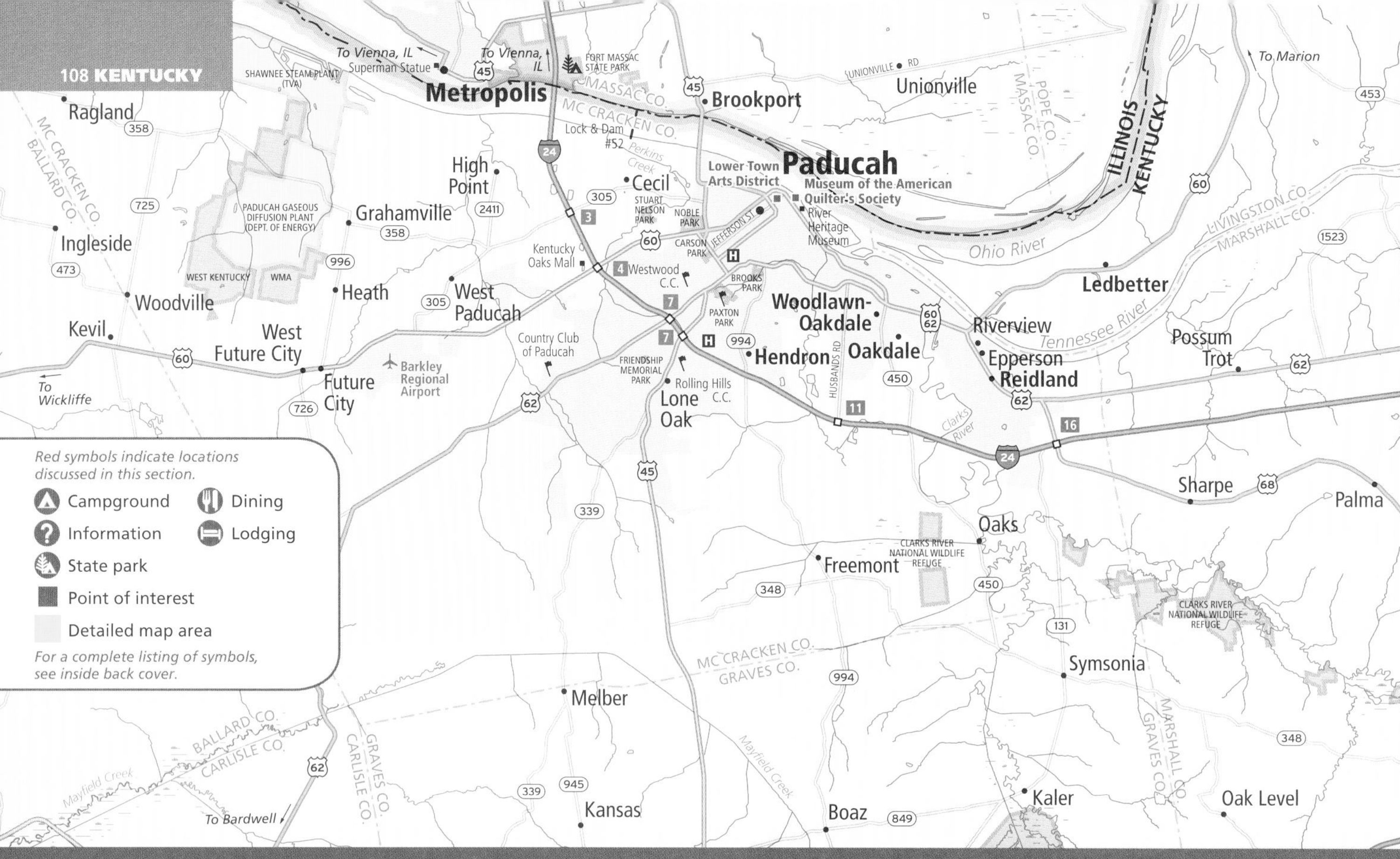

What to eat

Home-style cooking is the hallmark of local restaurants—country-cured ham with redeye gravy, sausage with fresh-baked biscuits and gravy, pork chops, catfish, grits, and homemade pies bursting with fruit. At Grand Rivers, at the north end of Kentucky Lake, **Patti's 1880's Settlement** (1793 J.H. O'Bryan Ave.) is known for its two-inch-thick pork chops, for specialty breads delivered in clay pots, and for pretty gazebos sometimes used for weddings. **Miss Scarlett's Restaurant** (off I-24 at exit 31) is known for its big pork chops and homemade desserts.

What to buy

Find all you ever wanted to know about quilting at the shop at the **Museum of the American Quilter's Society** (215 Jefferson St., Paducah). It carries more than 500 book titles on quilt history, techniques, and individual quilters, as well as novels and popular books related to quilting. Shop here, too, for fine handcrafted pottery, glass, fiber, wood, and jewelry by Kentucky and national artisans.

What to do

Pickin' Party, June.

Nature Station Hummingbird Festival, August.

For more details about these festivals, please see page 174.

Information

Kentucky Department of Tourism, (800) 225-8747, www.kentuckytourism.com.

Land Between The Lakes National Recreation Area, (270) 924-2000, www.lbl.org.

Lodging tips

State park lodges are a popular choice for comfortable accommodations. Views are stunning from **Lake Barkley State Resort Lodge**—built of western cedar, Douglas fir, and three-and-a-half acres of glass. In the main lodge, most of the 120 rooms and four suites have lake views. The resort has a 331-seat dining room and a state-of-the-art fitness center. Options at Kentucky Dam Village State Resort Park include **Village Inn Lodge** with 72 rooms, each with private patio or balcony. There also are 68 one-, two-, and three-bedroom cottages (with one or two baths) fully equipped with tableware, cooking utensils, and fresh linens daily. The resort has a 346-seat dining room, shops with a wide selection of handicrafts, and the largest marina in the park system.

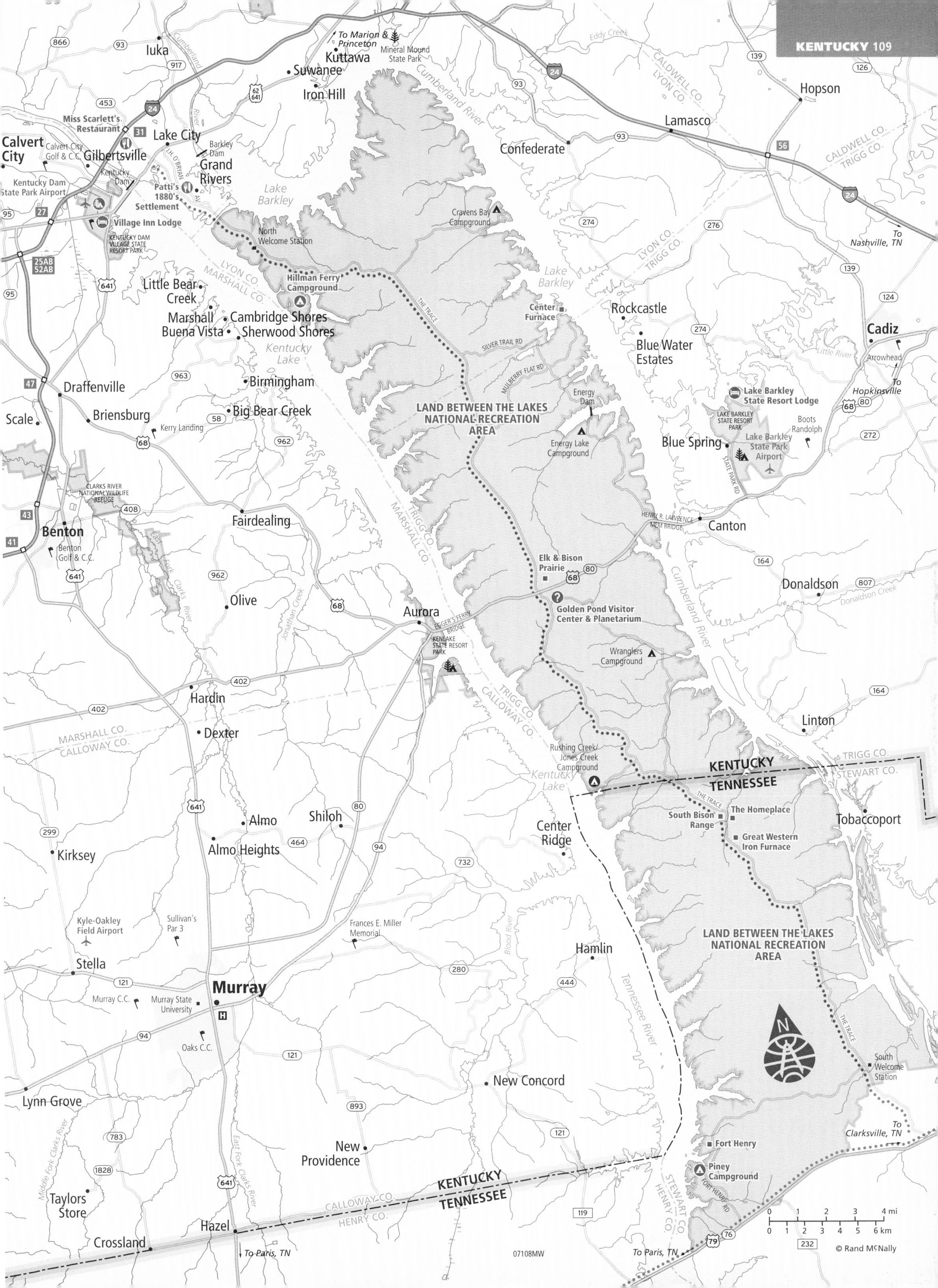

LAND BETWEEN THE LAKES NATIONAL RECREATION AREA
Lake Barkley
Kentucky Lake
Cumberland River
Tennessee River
Calvert City
Iuka
Kuttawa
Suwanee
Iron Hill
To Marion & Princeton
Mineral Mound State Park
Miss Scarlett's Restaurant
Lake City
Gilbertsville
Calvert City Golf & C.C.
Kentucky Dam
Barkley Dam
Grand Rivers
Kentucky Dam State Park Airport
Patti's 1880's Settlement
Village Inn Lodge
Kentucky Dam Village State Resort Park
North Welcome Station
Hillman Ferry Campground
Cravens Bay Campground
Confederate
Lamasco
Hopson
Little Bear Creek
Marshall
Buena Vista
Cambridge Shores
Sherwood Shores
Center Furnace
Rockcastle
Blue Water Estates
Cadiz
Arrowhead
To Nashville, TN
To Hopkinsville
Lake Barkley State Resort Lodge
Lake Barkley State Resort Park
Lake Barkley State Park Airport
Boots Randolph
Blue Spring
Draffenville
Birmingham
Big Bear Creek
Briensburg
Kerry Landing
Scale
Energy Dam
Energy Lake Campground
Clarks River National Wildlife Refuge
Benton
Benton Golf & C.C.
Fairdealing
Henry R. Lawrence Mem Bridge
Canton
Elk & Bison Prairie
Golden Pond Visitor Center & Planetarium
Olive
Aurora
Egger's Ferry Bridge
Kenlake State Resort Park
Donaldson
Wranglers Campground
Hardin
Dexter
Linton
Rushing Creek/Jones Creek Campground
KENTUCKY
TENNESSEE
The Homeplace
South Bison Range
Great Western Iron Furnace
Tobaccoport
Almo
Shiloh
Center Ridge
Kirksey
Almo Heights
Kyle-Oakley Field Airport
Sullivan's Par 3
Frances E. Miller Memorial
Hamlin
Stella
Murray
Murray C.C.
Murray State University
Oaks C.C.
South Welcome Station
New Concord
Lynn Grove
To Clarksville, TN
Fort Henry
Piney Campground
New Providence
Taylors Store
Hazel
Crossland
To Paris, TN
LYON CO.
MARSHALL CO.
TRIGG CO.
CALLOWAY CO.
CALDWELL CO.
STEWART CO.
HENRY CO.
The Trace
07108MW
© Rand McNally

Meeting Mountain Culture

Perched among the Appalachian foothills, **Berea** attracts thousands of visitors drawn to the self-dubbed "Folk Arts and Crafts Capital of Kentucky." They listen to the sweet sounds of a dulcimer and hear the clack of a weaver's shuttle as they soak up rich mountain culture and shop for heirloom-quality arts and crafts.

Uniting the architectural ambience of a colonial America college town (neo-Georgian buildings, a steepled church, and a commons) with the southern charm of Kentucky, **Berea College** serves its Appalachian community with social, cultural, and educational opportunities. About 10 percent of the students work in the school's crafts program, creating fine furniture, woven goods, ceramics, brooms, and wrought iron pieces that are sold at the **Berea College Log House Craft Gallery** (200 Estill St.). Berea's dozens of craft studios and galleries lie scattered along Chestnut Street, clustered together in Old Town, and lined up around the College Square. Some hide just off the beaten path. Others sit a short drive into the edge of the mountains. Most have one thing in common—an emphasis on quality handcrafted work.

In spring, crepe myrtle paint the woodlands with lavender flowers, spring-blooming redbud and dogwood add gaudy hues, and Berea begins its busy season of major craft fairs. But at any time of year travelers interested in crafts—and in a utopian lifestyle that has all but disappeared—head for **Shaker Village of Pleasant Hill** (3501 Lexington Rd., Harrodsburg), established 1805. The population of this former Shaker colony peaked in 1823 and flourished well into the 19th century. Kentucky Shakers no longer exist, driven to extinction by their practice of celibacy.

Shaker Village of Pleasant Hill, Harrodsburg

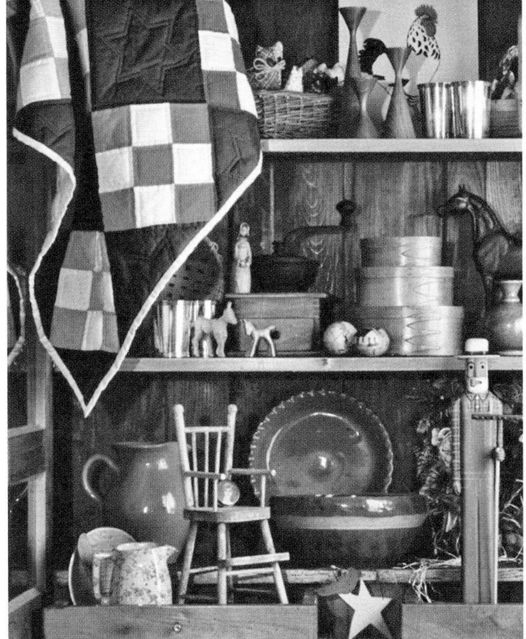

Shaker crafts

Today, **Shaker Village of Pleasant Hill** is a model of historic preservation. Costumed interpreters describe Shaker life and perform work associated with the Pleasant Hill of more than 100 years ago within 34 restored original buildings. Craft demonstrations include broom making, spinning, weaving, box making, and coopering. In the Meeting House, a cappella selections of Shaker music are performed four times a day, April through October. Shakers considered the voice the most perfect musical instrument and composed more than 20,000 songs telling of their dedication to hard work and worship. Other special music events are scheduled throughout the year.

Rolling bluegrass pastureland, bountiful orchards, and vegetable gardens surround the village's buildings. Buildings of handsome red brick and pale limestone cut from palisades along the Kentucky River display austere lines and strictly functional design. Inside are characteristic twin staircases, designed to avoid unnecessary interaction between the sexes. Heirloom farm breeds gather in the paddocks and fields—long-fleeced Bakewell sheep (a breed imported by the Shakers from England in the 1830s), Durham milking shorthorns, sturdy black Percheron draft horses, and varieties of poultry popular 100 years ago. Forty miles of multiple-use trails thread the village's 2,800 acres, some just for hikers, others for mountain bikes, horses, and carriages as well.

Seasonally, the brightly painted sternwheeler Dixie Belle departs from **Shaker Landing** to make three daily excursions down the Kentucky River. No roads, no marinas, and few powerboats disturb this quiet stretch of waterway. Its banks are heavily wooded with oak, maple, hickory, and sycamore. Great blue herons, egrets, kingfishers, and osprey feed on schools of shad while hawks ride the thermals high above the river. You may spot a muskrat or perhaps a 50-pound snapping turtle.

Nearby is the quaint village of **Harrodsburg**, Kentucky's first permanent settlement. The fort that James Harrod constructed in 1774 is re-created in **Old Fort Harrod State Park** (100 S. College St.). From mid-April to the end of October, costumed interpreters demonstrate frontier skills including weaving, blacksmithing, woodworking, and tinsmithing. Also on site are several monuments, the oldest cemetery west of the Allegheny Mountains, and a Civil War museum.

For a lively look at the musical side of mountain culture, head for **Renfro Valley**, which styles itself "Kentucky's Country Music Capital," bringing mountain music from front porches to modern stages and recording studios. It's where you'll find country music stars such as Loretta Lynn and The Oak Ridge Boys performing in headliner concert series and where you'll discover, depending on the time of year, the Monday night "Gospel Show," Tuesday's "Bluegrass Night," and signature "Renfro Valley Barn Dance." Trace country music history at the **Kentucky Music Hall of Fame and Museum** (2590 Richmond Rd.). You'll learn about the origins of bluegrass concerts on courthouse steps and at ball fields across the state, and you'll visit an instrument room where you're encouraged to see, touch, hear, and perform. Wannabes get their chance to sing and perform in a functioning sound booth.

Boone Tavern, Berea

What to eat

In Berea, **Boone Tavern** (100 Main St.) boasts "the best chess pie in Appalachia" and offers local specialties such as homemade spoonbread and "chicken flakes in a bird's nest" (creamed chicken served in a nest of potatoes with cinnamon-cranberry sauce).

What to buy

Shopping for crafts is a popular pastime among visitors to Berea. Many pieces are pricey (a handmade quilt can run $2,000), since you're paying for distinctive, quality work by internationally known artisans. But you can find inexpensive items, too. For a few dollars you can assemble your own bouquet of cornshuck flowers, made according to mountain tradition and sometimes dyed with Kool-Aid®. Less than $20 buys a pretty and unique arrangement.

What to do

Berea Craft Festival, Berea, mid-July.

For more details about this festival, please see page 174.

Information

Kentucky Department of Tourism,
(800) 225-8747, www.kentuckytourism.com.

Lodging tips

In the center of the Berea College campus, the **Boone Tavern Hotel and Restaurant** occupies a white-columned building dating from 1909. Out front stand 100-year-old holly trees. About 80 percent of its staff are students, and its 58 guestrooms feature student-made furniture. **The Inn at Shaker Village** has 81 overnight guestrooms in exquisitely restored buildings where Shaker folk lived and worked more than a century ago. Shaker reproduction furniture such as ladder-back chairs, hand-woven rag rugs on polished hardwood floors, and peg rails for hanging clothes furnish the rooms. Modern conveniences include air conditioning, television, and telephones.

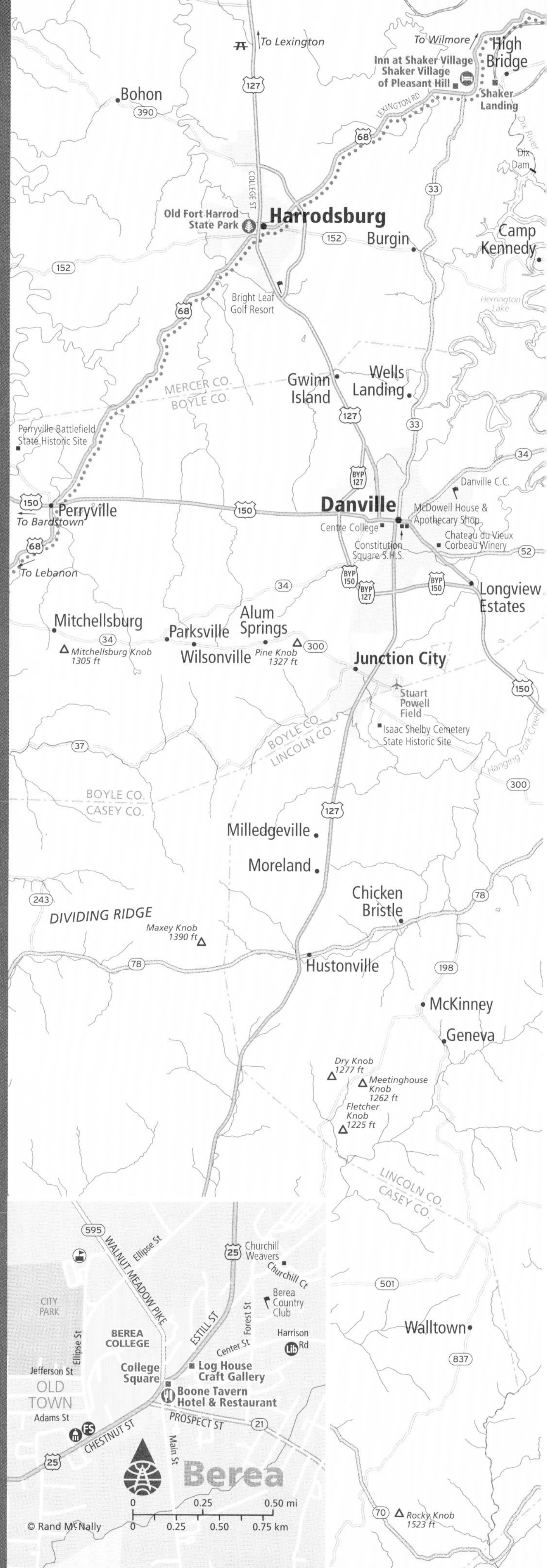

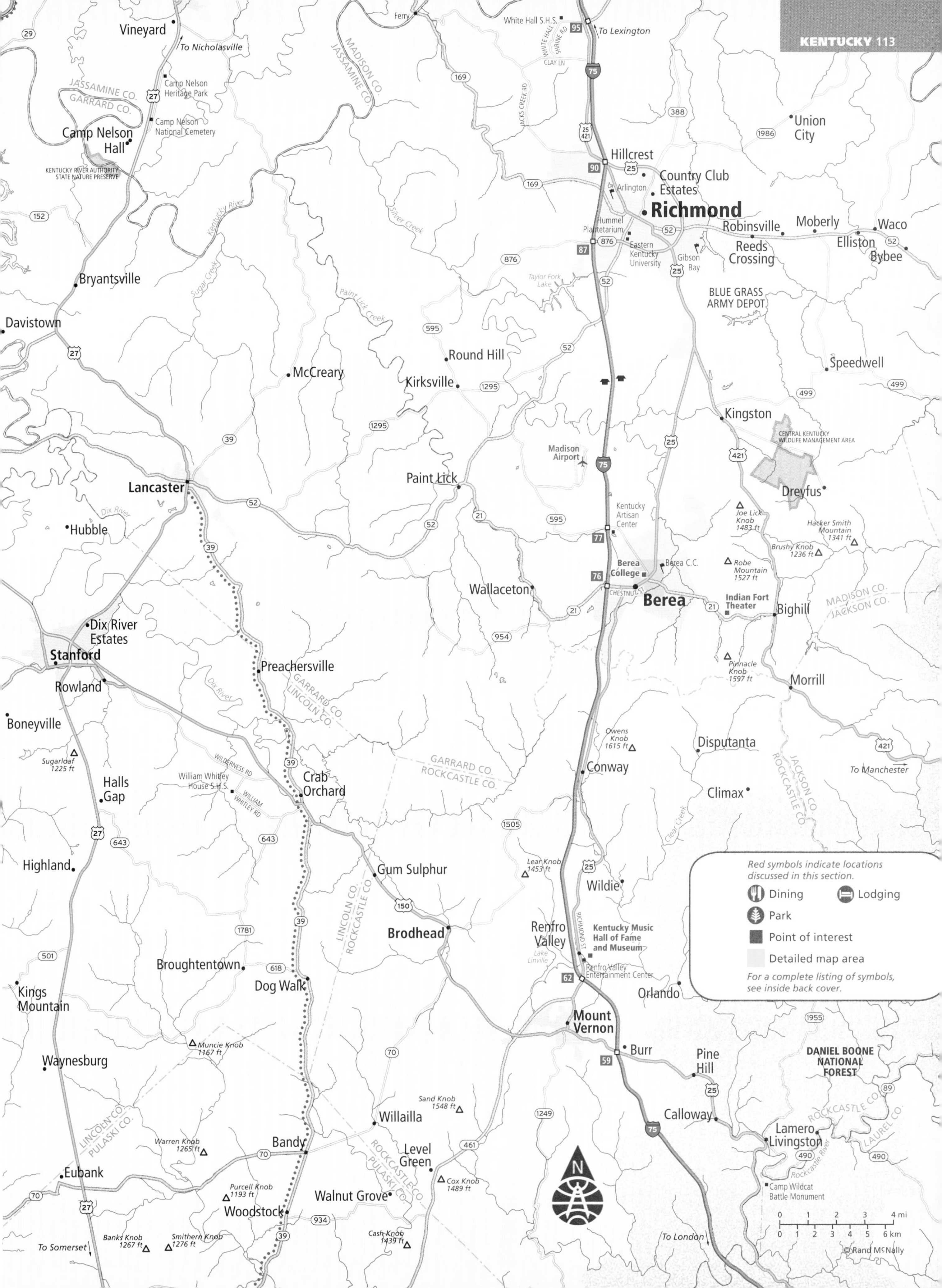

Vineyard
To Nicholasville
Camp Nelson Heritage Park
Camp Nelson National Cemetery
Camp Nelson
Hall
KENTUCKY RIVER AUTHORITY STATE NATURE PRESERVE
JASSAMINE CO.
GARRARD CO.
MADISON CO.
JASSAMINE CO.
Ferry
White Hall S.H.S.
To Lexington
CLAY LN
Union City
Hillcrest
Country Club Estates
Arlington
Richmond
Hummel Planetarium
Eastern Kentucky University
Gibson Bay
Robinsville
Moberly
Waco
Elliston
Bybee
Reeds Crossing
BLUE GRASS ARMY DEPOT
Bryantsville
Davistown
Kentucky River
Silver Creek
Sugar Creek
Paint Lick Creek
Taylor Fork Lake
Round Hill
Kirksville
McCreary
Speedwell
Kingston
CENTRAL KENTUCKY WILDLIFE MANAGEMENT AREA
Madison Airport
Paint Lick
Lancaster
Dix River
Hubble
Dreyfus
Joe Lick Knob 1483 ft
Hacker Smith Mountain 1341 ft
Brushy Knob 1236 ft
Kentucky Artisan Center
Berea College
Berea C.C.
Robe Mountain 1527 ft
Wallaceton
CHESTNUT ST
Berea
Indian Fort Theater
Bighill
MADISON CO.
JACKSON CO.
Dix River Estates
Stanford
Rowland
Preachersville
GARRARD CO.
LINCOLN CO.
Pinnacle Knob 1597 ft
Morrill
Boneyville
Owens Knob 1615 ft
Disputanta
Sugarloaf 1225 ft
WILDERNESS RD
William Whitley House S.H.S.
WILLIAM WHITLEY RD
Halls Gap
Crab Orchard
GARRARD CO.
ROCKCASTLE CO.
Conway
To Manchester
Climax
ROCKCASTLE CO.
JACKSON CO.
Clear Creek
Highland
Gum Sulphur
Lear Knob 1453 ft
Wildie
LINCOLN CO.
ROCKCASTLE CO.
Brodhead
Renfro Valley
RICHMOND ST
Kentucky Music Hall of Fame and Museum
Lake Linville
Renfro Valley Entertainment Center
Broughtentown
Dog Walk
Kings Mountain
Orlando
Mount Vernon
Muncie Knob 1167 ft
Waynesburg
Burr
Pine Hill
DANIEL BOONE NATIONAL FOREST
Sand Knob 1548 ft
Willailla
Calloway
LINCOLN CO.
PULASKI CO.
Warren Knob 1265 ft
Bandy
Level Green
ROCKCASTLE CO.
PULASKI CO.
Lamero
Livingston
ROCKCASTLE CO.
LAUREL CO.
Rockcastle River
Eubank
Purcell Knob 1193 ft
Cox Knob 1489 ft
Walnut Grove
Camp Wildcat Battle Monument
Woodstock
Banks Knob 1267 ft
Smithern Knob 1276 ft
Cash Knob 1439 ft
To Somerset
To London
N
Red symbols indicate locations discussed in this section.
Dining
Lodging
Park
Point of interest
Detailed map area
For a complete listing of symbols, see inside back cover.
0 1 2 3 4 mi
0 1 2 3 4 5 6 km
© Rand McNally

Anatomy of a Getaway

Anatomy of a Murder, a once-shocking 1959 courtroom drama starring gangly, affable Jimmy Stewart, not only earned seven Academy Award nominations, but also spawned a minor tourist industry. Fans curious about the region where the movie is set and where it was filmed head to **Marquette** and **Big Bay** on Michigan's Upper Peninsula, maybe to nostalgically recall Stewart's character's threat: "I'll punch you all the way out into the middle of Lake Superior!"

Another dark celebrity of this region: the SS *Edmund Fitzgerald*, the giant freighter that went down with all hands on November 9, 1975, during a fearsome storm on Lake Superior that was rated one of the worst of the century. Gordon Lightfoot memorialized the ship in his haunting folk ballad "The Wreck of the Edmund Fitzgerald." You can listen to Lightfoot's famous song and watch a video about the *Fitzgerald* at the **Marquette Maritime Museum** (300 Lakeshore Blvd.). Along with a former Coast Guard station and a lighthouse, the museum sits on a promontory poking out into Lake Superior at the most easterly point of the city of Marquette. It offers guided tours of the pretty red lighthouse and Coast Guard quarters. In the museum, a map shows Lake Superior's shoreline dotted with dark blue confetti that marks the graves of more than 550 lost ships. There's an especially large concentration around Whitefish Point, about 2½ hours east of Marquette in Paradise, Mich., where the *Edmund Fitzgerald* went down.

In some respects, Marquette, the largest city on Michigan's Upper Peninsula, evokes San Francisco. Hilly streets slope down to the water's edge, and Victorian mansions line a residential district once known as "Big Bug Hill" because of the lumber barons (the "big bugs") who built these fine homes. But most of Marquette is pure northern Michigan, with brownstone buildings on downtown streets, a distinctive red lighthouse, and a hulking iron-ore dock jutting into the harbor. An appealing downtown offers quality shopping in one-of-a-kind boutiques and galleries.

Marquette Harbor Lighthouse

The courtroom scenes for *Anatomy of a Murder* were filmed in Marquette's 1903 sandstone **county courthouse** (234 W. Baraga Ave.), which houses a display telling the story of the filming. The movie stemmed from local attorney John D. Voelker's best-selling novel, which was inspired by a real-life trial in which Voelker successfully defended a client accused of murder.

Lumberjack Tavern, Big Bay

The actual crime occurred in Big Bay, a tiny, former logging community on the shore of Lake Superior about 25 miles north of Marquette. The bar (The Lumberjack Tavern, at 202 Bensinger) is still there, a small, dark local hangout that remains—except for details your imagination may supply—a nondescript joint just like hundreds of other rural roadside watering holes. That didn't suit the moviemakers. Instead, filming took place a couple of blocks up the street at the **Thunder Bay Inn** (400 Bensinger), an inviting restaurant/pub that makes an interesting lunch stop. The pub was built in 1959 by the Hollywood film crew as an addition to a hotel dating back to 1911.

In the large dining room with knotty-pine décor and tan oilcloth tablecloths, order homemade thin-crust pizza, locally caught whitefish, or a steak. Or choose from the "Anatomy of our Sandwiches" menu (might as well milk celebrity all the way), which dubs a Reuben the "Otto Preminger" (the film's director) and a Philly steak sandwich the "Jimmy Stewart." On display are photographs, newsclips, magazine stories, movie posters, and other memorabilia relating to the real-life murder and the filming of the movie. Look for the photograph of Jimmy Stewart and author John Voelker lighting up cigars.

In downtown Marquette lies the evocatively named **Snowbound Books** (118 N. 3rd St.). This independent bookstore has a large section by Voelker (who used the pen name Robert Traver), including well-regarded titles about trout fishing. Shelves include first editions of *Anatomy of a Murder*.

Its name means "almost an island," but to those who flock to 323-acre **Presque Isle Park**, it most definitely is an island of simple pleasures in the city of Marquette. Bordered by beaches and sheer overhanging cliffs, it's a place to enjoy a band concert under the summer stars or to witness the wild beauty of Lake Superior acting up on a winter's day. It is a place, too, for watching autumn's colors and spring's blooms—and viewing Great Lakes freighters loading iron ore pellets from the LS&I railroad ore dock. Or shop for regional arts and crafts in the former LS&I depot and enjoy an ice cream cone from the Island Store.

At **Negaunee**, the **Michigan Iron Industry Museum** (73 Forge Rd.) marks the site of the first iron forge in the Lake Superior region. Through exhibits and activities both indoors and out, this free museum on the banks of the Carp River tells the story of how the region's iron-mining industry has been at the forefront since its beginnings in the 1840s.

Skiers may be interested in a side trip to **Ishpeming**, where the **U.S. National Ski Hall of Fame & Museum** (610 Palms Ave.) honors the men and women whose contributions and achievements have enriched the sport. Unusual topics include a display on modern ski warfare and the Soviet/Finnish War and a display of uphill lifts beginning with rope tows and leading to modern gondolas.

Outdoor lovers and photographers enjoy the bounty of the Marquette region's 11 notable waterfalls. West of Marquette lies the scenic, historic Keweenaw Bay area around **Baraga** and **L'Anse** with numerous photogenic falls. Hike through the wilderness of the Sturgeon River Gorge and venture to Point Abbaye for spectacular views of the Huron Mountains. The summits of Little Mountain and Silver Mountain in autumn provide a sweeping view of blazing oranges, reds, yellows, and golds of fall foliage. The top of **Mount Arvon** (1,979 ft.) is Michigan's highest point.

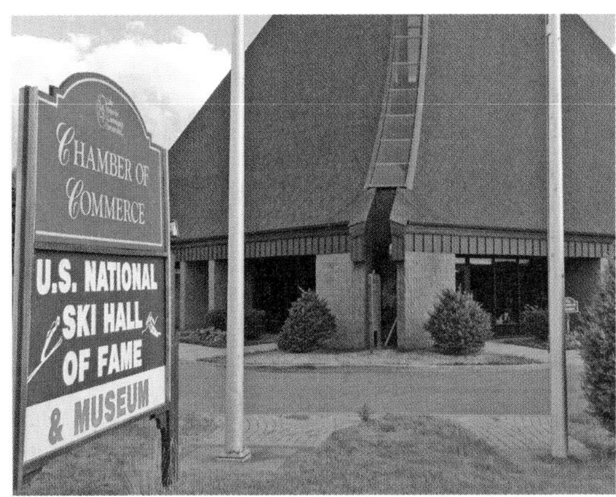

U.S. National Ski Hall of Fame & Museum, Ishpeming

What to eat

Stop for a Cornish pasty as a filling lunch or snack. The sturdy Cornish who came to the region to mine iron and copper brought the tradition of this hot pastry turnover filled with a mix of steak, potatoes, onion, and rutabaga. A miner could carry this perfect portable meal to work in his pocket and reheat it on the blade of a shovel. **Jean Kay's** (1635 Presque Isle, Marquette) has been baking pasties since 1976 and makes about 600 a day during peak season.

What to buy

Look for Norwegian sweaters and Swedish jewelry at **Scandinavian Gifts** (1025 N. Third St.) and chocolates and fudge at **Donckers** (137 W. Washington St.), which dates back to 1896. **Superior View** (156 W. Washington St.) photography museum and art gallery sells historic photos of Michigan, the U.S., and the world.

What to do

Art on the Rocks, Marquette, late July.

For more details about this festival, please see page 174.

Information

Marquette Country Convention and Visitors Bureau, (800) 544-4321, www.marquettecountry.org.

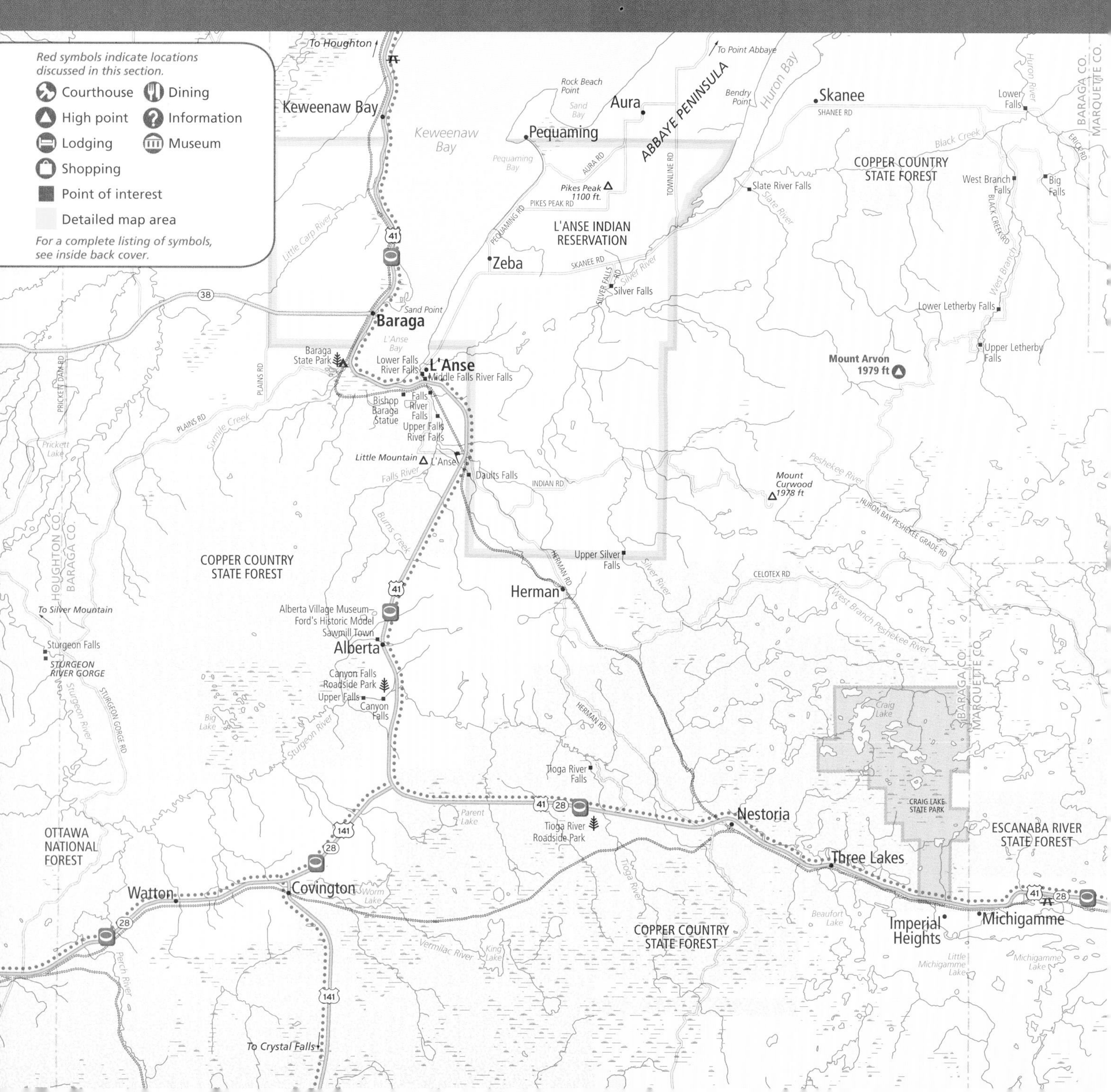

Lodging tips

The **Landmark Inn** opened in 1930 as the Hotel Northland and was the social center of Marquette until it closed in 1982. Fully restored, it reopened in 1997 and now belongs to the Historic Hotels of America, offering 62 rooms and suites, some with fireplaces and whirlpools. If you're up for staying in a former film set, check into the **Thunder Bay Inn**. It offers a dozen comfortable guest rooms furnished with antique and period-style furniture. You can buy a video of the movie in the hotel gift shop.

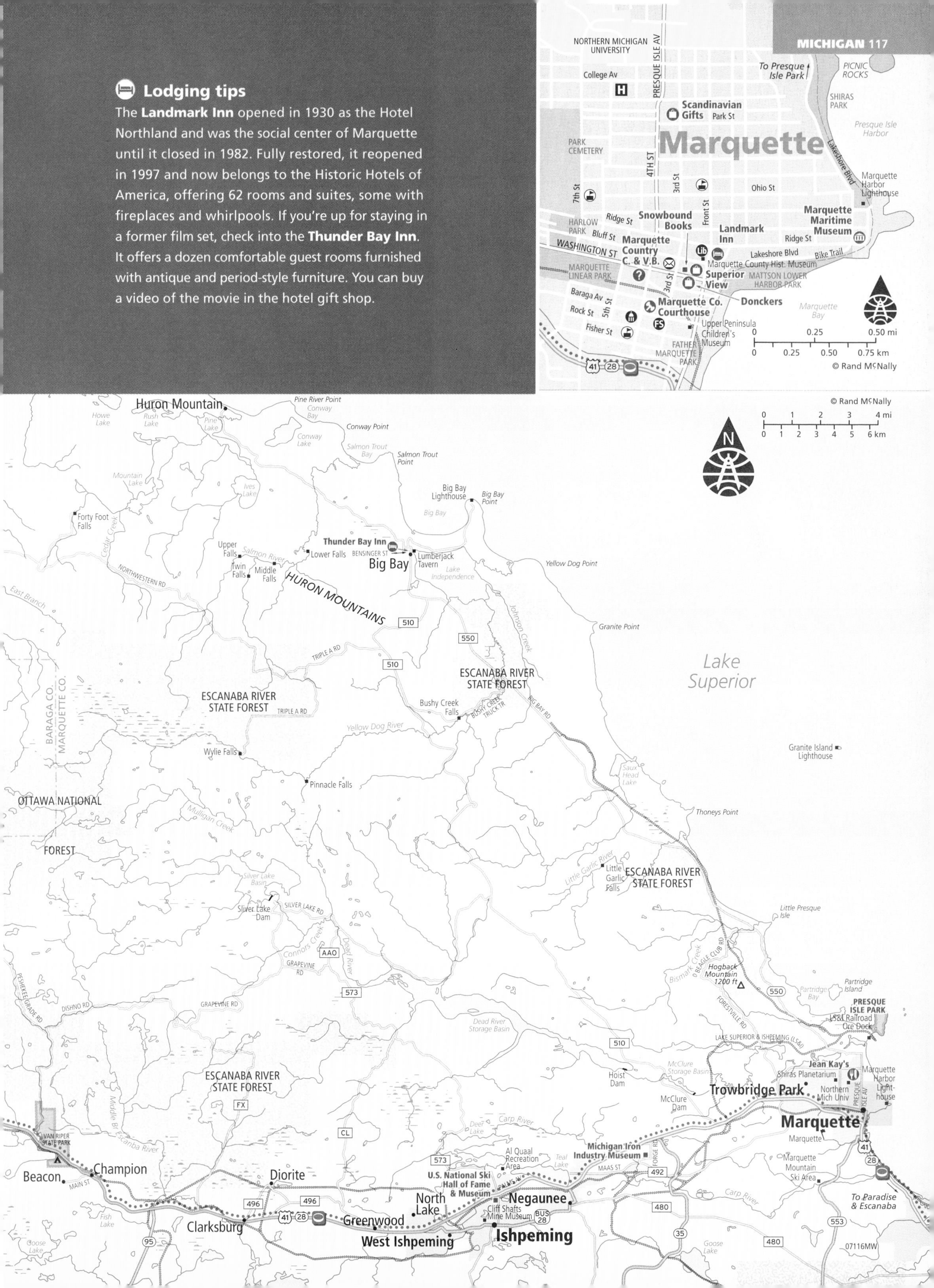

Finding Da Vinci **and Going Dutch**

Although its population numbers less than a quarter million, culturally **Grand Rapids** takes a back seat to no one. This clean-cut western Michigan city offers a clutch of major museums and a world-class botanic garden with iconic sculpture (including a da Vinci-inspired masterpiece). Lively performing arts, a landmark downtown hotel, and plenty of trendy restaurants round out the cultural scene. For good measure, travel about 30 miles west to **Holland** to enjoy wide expanses of beach and an occasionally kitschy, always-fun, chunk of Dutch culture.

Toward the end of a long winter, a cabin-bound Midwesterner's fancy turns to the outdoors and awakening gardens. Some hurry the season with a visit to **Frederik Meijer Gardens & Sculpture Park** (100 East Beltline Ave. NE). Meijer successfully blends art and nature, carefully positioning in natural settings world-renowned sculptures by masters. Mark di Suvero's *Scarlatti* rises above a wildflower meadow; Antony Gormley's *One and Other* peers through a wall of ash trees. With barely a decade behind it, Meijer is a mere infant in the world of botanical gardens. Yet is has come of age remarkably quickly, earning global recognition. Spread over 125 acres, Meijer features Michigan's largest tropical conservatory and one of the nation's largest children's gardens. It contains arid and Victorian gardens and the Midwest's most comprehensive outdoor sculpture experience, with significant works by Rodin, Oldenburg, and Moore. Inside are galleries with changing sculpture exhibitions, a café, and gift shops.

Pitcher plants at the Kenneth E. Nelson Carnivorous Plant House

Meijer's signature sculpture: *The American Horse* (Leonardo da Vinci's Horse), a 24-foot, 15-ton bronze work by Nina Akamu. Before da Vinci painted the *Mona Lisa* he dreamed of bringing to life a regal, towering horse referred to as Il Cavallo. He made the original sketches for the horse some 500 years ago, but never created the sculpture itself. Working from da Vinci's notes, Akamu completed the sculpture that eluded the Italian master. She actually cast two identical sculptures; the Meijer horse's twin is in Milan.

Visitors to the Gardens and Sculpture Park with a morbid fascination for Venus flytraps and the like love the Kenneth E. Nelson Carnivorous Plant House, whimsically dubbed "Little Greenhouse of Horrors." Dozens of carnivorous species call it home. The outdoor Amphitheater Garden, a concert venue, offers lawn seating and picnicking for 1,800. Beer and wine are available. Eclectic line-ups of performers often include the likes of Art Garfunkel, Buddy Guy, and Branford Marsalis.

Downtown Grand Rapids offers theater, concerts, and a splendid collection of public art. Museums such as the **Van Andel Museum Center of the Public Museum of Grand Rapids** (272 Pearl St. NW) and the **Grand Rapids Art Museum** (155 Division North) attract major traveling exhibitions.

The **Gerald R. Ford Presidential Museum** (303 Pearl St., NW) maintains a 1970s gallery akin to a time machine. It recalls the movie *Easy Rider* (featuring boyish Jack Nicholson), the best-selling book *Jonathan Livingston Seagull*, and popular TV commercials, as well as swimmer Mark Spitz's seven Olympic gold wins and the television show *The Mod Squad*. Visitors can watch events of those tumultuous years—George Wallace felled by assassin's bullets, National Guardsmen firing on students at Kent State University—on three TV monitors, which also show clips of Dr. Henry Kissinger receiving the Nobel Peace Prize and of kidnapped newspaper heiress Patty Hearst.

Architecture buffs delight in visiting **Heritage Hill**, one of the largest urban historic districts recognized by the National Register of Historic Places. The 1,300 homes in this neighborhood adjacent to downtown Grand Rapids date from 1848 and feature more than 60 architectural styles. The prairie-style design of Frank Lloyd Wright is represented by the **Meyer May House**, built in 1908 for the founder of May's of Michigan clothing stores. This completely restored house is free and open to the public on Tuesdays, Thursdays, and Sundays. A special time to visit is during the annual "Heritage Hill Weekend Tour of Homes" (October), when a number of privately owned homes also are open for tours.

About half an hour's drive away lies **Windmill Island** (7th St. at Lincoln Ave.) in Holland. Although blatantly touristy, it's a pretty park, planted with more than 150,000 tulips. The Amsterdam street organ, carousel, replica of a 14th-century Dutch inn, and distinctively Dutch redbrick architecture add to the atmosphere.

So does **"De Zwaan"** (The Swan), a windmill that began life in the Netherlands almost 250 years ago and was brought to Michigan in 1964. It's said to be the last authentic windmill to leave the Netherlands. (Dutch law now prohibits the sale of windmills, which are considered national monuments.) This graceful giant stands 12 stories high. Its sails were installed in 2000 to replace originals pocked with Nazi bullet holes. At this working mill, a miller produces whole-wheat graham flour that is packaged for sale into two-pound bags.

Fenn Valley (6130 122nd Ave.), a small family-owned vineyard and winery south of Holland in **Fennville**, made a big splash when its 2004 pinot grigio earned a double gold medal at the 2005 Tasters Guild International Wine Judging. It rose above 35 competitors from around the world. Owned by the Welsch family since it was established in 1973, the winery is located in the center of the vineyards and sells more than 90 percent of its production in the tasting room.

What to eat

Fried "perch burgers" lightly battered and served with tartar sauce on a toasted bun are a specialty at **Ottawa Beach Inn** (2155 Ottawa Beach Rd., Holland). Beach-goers stop to pick up orders of these delicious fish sandwiches. **Crane's Pie Pantry** (6054 124th Ave., Fennville) is located on an orchard that has been part of the family farm since 1917. It serves soups, sandwiches, and salads, along with signature cider donuts, fruit pies, apple dumplings, and tart rhubarb crisp. Fresh apple cider is the drink of choice, a bargain at a dollar a glass (refills free).

What to buy

Looking for an original piece of sculpted glass or a bronze sculpture? For one-of-a-kind gifts, check out the original and locally made selection in the **Meijer Gardens** Gift Shop. It also carries a wide selection of goods for green thumbs, including houseplants, tools, garden supplies, handmade pots, and art for the garden. You'll also find books on gardening and, in Kids Corner, educational books and toys. Some gardeners claim that wooden shoes make ideal footwear. Find them as you wander downtown Holland, along with such Dutch imports such as Delftware and intricate lace.

What to do

Foremost's Butterflies are Blooming, Grand Rapids, March-April.
Tulip Time, Holland,
first through second Saturdays in May.
For more details about these festivals, please see page 174.

Information

Grand Rapids/Kent County Convention and Visitors Bureau, (800) 678-9859, www.visitgrandrapids.org.
Holland Convention & Visitors Bureau, (800) 506-1299, www.holland.org.

Lodging tips

Downtown lodging choices in Grand Rapids include the **Amway Grand Plaza Hotel** (187 Monroe Ave. NW), which easily measures up to big-city luxury properties. Dating back to the early 1900s, this 682-room deluxe hotel definitely is the place to stay in Grand Rapids. In Holland, the **Haworth Inn & Conference Center** (225 College Ave.) sits downtown on the campus of Hope College. All the furniture in the 50-room hotel was custom-built by locally owned Haworth, Inc., a major manufacturer of office furniture.

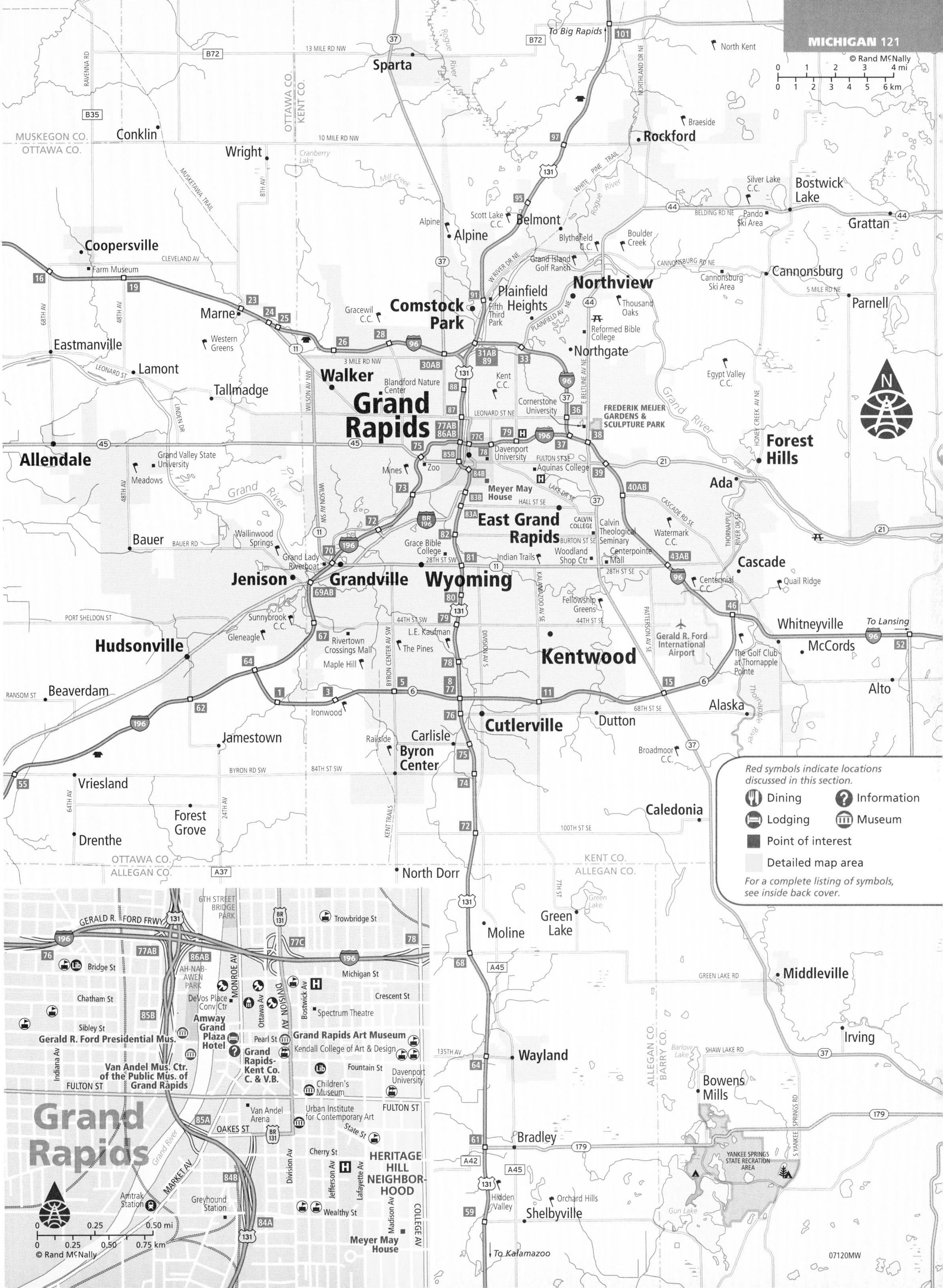
© Rand McNally
0 1 2 3 4 mi
0 1 2 3 4 5 6 km
Sparta
Rockford
Conklin
Wright
MUSKEGON CO.
OTTAWA CO.
OTTAWA CO.
KENT CO.
13 MILE RD NW
10 MILE RD NW
To Big Rapids
North Kent
Braeside
Cranberry Lake
Mill Creek
Rogue River
MUSKETAWA TRAIL
WHITE PINE TRAIL
Silver Lake C.C.
Bostwick Lake
Grattan
BELDING RD NE
Pando Ski Area
Belmont
Scott Lake C.C.
Alpine
Boulder Creek
Blythefield C.C.
Grand Island Golf Ranch
Coopersville
Farm Museum
CLEVELAND AV
CANNONSBURG RD NE
Cannonsburg
Cannonsburg Ski Area
Northview
Thousand Oaks
5 MILE RD NE
Parnell
Plainfield Heights
Fifth Third Park
Comstock Park
Gracewil C.C.
Marne
Western Greens
Reformed Bible College
Northgate
Eastmanville
Lamont
3 MILE RD NW
Walker
Blandford Nature Center
Kent C.C.
Egypt Valley C.C.
Tallmadge
Grand Rapids
Cornerstone University
LEONARD ST NE
FREDERIK MEIJER GARDENS & SCULPTURE PARK
Grand River
Allendale
Grand Valley State University
Meadows
Davenport University
FULTON ST SE
Aquinas College
Forest Hills
Ada
Mines
Zoo
Meyer May House
HALL ST SE
LAKE DR SE
East Grand Rapids
CALVIN COLLEGE
Calvin Theological Seminary
BURTON ST SE
Watermark C.C.
CASCADE RD SE
Bauer
BAUER RD
Wallinwood Springs
Grace Bible College
Grand Lady Riverboat
28TH ST SW
Indian Trails
Woodland Shop Ctr
Centerpointe Mall
28TH ST SE
Cascade
Centennial C.C.
Quail Ridge
Jenison
Grandville
Wyoming
Fellowship Greens
44TH ST SW
44TH ST SE
PORT SHELDON ST
Sunnybrook C.C.
Gleneagle
Rivertown Crossings Mall
L.E. Kaufman
The Pines
Maple Hill
Gerald R. Ford International Airport
Whitneyville
To Lansing
McCords
The Golf Club at Thornapple Pointe
Hudsonville
Kentwood
RANSOM ST
Beaverdam
Alto
Ironwood
68TH ST SE
Alaska
Cutlerville
Dutton
Jamestown
Railside
Carlisle
Byron Center
Broadmoor C.C.
BYRON RD SW
84TH ST SW
Vriesland
Forest Grove
Drenthe
KENT TRAILS
Caledonia
100TH ST SE
OTTAWA CO.
ALLEGAN CO.
North Dorr
KENT CO.
ALLEGAN CO.
Red symbols indicate locations discussed in this section.
Dining
Information
Lodging
Museum
Point of interest
Detailed map area
For a complete listing of symbols, see inside back cover.
Green Lake
Moline
GREEN LAKE RD
Middleville
Irving
Wayland
135TH AV
SHAW LAKE RD
Barlow Lake
ALLEGAN CO.
BARRY CO.
Bowens Mills
Bradley
YANKEE SPRINGS STATE RECREATION AREA
Hidden Valley
Orchard Hills
Shelbyville
Gun Lake
To Kalamazoo
07120MW
GERALD R. FORD FRWY
6TH STREET BRIDGE PARK
Trowbridge St
Bridge St
AH-NAB-AWEN PARK
MONROE AV
DIVISION AV
Michigan St
Chatham St
DeVos Place Conv Ctr
Ottawa Av
Bostwick Av
Crescent St
Spectrum Theatre
Sibley St
Amway Grand Plaza Hotel
Pearl St
Grand Rapids Art Museum
Gerald R. Ford Presidential Mus.
Kendall College of Art & Design
Grand Rapids-Kent Co. C. & V.B.
Indiana Av
Van Andel Mus. Ctr. of the Public Mus. of Grand Rapids
Fountain St
Davenport University
FULTON ST
Children's Museum
Urban Institute for Contemporary Art
FULTON ST
Van Andel Arena
OAKES ST
State St
Grand Rapids
Grand River
Cherry St
MARKET AV
Division Av
Jefferson Av
Lafayette Av
HERITAGE HILL NEIGHBORHOOD
Amtrak Station
Greyhound Station
Wealthy St
Madison Av
COLLEGE AV
0 0.25 0.50 mi
0 0.25 0.50 0.75 km
© Rand McNally
Meyer May House

Michigan's **Green Thumb**

The peninsula that juts out into Lake Huron halfway up the state's eastern shoreline, Eastern Michigan delivers glorious sunrises that begin with an orange orb peeking over Lake Huron's horizon. But if you're the sleeping-in sort, consider taking in the west-facing beaches and beautiful sunsets of "The Thumb."

Huron County's northernmost communities—**Port Austin, Caseville,** and **Port Hope**—lie a mere 130 miles north of Detroit, and the region differs dramatically from the playgrounds of western Michigan. Forget clusters of chain motels and slick condos; instead, look for small motels, rustic cabins, and homey restaurants that serve good food with no pretension on the side. Fishing, boating, canoeing, and other water sports (including diving) are popular activities, with snowmobiling in winter. Beaches and dunes contrast with vast tracts of cool, green forest.

With three miles of shoreline along **Saginaw Bay**, 565-acre **Port Crescent State Park** (1775 Port Austin Rd., five miles southwest of Port Austin) offers a mix of woods, wetlands, and the best sand dunes on the eastern side of the state. Scenic views stretch from a 900-foot-long shoreline boardwalk. Wildlife viewing is superb, especially during the spring hawk migration. Loons also migrate through this area in April, while bluebirds bring color and character to nearby fields. Wild turkeys, blue herons, and white-tailed deer are plentiful, with an occasional beaver or bald eagle.

Pointe Aux Barques Lighthouse

Gagetown's **Thumb Octagon Barn** (6948 Richie Rd.), a designated State of Michigan Historic Site, offers guided tours and an array of activities, May through October, including flea markets, antique fairs, ice cream socials, and live music. A major annual event, Fall Family Days (September) recaptures the color and moods of rural life in the early 20th century. Attend a workshop on dried flower arranging, basket weaving, or beginning knitting; visit a one-room schoolhouse, or sit down to a "farmers' breakfast" or Friday fish fry.

Thumb Octagon Barn

On summer Saturdays in agriculture-rich Huron County you'll find the Port Austin **farmers' market** and its free rides in a horse-drawn wagon. Local produce shows up on the tables of **The Farm Restaurant and School of Cooking** (699 Port Crescent Rd.), located just beyond the Port Austin city limits. It specializes in Heartland cuisine, using herbs and vegetables from its five-acre garden as it strives to honor the general principle of making things "from scratch": locally caught or reared meats, locally harvested vegetables, and fresh ingredients. Go for dinner and sample pan-seared whitefish with rock shrimp or farmer-style swiss steak with garlic mashed potatoes. Or join a "Culinary Weekend," a hands-on course for experienced as well as novice cooks. Each participant invites one guest to the Friday evening champagne and hors d'oeuvres reception; Saturday breakfast, lunch, and six-course dinner with wine; and Sunday, before departure, a full service breakfast. (Participants prepare the lunch and dinner.)

Lighthouse tours and shipwreck diving are popular attractions in Huron County. Passage on this region of Lake Huron can be treacherous, as several shipwrecks bear witness. The **Thumb Area Bottomland Preserve**, which covers about 276 square miles of lake bottom, is the resting place of 19 major shipwrecks. Here the steel freighter *John McGean* lies upside down, a victim of the Great Storm of November 7-12, 1913. Giant grindstones off the shore of Grindstone City, where they once were made, litter the area. At **Sanilac Shores Underwater Preserve**, divers can swim up to one of the legendary wrecks of the Great Lakes. Discovered in 1986, the *Regina* lies upside down 80 feet below the surface, victim of that same fierce 1913 storm. In 1847, President Polk ordered the **Pointe Aux Barques Lighthouse** be built to protect ships from some of the most treacherous shoals in the Great Lakes. Many sailing ships met their doom while "cutting the corner" into Saginaw Bay. The keeper's residence is preserved as a museum on grounds of lovely 120-acre **Lighthouse County Park** (7320 Lighthouse Rd., Port Hope).

Caseville offers miles of sandy beaches and those beautiful sunsets. Settled in 1836, it became a center for lumbering and shipbuilding. Visitors depart from here for 75-minute cruises to **Big Charity Island**, site of an 1857 lighthouse. The island has walking trails (with rare flora and fauna identified) and a picnic area with tables, grills, and a pavilion.

Lake Huron shoreline

What to eat

Lots of foodies insist the Leroy burger at the **Port Hope Hotel** (4405 Main St.) is the best and biggest anywhere on "The Thumb." Eighteen ounces of meat rest between the halves of a five-inch bun. It takes 25 minutes to prepare one with whichever toppings you prefer: cheese, mushroom, bacon, the works. Fully loaded, it can stand four inches tall on the plate.

What to buy

For a lasting keepsake, visit **Alchemy Stained Glass Studio** (6718 Vine St., Caseville). Consider ordering a custom-designed window or room divider—or select a free-hanging piece such as a lighthouse, sailboat, or colorful bird. To create your own stained-glass masterpiece, join a class in an outdoor studio during spring, summer, and fall.

What to do

Cheeseburger in Caseville, Caseville, August.
Michigan Sugar Festival, Sebewaing, mid-June
For more details about these festivals, please see page 174.

Information

Huron County Economic Development Corp., (800) 358-4862, www.huroncounty.com.

Lodging tips

For charming rustic cabins overlooking Lake Huron, look no further than **Lighthouse County Park**, where six two- and three-bedroom, fully furnished cabins overlook Pointe Aux Barques Lighthouse. More often than not, lovely sunsets arrive on cue. Cooking utensils are provided as well. Other choices include the 1830s **Garfield Inn** in Port Austin (8544 Lake St.), which features a French Second Empire design. President Garfield, a friend of the original owner, lumber baron Charles G. Learned, was a frequent guest. The inn has six guestrooms and a pub. **Krebs Beachside Cottages** (3478 Port Austin Rd.), owned by Sally and Marv Krebs since 1968, features eight waterfront units on Saginaw Bay in Port Austin. A large, elevated sundeck overlooks a 200-foot sandy beach.

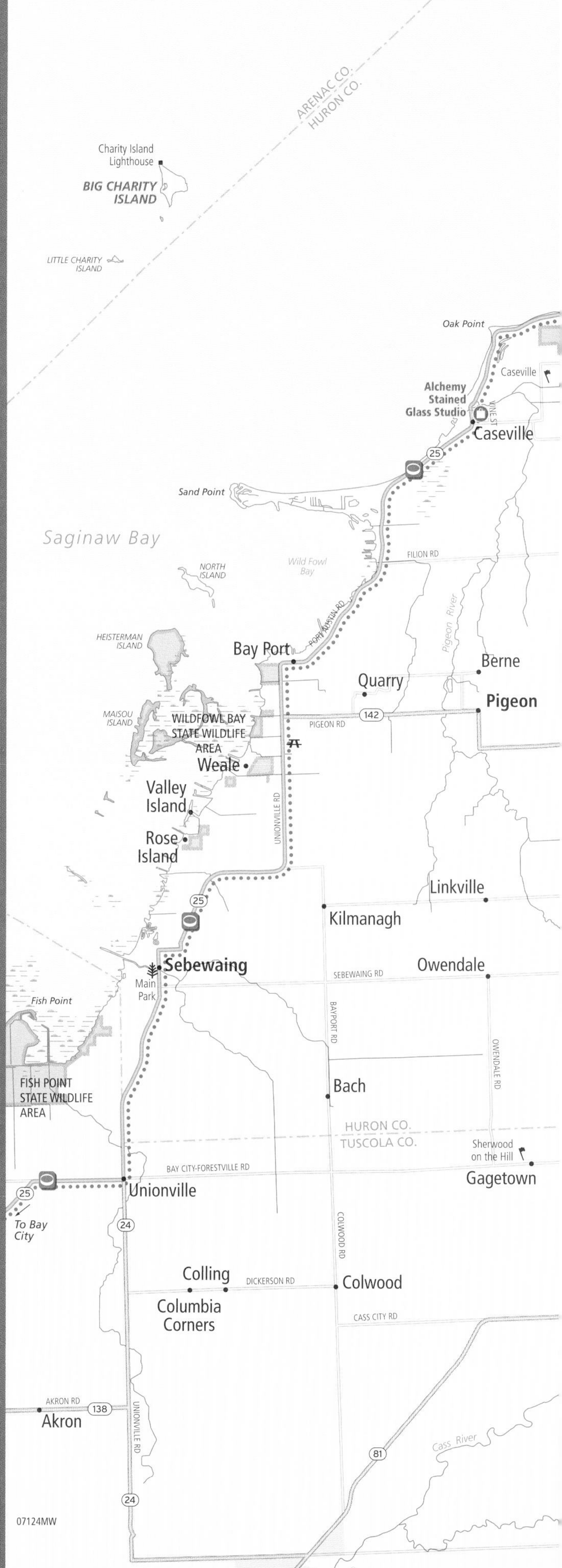

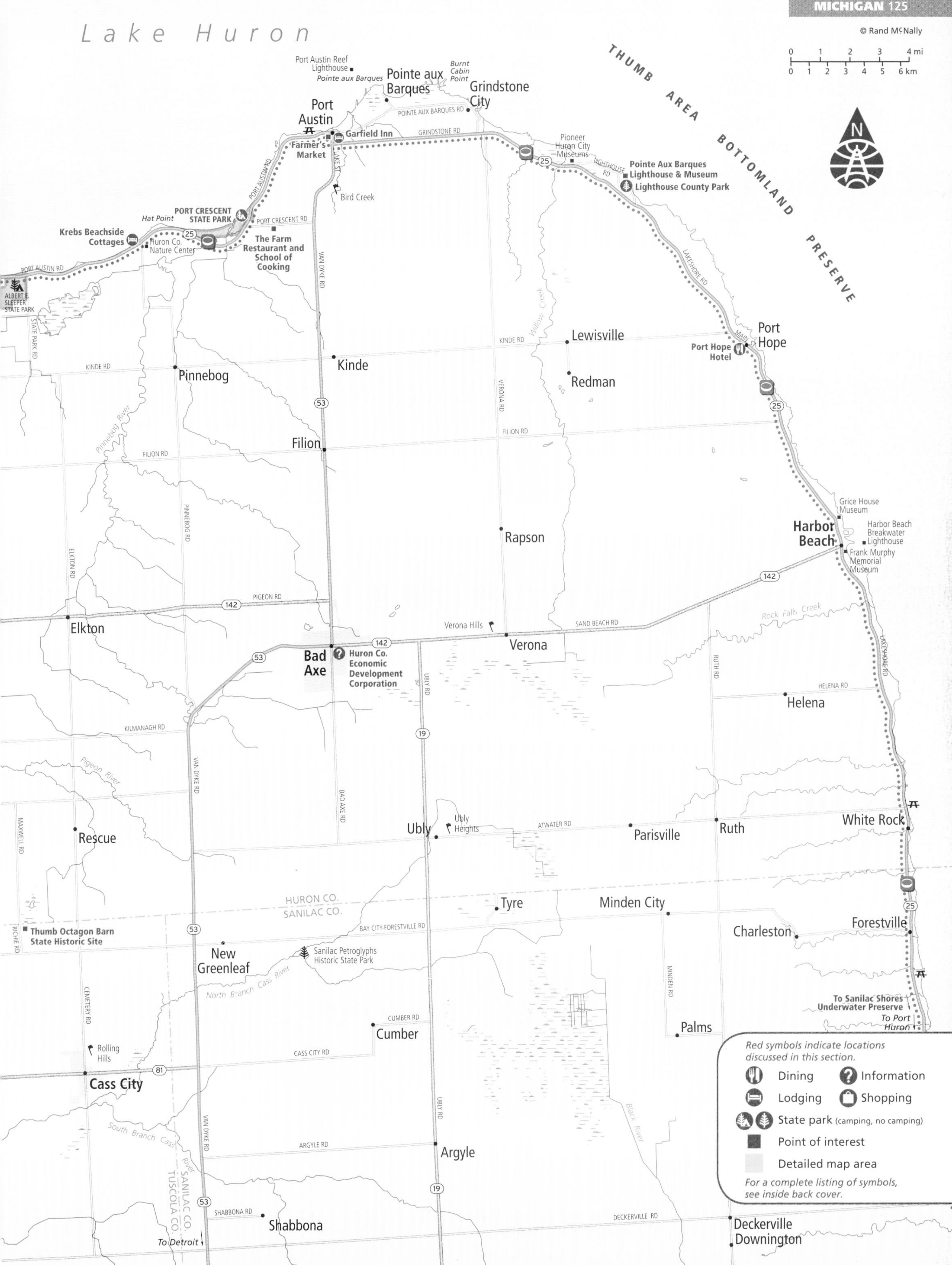
© Rand McNally
0 1 2 3 4 mi
0 1 2 3 4 5 6 km
Lake Huron
THUMB AREA BOTTOMLAND PRESERVE
Port Austin Reef Lighthouse
Pointe aux Barques
Pointe aux Barques
Burnt Cabin Point
Grindstone City
Port Austin
Garfield Inn
Farmer's Market
Pioneer Huron City Museums
Pointe Aux Barques Lighthouse & Museum
Lighthouse County Park
Bird Creek
PORT CRESCENT STATE PARK
Hat Point
Krebs Beachside Cottages
Huron Co. Nature Center
The Farm Restaurant and School of Cooking
ALBERT E. SLEEPER STATE PARK
Lewisville
Redman
Port Hope
Port Hope Hotel
Kinde
Pinnebog
Filion
Rapson
Grice House Museum
Harbor Beach
Harbor Beach Breakwater Lighthouse
Frank Murphy Memorial Museum
Elkton
Verona Hills
Verona
Bad Axe
Huron Co. Economic Development Corporation
Helena
Rescue
Ubly
Ubly Heights
Parisville
Ruth
White Rock
HURON CO.
SANILAC CO.
Tyre
Minden City
Charleston
Forestville
Thumb Octagon Barn State Historic Site
New Greenleaf
Sanilac Petroglyphs Historic State Park
To Sanilac Shores Underwater Preserve
To Port Huron
Cumber
Palms
Rolling Hills
Cass City
Argyle
SANILAC CO.
TUSCOLA CO.
Shabbona
To Detroit
Deckerville
Downington
Red symbols indicate locations discussed in this section.
Dining
Information
Lodging
Shopping
State park (camping, no camping)
Point of interest
Detailed map area
For a complete listing of symbols, see inside back cover.

Dorothy at Home

Though it's the birthplace of Frances Ethel Gumm—a.k.a. Judy Garland of *The Wizard of Oz*—you'll find no yellow brick road in northeastern Minnesota's Itasca County. This is big timber country, packed with deep forests. The Mississippi River, which flows through **Grand Rapids**, the county seat, helped create it and its logging industry. Today, tourists staying at the countless resorts and cabins that cluster around the shores of the county's 1,000 lakes visit Grand Rapids for shopping, dining, and entertainment.

One of the region's prettiest drives, particularly in fall: the 47-mile **Edge of the Wilderness Scenic Byway,** a winding stretch of MN 38 between Grand Rapids and Elfie that reaches into the rugged wilderness of the Chippewa National Forest. Enjoy towering pines and soaring bald eagles and detour to visit a lakeside resort or two.

Tourists also find their way to **Chisholm**, which movie buffs and baseball fans may remember from *Field of Dreams* as the town where Dr. Archibald "Moonlight" Graham gave up pro baseball for a career as a small-town doctor. Each July a festival fetes the local general physician who inspired the character. Chisholm is also home of **Ironworld Discovery Center** (801 SW US 169). Ride a 1928 vintage trolley as you learn about

View of Kremer Lake from Edge of the Wilderness Scenic Byway

Judy Garland Birthplace, Grand Rapids

the bands of iron ore that make up Minnesota's Iron Range and the immigrants who worked them. Find more mining history at **Hill Annex Mine State Park** (880 Gary St., Calumet). Activities include a 90-minute open-pit mine tour, a boat tour on a lake that once was a mine, and a fossil-hunting tour in search of 86-million-year-old sea life fossils such as shark's teeth and clams.

Logging camp at Forest History Center

The **Forest History Center** (2609 County Rd. 76, Grand Rapids) re-creates an early-1900s camp where loggers endured long winters in primitive quarters. Seventy-two men slept two to a bunk and survived on a steady diet of sow belly pork (sometimes known as salt or side pork), dried or smoked fish, beans, potatoes, and dried fruit. The cook used dried apples to make about 30 pies a day, which the loggers called "pregnant women" because of the way the apples plumped up. As you board the "wanigan"—the barge-like boat used as men and logs floated to mills downstream—you'll learn about spring log drives. Typically, they averaged little more than five miles a day and could take up to 70 days.

When the *Mississippi Melodie Showboat* comes to town, as it has every year since 1955, it reminds musicals fans of Captain Andy and other characters from *Show Boat*. After this showboat rounds a bend in the river, steam whistle blasting and paddlewheel churning, its captain brings it to dock at the **Grand Rapids Landing** (16th Ave. & 3rd St. NW). Adorned with patriotic flags and bunting, the steamboat becomes a stage, reminiscent of showboats that, more than a century ago, brought entertainment to small towns along the Mississippi. Music, songs, and dances of the showboat era, including a popular melodrama skit, entertain audiences in an outdoor amphitheater under a natural canopy of towering pines. Each year the last three full weekends of July bring new shows.

Though she lived in Grand Rapids for only four years, Judy Garland is a major local industry. Attractions include the former **Gumm home** where her parents lived for seven years and an adjacent museum of Garland and Oz memorabilia (2727 US 169 S.). Find more memorabilia at **Old Central School** (10 W. 5th St. NW), a restored 1895 brick schoolhouse. Classes ceased in 1972, and the school now houses shops and a local heritage museum. Judy's two older sisters went to school there. Auntie Em's Coffee Shop, known for its raspberry white chocolate scones, occupies a former classroom.

What to eat

Popovers, a big deal in Minnesota, resemble individual servings of that English favorite, Yorkshire pudding. As in Britain, they frequently arrive alongside roast beef. These light, hollow rolls swell or "pop" over their baking tin. Find them at the **Sawmill Inn's** Cedars Dining Room (2301 S. Pokegama Ave., Grand Rapids). Its kitchen has a deft hand with such standard northern fare as wild rice soup and walleye.

What to buy

For local stoneware pottery, birch bark baskets, and Minnesota food products, including wild rice soup mix, try **Jenny & Co.** (10 3rd St NW., Grand Rapids), housed in an old drugstore with exposed brick walls. **Hopperton's** (101 4th St. NW, Grand Rapids) has a selection of moccasins, cedar boxes, sterling jewelry, and Native American artifacts. **MacRostie Art Center** (405 First Ave. NW), once a Chevy dealership, displays the work of North Country artists.

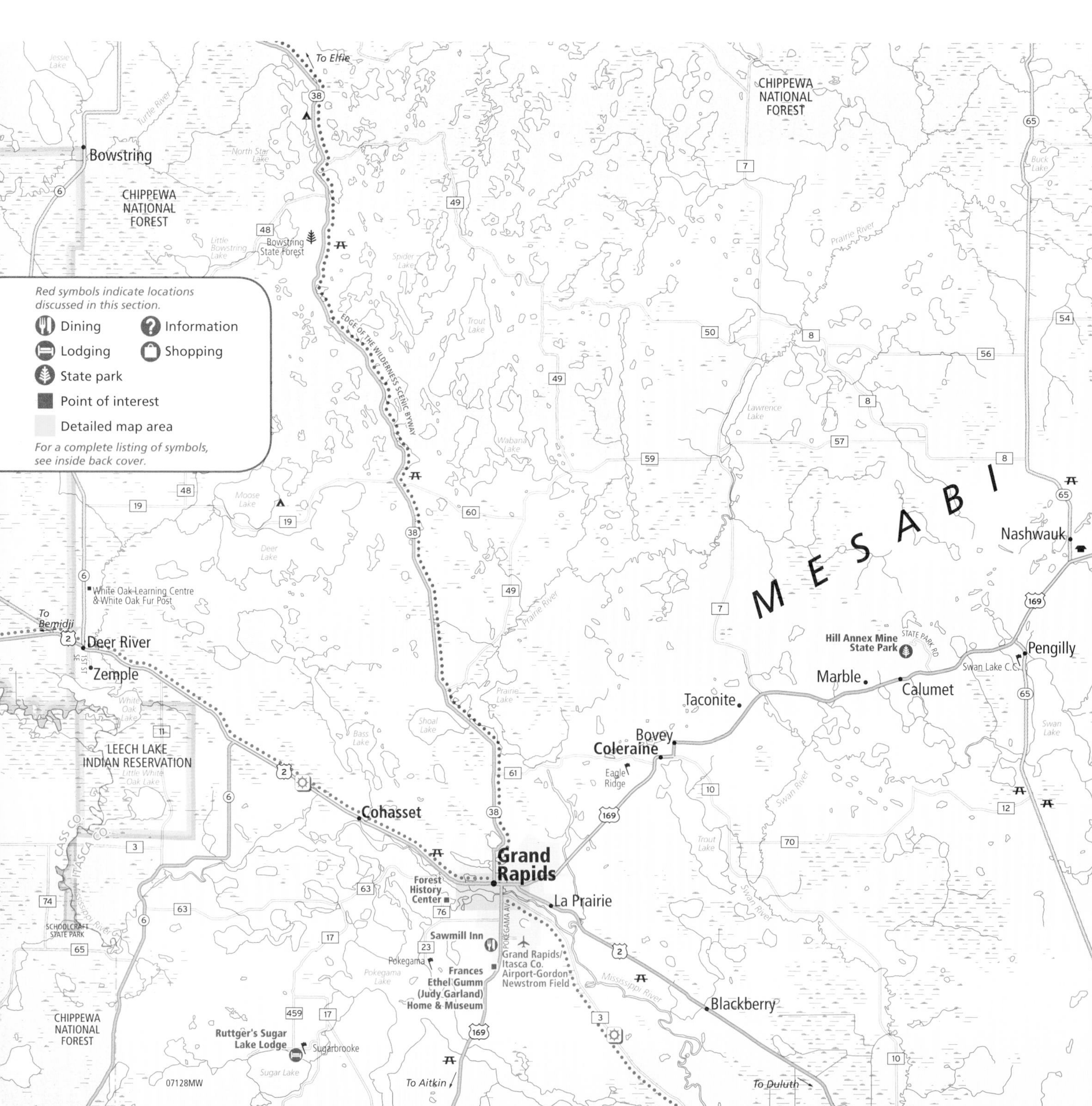

What to do

The Judy Garland Festival, Grand Rapids, late June.

White Oak Society Rendezvous, Deer River, August.

For more details about these festivals, please see page 174.

Information

Visit Grand Rapids,
(800) 355-9740, www.visitgrandrapids.com.

Lodging tips

Although hotels, motels, and bed-and-breakfasts crowd the region, the traditional North Woods resort or lakeside cabins are favorite lodging choices. Many repeat visitors favor Ruttger's Sugar Lake Lodge, with lakefront townhouses, suites, and cottages (southwest of Grand Rapids on County Rd. 17). Amenities include a beach, outdoor pool, tennis, free daily kids' camp, and the top-rated Sugarbrooke Golf Course.

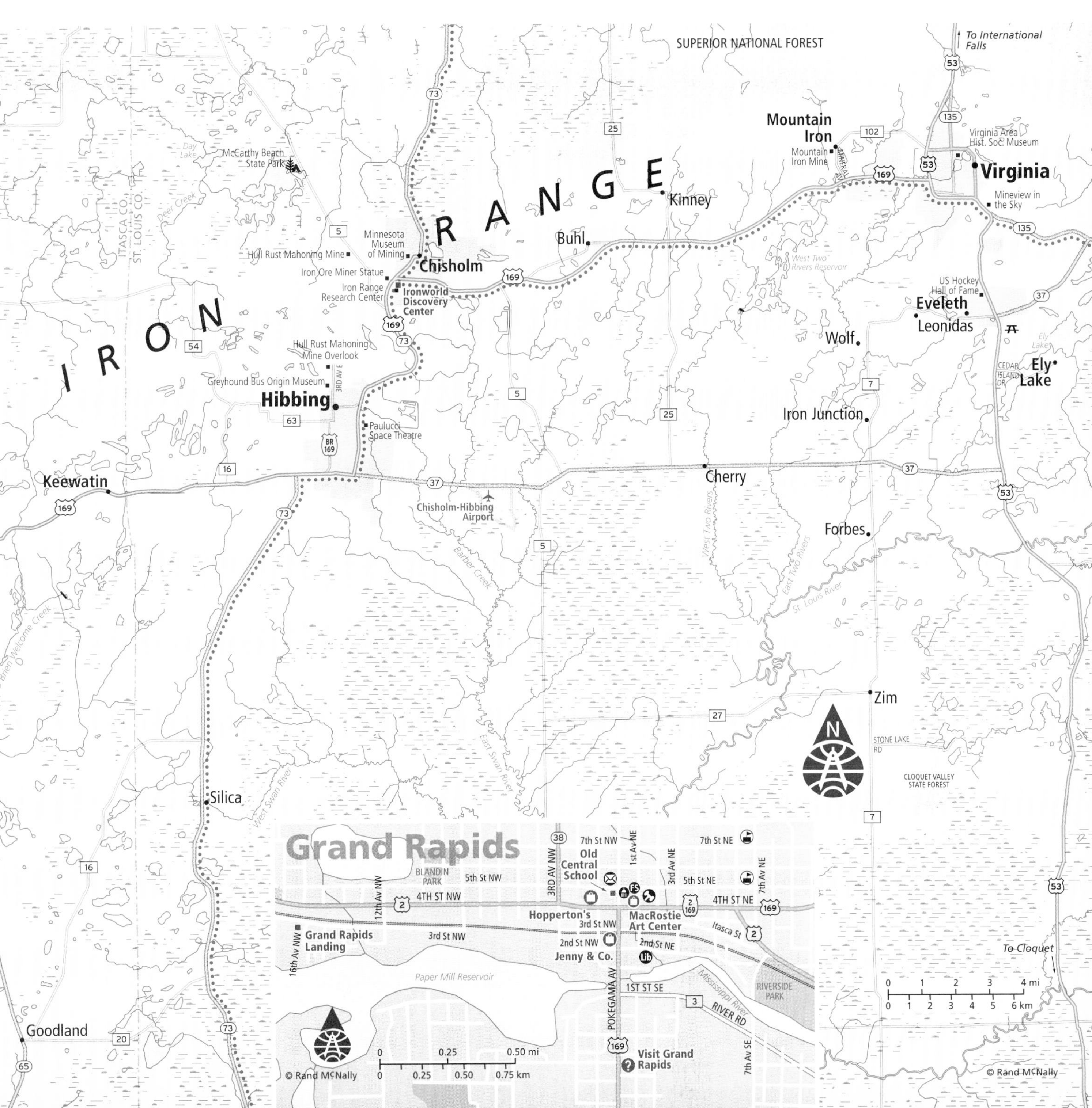

Minnesota **Twinship**

More than mere proximity makes **Saint Paul** and **Minneapolis** twins. Both commission cutting-edge architecture and emphasize the visual and performing arts. Both are sentimental, with sculptures honoring their favorite pop-culture icons—in Saint Paul's case, five of cartoonist Charles M. Schulz's *Peanuts* characters; in Minneapolis, Mary Richards, a.k.a. Mary Tyler Moore. While both offer splendid examples of the modern urban landscape, both also emphasize outdoor attractions practically in their backyards.

To start your Saint Paul exploration, hit **Grand Avenue**, the funky dining-and-drinking strip that originated as an 1870s transportation link between downtown and neighborhoods to the west. Although the streetcars are gone, the historic look and feel remains. An eclectic collection of independently owned and standard chain shops makes Grand Avenue a fun street for browsing.

Summit Avenue, described by F. Scott Fitzgerald as the city's "show street," offers a look at Saint Paul's showier side. With the nation's longest span of intact residential Victorian architecture, Summit presents a splendid urban drive, full of stately mansions with graceful pillars, stained-glass windows, and ornate wrought iron gates, surrounded by expansive lawns and landscaped gardens. **The governor's residence**, at No. 1006, is an English Tudor Revival house built in 1910. When wrestler-turned-governor Jesse Ventura moved in after his upset election victory in 1998, he displayed on the door the phrase "Dreams Do Come True." Docent-led tours are available by appointment.

Grand Avenue

Explore Saint Paul's cultural district, extending from pretty **Rice Park** (America's oldest urban park) to the **State Capitol** and the **Minnesota History Center**. You'll find museums, art galleries, historic sites, and theaters all within easy walking distance. Linger in Rice Park to admire the life-size bronze sculpture of literary giant F. Scott Fitzgerald. Nearby tourists rest on benches with maps and guidebooks; youngsters splash in a fountain. Not only was Fitzgerald born in Saint Paul in 1896, he also worked on two of his novels and many of his finest short stories here, often using the city as a locale.

Ordway Center for the Performing Arts

Across from the park lies the **Ordway Center for the Performing Arts** (345 Washington St.). An evening at this theater begins with a greeting from liveried footmen and continues as you climb a sweeping spiral staircase to the Grand Foyer and Upper Promenade, both with spectacular views of the city. The Ordway Center hosts the Minnesota Opera Company, the Schubert Club (one of the nation's oldest musical organizations), and the estimable Saint Paul Chamber Orchestra. It also brings the best of Broadway to Saint Paul. In fact, the Twin Cities offer more live-theater seats per capita than any city in the country except New York.

The buzz in Minneapolis? Its expanding arts scene. In just two years, it unveiled nearly a half-billion dollars of new arts infrastructure, recruiting some of the world's most celebrated architects to sculpt this expanding cultural landscape. Just as Chicago has its landmark Picasso sculpture, Minneapolis has its distinctive ***Spoonbridge and Cherry***, a huge, whimsical work that has been Minneapolis's signature sculpture since 1988. The giant spoon tips the scales at 5,800 pounds, and the bright red cherry weighs 1,200 pounds. Find it and more than 40 other permanent works at 11-acre **Minneapolis Sculpture Garden** (725 Vineland Pl.).

An early chapter of local history unfolds at **Historic Fort Snelling** (junction of MN 5 and MN 55), a stone fortress that overlooks the confluence of the Mississippi and Minnesota Rivers. Completed in 1825, this authentic living-history museum recaptures life on a frontier outpost, with stone barracks where soldiers slept two to a bunk. The firing of a cannon now is a popular daily ritual. Visitors can participate in the fort's everyday activities, such as mending clothing, shouldering a musket, or singing along with the soldiers.

Round tower and gatehouse at Historic Fort Snelling

A drive to **Lake Minnetonka**, west of Minneapolis, makes a popular day trip. Shop the boutiques in **Wayzata** and maybe have lunch at one of the town's stylish cafés. Ride the restored steamboat ***Minnehaha*** between Wayzata and **Excelsior**, home to America's oldest continuously running theater, the **Old Log Theater**. The century-old *Minnehaha* is a completely restored "streetcar boat," one of the original six built to extend the streetcar line into the lake. It lay at the bottom of the lake from its abandonment in 1926 until divers discovered it in 1980 and volunteers worked to restore its life.

What to eat

Although the Twin Cities offer a wide range of sophisticated dining, many locals also enjoy two Minnesota favorites: walleye and wild rice. Find them both at **Tavern on Grand** (656 Grand Ave., Saint Paul), which sports a planked pine North Woods décor. Mild-flavored walleye fillets arrive sautéed or deep-fried. Wild rice (which isn't really rice, but the seeds of an aquatic grass) shows up in soup. Traditionally, wild rice soup is made with creamy chicken stock, usually incorporating celery, carrots, and chopped onion.

What to buy

For millions, shopping in the Twin Cities is encapsulated in three magical words: **"Mall of America."** Dedicated shoppers should get a map and comfortable shoes, and allow at least half a day to wander around the nation's largest mall (520 stores, 20 sit-down restaurants). For a look at an unusual "big box" store, visit the **Target** in the middle of downtown Minneapolis. This flagship store of this Minnesota retailer is just down the street from Target Corporation's world headquarters. A special escalator accommodates shopping carts.

What to do

The Saint Paul Winter Carnival, Saint Paul, late January.

Minneapolis Aquatennial, Minneapolis, mid-July.

For more details about these festivals, please see page 174.

Information

Meet Minneapolis, (612) 767-8000, www.minneapolis.org.

Saint Paul River Centre Convention and Visitors Authority, (800) 627-6101, www.stpaulcvb.org.

Lodging tips

Besides the usual hotels and motels, the Twin Cities also offer unusual lodging choices, such as a floating bed-and-breakfast on the Mississippi River. The **Covington Inn** (Pier #1, Saint Paul), a retired and revamped 300-ton tugboat now permanently moored at Harriet Island, offers four staterooms, each with private bath and fireplace. Also alongside the Mississippi (only a few minutes from downtown Minneapolis) sits the 24-room **Nicollet Island Inn** (95 Merriam St.), occupying a converted 1893 factory building. For a splurge, the consensus choice is the **Saint Paul Hotel** (350 Market St.), elegant when built in 1910 and completely renovated into posh splendor in 2005. It is in the heart of Saint Paul, ready to pamper guests and their palates, too. Its St. Paul Grill, a power dining spot, offers prime steaks and single-malt Scotch and attracts the cream of local society.

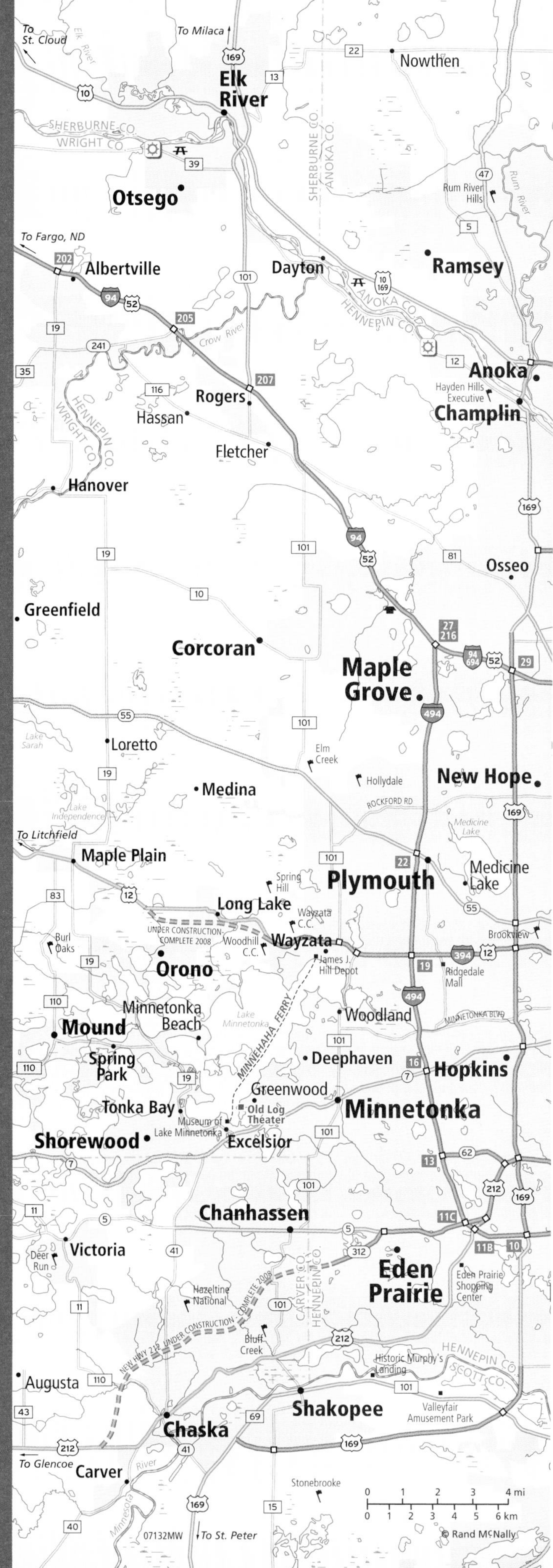

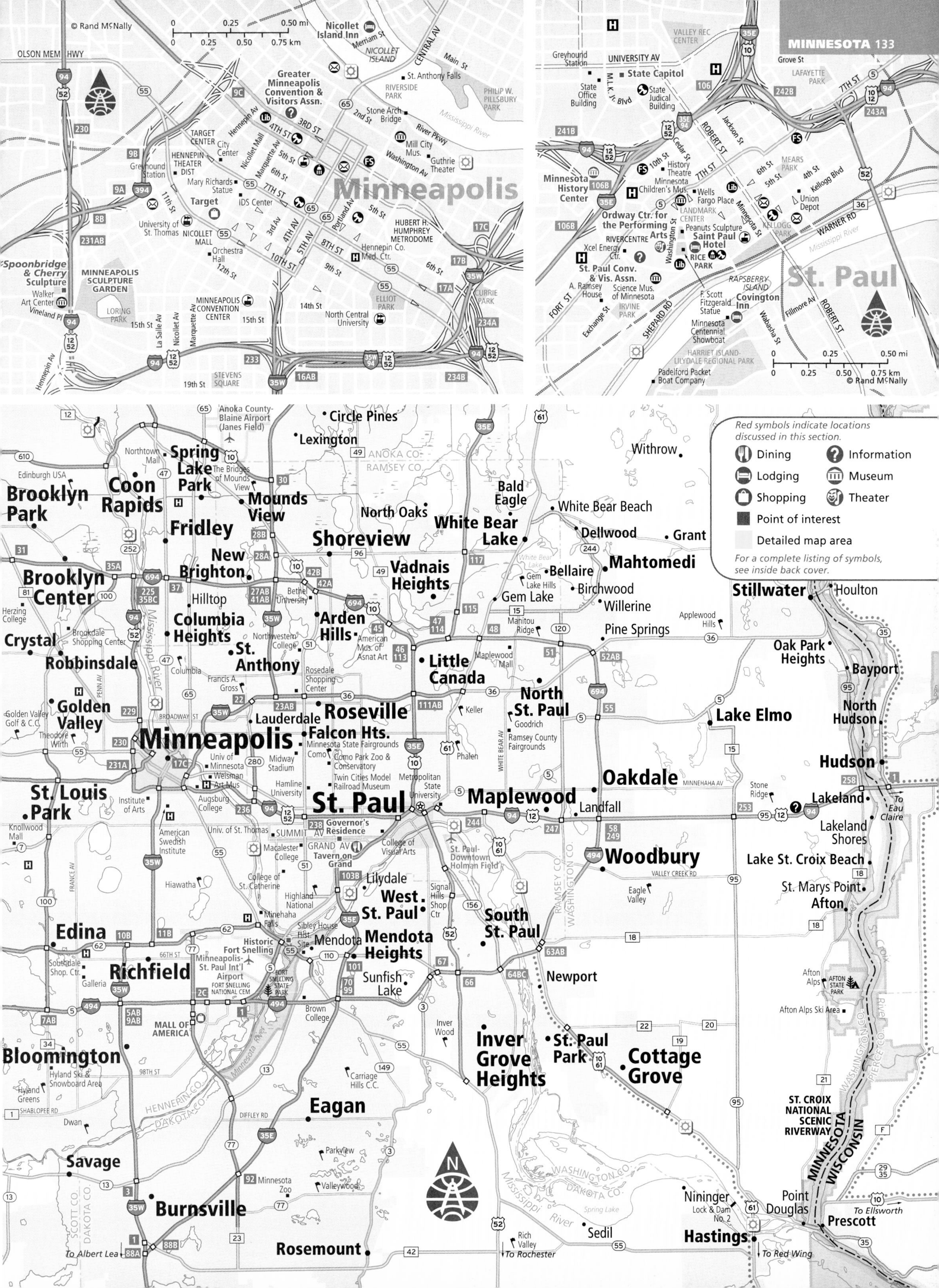
Minneapolis
St. Paul
Red symbols indicate locations discussed in this section.
Dining
Information
Lodging
Museum
Shopping
Theater
Point of interest
Detailed map area
For a complete listing of symbols, see inside back cover.
© Rand McNally

Relaxing in "Resort Country"

Brainerd, a former logging town, flourishes as a destination for relaxing North Woods getaways. With more than 450 lakes within a 30-mile radius and a concentration of resorts along their shores, the region is known as "resort country"—or to southern Minnesota urbanites, simply "up north." Loons cry hauntingly into the starry nights, piercing campfire reveries. This is the place for shore lunches and fish fries, for cruising in pontoon boats, and for paddling vacations by canoe or kayak.

About 22 miles north of Brainerd, the Whitefish Chain of Lakes comprises 14 connected lakes, with Norway red and billowy white pines edging 119 miles of shoreline. The lakes were created in 1884 when the Corps of Engineers constructed a dam at Cross Lake. Countless bays, inlets, and channels make for ideal boating and walleye fishing.

Typical of the two dozen or so resorts sprinkled around the lakes: rustic **Black Pine Beach Resort** (10732 County Rd. 16, Pequot Lakes) on **Lower Whitefish Lake** (also known as Pig Lake), with 13 housekeeping cabins tucked into pine woods dotted with distinctive silver birch. The resort has a sand beach and boats for guests. Cabins feature knotty-pine paneling, carpet, full kitchens, fireplaces (with wood provided), outdoor grills, and decks. Alongside the beach sits a large barbecue pit.

Fall foliage near Brainerd

Lower Whitefish Lake

Local wildlife includes white-tailed deer, fox, coyote, large porcupines, and a few black bear. In several nearby areas, bald eagles nest, raise their young, and gracefully ride the thermals searching for food. More commonly, you'll see loons diving for fish. Although loons—the Minnesota state bird—mate for life, they leave their young behind when they fly south. The young loons follow later, navigating on instinct. Because the region lies on the Mississippi flyway, spring and fall migrations bring a variety of warblers, waterfowl, and shorebirds such as sandpipers and plovers. Scores of white pelicans rest on larger lakes.

Tiny **Crosby** (pop. 2,275) is a hot collectibles destination, with more than a dozen antique shops. Facing buildings on Crosby's main street that once housed a department store and a mortuary now serve as antique emporiums, bringing together more than 40 dealers.

Deep, clear lakes formed from old mining pits pock this rugged Cuyuna Iron Range country. The pristine waters of these one-time mines draw diving clubs and fishing enthusiasts. Small, rustic mom-and-pop resorts are scattered along the deeply forested shores of Mille Lacs, the second-largest lake entirely within Minnesota. Nearby are a casino (with a 495-room hotel) and **Mille Lacs Indian Museum** (12 miles north of Onamia on US 169) where local Ojibwe provide first-hand narratives. Next door to the museum, a trading post sells quality Native American arts and crafts.

Hikers and bicyclists head for the **Paul Bunyan State Trail**, an ambitious rails-to-trails conversion. It occupies the railroad bed that the Burlington Northern Railroad built in 1893 and abandoned in 1983. This 100-mile-plus trail runs from Brainerd to Bemidji and is paved the entire route. The trail passes alongside 21 lakes, through scenic wetlands, and over several rivers and streams.

If you seek the giant statues of fabled lumberjack Paul Bunyan and Babe the Blue Ox that once occupied a prominent Brainerd intersection, you'll find them at their new home at **This Old Farm Pioneer Village** amusement park, seven miles east of town. (The woodsman is said to have created Minnesota's 10,000 lakes with his massive footprints.) A new Bunyan statue also stands outside the state-of-the-art **Brainerd Lakes Area Welcome Center**, opened in 2005. Although this version doesn't offer a personal greeting —as the original does—the 12-foot-high statue provides a fun photo op. Directly behind Paul, a putting green provides a teaser for the region's splendid golf courses. Golfers will find more than 25 courses within a 50-mile radius of Brainerd. Many are nationally acclaimed, built by a pantheon of famous designers that includes Robert Trent Jones, Jr. and Arnold Palmer.

What to eat

Sample walleye cakes, the North Woods' version of crab cakes, fashioned from mild, white walleye meat and wild rice. One place to try them: **Manhattan Beach Lodge** (39051 County Rd. 66, Manhattan Beach) on the eastern shore of Big Trout Lake.

What to buy

Shop for North Country crafts, especially birch bark products such as baskets and birdhouses. You'll find these at the 1930s Trading Post next door to the **Mille Lacs Indian Museum** (43411 Oodena Dr., Onamia). (Birch bark is hand-peeled from the tree and grows back in two or three years without damage to the tree.) Packages of wild rice also make nice gifts. Shop for these and other local food items at **Christmas Point Wild Rice Company** (14803 Edgewood Dr., Baxter).

What to do

Cider & Candlelight Tour, Crosslake, mid-September.

Taste of Pequot and Arts and Crafts Festival, Pequot Lakes, mid-September.

For more details about these festivals, please see page 174.

Information

Brainerd Lakes Area Chambers of Commerce, (800) 450-2838, www.explorebrainerdlakes.com.

Lodging tips

Lodging options range from old-style, family-operated resorts that attract repeat business year after year, to new full-service properties. The latter include **Grand View Lodge** (23521 Nokomis Ave., Nisswa), tucked into the shores of Gull Lake, where options range from cabins on the lake to golf course villas. Golf is a major preoccupation at this luxurious 269-room North Woods resort, which has three challenging courses. But this premier resort really does offer something for everyone—in addition to a social nine-hole golf course, you'll find a medley of restaurants and the luxurious Glacial Waters Spa, 1,500 feet of sand beach, tennis, boat rentals, horseback riding, and a heated indoor pool with hot tubs.

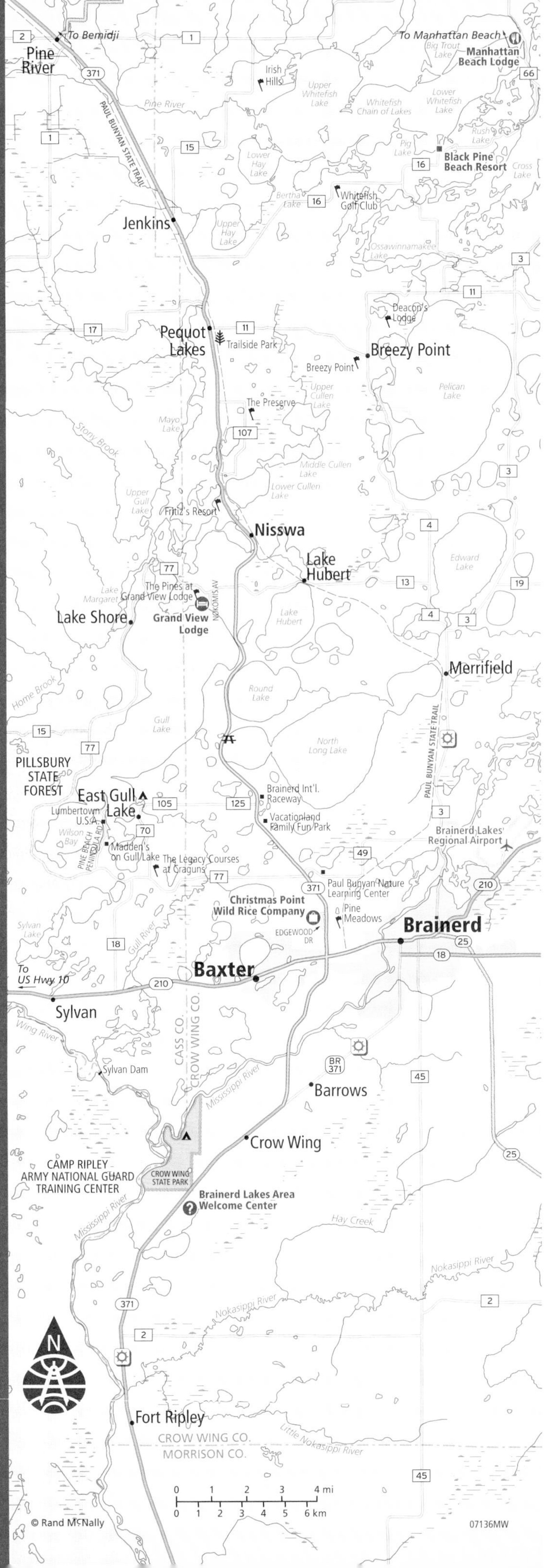

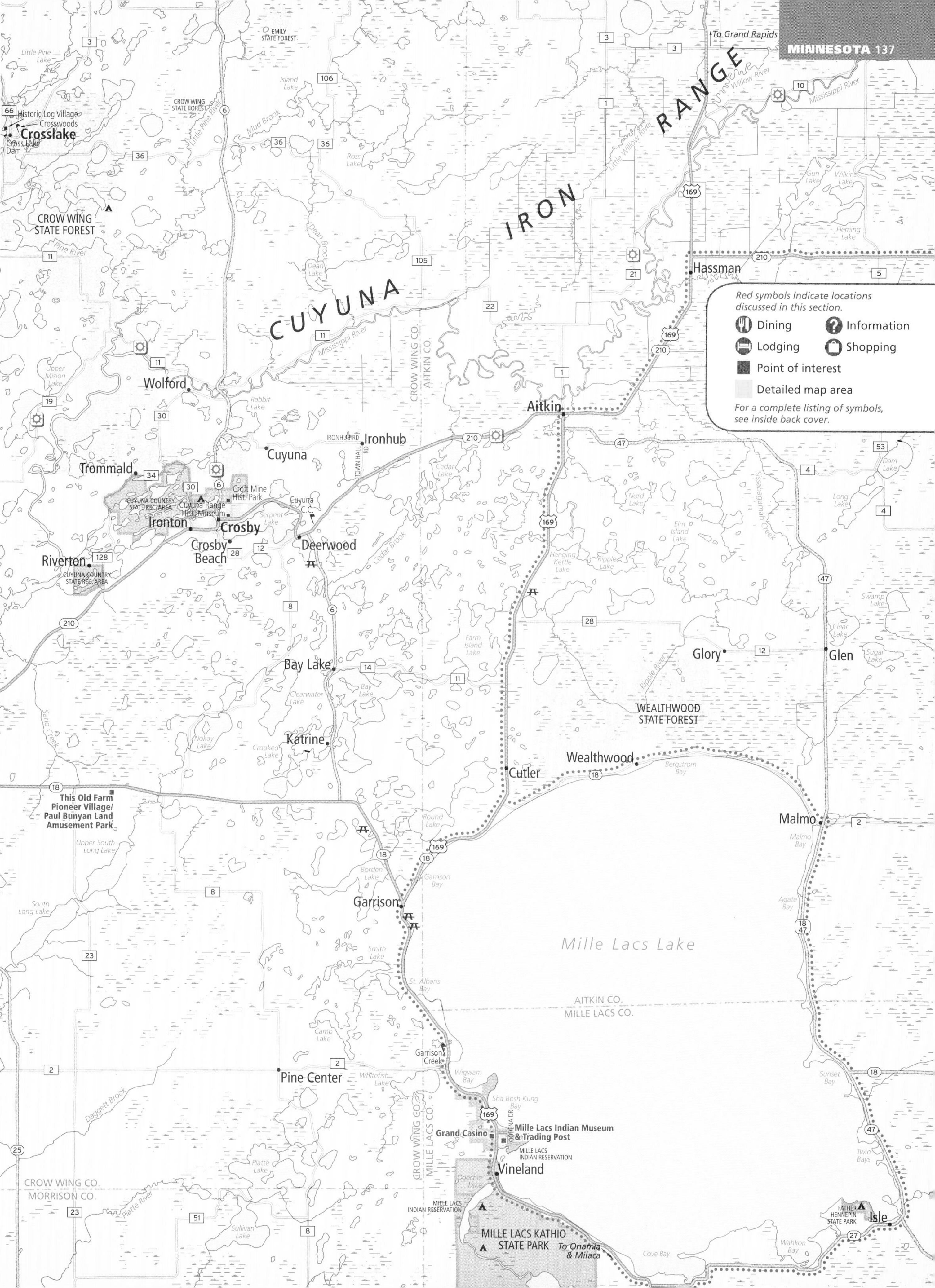
CUYUNA IRON RANGE
To Grand Rapids
Red symbols indicate locations discussed in this section.
Dining
Information
Lodging
Shopping
Point of interest
Detailed map area
For a complete listing of symbols, see inside back cover.
Historic Log Village
Crosswoods
Crosslake
Cross Lake Dam
CROW WING STATE FOREST
EMILY STATE FOREST
Wolford
Trommald
Cuyuna
Ironhub
Aitkin
Hassman
Croft Mine Hist. Park
Cuyuna Range Hist. Museum
CUYUNA COUNTRY STATE REC. AREA
Ironton
Crosby
Crosby Beach
Deerwood
Riverton
Bay Lake
Katrine
Cutler
Wealthwood
WEALTHWOOD STATE FOREST
Glory
Glen
Malmo
This Old Farm Pioneer Village/ Paul Bunyan Land Amusement Park
Garrison
Mille Lacs Lake
AITKIN CO.
MILLE LACS CO.
CROW WING CO.
MORRISON CO.
Pine Center
Garrison Creek
Grand Casino
Mille Lacs Indian Museum & Trading Post
MILLE LACS INDIAN RESERVATION
Vineland
MILLE LACS KATHIO STATE PARK
To Onamia & Milaca
FATHER HENNEPIN STATE PARK
Isle

Fine Fiddling and Fine Art

Long typecast as a haven for past-their-prime entertainers, **Branson**, Mo.—which has more theater seats than Broadway —is also an incubator of fresh young talent. More than 100 productions beckon up-and-comers seeking their big break. But there's plenty to do beyond the footlights, too, while exploring the scenic limestone foothills of the Ozarks.

With more than 750 miles of shoreline, Table Rock Lake provides boating opportunities along with many coves and underwater rock bluffs that attract divers. Outdoor adventures at **Dogwood Canyon Nature Park** (2038 West MO 86, Lampe) include cattle drives and fly-fishing clinics along trout streams. Explore this 10,000-acre park via hiking trails, rental bike, private jeep, or open-air tram. A two-hour tram ride travels deep into the park, which sprawls across the Arkansas state line about 20 miles southwest of Branson. It passes towering limestone bluffs, bowed ridges, tumbling waterfalls, and forest of oak, cedar, and pine sprinkled with towering sycamores. Picturesque stone bridges and spring-fed streams round out the landscape. In the upper reaches of the canyon, herds of Texas longhorns, American bison, and elk roam. Often, tram drivers park in the middle of a herd of bison grazing on open pastureland. The bison are comfortable with human intruders—even with their young around—though they'll quickly chase off a feisty razorback pig. Another way to see the park: private jeep tours that travel old logging roads. These guided tours also last about two hours (reservations required; maximum three passengers).

Fiddler at Silver Dollar City

Looking for something more rustic? City slickers can sign on for an abbreviated (one-day) cattle drive. With wide-brimmed hat and bandana in place, you'll help wranglers gather a herd of Texas longhorns and drive it to new pastures. Drives, available to groups of 10 to 20, may include breakfast, a chuckwagon barbecue, or a canyon cookout. On an overnight adventure, cowpokes-in-training help set up camp, cook over open flames, and enjoy music and entertainment around the campfire. Also offered: catch-and-release and catch-and-keep trout fishing and fly-fishing clinics. Guided kayak adventures on Table Rock Lake help newbies learn the basics.

Table Rock Lake, created by impounding the White River, is a major recreational area, with more than 100 resorts located nearby, as well a marina offering boat rentals—including ever-popular, easy-to-handle pontoon boats. Fishing can be excellent, especially in spring, for bass, crappie, and walleye. Submerged cedars and other trees provide a happy habitat, or "structure," for fish. Many visitors head for **Table Rock State Park** (5272 MO 165), where a busy public marina rents out personal watercraft, pontoon boats, ski boats, and fishing boats, as well as diving supplies. You also might try parasailing or take an excursion aboard a 48-foot catamaran.

Golfers will find challenging courses, such as the Tom Fazio-designed **Branson Creek** (1001 Branson Creek Blvd., Branson Creek), recognized as one of America's "100 Greatest Public Golf Courses" by *Golf Digest*. **Top of the Rock** (612 Devil's Pool Rd., Ridgedale), a sporty 18-hole, par-3 course designed by Jack Nicklaus, offers stunning views of Table Rock Lake.

Schedule a side trip to **Springfield's** art colony. Downtown Springfield takes on a carnival atmosphere the first Friday of each month, when thousands join Art Walk, an event that showcases the work of local artisans. Courted with free food, wine, and entertainment, visitors wander through clusters of shops and galleries that branch out from the central square. As Art Walk wraps up, nightlife slips into high gear with dueling-piano bars and clubs offering jazz, blues, rock, and bluegrass music.

Baseball fans say that **Hammons Field** (955 E. Trafficway), the $32-million, 8,000-seat ballpark that debuted in 2004, is a minor-league park with a major-league feel. Yet it has the attributes of minor-league baseball: affordability, availability of players to autograph-seeking fans, and the antics of Louie the Mascot as he interacts with spectators. Even the food is notable, such as the Hammons Hoagie Dog, a half-pound hot dog served with sauerkraut. Hammons Field is the latest chapter in a century of Springfield's baseball history—where legendary Stan "The Man" Musial played minor league ball until promotion to St. Louis in the 1930s. The Springfield Cardinals, a Texas League Double-A team, is affiliated with the St. Louis Cardinals.

Potter at Silver Dollar City

Civil War buffs journey to **Wilson's Creek National Battlefield** (6424 W. Farm Road 182). Fought 10 miles southwest of Springfield in 1861, this, the second major battle of the Civil War, was also the first major engagement west of the Mississippi. The Wilson's Creek Civil War Museum exhibits artifacts, including the sword belt and sash of Arkansas General Patrick Cleburne and the flag of the Confederate "Cherokee Braves." Also on site is the Ray House, the only surviving dwelling from the Battle of Wilson's Creek. It is open weekends through the summer, with interpreters dressed in period clothing.

Artillery firing demonstration at Wilson's Creek National Battlefield

MAP CONTINUED ON PAGE 141

Dogwood Canyon Nature Park

What to eat

North of Branson is Lambert's Café (1800 West MO J, Ozark), where folks stand in line to have food thrown at them. This quirky spot serves hearty down-home fare, including country ham, barbecued ribs, and chicken and dumplings, but it's best known for "throwed rolls"—made-from-scratch, freshly baked, toque-shaped dinner rolls that the "pitcher"on duty hurls across the dining room to seated customers.

What to buy

Woodsy, 1880s-themed Silver Dollar City (399 Indian Point Rd., Branson) emphasizes Ozark crafts. A colony of 100 resident artisans showcasing heritage crafts includes woodcarvers, glass-blowers, potters, basket makers, leather crafters, candle makers, and knife makers. Watch them at work explaining their techniques, and buy their products in adjoining shops.

What to do

Plumb Nellie Days, Branson, mid-May.

Branson Area Festival of Lights, Branson, November through December.

For more details about these festivals, please see page 174.

Information

Branson/Lakes Area Chamber of Commerce, (800) 214-3661, www.explorebranson.com.

Lodging tips

Bradford House Bed & Breakfast (296 Blue Meadows Rd., Branson), offering 20 guestrooms, combines the coziness of a bed-and-breakfast and the privacy of a hotel. Built as a Victorian-style guesthouse, it opened in 2001. Breakfasts, served in an airy room with mahogany furniture and marble-topped tables, feature blueberry pancakes, waffles, quiche, peach-stuffed French toast, omelets, and biscuits and gravy. If you prefer lodgings away from town, choose one of the resorts around Table Rock Lake. At one of the best known, Big Cedar Lodge, a full-service resort, choices include three distinctly different lodges, cozy knotty pine cottages, and log cabins.

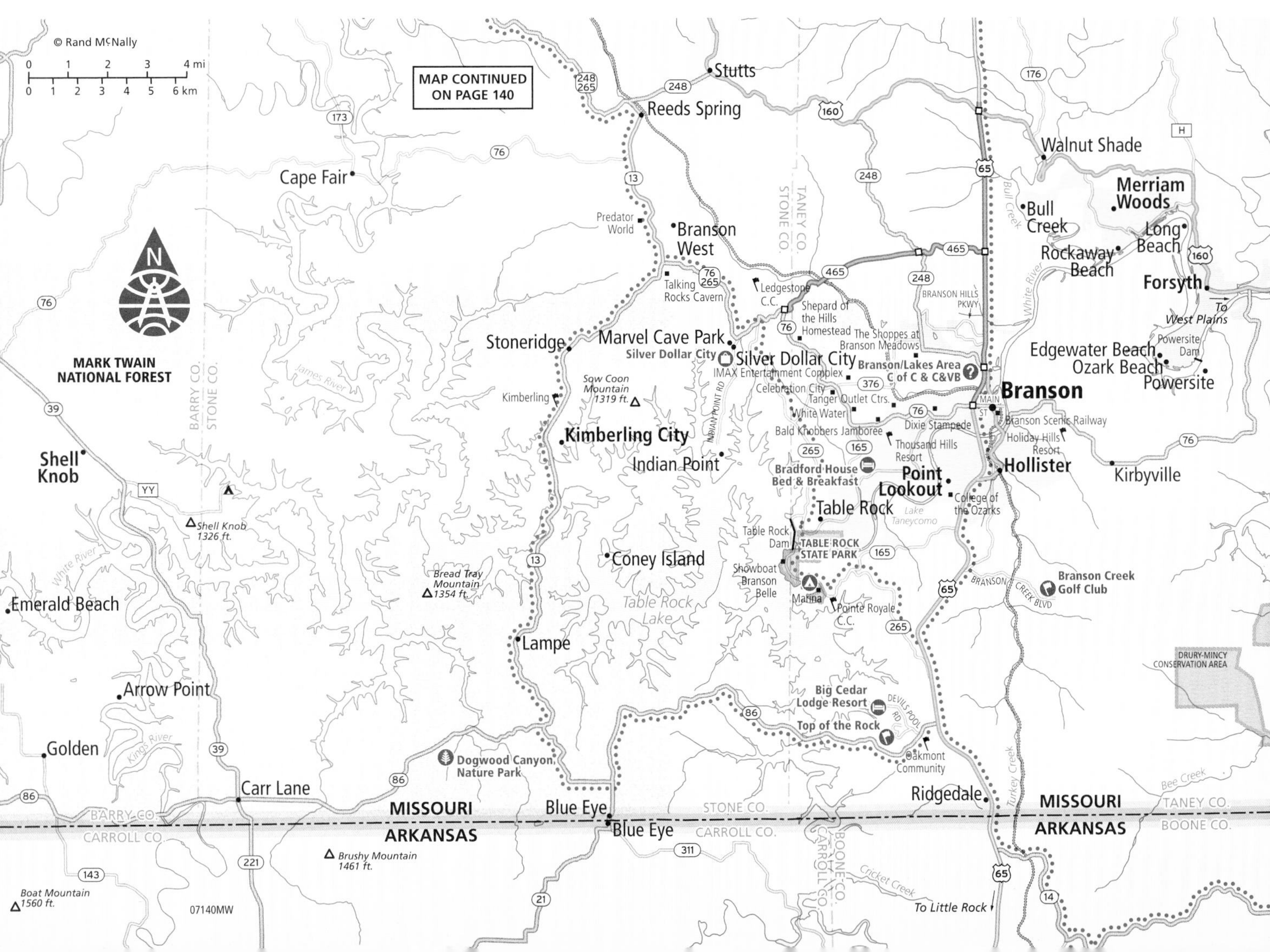

Midwest's Aquatic Playground

Wriggling across central Missouri, 92-mile-long Lake of the Ozarks offers 1,150-plus miles of shoreline, more than the entire coast of California. This artificial lake not only is a prime golfing and watersports destination, it also provides a wide range of accommodations, from rustic cabins to sleek condos. You can even spend an entire vacation on the water with a rental houseboat from **Lake of the Ozarks Marina** (North MO 5 at Niangua Bridge, Camdenton). Houseboats up to 65 feet long provide adventurous holidays afloat with comfortable living and sleeping quarters for as many as 12.

Though it provides so much pleasure nowadays, Lake of the Ozarks is a child of the Great Depression. Jobless men with hungry families traveled to central Missouri to find work with the Union Electric Company's Great Osage River Project, which created the Bagnell Dam, and the impoundment became the largest man-made lake in the world at that time. Despite long, grueling hours, these migrant workers welcomed the chance to earn from 35 cents to $1.25 an hour, at a time when you could load a car with groceries for $5.

Tan-Tar-A Resort

Willmore Lodge (1 Willmore Ln., Lake Ozark), built in 1930 as an administrative and entertainment center for Union Electric, embraces the popular Adirondack style, with white pine logs held together with square wooden pegs. Louis La Beaume, who worked on the 1904 Louisiana Purchase Exposition (a.k.a. the St. Louis World's Fair) designed it, using locally quarried stone for the fireplace and patio and incorporating a magnificent picture window providing eight-mile views of the lake. Modern conveniences included a state-of-the-art air-cooling machine.

Today, the rustic lodge houses a museum chronicling the dam and lake's creation. Listen to old-time radio broadcasts telling how the prospect of work attracted jobless from across the country; activate videotaped interviews with people who worked on the project. Willmore Lodge also hosts "Eagle Days," an annual event in early January. The vast Lake of the Ozarks region provides excellent habitat for the several hundred bald eagles that winter there, many congregating around the open waters of Bagnell Dam, where food is plentiful. High-powered viewing scopes stand on the deck of Willmore Lodge, with additional observation sites above and below the dam. Naturalists show injured birds recovered from the wild.

At **Ha Ha Tonka State Park** (1491 MO D), visitors find scenic overlooks and the ruins of a European-style "castle" built early in the last century by Scottish stonemasons. Mostly destroyed by fire in 1942, the ruins tower on a dramatic bluff over rugged surroundings as if straight out of a Gothic romance. Adventurous visitors climb a 300-step staircase from the docks to the site. While not for the faint of heart, the views make the trek worthwhile. Other photo ops in the 3,680-acre park: a natural bridge, caves, underground streams, and large springs (including one of Missouri's largest, which pumps nearly 48 million gallons of water daily). **Lake of the Ozarks State Park** is Missouri's largest, comprising 17,441 acres. It has 89 miles of shoreline, two swimming beaches, horseback riding, and more than 10 developed trails—one of which, the **Ozarks Aquatic Trail**, is designed for boaters, who can stop at 14 designated buoys along the shoreline. A free booklet, available at the park office, describes the significance of each stop. Take time for a guided group tour of **Ozark Caverns**, a park-operated cave, where you might spot the elusive blind grotto salamander.

An especially pretty season to visit: fall, when the landscape is daubed in shades of green, yellow, red, orange, and gold, and temperatures stay warm through September and beyond. (Even during winter, it's not unusual for daytime temperatures to warm

Ha Ha Tonka State Park castle ruins

Willmore Lodge, Lake Ozark

into the 50°-60°F range.) Boating remains popular—with traffic easier on and off the lake—and golf is splendid as trees start to turn, green fees drop, and tee times free up. This central Missouri resort area offers 288 holes on 17 golf courses chiseled into the Ozark hills.

What to eat

Local favorites include ham and white beans served with corn bread and sides of mashed potatoes and green beans. Blackberry and peach cobblers are popular desserts. Dining doesn't get more downhome than at **Tonka Hills Restaurant** (406 W. US 54, Linn Creek). This is the spot for belt-busting Ozark country breakfasts featuring ham, eggs, hash browns or grits, hot biscuits, and gravy.

What to buy

Determined shoppers pack the credit cards and head for **Osage Beach Premium Outlets** (4540 W. US 54, Osage Beach), where 110 brand-name stores occupy 13 buildings spread over 61 acres. Manufacturers' outlet stores even include a bible-factory outlet—since this is, after all, the "Bible Belt."

What to do

Dogwood Festival, Camdenton, mid-April.
Olde Tyme Apple Festival, Versailles, early October.

For more details about these festivals, please see page 174.

Information

Lake of the Ozarks Convention and Visitors Bureau, (800) 386-5253, www.funlake.com.

Lodging tips

Find accommodations in rustic cabins, lakeside cottages, and two full-service mega-resorts. **Tan-Tar-A Resort** (County Rd. KK at mile marker 26, Osage Beach) and **The Lodge of Four Seasons** (Horseshoe Bend Pkwy./County Rd. HH, Lake Ozark) brim with amenities such as tennis courts, spas, restaurants, lounges with entertainment, and programs for children. Another choice lodging option: **The Country Club Hotel & Spa** (Horseshoe Bend Parkway/County Road HH & Carol Rd., Lake Ozark), which offers live New Orleans-style jazz in its lounge four nights a week. Not all resorts are shiny new. Some offer quintessential old-style Lake of the Ozarks ambience—family-operated, comfortable, and as unpretentious as biscuits and gravy. Many visitors return year after year to their favorites where owners make guests feel like part of the family, such as **Bass Point Resort** (33510 Bass Point Rd., Gravois Mills).

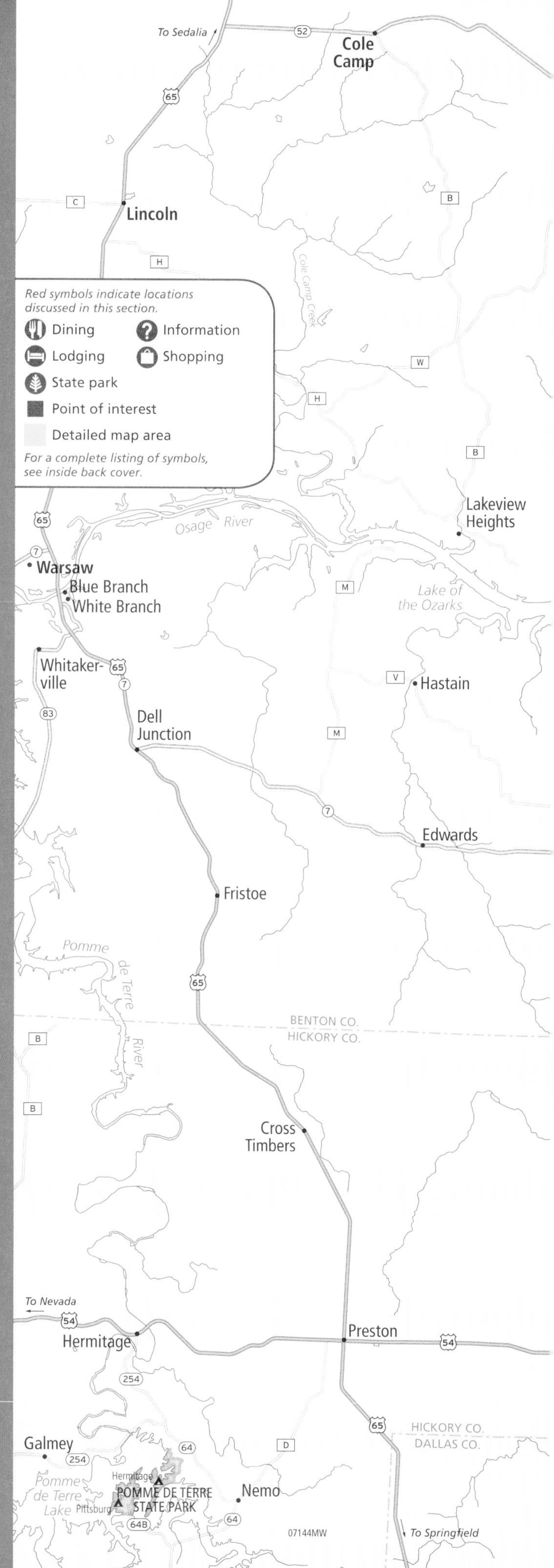

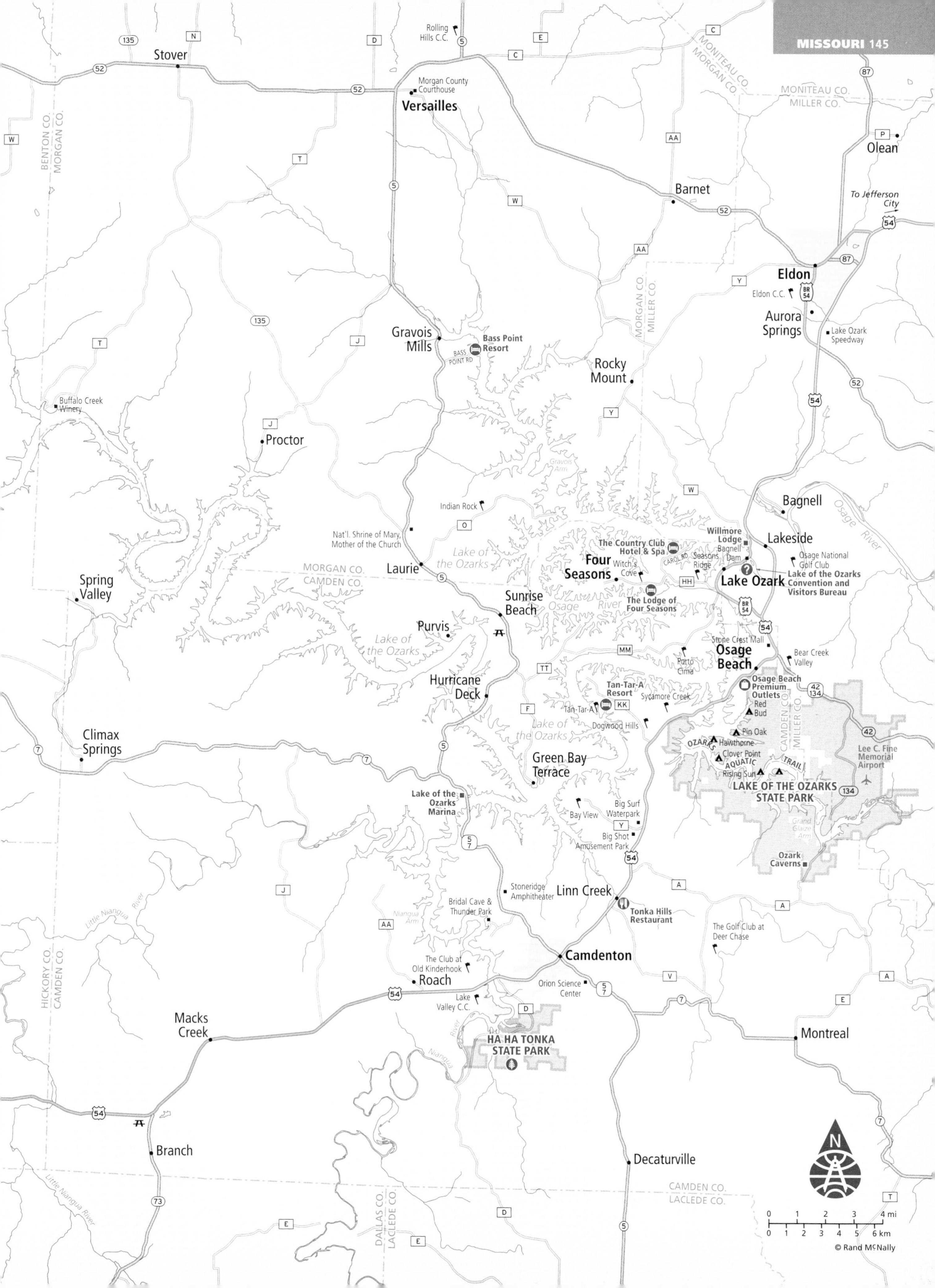

Stover
Versailles
Morgan County Courthouse
Rolling Hills C.C.
Barnet
Olean
To Jefferson City
Eldon
Eldon C.C.
Aurora Springs
Lake Ozark Speedway
Gravois Mills
Bass Point Resort
Rocky Mount
Buffalo Creek Winery
Proctor
Indian Rock
Nat'l. Shrine of Mary, Mother of the Church
Laurie
Lake of the Ozarks
Bagnell
Lakeside
Willmore Lodge
Bagnell Dam
The Country Club Hotel & Spa
Four Seasons
Witch's Cove
Seasons Ridge
Lake Ozark
Osage National Golf Club
Lake of the Ozarks Convention and Visitors Bureau
The Lodge of Four Seasons
Osage River
Spring Valley
Sunrise Beach
Purvis
Stone Crest Mall
Osage Beach
Bear Creek Valley
Porto Cima
Osage Beach Premium Outlets
Hurricane Deck
Tan-Tar-A Resort
Sycamore Creek
Red Bud
Dogwood Hills
Pin Oak
Hawthorne
Clover Point
Rising Sun
Ozarks Aquatic Trail
Climax Springs
Green Bay Terrace
Lee C. Fine Memorial Airport
LAKE OF THE OZARKS STATE PARK
Lake of the Ozarks Marina
Bay View
Big Surf Waterpark
Big Shot Amusement Park
Grand Glaize Arm
Ozark Caverns
Stoneridge Amphitheater
Linn Creek
Tonka Hills Restaurant
Bridal Cave & Thunder Park
The Golf Club at Deer Chase
Little Niangua River
Niangua Arm
Camdenton
The Club at Old Kinderhook
Roach
Orion Science Center
Lake Valley C.C.
Macks Creek
HA HA TONKA STATE PARK
Montreal
Branch
Decaturville
MONITEAU CO. MORGAN CO.
MONITEAU CO. MILLER CO.
BENTON CO. MORGAN CO.
MORGAN CO. MILLER CO.
MORGAN CO. CAMDEN CO.
CAMDEN CO. MILLER CO.
HICKORY CO. CAMDEN CO.
CAMDEN CO. LACLEDE CO.
DALLAS CO. LACLEDE CO.
0 1 2 3 4 mi
0 1 2 3 4 5 6 km
© Rand McNally

A Taste of Twain

Mark Twain is a major industry around **Hannibal**, Mo. You may encounter him wandering the streets, performing at a local theater in a one-man show, or even sitting at the breakfast table at your bed-and-breakfast inn. As you explore this hilly Mississippi river town, you'll also likely run into Tom Sawyer, complete with fishing pole, and Becky Thatcher, toting a parasol.

Twain, whose real name was Samuel Clemens, spent his formative years in Hannibal. The Clemens family moved to the river town in 1839 when Samuel was four. He lived there until age 18, providing invaluable insights into life on the Mississippi—particularly from the viewpoint of a small boy and young man.

A new cottage industry is flourishing in Hannibal and neighboring towns **Clarksville** and **Louisiana** as these small river communities join to offer **"50 Miles of Art."** The program connects professional artists, artisans, and galleries along Missouri's Route 79 Scenic Byway, which rides over steep bluffs stretching south from Hannibal and follows the winding river for some 50 miles.

Bronze statue of Huckleberry Finn and Tom Sawyer, Hannibal

Pick up or download a brochure for a self-guided tour of three charming riverfront communities, with directions to potters, cabinetmakers, stained-glass artisans, painters, sculptors, and retail galleries that offer high-grade work directly from the artists. There's also hand-forged antique iron, ceramics, quilts, handcrafted soaps, pewter, photography, and jewelry. Dozens of local artists and crafters are ready to greet visitors and talk about their work.

Allow plenty of time to stop at scenic lookouts. From atop high bluffs, they offer vast views of the forested Mississippi Valley and the flat farmlands across the river in Illinois. Egret, heron, and eagles are common.

Begin a tour along Hannibal's Main Street. The area is perking up with new businesses such as **Java Jive Coffee House** (211 N. Main), with inviting sofas and armchairs and jazz jam sessions that attract talented young musicians. The adjoining Fresh Ayers (209 N. Main), a project of local potter-entrepreneur Steve Ayers, offers an eclectic collection of gifts, including artwork, jewelry, and bath and body products. Neighboring Fresh Ayers Too (213 N. Main) showcases furniture handcrafted in the Midwest.

Nearby, occupying a former hardware store built in 1868, is the **Jam Factory** (207 N. Main), where a banjo rigged to the door welcomes visitors with a note or two of "Dueling Banjos" (from the movie *Deliverance*). Owner Chris Foss strums tunes himself on a hammered dulcimer or other string instrument that he skillfully fashions in a large workshop at the back of the store. Many of his creations are featured in jam sessions across the street in the **Breadeaux Pizza** parlor (200 N. Main).

In Hannibal, Tom Sawyer's irascible spirit and Samuel Clemens' irrepressible humor live on. You can visit the author's boyhood home and a museum that chronicles his life, and tour the caves in which Tom and his sweetheart Becky Thatcher were lost in *The Adventures of Tom Sawyer*.

Business establishments named after the author and his most famous characters are legion. You can stay at the **Hotel Clemens** (401 3rd St.), eat at the **Mark Twain Dinette** (400 N. 3rd St.), enjoy a shake or sundae at **Becky's Old Fashioned Ice Cream Parlor & Emporium** (318 N. Main St.), and ride the **Mark Twain Riverboat** (Central Street Landing). Photograph the bronze **Tom and Huck statue** that immortalizes two of his most memorable and mischievous characters, or climb the 244 steps of the **Mark Twain Memorial Lighthouse** for a panoramic view of Hannibal and Twain's beloved Mississippi River.

As for Mr. Clemens himself, check the **Planters Barn Theater** (319 N. Main St.) for Richard Garey's seasonal one-man show, "Mark Twain Himself." Or invite him to breakfast. Upon request, a local inn (**Reagan's Queen Anne Bed and Breakfast**) may be able to arrange a visit by Garey/Twain, who'll join you at the table and regale you with his wit. Should the discussion turn to food, ask for Mr. Clemens' opinion of cauliflower and await his famous riposte: "Cauliflower is nothing but cabbage with a college education."

In the tiny town of Louisiana, find art on the streets as well as in studios and galleries. More than a score of murals blossom on exterior walls around town. **Reflections of Missouri Gallery** (107 S. 9th St.) showcases the work of John Stoeckley, an artist specializing in pen, ink, and watercolor images of barns, lighthouses, wildlife, and historical sites. More than just a fine-dining restaurant, **Eagle's Nest Winery, Inn & Bistro** (221 Georgia St.) offers a bed-and-breakfast and their own wine, too. Stay in a room with a whirlpool tub, wrap up in a soft bathrobe, and get ready for a brunch of made-to-order omelets. Evenings feature live jazz and a menu of dishes such as veal piccata and ribs in house-made bourbon sauce.

In Clarksville, artists cluster along Second Street, facing the Mississippi River, and also along Howard Street. Among the town's galleries and shops, look for colonial-style Windsor chairs at the **Windsor Chair Shop** (307 S. Second St.), studio jewelry at **Sacre Bleu Gallery & Studio** (101 S. Front St.), pewter dishes and candle holders at **ASL Pewter Foundry** (114 Howard St.), hickory furniture at Gallery 24, and skin care and essential oils at **Bee Naturals** (108 Howard St.). Take time to visit **Lock & Dam No. 24**, where migrating eagles fish and nest by the hundreds during winter months.

Mark Twain Boyhood Home & Museum (on the right)

What to eat

Look for such staples as fried chicken, chicken-fried steak, and platters of baked turkey and ham. The Mark Twain Dinette (400 N. 3rd St.) is a fixture known for pork tenderloin sandwiches, catfish dinners, and frosty mugs of homemade root beer. At TJ's (211 Munger Ln.), a locally popular and extremely friendly supper club, prime rib gets top billing and steaks (mostly priced under $20) are a good choice. Barbecued baby back ribs, fried chicken, and chicken liver dinners are local favorites. Finish with blackberry cobbler with ice cream. Cavernous TJ's still manages to be warm and welcoming—probably because everyone seems to know each other. "Hey, Chuck, saw your truck outside, so I knew I'd find you here," is a typical greeting.

What to buy

In Hannibal, visit Ayers Pottery (308 N. Third), operated by Steve Ayers, a professional potter for 30 years whose work is recognized for its beautiful form and color-rich glazes. The Jam Factory creates exquisite hammered and mountain dulcimers and also carries entry-level guitars, fiddles, and banjos, as well as fun instruments such as tin whistles, nose flutes, and lap harps.

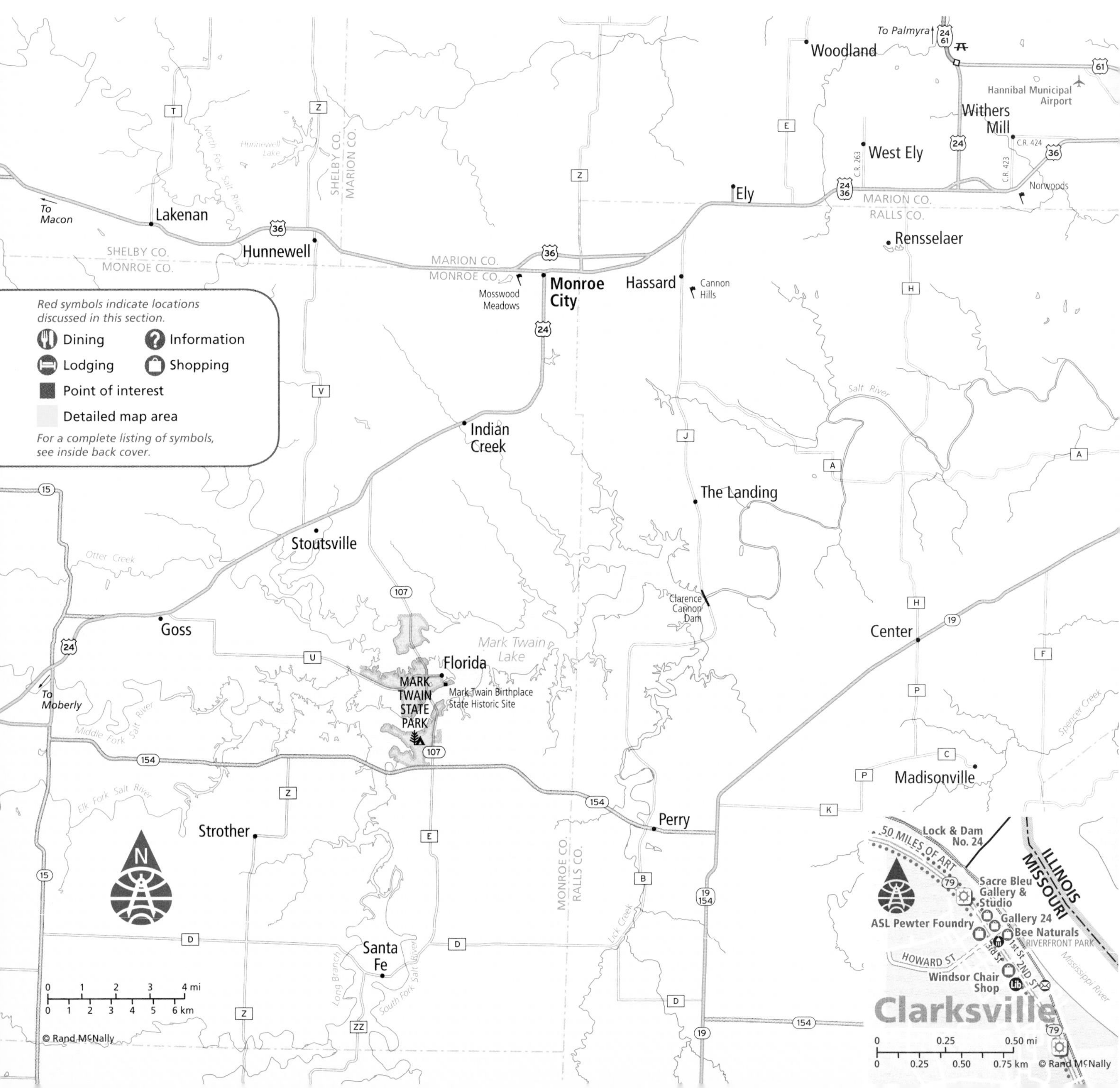

What to do

Eagle Days, Clarksville, late January.

National Tom Sawyer Days, Hannibal, Independence Day weekend.

For more details about these festivals, please see page 174.

Information

Hannibal Convention & Visitors Bureau, (866) 263-4825, www.visithannibal.com.

Lodging tips

Not unexpectedly, bed-and-breakfast properties are a popular lodging choice in what essentially is a small town; you'll find about a dozen to choose from. **Reagan's Queen Anne** (313 N. Fifth St.), the quintessential bed-and-breakfast inn, offers rockers on a porch and satisfying breakfasts.

If you prefer modern accommodations to the Victorians and painted ladies that typically house bed-and-breakfasts, there are numerous chains in the area, including Holiday Inn Express, Super 8, Travelodge, Days Inn, Econo Lodge, and Comfort Inn.

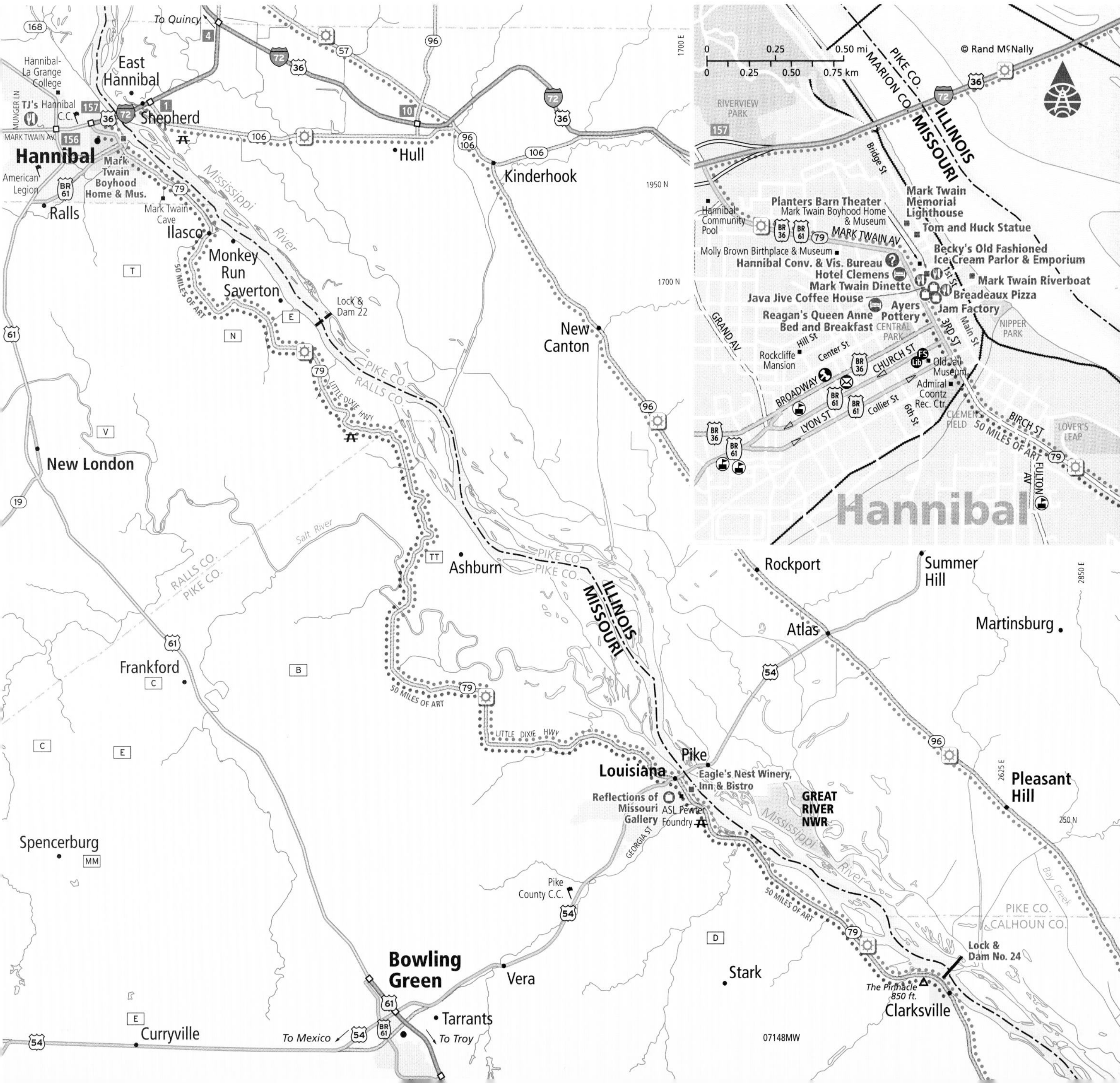

Dickens Did Not Sleep Here

Explore London, England, and you'll discover an improbably large number of inns where Charles Dickens reputedly quaffed ale and laid his head. Wander around **Lebanon**, Ohio, and you'll also find an inn that the illustrious novelist visited—but where he never took a drink nor stayed overnight. And therein, as he might himself have written, lies a tale.

As Ohio's oldest inn, dating back to 1803, the **Golden Lamb** has hosted 12 U.S. presidents and such prominent 19th-century figures as Harriet Beecher Stowe and Mark Twain. Charles Dickens visited the hostelry in 1842 and was heard eloquently bellowing uncomplimentary opinions about the United States. After objecting mightily at being unable to get a drink at the inn, which was owned by a temperance family, he's said to have left in a huff. Too bad he's not around to settle the quarrel with a glass of wine at the tavern and restaurant now on site.

This redbrick inn with broad white balconies offers lodgings in 18 overnight rooms furnished with antiques. Each room bears the name of a famous visitor from the inn's past. The Golden Lamb displays a fine collection of Shaker pieces and Currier & Ives prints.

The Golden Lamb, Lebanon

Lebanon, an early Shaker community founded in 1803 by Ichabod Corwin, flourished as stagecoaches rumbled through with settlers and travelers. Carefully preserved, it thrives as a popular destination for antique hunters. Spend a quiet afternoon browsing antique shops, specialty boutiques, art galleries, distinctive clothing stores, furniture shops, and cafés. Stroll wide streets and brick sidewalks lined with linden trees, enjoying the notable absence of neon, overhead wires, and overhanging signs. Admire the architectural mix of Federal, Greek Revival, and Victorian styles. Attractions include the **Warren County Historical Society Museum** (105 S. Broadway), which houses one of the nation's finest Shaker collections.

Neighboring **Waynesville** was designed in the manner of an English village, with formal parks and squares arranged around a central public square. In the early days there was flatboat trade with Cincinnati. After the building of the Miami Canal, farmers prospered as they efficiently moved produce to markets in Cincinnati. Today, sauerkraut (celebrated with an annual festival—see p. 174) and antiques are two major claims to fame of this picturesque town, which has charming historic buildings, brick sidewalks, window boxes spilling flowers, and plenty of benches for resting and people-watching. Packed into five blocks along the **"Old Main Street" historic district** are more than 70 antique and specialty stores and eight eateries (along with several inns and bed-and-breakfasts).

The Little Miami River, a state and National Scenic River, flows through the glacial hills of southwestern Ohio. Guided and unguided trips range from three to 18 miles and can last from one to seven hours. One of the region's premier outfitters, **Morgan's Canoe & Outdoor Centers** (5701 OH 350, Oregonia), offers canoe, kayak, and raft trips.

Morgan's sits deep in the Fort Ancient Gorge, along the most natural and undisturbed section of the river.

Waynesville's "Old Main Street" historic district

Paddlers enjoy wooded hillsides, frequent small rapids, and great swimming and picnic spots near 300- to 400-year-old mighty virgin-growth sycamore trees. In the fall, people harvest hickory nuts and walnuts. Indigenous wildlife includes the leatherback (or soft-shell) turtle, great blue heron, osprey hawk, and wild turkey. The Little Miami River region is popular with fossil hunters.

Atop a wooded bluff rising 235 feet above the Little Miami River, **Fort Ancient State Memorial** (6123 OH 350, Oregonia)—the largest prehistoric hilltop enclosure in North America—preserves 15,000 years of Native American history and culture. Tree-covered earthen walls, built 2,000 years ago by the Hopewell, enclose a modern museum with exhibits that bring to life the Ohio valley's ancient inhabitants.

Life-sized dioramas, collections of artifacts, and interactive exhibits illuminate Native American heritage. The exhibit "When Worlds Collide" chronicles the arrival of Europeans and its effect on Native Americans. A poignant display documents the impact of European diseases, especially smallpox. More Native Americans perished from these diseases than died in all of the warfare of that period. An outdoor re-creation of a prehistoric garden illustrates the development of agriculture (beginning circa 800 BC).

Lebanon City Park

Red symbols indicate locations discussed in this section.
Information
Lodging
Museum
Shopping
Point of interest
Detailed map area
For a complete listing of symbols, see inside back cover.
© Rand McNally
Miamisburg
Germantown
Sunbury
Chautauqua
Carlisle
Poast Town Heights
Franklin
Poast Town
Rickard Acres
West Middletown
Middletown
Stonyrill
Thorny Acres
Miltonville
Locust Grove
Trenton
Buena Vista
South Middletown
Excello
South Excello
Rockdale
Le Sourdsville
Monroe
Maustown
Huntsville
Jericho
Princeton
Bethany
Lakota Hills
Wetherington
Beckett Ridge
Maud
Port Union
Rialto
Olde West Chester
West Chester
Pisgah
Gano
Highpoint
Brecon
Sharonville
Glendale
Evendale
Lincoln Heights
Lockland
Blue Ash
Montgomery
Reading
Remington
Kenwood
Deer Park
Amberley
Silverton
Golf Manor
Madeira
Milford
Camp Dennison
Miamiville
The Village of Indian Hill
Terrace Park
Norwood
Fairfax
Mariemont
Shademore
Romohr Acres
Newtown
Summerside
Summerside Estates
Mount Carmel Heights
Mount Carmel
Turpin Hills
Dry Run
Fernell Heights
Mount Forest Trails
Glen Este
Willowville
Viking Village
Fort Thomas
Forestville
Fruit Hill
Cherry Grove
Withamsville
Olive Branch
Batavia
East Batavia Heights
Owensville
Stonelick
Perintown
Day Heights
Belfast
Wilshire
Mulberry
Mount Repose
Springvale
Eagles Nest
Goshen
Epworth Heights
Branch Hill
Twightwee
Loveland
Twenty Mile Stand
Loveland Park
Murdock
Landen
Socialville
Foster
Maineville
Hopkinsville
Zoar
South Lebanon
Kings Mills
Mason
Hageman
Hillcrest
Lebanon
Otterbien Home
Hunter
Wilshire Heights
Kay
Sterling Heights
Red Lion
Pekin
Flat Iron
Springboro
Five Points
Centerville
Bellview Estates
Bellbrook
Spring Valley
Mount Holly
Lytle
Shartz Road
Crosswick
Waynesville
Corwin
Ridgeville
Utica
Dodds
Harveysburg
Gurneyville
Kingman
Oakland
Genntown
Oregonia
Sligo
Ogden
Clarksville
Senior
Morrow
Roachester
Middleboro
Pansy
Midland
Butlerville
Windsor
Blanchester
Westboro
Pleasant Plain
Cozaddale
Woodville
Shiloh
Edenton
St. Martin
Modest
Fayetteville
To Dayton
To Washington Court House
To Hillsboro
To Cincinnati
MONTGOMERY CO.
BUTLER CO.
WARREN CO.
GREENE CO.
CLINTON CO.
CLERMONT CO.
BROWN CO.
HAMILTON CO.
OHIO
KY
Fort Ancient State Memorial
Morgan's Canoe & Outdoor Centers
Workshops of David T. Smith
Old Main St. Historic District
Caesar Creek State Park
Caesar's Creek Pioneer Village
Little Miami National Scenic River
Great Wolf Lodge
Indoor Waterpark
Paramount's Kings Island
Voice of America Radio Station
Dayton-Wright Brothers Airport
Lebanon Warren County Airport
Lebanon Raceway
Glendower State Memorial
Lebanon
Golden Lamb
Warren Co. Hist. Soc. Mus.
Golden Turtle Factory
Warren County C. & V.B.
Shaker Inn
Glendower State Memorial
Lebanon Mason Monroe (LM&M) Railroad
Harmon
07156MW

What to eat

Folks flock to the **Golden Lamb** for basic American food. Fried chicken is the most popular menu item, while family-style turkey and chicken dinners with all the trimmings draw sell-out crowds of 1,600-plus for Mother's Day and Thanksgiving. Lunches often feature Shaker specialties, such as bean salad, hot chicken salad, and sugar pie.

What to buy

At the **Workshops of David T. Smith** (3600 Shawhan Rd., Morrow), more than 40 artisans produce furniture, pottery, and kitchen cabinetry. Their specialty: careful reproductions of such classic pieces as a tavern table (circa 1760-1820), a Moravian design sugar jar, and a Pennsylvania German cupboard (circa 1720-1780). Chocoholics may want to check out the **Golden Turtle Factory** (120 S. Broadway, Lebanon), where popular items include buckeyes—chocolate-covered peanut butter balls resembling the state's best-known symbol.

What to do

Festival of American Crafts, Morrow, late June.
Ohio Sauerkraut Festival, Waynesville, second full weekend in October.

For more details about these festivals, please see page 174.

Information

Warren County Convention and Visitors Bureau, (800) 791-4386, www.ohio4fun.org.

Lodging tips

For a sense of early American history, reserve a room at Ohio's oldest inn, the **Golden Lamb** (27 S. Broadway). Other options in Lebanon include the 21-room, family-owned **Shaker Inn** (600 Cincinnati Ave.). Warren County offers about a dozen bed-and-breakfasts, while proximity to Kings Island theme park assures a wide variety of accommodations.

Workshops of David T. Smith, Lebanon

From the Cuyahoga **to Cleveland**

Revitalized **Cleveland** offers new generations of city dwellers homes in rehabbed lofts, factories, and warehouses. Galleries and studios, cutting-edge restaurants, lively nightlife, and thriving theater and other performing arts have followed the influx to the urban core. Visitors benefit from Cleveland's rejuvenation, but also enjoy exploring rural retreats along the Cuyahoga River. Hamlets with historic homes and barns dot the river valley framed by deep forests, rolling hills, and open farmlands. Native Americans named the river ka-ih-ogh-ha, which means "crooked," an apt description of the river's 90 twisting, turning miles.

Cuyahoga Valley National Park (15610 Vaughn Rd., Brecksville) preserves 33,000 acres along 22 miles of the Cuyahoga River between Cleveland and **Akron**. Two of many attractions: the tumbling cataracts of **Brandywine Falls** and the **Ohio & Erie Canal Towpath Trail**, which follows the valley alongside meadows, forest, and wetlands. At **Boston Store**, a restored historic structure houses a museum celebrating the area's rich canal boat-building history. The national park's landscapes vary. Pockets of evergreens punctuate hardwood forests; the forest floor features spring woodland wildflowers such as hepaticas and late-summer New England asters. In the wetlands, yellow and blue irises, cattails, and the American lotus bloom. Great blue herons—one of more than 100 species of birds—nest in rookeries high in the trees. Visitors have a chance to discover the landscapes while biking, hiking, golfing, horseback riding, skiing, and sledding.

North Coast Harbor Skyline, Cleveland

Blossom Music Center, Cuyahoga Valley National Park

It's not all nature in the national park. The **Cuyahoga Valley Scenic Railroad** has four boarding sites, in **Independence, Peninsula, Akron,** and Canton; it runs trains from February to December. A variety of excursions range from leisurely trips with unscheduled stops to view wildlife and wetlands, to bike and hike trips with a baggage car equipped to carry bicycles, and trips with rangers on board to discuss indigenous flora and fauna and the valley's history. **Hale Farm & Village** (2686 Oak Hill Rd., Bath), owned and operated by the Western Reserve Historical Society, contains the 1826 farmstead of Jonathan Hale, one of the region's earliest settlers. Through first-person interpretation, potters, blacksmiths, spinners, weavers, candlemakers, and glassblowers demonstrate crafts of the mid-19th century. They populate a village comprised of historic building from the region.

On pleasant summer evenings, folk from Cleveland and nearby Akron head for **Blossom Music Center** at Cuyahoga Falls (1145 W. Steels Corners Rd.). They spread out blankets, unfold chairs, and unpack picnic hampers as they prepare for a concert in a natural grass amphitheater under the stars (or in reserved pavilion seating). The estimable Cleveland Orchestra calls Blossom its summer home; the center also hosts jazz, pop, rock, and country music concerts.

Contrary to its rough-and-ready, blue-collar image, Cleveland can be a cultured, even black-tie kind of town. An important center for arts and entertainment, its orchestra regularly performs in Europe and at Carnegie Hall, and its two opera companies recently merged (2006) into Opera Cleveland, with performances at the **Cleveland Play House** and **Playhouse Square Center**. **University Circle**, gathering the nation's largest concentration of cultural arts and educational institutions within one square mile, hosts Severance Hall, where the Cleveland Orchestra performs.

Designed by renowned architect I.M. Pei, the **Rock & Roll Hall of Fame and Museum** (1 Key Plaza) pays homage to rock and its origins and derivatives. This vast music museum requires a good chunk of time to see. Whether it is viewing John Lennon's hand-written drafts of Beatles' classics or listening to the sweet harmony of the Ink Spots, it quickly engrosses even casual visitors. You'll find Madonna's gold stage costume from her Blonde Ambition tour, Bono's black "Fly" costume from U2's Zoo-TV tour, and historic early recordings, circa 1920, of Bessie Smith.

In the heart of downtown, the **Historic Warehouse District** throbs nightly with trendy restaurants, lounges, bars, and nightclubs. Similar nightlife hubs: the **Historic Gateway Neighborhood** and East Fourth Street, anchored by a branch of House of Blues. A downtown jewel is the renovated **Cleveland Arcade** (420 Superior Ave.). Dating from 1890, this five-story soaring atrium building with skylights is anchored by two nine-story towers and features ornamented brass and iron throughout. A Hyatt Regency hotel occupies the top three stories of the atrium and the towers, while the two lower atrium floors host typical mall shops.

Historic Warehouse District, Cleveland

What to eat

Stop for breakfast or lunch at Cleveland's colorful **West Side Market** (W 25th St. & Lorain Ave.), a cacophonous, aromatic old-world-style food bazaar, with an original red-tile floor and landmark medieval clock tower. Many booths have been in the same family for generations. Nearly 200 merchants represent a variety of ethnic groups and offer fresh produce, meats, cheeses, baked goods, and a range of specialty foods from pierogies to cannolies, kielbasa to bludwurst, in a vibrant, friendly setting.

What to buy

The name of this kitschy Cleveland shop says it all: **Big Fun** (1814 Coventry Rd.). Built for browsing and likely to prompt nostalgic memories, it's packed with collectibles, from lunch boxes and inflatable advertising gimmicks, to GI Joe's and classic toys (originals and reproductions). Prices range from a buck or so to hundreds of dollars.

What to do

Parade the Circle Celebration, Cleveland, June.
Twins Days Festival, Twinsburg,
first full weekend in August.
For more details about these festivals, please see page 174.

Information

The Convention and Visitors Bureau of Greater Cleveland, (800) 321-1001, www.travelcleveland.com.

Lodging tips

Stay in the heart of Cleveland's revitalized neighborhoods by checking into the **Hyatt Regency Cleveland at the Arcade** (420 Superior Ave.). It has 293 guestrooms, fitness center, state-of-the-art business amenities, and fine-dining restaurant, 1890 at the Arcade that is itself fast becoming a destination. The **Hilton Garden Inn Cleveland Downtown** (1100 Carnegie Ave.) offers 240 rooms and is across the street from Jacobs Field, home to the Cleveland Indians.

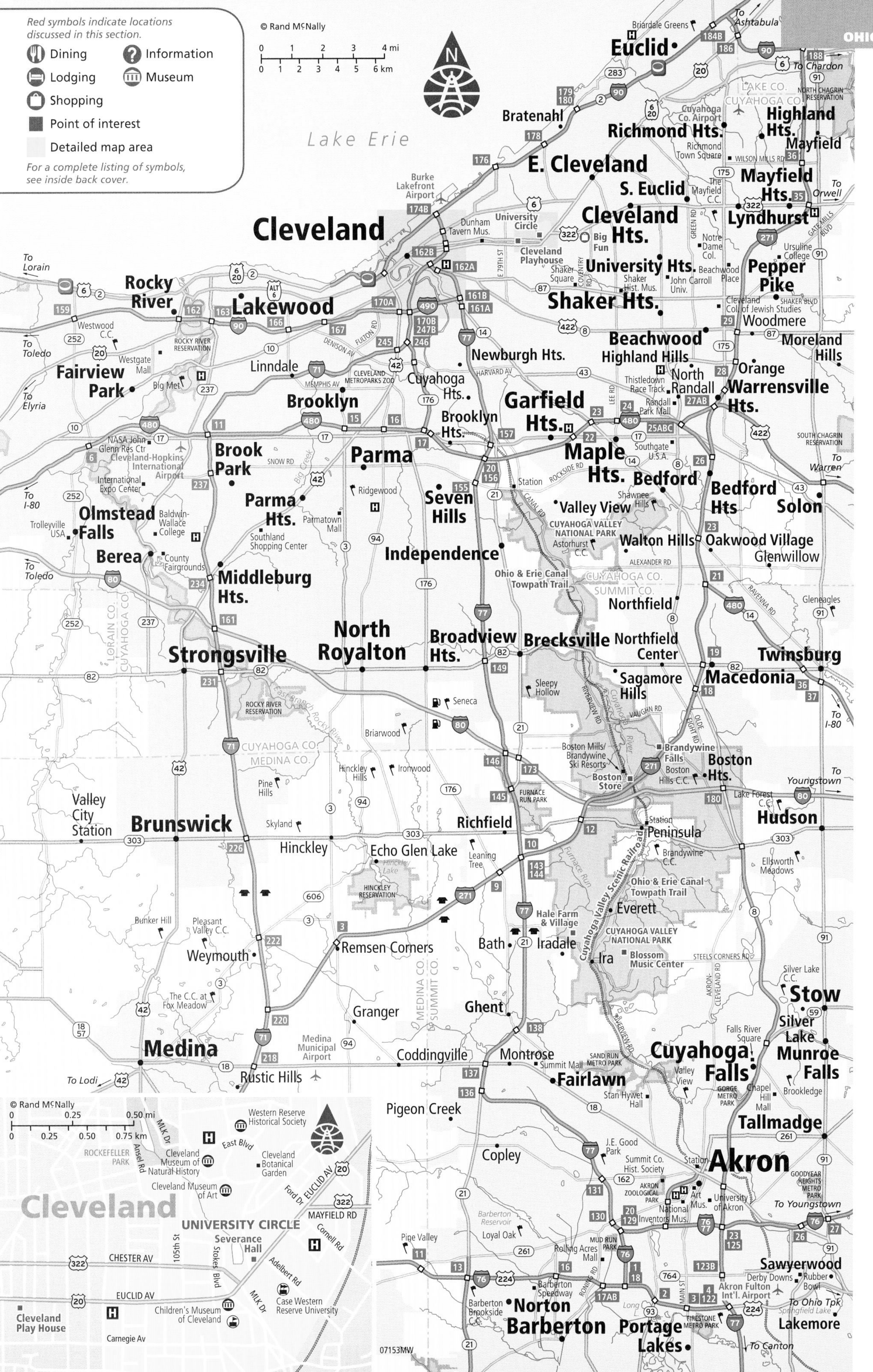
Red symbols indicate locations discussed in this section.
Dining
Information
Lodging
Museum
Shopping
Point of interest
Detailed map area
For a complete listing of symbols, see inside back cover.
© Rand McNally
Lake Erie
Cleveland
Euclid
Bratenahl
Richmond Hts.
Highland Hts.
Mayfield
E. Cleveland
S. Euclid
Mayfield Hts.
Cleveland Hts.
Lyndhurst
University Hts.
Pepper Pike
Shaker Hts.
Woodmere
Rocky River
Lakewood
Beachwood
Moreland Hills
Highland Hills
North Randall
Orange
Warrensville Hts.
Fairview Park
Linndale
Newburgh Hts.
Cuyahoga Hts.
Brooklyn
Garfield Hts.
Brooklyn Hts.
Maple Hts.
Brook Park
Parma
Bedford
Bedford Hts
Solon
Parma Hts.
Seven Hills
Valley View
Olmstead Falls
Walton Hills
Oakwood Village
Glenwillow
Berea
Independence
Middleburg Hts.
Northfield
North Royalton
Broadview Hts.
Brecksville
Northfield Center
Twinsburg
Strongsville
Sagamore Hills
Macedonia
Boston Hts.
Valley City Station
Brunswick
Richfield
Hudson
Hinckley
Echo Glen Lake
Peninsula
Everett
Weymouth
Remsen Corners
Bath
Iradale
Ira
Stow
Granger
Ghent
Silver Lake
Medina
Coddingville
Montrose
Cuyahoga Falls
Munroe Falls
Rustic Hills
Fairlawn
Pigeon Creek
Tallmadge
Copley
Akron
Sawyerwood
Norton
Barberton
Portage Lakes
Lakemore
CUYAHOGA VALLEY NATIONAL PARK
Ohio & Erie Canal Towpath Trail
Cuyahoga Valley Scenic Railroad
University Circle
Cleveland
UNIVERSITY CIRCLE
Western Reserve Historical Society
Cleveland Museum of Natural History
Cleveland Botanical Garden
Cleveland Museum of Art
Severance Hall
Case Western Reserve University
Children's Museum of Cleveland
Cleveland Play House
MAYFIELD RD
CHESTER AV
EUCLID AV
Carnegie Av
07153MW

Island-hopping on Lake Erie

Islands have their own rhythms, often several beats slower simply because people find themselves no longer in a hurry to get somewhere else. A good example: Kelleys Island, 2,800 acres of serene countryside and part of the Lake Erie islands archipelago. Boutiques, restaurants, and pubs cluster close to the village ferry docks. Golf carts, rentable by the hour, day, or week, are a fun way to explore. You also can rent a bicycle (or bring your own). Travel inland for a stop at **Glacial Grooves National Landmark** to see where a glacier scored limestone rocks about 18,000 years ago.

South Bass Island, home to the village of **Put-in-Bay**, is the most developed of Lake Erie's islands. As you travel the busy thoroughfares of popular Put-in-Bay, you'll hear music and singing escaping from a clutch of lively bars. There's a natural phenomenon here, too. **Heineman's Winery** (978 Catawba Ave.) offers tours of **Crystal Cave**, 35 feet below the surface and the largest known geode in the world. Hollow rocks lined with crystal or mineral deposits, geodes are usually seen in their fist-sized form. Crystal Cave stretches 30 feet across at its widest point and contains tons of crystals. At the surface, be sure to sample Heineman's award-winning Vidal Blanc.

Sailing regatta at Put-in-Bay

Perry's Victory and International Peace Memorial (93 Delaware Ave.) commemorates those who fought a pivotal battle in the War of 1812, as well as long-standing peace between the U.S., Great Britain, and Canada. On September 10, 1813, Commodore Oliver Hazard Perry defeated and captured a British fleet just a few miles northwest of Put-in-Bay. He also contributed to naval history one of its most enduring quotations: "We have met the enemy and they are ours ..." A landmark visible for miles, the 352-foot-tall memorial was built between 1912 and 1915 of pink granite topped by an 11-ton bronze urn. What does 352 feet mean? The Doric column reaches 47 feet taller than the Statue of Liberty's torch tip. An elevator takes visitors to an observation deck offering splendid views of the battle site and neighboring islands, as well as Canada, Cleveland, and Detroit on very clear days.

Catawba Avenue shops, Put-in-Bay

One of those islands is Middle Bass, another spot to find serenity. Cottages with private beaches and some campsites offer limited accommodations. Charter fishing for walleye and bass are popular. Ferry options abound for traveling between the mainland and the islands as well as for inter-island travel. You can ferry your car, though many prefer bicycles and golf carts for island travel.

Back on the mainland, **Lakeside** (founded in 1873) is a Chautauqua-style community dedicated to fostering Christian values in a lakeside vacation setting. Visitors settle into historic lodgings—or rent vacation houses or cottages—and spend time enjoying cultural and religious events and a range of recreational activities, from sailing lessons and bicycling on rental machines to fishing for Lake Erie's legendary walleye. Lakeside is a time-warp town where tidy Victorian cottages line narrow, leafy streets leading to a lakefront park and an ornate pavilion. Enjoy a treat at the ice-cream parlors, see family movies at a 1920s movie theater, drop a line off the fishing pier, and keep an eye open for community cookouts and impromptu sing-alongs on lakefront lawns.

At one time, more than 20 lighthouses dotted Ohio's Lake Erie shore. About half of these are gone or are in ruins. Those that remain cast a nostalgic light on days gone by, when steamers plied the waters and grand resorts graced the islands and the lakeshore. The oldest: **Marblehead Lighthouse** (110 Lighthouse Dr., Marblehead), completed in 1821, the third built on Lake Erie, and the oldest continuously operating light on the Great Lakes. Climb the 77-step spiral staircase to the lookout; visit a museum located in the keeper's house and operated by the Marblehead Lighthouse Historical Society; picnic on the grounds, enjoying views of Sandusky Bay and the islands. It's located in **Marblehead Lighthouse State Park**.

Sandusky's main claim to fame is **Cedar Point** (One Cedar Point Dr.), with its swimming beach and amusement park with 16 roller coasters (including its famed wooden models) and other extreme thrill rides. **Sandusky** also serves as home port for a number of ferries and excursion boats, including occasional service to Pelee Island, largest of the Lake Erie islands and a part of Canada.

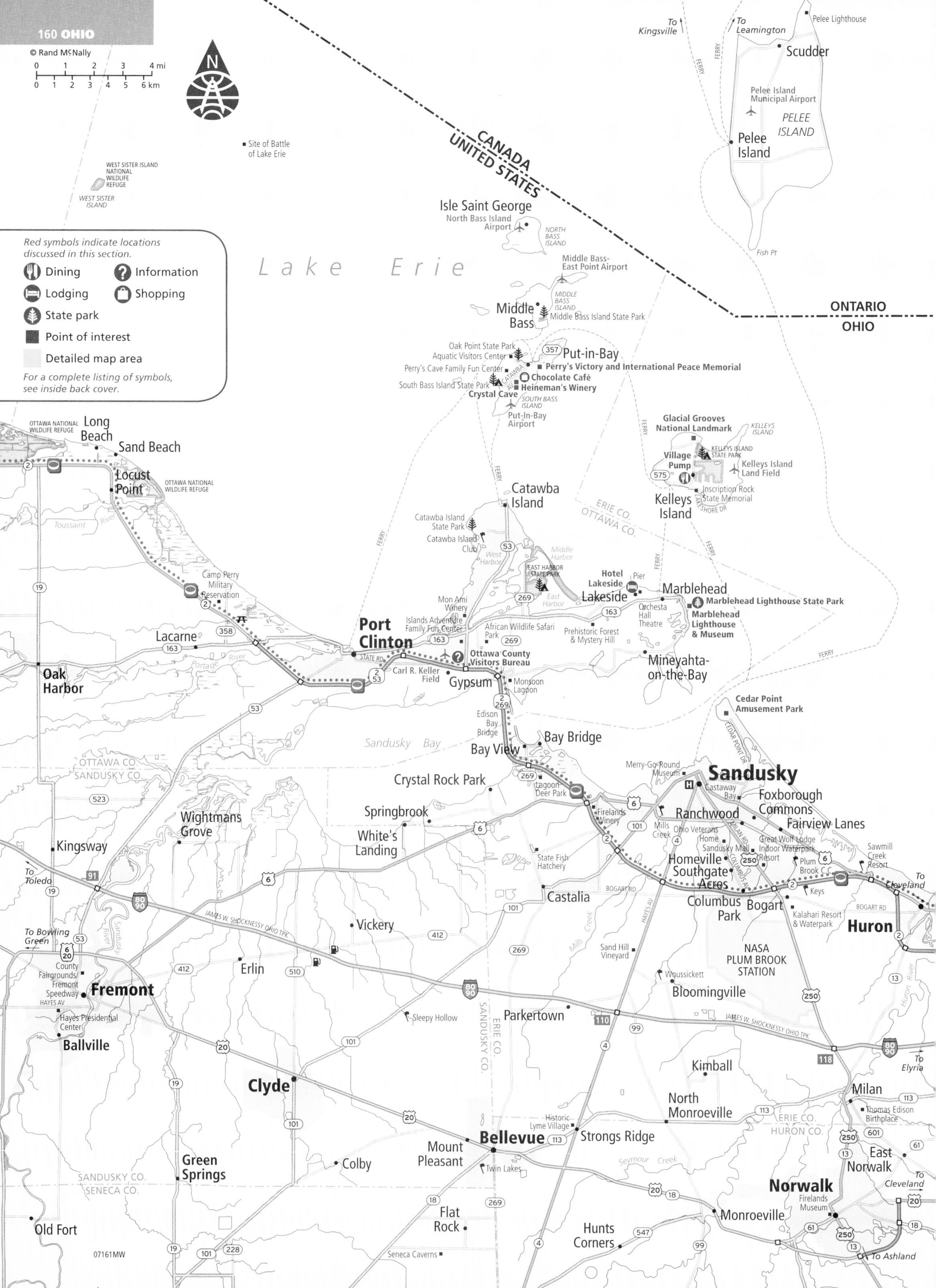
© Rand McNally
0 1 2 3 4 mi
0 1 2 3 4 5 6 km
N
Red symbols indicate locations discussed in this section.
Dining
Information
Lodging
Shopping
State park
Point of interest
Detailed map area
For a complete listing of symbols, see inside back cover.
Lake Erie
CANADA
UNITED STATES
ONTARIO
OHIO
To Kingsville
To Leamington
Pelee Lighthouse
Scudder
Pelee Island Municipal Airport
PELEE ISLAND
Pelee Island
Fish Pt
FERRY
Site of Battle of Lake Erie
WEST SISTER ISLAND NATIONAL WILDLIFE REFUGE
WEST SISTER ISLAND
Isle Saint George
North Bass Island Airport
NORTH BASS ISLAND
Middle Bass-East Point Airport
MIDDLE BASS ISLAND
Middle Bass
Middle Bass Island State Park
Oak Point State Park
Aquatic Visitors Center
Perry's Cave Family Fun Center
South Bass Island State Park
Crystal Cave
Put-in-Bay
Perry's Victory and International Peace Memorial
Chocolate Café
Heineman's Winery
SOUTH BASS ISLAND
Put-In-Bay Airport
CATAWBA AV
Glacial Grooves National Landmark
KELLEYS ISLAND
KELLEYS ISLAND STATE PARK
Village Pump
Kelleys Island Land Field
Inscription Rock State Memorial
LAKESHORE DR
Kelleys Island
ERIE CO.
OTTAWA CO.
OTTAWA NATIONAL WILDLIFE REFUGE
Long Beach
Sand Beach
Locust Point
Toussaint River
Catawba Island
Catawba Island State Park
Catawba Island Club
West Harbor
Middle Harbor
EAST HARBOR STATE PARK
East Harbor
Hotel Lakeside
Pier
Lakeside
Marblehead
Marblehead Lighthouse State Park
Marblehead Lighthouse & Museum
Orchesta Hall Theatre
Prehistoric Forest & Mystery Hill
Mineyahta-on-the-Bay
Camp Perry Military Reservation
Mon Ami Winery
Islands Adventure Family Fun Center
African Wildlife Safari Park
Lacarne
Portage River
Port Clinton
STATE RD
Ottawa County Visitors Bureau
Carl R. Keller Field
Gypsum
Monsoon Lagoon
Oak Harbor
Edison Bay Bridge
Sandusky Bay
Bay Bridge
Bay View
Cedar Point Amusement Park
CEDAR POINT DR
OTTAWA CO.
SANDUSKY CO.
Crystal Rock Park
Lagoon Deer Park
Merry-Go-Round Museum
Sandusky
Castaway Bay
Foxborough Commons
Ranchwood
Fairview Lanes
Firelands Winery
Mills Creek
Ohio Veterans Home
Great Wolf Lodge
Sandusky Mall
Indoor Waterpark Resort
Homeville
Southgate Acres
Plum Brook C.C.
Sawmill Creek Resort
Keys
To Cleveland
Wightmans Grove
Springbrook
White's Landing
Kingsway
To Toledo
State Fish Hatchery
Castalia
BOGART RD
Columbus Park
Bogart
Kalahari Resort & Waterpark
Huron
HAYES AV
COLUMBUS AV
MILAN RD
JAMES W. SHOCKNESSY OHIO TPK
Vickery
To Bowling Green
Sandusky River
County Fairgrounds/ Fremont Speedway
Fremont
HAYES AV
Hayes Presidential Center
Ballville
Erlin
Mills Creek
Sand Hill Vineyard
NASA PLUM BROOK STATION
Wussickett
Bloomingville
Huron River
Sleepy Hollow
Parkertown
SANDUSKY CO.
ERIE CO.
To Elyria
Kimball
Milan
Thomas Edison Birthplace
Clyde
North Monroeville
ERIE CO.
HURON CO.
Historic Lyme Village
Strongs Ridge
Bellevue
Mount Pleasant
Twin Lakes
Seymour Creek
East Norwalk
Green Springs
Colby
SANDUSKY CO.
SENECA CO.
Norwalk
Firelands Museum
To Cleveland
Flat Rock
Monroeville
Hunts Corners
Old Fort
Seneca Caverns
To Ashland
07161MW

What to eat

Fishing Lake Erie for walleye, bass, and perch is legendary—which makes it an ideal location to sample a perch dinner or perch sandwich. These are specialties of the **Village Pump** (103 W. Lakeshore Dr.,) on Kelleys Island, where hand-dipped onion rings are a favored accompaniment.

What to buy

Please a chocolate-fancier with a gift from the Put-in-Bay branch of the estimable South Bend Chocolate Company's **Chocolate Café** (820 W. Catawba St.). The café offers coffee and chocolate drinks, while a museum chronicles the 2,000-year-old history of chocolate. The Indiana chocolatier offers more than 100 different kinds of chocolates and a gift shop that sells glassware, T-shirts, books, and other chocolate-related items.

What to do

Historical Weekend at Put-in-Bay, Put-in-Bay, September.

Marblehead Lighthouse Festival, Marblehead, October.

For more details about these festivals, please see page 174.

Information

Ottawa County Visitors Bureau,
(800) 441-1271, www.lake-erie.com.

Lodging tips

Bed-and-breakfast inns are a popular lodging choice on the islands, while the mainland has a wide range of motels, hotels, and full-service resorts. Lakeside contains more than half a dozen bed-and-breakfast inns, many in 19th-century houses, and also has the **Hotel Lakeside** (236 Walnut Ave.), offering 70 guest rooms. Built in 1874, it is a restored Victorian hostelry overlooking Lake Erie.

The Chocolate Café and Museum, Put-in-Bay

Cranberry Country Caper

The countryside around **Wisconsin Rapids** takes its color cue from the thousands of acres of cranberry marshes for which the region is famous. Summer brings a carpet of dainty pink blossoms; in fall, bright red berries bob on the surface. Winter is the season when the marshes wear a white mantel and project a stark beauty.

Wisconsin, a national leader in cranberry farming, produces about 375 million pounds annually—more than one-half of the cranberries that Americans consume. Cultivation began in Wisconsin in the mid-19th century, but long before that Native Americans used cranberries to dye blankets and rugs and make pemmican, a winter staple of fruit and dried meat. Some marshes have successfully produced crops for more than a century.

In fall, motorists enjoy traveling the **"Cranberry Highway,"** perhaps stopping for a cranberry shake at **Herschleb's Restaurant & Ice Cream** (640 16th St. N., Wisconsin Rapids), a cranberry muffin at the **Hotel Mead** (see Lodging Tips), or some "cran-jack" cheese, studded with dried fruit, at **Wisconsin Dairy State Cheese Company** (6860 WI 34, Rudolph). The self-guided route runs almost 50 miles alongside marshland, historic sites, museums, markets, shops, and restaurants. An outline of the route is available from www.visitwisrapids.com. A companion route, the "Cranberry Biking Trail," takes bicyclists on a 29-mile journey. At harvest time (late September through early November), stop at the visitor center of **Glacial Lake Cranberries** (2480 County Rd. D) for history, videos, cranberry gifts, and tours of one of the oldest cranberry marshes in central Wisconsin.

Cranberry harvest

Fall is also prime time for bird watching. Geese and other migratory waterfowl head south for the winter, their sheer numbers darkening skies of Midwest flyways. Many stop to rest and feed at **Necedah National Wildlife Refuge** (four miles west of **Necedah** on WI 21). Every autumn, this 43,696-acre preserve attracts thousands of migrating Canada geese, tundra swans, canvasbacks, mallards, teal, and a variety of other species. Visitors drive miles of roads that thread through the refuge. The best month for viewing: October. The refuge is part of the Great Central Wisconsin Swamp, created 10,000 years ago by retreating glaciers. This complex of wetlands, open lands, and woodlands provides a splendid habitat for wildlife, including many endangered species. The southernmost gray wolf habitat in Wisconsin, it's also a refuge for bald eagles, black bear, wild turkeys, ruffed grouse, and an abundance of white-tailed deer. Sandhill cranes are common on the refuge and can be seen near wetlands or in open fields. They arrive in March and depart for warmer climates in October and November.

Whooping crane at Necedah National Wildlife Refuge

Golfers tired of shelling out hefty greens fees will appreciate the lower costs at the region's championship courses. At **The Ridges Golf Course** in Wisconsin Rapids (2311 Griffith Ave.), golfers pay only $42 in the summer ($26-$35 in fall) to play an 18-hole course with challenging elevations and plenty of water and woods—white birch, green willows, and tall pines. Sit in the clubhouse restaurant and watch golfers tee-off on the back nine with a shot that begins on an 80-foot-high ridge overlooking a tree-flanked valley, Buena Vista Creek snaking across the valley floor.

The Pines course at the **Lake Arrowhead Resort** complex (1195 Apache Ln., Rome), ranked by *Golf Digest* as one of the best golf values in America, charges only $50 per round ($32 during off-peak seasons). Lofty oaks and pines flank its fairways, which are dotted with five water holes.

Winter brings solitude to the cranberry marshes and stillness to the countryside. Diversions include snowshoeing, winter hiking, and excellent cross-country skiing on hundreds of miles of well-marked trails. **Powers Bluff County Park's** winter sports area (6990 Bluff Dr., Arpin), a 160-acre park 17 miles northwest of Wisconsin Rapids, offers downhill and cross-country skiing, tubing, snowmobiling, and snowshoeing. A two-story stone shelter contains a warming house with concessions and ski and snowboarding rentals. A delightful winter getaway spot, **The Stone Cottage** (see Lodging Tips) stands on the grounds of Glacial Lake Cranberries. It sits in the historic township of Cranmoor, about 15 miles west of Wisconsin Rapids along the Cranberry Highway. The estate has been in the family of Phil and Mary Brown for more than a century, and its cozy Stone Cottage, with a wood-burning fireplace and screened porch, offers a one-of-a-kind escape. At its doorstep lies a vast expanse of cranberry marshes, excellent for cross-country skiing, snowshoeing, and hiking. Typical Wisconsin wildlife—white-tailed deer, wild turkeys—can be spotted during quiet sojourns across the snow.

The Stone Cottage

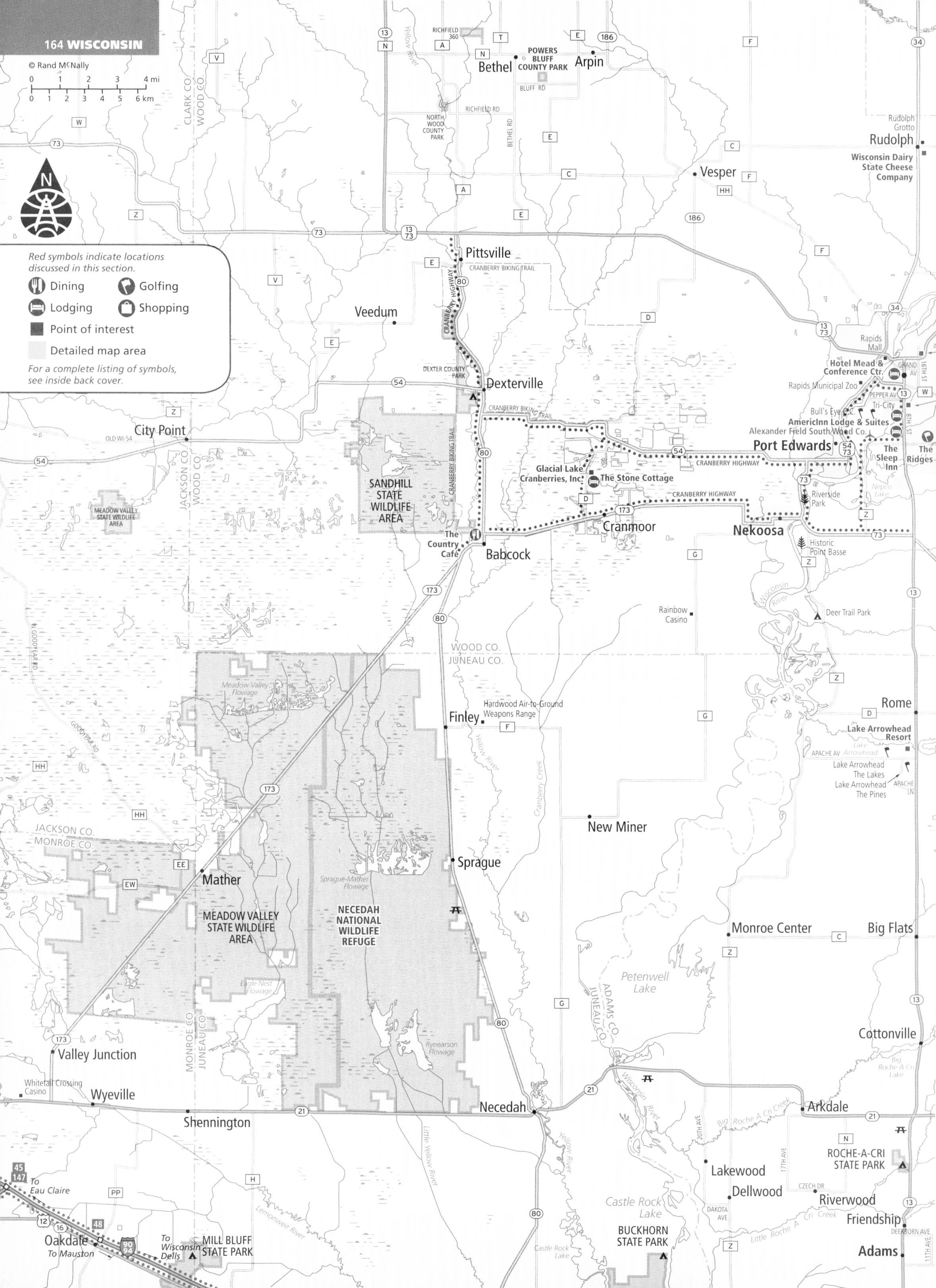

© Rand McNally
Red symbols indicate locations discussed in this section.
Dining
Golfing
Lodging
Shopping
Point of interest
Detailed map area
For a complete listing of symbols, see inside back cover.
Bethel
Arpin
POWERS BLUFF COUNTY PARK
NORTH WOOD COUNTY PARK
Rudolph
Rudolph Grotto
Wisconsin Dairy State Cheese Company
Vesper
Pittsville
CRANBERRY BIKING TRAIL
CRANBERRY HIGHWAY
Veedum
Rapids Mall
Hotel Mead & Conference Ctr.
DEXTER COUNTY PARK
Dexterville
Rapids Municipal Zoo
Tri-City
Bull's Eye C.C.
AmericInn Lodge & Suites
Alexander Field South Wood Co.
City Point
Port Edwards
The Sleep Inn
The Ridges
Glacial Lake Cranberries, Inc.
The Stone Cottage
SANDHILL STATE WILDLIFE AREA
MEADOW VALLEY STATE WILDLIFE AREA
Riverside Park
Cranmoor
Nekoosa
The Country Café
Babcock
Historic Point Basse
Rainbow Casino
Deer Trail Park
Wisconsin River
WOOD CO.
JUNEAU CO.
Meadow Valley Flowage
Rome
Hardwood Air-to-Ground Weapons Range
Finley
Lake Arrowhead Resort
Lake Arrowhead The Lakes
Lake Arrowhead The Pines
Yellow River
Cranberry Creek
New Miner
JACKSON CO.
MONROE CO.
Sprague
Mather
Sprague-Mather Flowage
MEADOW VALLEY STATE WILDLIFE AREA
NECEDAH NATIONAL WILDLIFE REFUGE
Monroe Center
Big Flats
Petenwell Lake
Eagle Nest Flowage
ADAMS CO.
JUNEAU CO.
Cottonville
Valley Junction
Rynearson Flowage
Big Roche A Cri Lake
Whitetail Crossing Casino
Wyeville
Necedah
Arkdale
Shennington
Big Roche A Cri Creek
ROCHE-A-CRI STATE PARK
Lakewood
Dellwood
Riverwood
To Eau Claire
Little Yellow River
Castle Rock Lake
Friendship
Oakdale
To Mauston
To Wisconsin Dells
MILL BLUFF STATE PARK
Lemonweir River
BUCKHORN STATE PARK
Castle Rock Lake
Little Roche A Cri Creek
Adams

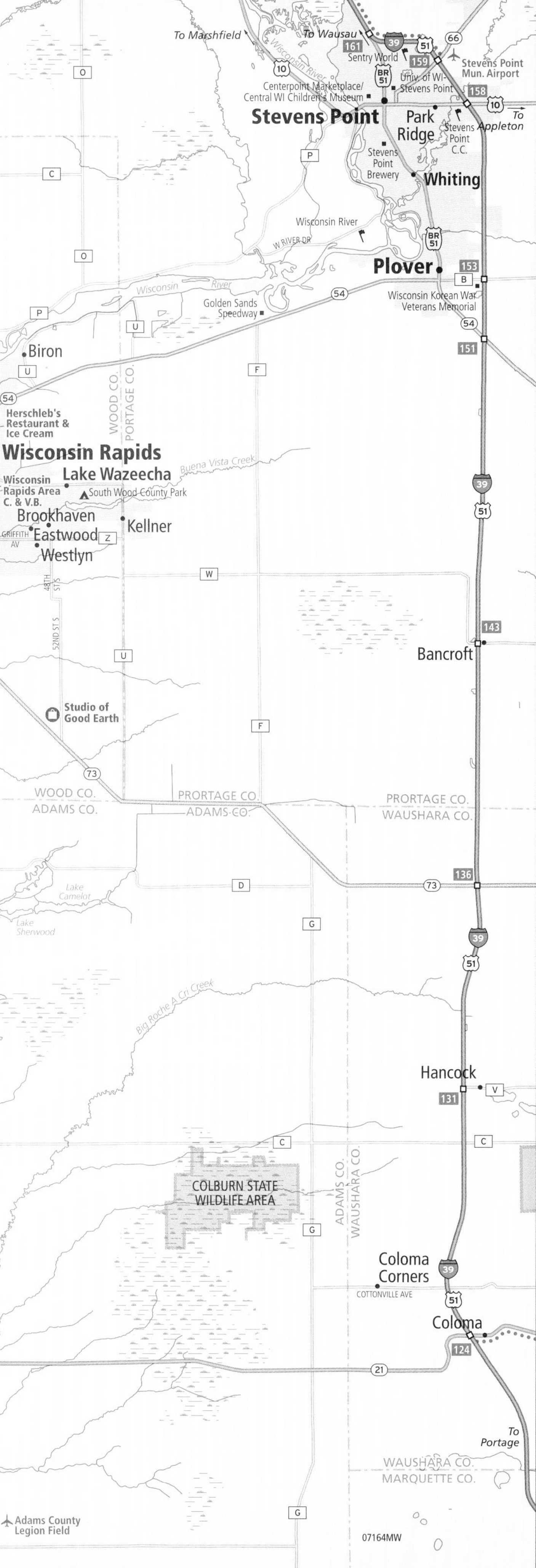

What to eat

If you'd like to eat the local food and support the local economy, the byword is, of course, cranberries. Choices include cranberry shakes, cranberry muffins, and cranberry-walnut pie (a fall favorite). Find these specialties at **The Country Café** at **Babcock** (1699 WI 80), known for its cranberry/raisin pies and cranberry muffins, and **Hotel Mead**, where the cranberry French toast is ambrosial.

What to buy

Shoppers will find it well worth the effort to search out the **Studio of Good Earth** (12410 52nd St. S., Wisconsin Rapids). Operated by William and Annette Gudim, it offers the work of more than 45 artists and craftspeople (including the Gudims themselves), ranging from paintings, calligraphy, and baskets to weavings, handmade paper, and stained glass. Prices are remarkably lower than those at well-traveled resorts. Take time to enjoy the Gudims' beautiful flower gardens.

What to do

Ice Harvest, Nekoosa, late January.
Giant Pumpkin Festival, Nekoosa, first weekend in October.
For more details about these festivals, please see page 174.

Information

Wisconsin Rapids Area Convention and Visitors Bureau, (800) 554-4484, www.visitwisrapids.com.

Lodging tips

The luxurious **Hotel Mead and Conference Center** (451 E. Grand Ave.), built with paper-industry money and managed by Marcus Hotels and Resorts, is as fine a hostelry as you'll find outside a major metropolitan area. After a $14-million renovation and addition, it offers 157 indulgent guestrooms and suites, two restaurants, and an indoor pool, sauna, and fitness center. Also recommended: **The Sleep Inn** and **AmericInn Lodge & Suites**. All three are in Wisconsin Rapids. For a totally offbeat lodging choice, consider **The Stone Cottage** (2480 County Rd. D) about 15 miles west of town, a peaceful retreat that sleeps four.

Rambling through
Rambler's Birthplace

Most motorists driving the interstate between Chicago and Milwaukee feel neither need nor inclination to travel the half-dozen miles or so east to **Racine** and **Kenosha**. More's the pity, because these towns, tucked away in southeast Wisconsin along the Lake Michigan shoreline, hold some of the region's best-kept travel secrets.

Art lovers welcomed the 2003 opening of the **Racine Art Museum** (441 Main St.), which incorporates a former bank building (famously robbed in 1933 by John Dillinger). Parts of the original building date from the Civil War, and the new museum is a striking adaptation of urban space. At night, it glows like a lantern, thanks to the back-lit transluscent acrylic panels that wrap it. The museum holds the nation's largest collections of contemporary jewelry and ceramic teapots as well as one of North America's most extensive contemporary basket collections.

A natural gem: Racine's **North Beach** (Michigan Blvd. & Kewaunee St.), covering 46 acres and offering 3,400 feet of sandy shoreline. Awarded "Blue Wave" certification from the Clean Beaches Council as clean, healthy, and environmentally well managed, it's the only beach in the state to receive that designation.

With a flowing cloak and a leonine mane of white hair, Frank Lloyd Wright burst upon the scene in 1930s Racine, flattering H.F. Johnson and snatching away from another architect the job of designing company headquarters. The result is the **SC Johnson Wax Administration Building** (1525 Howe St.), built from 1936 to 1939, which attracts Wright devotees from around the world. It features a forest of dendriform columns and 43 miles of glass tubing for both natural and artificial light, and contains Wright-designed furniture.

Racine waterfront

SC Johnson Wax Administration Building, Racine

Also on site are a 153-foot cantilevered research tower and the **Golden Rondelle**, which originally stood on the site of the 1964-1965 New York's World's Fair. The Taliesen architectural group, founded by Wright, redesigned it to complement existing Wright buildings. Tours are available by reservation. Wright also designed the Johnson family home, regarded as the last of the architect's "prairie homes" and now incorporated into the **Wingspread Conference Center**. Located north of the city, it's open to limited tours (Tuesday-Thursday only) when no conference is in session.

Racine, once an important point for slaves fleeing to Canada, is creating the "Underground Railroad Heritage Trail," with sites and commemorative markers. The language of freedom comes into subtle play with a display of patterned quilts at the **Racine Arts Council** (505 Sixth Street). Some say the quilts contained hidden messages in the design and were hung on clotheslines or in windows to provide advice, directions, inspiration, and resolve to runaway slaves. Racine quilters have replicated quilts "encoded" with navigational themes such as a log cabin pattern to indicate a safe house.

On selected dates during the year, visitors give their stairclimbers a rest and opt to do the Tour to the Top, a climb up 144 steps to the top of **Wind Point Lighthouse** (4725 Lighthouse Dr., between Three and Four Mile Rds.). It's the oldest and tallest lighthouse on Lake Michigan, and climbers can venture out on its catwalk to enjoy the view. Twelve people are permitted to climb the stairs every 20 minutes, from 10 a.m. to 4 p.m. The event raises funds to preserve and maintain the 108-foot structure, which was built in 1880. Reservations are accepted at (262) 639-3524.

Visitors "of a certain age" from Toronto, Pittsburgh, Cincinnati, and Chicago may experience déjà vu when they see streetcars, circa 1951, clanking along Kenosha's revitalized lakefront. Refurbished and repainted, they sport the original color schemes of streetcars in those cities. One bears the orange-and-white design of the Electric Streetcar Circulator system that served Kenosha from the 1930s to the 1950s.

In 2001, the **Kenosha Public Museum** (5500 First Ave.) got a new home. After 67 years in an old post office building, it moved into brand-new quarters. With a towering copper-and-glass lobby, the museum is an architectural metaphor of a glacier cutting through the Wisconsin landscape. Permanent exhibits focus on the Wisconsin story beginning 425 million years ago and continuing through the early 1800s. Visitors walk through a timeline of galleries, experiencing the flora, fauna, and people of the region through millions of years of history. Highlights include the Schaefer mammoth, locally excavated in 1992-93 and documented as the earliest evidence of mammoth-human interaction east of the Mississippi River and one of the earliest sites in the Americas.

Another newcomer to the harbor front is the **Kenosha History Center** (220 51st Pl.), opened in 2001. It chronicles the golden days of Kenosha's auto-making history, when the city was home to the Jeffery, Nash, and American Motors Corp. car manufacturers. One gallery salutes local production of the enormously popular Rambler. Adjoining the museum is historic 1866 **Southport Light Station**, where restoration continues on the lighthouse and the keeper's dwelling.

What to eat

No trip to this region is complete without sampling kringle, the original Danish pastry. In the late 19th century, Racine County was among the most prominent Danish-settled regions of the United States. Populated by many family-run Danish bakeries, West Racine became known as "Kringleville." A handful remain, including **Larsen Bakery** (3311 Washington Ave.) and **O & H Danish Bakery** (1841 Douglas Ave./ 4006 Durand Ave.). Kringles are delicately flaky, made with up to a dozen layers of buttery pastry. Shaped into a ring, they're filled with nuts, custard, and fruit such as apples, apricots, cherries, prunes, or various berries, then topped with creamy icing or glazed sugar.

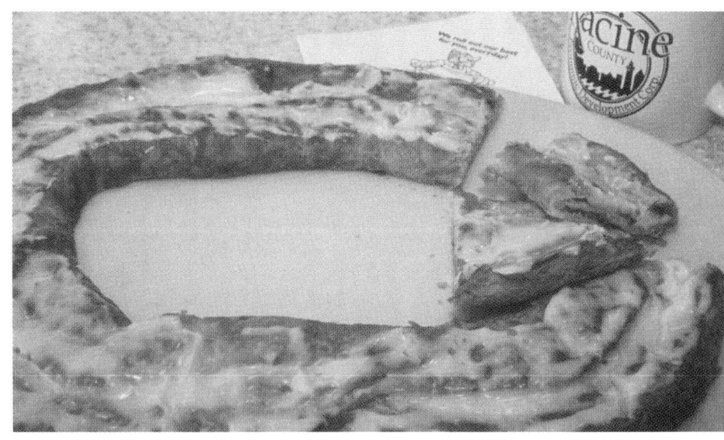

Kringle

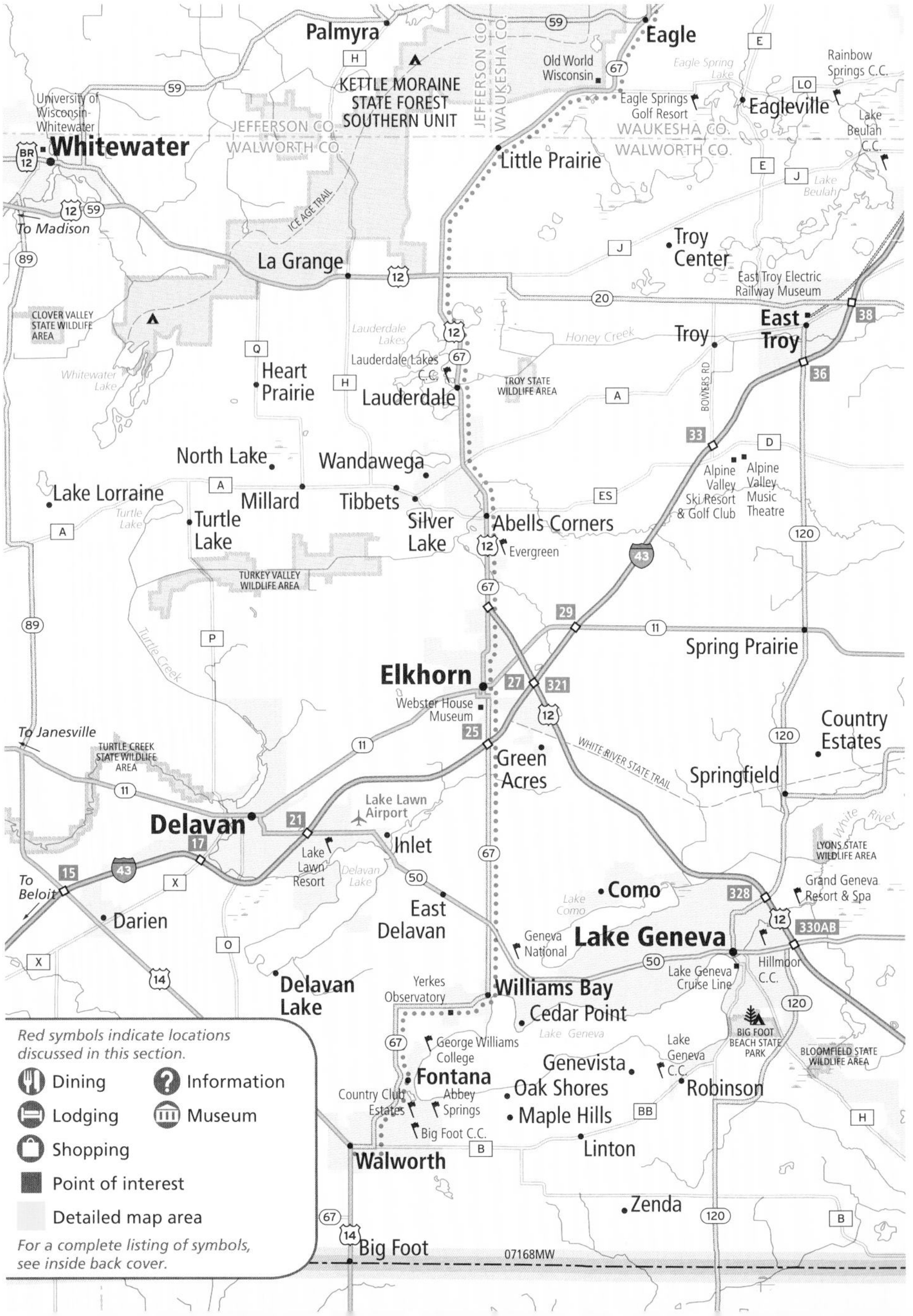

Red symbols indicate locations discussed in this section.

Dining · Information · Lodging · Museum · Shopping · Point of interest · Detailed map area

For a complete listing of symbols, see inside back cover.

07168MW

What to buy

The **Racine Art Museum** store is well worth a stop. While many museum stores stock only reproductions of artwork displayed in the galleries, this shop—because RAM focuses on contemporary artists—offers original work. Also check out the unusual garden ornaments and decorating accessories, including dried and silk arrangements, at **Milaeger's** (4838 Douglas Ave., Racine), one of the Midwest's largest nurseries.

What to do

Great Midwest Dragon Boat Festival, Racine, July.
Great Lakes Brew Fest, Racine, September.
For more details about these festivals, please see page 174.

Information

Racine County Convention and Visitors Bureau, (800) 272-2463, www.racine.org.
Kenosha Area Convention & Visitors Bureau, (800) 654-7309, www.kenoshacvb.com.

Lodging tips

For lodging with harbor views, choose the **Radisson Inn Harbourwalk** (233 Gaslight Circle, Racine), where you can watch glorious sunrises (request a lakeview room) and swim in an indoor pool with picture windows looking out onto the water. Racine and Kenosha are well stocked with hotel/motel chains and have a handful of bed-and-breakfasts.

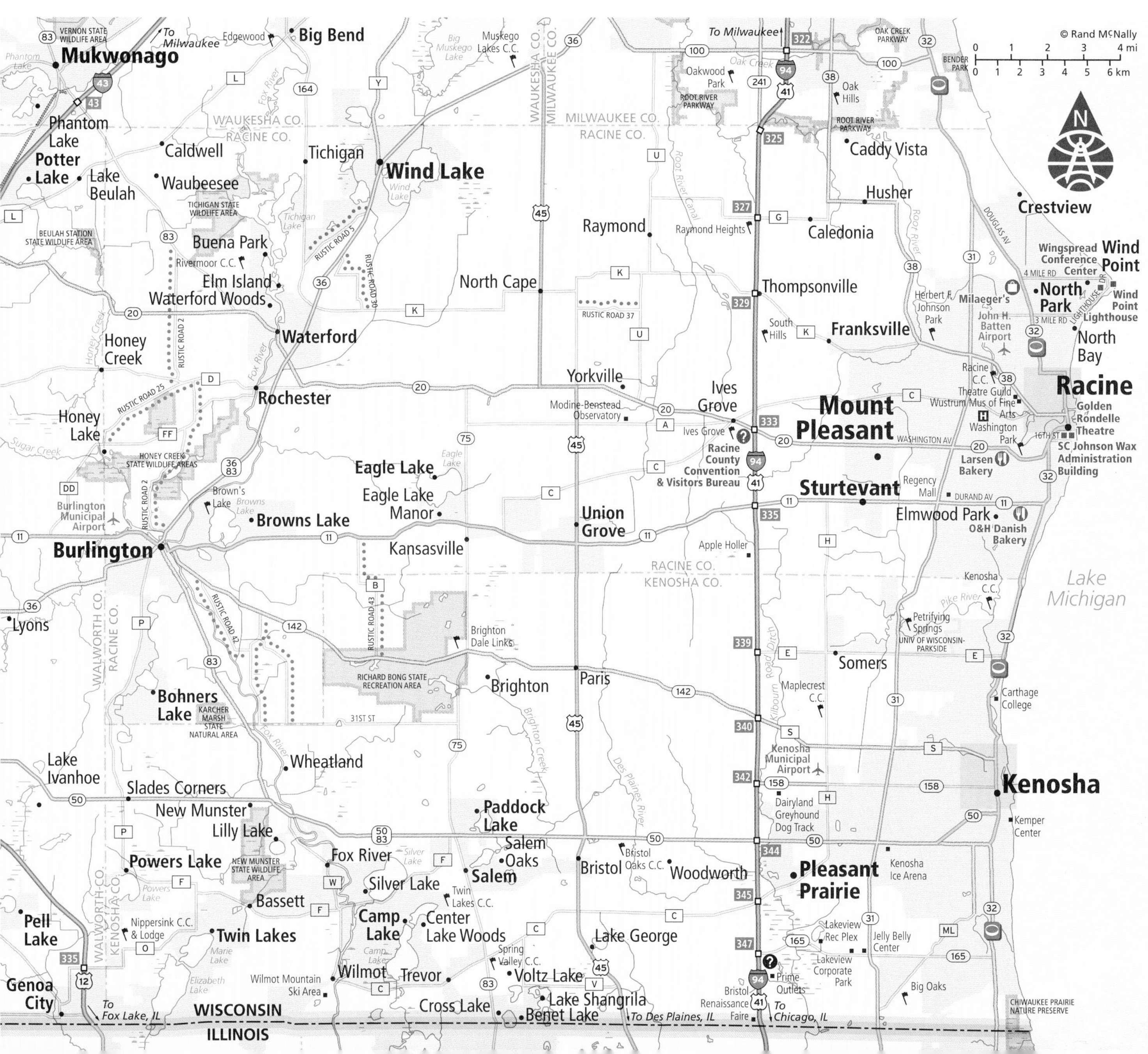

You Can't Miss **the Swiss**

Early last century, more than 200 cheese factories dotted the tucked-away valleys of southwest Wisconsin. Although most have disappeared, about a dozen remain in Green County, including three in **Monroe**, the county seat. In fact, cows still outnumber people in Green County. Tasting and shopping for freshly made cheese attracts foodies—and not a few chefs and restaurant owners—to the region. Other magnets include charming Swiss culture and traditions (with plenty of yodeling and alpenhorn playing), float trips on Sugar River, and a number of well-maintained hiking and biking trails. Many visitors simply tour this appropriately named "Hidden Valleys" region, through countryside where wooded hillsides are etched with rocky outcroppings and dairy cows graze in lush meadows.

Monroe has a Romanesque-style 1891 courthouse as well as **Turner Hall**, home of many Swiss-style community events. A walking tour showcases a variety of 19th-century homes in a melange of architectural styles ranging from Greek Revival and French Empire to Queen Anne Victorian. Decorative Swiss folk art adorns many buildings, inside and out.

Swiss-costumed yodelers in Monroe

Stops in Monroe include the **Joseph Huber Brewery** (1208 14th Ave.), which offers tours and sampling. Its hospitality center features an introductory video and cold suds on tap. The former Monroe Depot of the Chicago, Milwaukee and St. Paul Railroad, circa 1888, now serves as the **Historic Cheesemaking Center** (2108 7th Ave.). On the front lawn are two massive copper cheesemaking kettles; inside the center, you'll learn about the region's rich Swiss heritage and master cheesemakers, brewers, and dairy farmers. Exhibits trace the process of cheesemaking from the arrival at the factory of 10- and 30-gallon cans of fresh milk until the finished product is ready for sale as cured cheese.

Green County Courthouse, Monroe

Snuggled in the Little Sugar River Valley, surrounded by hills and meadows where dairy herds of Swiss browns graze, picturesque **New Glarus** resembles a Swiss mountain town. A group of 108 colonists from the canton of Glarus in Switzerland, fleeing economic hard times in their homeland, founded the town in 1845. Chalet-style buildings feature carved balconies decorated with colorful coats of arms, Swiss flags, and banners. The clank of cowbells announces visitors at shops selling cheese, chocolate, and Swiss imports.

The **Swiss Historical Village and Museum** (612 7th Ave.) is a replica pioneer village with log cabins, a log church, and a one-room schoolhouse. Operated by the local historical society, it preserves the history and records of New Glarus and tells the story of Swiss immigration and colonization as well as early colonial life in the town.

In the neatly kept town of **Brodhead**, find the collected works of more than 50 folk artists from around the United States at **Artisans on the Square Folk Art Gallery** (923 W. Exchange St.). Stop at nearby **Courtyard Coffee House** (1008 1st Center Ave.) for cherry-almond muffins, caramel-apple bars, and espressos, mochas, and lattes. More substantial offerings include organic bread and soups made from scratch (try black bean or French onion).

In addition to everyday car traffic, squat black buggies of the Amish roll through the surrounding countryside. At **Albany**, about five miles north of Brodhead on WI 104, are a couple of Amish shops. **Detweiler Bulk Foods** carries homemade jams, and **Detweiler & Kaufman Furniture** offers sturdily crafted home furnishings. The **Albany Historical Society Museum** (117 N. Water St.), open on Saturdays, features the history of the Sugar River, including the once-thriving pearl-button industry that punched buttons out of the shells of freshwater mussels. The river still yields pink, gray, and white shells occasionally.

To take a float trip—by canoe, kayak, or inner tube—down this slow-moving river, head for Brodhead, where a riverside campground provides rentals and shuttle service. They'll drop customers off upstream to paddle or float back to the campgrounds. **Crazy Horse Campground** (N3201 Crazy Horse Ln.) offers two-, three-, and four-hour trips. **S&B Tubing** (100 E. Main St., Albany) also rents equipment, including "cooler tubes" for conveying lunch and refreshments. The serene river flows through bucolic farmlands with tree-thick banks on either side. Sandbars invite you to pull out of the current and spread out a picnic lunch.

After reaching an all-time low, Wisconsin's bald eagle population has rebounded sufficiently enough that the species has been removed from the state's endangered-species list. These raptors are one of the attractions of a float trip down Sugar River. Of course, they'll see you long before you spot them. Eagles have vision several times more powerful than that of humans.

Painted Swiss cow in New Glarus

What to eat

Find a seat on the balcony of the **New Glarus Hotel** (100 6th Ave.) and sample such Swiss specialties as raclette, which features medium-aged Raclette cheese melted over boiled potatoes and garnished with tiny pickles. Tender veal appears in a number of dishes, including geschnetzlets (thin slices lightly browned and served with a white wine sauce). Tortes are baked on the premises—don't miss the rhubarb-custard version. At **Baumgartner's Cheese Store & Tavern** on Courthouse Square (1023 16th Ave.), the local sport is persuading visitors to sample a sandwich featuring pungent Limburger cheese and watching their reaction. This is the spot for well-made sandwiches, homemade soups, and the world's second-best chili. For those who inevitably ask, it's second best because "Mom makes the best chili, and you don't want to mess with Mom."

What to buy

Browse the shops of New Glarus for lace and embroidery, Swiss chocolates, and perhaps an imported raclette pan. Cheese is a popular purchase throughout Green County. Stop at **Roth Käse** (657 Second St., Monroe), the nation's only manufacturer of Gruyere. It uses traditional methods with copper vats and special curing cellars and ages the cheese for up to nine months. Similarly, **Chalet Cheese Cooperative** (N 4858 County Rd. N) is the only factory in the country still making Limburger. Once you get past the odor, you'll taste a piece of history. Admittedly, the intensely flavored cheese is an acquired taste, but many find it quite palatable on dark rye with a slice of raw onion and mustard.

What to do

Monroe Balloon Rally, Monroe, mid-June.
Heidi Festival, New Glarus, last weekend in June.
For more details about these festivals, please see page 174.

Information

Green County Tourism,
(888) 222-9111, www.greencounty.org.

Lodging tips

In New Glarus, the **Chalet Landhaus Inn** (801 WI 69 S.) serves as a convenient headquarters hotel for exploring Green County. This Bernese-style chalet, festooned with geraniums spilling from planters attached to wooden balconies, is comfortable and companionable, with a log fire blazing in a stone fireplace in the lobby and hand-painted Swiss murals. Otherwise, lodging options are mainly bed-and-breakfast inns and budget chain motels, such as **AmericInn** and **Super 8** (both in Monroe).

Baumgartner's Cheese Store, Monroe

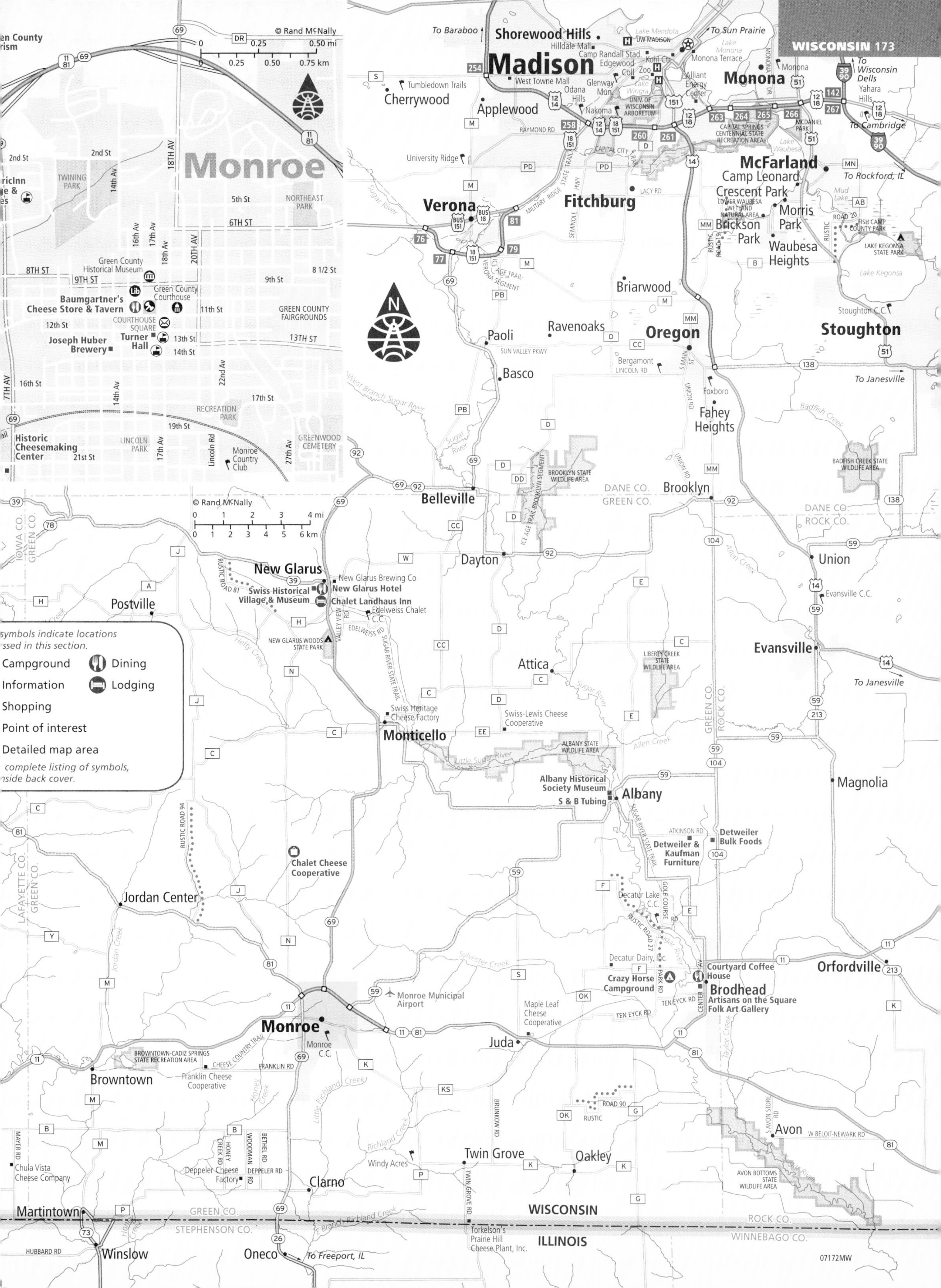
Monroe
© Rand McNally
0.25
0.50 mi
0.25
0.50
0.75 km
2nd St
TWINING PARK
14th Av
18TH AV
5th St
NORTHEAST PARK
6TH ST
16th Av
17th Av
18th Av
20TH AV
8TH ST
9TH ST
Green County Historical Museum
9th St
8 1/2 St
Baumgartner's Cheese Store & Tavern
Green County Courthouse
11th St
GREEN COUNTY FAIRGROUNDS
12th St
COURTHOUSE SQUARE
Joseph Huber Brewery
Turner Hall
13th St
14th St
13TH ST
22nd Av
16th St
17th St
RECREATION PARK
19th St
Historic Cheesemaking Center
21st St
LINCOLN PARK
Lincoln Rd
Monroe Country Club
27th Av
GREENWOOD CEMETERY
To Baraboo
Shorewood Hills
Hilldale Mall
Madison
UW-MADISON
Camp Randall Stad.
Edgewood Coll
Zoo
Kohl Ctr
West Towne Mall
Odana Hills
Glenway Mun.
Nakoma
UNIV. OF WISCONSIN ARBORETUM
To Sun Prairie
Monona Terrace
Alliant Energy Center
Monona
To Wisconsin Dells
Yahara Hills
To Cambridge
Tumbledown Trails
Cherrywood
Applewood
RAYMOND RD
CAPITAL SPRINGS CENTENNIAL STATE RECREATION AREA
McDANIEL PARK
University Ridge
CAPITAL CITY
McFarland
Camp Leonard
Crescent Park
To Rockford, IL
LACY RD
Verona
Fitchburg
MILITARY RIDGE STATE TRAIL
SEMINOLE HWY
LOWER WAUBESA WETLAND NATURAL AREA
Morris Park
Brickson Park
Waubesa Heights
FISH CAMP COUNTY PARK
LAKE KEGONSA STATE PARK
Lake Kegonsa
ICE AGE TRAIL-VERONA SEGMENT
Sugar River
Briarwood
Paoli
Ravenoaks
Oregon
Stoughton
Stoughton C.C.
SUN VALLEY PKWY
Bergamont
LINCOLN RD
Basco
To Janesville
Foxboro
Fahey Heights
West Branch Sugar River
Badfish Creek
BADFISH CREEK STATE WILDLIFE AREA
BROOKLYN STATE WILDLIFE AREA
ICE AGE TRAIL BROOKLYN SEGMENT
DANE CO.
GREEN CO.
Brooklyn
Belleville
DANE CO.
ROCK CO.
IOWA CO.
GREEN CO.
© Rand McNally
0 1 2 3 4 mi
0 1 2 3 4 5 6 km
New Glarus
New Glarus Brewing Co
New Glarus Hotel
Swiss Historical Village & Museum
Chalet Landhaus Inn
Edelweiss Chalet C.C.
Dayton
Union
Evansville C.C.
Postville
NEW GLARUS WOODS STATE PARK
SUGAR RIVER STATE TRAIL
Evansville
To Janesville
Attica
LIBERTY CREEK STATE WILDLIFE AREA
Swiss Heritage Cheese Factory
Swiss-Lewis Cheese Cooperative
Monticello
Little Sugar River
ALBANY STATE WILDLIFE AREA
Allen Creek
Magnolia
Albany Historical Society Museum
Albany
S & B Tubing
Campground
Dining
Information
Lodging
Shopping
Point of interest
Detailed map area
LAFAYETTE CO.
GREEN CO.
RUSTIC ROAD 94
Chalet Cheese Cooperative
Detweiler Bulk Foods
Detweiler & Kaufman Furniture
ATKINSON RD
Jordan Center
Jordan Creek
Decatur Lake C.C.
RUSTIC ROAD 27
GOLF COURSE RD
Sylvester Creek
Decatur Dairy, Inc.
Crazy Horse Campground
Courtyard Coffee House
Brodhead
Artisans on the Square Folk Art Gallery
Orfordville
Monroe Municipal Airport
Maple Leaf Cheese Cooperative
TEN EYCK RD
Monroe
Monroe C.C.
Juda
BROWNTOWN-CADIZ SPRINGS STATE RECREATION AREA
CHEESE COUNTRY TRAIL
FRANKLIN RD
Browntown
Franklin Cheese Cooperative
Little Richland Creek
BRUNKOW RD
RUSTIC ROAD 90
Avon
W BELOIT-NEWARK RD
MAYER RD
HONEY CREEK RD
WOODMAN RD
BETHEL RD
Chula Vista Cheese Company
Deppeler Cheese Factory
DEPPELER RD
Windy Acres
Twin Grove
Oakley
AVON BOTTOMS STATE WILDLIFE AREA
Clarno
TWIN GROVE RD
Martintown
GREEN CO.
STEPHENSON CO.
WISCONSIN
ILLINOIS
ROCK CO.
WINNEBAGO CO.
Torkelson's Prairie Hill Cheese Plant, Inc.
HUBBARD RD
Winslow
Oneco
To Freeport, IL
07172MW

FESTIVAL INFORMATION

More details about all the festivals listed earlier in the book can be found on these pages. The festivals are grouped by state, then arranged alphabetically by title. Even more details about the festivals can be found by contacting state or local tourism boards.

ILLINOIS

Bald Eagle Days

(see page 70 for destination details)

Celebrate eagle migration at **Grafton's** Pere Marquette State Park. Nearly 1,000 eagles, many reclaiming winter nests along the Great River Road, return to the region. Numerous programs let visitors witness these magnificent birds. These include day-long guided eagle-watching tours throughout the region and 75-minute eagle-watching opportunities (available most weekends). Pick up a copy of the "Eagle Watcher's Guide" for listings. www.visitalton.com **Late December through February**

Great Rivers Towboat Festival

(see page 70 for destination details)

Held along **Grafton's** riverfront, the festival features music, food, and tours of working towboats. Festivalgoers enjoy historical and educational displays about the Mississippi River, and artwork and photography from local artists. Adjacent to the festival grounds, the Historic Boatworks is the venue for one of the region's largest flea markets. **Last weekend in June**

International Route 66 Mother Road Festival

(see page 74 for destination details)

Every year about 60,000 Route 66 and car enthusiasts from across North America and around the globe come to **Springfield** for this annual event. It features celebrity appearances, food and drink, free outdoor concerts, and nearly 1,000 classic and vintage cars. www.route66fest.com **September**

New Salem Candlelight Tour

(see page 74 for destination details)

Costumed interpreters engage in cooking, needlework, and other pioneer activities at the **New Salem State Historic Site**. This subdued, picturesque evening event is conducted by candlelight and firelight, for two nights only each year. It's the only evening event held at the village. www.lincolnsnewsalem.com **Early October**

Nouveau Wine Festival

(see page 66 for destination details)

Galena Cellars, a local winery (one of 33 in Illinois), celebrates the release of each year's Beaujolais Nouveau. A horse-drawn wagon delivers cases of the young wine to shops along **Galena's** Main Street, and local restaurants serve traditional French stew (with wine and cheese parties at various downtown locations). **Weekend before Thanksgiving**

Stephenson County Barn Tour

(see page 66 for destination details)

Stephenson County is home to seven round barns and a few polygonal specimens. See them on a tour that takes you through scenic Illinois countryside. **Mid-October**

INDIANA

Indian Market

(see page 82 for destination details)

Nearly 200 artists from across the country converge on **Indianapolis's** Eiteljorg Museum to participate in this art festival. It's one of the nation's largest juried shows and sale of authentic Native American art, pottery, sculpture, and jewelry. Dancers, storytellers, singers, and food are also featured. **Late June**

Indy Jazz Fest

(see page 82 for destination details)

Celebrate **Indy's** deep jazz heritage at this annual, three-day fundraiser in Military Park. It has become one of the Midwest's largest music events. Big-name musical headliners (past artists have included Ray Charles, Aretha Franklin, and Shaggy) perform a variety of musical genres, including jazz, blues, reggae, R&B, and gospel. This family-oriented event includes local food favorites, activities for children, and even health screenings; admission for children 14 and under is free. www.indyjazzfest.net **June**

Madison Chautauqua Festival of Art

(see page 78 for destination details)

The annual juried outdoor fine arts and crafts show in **Madison** features 280-plus artists and their variety of work: sculpture, stained glass, painting, and textiles. A kids' activities tent, the Riverfront Food Fest, and live entertainment round out the offerings. www.madisonchautauqua.com **Late September**

Madison in Bloom

(see page 78 for destination details)

Private gardens in **Madison's** downtown historic district open to the public during the spring garden tours, the highlight of the Madison in Bloom festival. Many other gardens can be seen by strolling the streets. **Mid-May**

Maple Syrup Time

(see page 86 for destination details)

For two consecutive weekends, **Deep River County Park** offers demonstrations of tapping maple trees, gathering sap, and turning it into syrup via wood-fired evaporation in a sugar shack. Activities include voyageur-era-clad volunteers making maple syrup over a campfire and a workshop to guide you through the process of making your own. Visitors can also see a quilting demonstration or purchase a bottle of maple syrup to take home. **Early March**

FESTIVAL INFORMATION

IOWA

Grant Wood Art Festival

(see page 98 for destination details)

This annual festival is held in **Stone City** and **Anamosa**, about 30 miles east of Cedar Rapids, a region set amid the hills and valleys of "Grant Wood Country." Juried artists (a jury of peers judges entrants worthy of the right to display) and entertainers come from around the Midwest to participate. Look for replicas of the colorfully painted horse-drawn wagons that once housed students participating in Grant Wood's art colony in 1932-33. **Early June**

Grand Celebration of Brass Bands

(see page 98 for destination details)

Flugelhorns, cornets, and euphoniums join trumpets and trombones, among others, for rousing renditions of brass band favorites. Hosted by the Eastern Iowa Brass Band, the event attracts brass bands from across America to **Cedar Rapids**. Find a shady spot in picturesque Ushers Ferry Historic Village, quite the appropriate setting, and enjoy the concerts, which are usually scheduled over the course of one long afternoon. www.eibb.org/gcobb.php **Mid-June**

Lakefest

(see page 90 for destination details)

City Park, on the waterfront in downtown **Clear Lake**, hosts three arts festivals on the same weekend. Lakefest includes the Iowa Storytelling Festival, featuring professional storytellers of regional and national reputation; DixieFest, showcasing Dixieland jazz at free concerts; and the Art "Sail," offering pottery, prints, jewelry, and other media from more than 75 artists at a juried show. www.clearlakeiowa.com **Late July**

Nordic Fest

(see page 94 for destination details)

Decorah hosts a massive annual Nordic festival. It includes an antique, artisan, and crafts show featuring more than 100 exhibitors and offers juried rosemaling, weaving, and woodcarving exhibitions, as well as demonstrations of those crafts. Downtown streets are blocked off to traffic for activities that include Scandinavian folkloric music and dance, a grand parade, and food demonstrations and tastings. The annual rock throw is an entertaining event dating back to Viking times, with participants challenged to hurl a 100-pound rock. www.nordicfest.com **Late July**

North Iowa Band Festival

(see page 90 for destination details)

Marching bands converge upon **Mason City** for the annual North Iowa Band Festival. While the highlight is the parade of marching bands—at least 20,000 spectators line the streets—the festival also features music, free entertainment, a carnival, a car show, and plenty of food. It's been held since 1928. www.bigimedia.biz/bandfest **Late May**

KENTUCKY

Berea Craft Festival

(see page 110 for destination details)

Head for the **Berea College Forest** and its historic Indian Fort Theater to find the three-day festival. It's an important national craft showcase attracting more than 120 artists and crafters from across the country. Strolling musicians with dulcimers and fiddles entertain while craftspeople demonstrate woodturning, basket-making, and other arts. www.bereacraftfestival.com **Mid-July**

Festival Latino de Lexington

(see page 102 for destination details)

Courthouse Plaza in downtown **Lexington** hosts the two-day festival, where visitors sample authentic food, listen to Latin music, and absorb the culture through presentations about Hispanic countries. The festival concludes with all-star soccer and baseball games followed by a fireworks show. **September**

Nature Station Hummingbird Festival

(see page 106 for destination details)

Celebrate these tiny, migratory creatures as hundreds pass through **Land Between The Lakes** each day for the long journey south. Festivities include crafts and games, as well as workshops about hummingbird science and how to lure them to your own backyard. **August**

Pickin' Party

(see page 106 for destination details)

This annual **Land Between The Lakes** event attracts country pickers and cloggers from around the region. Musicians bring instruments such as fiddles, guitars, and banjos to participate in open-mic and pickin' sessions, while music lovers sing and clap along with traditional country tunes. Games, toys, and sing-alongs are offered for children, and food and beverages are available. **June**

Woodland Art Fair

(see page 102 for destination details)

Held in **Lexington's** Woodland Park, the two-day event draws a crowd of more than 60,000 people. Nearly 200 juried artists exhibit and sell every type of art, from watercolor to jewelry to sculpture. Visitors enjoy food, bands, the Family/Children's Project area, and a beer garden. www.lexingtonartleague.org/woodland.htm **Third weekend in August**

FESTIVAL INFORMATION

MICHIGAN

Art on the Rocks

(see page 114 for destination details)

The Lake Superior Art Association's annual outdoor show takes place in **Marquette's** Presque Isle Park, along the Lake Superior shore. Join more than 15,000 visitors on the wooded lakefront as they view 200 booths showcasing the work of 150 artists.
www.lakesuperiorartassociation.org **Late July**

Cheeseburger in Caseville

(see page 122 for destination details)

Every August, **Caseville** transforms itself into "Margaritaville" as it celebrates summertime. The music tends toward Jimmy Buffet; the general atmosphere resembles nothing so much as Key West. The festival brings together more than a dozen performers and bands (including reggae) and serves its eponymous food in a variety of guises. Call it Key North.
www.cheeseburgerincaseville.com **August**

Foremost's Butterflies are Blooming

(see page 118 for destination details)

For eight weeks in early spring, more than 6,000 butterflies representing about 40 species flutter through the Lena Meijer Conservatory (in **Grand Rapids'** Frederik Meijer Gardens), drinking nectar from flowers and alighting upon visitors' shoulders—and sometimes on their noses. This annual event is the largest temporary tropical butterfly exhibition in the United States. Kids' activities are held at the Family Fun Center and the Lena Meijer Children's Garden.
www.foremostbutterflies.com **March-April**

Michigan Sugar Festival

(see page 122 for destination details)

Huron County celebrates its sugar beet crop in **Sebewaing's** Main Park. A main event: the coronation of the Michigan Sugar Queen. There's also a parade, a tasty chicken barbecue, fireworks, entertainment, carnival, and a midway. **Mid-June**

Tulip Time

(see page 118 for destination details)

Holland's massive annual festival, full of pageantry and entertainment, is a local rite of spring. Attendees enjoy headliners on the main stage and a trio of parades, the latter preceded by hundreds of Dutch-costumed townsfolk equipped with brooms and pails scrubbing the parade route clean. Find klompen dancing, a military cavalry demonstration, a quilt show, a Dutch marketplace, and trolley rides. Adding to the theme are organ recitals, Dutch-language church services, an arts-and-crafts fair, a flower show, and a beer festival with entertainment.
www.tuliptime.com
First through second Saturdays in May

MINNESOTA

Cider & Candlelight Tour

(see page 134 for destination details)

Take an evening candlelight tour of the Historic Log Village in **Crosslake**. Participants drink cider and ride in horse-drawn wagons as the smell of wood smoke fills the air. www.explorebrainerdlakes.com **Mid-September**

Good Samaritan's Festival of Trees

Madden's Town Hall in **Brainerd** turns magical with displays of Christmas trees sponsored by families and organizations. The holiday fundraiser tradition includes a gala reception, holiday brunch, wine and cheese tasting, and artisans' fair.
www.good-sambrainerdpineriver.com/festival.html
The week of Thanksgiving

Judy Garland Festival

(see page 126 for destination details)

Grand Rapids celebrates its favorite daughter, complete with film screenings, visits with an original Munchkin or two (although the years have taken a toll on their numbers), and an auction of *Wizard of Oz* memorabilia. Take a tour of Judy's birthplace home, and wander through the museum honoring the accomplishments of the famous actress. www.judygarlandmuseum.com
June

Minneapolis Aquatennial

(see page 130 for destination details)

This **Minneapolis** festival originated in 1940, with singing cowboy Gene Autry as a guest performer. It hosts races with boats fashioned from milk cartons, plus parades, fireworks, a free outdoor concert, an art fair at the beach, and a giant block party. www.aquatennial.org **Mid-July**

The Saint Paul Winter Carnival

(see page 130 for destination details)

Dating back to 1886, the carnival began after Eastern newspapers snubbed the city as "another Siberia," unfit for human habitation. In response, **Saint Paul** launched a carnival featuring ice castles lit with Edison's newly invented electric light. Today, the fun includes fast toboggan runs, ice carving, snow sculpture, parades, bonfires, fireworks, kite flying, and winter-adapted sporting events such as golf and baseball played on ice and snow. www.winter-carnival.com
Late January–early February

Taste of Pequot and Arts and Crafts Festival

(see page 134 for destination details)

The annual festival in **Pequot Lakes** features more than 100 crafters and local restaurants showcasing signature dishes. Walk along the Paul Bunyan Trail and peruse everything from herbal soaps to handcrafted furniture.
www.explorebrainerdlakes.com **Mid-September**

FESTIVAL INFORMATION

MINNESOTA *(cont.)*

White Oak Society Rendezvous

(see page 126 for destination details)

A three-day reenactment of a 1798 Northwest Company fur post breathes life into history in the city of **Deer River**. An encampment of more than 200 tents rises along the river as some 1,000 reenactors narrate the lives of fur trappers. Find food, music, crafts, and a variety of competitions, such as black-powder shooting. www.whiteoak.org **Early August**

MISSOURI

Branson Area Festival of Lights

(see page 138 for destination details)

More than 500,000 light bulbs stretched over nine miles power the annual display. To see the Parkway aglow for the holidays, take one of three drives through the **Branson** area. Details of the drive are available online at www.bransonchamber.com and at the Branson/Lakes Area Chamber of Commerce and CVB Visitor Centers. www.bransontourismcenter.com **November through December**

Dogwood Festival

(see page 142 for destination details)

For more than a half century, **Camdenton** has greeted spring's arrival to the Lake of the Ozarks with its popular celebration. The Chamber of Commerce hands out blooming dogwoods (Missouri's state tree), and pooches perform in the Dog Contest. Other activities include a fine-art show and sale, live entertainment, a golf tournament, and a variety of foods. www.camdentonchamber.com/dogwood.htm **Mid-April**

Eagle Days

(see page 146 for destination details)

Take a side trip to **Clarksville**, a town that's considered to be among the top eagle-spotting areas in the nation. The annual winter celebration honors the species with spotting scopes, special programs, exhibits, children's activities, and refreshments. Be sure to bundle up! www.greatriverroad.com/hannibal/hanevents/eagledays.htm **Late January**

National Tom Sawyer Days

(see page 146 for destination details)

The annual nostalgic event attracts more than 100,000 visitors to **Hannibal**, the town where Samuel Clemens grew up. In addition to frenzied fence-painting and frog-jumping contests, there's a Tom and Becky contest, entertainment, and food. www.hannibaljaycees.org **July (Independence Day weekend)**

Olde Tyme Apple Festival

(see page 142 for destination details)

Juicy red apples, crisp fall weather, and a rainbow of autumn colors herald the fall favorite in **Versailles**. You'll find continuous entertainment at the historic Morgan County Courthouse. Attractions include a parade, apple-pie auction, fiddle contest, museum tours, and craft and food booths. www.versailleschamber.org **Early October**

Plumb Nellie Days

(see page 138 for destination details)

While **Branson** always offers traditional crafts, they virtually take over the entire town during this festival, with Main Street blocked off and filled with vendors. Country fiddlers entertain while food vendors offer traditional southern favorites. www.bransontourismcenter.com **Mid-May**

OHIO

Festival of American Crafts

(see page 150 for destination details)

More than 50 early American folk artists from across the country come to **Morrow** to demonstrate and sell their wares at The Workshops of David T. Smith. The festival includes a tent sale with handmade items discounted 20-60% and live music and food. www.davidsmith.com **Late June**

Historical Weekend at Put-in-Bay

(see page 158 for destination details)

The **Put-in-Bay** area continues its tradition of honoring history by commemorating the War of 1812's Battle of Lake Erie at this annual event at the Perry Memorial. Along with art and music, the festival includes a parade, musket and cannon firing demonstrations, and a military encampment with hundreds of participating reenactors. www.put-in-bay.com **September**

Marblehead Lighthouse Festival

(see page 158 for destination details)

Snap a picture of the most photographed lighthouse in the Great Lakes region at this festival in **Marblehead**. Tour the lighthouse and Keeper's House museum, and enjoy bean soup, cornbread, and other goodies. Among the many activities are Revolutionary War–era reenactments of the first family to settle on the peninsula and serve as keepers of the lighthouse. www.thekeepershouse.org **October**

FESTIVAL INFORMATION

OHIO *(cont.)*

Ohio Sauerkraut Festival
(see page 150 for destination details)

This **Waynesville** festival began in 1969 and now draws 300,000 visitors each year to browse 450-plus craft booths and 30 food booths. It's where you'll find such quirky offerings as sauerkraut ice cream, sauerkraut cake with chocolate frosting, and sauerkraut cookies studded with chocolate chips and cashew nuts.
www.sauerkrautfestival.com

Second full weekend in October

Parade the Circle Celebration
(see page 154 for destination details)

More than 30,000 people converge in **Cleveland** for this free community arts event. Cleveland's renowned University Circle sponsors music, dance, and interactive activities, while the Cleveland Museum of Art hosts a parade. **June**

Twins Days Festival
(see page 154 for destination details)

You will be seeing double at this annual celebration in **Twinsburg**. More than 2,000 sets of twins register for contests, talent shows, and other events. The "Double Take Parade" is a festival highlight, alongside food, entertainment, and crafts. www.twinsdays.org
First full weekend in August

WISCONSIN

Giant Pumpkin Fest and Official Central Wisconsin Pumpkin Growers Weigh-in
(see page 162 for destination details)

Orange splashes among the crimson in **Nekoosa** as growers from across Wisconsin and beyond gather to showcase their giant pumpkins. Not long ago, the Holy Grail was a 500-pound pumpkin; these days the top 10 contenders are likely to average well over 700 pounds each, and the record is for a 1,000-pounder. Along with a classic car show and a variety of pumpkin-related events, the festival features weigh-ins for oversized squash and watermelons. www.nekoosagiantpumpkinfest.com
First weekend in October

Great Lakes Brew Fest
(see page 166 for destination details)

Celebrate the region known for beer by raising a glass at this annual celebration in **Racine**. More than 75 brewers offer unlimited samplings of 200+ brews. Live music and food add to the lakefront festivities. Patrons must be at least 21 years of age.
www.greatlakesbrewfest.com **September**

Great Midwest Dragon Boat Festival
(see page 166 for destination details)

This ritualistic event honors an ancient Chinese water race of brightly decorated dragon boats. The long, sleek, canoe-like boats race all day on Lake Michigan, off **Racine**, while festival patrons enjoy music, Asian food, and children's activities. The celebration includes a parade and a special ceremony featuring lion dancers.
www.midwestdragonboatfestival.com **July**

Heidi Festival
(see page 170 for destination details)

New Glarus is so unabashedly Swiss that you almost expect to see Heidi skipping through town. Visit in June and you won't be disappointed. The annual festival honoring the little girl in braids includes a stage version of Johanna Spyri's classic tale. The celebration is anchored by Taste & Treasures, featuring foods for sampling and bargains for shopping.
www.swisstown.com/festivals.shtml
Last weekend in June

Ice Harvest
(see page 162 for destination details)

Bundle up and head to Nepco Lake for the annual historic reenactment of harvesting ice at Historic Point Basse in **Nekoosa**. Participants dressed in period costume harvest the ice, pack it in sawdust, and store it away for the warmer months. The event is part of the Port Edwards Lions' Annual Fisheree, which includes ice fishing, a raffle, family activities, and refreshments such as hot cocoa and cider. www.historicpointbasse.com **Late January**

Monroe Balloon Rally
(see page 170 for destination details)

Champion pilots from around the world fill the sky above the Green County Fairgrounds with colorful hot-air balloons all weekend long. The city of **Monroe** incorporates an arts and crafts fair, the "Taste of Monroe" in Courthouse Square, a pig cookout, and pancake breakfasts. www.monroechamber.org **Mid-June**

Best of the Road™

bus Beckley **Dubuque** Saint Paul **Duluth** Thunder Bay **New Harmony** Cairo **La Crosse** Hibbing **Story** Fayetteville **Wabasha** Grand Marais **French Lic**

Rappeling, New River Gorge

Climbing the Hills

Columbus, Ohio to Beckley, West Virginia

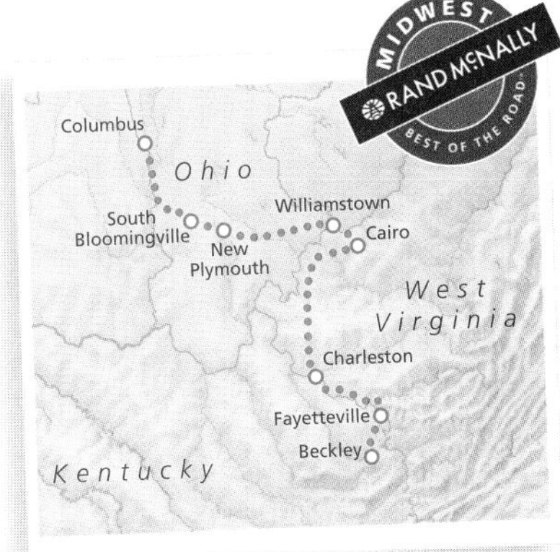

Beginning in Columbus, Ohio, the drive to Beckley, West Virginia, meanders through some of the prettiest farmland and rolling hills anywhere. It crosses the Ohio River, lined by river towns with rich Victorian architecture and industrial history, and on into the steep foothills of the Appalachians. Loaded with outdoor recreation opportunities, natural attractions, museums, and down-home dining, it's a deep dive into the heart of American culture and history.

A few blocks from the heart of downtown Columbus, German Village hums with activity. Built in the 1860s by German immigrants, the trendy neighborhood is one of the nation's oldest historic districts. The sturdy brick streets are lined with boutiques, upscale restaurants, pubs, and coffee shops like Cup O' Joe, a local hangout.

Students from Ohio State and neighborhood residents browse through the 32 rooms of the Book Loft, an independent bookstore filled with books, music, and lots of crannies in which to read. Open six days a week, the Visitor's Center at the Meeting Haus offers tours of the neighborhood.

The district north of downtown, the Arena District and Short North, is home to the Columbus Blue Jackets hockey arena, bars, shops, and art galleries. At the North Market, stalls selling Jeni's ice cream (made in Columbus), Vietnamese, Indian, and deli food, cheese, wines, honey, fruits, and even fresh flowers compete for shoppers.

South of Columbus, the drive quickly passes into farmland and wooded areas. In the Hocking Hills, lodging options range from simple campsites and motels to cabins at upscale resorts like Glenlaurel Inn and Inn at Cedar Falls. Dinner at the Scottish-style Glenlaurel Inn is a five-course affair for $49 plus tax and tip. Entrees vary, but may include filet mignon, salmon, or rack of lamb, served in the castle-motif dining room.

Hocking Hills State Park, with more than two million visitors a year, packs in families at familiar sites like Old Man's Cave. Guided tours by local historians provide an in-depth perspective of the land, while that of Mimi Morrison of Touch the Earth Adventures explores Lake Logan via kayak to spot vultures and eagles.

Just outside the park in Logan, Columbus Washboard Factory shows visitors how washboards can be assembled in just 45 seconds. See original 1800s equipment, buy a washboard souvenir, and then check out the world's largest washboard at 24 feet outside.

En route east towards West Virginia on US 33 and OH 550, Etta's Lunchbox serves up more than pizza and sandwiches. The walls and ceiling of this café and general store are covered with owner Ledora Ousley's collection of lunchboxes dating from the 1940s.

Etta's Lunchbox

Across the Ohio River, Parkersburg, West Virginia, wears its age well. At the Visitors Center, detailed brochures are available for a tour of the Julia-Ann Square Historic District. Right in downtown Parkersburg, oil rigs litter the grounds of the Oil and Gas Museum. Inside, visitors find a wealth of equipment, exhibits, and historic photos about the oil boomtowns and the tumultuous Civil War history here.

Near the Oil and Gas Museum, the Blennerhassett Museum of Regional History sells tickets to Blennerhasset Island State Park. The island, purchased in 1798 by wealthy Irish immigrants Harman and Margaret Blennerhasset, can be accessed via a paddlewheel boat in summer. Its original mansion, which burned in 1811, has been re-created, and docents dressed in period costume lead tours through the magnificent home. Families enjoy taking the horse-drawn carriage ride around part of the 169-acre grounds, which once served as training grounds for a secret army formed by Aaron Burr.

Upriver in Williamstown, Fenton Art Glass remains one of the last of a long line of glass operations in West Virginia. It is still owned by the Fenton family, which founded it in 1905. Up to eight factory tours a day and an extensive gift shop that also sells factory seconds draw visitors and collectors from all over the world. After a factory tour, many stop at DaVinci's Italian Restaurant. Famed for its surprisingly tasty German pizza (made with sauerkraut), the restaurant is packed on Sundays for purely American fare of ham, baked potatoes, and more.

A favorite Vienna stop is Holl's Swiss Chocolate. Founded by Fritz Holl and currently run by his son Dominic, the company hand-crafts, decorates, and hand-packs the confections, which are artfully displayed in cases.

Half an hour east of Parkersburg in Cairo, just off US 50, the 72-mile North Bend Rail Trail includes thirteen tunnels for bikers to pass through, including one purported to be haunted. Country Trails Bikes, just off Main Street in Cairo, rents bikes by the hour ($4) or day ($32), services them, and sells bike supplies. One popular route burrows through three tunnels, past a gazebo, and on to an ice cream shop for a sweet finale.

Scenic US 60 jogs east along the Midland Trail into the New River Gorge area. A platform at Hawks Nest State Park, in Ansted, overlooks the New River. Here, an aerial tram brings park guests to New River Jetboat Tours, a 30-minute wet and wild ride upstream to the New River Gorge Bridge towering 876 feet above.

Most summer visitors to the area come for the river rafting. Eleven companies offer raft trips ranging from a half day to overnight at www.wvawhitewater.com. There are gentle rapids on the Upper New River for families with small children, and big rapid rides on the New and Gauley Rivers. Because the river action is somewhat dictated by the amount of rainfall each season, the ride is different each time.

A perhaps lesser-known sport in the area is rock climbing. With more than 1,600 sport climbing and traditional climbing routes, rock rats scramble up terrain as provocative as the route names: Nude Scientist, Party in My Mind, Cotton Mouth, and Satisfaction Guaranteed. Most routes are 80-100 ft., rated from 5.5 to 5.14—which for the uninitiated means pretty tough—from spots where there are two hand and foot holds for every move to real Spiderman stuff.

Mountain bikers also love the gorge. Bike rentals and guides are available at New River Bike and Touring Company.

Many bikers, rafters, and guides end their day's outing at Pies and Pints pizzeria in Fayetteville. On Tuesdays, an $8 all-you-can-eat pizza special includes their favorite spicy chicken chipotle pizza topped with chicken, red onions, cilantro, and crème fraîche. Brews are extra.

Most people wander down to Beckley during their visit due to the more extensive lodging, dining, and entertainment options. Learn about West Virginia's coal mining at the Beckley Exhibition Mine. Retired mine workers ferry visitors 1,550 feet underground via authentic "man cars" (akin to a miniature train) through the former working mine of the Phillips Coal Company. The half-hour tour details the history of the dangerous, dark, wet, and lonely business of mining. The site also has a number of historic buildings with period furniture, such as the Superintendent's Home, a coal worker's shanty, and the Pemberton Coal Camp Church.

Also in Beckley, Tamarack: The Best of West Virginia sits right off I-64. Six artisans work on site carving wooden instruments, designing cornhusk dolls, weaving baskets, and making other crafts. Works from these and nearly 2,000 other juried West Virginian craftspeople are sold here, including textiles, agricultural products, glass, pottery, wood, metal, jewelry, quilts, and wearable art. Hungry shoppers make their way to the food court, which is operated by the chef of the highly rated Greenbrier Resort. It's a tasty end to an adventurous trip.

Country Trails Bikes

Dubuque County Courthouse

The Great River Road

Dubuque, Iowa to Saint Paul, Minnesota

Start your engine in Dubuque, Iowa, and follow the Great River Road north to Saint Paul, Minn. Thanks to a glacial detour, this part of northern Iowa, western Wisconsin, and eastern Minnesota boasts a landscape replete with rolling countryside, dense wetlands, and towering bluffs. By following road signs identified by a river pilot's wheel, the Great River Road leads to one charming river town after another.

In Dubuque, silhouettes of Victorian homes perched on precipitous bluffs form a dramatic skyline, and an elevated one. The Fenelon Place Elevator, originally built in 1882, provides a ride in a four-seat lift to the top of the bluffs (and down). Called the world's shortest and steepest scenic railway, the Fenelon ascends 189 feet via ropes and pulleys to a wooden platform nestled in a neighborhood of restored homes. The unrestricted views of Wisconsin, Illinois, the downtown, and the Port of Dubuque are well worth the shake, rattle, and roll of the ride.

Private homes aren't the only structures being restored in Dubuque. Much of downtown has been converted into trendy shops and eateries. Café Manna Java is located in a restored storefront. Luncheon menu favorite: Hot panini sandwich served with a choice of homemade sauces, like the béchamel made for a croque monsieur.

An hour-long narrated tour via Trolleys of Dubuque covers the city's historic section and provides an alternative way to get to the top of the bluffs. With hop-on and hop-off service, riders can walk or ride from downtown to America's River, a tourism development set on the banks of the Mississippi.

As the Great River Road heads north out of Dubuque, it rolls through hilly farmland before curving toward the state line, in this case, the Mississippi River. Crossing the river, it continues on the Wisconsin side at Prairie du Chien.

The Prairie du Chien Tourism Center is just across the bridge. Anyone there will know how to find Willy & Nellie's Place, a local root beer stand that serves draft root beer along with ice cream, hot dogs, and freshly popped corn. Willy's is just this side of the tributary to St. Feriole Isle, where Villa Louis, a Victorian estate built in the 1840s, continues to be restored to its original splendor.

The Great River Road is so clearly marked that driving into La Crosse, even at dusk, is easy. The height of the bluffs along the Mississippi peaks at La Crosse, stretching to more than 500 feet at Granddad Bluff. Granddad's is a terrific spot to look over the city, back at Iowa, and into Minnesota. On the way to the lookout, it's difficult to miss Rudy's Drive-In; it is the largest in the Midwest. The red hots are boiled hot dogs served as you like them and delivered to the driver's side window by roller-skating waitresses.

Granddad Bluff

The drive between La Crosse and Trempealeau alternates between wide-open spaces and canyon-like passes with bluffs encroaching on both sides of the river. The restored-to-period downtown stretches about four blocks before reaching the river. The kitchen at the Trempealeau Hotel, a wooden clapboard building, serves a veggie burger made with ground walnuts, which patrons can enjoy in the dining room or outside on a broad expanse of lawn overlooking the river.

Before crossing into Minnesota, stop at the Trempealeau National Wildlife Refuge. Auto tours are clearly marked, or visitors can walk or cycle any number of trails within the 6,220 acres. Depending on the time of year, there are red-shouldered hawks and bald eagles, bluebirds and yellow-breasted chats, grebes and geese.

Entering Minnesota, the Great River Road turns north toward Winona. The Winona County Historical Society Museum has three levels of exhibits, including a full-size reconstructed Main St. from the early 20th century. The Watkins Heritage Museum and Store offers a brief look at the history of the home-remedy giant while the Polish Cultural Institute honors the contributions made by Polish laborers.

While in Winona, grab a bite to eat at the Jefferson Pub and Grill, located along the railroad tracks. Jefferson's offers world-class burgers of both beef and vegetarian variety.

Continuing north, the Great River Road curves along flat lowland, then stretches east toward the river into Wabasha. The confluence of the Mississippi and Chippewa rivers is located at Wabasha, and the force from the two rivers is so great that the water never freezes. That's lucky for the bald eagles that are able to overwinter—luckier still for residents, as eagle sightings are part of everyday life.

The drive to Red Wing is all uphill. Red Wing is built into hills in the west and onto the banks of the Mississippi in the east. Annually rated as one of the best small towns in America, Red Wing is well known for it historic architecture, antiques, pottery, and Red Wing shoes. The St. James Hotel opened in 1875 and still anchors the downtown. Across from the railroad station and a stone's throw from the Mississippi, its décor and ambience are closely associated with both. Each of the 61 elegantly appointed rooms is named after a riverboat, and photographs and information on the boats are displayed in the rooms.

One of the town's treasures is the Tale of Two Sisters Tea Room and Gift Shoppe, where tea and its accoutrements are served in one of Red Wing's historic homes. There's

Tale of Two Sisters Tea Room

Science Museum of Minnesota

shopping at the tearoom, too: trimmings for the table, accessories for the home, and a selection of choice teas including several cut exclusively for the two sisters. Many private homes have been restored to turn-of-the-last-century grandeur. The Sheldon, circa 1904, is a showcase, both as a building with delicately painted murals, marble columns, and gilded plaster, and as a venue for performances, concerts, and theater. Group tours for 10 or more are given with advance reservation.

North of Red Wing, the Great River Road curves toward Saint Paul. The section of the river that runs through the city is part of the National Park Service. Park service rangers staff an information center for the Mississippi National River and Recreation Area inside the Science Museum of Minnesota (SMM).

The SMM's façade soars as high as a river bluff between the Mississippi's banks and Kellogg Blvd. Visitors are greeted by Iggy, a 10-foot iguana sculpture at the school group entrance to the museum. A towboat riverside serves as a viewing platform overlooking the river. The boat isn't in the water; it is located 75 feet off the ground on the balcony of the Mississippi River Gallery. Visitors can board and explore it to clang bells and take pretend trips along the world's fourth-longest river all the way to the Gulf of Mexico. Interactive exhibits are the hallmark of the SMM.

On weekend mornings, the most popular spot in town is the Saint Paul Farmer's Market. Starting at 6 a.m., local farmers' best is offered in stalls that fill an entire city block. The market is a primary outlet for PanDau, story cloth made by the women of the local Hmong community. Through stitching, story cloths depict daily life in Laos, usually farming or celebrations, while some recount stories of political unrest.

Saint Paul was founded as a riverboat landing long before it was named territorial capital in 1849. Then it served as a port of call for adventurers, an opportunity for settlers, and, much like our drive along the Great River Road, a final destination.

Into the Woods

Duluth, Minnesota to Thunder Bay, Ontario

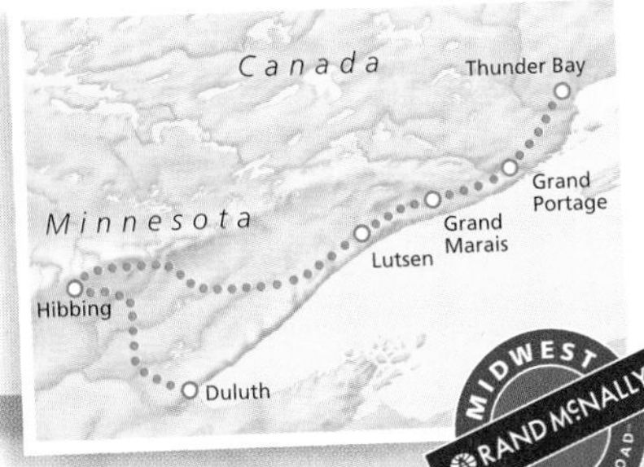

Located on the westernmost edge of Lake Superior, MN 61 rises between the storied waters of Gitchee Gumee and the highest peaks in Minnesota. Locals call this winding, two-lane road the "North Shore." Natural wonders, charming shops, and terrific restaurants dot the route.

Tettegouche State Park on the edge of Lake Superior

This trip starts on Skyline Drive, 600 feet above Duluth. The view of the metropolitan area as it stretches 25 miles along the water is spectacular. On the gray-blue horizon, Duluth's landmark Aerial Lift Bridge anchors the working harbor, which welcomes more than 1,000 freighters annually.

This area high above Duluth is called Hawk Ridge. For 33 years, a full-time raptor count has been conducted at Hawk Ridge Nature Reserve. In the fall, it is not uncommon for Doppler radar to mistakenly warn of storms approaching from Canada. In truth, the mass picked up by radar systems will be the shadow of huge kettles of migrating raptors. On Sept. 14, 2003, due to a combination of weather fronts and the far-reaching effects of Hurricane Isabel, more than 100,000 raptors flew over Duluth. Back on the ground below, Duluth bustles with trendy shops, tempting restaurants, and cultural centers along the downtown lakefront. At Union Depot, restored cars from the North Shore Scenic Railroad (NSRR) sit trackside at the Lake Superior Railroad Museum. The NSSR offers theme rides, such as the Pizza Train, which serves fresh, hot pizza delivered on board. The excursion along the lake and into the northwoods lasts about 90 minutes and is hosted by an interpreter dressed as a conductor.

The center of Minnesota's iron range is Hibbing, home of the Hull Rust Mahoning Mine, the world's largest open pit iron mine. The pit stretches for more than three miles in length, and is two miles wide and 600 feet deep. Because of its size, it is often referred to as the "Grand Canyon of the North."

Since the mid-1960s, Hibbing has gained international recognition as the hometown of singer and songwriter Bob Dylan. One must-see stop is Zimmy's & the Atrium Restaurant. Housed in the town's first trolley station, the restaurant boasts the largest-known collection of Dylan memorabilia as well as an extensive menu named after his songs, like "Forever Young" veggie burgers.

Driving back toward the shore, the route passes Chisholm, where the Ironworld Discovery Center commemorates the struggle of the immigrants who came to work the mines. And in Eveleth, visitors at the United States Hockey Hall of Fame, located on Hat Trick Drive, can relive the thrill of the 1980 match between the U.S. Olympic hockey team and the Soviet Union.

The Superior National Forest Scenic Byway starts at nearby Aurora and connects the Iron Range to the North Shore. The byway is wide and smooth with broad shoulders that allow unobstructed views of the boreal forest and occasional marshland. Moose sightings are common. This serene 61-mile stretch offers access to a variety of recreation areas including the Iron Range Off-Highway Vehicle Recreation Area, Minnesota's only recreational area for all-terrain vehicles, off-road motorcycles, and 4x4's.

The byway ends at Silver Bay, where Split Rock Lighthouse State Park provides an impressive view of Lake Superior. Visitors can blast a foghorn that can be heard for five miles and climb to the top of the lighthouse to see its original Fresnel lens.

North on MN 61 at Sawtooth Mountain Park in Lutsen, the summit of Moose Mountain is open all year, thanks to an aerial gondola service. The view from the top of the surrounding Sawtooth Mountains and its maple canopy is dazzling. Visitors can enjoy the mountain by hiking any number of well-marked trails, riding one of the lift-accessed mountain bike trails, or simply enjoying the return ride on the four-seat, enclosed gondola.

Caribou Trail, located just east of Lutsen, is the starting point for one of the North Shore's favorite fall color drives. It also inspired the name of an blue-ribbon-winning maple syrup called Caribou Cream. Herb Wills and Sonja Helland produce the syrup in a refitted garage located on their property about a mile from MN 61.

Grand Marais's reputation as an art colony is well founded. Both local art and Inuit art is represented on canvas and in crafts and sculpture. There's a wealth of artwork available at many downtown galleries and at the Joynes Ben Franklin Store where, for more than 60 years, it has been as easy to buy an original watercolor as a tube of toothpaste.

The Angry Trout Café at the Grand Marais harbor features an eclectic ambience as special as its partially organic menu. So many diners ask about the décor that laminated flyers identifying which local artisan made the chairs, who created the mosaic mural in the unisex bathroom, and the like are placed on the tables. The locally caught lake trout is expertly grilled and served with wild rice mixed with peas, shiitake mushrooms, and cranberries alongside an ear of roasted calico corn.

Grand Portage

In the 18th century, afternoon tea was served with sandwiches and sweets at what is now Grand Portage National Monument, 26 miles east of Grand Marais, but only when officers of the North West Company were attending the Rendezvous at the depot. Held each July for more than 40 years, the Rendezvous brought together voyageurs from the north with their stock of fur pelts to be exchanged for goods brought from the east by the men from Montreal. Visitors can see a fur press in action, examine trade goods, visit with the fort cook in the kitchen, and watch craftsmen building birch bark canoes.

Crossing the border into Canada, MN 61 becomes Kings Highway 61, making the transition to Ontario as easy as showing proof of citizenship and automobile registration to the border guard. (Beginning January 1, 2008, U.S. citizens will need to carry a passport or other secure document to re-enter the United States.)

Thunder Bay (pop. 120,000) has a small-town feel to it. Must-see stops include Fort William Historical Park, which replaced Grand Portage as the meeting place for trading in the early 19th century. Costumed interpreters bring the fort to life at Trades Square, in the Great Hall kitchen, and at the pharmacy, where the goodly doctor prescribes questionable treatments. Reenactors escort 90-minute tours, nine times a day, all year long.

Fireweed

Downtown there's plenty of shopping in trendy neighborhoods, like Victoria Street. In the Bay/Algoma Street area, stop at the Finn-Tastic Sauna Shop (pronounced "sow-na" in Canada just as in Finland) or at the Fireweed cooperative, which sells Canadian handicrafts.

North America's largest vein of amethyst is a short drive north of town at The Amethyst Mine Panorama. Following a brief instructional tour, visitors grab a bucket, select a pick, and dig for gemstones in great mounds of dirt, debris, and sparkling purple amethyst. Price for any found amethyst is based on the weight of the bucket and the day's market. The gift shop has a wealth of gemstones already cleaned and polished.

On the south side of Thunder Bay, the province's only Gouda cheese farm draws visitors from all over the world. In addition to making traditional Gouda, owners Margaret and Jacob Schep flavor some of their cheese with herbs—not just culinary herbs, but those found in folklore. One cheese includes seeds from fenugreek, an herb used in some folk medications to reportedly control diabetes and cholesterol. Mrs. Schep will vacuum-seal rounds or wedges for the trip home. And she promises that the border guard will not confiscate the package. (She is correct.) Much like the rest of the trip along the North Shore, this day at Thunder Oak Cheese Farm ends with a smile. Say cheese!

Bartholomew County Courthouse and the Veterans Memorial, Columbus

Wooded Hills, Grand Architecture

Columbus, Indiana to New Harmony, Indiana

From architectural marvels and national forest land to soothing spa waters and utopian communities, southern Indiana offers a surprising bounty of roadside stops. Begin your drive in Columbus, a city loaded with stylish buildings designed by famed architects—more than 65 in all, one for every 600 residents. Visitors can take a two-hour tour of these gems, guided by local volunteers who add personal footnotes to their patter. You'll see works by Robert A.M. Stern, Eero Saarinen, I. M. Pei—churches, schools, commercial buildings, and a hospital.

From Columbus, head west on IN 46 towards Nashville. The flat cornfields quickly give way to the rolling hills that mark southern Indiana. If you have time, stop in Gnaw Bone at one of the little flea markets along the road. You can buy the usual flea market items, but the real buys are the local goods, such as homemade jams, sorghum, fresh-baked breads, or perhaps a bunch of bittersweet in the fall. Hoards descend on the shops of Nashville on the weekends. Tucked among the kitschy craft stores and other shops are a few genuine art galleries. Look for potters, weavers, and leather craftsmen. One shop worth checking out: Acorn Cottage Gallery, 91 W. Franklin, which features local artisans' works at reasonable prices. If you're hungry, options include the always-busy Nashville House, at Main and Van Buren Sts., specializing in country fried steak, fried biscuits, and baked apple butter, or Hobnob Corner Restaurant (also at Main and Van Buren Sts.) for soups, salads, and sandwiches.

If you have kids in tow, the 20-minute Melchior Marionette Theater show on Saturdays and Sundays in June, July, September, and October, is worth the stop. (It's located between the Olde Bartley House and Summer Kitchen on IN 135). Peggy Melchior, the puppeteer, designs the intricate, humorous puppets herself.

Drive north of Nashville on IN 135 towards Beanblossom. Just past Greasy Creek Road, you'll find a turnoff for the Bean Blossom Bridge, built in 1880. Indiana's loaded with covered bridges, but this one is special because of its remote location.

It's time to drive south, back towards Nashville and east on IN 46 to the turnoff for IN 135. If it's time for dinner, Tuesday through Sunday, stop at the Story Inn in Story. The walls and shelves are lined with antiques and bric-a-brac, but the dining is very upscale American. A bed-and-breakfast occupies the second floor of the establishment.

Turn west on IN 56, and south on IN 145. A magnificent domed wonder, the West Baden Springs Hotel, looms ahead. Built in 1902 as a modern hotel with every convenience (bank, stock ticker, barber shop, beauty salon, spas, bicycle track, and more), it was a popular spot for the wealthy to enjoy drinking and soaking in the famed spring waters, and to gamble nearby. In the '20s, the town was also a place to imbibe forbidden alcohol. After the stock market crash, the hotel became a Jesuit seminary, then a private college, and fell into disrepair in the '80s.

Nashville

An Indiana industrialist saved it from the wrecking ball, and it has been re-opened as a resort once more. You can tour this gorgeous, semi-restored structure and reminisce about the days when gangsters and high society mingled. Stop by the shop at the end of the tour for period gifts like '20s-style reading glasses or a cowboy-shaped iron bottle opener.

Right next to West Baden Springs, the town of French Lick survived a bit more elegantly. Here you can take an old-fashioned train ride from the Indiana Railway Museum. Beechwood Inn, a popular bed-and-breakfast, also serves an elegant dinner for the general public.

Comfy rockers line the broad porch of the sprawling French Lick Springs Resort & Spa. The grand old dame, once the rival of West Baden Springs Hotel but now owned by the same people, features a host of activities, such as bowling, golf, horseback riding, tennis, swimming, and more. A special treat awaits spa-goers: immersion in a bubbling tub of odoriferous spring water. Don't be alarmed as the foam turns gray to black: It's just the heavy mineral content. Lie back and admire the marble walls and décor of the recently redecorated spa. The resort has recently expanded to include a casino, conference center, and entertainment venue.

Monastery Immaculate Conception

IN 145 south continues through Hoosier National Forest, past several state recreation areas that are busy with boaters and hikers in the warm months. Turn west on IN 64 and south on IN 162. Wondering what that big dome is perched high on the hill in the town of Ferdinand? It's home to Monastery Immaculate Conception, and free tours do not require religious instruction. Get some exercise descending the steps to the crypt, which isn't creepy or lined with bones. The church, in the process of restoration, was begun in 1915 and completed in 1924. A gift shop on site features crafts by the nuns.

It's Christmas all year round in Santa Claus, a few miles south of Ferdinand, where streets with names like Candy Castle Road and shops like the Holly Tree keep the Yule spirit glowing. The town is also home of Holiday World and Splashin' Safari, a theme and water park that has been voted the cleanest and friendliest park in the nation by Amusement Today. Santa Claus is on hand to greet the kids, both in person and as a statue at the front of the park.

The other famous fellow in this part of the state, Abraham Lincoln, lived here from ages 7-21, arriving when Indiana became a state in 1816. En route to Lincoln's boyhood home, now a national monument, stop for a buffalo burger at the Buffalo Run Grill just a few miles west of Santa Claus on IN 162. The owners of the Buffalo Run, Kathleen and Michael Crews, believe in sustainable living and raise buffalo and ostrich on the ranch out behind the restaurant. In the gift shop—a kid's dream—they sell buffalo teeth, hair, horns, and deer antlers.

The Lincoln Boyhood National Memorial bustles with visitors from April through September, when docents demonstrate the hard life of farming in the early 1800s. The buildings are replicas built on the original foundations. If you haven't had your fill of Lincoln lore by now, cross the road to the Lincoln Amphitheatre, which presents a play in the summer season on Lincoln's life.

Driving south on US 231 towards the Ohio River, then west on IN 66, brings you along a scenic stretch towards Evansville. Keep heading west, right into New Harmony, a spiritual community founded in 1814 by George Rapp. The dormitory where men and women lived still stands, as do a number of other buildings from this early period. Rapp and his followers sold the town they built in 1824 to Robert Owen and a group of philosophers, doctors, and intellectuals, who then established a utopian society. Several buildings from Owen's time also survive, some of which are private homes, and some of which are public and open for tours. New Harmony never really expanded, and historic buildings underwent several reincarnations without being torn down. Sample the gourmet fare at the Red Geranium, meditate while you walk the labyrinth, or buy some garden seeds at Earthcare at the Depot.

The Athenaeum, New Harmony

If you're up early, head over to the Main Café, 520 N. Main, for eggs and toast. The restaurant has high ceilings with pressed tin panels, but that's not all that's old fashioned. You'll get yesterday's prices and today's gossip from the farmers gathered for coffee. It's pure Hoosier.

"Big Red," the Holland Harbor Lighthouse, Holland, Michigan

Indexes and Reference

uction/Conditions Mileage Chart Point of Interest Index Lodging Resources City Index Drive Time Map Mileage Map Road Construction/Condit

POINTS OF INTEREST

This index lists all points of interest that fall on the regional maps. To see that area, turn to the inside front cover.

AIRPORTS

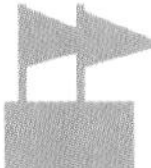

COLLEGES & UNIVERSITIES

Colleges & Universities - Parks, Forests & Wildlife Spaces

COLLEGE / UNIVERSITY	Page	Grid
MISSOURI		
Central Methodist College	46	G1
Central Missouri State University	45	H9
Culver-Stockton College	46	C4
Kirksville College of Osteopathic Medicine	46	C1
Missouri Valley College	45	G11
Northwest Missouri State University	45	B6
Southeast Missouri State University	57	E10
Southwest Baptist University	55	D10
Truman State University	46	C2
University of Missouri-Rolla	56	C4
Westminster College	46	H3
William Woods University	46	H3
NEBRASKA		
Bellevue University	34	G3
Dana College	34	F3
Midland Lutheran College	34	F1
Peru State College	44	A4
NEW YORK		
Alfred University	43	C10
Hobart and William Smith Colleges	33	I11
Houghton College	43	C9
Keuka College	43	B12
Roberts Wesleyan College	33	H9
Rochester Institute of Technology	33	H9
St. Bonaventure University	43	D8
State University of New York at Fredonia	43	B6
State University of New York College at Brockport	33	H8
State University of New York College at Geneseo	43	A10
State University of New York College at Oswego	33	G12
NORTH DAKOTA		
Mayville State University	10	H1
University of North Dakota	10	G2
OHIO		
Antioch University	50	D5
Ashland University	41	I8
Baldwin-Wallace College	41	G10
Bluffton University	40	H4
Bowling Green State University	40	F4
Cedarville University	50	D5
Central State University	50	D5
Circleville Bible College	51	E7
College of Wooster, The	41	I9
Defiance College	40	G2
Denison University	51	C9
Franciscan University of Steubenville	52	B3
Heidelberg College	41	H6
Hiram College	41	G12
Kent State University	41	G11
Kenyon College	51	B9
Lake Erie College	41	E11
Lourdes College	40	E4
Marietta College	51	F12
Miami University	50	E2
Mount Union College	41	H12
Mount Vernon Nazarene University	51	B9
Oberlin College	41	G8
Ohio Northern University	40	I4
Ohio State University at Lima, The	40	I3
Ohio State University at Marion, The	51	A7
Ohio State University Mansfield Campus, The	41	I8
Ohio State University Newark Campus, The	51	C9
Ohio University	51	F10
Ohio Wesleyan University	51	B7
Otterbein College	51	C7
Shawnee State University	51	H7
Tiffin University	41	G6
University of Akron, The	41	H11
University of Findlay, The	40	H4
University of Rio Grande	51	H9
Urbana University	50	C5
Walsh University	41	H11
Wilberforce University	50	D5
Wilmington College	50	F5
Youngstown State University	42	H2
OKLAHOMA		
Oklahoma Wesleyan University	54	G2
PENNSYLVANIA		
Allegheny College	42	E3
California University of Pennsylvania	52	C5
Clarion University of Pennsylvania	42	G5
Edinboro University of Pennsylvania	42	E3
Geneva College	42	I3
Grove City College	42	G3
Indiana University of Pennsylvania	53	A7
Juniata College	53	B11
Lock Haven University of Pennsylvania	43	G11
Lycoming College	43	G12
Mansfield University of Pennsylvania	43	E12
Pennsylvania State University	43	I10
Robert Morris University	52	A4
St. Francis University	53	B9
St. Vincent College	53	B7
Seton Hill University	53	B6
Shippensburg University	53	C12
Slippery Rock University of Pennsylvania	42	H4
Thiel College	42	F3
University of Pittsburgh at Bradford	43	D7
University of Pittsburgh at Johnstown	53	B8
Washington and Jefferson College	52	C4
Waynesburg College	52	D4
Westminster College	42	G3
Wilson College	53	D12
SOUTH DAKOTA		
Flandreau Indian School	24	D2
South Dakota State University	24	D1
TENNESSEE		
Austin Peay State University	59	H6
Eastern Tennessee State University	61	I10
King College	61	H10
Lincoln Memorial University	61	H6
Milligan College	61	I10
University of Tennessee at Martin	58	I1
VIRGINIA		
Eastern Mennonite University	53	I8
Emory & Henry College	61	G11
George Washington University-Virginia Campus	53	G12
Shenandoah University	53	G10
University of Virginia's College at Wise, The	61	G9
Virginia Intermont College	61	H10
WEST VIRGINIA		
Alderson-Broaddus College	52	G5
Bethany College	52	C3
Davis & Elkins College	52	G5
Fairmont State University	52	E4
Glenville State College	52	G2
Marshall University	61	A10
Ohio Valley University	51	F12
Salem International University	52	F3
Shepherd University	53	F11
University of Charleston	61	A12
West Liberty State College	52	C3
West Virginia State University	61	A11
West Virginia University	52	E5
West Virginia University at Parkersburg	51	F12
West Virginia Wesleyan College	52	G4
WISCONSIN		
Lakeland College	28	F3
Marian College of Fond du Lac	28	F2
Northland College	19	D6
Ripon College	27	F12
Silver Lake College	28	E4
University of Wisconsin-Eau Claire	26	B5
University of Wisconsin-La Crosse	26	F5
University of Wisconsin-Parkside	38	B4
University of Wisconsin Pigeon Lake Field Station	18	D5
University of Wisconsin-Platteville	37	A7
University of Wisconsin-River Falls	26	B1
University of Wisconsin-Stevens Point	27	C10
University of Wisconsin-Stout	26	B3
University of Wisconsin-Whitewater	37	A12
Viterbo University	26	F5

PARKS, FORESTS & WILDLIFE SPACES

PARK / FOREST / WILDLIFE SPACE	Page	Grid
ARKANSAS		
Bald Knob National Wildlife Refuge	62	E4
Big Lake National Wildlife Refuge	63	B9
Buffalo National River	62	A1
Bull Shoals - White River State Park	56	I1
Cache River National Wildlife Refuge	62	E5
Crowley's Ridge State Park	63	B7
Hampson Museum State Park	63	C9
Herman Davis Monument State Park	63	B9
Hobbs State Park - Conservation Area	55	I8
Jacksonport State Park	62	C5
Jenkins' Ferry Battlefield State Park	62	I1
Lake Charles State Park	62	A5
Lake Frierson State Park	63	B7
Lake Poinsett State Park	63	D7
Louisiana Purchase Monument State Park	63	G6
Mammoth Spring State Park	56	H4
Old Davidsonville State Park	63	A6
Ozark Folk Center State Park	62	B2
Ozark National Forest	62	A2
Parkin Archeological State Park	63	D7
Pea Ridge National Military Park	55	H8
Pinnacle Mountain State Park	62	F1
Plantation Agriculture Museum State Park	62	G2
Powhatan Court House State Park	63	A6
Prairie County Museum State Park	62	F4
St. Francis National Forest	63	G7
Toltec Mounds Archeological State Park	62	G3
Village Creek State Park	63	E7
Wapanocca National Wildlife Refuge	63	D9
White River National Wildlife Refuge	63	H6
Woolly Hollow State Park	62	D2
ILLINOIS		
Anderson Lake State Fish & Wildlife Area	47	C9
Apple River Canyon State Park	37	C9
Argyle Lake State Park	47	B7
Banner Marsh State Fish & Wildlife Area	47	A10
Beall Woods State Park	58	A4
Beaver Dam State Park	47	F9
Big Bend State Fish and Wildlife Area	37	E9
Buffalo Rock State Park	37	G12
Cache River State Natural Area	57	E12
Carlyle Lake State Fish & Wildlife Area	47	H12
Castle Rock State Park	37	D11
Cave-in-Rock State Park	58	D3
Chain O'Lakes State Park	38	B3
Channahon State Park	38	F3
Chautauqua National Wildlife Refuge	47	B9
Chautauqua National Wildlife Refuge (Cameron Division)	37	H10
Clinton Lake State Recreation Area	48	C1
Coffeen Lake State Fish & Wildlife Area	47	G11
Crab Orchard National Wildlife Refuge	57	D12
Crawford County State Fish & Wildlife Area	48	G5
Cypress Creek National Wildlife Refuge	57	F11
Danville National Cemetery	48	C5
Delabar State Park	37	H6
Des Plaines Fish & Wildlife Area	38	G3
Dixon Springs State Park	58	E2
Donnelley State Fish & Wildlife Area	37	G11
Eagle Creek State Recreation Area	48	E2
Edward R. Madigan State Park	47	C11
Eldon Hazlet State Park	47	H11
Emiquon National Wildlife Refuge	47	B9
Ferne Clyffe State Park	57	D12
Fort Defiance State Park	57	F12
Fort Massac State Park	58	F2
Fox Ridge State Park	48	F3
Franklin Creek State Natural Area	37	E11
Gebhard Woods State Park	38	G2
Giant City State Park	57	D11
Golconda Marina State Recreation Area	58	E2
Goose Lake Prairie State Natural Area	38	G2
Great River National Wildlife Refuge (Delair Division)	47	E6
Great River National Wildlife Refuge (Long Island Division)	46	C4
Green River State Wildlife Area	37	F10
Hamilton County State Fish & Wildlife Area	58	B3
Henderson County Conservation Area	37	I6
Hennepin Canal Parkway State Park	37	G10
Hidden Springs State Forest	48	F2
Horseshoe Lake State Fish & Wildlife Area	57	F11
Illini State Park	38	G1
Illinois and Michigan Canal State Trail	38	F3
Illinois Beach State Park	38	C4
Illinois Caverns State Natural Area	57	B9
Iroquois County State Wildlife Area	38	H4
Jim Edgar Panther Creek State Fish & Wildlife Area	47	D9
Johnson-Sauk Trail State Recreation Area	37	G9
Jubilee College State Park	37	I9
Kankakee River State Park	38	G3
Kaskaskia River State Fish & Wildlife Area	57	B9
Kickapoo State Park	48	C5
Lake Le-Aqua-Na State Park	37	C9
Lake Murphysboro State Park	57	C11
LaSalle Lake State Fish & Wildlife Area	38	G1
Lincoln Trail Homestead State Memorial	47	D12
Lincoln Trail State Recreation Area	48	F5
Lowden-Miller State Forest	37	D11
Lowden State Park	37	D11
Mackinaw River State Fish & Wildlife Area	47	A11
Marshall State Fish & Wildlife Area	37	H10
Matthiessen State Park	37	G12
Mautino State Fish & Wildlife Area	37	G10
Mazonia / Braidwood State Fish & Wildlife Area	38	G2
Meredosia National Wildlife Refuge	47	D7
Mermet Lake State Fish & Wildlife Area	58	E1
Middle Fork State Fish & Wildlife Area	48	B4
Middle Mississippi River National Wildlife Refuge	57	C10
Midewin National Tallgrass Prairie	38	G3
Mississippi Palisades State Park	37	D8
Mississippi River State Fish &Wildlife Area	47	G8
Moraine Hills State Park	38	C3
Moraine View State Park	48	B2
Morrison-Rockwood State Park	37	E9
Mound City National Cemetery	57	F11
Nauvoo State Park	46	A5
Newton Lake State Fish & Wildlife Area	48	G3
Peabody River King State Fish & Wildlife Area	57	A9
Pere Marquette State Park	47	G8
Port Louisa National Wildlife Refuge (Keithsburg Division)	37	G6
Prophetstown State Park	37	E9
Pyramid State Recreation Area	57	B11
Quincy National Cemetery	46	D5
Ramsey Lake State Recreation Area	47	G12
Randolph County State Recreation Area	57	C10
Ray Norbut State Fish & Wildlife Area	47	E7
Red Hills State Park	48	H4
Rend Lake State Fish & Wildlife Area	57	B12
Rice Lake State Fish & Wildlife Area	47	B9
Rock Cut State Park	37	C12
Rock Island Trail State Park	37	H9
Saline County State Fish & Wildlife Area	58	D3
Sam Dale Lake State Fish & Wildlife Area	48	I2
Sam Parr State Fish & Wildlife Area	48	G3
Sand Ridge State Forest	47	B9
Sanganois State Fish & Wildlife Area	47	C8
Sangchris Lake State Park	47	E11
Shabbona Lake State Park	37	E12
Shawnee National Forest	58	D2
Shelbyville State Fish & Wildlife Area	48	E2
Siloam Springs State Park	47	D6
Silver Springs State Park	38	E2
Snakeden Hollow State Fish & Wildlife Area	37	H9
South Shore State Park	47	I11
Spitler Woods State Natural Area	48	D1
Spring Lake State Fish & Wildlife Area	47	B9
Starved Rock State Park	37	G12
Stephen A. Forbes State Recreation Area	48	H1
Ten Mile Creek State Fish & Wildlife Area	58	B2
Trail of Tears State Forest	57	E11
Turkey Bluffs State Fish & Wildlife Area	57	C10
Two Rivers National Wildlife Refuge (Batchtown Division)	47	G7
Two Rivers National Wildlife Refuge (Calhoun Division)	47	H8
Union County State Fish & Wildlife Area	57	E11
Upper Mississippi River Wildlife and Fish Refuge	26	G5
Walnut Point State Fish & Wildlife Area	48	E4
Washington County State Recreation Area	57	B11
Wayne Fitzgerrell State Park	57	B12
Weinberg-King State Park	47	B6
Weldon Springs State Park	47	C12
White Pines Forest State Park	37	D10
William G. Stratton State Park	38	G2
William W. Powers State Conservation Area	38	E5
Wolf Creek State Park	48	E2
Woodford State Fish & Wildlife Area	37	H10
INDIANA		
Big Oaks National Wildlife Refuge	49	G11
Brown County State Park	49	G9
Chain O'Lakes State Park	39	G11
Charlestown State Park	59	A11
Clark State Forest	49	I10
Clifty Falls State Park	49	H11
Deam Lake State Recreation Area	49	I10
Fairfax State Recreation Area	49	G8
Ferdinand State Forest	59	B8
Fort Harrison State Park	49	D10
Frances Slocum State Recreation Area	39	I9
George Rogers Clark National Historic Park	48	I5
Greene-Sullivan State Forest	49	G6
Hardin State Recreation Area	49	G8
Hardy Lake State Recreation Area	49	H10
Harmonie State Park	58	B4
Hoosier National Forest	59	C8
Indiana Dunes National Lakeshore	39	E6
Indiana Dunes State Park	39	E6
Jackson State Recreation Area	49	I8
Jackson-Washington State Forest	49	H10
Kil-So-Quah State Recreation Area	39	I11
Lick Fork State Recreation Area	49	I8
Lieber State Recreation Area	49	E7
Lincoln State Park	59	B7
Little Turtle State Recreation Area	39	I11
Lost Bridge State Recreation Area	39	I10
Martin State Forest	49	H7
McCormick's Creek State Park	49	F8
Miami State Recreation Area	39	I9
Morgan-Monroe State Forest	49	F8
Mounds State Park	49	C11
Mounds State Recreation Area	50	E1
Muscatatuck National Wildlife Refuge	49	G10
Newton-Stewart State Recreation Area	59	A8
Ouabache State Park	39	I12
Owen-Putnam State Forest	49	F7
Patoka River National Wildlife Refuge	59	A6
Paynetown State Recreation Area	49	G8
Pike State Forest	59	A6
Pokagon State Park	39	E12
Potato Creek State Park	39	F8
Quakertown State Recreation Area	50	E1
Raccoon State Recreation Area	49	D6
Red Bridge State Recreation Area	39	I9
Salamonie River State Forest	39	I10
Selmier State Forest	49	G11
Shades State Park	49	D6
Shakamak State Park	49	G6
Spring Mill State Park	49	H8
Starve Hollow State Recreation Area	49	H10
Summit Lake State Park	49	C12
Tillery Hill State Recreation Area	59	A8
Tippecanoe River State Park	39	H7
Turkey Run State Park	49	D6
Versailles State Park	49	G12
Whitewater Memorial State Park	50	E1
Wyandotte Caves State Recreation Area	59	B9
Wyandotte Woods State Recreation Area	59	B9
Yellowwood State Forest	49	G9
IOWA		
Ambrose A. Call State Park	25	I8
Backbone State Park	36	B4
Badger Creek State Recreation Area	35	F9
Banner Lakes at Summerset State Park	35	F10
Beeds Lake State Park	35	A11
Bellevue State Park	37	C8
Big Creek State Park	35	E9
Bixby State Preserve	36	B5
Black Hawk State Park	35	C6
Boyer Chute National Wildlife Refuge	34	F3
Brush Creek Canyon State Preserve	36	A4
Brushy Creek State Recreation Area	35	C9
Cayler Prairie State Preserve	24	G5
Clear Lake State Park	25	H11
DeSoto National Wildlife Refuge	34	F3
Dolliver Memorial State Park	35	C8
Echo Valley State Park	26	I4

Parks, Forests & Wildlife Spaces

PARK / FOREST / WILDLIFE SPACE	Page	Grid
Effigy Mounds National Monument	26	H5
Elinor Bedell State Park	25	G6
Elk Rock State Park	35	F11
Emerson Bay State Recreation Area	25	G6
Fairport State Recreation Area	37	F6
Fort Atkinson State Preserve	26	H3
Fort Defiance State Park	25	G6
Geode State Park	36	I5
George Wyth Memorial State Park	36	B2
Gitchie Manitou State Preserve	24	G2
Green Valley State Park	35	H8
Gull Point State Park	25	G6
Hartman Reserve Nature Center	36	B2
Hayden Prairie State Preserve	26	G2
Holst State Forest	35	D9
Honey Creek State Park	35	H12
Kalsow Prairie State Preserve	35	B7
Lacey- Keosauqua State Park	36	I3
Lake Ahquabi State Park	35	G10
Lake Anita State Park	35	F6
Lake Darling State Park	36	G3
Lake Keomah State Park	36	G1
Lake Macbride State Park	36	E4
Lake Manawa State Park	34	G3
Lake of Three Fires State Park	35	I7
Lake Wapello State Park	36	I1
Ledges State Park	35	D9
Lewis and Clark State Park	34	D2
Maquoketa Caves State Park	37	D7
Marble Beach State Recreation Area	25	G6
McIntosh Woods State Park	25	H10
Mines of Spain State Recreation Area	37	B7
Mini-Wakan State Park	25	G6
Neal Smith National Wildlife Refuge	35	F11
Nine Eagles State Park	45	A9
Okamanpedan State Park	25	G7
Palisades-Kepler State Park	36	E5
Pikes Peak State Park	26	I5
Pikes Point State Park	25	G6
Pillsbury Point State Park	25	G6
Pilot Knob State Park	25	H10
Pine Lake State Park	35	C11
Pleasant Creek State Recreation Area	36	D4
Port Louisa National Wildlife Refuge (Horseshoe Bend Division)	37	H6
Port Louisa National Wildlife Refuge (Iowa River Corridor Division)	36	E3
Port Louisa National Wildlife Refuge (Louisa Division)	37	G6
Prairie Rose State Park	34	F5
Preparation Canyon State Park	34	E3
Red Haw State Park	35	H11
Rice Lake State Park	25	G10
Rock Creek State Park	35	E12
Sheeder Prairie State Preserve	35	E7
Shimek State Forest	36	I4
Springbrook State Park	35	E7
Stephens State Forest	35	H12
Stone State Park	34	B2
Trappers Bay State Park	24	G5
Twin Lakes State Park	35	B7
Union Grove State Park	35	D12
Union Slough National Wildlife Refuge	25	H9
Upper Mississippi River Wildlife and Fish Refuge	26	G5
Viking Lake State Park	35	H6
Volga River State Recreation Area	26	I4
Wanata State Park	34	A5
Wapsipinicon State Park	36	D5
Waubonsie State Park	34	I4
Wildcat Den State Park	37	F6
Wilson Island State Recreation Area	34	F3
Yellow River State Forest	26	H5

KANSAS

PARK / FOREST / WILDLIFE SPACE	Page	Grid
Clinton State Park	44	G4
Crawford State Park	55	D6
Cross Timbers State Park	54	C2
Eisenhower State Park	44	I3
Elk City State Park	54	E3
Fall River State Park	54	D2
Flint Hills National Wildlife Refuge	54	A2
Fort Scott National Cemetery	55	C6
Hillsdale State Park	45	I6
La Cygne Lake and Wildlife Area	55	A6
Marais des Cygnes National Wildlife Refuge	55	B6
Mine Creek Battlefield Park	55	B6
Mined Land Wildlife Area	55	E6
Nebo State Fishing Lake	44	E4
Nemaha State Fishing Lake	44	D3
Neosho Wildlife Area	54	E5
Perry State Park	44	G4
Pomona State Park	44	H4
Tallgrass Prairie National Preserve	44	I1
Tuttle Creek State Park	44	F1

KENTUCKY

PARK / FOREST / WILDLIFE SPACE	Page	Grid
Barren River Lake State Resort Park	59	G10
Ben Hawes State Park	59	C6
Bernheim Forest	59	C11
Big Bone Lick State Park	50	H2
Big South Fork National River and Recreation Area	60	H3
Blue Licks Battlefield State Resort Park	60	A5
Buckhorn Lake State Resort Park	61	E6
Camp Nelson National Cemetery	60	C3
Carr Creek State Park	61	E8
Carter Caves State Resort Park	61	A7
Clarks River National Wildlife Refuge	58	G3
Columbus-Belmont State Park	57	G12
Cumberland Falls State Resort Park	60	G4
Cumberland Gap National Historical Park	61	G6
Dale Hollow Lake State Resort Park	59	H12
Daniel Boone National Forest	60	F4
E.P. "Tom" Sawyer State Park	59	A11
Fishtrap Lake State Park	61	E10
Fort Boonesborough State Park	60	C4
General Burnside Island State Park	60	F3
General Butler State Resort Park	49	H12
Grayson Lake State Park	61	B8
Greenbo Lake State Resort Park	51	I8
Green River Lake State Park	59	E12
Green River State Forest	58	C5
Jefferson National Forest	61	F9
Jenny Wiley State Resort Park	61	D9
John James Audubon State Park	58	C5
Kenlake State Resort Park	58	G3
Kentenia State Forest	61	G7
Kentucky Dam Village State Resort Park	58	F3
Kentucky Ridge State Forest	60	H5
Kincaid Lake State Park	50	H3
Kingdom Come State Park	61	F8
Lake Barkley State Resort Park	58	G4
Lake Cumberland State Resort Park	60	G2
Lake Malone State Park	59	F7
Land Between the Lakes	58	G4
Levi Jackson Wilderness Road State Park	60	F5
Lincoln Homestead State Park	59	C12
Mammoth Cave National Park	59	F10
Mineral Mound State Park	58	F4
My Old Kentucky Home State Park	59	C11
National Scenic River	61	C6
Natural Bridge State Resort Park	61	D6
Nolin Lake State Park	59	E9
Old Fort Harrod State Park	60	C2
Paintsville Lake State Park	61	C8
Pennyrile Forest State Resort Park	58	F5
Pine Mountain State Resort Park	61	G6
Rough River Dam State Resort Park	59	D8
Taylorsville Lake State Park	59	B12
Tygarts State Forest	61	A7
Yatesville Lake State Park	61	B9

MANITOBA

PARK / FOREST / WILDLIFE SPACE	Page	Grid
Northwest Angle Provincial Forest	11	B7
St. Malo Provincial Park	10	A3
Sandilands Provincial Forest	10	A5

MARYLAND

PARK / FOREST / WILDLIFE SPACE	Page	Grid
Antietam National Battlefield	53	F12
Big Run State Park	53	E7
Catoctin Mountain Park	53	E12
Cunningham Falls State Park	53	E12
Deep Creek Lake State Park	53	E7
Fort Frederick State Park	53	E11
Gambrill State Park	53	E12
Garrett State Forest	53	F7
Greenbrier State Park	53	E12
Green Ridge State Forest	53	E9
Harpers Ferry National Historical Park	53	F11
Herrington Manor State Park	53	F6
New Germany State Park	53	E7
Potomac State Forest	53	F7
Rocky Gap State Park	53	E9
Savage River State Forest	53	E7
Swallow Falls State Park	53	E7

MICHIGAN

PARK / FOREST / WILDLIFE SPACE	Page	Grid
Albert E. Sleeper State Park	30	E5
Algonac State Park	41	B8
Aloha State Park	21	H12
Bald Mountain State Recreation Area	41	A6
Baraga State Park	20	C1
Bay City State Recreation Area	30	F3
Bewabic State Park	20	E1
Brighton State Recreation Area	40	B4
Brimley State Park	21	D12
Burt Lake State Park	21	H12
Cambridge Junction Historic State Park	40	D3
Charles Mears State Park	29	F7
Cheboygan State Park	21	G12
Clear Lake State Park	22	I2
Coldwater Lake State Park (Undeveloped)	39	E12
Craig Lake State Park (Undeveloped)	20	C2
Duck Lake State Park	29	H8
Fayette Historic State Park	21	G6
Fisherman's Island State Park	21	H10
F.J. McLain State Park	14	I1
Fort Custer State Recreation Area	39	C11
Fort Wilkins Historic State Park	14	I3
Grand Haven State Park	29	I8
Grand Island National Recreation Area	21	C6
Grand Mere State Park	39	D7
Harbor Island National Wildlife Refuge	22	E3
Harrisville State Park	30	B5
Hart-Montague Trail State Park	29	F8
Hartwick Pines State Park	29	B12
Hiawatha National Forest	21	E7
Highland State Recreation Area	40	B5
Holland State Park	39	A8
Holly State Recreation Area	40	I4
Huron National Forest	30	C3
Huron National Wildlife Refuge	20	B3
Indian Lake State Park	21	F7
Indian Lake State Park (West Unit)	21	F7
Interlochen State Park	29	C9
Ionia State Recreation Area	29	I11
Island Lake State Recreation Area	40	B4
Isle Royale National Park	14	G1
J.W. Wells State Park	20	H4
Kal-Haven Trail State Park	39	C9
Kirtland's Warbler National Wildlife Refuge	30	B2
Lake Gogebic State Park	19	D10
Lake Hudson State Recreation Area	40	E3
Lakeport State Park	31	H7
Leelanau State Park	21	I9
Ludington State Park	29	E7
Mackinac Island State Park	21	F12
Manistee National Forest	29	F8
Maybury State Park	40	C5
Metamora-Hadley State Recreation Area	30	I5
Michigan Islands National Wildlife Refuge	21	G10
Mill Creek Historic State Park	21	G12
Muskallonge Lake State Park	21	C9
Muskegon State Park	29	H8
Negwegon State Park (Undeveloped)	30	B5
Newaygo State Park	29	G10
North Higgins Lake State Park	29	C12
Onaway State Park	22	H1
Orchard Beach State Park	29	D8
Ortonville State Recreation Area	30	I4
Otsego Lake State Park	29	A12
Ottawa National Forest	19	D12
Palms Book State Park	21	F7
Petoskey State Park	21	H11
P.H. Hoeft State Park	22	H2
Pictured Rocks National Lakeshore	21	C7
Pinckney State Recreation Area	40	C3
P.J. Hoffmaster State Park	29	H8
Porcupine Mountains Wilderness State Park	19	C9
Port Crescent State Park	30	E5
Proud Lake State Recreation Area	40	B5
Rifle River State Recreation Area	30	C3
Rochester-Utica State Recreation Area	41	B6
Sanilac Petroglyphs Historic State Park	30	F5
Saugatuck Dunes State Park	39	B8
Seney National Wildlife Refuge	21	E8
Seven Lakes State Park	40	A4
Shiawassee National Wildlife Refuge	30	H3
Silver Lake State Park	29	F7
Sleeping Bear Dunes National Lakeshore	29	B8
Sleepy Hollow State Park	30	I2
South Higgins Lake State Park	30	C1
Sterling State Park	40	D5
Straits State Park	21	F12
Tahquamenon Falls State Park	21	D10
Tawas Point State Park	30	D4
Thompson's Harbor State Park (Undeveloped)	22	H3
Thunder Bay National Marine Sanctuary and Underwater Preserve	30	A5
Traverse City State Park	29	B10
Twin Lakes State Park	19	B12
Upper Peninsula Experimental Forest	20	D5
Van Buren State Park	39	C8
Van Riper State Park	20	D3
Walter J. Hayes State Park	40	D3
Warren Dunes State Park	39	D7
Warren Woods State Park	39	E7
Waterloo State Recreation Area	40	C3
W.C. Wetzel State Park (Undeveloped)	41	A7
Wilderness State Park	21	G11
William Mitchell State Park	29	D10
Wilson State Park	29	E12
Yankee Springs State Recreation Area	39	B10
Young State Park	21	I11

MINNESOTA

PARK / FOREST / WILDLIFE SPACE	Page	Grid
Afton State Park	26	B1
Agassiz National Wildlife Refuge	10	E5
Badoura State Forest	17	B7
Banning State Park	17	E12
Battleground State Forest	17	A9
Bear Head Lake State Park	12	G4
Bear Island State Forest	12	G4
Beaver Creek Valley State Park	26	F4
Beltrami Island State Forest	11	D7
Big Fork State Forest	11	G10
Big Stone Lake State Park	16	H2
Big Stone National Wildlife Refuge	16	I3
Birch Lakes State Forest	17	G7
Blackduck State Forest	11	H9
Blue Mounds State Park	24	F3
Bowstring State Forest	11	H11
Buena Vista State Forest	11	G8
Buffalo River State Park	16	B3
Burntside State Forest	12	F4
Camden State Park	24	C4
Caribou Falls State Wayside	13	H6
Carley State Park	26	D3
Cascade River State Park	13	G8
Charles A. Lindbergh State Park	17	F8
Chengwatana State Forest	18	F1
Chippewa National Forest	11	H10
Cloquet Valley State Forest	18	A3
Crane Meadows National Wildlife Refuge	17	F9
Cross River State Wayside	13	H7
Crow Wing State Forest	17	C9
Crow Wing State Park	17	E8
D.A.R. State Forest	18	E1
Emily State Forest	17	C9
Father Hennepin State Park	17	E11
Finland State Forest	12	H5
Flandrau State Park	25	D8
Flood Bay State Wayside	18	B4
Fond du Lac State Forest	17	C12
Foot Hills State Forest	17	C7
Forestville/Mystery Cave State Park	26	F2
Fort Ridgely State Park	25	C7
Franz Jevne State Park	11	D10
Frontenac State Park	26	C2
General C.C. Andrews State Forest	17	D12
George Crosby Manitou State Park	13	I6
George Washington State Forest	11	G12
Glacial Lakes State Park	16	G5
Glendalough State Park	16	D5
Golden Anniversary State Forest	17	A11
Gooseberry Falls State Park	18	A5
Grand Portage National Monument	13	F10
Grand Portage State Forest	13	G9
Grand Portage State Park	13	F10
Great River Bluffs State Park	26	E5
Hamden Slough National Wildlife Refuge	16	B4
Hayes Lake State Park	11	D6
Hill Annex Mine State Park	11	I12
Hill River State Forest	17	B11
Huntersville State Forest	17	C7
Inspiration Peak State Wayside	16	E5
Insula Lake State Forest	13	G6
Itasca State Park	17	A6
Jay Cooke State Park	18	C2
John Latsch State Park	26	D3
Joseph R. Brown State Wayside	24	B5
Judge C.R. Magney State Park	13	G9
Kabetogama State Forest	12	E1
Kilen Woods State Park	25	F6
Kodonce River State Wayside	13	G9
Koochiching State Forest	11	F11
Lac qui Parle State Park	16	I4
Lake Bemidji State Park	11	H8
Lake Bronson State Park	10	C3
Lake Carlos State Park	17	F6
Lake Isabella State Forest	13	G6
Lake Jeanette State Forest	12	F3
Lake Louise State Park	26	G2
Lake Maria State Park	17	H9
Lake Shetek State Park	24	E4
Land O'Lakes State Forest	17	B9
Lost River State Forest	11	C6
Lyons State Forest	17	D7
Maplewood State Park	16	D4
McCarthy Beach State Park	12	H1
Mille Lacs Kathio State Park	17	E10
Minneopa State Park	25	D8
Minnesota Valley National Wildlife Refuge	25	B10
Minnesota Valley State Recreation Area	25	B10
Mississippi Headwaters State Forest	11	I7
Mississippi National River and Recreation Area	17	I11
Monson Lake State Park	17	H6
Moose Lake State Park	18	D1
Myre-Big Island State Park	25	F11
Nemadji State Forest	18	E2
Nerstrand Big Woods State Park	25	D11
North/South Continental Divide	16	G2
Northwest Angle State Forest	11	B7
Old Mill State Park	10	E3
Pat Bayle State Forest	13	G7
Paul Bunyan State Forest	11	I7
Pillsbury State Forest	17	D8
Pine Island State Forest	11	E9
Pipestone National Monument	24	E2
Ray Berglund State Wayside	13	H7
Red Lake State Forest	11	F9
Remer State Forest	17	B10
Rice Lake National Wildlife Refuge	17	D11
Rice Lake State Park	25	E12
Richard J. Dorer Memorial Hardwood State Forest	26	E4
Rum River State Forest	17	F10
Rydell National Wildlife Refuge	10	G5
Saint Croix National Scenic Riverway	18	E3
St. Croix State Forest	18	F2
St. Croix State Park	18	F2
Sakatah Lake State Park	25	D10
Sand Dunes State Forest	17	H10
Savanna Portage State Park	17	B11
Savanna State Forest	17	B11
Scenic State Park	11	G11
Schoolcraft State Park	17	A10
Sherburne National Wildlife Refuge	17	H10
Sibley State Park	17	H6
Smokey Bear State Forest	11	E11
Smoky Hills State Forest	17	B6
Snake River State Forest	17	E11
Solana State Forest	17	E11
Soudan Underground Mine State Park	12	G3
Split Rock Creek State Park	24	E2
Split Rock Lighthouse State Park	18	A5
Sturgeon River State Forest	12	G2
Superior National Forest	13	G7
Tamarac National Wildlife Refuge	16	B5
Temperance River State Park	13	H7
Tettegouche State Park	13	I6
Two Inlets State Forest	17	B6
Upper Mississippi River Wildlife and Fish Refuge	26	G5
Upper Sioux Agency State Park	24	B5
Voyageurs National Park	12	D2
Wealthwood State Forest	17	D10
Welsh Lake State Forest	11	I8
White Earth State Forest	11	I6
Whiteface River State Forest	18	B2
Whitewater State Park	26	E3
Wild River State Park	18	G1
William O'Brien State Park	18	I1
Zippel Bay State Park	11	C8

MISSISSIPPI

PARK / FOREST / WILDLIFE SPACE	Page	Grid
George P. Cossar State Park	63	I10
Holly Springs National Forest	63	F11
John W. Kyle State Park	63	H10
Tallahatchie National Wildlife Refuge (Black Bayou Unit)	63	I9
Wall Doxey State Park	63	G11

MISSOURI

PARK / FOREST / WILDLIFE SPACE	Page	Grid
Arrow Rock State Historic Site	45	G12
Babler Memorial State Park	47	I7
Battle of Athens State Historic Site	46	A4
Bennett Spring State Park	55	D12
Big Lake State Park	44	C5
Big Muddy National Fish and Wildlife Refuge	45	G12
Big Oak Tree State Park	57	H11
Big Sugar Creek State Park	55	H7
Castlewood State Park	47	I8
Clarence Cannon National Wildlife Refuge	47	F7
Coldwater State Forest	57	E8
Crowder State Park	45	C9
Cuivre River State Park	47	G6
Daniel Boone Memorial Forest	46	H5
Deer Run State Forest	57	F6
Elephant Rocks State Park	57	D7
Eleven Point National Wild and Scenic River	56	G5
Finger Lakes State Park	46	G2
Fourche Creek State Forest	57	H6
George W. Carver National Monument	55	F7
Graham Cave State Park	46	G4
Grand Gulf State Park	56	H4
Great River National Wildlife Refuge (Fox Island Division)	46	B5

Parks, Forests & Wildlife Spaces

PARK / FOREST / WILDLIFE SPACE	Page	Grid
Ha Ha Tonka State Park	55	C12
Harry S. Truman State Park	55	B10
Hawn State Park	57	C8
Huckleberry Ridge State Forest	55	H7
Indian Trail State Forest	56	D5
Johnson's Shut-Ins State Park	57	D6
Katy Trail State Park	45	G12
Katy Trail State Park	46	I3
Katy Trail State Park	47	H6
Katy Trail State Park	45	H11
Katy Trail State Park	55	A9
Knob Noster State Park	45	H10
Lake of the Ozarks State Park	55	B12
Lake Wappapello State Park	57	G8
Lewis and Clark State Park	44	E5
Long Branch State Park	46	D2
Mark Twain National Forest	57	C6
Mark Twain State Park	46	E4
Meramec State Park	57	B6
Mingo National Wildlife Refuge	57	F8
Missouri State Forest	56	F5
Montauk State Park	56	E4
Onondaga Cave State Park	56	B5
Ozark National Scenic Riverways	56	E5
Pershing State Park	45	D11
Pomme de Terre State Park	55	C10
Prairie State Park	55	D6
Reifsnider State Forest	47	H6
Roaring River State Park	55	H9
Robertsville State Park	57	A6
Rock Bridge Memorial State Park	46	H2
St. Francois State Park	57	C7
St. Joe State Park	57	C7
Sam A. Baker State Park	57	E7
Squaw Creek National Wildlife Refuge	44	C5
Stockton State Park	55	D9
Swan Lake National Wildlife Refuge	45	E11
Table Rock State Park	55	H10
Taum Sauk Mountain State Park	57	D7
Thousand Hills State Park	46	C1
Trail of Tears State Park	57	E11
Van Meter State Park	45	F11
Wakonda State Park	46	C5
Wallace State Park	45	E8
Washington State Park	57	B7
Watkins Mill State Historic Site and State Park	45	F8
Weston Bend State Park	45	F6
Wilson's Creek National Battlefield	55	F10

NEBRASKA

PARK / FOREST / WILDLIFE SPACE	Page	Grid
Boyer Chute National Wildlife Refuge	34	F3
Brownville State Recreation Area	44	B4
Dead Timber State Recreation Area	34	E1
DeSoto National Wildlife Refuge	34	F3
Eugene T. Mahoney State Park	34	H2
Fremont Lakes State Recreation Area	34	F1
Indian Cave State Park	44	B4
Louisville State Recreation Area	34	H2
Memphis State Recreation Area	34	H2
Pelican Point State Recreation Area	34	E3
Pioneer State Recreation Area	34	H1
Platte River State Park	34	H2
Ponca State Park	34	B1
Riverview Marina State Recreation Area	34	I3
Rockford Lake State Recreation Area	44	B1
Schramm Park State Recreation Area	34	H2
Stagecoach State Recreation Area	44	A1
Summit Lake State Recreation Area	34	E2
Two Rivers State Recreation Area	34	G2
Verdon State Recreation Area	44	C3
Wagon Train State Recreation Area	34	I1

NEW YORK

PARK / FOREST / WILDLIFE SPACE	Page	Grid
Allegany State Park	43	D7
Big Six Mile Creek Marina	32	I5
Cayuga Lake State Park	33	I12
Chimney Bluffs State Park	33	H11
Darien Lakes State Park	33	I7
Earl W. Brydges Artpark State Park	32	H5
Evangola State Park	43	B6
Fair Haven Beach State Park	33	G12
Fort Niagara State Park	32	H5
Four Mile Creek State Park	32	H5
Golden Hill State Park	33	G7
Hamlin Beach State Park	33	G8
Harriet H. Spencer State Recreation Area	43	B11
Irondequoit Bay State Marine Park	33	H9
Iroquois National Wildlife Refuge	33	H7
Joseph Davis State Park	32	H5
Keuka Lake State Park	43	B12
Knox Farm State Park	43	A7
Lake Erie State Park	42	C5
Lakeside Beach State Park	33	G7
Letchworth State Park	43	A9
Long Point State Park on Lake Chautauqua	42	C5
Montezuma National Wildlife Refuge	33	I11
Niagara Reserve State Park	32	H5
Oak Orchard State Marine Park	33	G8
Pinnacle State Park	43	D12
Sampson State Park	43	A12
Seneca Lake State Park	33	I11
Silver Lake State Park	43	B9
Stony Brook State Park	43	B10
Wilson-Tuscarora State Park	33	G6
Women's Rights National Historic Park	33	I12

NORTH CAROLINA

PARK / FOREST / WILDLIFE SPACE	Page	Grid
Cherokee National Forest	61	I11

NORTH DAKOTA

PARK / FOREST / WILDLIFE SPACE	Page	Grid
Ardoch National Wildlife Refuge	10	E2
Kellys Slough National Wildlife Refuge	10	F2
Sheyenne National Grassland	16	D1
Turtle River State Park	10	F1

OHIO

PARK / FOREST / WILDLIFE SPACE	Page	Grid
Adams Lake State Park	51	H6
Alum Creek State Park	51	C7
A.W. Marion State Park	51	E8
Barkcamp State Park	52	C2
Beaver Creek State Forest	42	I2
Beaver Creek State Park	42	I2
Blue Rock State Forest	51	D11
Blue Rock State Park	51	D11
Brush Creek State Forest	51	G6
Buck Creek State Park	50	D5
Buckeye Lake State Park	51	D9
Burr Oak State Park	51	E10
Caesar Creek State Park	50	E4
Catawba Island State Park	41	F7
Cedar Point National Wildlife Refuge	40	E5
Cowan Lake State Park	50	F5
Crane Creek State Park	41	F6
Cuyahoga Valley National Park	41	G11
Dean State Forest	51	H8
Deer Creek State Park	51	E7
Delaware State Park	51	B7
Dillon State Park	51	C10
East Fork State Park	50	G4
East Harbor State Park	41	F7
Fallen Timbers Battlefield and Fort Miamis National Historic Park	40	F4
Fernwood State Forest	52	B3
Findley State Park	41	H9
Forked Run State Park	51	G11
Geneva State Park	41	E12
Gifford State Forest	51	E10
Grand Lake St. Marys State Park	50	A3
Great Seal State Park	51	F7
Guilford Lake State Park	41	I12
Harrison Lake State Park	40	E2
Harrison State Forest	52	B2
Headlands Beach State Park	41	E11
Hocking Hills State Park	51	F9
Hocking State Forest	51	F9
Hopewell Culture National Historical Park	51	F7
Hueston Woods State Park	50	E2
Independence Dam State Park	40	G3
Indian Lake State Park	50	B5
Jackson Lake State Park	51	H8
Jefferson Lake State Park	52	B3
John Bryan State Park	50	D5
Kelleys Island State Park	41	F7
Kiser Lake State Park	50	C4
Lake Alma State Park	51	G9
Lake Hope State Park	51	F9
Lake Logan State Park	51	E9
Lake Loramie State Park	50	B3
Lake Milton State Park	41	H12
Lake White State Park	51	G7
Little Miami State Park	50	E4
Madison Lake State Park	51	D6
Malabar Farm State Park	41	I8
Marblehead Lighthouse State Park	41	F7
Mary Jane Thurston State Park	40	F4
Maumee Bay State Park	40	E5
Maumee State Forest	40	F4
Middle Bass Island State Park	41	E7
Mohican-Memorial State Forest	51	A9
Mohican State Park	51	A9
Mosquito Lake State Park	42	G1
Mount Gilead State Park	51	A8
Muskingum River Parkway State Park	51	C10
Nelson-Kennedy Ledges State Park	41	G12
Oak Point State Park	41	E7
Ottawa National Wildlife Refuge	41	E6
Paint Creek State Park	51	F6
Perry State Forest	51	D10
Pike Lake State Park	51	G7
Pike State Forest	51	G6
Portage Lakes State Park	41	H10
Punderson State Park	41	F11
Pymatuning State Park	42	F2
Quail Hollow State Park	41	H11
Richland Furnace State Forest	51	G8
Rocky Fork State Park	51	F6
Salt Fork State Park	51	C12
Scioto Trail State Forest	51	F7
Scioto Trail State Park	51	F7
Shade River State Forest (Undeveloped)	51	G11
Shawnee State Forest	51	H7
Shawnee State Park	51	H7
South Bass Island State Park	41	F7
Stonelick State Park	50	F4
Strouds Run State Park	51	F10
Sunfish Creek State Forest	52	D2
Sycamore State Park	50	D3
Tar Hollow State Forest	51	F8
Tar Hollow State Park	51	F8
Tinkers Creek State Park	41	G11
Van Buren State Park	40	G5
Wayne National Forest	51	E10
West Branch State Park	41	G12
West Sister Island National Wildlife Refuge	41	E6
Wolf Run State Park	51	D12
Yellow Creek State Forest	52	A2
Zaleski State Forest	51	F9
Oklahoma		
Bernice State Park	54	H5
Cherokee State Park	54	H5
Disney / Little Blue State Park	54	H5
Honey Creek State Park	55	H6
Lake Eucha State Park	55	I6
Osage Hills State Park	54	G1
Snowdale State Park	54	I4
Spavinaw State Park	54	I5
Spring River State Park	55	F6
Twin Bridges State Park	55	G6
Wah-Sha-She State Park	54	G2
Walnut Creek State Park	54	I1

ONTARIO

PARK / FOREST / WILDLIFE SPACE	Page	Grid
Awanda Provincial Park	32	B3
Balsam Lake Provincial Park	33	B6
Bass Lake Provincial Park	32	C4
Batchawana Bay Provincial Park	21	B12
Bon Echo Provincial Park	33	A10
Bronte Creek Provincial Park	32	G3
Bruce Peninsula National Park	23	I9
Caliper Lake Provincial Park	11	B10
Chutes Provincial Park	23	E7
Craigleith Provincial Park	32	C2
Darlington Provincial Park	33	E6
Earl Rowe Provincial Park	32	D3
Emily Provincial Park	33	D7
Fairbank Provincial Park	23	D9
Fathom Five National Marine Park	23	H9
Ferris Provincial Park	33	D9
Fort William Historic Park	13	E10
Frontenac Provincial Park	33	C12
Grundy Lake Provincial Park	23	F11
Halfway Lake Provincial Park	23	B8
Inverhuron Provincial Park	31	D9
John E. Pearce Provincial Park	41	B11
Kakabeka Falls Provincial Park	13	E10
Kilbear Provincial Park	23	H12
Killarney Provincial Park	23	E9
Lake of the Woods Provincial Park	11	B9
Lake on the Mountain Provincial Park	33	E11
Lake Superior Provincial Park	15	H11
Long Point Provincial Park	42	B3
MacGregor Point Provincial Park	31	C10
Mara Provincial Park	32	C4
Mark S. Burnham Provincial Park	33	D7
Massasauga Provincial Park	32	A3
McRae Point Provincial Park	32	C5
Mississagi Provincial Park	23	C6
Nagagamisis Provincial Park	15	A11
Neys Provincial Park	15	C6
North Beach Provincial Park	33	E9
Obatanga Provincial Park	15	E10
Pancake Bay Provincial Park	21	B11
Petroglyphs Provincial Park	33	C8
Pigeon River Provincial Park	13	F10
Point Farms Provincial Park	31	F9
Point Pelee National Park	41	D8
Port Bruce Provincial Park	41	B12
Port Burwell Provincial Park	42	B1
Potholes Provincial Park	15	G12
Presqu'ile Provincial Park	33	E9
Pukaskwa National Park	15	E8
Quetico Provincial Park	12	E5
Quimet Canyon Provincial Park	14	C1
Rainbow Falls Provincial Park	14	C5
Rock Point Provincial Park	32	I4
Rondeau Provincial Park	41	C10
Sandbanks Provincial Park	33	E10
Sauble Falls Provincial Park	31	B10
Selkirk Provincial Park	42	A4
Serpent Mounds Provincial Park	33	D8
Sharbot Lake Provincial Park	33	B12
Sibbald Point Provincial Park	32	D4
Silent Lake Provincial Park	33	A8
Silver Lake Provincial Park	33	B12
Sioux Narrows Provincial Park	11	A10
Six Mile Lake Provincial Park	32	A3
Sleeping Giant Provincial Park	13	E12
Springwater Provincial Park	32	C3
Sturgeon Bay Provincial Park	23	G12
The Pinery Provincial Park	31	H9
Turkey Point Provincial Park	42	A3
Wasaga Beach Provincial Park	32	C2
Wheatley Provincial Park	41	D8
White Lake Provincial Park	15	D9
Windy Lake Provincial Park	23	C9

PENNSYLVANIA

PARK / FOREST / WILDLIFE SPACE	Page	Grid
Alan Seeger	43	I10
Allegheny National Forest	43	E7
Allegheny National Recreation Area	43	E6
Bald Eagle State Forest	43	H11
Bald Eagle State Park	43	H10
Bendigo State Park	43	F8
Big Spring State Park	53	B12
Black Moshannon State Park	43	H9
Blue Knob State Park	53	B9
Buchanan's Birthplace State Park	53	D11
Buchanan State Forest	53	C10
Bucktail State Park	43	G10
Caledonia State Park	53	D12
Canoe Creek State Park	53	B10
Chapman State Park	43	E6
Cherry Springs State Park	43	E10
Clear Creek State Forest	42	G4
Clear Creek State Park	43	G6
Colton Point State Park	43	E11
Cook Forest State Park	43	G6
Cowans Gap State Park	53	C11
Denton Hill State Park	43	E10
Elk State Forest	43	F9
Elk State Park	43	F8
Erie National Wildlife Refuge	42	F4
Forbes State Forest	53	C7
Fort Necessity National Battlefield	53	D6
Fowlers Hollow State Park	53	B12
Gallitzin State Forest	53	C9
Greenwood Furnace State Park	43	I10
Hills Creek State Park	43	E12
Hyner Run State Park	43	G10
Hyner View State Park	43	G10
Jennings Environmental Education Center	42	H3
Kettle Creek State Park	43	F9
Keystone State Park	53	B7
Kinzua Bridge State Park	43	E8
Kooser State Park	53	C7
Laurel Mountain State Park	53	C7
Laurel Ridge State Park	53	D7
Leonard Harrison State Park	43	E11
Linn Run State Park	53	C7
Little Pine State Park	43	G11
Lyman Run State Park	43	E10
Maurice K. Goddard State Park	42	F3
McCall Dam State Park	43	H12
McConnell's Mill State Park	42	H3
Michaux State Forest	53	D12
Mont Alto State Park	53	D12
Moraine State Park	42	H3
Moshannon State Forest	43	G8
Ohiopyle State Park	53	D6
Oil Creek State Park	42	F5
Ole Bull State Park	43	F10
Parker Dam State Park	43	G8
Patterson State Park	43	E10
Penn Roosevelt State Park	43	I10
Poe Paddy State Park	43	I11
Poe Valley State Park	43	I11
Presque Isle State Park	42	D3
Prince Gallitzin State Park	43	I8
Prouty Place State Park	43	E10
Pymatuning State Park	42	F2
Raccoon Creek State Park	52	A4
Ravensburg State Park	43	H12
Raymond B. Winter State Park	43	H12
Reeds Gap State Park	43	I11
Rothrock State Forest	43	I10
Ryerson Station State Park	52	D4
Sand Bridge State Park	43	H12
S.B. Elliott State Park	43	H8
Shawnee State Park	53	C9
Sinnemahoning State Park	43	F9
Sizerville State Park	43	F9
Sproul State Forest	43	G10
Susquehanna State Park	43	G12
Susquehannock State Forest	43	F10
Tiadaghton State Forest	43	F11
Tioga State Forest	43	F11
Trough Creek State Park	53	B10
Tuscarora State Forest	53	B12
Upper Pine Bottom State Park	43	G11
Warriors Path State Park	53	C10
Whipple Dam State Park	43	I10
Yellow Creek State Park	53	A8

SOUTH DAKOTA

PARK / FOREST / WILDLIFE SPACE	Page	Grid
Adams Homestead and Nature Preserve	34	B1
Big Sioux State Recreation Area	24	F2
Hartford Beach State Park	16	H2
Lake Alvin State Recreation Area	24	G2
Lake Cochrane State Recreation Area	24	B2
Lake Hendricks Lakeside Use Area	24	C2
Newton Hills State Park	24	H2
Oakwood Lakes State Park	24	C1
Palisades State Park	24	F2
Union Grove State Park	24	I1

TENNESSEE

PARK / FOREST / WILDLIFE SPACE	Page	Grid
Big Ridge State Park	60	I5
Big South Fork National River and Recreation Area	60	H3
Bledsoe Creek State Park	59	I9
Cherokee National Forest	61	I11
Chickasaw National Wildlife Refuge	63	B10
Cordell Hull Birthplace and Museum State Park	60	H1
Cove Lake State Park	60	I4
Cross Creeks National Wildlife Refuge	58	H5
Cumberland Gap National Historical Park	61	G6
Dunbar Cave State Natural Area	59	H6
Fort Donelson National Battlefield	58	H4
Hatchie National Wildlife Refuge	63	D12
Indian Mountain State Park	60	H4
Lake Isom National Wildlife Refuge	57	I11
Lower Hatchie National Wildlife Refuge	63	C10
Meeman-Shelby Forest State Park	63	D9
Paris Landing State Park	58	H3
Pickett State Park	60	H2
Reelfoot Lake State Park	57	I11
Reelfoot National Wildlife Refuge	57	I11
Standing Stone State Park	59	H12
Stewart State Forest	58	I5
Sycamore Shoals State Historic Area	61	I10
Tennessee National Wildlife Refuge (Big Sandy Unit)	58	I4
T.O. Fuller State Park	63	E9
Warriors Path State Park	61	H9

VIRGINIA

PARK / FOREST / WILDLIFE SPACE	Page	Grid
Breaks Interstate Park	61	E10
Cumberland Gap National Historical Park	61	G6
George Washington National Forest	53	I8
Grayson Highlands State Park	61	H12
Hungry Mother State Park	61	G12
Jefferson National Forest	61	F9
Manassas National Battlefield Park	53	H12
Mount Rogers National Recreation Area	61	H12
Natural Tunnel State Park	61	H9
Shenandoah National Park	53	H10
Shenandoah River "Andy Guest" State Park	53	H10
Sky Meadows State Park	53	G11
Wilderness Road State Park	61	H6

WEST VIRGINIA

PARK / FOREST / WILDLIFE SPACE	Page	Grid
Audra State Park	52	G5
Beech Fork State Park	61	B10
Berkeley Springs State Park	53	E10
Blackwater Falls State Park	53	G6
Blackwater Outdoor Center	53	G6
Blennerhassett Island Historic State Park	51	F11
Cabwaylingo State Forest	61	C10
Cacapon Resort State Park	53	E10
Canaan Valley National Wildlife Refuge	53	G7
Canaan Valley Resort State Park	53	G6
Cathedral State Park	53	F6
Cedar Creek State Park	52	H2
Chief Logan State Park	61	C11
Coopers Rock State Forest	53	E6
Fairfax Stone Historic Monument State Park	53	F6
Holly River State Park	52	H4
Kanawha State Forest	61	B12
Kumbrabow State Forest	52	I4
Lost River State Park	53	H8
Monongahela National Forest	53	G6
North Bend State Park	52	F1

Parks, Forests & Wildlife Spaces - Museums & More

MUSEUMS, HISTORIC SITES, SKI AREAS & MORE

Museums, Historic Sites, Ski Areas & More

CITIES AND TOWNS

Population figures are from the latest available census or are Rand McNally estimates

Arkansas

CITY, Population	Page	Grid
Alco, 30	62	B2
Alicia, 145	63	B6
Allison	62	B2
Allport, 127	62	G3
Almyra, 319	62	H5
Alpena, 371	55	I10
Altheimer, 1,192	62	H3
Amagon, 95	63	C6
Anthonyville, 250	63	E8
Apt, 295	63	C7
Armorel, 70	63	B10
Ash Flat, 977	62	A4
Atkins Lake, 30	62	I3
Attica	57	I6
Aubrey, 221	63	G6
Augusta, 2,665	62	E5
Auvergne, 75	62	D5
Balch, 50	63	D6
Bald Knob, 3,210	62	D4
Barton, 200	63	G7
Bassett, 168	63	D9
Batavia, 155	55	I10
Batesville, 9,445	62	C4
Bauxite, 432	62	G1
Bay, 1,800	63	C7
Bayou Meto	62	I4
Bay Village, 80	63	D7
Bear Creek Springs, 25	55	I11
Beebe, 4,930	62	E3
Bee Branch, 130	62	D2
Beedeville, 105	63	D6
Bella Vista, 16,582	55	H7
Ben	62	C3
Benton, 21,906	62	G1
Bentonville, 19,730	55	I7
Bergman, 407	55	I11
Berryville, 4,433	55	I9
Bethesda, 55	62	C3
Bexar, 10	56	I3
Bigelow, 329	62	F1
Big Flat, 104	62	B2
Biggers, 355	57	I7
Black Oak, 286	63	B8
Black Oak, 50	63	D8
Black Rock, 717	63	A6
Blackton, 30	63	G6
Blytheville, 18,272	63	B9
Bono, 1,512	63	B7
Boswell	62	B3
Botkinburg	62	C1
Boydsville, 30	57	I8
Bradford, 800	62	D4
Brasfield, 70	62	F5
Brickeys, 60	63	F7
Brinkley, 3,940	62	F5
Brookland, 1,332	63	B7
Brownsville, 60	62	C3
Bryant, 9,764	62	G1
Buffalo City, 40	62	A1
Bull Shoals, 2,000	56	I1
Burdette, 129	63	B9
Burlington, 70	55	I10
Butlerville, 180	62	F3
Cabot, 15,261	62	F3
Calamine	62	B5
Caldwell, 465	63	E6
Calico Rock, 991	62	A2
Camp, 200	56	I4
Caney, 100	62	E2
Caraway, 1,349	63	C8
Carlisle, 2,304	62	F4
Carthage, 442	62	I1
Cash, 294	63	C6
Casscoe, 134	62	G5
Catholic Point, 50	62	D1
Cato, 200	62	F2
Cave City, 1,946	62	B4
Cave Springs, 1,103	55	I7
Center, 100	62	A4
Center Hill, 145	62	E3
Center Ridge, 150	62	D1
Centerton, 2,146	55	I7
Charlotte, 100	62	B5
Chatfield, 40	63	F8
Cherokee Village, 4,648	56	I4
Cherry Valley, 704	63	D7
Choctaw, 230	62	D1
Clarendon, 1,960	62	G5
Clarkedale, 200	63	D8
Clifty, 60	55	I9
Clinton, 2,283	62	C1
Coldwater	63	D7
College City, 269	63	A6
Colt, 368	63	E7
Concord, 255	62	C3
Congo, 60	62	G1
Conway, 43,167	62	E1
Cord, 200	62	C5
Corning, 3,679	57	I7
Cotter, 921	56	I1
Cotton Plant, 960	62	F5
Coy, 116	62	G3
Cozahome, 40	62	B1
Crabtree	62	C1
Crawfordsville, 514	63	E8
Crocketts Bluff, 50	62	H5
Crossroads	62	D2
Crumrod, 30	63	I6
Cushman, 461	62	B4
Damascus, 306	62	D2
Decatur, 1,314	55	I7
Deerfield, 20	63	I6
Delaplaine, 127	63	A7
Dell, 251	63	B9
Denmark	62	D4
Dennard, 120	62	C1
Denwood, 40	63	D8
Des Arc, 1,933	62	F4
Desha, 750	62	C4
De Valls Bluff, 783	62	F4
De Witt, 3,552	62	H5
Diamond City, 730	55	H11
Diaz, 1,284	62	C5
Dixie, 100	63	B8
Dixie, 30	62	E5
Dolph, 350	62	A2
Douglas	62	I4
Drasco, 125	62	C3
Dyess, 515	63	C8
Earle, 3,036	63	E8
East End, 5,623	62	G2
Edgemont, 140	62	C2
Edmondson, 513	63	E8
Egypt, 101	63	B6
Elaine, 865	63	H6
Elizabeth, 95	56	I3
Elm Store	56	H5
El Paso, 300	62	E2
Emanuel	62	H5
Enders, 30	62	D2
England, 3,016	62	G3
Enola, 188	62	E2
Ethel, 40	62	H5
Etowah, 366	63	C8
Eureka Springs, 2,278	55	I9
Evening Shade, 465	62	B4
Fairfield Bay, 2,460	62	C2
Fairmount	62	G4
Fair Oaks, 100	63	E6
Fargo, 118	62	F5
Felton	63	F7
Ferndale	62	F1
Fiftysix, 163	62	B3
Fisher, 265	63	D6
Fitzhugh	62	D5
Flippin, 1,357	56	I1
Floral, 160	62	C4
Floyd, 130	62	E3
Formosa, 90	62	D1
Forrest City, 14,774	63	F7
Fox, 100	62	B3
Franklin, 184	62	A4
Fredonia (Bisco), 476	62	F5
Furlow, 80	62	F3
Gamaliel, 200	56	H2
Garfield, 490	55	I8
Garner, 284	62	E3
Gassville, 1,706	56	I1
Gentry, 2,165	55	I7
Georgetown, 126	62	E4
Gepp, 30	56	I3
Gieseck	63	E7
Gillett, 819	62	I5
Gilmore, 292	63	D8
Glencoe, 200	56	I4
Gold Creek, 300	62	F1
Gosnell, 3,968	63	B9
Grady, 523	62	I4
Grandview, 65	55	I9
Grapevine, 90	62	I2
Gravette, 1,810	55	I7
Grays, 30	62	E5
Greenbrier, 3,042	62	E2
Greenfield, 60	63	C7
Green Forest, 2,717	55	I10
Greenway, 244	57	I8
Greers Ferry, 930	62	C2
Gregory, 50	62	E5
Griffithville, 262	62	E4
Grubbs, 438	63	C6
Guion, 90	62	B3
Guy, 202	62	D2
Hardin, 125	62	H2
Hardy, 754	56	I4
Hargrave Corner, 30	57	I8
Harriet, 50	62	B1
Harrisburg, 2,192	63	C7
Harrison, 12,152	55	I11
Haskell, 2,645	62	G1
Haynes, 214	63	F7
Hazen, 1,637	62	F4
Heber Springs, 6,432	62	D3
Helena, 6,323	63	G7
Heth, 20	63	E8
Hickoria	57	I8
Hickory Plains, 90	62	F4
Hickory Ridge, 384	63	D6
Highfill, 379	55	I7
Highland, 986	56	I4
Hillemann, 30	63	E6
Hiwasse, 125	55	I7
Holiday Island, 200	55	H9
Holland, 577	62	E2
Holly Grove, 722	62	G5
Hooker	63	A7
Hooker, 100	62	I3
Horseshoe Bend, 2,278	56	I4
Horseshoe Lake, 321	63	F8
Horseshoe Lake, 50	62	E5
Hough, 150	55	I10
Howell, 30	62	E5
Hoxie, 2,817	63	B6
Hughes, 1,867	63	F8
Humnoke, 280	62	G4
Humphrey, 806	62	H4
Hunter, 152	63	E6
Ico, 110	62	H2
Imboden, 684	62	A5
Indian Bay, 40	63	H6
Indian Springs, 1,075	62	G1
Iron Springs, 500	62	G2
Jacksonport, 235	62	C5
Jacksonville, 29,916	62	F2
Jefferson, 150	62	H2
Jennette, 124	63	E8
Joiner, 540	63	D9
Jonesboro, 55,515	63	B7
Joy	62	D3
Judsonia, 1,982	62	E4
Julius, 60	63	E8
Keiser, 808	63	C9
Kensett, 1,791	62	E4
Keo, 235	62	G3
Knob	57	I8
Knobel, 358	57	I7
Lafe, 385	63	A7
LaGrange, 122	63	G7
Lake City, 1,956	63	B8
Lake Poinsett, 200	63	D7
Lakeside Terrace, 170	56	I2
Lakeview, 531	63	H7
Lambrook, 50	63	H6
Lazy Acres, 90	55	H12
Leachville, 1,981	63	B8
Lead Hill, 287	55	I11
Lennie	63	C8
Leola, 515	62	I1
Lepanto, 2,133	63	C8
Leslie, 482	62	B1
Letona, 201	62	D3
Lexa, 331	63	G7
Light, 80	63	B7
Little Flock, 2,585	55	I8
Little Rock, 183,133	62	G2
Lodge Corner	62	H4
Lonoke, 4,287	62	F3
Lorado, 120	63	B7
Lost Bridge Village, 270	55	I8
Lowell, 5,013	55	I8
Lunsford, 75	63	C8
Luxora, 1,317	63	C9
Lynn, 315	62	B5
Macon, 960	62	F2
Madison, 987	63	E7
Mammoth Spring, 1,147	56	H4
Manila, 3,055	63	B8
Marcella, 80	62	C3
Marianna, 5,181	63	F7
Marion, 8,901	63	E8
Marked Tree, 2,800	63	D8
Marmaduke, 1,158	63	A8
Marshall, 1,313	62	B1
Marvell, 1,395	63	G6
Maumelle, 10,557	62	F2
Mayflower, 1,631	62	F1
Maynard, 381	57	I6
Maysville, 200	55	I6
McAlmont, 1,922	62	F2
McCormick, 50	63	C7
McCreanor, 50	62	F3
McCrory, 1,850	62	E5
McDougal, 195	57	I8
McGintytown, 50	62	E2
McRae, 661	62	E3
Meadow Cliff, 165	63	E7
Melbourne, 1,673	62	B3
Mellwood, 100	63	I6
Menifee, 311	62	E1
Midway, 330	56	I1
Midway, 90	63	C6
Mimosa Circle, 40	56	I4
Minturn, 114	63	B6
Moark, 20	57	H7
Moko, 30	56	H3
Monette, 1,179	63	B8
Monroe, 110	63	G6
Morning Star, 30	62	B1
Moro, 241	63	F6
Morton, 140	63	E6
Moscow, 200	62	I3
Mounds	63	A8
Mountain Home, 11,012	56	I2
Mountain View, 2,876	62	B2
Mount Olive	62	B3
Mount Pleasant, 401	62	B4
Mount Vernon, 144	62	E2
Mount Zion, 30	62	I2
Newark, 1,219	62	C5
Newburg, 50	62	A3
Newport, 7,811	62	C5
New Salem, 30	63	F6
Newtown, 300	62	H3
Nimmons, 100	57	I9
Noble Lake, 50	62	I3
Norfork, 484	62	A2
North Little Rock, 60,433	62	F2
Oak Forest	63	F6
Oak Grove, 376	55	H10
Oak Grove, 50	62	F3
Oak Grove Heights, 727	63	A7
Oakland, 60	56	H1
Oil Trough, 218	62	C5
O'Kean, 201	63	A6
Olmstead, 30	62	F2
Olyphant, 30	62	D5
Omaha, 165	55	H11
Osceola, 8,875	63	C9
Otwell, 140	63	C6
Oxford, 642	62	A3
Oxley	62	B1
Ozark Acres, 760	56	I5
Palatka	57	H7
Palestine, 741	63	F6
Pangburn, 654	62	D3
Paragould, 22,017	63	B7
Park Grove, 30	62	G5
Parkin, 1,602	63	E7
Parmenter Addition, 200	63	B9
Patterson, 467	62	E5
Peach Orchard, 195	57	I7
Pea Ridge, 2,346	55	H8
Peel, 85	55	I12
Pettus	62	G3
Philadelphia, 350	63	B7
Piggott, 3,894	57	I8
Pinebergen, 60	62	I3
Pine Bluff, 55,135	62	I3
Pine City, 110	63	G6
Pinetree	63	E6
Pineville, 246	62	A2
Pleasant Grove, 220	62	B3
Pleasant Plains, 267	62	D4
Plumerville, 854	62	E1
Pocahontas, 6,518	57	I6
Pollard, 240	57	I8
Poplar Grove, 200	63	G6
Portia, 483	63	A6
Possum Grape, 130	62	D5
Poughkeepsie, 200	62	B4
Prattsville, 282	62	H1
Preston Ferry	62	G5
Prim	62	C2
Proctor, 60	63	E8
Providence, 100	62	D4
Pyatt, 253	55	I12
Quitman, 714	62	D2
Raggio	63	F7
Rainbow Island, 200	62	D3
Ratio, 30	63	H6
Ravenden, 511	62	A5
Ravenden Springs, 137	56	I5
Rea Valley	62	A1
Rector, 2,017	57	I8
Redfield, 1,157	62	H2
Reydell, 50	62	I4
Reyno, 484	57	I7
Rivercliff Estates, 260	55	I8
Riverview, 600	62	C4
Roe, 124	62	G5
Rogers, 38,829	55	I8
Roland, 200	62	F1
Romance, 60	62	E3
Rondo, 237	63	G6
Rose Bud, 429	62	D3
Roseland, 50	63	B9
Rosie, 300	62	C4
Round Pond, 250	63	E7
Rushing	62	C2
Russell, 228	62	D4
Saffell, 150	62	B5
Sage, 80	62	B3
St. Charles, 261	63	H6
St. Francis, 250	57	H9
Salado, 370	62	C4
Salem, 1,591	56	I3
Salem, 2,789	62	G1
Salesville, 437	56	I2
Sandtown	62	B4
Scotland, 130	62	D1
Scott, 94	62	G2
Searcy, 18,928	62	E4
Sedgwick, 112	63	B6
Shannon	63	A6
Shannon Hills, 2,005	62	G2
Sheridan, 3,872	62	H1
Sherrill, 126	62	H3
Sherwood, 21,511	62	F2
Shirley, 337	62	C2
Sidney, 275	62	B4
Sidon	62	D3
Sitka	62	A5
Slabtown, 430	62	H1
Slovak, 50	62	G4
Smithville, 73	62	A5
Snow Lake	63	I6
Soudan	63	F7
South Bend, 950	62	F3
South Lead Hill, 88	55	I11
Springfield, 185	62	E1
Stacy, 30	63	C7
Stanford, 250	63	A7
Staves, 135	62	I2
Stokes	57	I6
Strawberry, 283	62	B5
Sturkie, 35	56	H3
Stuttgart, 9,745	62	G4
Success, 180	57	H7
Sulphur Rock, 421	62	C4
Sulphur Springs, 671	55	H7
Sulphur Springs, 100	62	I2
Summit, 586	55	I12
Sunnydale	62	D4
Sunset, 348	63	E8
Supply	57	H6
Swan Lake, 40	62	I4
Swifton, 871	63	B6
Thida, 110	62	C4
Three Brothers	56	H1
Tichnor, 85	62	I5
Tilton, 70	63	D6
Timbo, 240	62	B2
Toad Suck, 90	62	E1
Tollville	62	G4
Tomato, 30	63	B10
Trumann, 6,889	63	C7
Tucker, 285	62	H3
Tuckerman, 1,757	62	C5
Tull, 358	62	H1
Tumbling Shoals, 280	62	D3
Tupelo, 177	62	D5
Turner, 50	63	H6
Turrell, 957	63	D8
Twist, 50	63	D7
Tyronza, 918	63	D8
Ulm, 205	62	G4
Union	56	I3
Vanndale, 225	63	D7
Varner, 45	62	I4
Victoria, 59	63	C9
Vilonia, 2,106	62	E2
Viola, 381	56	I3
Wabash, 60	63	H6
Wabbaseka, 323	62	H3
Walcott, 170	63	B7
Waldenburg, 80	63	C6
Walnut Ridge, 4,925	63	B6
Ward, 2,580	62	E3
Warm Springs, 30	57	H6
Weber, 30	62	I5
Weiner, 760	63	C6
Weldon, 100	62	D5
West Helena, 8,689	63	G7
West Memphis, 27,666	63	E9
Wheatley, 372	63	F6
White Hall, 4,732	62	H2
Whitehall, 50	63	D7
Widener, 335	63	F7
Wilburn, 75	62	D3
Williford, 63	56	I5
Wilson, 939	63	C9
Wirth	56	I5
Wolf Bayou, 70	62	C3
Woodson, 445	62	G2
Wooster, 516	62	E1
Wright, 350	62	H3
Wrightsville, 1,368	62	G2
Wynne, 8,615	63	E7
Yellville, 1,312	55	I12
Zinc, 76	55	I11
Zion, 135	62	A4

Illinois

CITY, Population	Page	Grid
Abingdon, 3,612	37	I8
Adair, 230	47	B8
Addieville, 267	57	A10
Aetna, 60	48	F2
Akin, 110	58	C2
Albany, 895	37	E8
Albion, 1,933	58	A4
Aledo, 3,613	37	G7
Alexander, 300	47	D9
Alexis, 863	37	H7
Alhambra, 638	47	H10
Allendale, 528	48	I5
Allenville, 154	48	E2
Allerton, 293	48	D4
Alpha, 726	37	G8
Altamont, 2,283	48	G1
Alton, 30,504	47	H9
Altona, 570	37	H8
Alvin, 316	48	B5
Amboy, 2,561	37	E11
Andalusia, 1,050	37	F7
Anderson Lake, 60	47	C8
Andover, 594	37	G8
Anna, 5,136	57	E11
Annapolis, 150	48	G4
Annawan, 868	37	F9
Antioch, 8,788	38	B3
Apple River, 379	37	B8
Arcola, 2,652	48	E3
Arenzville, 419	47	D8
Argenta, 921	48	C1
Argo Fay, 100	37	D9
Arlington Heights, 76,079	38	D3
Armington, 368	47	B11
Arthur, 2,203	48	D2
Ashkum, 724	38	H3
Ashland, 1,361	47	D9
Ashley, 613	57	A11
Ashmore, 809	48	E4
Ashton, 1,142	37	E11
Assumption, 1,261	47	E12
Astoria, 1,193	47	C8
Athens, 1,726	47	D10
Athensville, 50	47	E9
Atkinson, 1,001	37	F9
Atlanta, 1,649	47	B11
Atwood, 1,290	48	D2
Auburn, 4,317	47	E10
Augusta, 657	47	C6
Aurora, 142,990	38	E2
Ava, 662	57	C10
Avon, 915	37	I8
Baldwin, 434	57	B9
Banner, 149	47	A9
Bardolph, 253	47	B7
Barnhill, 80	58	A3
Barry, 1,368	47	E6
Bartlett, 36,706	38	D3
Bartonville, 6,310	47	A10
Basco, 107	47	B6
Batavia, 23,866	38	E2
Bath, 310	47	C9
Beardstown, 5,766	47	C8
Beason, 250	47	C11
Beaucoup, 80	57	A11
Beaver Creek, 35	47	H11
Beaverville, 391	38	H4
Beecher, 2,033	38	G4
Beecher City, 493	48	F1
Belle Prairie City, 60	58	B2
Belleview, 25	47	F7
Belleville, 41,410	47	I9
Bellflower, 408	48	B2
Bellmont, 297	58	A4
Belvidere, 20,820	37	C12
Bement, 1,784	48	D2
Benson, 408	37	I11
Benton, 6,879	57	C12
Berlin, 149	47	D9
Berwick, 160	37	I7
Bethalto, 9,454	47	H9
Bethany, 1,287	48	E2
Bible Grove, 100	48	H2
Biggsville, 343	37	I6
Bishop Hill, 125	37	G9
Bismarck, 542	48	B5
Blackstone, 100	38	H1
Blandinsville, 777	47	A7
Bloomington, 64,808	47	A12
Blue Mound, 1,129	47	E12
Bluff City, 300	47	G12
Bluffs, 748	47	D7
Bluff Springs, 120	47	C8
Bluford, 785	58	A2
Bogota, 60	48	G3
Boles, 90	57	E12
Bolingbrook, 56,321	38	E3
Bonfield, 364	38	G3
Bonnie, 424	57	B12
Boskydell, 30	57	D11
Boulder, 100	47	H11
Bourbonnais, 15,256	38	G4
Bradford, 787	37	G10
Bradley, 12,784	38	G4
Braidwood, 5,203	38	G3
Breese, 4,048	47	I11
Bridgeport, 2,168	48	H4
Brighton, 2,196	47	G9
Brimfield, 933	37	I9
Broadwell, 169	47	C11
Brocton, 322	48	D4
Brooklyn, 100	47	C7
Broughton, 193	58	C2
Brownfield, 75	58	E2
Brownstown, 705	47	G12
Brussels, 141	47	G7
Buckley, 593	48	A4
Buffalo, 491	47	D11
Buffalo Prairie, 60	37	G6
Bunker Hill, 1,801	47	G9
Bureau, 368	37	G11
Bushnell, 3,221	47	A8
Byron, 2,917	37	D11
Cabery, 263	38	H3
Cable, 120	37	G7
Cahokia, 16,391	47	I9
Cairo, 3,632	57	F11
Calhoun, 222	48	I4
Camargo, 469	48	D3
Cambridge, 2,180	37	G8
Camden, 97	47	C7
Cameron, 200	37	H7
Camp Point, 1,244	47	C6
Canton, 15,288	47	A9
Cantrall, 139	47	D10
Capron, 961	37	C12
Carbondale, 25,597	57	D11
Carlinville, 5,685	47	F9
Carlock, 456	47	A12
Carlyle, 3,406	47	I11
Carmi, 5,422	58	B3
Carpentersville, 30,579	38	D3
Carrier Mills, 1,886	58	D2
Carrollton, 2,605	47	F8
Carterville, 4,616	57	C12
Carthage, 2,725	47	B6
Casey, 2,942	48	F4
Cave-In-Rock, 346	58	E3
Cedarville, 719	37	C10
Centerville, 50	58	B3
Central City, 1,371	47	I12
Centralia, 14,136	47	I12
Centreville, 5,951	47	I9
Cerro Gordo, 1,436	48	D2
Chadwick, 505	37	D9
Champaign, 67,959	48	C3
Chandlerville, 704	47	C9
Channahon, 7,344	38	F3
Chapin, 592	47	D8
Charleston, 21,149	48	E3
Charlotte, 25	38	I2
Chatham, 8,583	47	E10

Illinois

Illinois - Indiana

Indiana

Indiana - Iowa

Iowa

CITY, Population Page Grid

Iowa

Iowa - Kentucky

Kansas

Kentucky

Kentucky - Michigan

Manitoba

Maryland

Michigan

Michigan

Michigan - Minnesota

Michigan Center, 4,641 ... 40 C3
Middle Village, 30 ... 21 G10
Middleville, 2,721 ... 39 A10
Midland, 41,685 ... 30 F2
Mikado, 150 ... 30 C4
Milan, 4,775 ... 40 D4
Milford, 6,272 ... 40 B5
Millbrook, 110 ... 29 G11
Millecoquins, 50 ... 21 E9
Millersburg, 263 ... 22 H2
Millgrove ... 39 B9
Millington, 1,137 ... 30 H4
Minden City, 242 ... 31 F6
Mio, 2,016 ... 30 B2
Moddersville ... 29 D11
Mohawk, 600 ... 14 I2
Moline, 750 ... 39 A10
Monroe, 22,076 ... 40 E5
Montague, 2,407 ... 29 G8
Montrose, 1,619 ... 30 H3
Moorestown, 100 ... 29 C11
Mooreville, 70 ... 40 D4
Moran, 200 ... 21 F11
Morenci, 2,398 ... 40 E3
Morley, 495 ... 29 G10
Morrice, 882 ... 40 A3
Moscow, 190 ... 40 D2
Mottville, 200 ... 39 E10
Mount Clemens Southeast, 13,500 ... 41 B7
Mount Morris, 3,194 ... 30 H4
Mount Pleasant, 25,946 ... 29 F12
Muir, 634 ... 29 I11
Mullet Lake, 250 ... 21 G12
Mulliken, 557 ... 39 A12
Munger, 200 ... 30 G3
Munising, 2,539 ... 21 D6
Muskegon, 40,105 ... 29 H8
Muskegon Heights, 12,049 ... 29 H8
Nadeau, 260 ... 20 G4
Nagel Corner, 30 ... 22 H3
Nahma, 210 ... 21 F6
Napoleon, 1,254 ... 40 D3
Nashville, 1,684 ... 39 B11
Nathan ... 20 G3
National City, 80 ... 30 D4
Naubinway, 350 ... 21 E10
Negaunee, 4,576 ... 20 D4
Nellsville, 180 ... 29 D12
Nessen City, 40 ... 29 C9
Newaygo, 1,670 ... 29 G9
New Baltimore, 7,405 ... 41 B7
Newberry, 1,749 ... 21 D9
New Boston, 1,300 ... 40 D5
New Buffalo, 2,200 ... 39 E7
New Era, 461 ... 29 G8
New Greenleaf, 30 ... 30 F5
New Haven, 3,071 ... 41 A7
New Hudson, 110 ... 40 B5
New Lothrop, 603 ... 30 H3
New Richmond, 180 ... 39 B9
Niles, 12,204 ... 39 E8
Nisula, 100 ... 19 C12
North Adams, 514 ... 40 D2
North Bradley, 70 ... 30 F1
North Branch, 1,027 ... 30 H5
North Epworth ... 29 E7
North Lake, 380 ... 30 H4
North Lakeport, 300 ... 31 H7
Northland, 60 ... 20 E4
North Manitou, 170 ... 21 I8
North Morenci, 90 ... 40 E3
North Paynesville ... 19 D11
Northport, 648 ... 21 I9
North Star, 300 ... 30 H1
Northview, 14,730 ... 29 I10
Northville, 6,459 ... 40 C5
North Wheeler ... 30 G2
Norton Shores, 22,527 ... 29 H8
Norway, 2,959 ... 20 F3
Norwood, 100 ... 21 I10
Novi, 47,386 ... 40 B5
Nunica, 360 ... 29 H8
Oak Grove, 150 ... 40 A4
Oak Hill, 920 ... 29 D8
Oakhurst, 50 ... 30 F4
Oakley, 339 ... 30 H2
Oak Park, 29,793 ... 41 B6
Ocqueoc, 90 ... 22 H2
Oden, 350 ... 21 H11
Oil City ... 30 F1
Okemos, 22,805 ... 40 A2
Old Mission, 300 ... 29 A10
Olivet, 1,758 ... 39 B12
Omena, 60 ... 29 A10
Omer, 337 ... 30 E3
Onaway, 993 ... 22 H2
Onekama, 647 ... 29 D8
Onondaga, 250 ... 40 B2
Onsted, 813 ... 40 D3
Ontonagon, 1,769 ... 19 B10
Orangeville, 250 ... 39 B10
Orchard Lake, 2,215 ... 40 B5
Ortonville, 1,535 ... 30 I4
Oscoda, 992 ... 30 C5
Ossineke, 1,059 ... 30 A4
Otisville, 882 ... 30 H4
Otsego, 3,933 ... 39 B10
Otter Lake, 437 ... 30 H4
Ovid, 1,514 ... 30 I2
Owendale, 296 ... 30 F5
Owosso, 15,713 ... 30 I2
Oxford, 3,540 ... 41 A6
Ozark ... 21 E11
Painesdale, 450 ... 19 B12
Palmyra, 370 ... 40 E4
Palo, 250 ... 29 H11
Paradise, 340 ... 21 C11
Paris, 230 ... 29 F10
Parkdale, 550 ... 29 D8
Parkville, 140 ... 39 D10
Parma, 907 ... 40 C2
Parshallville, 80 ... 40 B4
Paulding, 100 ... 19 D11
Paw Paw, 3,363 ... 39 C9
Paw Paw Lake, 3,944 ... 39 C8
Payment, 110 ... 22 D2
Paynesville, 30 ... 19 D11
Peacock, 60 ... 29 E9
Pearl Beach, 3,224 ... 41 B7
Peck, 599 ... 31 H6
Pelkie, 160 ... 19 B12
Pellston, 771 ... 21 G11
Pentoga ... 20 F1
Pentwater, 958 ... 29 F7
Pequaming, 30 ... 20 B2
Perkins, 400 ... 20 F5
Perrinton, 439 ... 29 H12
Perronville, 60 ... 20 F4
Perry, 2,065 ... 40 A3
Peshawbestown, 90 ... 29 A10
Peters, 50 ... 41 A7
Petersburg, 1,157 ... 40 E4
Petoskey, 6,080 ... 21 H11
Pewamo, 560 ... 29 I12
Phoenix, 20 ... 14 I2
Pickford, 450 ... 22 E1
Pigeon, 1,207 ... 30 F5
Pinckney, 2,141 ... 40 B4
Pinconning, 1,386 ... 30 E3
Pine Stump Junction, 15 ... 21 D9
Piney Woods, 500 ... 29 E12
Pinnebog, 60 ... 30 E5
Pittsford, 530 ... 40 E2
Plainwell, 3,933 ... 39 B10
Pleasant Lake, 710 ... 40 C4
Pleasant Lake, 160 ... 40 C4
Pogy ... 29 F10
Point Nipigon ... 21 G12
Ponchartrain Shores, 50 ... 21 E12
Ponshewaing, 290 ... 21 H11
Pontiac, 67,506 ... 40 B5
Portage, 44,897 ... 39 C10
Port Austin, 737 ... 31 E6
Port Hope, 310 ... 31 E6
Port Huron, 32,338 ... 31 I7
Portland, 3,789 ... 29 I12
Port Sanilac, 658 ... 31 G7
Port Sheldon, 180 ... 29 I8
Posen, 292 ... 22 H3
Potterville, 2,168 ... 40 B1
Powers, 430 ... 20 G4
Prattville, 200 ... 40 E2
Prescott, 286 ... 30 D3
Presque Isle, 120 ... 22 H4
Princeton, 180 ... 20 E4
Prudenville, 1,737 ... 29 D12
Pullman, 600 ... 39 B9
Quanicassee, 130 ... 30 F4
Quincy, 1,701 ... 39 D12
Raco, 50 ... 21 D11
Ralph, 60 ... 20 E3
Ramsay, 1,080 ... 19 D9
Randville, 30 ... 20 F3
Rapid City, 420 ... 29 B10
Rapid River, 800 ... 20 F5
Rapson, 60 ... 31 E6
Rathbone ... 30 G2
Ravenna, 1,206 ... 29 H9
Reading, 1,134 ... 40 E1
Redman ... 31 E6
Red Oak ... 30 B2
Redridge, 40 ... 19 A12
Reed City, 2,430 ... 29 E10
Reeman, 110 ... 29 G8
Reese, 1,375 ... 30 G4
Remus, 480 ... 29 F11
Republic, 614 ... 20 D3
Rexton, 160 ... 21 E10
Rhodes, 130 ... 30 E2
Richland, 593 ... 39 C10
Richmond, 4,897 ... 41 A7
Richmondville, 30 ... 31 G7
Richville, 370 ... 30 G4
Ridgeway, 200 ... 40 D4
Riga, 400 ... 40 E4
Riley Center, 60 ... 31 I6
Riverdale, 400 ... 29 G12
Rives Junction, 450 ... 40 C2
Roberts Landing, 50 ... 41 B8
Rochester Hills, 68,825 ... 41 B6
Rock, 440 ... 20 E5
Rockford, 4,626 ... 29 H10
Rockland, 270 ... 19 C11
Rockwood, 3,442 ... 41 D6
Rodney, 160 ... 29 F10
Rogers City, 3,322 ... 22 H3
Romeo, 3,721 ... 41 A6
Romulus, 22,979 ... 40 C5
Roscommon, 1,133 ... 29 C12
Rosebush, 379 ... 29 F12
Rose City, 721 ... 30 C2
Rousseau ... 19 C11
Royal Oak, 60,062 ... 41 B6
Ruby, 220 ... 31 I7
Rudyard, 1,100 ... 21 E12
Rumely, 90 ... 20 D5
Rust, 50 ... 30 A3
Ruth, 230 ... 31 F6
Sac Bay, 20 ... 21 G6
Saginaw, 61,792 ... 30 G3
Sagola, 180 ... 20 E2
St. Charles, 2,215 ... 30 H2
St. Clair, 5,802 ... 41 A8
St. Clair Shores, 63,096 ... 41 B7
St. Helen, 2,993 ... 30 C2
St. Ignace, 2,678 ... 21 F11
St. Jacques, 30 ... 21 F6
St. Johns, 7,744 ... 30 I1
St. Joseph, 8,789 ... 39 D8
St. Louis, 5,453 ... 29 G12
Salem, 350 ... 40 C5
Saline, 8,034 ... 40 D4
Sand Lake, 492 ... 29 H10
Sand River, 80 ... 20 D5
Sands, 60 ... 20 D4
Sandusky, 2,745 ... 31 G6
Sanford, 943 ... 30 F2
Saranac, 1,326 ... 29 I11
Saugatuck, 1,065 ... 39 B8
Sault Ste. Marie, 14,324 ... 22 D1
Sawyer Lake, 80 ... 20 E3
Schaffer, 150 ... 20 G5
Schoolcraft, 1,587 ... 39 D10
Schultz, 301 ... 39 B11
Scottville, 1,266 ... 29 E8
Sears, 90 ... 29 E11
Sebewaing, 1,974 ... 30 F4
Selkirk, 40 ... 30 D3
Seney, 200 ... 21 D8
Seven Harbors, 4,700 ... 40 B5
Shabbona, 90 ... 30 G5
Shaftsburg, 270 ... 40 A3
Sharon Hollow ... 40 C3
Shelby, 65,159 ... 41 B6
Shelby, 1,914 ... 29 F7
Shepherd, 1,536 ... 29 G12
Sheridan, 705 ... 29 H11
Sherman City, 30 ... 29 F11
Sherwood, 324 ... 39 D11
Shields, 6,590 ... 30 G3
Shingleton, 320 ... 21 D7
Sidnaw, 300 ... 19 D12
Sidney, 120 ... 29 H11
Sigma, 100 ... 29 B11
Silver City, 60 ... 19 C10
Sister Lakes, 1,780 ... 39 D8
Six Lakes, 420 ... 29 G11
Skandia, 300 ... 20 D5
Skanee, 100 ... 20 B2
Skeels ... 29 E12
Skidway Lake, 3,147 ... 30 D3
Slapneck, 40 ... 21 D6
Smyrna, 150 ... 29 I11
Snover, 300 ... 31 G6
Somerset Center, 440 ... 40 D2
South Boardman, 250 ... 29 B10
South Branch, 150 ... 30 C3
Southfield, 78,296 ... 40 B5
South Haven, 5,021 ... 39 C8
South Ionia, 100 ... 29 I11
South Lyon, 10,036 ... 40 B4
South Monroe, 6,370 ... 40 E5
South Riley ... 29 I12
Spalding, 590 ... 20 G4
Sparr, 30 ... 29 A12
Sparta, 4,159 ... 29 H9
Spencer, 70 ... 29 B11
Spring Arbor, 2,188 ... 40 C2
Springfield, 5,189 ... 39 C11
Spring Lake, 2,514 ... 29 H8
Springport, 704 ... 40 C1
Spruce, 120 ... 30 B4
Stalwart, 60 ... 22 E2
Standish, 2,096 ... 30 E3
Stanton, 1,504 ... 29 H11
Stanwood, 204 ... 29 G10
Stephenson, 875 ... 20 H4
Sterling, 533 ... 30 E3
Sterling Heights, 124,471 ... 41 B6
Steuben, 70 ... 21 E7
Stevensville, 1,191 ... 39 D7
Stockbridge, 1,260 ... 40 B3
Stony Lake, 50 ... 29 G7
Stony Point, 1,775 ... 41 D6
Strongs, 380 ... 21 D11
Sturgis, 11,285 ... 39 E11
Sullivan, 100 ... 29 H8
Summit City, 50 ... 29 C10
Sunfield, 591 ... 39 A12
Suttons Bay, 589 ... 29 A9
Swartz Creek, 5,102 ... 30 I3
Sylvan Lake, 1,735 ... 40 B5
Tawas City, 2,005 ... 30 D4
Taylor, 65,868 ... 41 C6
Tecumseh, 8,574 ... 40 D4
Tekonsha, 712 ... 39 D12
Temperance, 7,757 ... 40 E5
Temple, 300 ... 29 E11
Texas Corners, 270 ... 39 C10
Thomaston, 80 ... 19 D9
Thompson, 200 ... 21 F7
Thompsonville, 457 ... 29 C9
Thornville, 60 ... 30 I5
Three Lakes, 150 ... 20 D2
Three Oaks, 1,829 ... 39 E7
Three Rivers, 7,328 ... 39 D10
Tipton, 200 ... 40 D3
Toivola, 130 ... 19 B12
Tompkins, 60 ... 40 C2
Topaz ... 19 D10
Topinabee, 400 ... 21 H12
Torch River, 410 ... 29 B10
Tower, 300 ... 22 H1
Traunik, 100 ... 20 E5
Traverse Bay, 40 ... 20 A2
Traverse City, 14,532 ... 29 B9
Trenary, 300 ... 20 E5
Trenton, 19,584 ... 41 D6
Trimountain, 220 ... 19 B12
Trombly, 40 ... 20 F5
Trout Creek, 230 ... 19 D11
Trout Lake, 370 ... 21 E11
Trowbridge Park, 2,012 ... 20 D4
Troy, 80,959 ... 41 B6
Trufant, 500 ... 29 H10
Turner, 139 ... 30 D3
Tustin, 237 ... 29 E10
Twining, 192 ... 30 D3
Twin Lake, 1,613 ... 29 G8
Twin Lakes, 150 ... 19 B12
Tyre, 40 ... 31 F6
Ubly, 873 ... 31 F6
Unadilla, 100 ... 40 C3
Union, 200 ... 39 E9
Union City, 1,804 ... 39 D11
Union Lake, 8,500 ... 40 B5
Unionville, 605 ... 30 F4
Vandalia, 429 ... 39 D9
Vanderbilt, 587 ... 21 I12
Vandercook Lake, 4,809 ... 40 C2
Van Meer, 60 ... 21 D7
Vantown, 30 ... 40 B3
Vassar, 2,823 ... 30 G4
Vermontville, 789 ... 39 B12
Vernon City, 500 ... 29 F12
Verona, 80 ... 31 F6
Vestaburg, 420 ... 29 G12
Vicksburg, 2,320 ... 39 D10
Vienna, 30 ... 30 A2
Vogel Center, 110 ... 29 D11
Volney, 30 ... 29 F8
Wagarville, 30 ... 30 E1
Wakefield, 2,085 ... 19 D9
Waldron, 590 ... 40 E2
Walhalla, 380 ... 29 E8
Walker, 21,842 ... 29 I9
Walkerville, 254 ... 29 F8
Wallace, 150 ... 20 H4
Walled Lake, 6,713 ... 40 B5
Walloon Lake, 240 ... 21 H11
Waltz, 500 ... 40 D5
Warren, 138,247 ... 41 B6
Washington, 1,850 ... 41 A6
Waterford, 71,981 ... 40 A5
Waterloo, 190 ... 40 C3
Waters, 150 ... 29 B12
Watersmeet, 800 ... 19 E11
Watertown, 100 ... 31 G6
Watervliet, 1,843 ... 39 C8
Watrousville, 200 ... 30 G4
Watton, 150 ... 19 D12
Waucedah, 50 ... 20 G3
Wayland, 3,939 ... 39 B10
Wayne, 19,051 ... 40 C5
Webberville, 1,503 ... 40 B3
Weidman, 879 ... 29 F11
Wells, 1,000 ... 20 G5
Wellston, 320 ... 29 D9
West Branch, 1,926 ... 30 D2
West Ishpeming, 2,792 ... 20 D4
Westland, 86,602 ... 40 C5
West Olive, 200 ... 29 I8
Weston, 300 ... 40 E3
Westphalia, 876 ... 29 I12
Wetmore, 480 ... 21 D6
White Cloud, 1,420 ... 29 G9
Whitefish Point, 50 ... 21 C11
Whitehall, 2,884 ... 29 G8
White Lake, 3,200 ... 40 B5
White Pigeon, 1,627 ... 39 E10
White Pine, 910 ... 19 C10
White Rock, 50 ... 31 F7
Whites Beach, 150 ... 30 E3
Whitmore Lake, 6,574 ... 40 C4
Whittemore, 476 ... 30 D3
Wildwood ... 21 H12
Wildwood, 80 ... 29 C8
Willard ... 30 F2
Williamsburg, 400 ... 29 B10
Williamston, 3,441 ... 40 B3
Willis, 300 ... 40 D5
Winegars ... 30 E2
Winn, 450 ... 29 G12
Winona, 40 ... 19 B11
Witch Lake, 80 ... 20 E3
Wixom, 13,263 ... 40 B5
Wolf Lake, 4,455 ... 29 H8
Wolverine, 359 ... 21 H12
Woodbury, 80 ... 39 A12
Wooden Shoe Village, 330 ... 30 E2
Woodland, 495 ... 39 A11
Woodland Park, 200 ... 29 F9
Woodville, 50 ... 29 F9
Wyandotte, 28,006 ... 41 C6
Wyman, 50 ... 29 G11
Wyoming, 69,368 ... 29 I9
Yale, 2,063 ... 31 H6
Ypsilanti, 22,237 ... 40 C5
Yuma, 80 ... 29 D9
Zeba, 130 ... 20 C2
Zeeland, 5,805 ... 39 A9

Minnesota

CITY, Population ... Page Grid

Ada, 1,657 ... 10 I3
Adams, 800 ... 26 G1
Adrian, 1,234 ... 24 F4
Afton, 2,839 ... 26 A1
Ah-gwah-ching, 50 ... 17 B8
Aitkin, 1,984 ... 17 D10
Akeley, 412 ... 17 B7
Albany, 1,796 ... 17 G8
Alberta, 142 ... 16 G4
Albert Lea, 18,356 ... 25 F11
Albertville, 3,621 ... 17 I10
Albion Center, 35 ... 17 I9
Alborn, 200 ... 18 B2
Alden, 652 ... 25 F10
Aldrich, 53 ... 17 D7
Alexandria, 8,820 ... 17 F6
Alida, 20 ... 11 I7
Almelund, 150 ... 18 H1
Almora, 50 ... 17 E6
Alpha, 126 ... 25 F6
Altura, 417 ... 26 E3
Alvarado, 371 ... 10 F2
Alvwood ... 11 G9
Amboy, 575 ... 25 E8
Amiret, 60 ... 24 D4
Amor ... 16 D5
Andover, 26,588 ... 17 I11
Angle Inlet, 75 ... 11 A7
Angora, 100 ... 12 G2
Angus, 50 ... 10 F3
Annandale, 2,684 ... 17 I9
Anoka, 18,076 ... 17 I11
Appleton, 2,871 ... 16 I4
Apple Valley, 45,527 ... 25 B11
Arco, 100 ... 24 C3
Argyle, 656 ... 10 E3
Arlington, 2,048 ... 25 C9
Armstrong, 30 ... 25 F10
Arnesen ... 11 C7
Arnold, 3,032 ... 18 B3
Ashby, 472 ... 16 E4
Ash Creek, 25 ... 24 G3
Ash Lake, 30 ... 12 F1
Askov, 368 ... 18 E1
Atwater, 1,079 ... 17 I7
Audubon, 445 ... 16 B4
Aurora, 1,850 ... 12 H3
Austin, 23,314 ... 25 F12
Averill, 40 ... 16 B3
Avoca, 146 ... 24 E4
Avon, 1,242 ... 17 G8
Babbitt, 1,670 ... 12 H4
Backus, 311 ... 17 C8
Badger, 470 ... 10 C5
Bagley, 1,235 ... 11 H6
Baker, 90 ... 16 C2
Balaton, 637 ... 24 D4
Ball Club, 75 ... 11 I10
Bancroft, 30 ... 25 F11
Barnesville, 2,173 ... 16 C3
Barnum, 525 ... 18 D1
Barrett, 355 ... 16 F4
Barry, 25 ... 16 G2
Bassett, 50 ... 12 I4
Battle Lake, 747 ... 16 E5
Baudette, 1,104 ... 11 D8
Baxter, 5,555 ... 17 D8
Bay Lake, 80 ... 17 D10
Beardsley, 262 ... 16 G2
Bear River ... 11 G12
Beauford, 60 ... 25 E9
Beaulieu, 30 ... 10 I5
Beaver Bay, 175 ... 13 I6
Beaver Creek, 250 ... 24 F2
Becida ... 11 I7
Becker, 2,673 ... 17 H10
Bejou, 94 ... 10 I5
Belgrade, 750 ... 17 H7
Bellechester, 172 ... 26 D2
Belle Plaine, 3,789 ... 25 C10
Belle Prairie, 500 ... 17 F8
Bellingham, 205 ... 16 I3
Beltrami, 101 ... 10 H3
Belview, 412 ... 24 C5
Bemidji, 11,917 ... 11 H8
Bena, 110 ... 11 I9
Benedict, 90 ... 17 A7
Benson, 3,376 ... 16 H5
Bergen, 35 ... 25 F6
Bergville ... 11 G9
Bernadotte, 25 ... 25 C8
Berner ... 11 G6
Beroun, 100 ... 17 F12
Bertha, 470 ... 17 E6
Bethel, 443 ... 17 H11
Big Bend City, 60 ... 16 I4
Bigelow, 231 ... 24 G4
Big Falls, 264 ... 11 F10
Bigfork, 469 ... 11 G11
Big Lake, 6,063 ... 17 H10
Bingham Lake, 167 ... 25 E6
Birchdale, 30 ... 11 D10
Bird Island, 1,195 ... 25 B6
Biscay, 114 ... 25 B8
Biwabik, 954 ... 12 H3
Bixby, 100 ... 25 E11
Blackberry, 50 ... 17 A11
Blackduck, 696 ... 11 G9
Black Hammer, 50 ... 26 F4
Blaine, 45,014 ... 17 I11
Blakeley, 100 ... 25 C9
Blomford ... 17 H12
Blomkest, 186 ... 25 A6
Blooming Prairie, 1,933 ... 25 E12
Bloomington, 85,172 ... 25 B11
Blue Earth, 3,621 ... 25 F9
Blue Grass, 20 ... 17 D7
Bluffton, 210 ... 17 D6
Bock, 106 ... 17 G10
Bois Fort, 350 ... 11 F12
Borup, 91 ... 16 A3
Bovey, 662 ... 11 I11
Bowlus, 260 ... 17 F8
Bowstring, 25 ... 11 H10
Boyd, 210 ... 24 B4
Boy River, 38 ... 17 A9
Bradford, 40 ... 17 H11
Braham, 1,276 ... 17 G11
Brainerd, 13,382 ... 17 D9
Brandon, 450 ... 16 F5
Breckenridge, 3,559 ... 16 E2
Breezy Point, 979 ... 17 C9
Brennyville, 35 ... 17 F9
Brevik, 30 ... 17 B8
Brewster, 502 ... 24 F5
Bricelyn, 379 ... 25 G9
Brimson, 40 ... 12 I4
Bristol ... 26 G3
Britt, 80 ... 12 H2
Brook Park, 156 ... 17 F12
Brooks, 141 ... 10 G5
Brookston, 98 ... 18 B2
Brooten, 649 ... 17 H6
Browerville, 735 ... 17 E7
Brownsdale, 718 ... 25 F12
Browns Valley, 690 ... 16 G2
Brownsville, 517 ... 26 F5
Brownton, 807 ... 25 B8
Bruno, 102 ... 18 E1
Brunswick, 80 ... 17 G11
Buckman, 208 ... 17 F9
Buffalo, 10,097 ... 17 I10
Buffalo Lake, 768 ... 25 B7
Buhl, 983 ... 12 H2
Bunde, 25 ... 24 A5
Burr, 20 ... 24 B3
Burtrum, 146 ... 17 F7
Butler ... 17 C6
Butterfield, 564 ... 25 E7
Butternut, 30 ... 25 D8
Buyck, 25 ... 12 F2
Bygland ... 10 G2
Byron, 3,500 ... 26 E1
Caledonia, 2,965 ... 26 F5
Callaway, 200 ... 16 B4
Calumet, 383 ... 11 I12
Cambria, 80 ... 25 D8
Cambridge, 5,520 ... 17 G11
Campbell, 241 ... 16 E3
Canby, 1,903 ... 24 B3
Cannon City, 60 ... 25 D11
Cannon Falls, 3,795 ... 25 C12
Canton, 343 ... 26 G3
Canyon, 70 ... 18 B2
Carlisle, 30 ... 16 D3
Carlos, 329 ... 17 F6
Carlton, 810 ... 18 C2
Carver, 1,266 ... 25 B10
Cass Lake, 860 ... 11 I8
Castle Danger, 35 ... 18 A5
Castle Rock, 150 ... 25 C11
Cedar, 150 ... 17 H11
Cedar Mills, 53 ... 25 A7
Central ... 17 D7
Ceylon, 413 ... 25 G7
Chandler, 276 ... 24 E4
Chaska, 17,449 ... 25 B10
Chatfield, 2,394 ... 26 F3
Cherry, 100 ... 12 I2
Cherry Grove, 70 ... 26 G2
Chester, 200 ... 26 E2
Chickamaw Beach, 148 ... 17 C8
Chisago City, 2,622 ... 17 H12
Chisholm, 4,960 ... 12 H1
Chokio, 443 ... 16 G3
Clara City, 1,393 ... 24 A5
Claremont, 620 ... 25 E12
Clarissa, 609 ... 17 E7
Clarkfield, 944 ... 24 B4
Clarks Grove, 734 ... 25 F11
Clearbrook, 551 ... 11 H6
Clear Lake, 266 ... 17 H9
Clearwater, 858 ... 17 H9
Clements, 191 ... 25 C6
Clementson, 20 ... 11 D9
Cleveland, 673 ... 25 D9
Climax, 243 ... 10 H3
Clinton, 453 ... 16 H3
Clinton Falls, 40 ... 25 D11
Clitherall, 118 ... 16 E5
Clontarf, 173 ... 16 H5
Cloquet, 11,201 ... 18 C2
Clotho, 25 ... 17 F6

Minnesota

Minnesota - Missouri

Ramey, 50 17 F9
Ramsey, 18,510 17 H11
Randall, 535 17 E8
Randolph, 318 25 C12
Ranier, 188 11 D12
Ray, 80 11 E12
Raymond, 803 25 A6
Reading, 150 24 F4
Redby, 957 11 G8
Red Lake, 1,430 11 G7
Red Lake Falls, 1,590 10 G4
Redtop 17 E11
Red Wing, 16,116 26 C2
Redwood Falls, 5,459 25 C6
Regal, 40 17 H7
Remer, 372 17 B9
Reno, 40 26 G5
Renville, 1,323 25 B6
Revere, 100 24 D5
Rice, 711 17 G9
Rice Lake, 226 11 I6
Richmond, 1,213 17 H8
Richville, 124 16 D5
Richwood, 100 16 B4
Rindal, 25 10 H4
Robbin, 30 10 D2
Rochert, 100 16 B5
Rochester, 85,806 26 E2
Rock Creek, 1,119 17 G12
Rock Dell, 40 26 E1
Rockford, 3,484 17 I10
Rockville, 1,253 17 H8
Rollag, 30 16 C3
Rollingstone, 697 26 E4
Rollins 12 I4
Roosevelt, 166 11 C7
Roscoe, 116 17 H7
Roseau, 2,756 10 C5
Rose City, 40 17 E6
Rose Creek, 354 26 F1
Roseland, 250 25 A6
Rosemount, 14,619 25 B11
Rosen, 40 16 I3
Rosendale 25 A7
Roseville, 33,690 25 A11
Rosewood, 25 10 F4
Ross, 20 10 C5
Rothsay, 497 16 D3
Round Lake, 424 24 G5
Round Prairie, 30 17 F7
Royalton, 816 17 F8
Roy Lake, 100 11 I6
Rush City, 2,102 17 G12
Rushford, 1,696 26 F4
Rushford Village, 714 26 F4
Rushmore, 376 24 F4
Russell, 371 24 D4
Rustad, 40 16 C2
Ruthton, 284 24 D3
Rutledge, 196 17 E12
Sabin, 421 16 C2
Sacred Heart, 549 24 B5
Saginaw, 100 18 B2
St. Anthony, 90 17 G8
St. Charles, 3,295 26 E3
St. Clair, 827 25 E9
St. Cloud, 59,111 17 G9
St. Francis, 4,910 17 H11
St. George, 60 25 C7
St. Hilaire, 272 10 F4
St. James, 4,695 25 E7
St. Killian, 40 24 F4
St. Leo, 106 24 B3
St. Martin, 278 17 H7
St. Michael, 9,099 17 I10
St. Patrick, 50 25 C10
St. Paul, 286,840 25 A11
St. Peter, 9,761 25 D9
St. Stephen, 860 17 G8
St. Thomas, 40 25 C10
St. Vincent, 117 10 B2
St. Wendel, 50 17 G8
Salol, 80 11 C6
Sanborn, 434 25 D6
Sandstone, 2,396 17 E12
Santiago, 75 17 G10
Saratoga, 30 26 E3
Sartell, 9,641 17 G9
Sauk Centre, 3,930 17 G7
Sauk Rapids, 10,213 17 G9
Saum, 40 11 F8
Savage, 21,115 25 B11
Sawyer, 200 18 C2
Scandia, 250 18 I1
Schley 11 I9
Schroeder, 350 13 H7
Seaforth, 77 24 C5
Searles, 150 25 D8
Sebeka, 710 17 C6
Sedan, 65 17 G6
Shafer, 343 18 H1
Shakopee, 20,568 25 B10
Sheldon, 50 26 F4
Shelly, 266 10 H3
Sherack 10 F3
Sherburn, 1,082 25 F7
Shevlin, 160 11 H7
Shieldsville 25 D10
Shooks, 30 11 G9
Shoreview, 25,924 17 I12
Shorewood, 7,400 25 B10
Shotley 11 F8
Side Lake, 180 12 H1
Silica, 50 12 I1
Silver Bay, 2,068 13 I6
Silverdale 11 F12
Silver Lake, 761 25 B8
Simpson, 90 26 E2
Sioux Valley, 30 24 G5
Skibo 12 H4
Skyburg 25 D12
Slayton, 2,072 24 E4
Sleepy Eye, 3,644 25 D7
Smiths Mill, 50 25 D10
Snellman, 20 16 B5
Sobieski, 196 17 F8
Sogn, 30 25 C12
Solway, 69 11 H7
Soudan, 900 12 G3
South Haven, 204 17 H9
Spafford 24 F5
Spicer, 1,126 17 I7
Springfield, 2,215 25 D6
Spring Grove, 1,304 26 G4
Spring Lake, 50 11 H10
Spring Valley, 2,518 26 F2
Spruce Center, 25 17 E6
Squaw Lake, 99 11 H10
Stacy, 1,278 17 H12
Stanchfield, 200 17 G12
Stanton, 50 25 C12
Staples, 3,104 17 D7
Starbuck, 1,314 16 G5
Stephen, 708 10 E3
Stewart, 564 25 B8
Stewartville, 5,411 26 F2
Stillwater, 15,323 26 A1
Stockholm, 25 25 A8
Storden, 274 24 E5
Strandquist, 88 10 D4
Strathcona, 29 10 D4
Sturgeon, 30 12 G2
Sturgeon Lake, 347 17 D12
Sunburg, 110 17 H6
Sundal 10 H4
Sunrise, 120 17 G12
Svea, 100 25 A6
Sveadahl 25 E7
Swan River, 50 17 B11
Swanville, 351 17 F7
Swatara, 50 17 B10
Swift, 30 11 C7
Swift Falls, 70 16 H5
Syre 16 A3
Tabor, 40 10 F3
Taconite, 315 11 I12
Taconite Harbor 13 H7
Talmoon, 60 11 H11
Tamarack, 59 17 C12
Taopi, 93 26 G1
Taunton, 207 24 C3
Tenney, 6 16 E3
Tenstrike, 195 11 H8
Terrace, 40 17 H6
Terrebonne, 25 10 G4
Theilman, 70 26 D3
Thief River Falls, 8,410 10 F4
Thomson, 153 18 C2
Thorhult 11 E7
Tintah, 79 16 F3
Tofte, 250 13 H7
Togo 11 G12
Toivola, 30 17 A12
Tower, 479 12 G3
Tracy, 2,268 24 D4
Trail, 62 11 G6
Trimont, 754 25 F7
Trommald, 125 17 D9
Trosky, 116 24 E3
Truman, 1,259 25 F8
Turtle River, 75 11 H8
Twig, 200 18 B2
Twin Lakes, 168 25 G11
Twin Valley, 865 10 I4
Two Harbors, 3,613 18 B4
Two Inlets, 30 17 B6
Tyler, 1,218 24 D3
Ulen, 532 16 B3
Underwood, 319 16 E4
Upsala, 424 17 F8
Urbank, 59 16 E5
Utica, 230 26 E3
Vasa, 70 26 C1
Verdi, 70 24 D2
Vergas, 311 16 C4
Vermillion, 437 25 B12
Verndale, 575 17 D7
Vernon Center, 359 25 E8
Veseli, 200 25 C10
Vesta, 339 24 C5
Viking, 92 10 E4
Villard, 244 17 G6
Vineland, 607 17 E10
Vining, 68 16 E5
Viola, 90 26 E2
Virginia, 9,157 12 H2
Wabasha, 2,599 26 D3
Wabasso, 682 24 C5
Wabedo, 30 17 B9
Waconia, 6,814 25 B9
Wadena, 4,294 17 D6
Wahkon, 314 17 E11
Waite Park, 6,568 17 G9
Waldorf, 242 25 E10
Walker, 1,069 17 A8
Walnut Grove, 599 24 D5
Walters, 88 25 F10
Waltham, 196 25 F12
Wanamingo, 1,007 26 D1
Wanda, 103 25 D6
Wannaska, 90 11 D6
Warba, 183 17 A11
Ward Springs, 60 17 G7
Warman, 30 17 E11
Warren, 1,678 10 F3
Warroad, 1,722 11 C7
Warsaw, 250 25 D11
Waseca, 9,611 25 E10
Wasioja, 70 26 E1
Waskish, 75 11 F9
Waterford, 75 25 C11
Watertown, 3,029 25 A9
Waterville, 1,833 25 D10
Watkins, 880 17 H8
Watson, 209 24 A4
Waubun, 403 16 A4
Waverly, 732 17 I9
Wawina, 25 17 B12
Wayzata, 4,113 25 A10
Wealthwood, 30 17 D10
Weaver, 50 26 D3
Webster, 150 25 C11
Wegdahl, 100 24 B4
Welch, 80 26 C1
Welcome, 721 25 F7
Wells, 2,494 25 F10
Wendell, 177 16 F4
West Albany, 40 26 D2
Westbrook, 755 24 E5
Westbury 16 B4
West Concord, 836 25 D12
Westport, 72 17 G6
West Union, 87 17 F6
Whalan, 64 26 F3
Wheaton, 1,619 16 F3
Wheeler's Point, 220 11 C8
Whipholt, 130 17 B8
White Bear Lake, 24,325 17 I12
White Earth, 424 16 A4
White Rock, 50 26 C1
Wilbert, 40 25 G7
Wilder, 69 25 F6
Wilkinson 11 I8
Williams, 210 11 C8
Willmar, 18,488 17 I6
Willow River, 309 17 D12
Wilmont, 332 24 F4
Wilno, 35 24 C3
Wilson, 40 26 E4
Wilton, 186 11 H7
Windom, 4,490 25 E6
Winger, 205 10 H5
Winnebago, 1,487 25 F8
Winona, 27,069 26 E4
Winsted, 2,094 25 A9
Winthrop, 1,367 25 C8
Winton, 185 12 G4
Wirock, 25 24 E4
Wirt, 30 11 G10
Witoka, 90 26 E4
Wolf Lake, 31 17 C6
Wolverton, 122 16 C2
Woodbury, 46,463 25 A12
Wood Lake, 436 24 B5
Woodland 17 E11
Woodstock, 132 24 E3
Worthington, 11,283 24 F4
Wrenshall, 308 18 C2
Wright, 93 17 C12
Wrightstown, 30 17 E6
Wykoff, 460 26 F2
Wyoming, 3,048 17 H12
Zerkel 11 I6
Zim, 100 12 I2
Zimmerman, 2,851 17 H10
Zumbro Falls, 177 26 D2
Zumbrota, 2,789 26 D1

Mississippi

CITY, Population Page Grid
Abbeville, 423 63 G11
Algoma, 508 63 I12
Alligator, 220 63 I7
Arkabutla, 380 63 G9
Ashland, 577 63 F12
Austin, 70 63 G8
Banner, 100 63 I11
Barton, 60 63 F10
Batesville, 7,113 63 H9
Belen, 250 63 H8
Bethlehem, 120 63 G11
Bett 63 G10
Blue Mountain, 670 63 G12
Bobo, 100 63 I7
Brazil 63 I8
Buena Vista Lakes, 380 63 G9
Burgess, 50 63 H10
Byhalia, 706 63 F10
Canaan, 40 63 F12
Central Academy, 90 63 H10
Clarksdale, 20,645 63 I7
Coahoma, 325 63 H7
Cockrum, 200 63 F10
Coldwater, 1,674 63 G9
College Hill, 200 63 H10
College Hill Station, 80 63 H11
Como, 1,310 63 G9
Cornersville 63 G11
Courtland, 460 63 H9
Crenshaw, 916 63 G8
Crowder, 766 63 I9
Curtis Station, 140 63 H9
Darling, 230 63 H8
Dubbs 63 G8
Duncan, 578 63 I7
Dundee, 200 63 G8
Early Grove, 50 63 F11
Ecru, 947 63 H12
Enterprise, 200 63 H12
Etta 63 H12
Eudora, 200 63 F9
Falcon, 317 63 H8
Farrell, 250 63 H7
Friars Point, 1,480 63 H7
Gault, 80 63 H11
Gravestown, 200 63 G12
Harmontown, 200 63 G10
Hernando, 6,812 63 F9
Hickory Flat, 565 63 G12
Hideaway Hills, 50 63 H10
Holly Springs, 7,957 63 F11
Hollywood, 80 63 G8
Horn Lake, 14,099 63 F9
Hurricane, 200 63 H12
Independence, 350 63 G10
Ingomar, 250 63 H12
Jonestown, 1,701 63 H8
Lake Center, 370 63 G11
Lake Cormorant, 270 63 F8
Lamar, 150 63 F11
Lambert, 1,967 63 I8
Laws Hill, 170 63 G10
Longtown, 250 63 G9
Looxahoma, 110 63 G10
Lula, 370 63 H8
Lurand, 130 63 I7
Lynchburg, 2,959 63 F9
Lyon, 418 63 I7
Marks, 2,047 63 H8
Mattson, 150 63 I7
Michigan City, 250 63 F11
Mount Pleasant, 400 63 F11
Myrtle, 407 63 G12
New Albany, 7,607 63 H12
New Houlka, 710 63 I12
Norfolk, 30 63 F8
North Haven, 270 63 G12
North Tunica, 1,450 63 G8
Oakland, 586 63 I9
Old Houlka, 30 63 I12
Olive Branch, 21,054 63 F10
Oxford, 11,756 63 H11
Paris, 160 63 I11
Pleasant Grove, 110 63 H9
Pontotoc, 5,253 63 H12
Pope, 241 63 I9
Potts Camp, 494 63 G11
Prichard, 30 63 G8
Pumpkin Center, 70 63 G12
Randolph, 400 63 I12
Red Banks, 580 63 F11
Rena Lara, 270 63 I7
Robbs, 100 63 I12
Robinsonville, 260 63 F8
Roundlake, 100 63 I6
Sardis, 2,038 63 H9
Sarepta, 50 63 I11
Savage, 160 63 G8
Senatobia, 6,682 63 G9
Senatobia Lakes, 200 63 G9
Sherard, 150 63 I7
Slayden, 120 63 F11
Sledge, 529 63 H8
Snow Lake Shores, 300 63 F11
Southaven, 28,977 63 F9
Splinter, 30 63 H10
Springville, 80 63 H12
Stovall, 30 63 H7
Strayhorn, 250 63 G9
Taylor, 289 63 H10
Thaxton, 513 63 H12
Toccopola, 189 63 H12
Tula, 120 63 H11
Tunica, 1,132 63 G8
Twin Lakes, 4,700 63 F9
Tyro, 100 63 G10
Vance, 250 63 I8
Victoria, 570 63 F10
Walls, 480 63 F9
Waterford, 350 63 G11
Water Valley, 3,677 63 I10
West Marks, 300 63 H8
Wyatte 63 G10
Yocona, 150 63 H11

Missouri

CITY, Population Page Grid
Acorn Ridge, 30 57 G9
Adrian, 1,780 55 A7
Advance, 1,244 57 F9
Agency, 599 45 E6
Albany, 1,937 45 B8
Aldrich, 75 55 D9
Alexandria, 166 46 B5
Alley Spring 56 F5
Alma, 399 45 G10
Almartha 56 G1
Altamont, 218 45 D8
Altenburg, 309 57 D10
Alton, 668 56 H5
Amoret, 211 55 B6
Amsterdam, 281 55 A6
Anderson, 1,856 55 H7
Annapolis, 310 57 E7
Anniston, 285 57 G11
Anthonies Mill 57 B6
Anutt, 60 56 D4
Appleton City, 1,314 55 B8
Arab, 130 57 F9
Arbyrd, 528 63 B8
Arcadia, 567 57 D7
Archie, 890 45 I8
Arcola, 45 55 D8
Argyle, 164 56 A3
Arkoe, 58 45 B6
Armstrong, 287 46 F1
Arnold, 19,965 57 A8
Arrow Rock, 79 45 G12
Asbury, 218 55 E6
Ashburn, 51 47 E6
Asherville, 40 57 G8
Ash Grove, 1,430 55 E9
Ashland, 2,201 46 H2
Ashley, 150 46 F5
Atlanta, 450 46 D2
Augusta, 218 47 I6
Aurora, 7,014 55 G9
Austin, 150 45 I8
Auxvasse, 901 46 G3
Ava, 3,021 55 G12
Avalon, 70 45 E10
Avilla, 137 55 F8
Bahner 45 I11
Bakersfield, 285 56 H2
Bakerville 57 I9
Ballard, 80 55 A8
Ballwin, 31,283 47 I7
Bardley 57 H6
Baring, 159 46 B3
Barnard, 257 45 C6
Barnett, 207 55 A12
Barnhart, 6,108 57 A8
Bartlett 56 F5
Battlefield, 2,385 55 F10
Beaufort, 260 56 A5
Belfast, 220 55 G7
Belgrade, 250 57 C6
Bell City, 461 57 F10
Belle, 1,344 56 B4
Belleview, 200 57 D7
Bellflower, 427 46 G5
Belton, 21,730 45 H7
Bem 56 B5
Bennett Springs, 100 55 D12
Benton, 732 57 F10
Benton City, 122 46 G4
Berger, 206 46 H5
Bernie, 1,777 57 H9
Berryman 57 C6
Bertrand, 740 57 G11
Bethany, 3,087 45 B8
Bethel, 121 46 D3
Bevier, 723 46 D2
Bigelow, 38 44 C5
Big Lake, 127 44 C5
Big Spring, 120 46 H5
Billings, 1,091 55 F9
Birch Tree, 634 56 F4
Bismarck, 1,470 57 D7
Bixby, 100 57 D6
Black, 210 57 D6
Blackburn, 284 45 G10
Blackwater, 199 45 G12
Blairstown, 141 45 I9
Bland, 565 56 A4
Bloomfield, 1,952 57 G9
Bloomsdale, 419 57 C8
Blue Eye, 129 55 H10
Blue Springs, 48,080 45 G8
Blythedale, 233 45 B9
Bogard, 234 45 E10
Bois D'Arc, 500 55 E10
Bolivar, 9,143 55 D10
Bona, 30 55 D9
Bonne Terre, 4,039 57 C7
Boonesboro, 60 45 G12
Boonville, 8,202 45 G12
Boss, 100 56 D5
Bosworth, 382 45 E11
Bourbon, 1,348 56 B5
Bowling Green, 5,166 47 F6
Bowmansville, 250 45 H9
Bradleyville, 100 55 G11
Bragg City, 189 57 I9
Branch, 200 55 C11
Brandon 45 I10
Brandsville, 174 56 H4
Branson, 6,050 55 H11
Branson West, 408 55 H10
Braymer, 910 45 E9
Breckenridge, 454 45 D9
Brewer, 115 57 C9
Briar 57 H6
Brinktown, 100 56 B3
Bronaugh, 245 55 D7
Brookfield, 4,769 45 D11
Broseley, 200 57 H8
Brownbranch 55 G12
Browning, 317 45 C11
Brownington, 119 55 B9
Brownwood, 200 57 F9
Brumley, 102 56 B1
Brunswick, 925 45 F11
Brush Creek, 100 55 D12
Buckhorn 57 E8
Buckhorn, 300 56 C2
Bucklin, 524 45 D12
Buckner, 2,725 45 G8
Bucyrus, 50 56 E3
Buell, 70 46 G5
Buffalo, 2,781 55 D11
Bunceton, 348 45 H12
Bunker, 427 56 E5
Burfordville, 80 57 E10
Burlington Junction, 632 44 B5
Butler, 4,209 55 B7
Bynumville, 50 45 E12
Byrnes Mill, 2,376 57 A7
Cabool, 2,168 56 F3
Cainsville, 370 45 B9
Cairo, 293 46 E2
Caledonia, 158 57 D7
Calhoun, 491 45 I10
California, 4,005 46 I1
Callao, 291 46 D1
Calwood, 100 46 H4
Camdenton, 2,779 55 C12
Cameron, 9,788 45 D8
Campbell, 1,883 57 H9
Canalou, 348 57 G10
Cane Hill, 80 55 D9
Canton, 2,557 46 C5
Cape Fair, 600 55 G10
Cape Girardeau, 35,349 57 E10
Cardwell, 789 63 B8
Carl Junction, 5,294 55 F6
Carr Lane, 80 55 H9
Carrollton, 4,122 45 F10
Carthage, 12,668 55 F7
Caruth, 100 63 A9
Caruthersville, 6,760 63 A10
Cascade 57 E8
Cassville, 2,890 55 H8
Caulfield, 110 56 H3
Cedarcreek, 100 55 H11
Cedar Gap, 40 55 F12
Cedar Hill, 1,703 57 A7
Cedar Springs, 85 55 C8
Center, 644 46 E5
Centerview, 249 45 H9
Centerville, 171 57 E6
Centralia, 3,774 46 F3
Chadwick, 190 55 G11
Chaffee, 3,044 57 F10
Chamois, 456 46 H4
Charity, 120 55 D11
Charleston, 4,732 57 G11
Cherokee Pass, 300 57 E8
Cherryville, 135 56 C5
Chesapeake, 100 55 F9
Chesterfield, 46,802 47 I7
Chestnutridge, 150 55 G10
Chilhowee, 329 45 I9
Chillicothe, 8,968 45 D10
Chula, 198 45 D10
Clarence, 915 46 D2
Clark, 275 46 F2
Clarksburg, 375 46 H1
Clarksdale, 351 45 D7
Clarksville, 490 47 F6
Clarkton, 1,330 57 H9
Clearmont, 191 45 A6
Cleveland, 592 45 H7
Clever, 1,010 55 F10
Clifton Hill, 124 46 E1
Climax Springs, 80 55 B11
Clinton, 9,311 55 A9
Cliquot, 100 55 D10
Coal 55 A9
Cobalt Village, 189 57 D8
Coffman, 80 57 C8
Coldspring 56 F2
Coldwater 57 E8
Cole Camp, 1,028 45 I11
College Mound, 50 46 E1
Collins, 176 55 C9
Columbia, 84,531 46 G2
Columbus, 100 45 H9
Commerce, 110 57 F11
Competition 56 E2
Conception Junction, 202 45 B7
Concordia, 2,360 45 G10
Connelsville, 120 45 B12
Conran, 100 57 H10
Conway, 743 55 D12
Cook Station 56 C5
Cooper Hill, 60 56 A4
Corder, 427 45 G10
Corning, 21 44 B4
Corridon, 50 57 E6
Cosby, 143 45 D7
Cottonwood Point, 30 63 B10
Couch, 80 56 H5
Country Club Village, 1,846 45 D6
Cowgill, 247 45 E9
Craig, 309 44 C5

Missouri

Missouri - New York

Nebraska

New York

North Carolina

North Dakota

Ohio

Ohio - Ontario

Mount Liberty, 250 ... 51 B8
Mount Orab, 2,307 ... 50 G5
Mount Perry, 220 ... 51 D10
Mount Pleasant, 70 ... 51 F9
Mount Sterling, 1,865 ... 51 D6
Mount Vernon, 15,256 ... 51 B9
Mount Victory, 600 ... 51 A6
Mowrystown, 373 ... 50 G5
Moxahala, 300 ... 51 E10
Nankin, 400 ... 41 H8
Napoleon, 9,318 ... 40 F3
Nashport, 260 ... 51 C10
Nashville, 172 ... 51 A10
Neelysville, 40 ... 51 E11
Negley, 900 ... 42 I2
Nelsonville, 5,230 ... 51 E9
Nettle Lake, 200 ... 40 E1
Nevada, 814 ... 41 I6
New Albany, 3,711 ... 51 C8
Newark, 46,275 ... 51 C9
New Bavaria, 78 ... 40 G3
New Boston, 2,340 ... 51 H7
New Bremen, 2,909 ... 50 B3
New Carlisle, 5,735 ... 50 D4
Newcastle, 100 ... 51 B10
Newcomerstown, 4,008 ... 51 B11
New Concord, 2,651 ... 51 C11
New Dover, 130 ... 51 B6
New Holland, 785 ... 51 E6
New Hope, 150 ... 50 D2
New Jasper, 100 ... 50 E5
New Knoxville, 891 ... 50 A3
New Lebanon, 4,231 ... 50 D3
New Lexington, 4,689 ... 51 D10
New London, 2,696 ... 41 H8
New Madison, 817 ... 50 C2
New Paris, 1,623 ... 50 D2
New Philadelphia, 17,056 ... 51 A12
New Pittsburg, 270 ... 41 I9
New Plymouth, 120 ... 51 F9
Newport, 180 ... 51 D6
Newport, 700 ... 52 F1
New Richmond, 2,219 ... 50 G3
New Riegel, 226 ... 40 H5
New Straitsville, 774 ... 51 E9
Newton Falls, 5,002 ... 41 G12
Newtonsville, 492 ... 50 G4
New Vienna, 1,294 ... 50 F5
New Washington, 987 ... 41 H7
New Waterford, 1,391 ... 42 I2
Ney, 364 ... 40 F2
Niles, 20,932 ... 42 G1
Nipgen, 100 ... 51 F7
North Baltimore, 3,361 ... 40 G4
North Bloomfield, 500 ... 42 F1
North Canton, 16,369 ... 41 H11
North Fork Village, 1,726 ... 51 F7
Northgate, 8,016 ... 50 F3
North Hampton, 370 ... 50 C4
North Lewisburg, 1,588 ... 51 C6
North Madison, 8,451 ... 41 E12
North Olmsted, 34,113 ... 41 F9
Northridge, 6,853 ... 50 C5
North Royalton, 28,648 ... 41 G10
North Zanesville, 3,013 ... 51 C10
Norwalk, 16,238 ... 41 G7
Norwood, 21,675 ... 50 G3
Nova, 430 ... 41 H8
Oak Harbor, 2,841 ... 41 F6
Oak Hill, 1,685 ... 51 H9
Oak Shade, 100 ... 40 E3
Oakwood, 607 ... 40 H2
Oberlin, 8,195 ... 41 G9
Obetz, 3,977 ... 51 D7
Ohio City, 784 ... 40 I2
Okolona, 140 ... 40 G3
Old Washington, 265 ... 51 C12
Olena, 350 ... 41 G8
Olive Green, 65 ... 51 B8
Ontario, 5,303 ... 41 I7
Oregon, 19,355 ... 40 F5
Oregonia, 100 ... 50 E4
Orrville, 8,551 ... 41 I10
Orwell, 1,519 ... 42 F1
Osgood, 255 ... 50 B3
Ostrander, 405 ... 51 B7
Otsego, 50 ... 51 C11
Ottawa, 4,367 ... 40 H3
Ottoville, 873 ... 40 H2
Owensville, 816 ... 50 G4
Oxford, 21,943 ... 50 E2
Padua, 70 ... 50 A2
Pagetown, 40 ... 51 B8
Painesville, 17,503 ... 41 E11
Palmyra, 240 ... 41 H12
Pancoastburg, 150 ... 51 E6
Pandora, 1,188 ... 40 H4
Parma, 85,655 ... 41 F10
Pataskala, 10,249 ... 51 C8
Patriot, 140 ... 51 H9
Paulding, 3,595 ... 40 G2
Pavonia, 100 ... 41 I8
Payne, 1,166 ... 40 H1
Peebles, 1,739 ... 51 G6
Pemberville, 1,365 ... 40 F5
Peninsula, 602 ... 41 G10
Peoli, 30 ... 51 C12
Perrysburg, 16,945 ... 40 F5
Perrysville, 816 ... 41 I8
Phillipsburg, 628 ... 50 D3
Philo, 769 ... 51 D10
Pickerington, 9,792 ... 51 D8
Pierpont, 420 ... 42 E2
Piketon, 1,907 ... 51 G7
Pioneer, 1,460 ... 40 E2
Piqua, 20,738 ... 50 C4
Pitsburg, 392 ... 50 C3
Plain City, 2,832 ... 51 C6
Plainfield, 158 ... 51 C11
Plantsville, 25 ... 51 E11
Pleasant Grove, 2,016 ... 51 D10
Pleasant Hill, 1,134 ... 50 C3
Pleasant Home, 200 ... 41 H9
Plumwood, 280 ... 51 C6
Plymouth, 1,852 ... 41 H7
Pomeroy, 1,966 ... 51 G10
Portage Lakes, 9,870 ... 41 H11
Port Clinton, 6,391 ... 41 F6
Port Jefferson, 321 ... 50 B4
Portsmouth, 20,909 ... 51 H7
Port Washington, 552 ... 51 B12
Port William, 258 ... 50 E5
Powell, 6,247 ... 51 C7
Powhatan Point, 1,744 ... 52 D2
Prattsville, 30 ... 51 F9
Prospect, 1,191 ... 51 B7
Put In Bay, 131 ... 41 E7
Pyro, 150 ... 51 G9
Quaker City, 563 ... 51 C12
Quincy, 734 ... 50 B4
Radcliff, 150 ... 51 G9
Radnor, 250 ... 51 B7
Rainsboro, 280 ... 51 F6
Randolph, 750 ... 41 H11
Rarden, 176 ... 51 H7
Ravenna, 11,771 ... 41 G11
Rawson, 465 ... 40 H4
Ray, 100 ... 51 F8
Raymond, 300 ... 51 B6
Reading, 11,292 ... 50 F3
Reedsville, 300 ... 51 G11
Reinersville, 100 ... 51 E11
Reno Beach, 430 ... 41 E6
Republic, 614 ... 41 H6
Revenge ... 51 E8
Reynoldsburg, 32,069 ... 51 D8
Richfield Center, 110 ... 40 E4
Richmond, 471 ... 52 B3
Richmond Dale, 700 ... 51 F8
Richwood, 2,156 ... 51 B6
Ridgeland, 50 ... 51 G9
Ridgeway, 354 ... 51 A6
Ringgold, 25 ... 51 E10
Rio Grande, 915 ... 51 H9
Ripley, 1,745 ... 50 H5
Rittman, 6,314 ... 41 H10
Riverside, 23,545 ... 50 D4
Roaming Shores, 1,239 ... 42 F1
Rockbridge, 450 ... 51 E9
Rock Creek, 584 ... 42 E1
Rockford, 1,126 ... 40 I2
Rocky Ridge, 389 ... 41 F6
Rootstown, 650 ... 41 H11
Rosedale, 180 ... 51 C6
Roseland, 2,150 ... 41 I8
Roseville, 1,936 ... 51 D10
Rossburg, 224 ... 50 B2
Rossford, 6,406 ... 40 F5
Rudolph, 500 ... 40 G4
Ruraldale, 60 ... 51 D11
Rushsylvania, 543 ... 50 B5
Rushville, 268 ... 51 D9
Russells Point, 1,619 ... 50 B5
Russellville, 453 ... 50 H5
Russia, 551 ... 50 B3
Sabina, 2,780 ... 50 E5
St. Clairsville, 5,057 ... 52 C2
St. Henry, 2,271 ... 50 B2
St. Johns, 200 ... 50 A4
St. Louisville, 346 ... 51 C9
St. Marys, 8,342 ... 50 A3
St. Paris, 1,998 ... 50 C4
Salem, 12,197 ... 42 H1
Salineville, 1,397 ... 52 A2
Sandusky, 27,844 ... 41 F7
Scott, 322 ... 40 H2
Scottown, 100 ... 51 I9
Seaman, 1,039 ... 51 G6
Sebring, 4,912 ... 41 H12
Sedalia, 274 ... 51 D6
Senecaville, 453 ... 51 D12
Seven Mile, 678 ... 50 E3
Seville, 2,160 ... 41 H10
Shade, 120 ... 51 F10
Shaker Heights, 29,405 ... 41 F10
Shalersville, 220 ... 41 G11
Shandon, 400 ... 50 F2
Sharonville, 13,804 ... 50 F3
Shauck, 200 ... 51 A8
Shawnee, 608 ... 51 E10
Sheffield Lake, 9,371 ... 41 F9
Shelby, 9,821 ... 41 H7
Shenandoah, 100 ... 41 H8
Sherrodsville, 316 ... 51 A12
Sherwood, 801 ... 40 G2
Sherwood Park, 750 ... 40 I3
Shiloh, 721 ... 41 H7
Shreve, 1,582 ... 41 I9
Sidney, 20,211 ... 50 B4
Sinking Spring, 158 ... 51 G6
Smithfield, 867 ... 52 B3
Smithville, 1,333 ... 41 H10
Solon, 21,802 ... 41 F11
Somerset, 1,549 ... 51 D9
Somerton, 180 ... 52 D2
Somerville, 294 ... 50 E2
South Amherst, 1,863 ... 41 G8
South Bloomingville, 40 ... 51 F8
South Charleston, 1,850 ... 50 D5
Southington, 400 ... 41 G12
South Lebanon, 2,538 ... 50 F4
South Russell, 4,022 ... 41 F11
South Salem, 213 ... 51 F6
South Solon, 405 ... 50 D5
South Vienna, 469 ... 50 D5
South Webster, 764 ... 51 H8
Spencer, 747 ... 41 H9
Spencerville, 2,235 ... 40 I2
Springboro, 12,380 ... 50 E4
Springfield, 65,736 ... 50 D5
Springhills, 150 ... 50 B5
Spring Valley, 510 ... 50 E4
Stafford, 86 ... 51 D12
Steinersville, 200 ... 52 D2
Steubenville, 19,941 ... 52 B3
Stewart, 250 ... 51 F11
Stockdale, 200 ... 51 G8
Stockport, 540 ... 51 E11
Stone Creek, 184 ... 51 B11
Stoutsville, 581 ... 51 E8
Stow, 32,139 ... 41 G11
Strasburg, 2,310 ... 51 A12
Stratford, 80 ... 51 B7
Streetsboro, 12,311 ... 41 G11
Strongsville, 43,858 ... 41 G10
Struthers, 11,756 ... 42 H2
Stryker, 1,406 ... 40 F2
Sugarcreek, 2,174 ... 51 A11
Sulphur Springs, 300 ... 41 H7
Summerfield, 296 ... 51 D12
Summerford, 250 ... 51 D6
Sunbury, 2,630 ... 51 B8
Sunshine ... 51 H6
Swanton, 3,307 ... 40 F4
Sycamore, 914 ... 41 H6
Sylvania, 18,670 ... 40 E4
Tallmadge, 16,390 ... 41 H11
Tarlton, 298 ... 51 E8
Terre Haute, 180 ... 50 C5
The Plains, 2,931 ... 51 F10
Thompson, 370 ... 41 E12
Thornville, 731 ... 51 D9
Tiffin, 18,135 ... 41 H6
Tipp City, 9,221 ... 50 D4
Tippecanoe, 200 ... 51 B12
Tiro, 281 ... 41 H7
Tiverton, 80 ... 51 B10
Toledo, 313,782 ... 40 E5
Torch, 300 ... 51 F11
Toronto, 5,676 ... 52 B3
Trenton, 8,746 ... 50 E3
Triadelphia, 40 ... 51 E10
Trotwood, 27,420 ... 50 D3
Troy, 21,999 ... 50 C4
Trumbull, 200 ... 41 E12
Tuppers Plains, 350 ... 51 G11
Uhrichsville, 5,662 ... 51 B12
Unionville Center, 299 ... 51 C6
Upper Arlington, 33,686 ... 51 C7
Upper Sandusky, 6,533 ... 40 I5
Urbana, 11,613 ... 50 C5
Utica, 2,141 ... 51 C9
Utopia, 70 ... 50 H4
Valley Hi, 244 ... 50 B5
Vandalia, 14,603 ... 50 D4
Vanlue, 371 ... 40 H5
Van Wert, 10,690 ... 40 H2
Vaughnsville, 350 ... 40 H3
Venedocia, 160 ... 40 I2
Vermilion, 10,927 ... 41 F8
Versailles, 2,589 ... 50 C3
Vickery, 200 ... 41 F6
Vincent, 400 ... 51 F11
Vinton, 324 ... 51 G9
Wabash, 70 ... 50 A2
Wacker Heights, 750 ... 51 D8
Wadsworth, 18,437 ... 41 H10
Wakefield, 140 ... 51 G7
Wakeman, 951 ... 41 G8
Waldo, 332 ... 51 B7
Wamsley, 90 ... 51 H6
Wapakoneta, 9,474 ... 50 A4
Warner, 130 ... 51 E12
Warren, 48,224 ... 42 G1
Warsaw, 781 ... 51 B10
Washington Court House, 13,524 ... 51 E6
Waterford, 600 ... 51 E11
Waterloo, 150 ... 51 H9
Watertown, 220 ... 51 E11
Waterville, 4,828 ... 40 F4
Wauseon, 7,091 ... 40 F3
Waverly, 4,433 ... 51 G7
Wayne, 842 ... 40 G5
Wayne Lakes, 684 ... 50 C2
Waynesfield, 803 ... 50 A4
Waynesville, 2,558 ... 50 E4
Wellington, 4,511 ... 41 G9
Wellston, 6,078 ... 51 G9
Wellsville, 4,133 ... 52 A3
West Alexandria, 1,395 ... 50 D3
West Carlisle, 30 ... 51 C10
Westerville, 35,318 ... 51 C7
West Farmington, 519 ... 41 F12
Westfield, 110 ... 51 B7
West Independence, 40 ... 40 H5
West Jefferson, 4,331 ... 51 D6
West Lafayette, 2,313 ... 51 B11
Westlake, 31,719 ... 41 F9
West Liberty, 1,813 ... 50 B5
West Lodi, 80 ... 41 G6
West Logan, 440 ... 51 E9
West Manchester, 433 ... 50 D2
West Mansfield, 700 ... 51 B6
West Milton, 4,645 ... 50 D3
Westminster, 100 ... 40 I3
Weston, 1,659 ... 40 G4
West Salem, 1,501 ... 41 H9
West Sonora, 100 ... 50 D3
West Union, 2,903 ... 51 H6
West Unity, 1,790 ... 40 F2
Westville, 200 ... 50 C5
Wharton, 409 ... 40 H5
Wheelersburg, 6,471 ... 51 H8
Whitehall, 19,201 ... 51 D8
Whitehouse, 2,733 ... 40 F4
Wilkesville, 151 ... 51 G9
Willard, 6,806 ... 41 H7
Williamsburg, 2,358 ... 50 G4
Williamsfield, 400 ... 42 F2
Williamsport, 70 ... 51 A8
Williamsport, 1,002 ... 51 E7
Willoughby, 22,621 ... 41 F11
Willowick, 14,361 ... 41 F11
Willshire, 463 ... 40 I1
Wilmington, 11,875 ... 50 F5
Winchester, 1,025 ... 50 G5
Winchester, 50 ... 51 G9
Windham, 2,806 ... 41 G12
Wingett Run, 40 ... 52 E1
Winterset, 150 ... 51 C12
Wintersville, 4,067 ... 52 B3
Woodsfield, 2,598 ... 52 D2
Woodstock, 317 ... 51 C6
Woodville, 1,977 ... 40 F5
Wooster, 24,811 ... 41 I9
Worthington, 14,125 ... 51 C7
Wren, 199 ... 40 I1
Xenia, 24,164 ... 50 E5
Yellow Springs, 3,761 ... 50 D5
Young Hickory ... 51 D11
Youngs, 110 ... 51 H7
Youngstown, 82,026 ... 42 H2
Zaleski, 375 ... 51 F9
Zanesville, 25,586 ... 51 D10
Zoar, 193 ... 51 A12

Oklahoma

CITY, Population ... Page Grid
Adair, 704 ... 54 I4
Afton, 1,118 ... 54 H5
Avant, 372 ... 54 H2
Barnsdall, 1,325 ... 54 H1
Bartlesville, 34,748 ... 54 G2
Bernice, 504 ... 54 H5
Big Cabin, 293 ... 54 H4
Bluejacket, 274 ... 54 G5
Boatman, 100 ... 54 I4
Bowring, 100 ... 54 G2
Bushyhead, 1,203 ... 54 H3
Centralia, 35 ... 54 G4
Chelsea, 2,136 ... 54 H4
Childers, 40 ... 54 G3
Claremore, 15,873 ... 54 I3
Cleora, 1,113 ... 54 H5
Colcord, 819 ... 55 I6
Collinsville, 4,077 ... 54 I2
Commerce, 2,645 ... 54 G5
Copan, 796 ... 54 G2
Copeland, 1,448 ... 55 H6
Delaware, 456 ... 54 G3
Dennis, 185 ... 54 H5
Dewey, 3,179 ... 54 G2
Disney, 226 ... 54 H5
Eucha, 150 ... 54 I5
Fairland, 1,025 ... 55 G6
Grove, 5,131 ... 55 H6
Hominy, 3,795 ... 54 I1
Jay, 2,482 ... 55 I6
Justice, 1,311 ... 54 I3
Kellyville, 50 ... 55 G6
Kenwood, 120 ... 54 I5
Langley, 669 ... 54 H5
Lenapah, 298 ... 54 G3
Limestone, 745 ... 54 I3
Lynn Addition, 350 ... 54 H1
Miami, 13,704 ... 54 G5
New Alluwe, 95 ... 54 H4
Nowata, 3,971 ... 54 H3
Ochelata, 494 ... 54 H2
Oglesby, 100 ... 54 H2
Okesa, 120 ... 54 G2
Oologah, 883 ... 54 H3
Owasso, 18,502 ... 54 I2
Patton, 100 ... 54 H4
Pawhuska, 3,629 ... 54 H1
Peoria, 141 ... 55 G6
Pershing, 50 ... 54 H1
Picher, 1,640 ... 55 F6
Prue, 433 ... 54 I1
Pryor Creek, 8,659 ... 54 I4
Pyramid Corners, 45 ... 54 G5
Quapaw, 984 ... 55 G6
Ramona, 564 ... 54 H2
Salina, 1,422 ... 54 I5
Sequoyah, 671 ... 54 I3
Skiatook, 5,396 ... 54 I2
South Coffeyville, 790 ... 54 F3
Spavinaw, 563 ... 54 I5
Sperry, 981 ... 54 I2
Sycamore, 183 ... 55 I6
Talala, 270 ... 54 H3
Turley, 3,231 ... 54 I2
Vera, 188 ... 54 H2
Verdigris, 223 ... 54 I3
Vinita, 6,062 ... 54 H5
Wann, 132 ... 54 G3
Watova, 150 ... 54 H3
Welch, 597 ... 54 G5
Whippoorwill, 100 ... 54 G2
White Oak, 100 ... 54 H4
Wolco, 30 ... 54 H2
Wyandotte, 363 ... 55 G6
Wynona, 531 ... 54 H1

Ontario

CITY, Population ... Page Grid
Actinolite, 119 ... 33 C10
Acton ... 32 F2
Ailsa Craig, 1,065 ... 31 H10
Ajax, 73,753 ... 32 E5
Alban ... 23 E11
Algoma Mills, 198 ... 22 E5
Allenford, 345 ... 31 C11
Alliston, 6,700 ... 32 D3
Alma, 444 ... 31 F12
Alton, 955 ... 32 E2
Alvinston, 1,022 ... 41 A9
Amberly, 32 ... 31 E9
Ameliasburg, 198 ... 33 E10
Amherstburg, 20,339 ... 41 D6
Amherstview ... 33 D12
Angus ... 32 D3
Appin, 244 ... 41 A10
Apsley, 331 ... 33 B8
Arbor-Vitae ... 11 C9
Arden, 239 ... 33 B11
Argyle, 92 ... 33 C5
Ariss, 125 ... 32 F2
Arkona, 464 ... 31 H9
Arthur, 2,284 ... 31 E12
Arva, 25 ... 31 H10
Atherley, 175 ... 32 C4
Atikokan, 3,632 ... 12 D5
Atwood, 877 ... 31 F11
Auburn, 244 ... 31 F10
Aurora, 40,167 ... 32 E4
Avening, 70 ... 32 D2
Avon, 32 ... 31 I11
Aylmer, 7,126 ... 41 A12
Ayr ... 32 H1
Ayton, 606 ... 31 E11
Bailieboro, 294 ... 33 D7
Bala, 490 ... 32 A4
Balm Beach ... 32 B3
Baltimore, 261 ... 33 E8
Bancroft, 2,546 ... 33 A8
Bannockburn, 94 ... 33 B9
Baptiste ... 33 A8
Barrie, 103,710 ... 32 C3
Barrow Bay, 86 ... 31 A10
Barwick, 102 ... 11 D10
Batawa, 274 ... 33 D9
Batchawana Bay, 150 ... 21 B12
Bath, 1,583 ... 33 D11
Bayfield, 909 ... 31 G9
Bayside, 56 ... 33 D10
Beachville, 875 ... 31 H12
Beaverton ... 32 C5
Beeton ... 32 E3
Belle River, 4,887 ... 41 C7
Belleville, 45,986 ... 33 D10
Belmont, 1,819 ... 31 I11
Belwood, 304 ... 32 F2
Bergland, 72 ... 11 C9
Berkeley, 158 ... 31 C12
Bethany, 603 ... 33 D7
Bewdley, 825 ... 33 E7
Big Bay, 22 ... 31 B11
Big Bay Point ... 32 C4
Bigwood ... 23 E11
Binbrook ... 32 H3
Bismarck, 35 ... 32 I4
Black Hawk ... 11 C10
Blenheim, 4,780 ... 41 C9
Blind River, 3,969 ... 22 E5
Bloomfield, 643 ... 33 E10
Bluevale, 174 ... 31 E10
Blyth, 987 ... 31 F10
Blytheswood, 87 ... 41 D7
Bobcaygeon, 2,854 ... 33 C7
Bolton ... 32 E3
Bornholm, 49 ... 31 G11
Bothwell, 1,002 ... 41 B9
Bowmanville ... 33 E6
Bracebridge, 13,751 ... 32 A5
Bradford, 15,000 ... 32 D4
Brampton, 325,428 ... 32 F3
Brantford, 86,417 ... 32 H2
Brechin ... 32 C5
Bridgenorth ... 33 C7
Brigden ... 41 A8
Bright, 323 ... 31 H12
Brighton, 9,449 ... 33 E9
Brights Grove ... 31 I8
Britt, 19 ... 23 F11
Brodhagen, 136 ... 31 G10
Bronte ... 32 G3
Brooklin ... 32 E5
Brookville, 147 ... 32 G2
Brucefield, 212 ... 31 G10
Bruce Mines, 627 ... 22 D3
Brussels, 1,143 ... 31 F10
Buckhorn, 69 ... 33 C7
Burford, 1,685 ... 32 H1
Burgessville, 493 ... 31 I12
Burleigh Falls, 98 ... 33 C7
Burlington, 150,836 ... 32 G3
Burnt River, 41 ... 33 B6
Byng Inlet, 101 ... 23 F11
Caesarea ... 33 D6
Cairo, 26 ... 41 A9
Caistorville, 52 ... 32 H3
Caledon, 50,595 ... 32 E3
Caledon East, 848 ... 32 E3
Caledonia, 1,424 ... 32 H3
Cambridge, 110,372 ... 32 G2
Camden East, 306 ... 33 C11
Camilla, 110 ... 32 E2
Camlachie, 208 ... 31 I8
Campbellford, 3,517 ... 33 D9
Canborough ... 32 I3
Cannifton, 271 ... 33 D10
Cannington, 1,623 ... 32 C5
Cape Croker ... 31 A11
Capreol, 3,486 ... 23 C10
Cardiff, 542 ... 33 A8
Carlisle ... 32 G3
Carnarvon, 126 ... 33 A6
Carrying Place, 144 ... 33 E9
Cartier, 472 ... 23 C9
Castleton, 356 ... 33 D8
Cathcart ... 31 H12
Cedar Point, 18 ... 32 B2
Cedar Springs, 343 ... 41 C9
Centralia, 235 ... 31 H10
Ceylon, 77 ... 31 D12
Charing Cross, 431 ... 41 C9
Chatham, 43,690 ... 41 C9
Chatsworth, 517 ... 31 C11
Chelmsford ... 23 C10
Chepstow, 219 ... 31 D10
Cherry Valley ... 33 E10
Chesley, 1,880 ... 31 D11
Clandeboye, 30 ... 31 H10
Clarington, 69,834 ... 33 E6
Clarkson ... 32 G4
Clear Creek, 37 ... 42 B2
Clifford, 792 ... 31 E11
Clinton, 3,117 ... 31 F10
Cloud Bay ... 13 F10
Cloyne, 78 ... 33 B10
Coboconk, 423 ... 33 B6
Cobourg, 17,172 ... 33 E8
Coe Hill, 56 ... 33 B8
Colborne, 2,040 ... 33 E8
Colchester, 771 ... 41 D7
Coldstream, 315 ... 31 I10
Coldwater, 1,254 ... 32 B4
Collingwood, 16,039 ... 32 C2
Collins Bay ... 33 D12
Comber, 1,480 ... 41 C8
Conestogo, 692 ... 32 G1
Coniston ... 23 D11
Conn, 125 ... 31 E12
Consecon, 353 ... 33 E9
Cookstown ... 32 D3
Copenhagen, 201 ... 41 B12
Copper Cliff ... 23 D10
Corbett, 55 ... 31 H9
Corbetton, 91 ... 32 D2
Corunna ... 31 I7
Cottam, 723 ... 41 D7
Courtland, 917 ... 31 I12
Courtright ... 41 A8
Craighurst, 90 ... 32 C3
Crediton, 380 ... 31 H10
Creemore, 1,327 ... 32 D2
Crooked Bay ... 32 A3
Crow Lake ... 11 B10
Crystal Beach ... 32 I5
Damascus, 118 ... 32 E1
Dashwood, 171 ... 31 G9
Delaware, 1,198 ... 31 I10
Delhi, 16,365 ... 32 I1
Deloro, 159 ... 33 C9
Denfield, 111 ... 31 H10
Desbarats, 298 ... 22 D2
Desboro, 85 ... 31 C11
Deseronto, 1,796 ... 33 D11
Devlin, 678 ... 11 D11
Dobbinton, 53 ... 31 C11
Dorchester ... 31 I11
Dorion ... 14 C2
Dorking, 100 ... 31 F12
Drayton, 1,520 ... 31 F12
Dresden, 2,572 ... 41 B9
Drumbo, 531 ... 31 H12
Duart, 121 ... 41 B10
Dublin, 255 ... 31 G10
Dubreuilville ... 15 E12
Dundalk, 1,972 ... 32 D1
Dungannon, 239 ... 31 E9
Dunnville, 12,581 ... 32 I4
Dunsford, 201 ... 33 C6
Duntroon ... 32 C2
Durham, 2,647 ... 31 D12
Dutton, 1,374 ... 41 B11

Ontario - Pennsylvania

Pennsylvania

CITY, Population Page Grid

Pennsylvania - Tennessee

South Dakota

Tennessee

Tennessee - West Virginia

Virginia

West Virginia

West Virginia - Wisconsin

Wisconsin

Wisconsin

This map shows both the distance and the approximate driving time between many cities across the Midwest region.
You can get even more mileages and driving times at **randmcnally.com**

MILEAGES

277 Black numerals indicate mileage in statue miles.

DRIVE TIMES

7:55 Blue numbers indicate driving time. Driving time shown is approximate under normal conditions. Consideration has been given to topography, number of towns along the route, congested urban areas, and the speed limit imposed by each state. Allowances should be made for night driving and unusually fast or slow drivers.

POINTS OF INTEREST

1. Amana Colonies E-4
2. Amish Acres. E-7
3. Apostle Islands National Lakeshore B-4
4. Cuyahoga Valley National Park E-9
5. Cumberland Gap National Historic Park. H-8
6. Isle Royale National Park A-5
7. Madison County Covered Bridges . . E-3
8. Mammoth Cave National Park. H-7
9. Neil Armstrong Air and Space Museum E-8
10. Pictured Rocks National Lakeshore. . B-6
11. Sleeping Bear Dunes National Lakeshore C-7
12. St. Croix National Scenic Riverway . . C-4

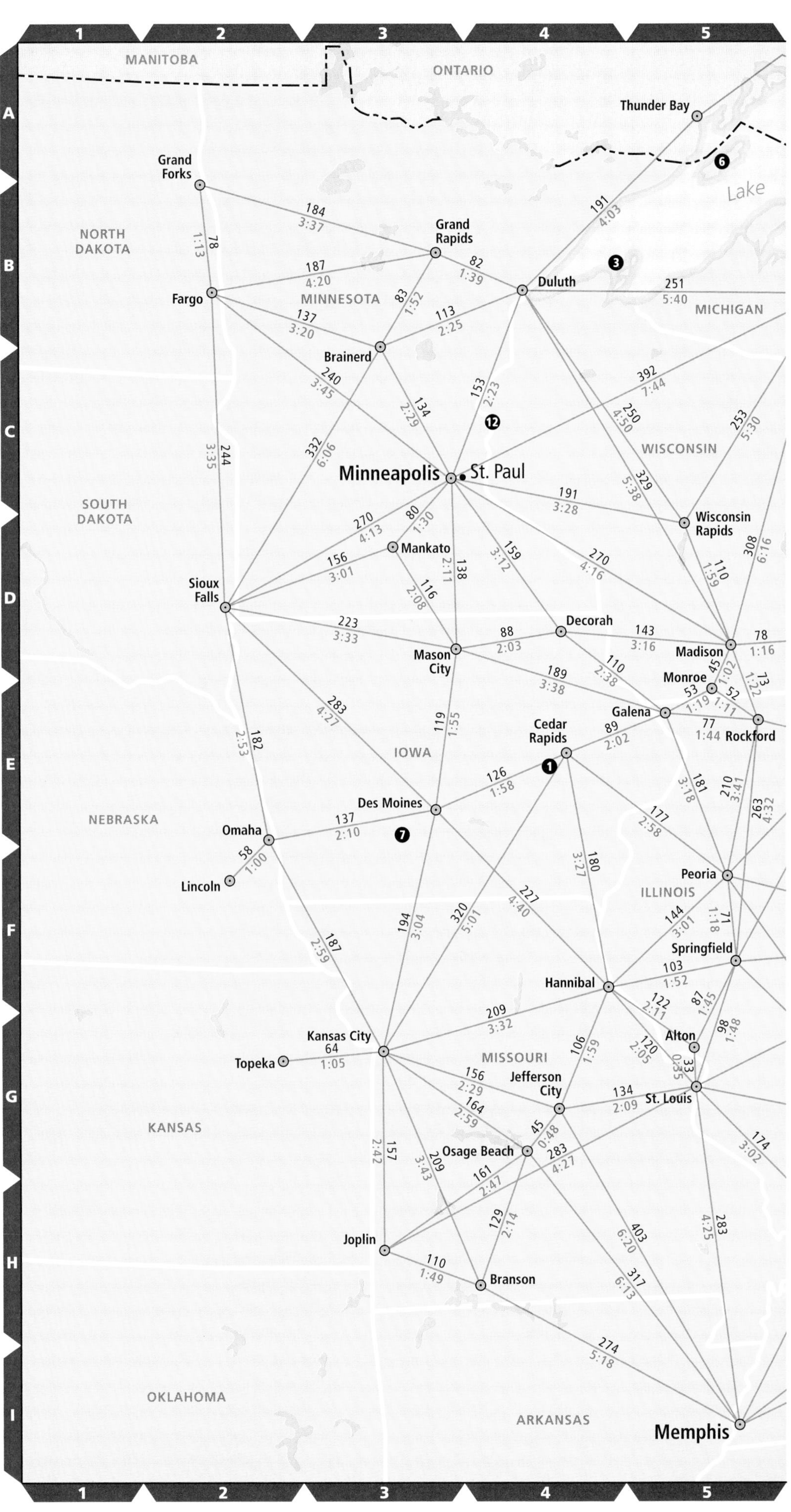

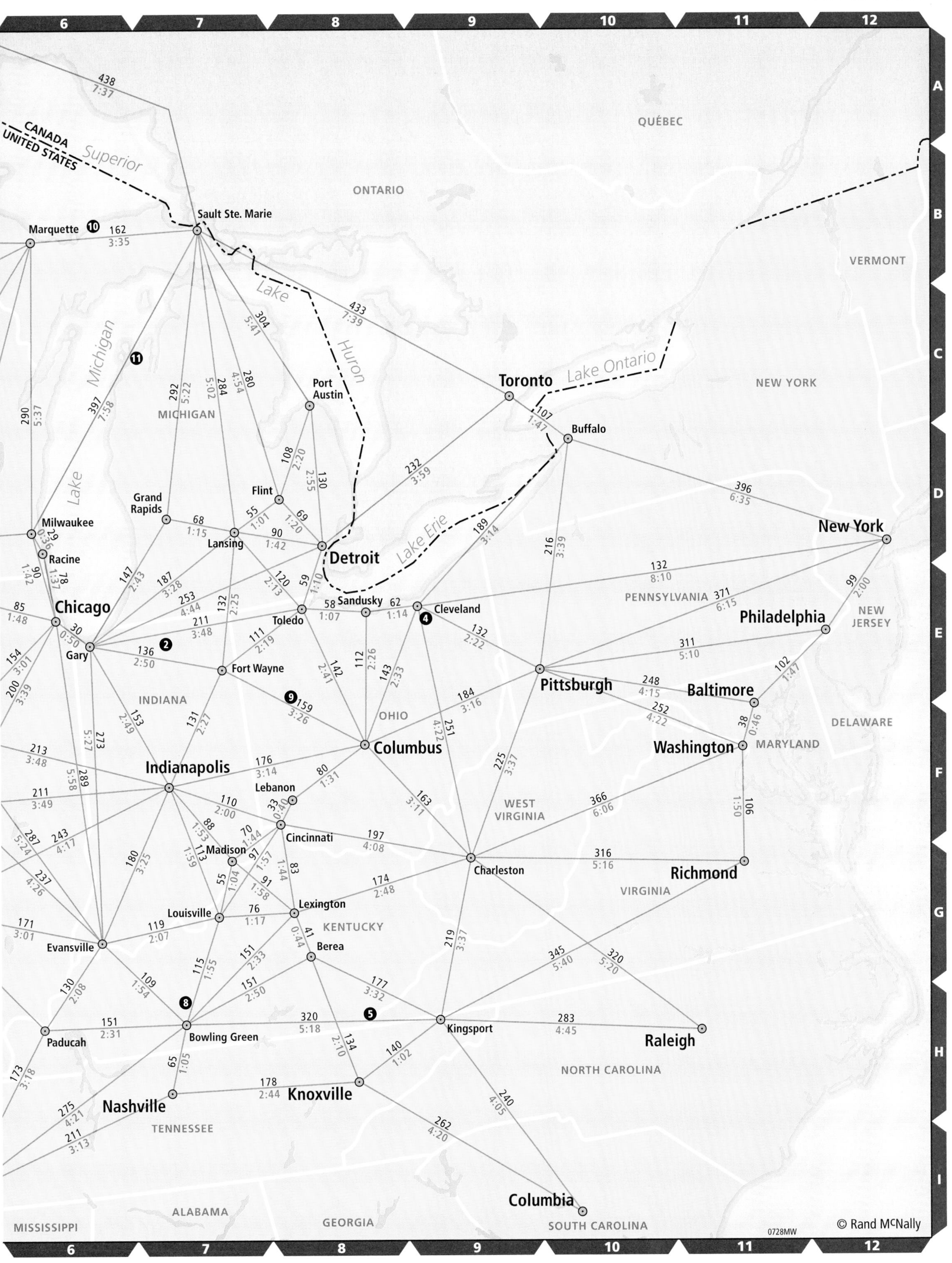
QUÉBEC
ONTARIO
CANADA
UNITED STATES
Lake Superior
Lake Michigan
Lake Huron
Lake Ontario
Lake Erie
MICHIGAN
NEW YORK
VERMONT
PENNSYLVANIA
NEW JERSEY
OHIO
INDIANA
DELAWARE
MARYLAND
WEST VIRGINIA
VIRGINIA
KENTUCKY
TENNESSEE
NORTH CAROLINA
SOUTH CAROLINA
GEORGIA
ALABAMA
MISSISSIPPI
Sault Ste. Marie
Marquette
Toronto
Buffalo
Port Austin
Flint
Grand Rapids
Lansing
Detroit
Milwaukee
Racine
Chicago
Gary
Toledo
Sandusky
Cleveland
Fort Wayne
New York
Philadelphia
Pittsburgh
Baltimore
Washington
Columbus
Indianapolis
Lebanon
Cincinnati
Madison
Charleston
Richmond
Louisville
Lexington
Evansville
Berea
Paducah
Bowling Green
Kingsport
Raleigh
Nashville
Knoxville
Columbia
0728MW

Grid references following the city names refer to locations on the mileage and driving times map on pages 220 – 221.

	Alton, IL (G-5)	Berea, KY (G-8)	Bowling Green, KY (H-7)	Brainerd, MN (C-3)	Branson, MO (H-4)	Cedar Rapids, IA (E-4)	Charleston, WV (G-9)	Chicago, IL (E-6)	Cincinnati, OH (F-8)	Cleveland, OH (E-9)	Columbus, OH (F-8)	Decorah, IA (D-4)	Des Moines, IA (E-3)	Detroit, MI (D-8)	Duluth, MN (B-4)	Evansville, IN (G-6)	Flint, MI (D-8)	Fort Wayne, IN (E-7)	Galena, IL (E-5)	Gary, IN (E-6)	Grand Forks, ND (B-2)	Grand Rapids, MI (D-7)	Grand Rapids, MN (B-3)	Hannibal, MO (F-4)	Indianapolis, IN (F-7)	Jefferson City, MO (G-4)	Joplin, MO (H-3)	Kansas City, MO (G-3)	Kingsport, TN (H-9)
Alton, IL (G-5)		392	297	742	273	299	523	285	351	564	422	406	347	534	669	188	530	377	337	291	933	434	749	122	244	137	305	252	602
Berea, KY (G-8)	392		151	955	625	613	192	411	119	380	237	699	699	398	881	231	440	327	576	381	1137	476	961	492	225	506	657	622	177
Bowling Green, KY (H-7)	297	151		955	476	573	326	411	210	472	329	659	622	490	882	109	531	352	565	381	1137	482	962	397	225	412	517	527	321
Brainerd, MN (C-3)	742	955	955		775	408	1036	540	838	889	899	291	374	829	113	842	817	707	459	579	222	722	83	587	727	644	723	568	1128
Branson, MO (H-4)	273	625	476	775		457	757	547	601	813	671	602	401	784	794	421	791	626	529	553	894	696	832	280	493	174	110	209	739
Cedar Rapids, IA (E-4)	299	613	573	408	457		702	247	499	574	569	106	126	514	426	464	503	392	89	264	590	407	465	180	390	283	475	320	787
Charleston, WV (G-9)	523	192	326	1036	757	702		492	197	251	163	788	788	354	962	362	408	326	657	462	1218	486	1042	624	314	638	789	753	219
Chicago, IL (E-6)	285	411	411	540	547	247	492		294	343	355	286	332	283	467	289	272	162	162	30	722	177	547	300	183	393	579	527	584
Cincinnati, OH (F-8)	351	119	210	838	601	499	197	294		252	108	584	584	263	764	215	305	183	460	264	1020	355	845	420	110	474	633	589	292
Cleveland, OH (E-9)	564	380	472	889	813	574	251	343	252		143	634	659	168	815	476	220	214	510	313	1071	298	895	616	318	687	846	802	471
Columbus, OH (F-8)	422	237	329	899	671	569	163	355	108	143		655	655	191	825	333	245	159	520	325	1081	323	905	491	176	544	703	660	319
Decorah, IA (D-4)	406	699	659	291	602	106	788	286	584	634	655		201	574	297	549	563	453	110	325	473	468	336	286	474	389	550	395	871
Des Moines, IA (E-3)	347	699	622	374	401	126	788	332	584	659	655	201		599	392	513	588	478	213	350	556	493	431	227	475	324	349	194	872
Detroit, MI (D-8)	534	398	490	829	784	514	354	283	263	168	191	574	599		755	494	69	173	450	253	1011	158	835	556	288	657	816	772	509
Duluth, MN (B-4)	669	881	882	113	794	426	962	467	764	815	825	297	392	755		768	640	634	358	506	266	649	82	606	654	662	741	586	1055
Evansville, IN (G-6)	188	231	109	842	421	464	362	289	215	476	333	549	513	494	768		492	313	456	273	1024	414	848	288	180	303	454	418	426
Flint, MI (D-8)	530	440	531	817	791	503	408	272	305	220	245	563	588	69	640	492		187	439	242	1000	113	720	545	310	637	824	753	563
Fort Wayne, IN (E-7)	377	327	352	707	626	392	326	162	183	214	159	453	478	173	634	313	187		333	136	894	180	718	403	131	500	659	615	455
Galena, IL (E-5)	337	576	565	459	529	89	657	162	460	510	520	110	213	450	358	456	439	333		201	641	344	438	250	349	355	562	407	750
Gary, IN (E-6)	291	381	381	579	553	264	462	30	264	313	325	325	350	253	506	273	242	136	201		761	147	586	307	153	399	585	514	554
Grand Forks, ND (B-2)	933	1137	1137	222	894	590	1218	722	1020	1071	1081	473	556	1011	266	1024	1000	894	641	761		905	184	770	910	837	827	678	1311
Grand Rapids, MI (D-7)	434	476	482	722	696	407	486	177	355	298	323	468	493	158	649	414	113	180	344	147	905		729	450	260	542	728	658	650
Grand Rapids, MN (B-3)	749	961	962	83	832	465	1042	547	845	895	905	336	431	835	82	848	720	718	438	586	184	729		644	734	701	780	625	1135
Hannibal, MO (F-4)	122	492	397	587	280	180	624	300	420	616	491	286	227	556	606	288	545	403	250	307	770	450	644		312	106	312	209	703
Indianapolis, IN (F-7)	244	225	225	727	493	390	314	183	110	318	176	474	475	288	654	180	310	131	349	153	910	260	734	312		366	526	482	398
Jefferson City, MO (G-4)	137	506	412	644	174	283	638	393	474	687	544	389	324	657	662	303	637	500	355	399	837	542	701	106	366		206	156	717
Joplin, MO (H-3)	305	657	517	723	110	475	789	579	633	846	703	550	349	816	741	454	824	659	562	585	827	728	780	312	526	206		157	781
Kansas City, MO (G-3)	252	622	527	568	209	320	753	527	589	802	660	395	194	772	586	418	753	615	407	514	678	658	625	209	482	156	157		833
Kingsport, TN (H-9)	602	177	321	1128	739	787	219	584	292	471	319	871	872	509	1055	426	563	455	750	554	1311	650	1135	703	398	717	781	833	
Lansing, MI (D-7)	475	450	476	763	737	448	418	217	315	230	255	508	533	90	689	437	55	137	384	187	945	68	769	490	255	582	769	698	574
Lebanon, OH (F-8)	370	162	254	856	619	517	194	312	33	223	80	602	603	236	783	258	278	153	478	282	1039	328	863	439	128	492	651	607	336
Lexington, KY (G-8)	351	41	151	914	584	573	174	370	83	344	201	657	658	362	841	190	404	245	536	340	1096	440	921	451	184	466	617	581	214
Louisville, KY (G-7)	280	112	115	843	513	502	244	299	97	359	215	586	587	376	770	119	418	240	465	269	1025	370	850	380	113	395	546	510	286
Madison, IN (G-7)	334	127	168	818	567	477	258	274	70	321	178	562	562	328	745	173	369	199	440	244	1001	345	825	399	88	448	599	564	300
Madison, WI (D-5)	349	561	561	402	610	168	642	147	444	495	505	143	292	435	329	448	424	318	93	185	585	329	409	364	334	456	643	486	735
Mankato, MN (D-3)	553	846	846	203	621	254	927	431	729	780	790	157	220	720	233	718	709	603	304	470	385	613	248	433	618	489	568	414	1019
Marquette, MI (B-6)	658	798	799	362	920	479	792	380	682	604	629	441	625	455	251	672	389	528	404	410	515	402	331	673	571	765	952	819	972
Mason City, IA (D-3)	437	751	711	270	520	138	840	385	637	712	707	88	119	652	288	602	641	535	189	402	452	545	327	318	528	389	468	313	925
Memphis, TN (I-5)	314	423	275	973	274	565	597	534	482	743	600	672	613	761	964	288	778	599	632	534	1199	677	1044	388	466	403	352	518	491
Milwaukee, WI (D-6)	368	509	509	468	630	286	590	90	392	443	453	222	371	383	395	382	371	266	161	120	651	276	475	384	281	476	662	565	682
Minneapolis, MN (C-3)	610	822	822	134	643	276	903	408	705	756	766	159	242	696	153	709	685	579	326	447	317	590	192	455	595	512	591	436	996
Monroe, WI (E-5)	331	543	543	451	593	135	624	129	426	477	487	146	259	417	377	430	406	300	53	168	633	311	458	290	316	395	625	453	717
Omaha, NE (E-2)	442	811	717	511	402	263	943	470	722	797	792	338	137	737	530	608	725	620	351	487	497	630	568	324	613	346	336	187	1022
Osage Beach, MO (G-4)	182	539	444	707	129	328	670	437	519	731	589	434	332	702	725	335	682	545	399	444	845	587	764	150	411	45	161	164	749
Paducah, KY (H-6)	191	299	151	880	328	468	431	373	315	577	434	571	516	595	807	130	617	438	490	373	1063	516	887	291	305	306	369	421	415
Peoria, IL (F-5)	157	436	396	585	419	177	525	154	322	470	392	262	263	410	530	287	399	260	181	160	768	303	610	144	213	264	451	352	610
Pittsburgh, PA (E-10)	606	417	509	1006	855	691	225	461	289	132	184	752	777	285	933	514	337	321	628	430	1188	415	1013	675	359	728	887	843	402
Port Austin, MI (C-8)	637	526	617	774	899	610	481	380	390	296	319	671	696	130	662	600	108	299	547	349	1107	194	743	653	417	745	931	860	637
Racine, WI (D-6)	349	496	496	495	611	284	577	78	379	430	440	249	370	370	422	370	359	253	160	108	678	264	502	365	268	457	643	564	670
Rockford, IL (E-5)	283	499	491	467	545	200	580	85	382	433	443	187	286	373	393	382	362	256	77	123	649	267	474	298	272	390	577	480	673
St. Louis, MO (G-5)	33	375	280	705	251	297	506	296	350	563	421	403	345	533	680	171	541	376	349	303	931	446	760	120	243	134	283	250	585
St. Paul, MN (C-3)	601	814	814	143	645	278	895	399	697	748	758	150	244	688	149	700	676	571	283	438	325	581	187	457	586	513	592	438	987
Sandusky, OH (E-8)	515	349	441	836	765	521	297	290	221	62	112	581	606	115	762	445	166	160	457	260	1018	244	842	563	269	638	797	753	431
Sault Ste. Marie, MI (B-7)	727	715	759	525	989	587	682	469	579	494	520	546	785	346	413	720	280	419	512	439	677	292	493	742	537	834	1021	950	838
Sioux Falls, SD (D-2)	618	988	893	332	579	361	1119	573	868	922	938	272	283	862	420	784	851	745	412	612	319	755	459	500	759	522	512	363	1198
Springfield, IL (F-5)	87	434	346	657	349	249	523	200	320	516	390	333	334	455	583	237	444	302	252	206	839	349	664	103	211	195	381	311	651
Thunder Bay, ON (A-5)	859	1072	1072	304	984	617	1120	657	955	932	957	488	583	784	191	959	718	857	548	696	442	730	272	796	844	853	932	777	1246
Toledo, OH (E-8)	474	337	428	787	723	472	304	242	201	111	142	533	558	59	714	433	110	111	409	212	970	188	794	515	227	596	755	711	460
Toronto, ON (C-9)	764	628	720	1060	1014	745	535	514	493	290	426	805	830	232	847	724	249	402	681	484	1242	362	927	787	518	887	1046	1002	711
Wisconsin Rapids, WI (D-5)	449	662	662	323	711	247	743	248	545	596	606	160	363	536	250	549	525	419	172	286	505	430	330	465	434	557	712	557	836

Grid references following the city names refer to locations on the mileage and driving times map on pages 220 – 221.

	Lexington, KY (G-8)	Louisville, KY (G-7)	Madison, IN (G-7)	Madison, WI (D-5)	Mankato, MN (D-3)	Marquette, MI (B-6)	Mason City, IA (D-3)	Memphis, TN (I-5)	Milwaukee, WI (D-6)	Minneapolis, MN (C-3)	Monroe, WI (E-5)	Omaha, NE (E-2)	Osage Beach, MO (G-4)	Paducah, KY (H-6)	Peoria, IL (F-5)	Pittsburgh, PA (E-10)	Port Austin, MI (C-8)	Racine, WI (D-6)	Rockford, IL (E-5)	St. Louis, MO (G-5)	St. Paul, MN (C-3)	Sandusky, OH (E-8)	Sault Ste. Marie, MI (B-7)	Sioux Falls, SD (D-2)	Springfield, IL (F-5)	Thunder Bay, ON (A-5)	Toledo, OH (E-8)	Toronto, ON (C-9)	Wisconsin Rapids, WI (D-5)
Alton, IL (G-5)	351	280	334	349	553	658	437	314	368	610	331	442	182	191	157	606	637	349	283	33	601	515	727	618	87	859	474	764	449
Berea, KY (G-8)	41	112	127	561	846	798	751	423	509	822	543	811	539	299	436	417	526	496	499	375	814	349	715	988	434	1072	337	628	662
Bowling Green, KY (H-7)	151	115	168	561	846	799	711	275	509	822	543	717	444	151	396	509	617	496	491	280	814	441	759	893	346	1072	428	720	662
Brainerd, MN (C-3)	914	843	818	402	203	362	270	973	468	134	451	511	707	880	585	1006	774	495	467	705	143	836	525	332	657	304	787	1060	323
Branson, MO (H-4)	584	513	567	610	621	920	520	274	630	643	593	402	129	328	419	855	899	611	545	251	645	765	989	579	349	984	723	1014	711
Cedar Rapids, IA (E-4)	573	502	477	168	254	479	138	565	286	276	135	263	328	468	177	691	610	284	200	297	278	521	587	361	249	617	472	745	247
Charleston, WV (G-9)	174	244	258	642	927	792	840	597	590	903	624	943	670	431	525	225	481	577	580	506	895	297	682	1119	523	1120	304	535	743
Chicago, IL (E-6)	370	299	274	147	431	380	385	534	90	408	129	470	437	373	154	461	380	78	85	296	399	290	469	573	200	657	242	514	248
Cincinnati, OH (F-8)	83	97	70	444	729	682	637	482	392	705	426	722	519	315	322	289	390	379	382	350	697	221	579	868	320	955	201	493	545
Cleveland, OH (E-9)	344	359	321	495	780	604	712	743	443	756	477	797	731	577	470	132	296	430	433	563	748	62	494	922	516	932	111	290	596
Columbus, OH (F-8)	201	215	178	505	790	629	707	600	453	766	487	792	589	434	392	184	319	440	443	421	758	112	520	938	390	957	142	426	606
Decorah, IA (D-4)	657	586	562	143	157	441	88	672	222	159	146	338	434	571	262	752	671	249	187	403	150	581	546	272	333	488	533	805	160
Des Moines, IA (E-3)	658	587	562	292	220	625	119	613	371	242	259	137	332	516	263	777	696	370	286	345	244	606	785	283	334	583	558	830	363
Detroit, MI (D-8)	362	376	328	435	720	455	652	761	383	696	417	737	702	595	410	285	130	370	373	533	688	115	346	862	455	784	59	232	536
Duluth, MN (B-4)	841	770	745	329	233	251	288	964	395	153	377	530	725	807	530	933	662	422	393	680	149	762	413	420	583	191	714	847	250
Evansville, IN (G-6)	190	119	173	448	718	672	602	288	382	709	430	608	335	130	287	514	600	370	382	171	700	445	720	784	237	959	433	724	549
Flint, MI (D-8)	404	418	369	424	709	389	641	778	371	685	406	725	682	617	399	337	108	359	362	541	676	166	280	851	444	718	110	249	525
Fort Wayne, IN (E-7)	245	240	199	318	603	528	535	599	266	579	300	620	545	438	260	321	299	253	256	376	571	160	419	745	302	857	111	402	419
Galena, IL (E-5)	536	465	440	93	304	404	189	632	161	326	53	351	399	490	181	628	547	160	77	349	283	457	512	412	252	548	409	681	172
Gary, IN (E-6)	340	269	244	185	470	410	402	534	120	447	168	487	444	373	160	430	349	108	123	303	438	260	439	612	206	696	212	484	286
Grand Forks, ND (B-2)	1096	1025	1001	585	385	515	452	1199	651	317	633	497	845	1063	768	1188	1107	678	649	931	325	1018	677	319	839	442	970	1242	505
Grand Rapids, MI (D-7)	440	370	345	329	613	402	545	677	276	590	311	630	587	516	303	415	194	264	267	446	581	244	292	755	349	730	188	362	430
Grand Rapids, MN (B-3)	921	850	825	409	248	331	327	1044	475	192	458	568	764	887	610	1013	743	502	474	760	187	842	493	459	664	272	794	927	330
Hannibal, MO (F-4)	451	380	399	364	433	673	318	388	384	455	290	324	150	291	144	675	653	365	298	120	457	563	742	500	103	796	515	787	465
Indianapolis, IN (F-7)	184	113	88	334	618	571	528	466	281	595	316	613	411	305	213	359	417	268	272	243	586	269	537	759	211	844	227	518	434
Jefferson City, MO (G-4)	466	395	448	456	489	765	389	403	476	512	395	346	45	306	264	728	745	457	390	134	513	638	834	522	195	853	596	887	557
Joplin, MO (H-3)	617	546	599	643	568	952	468	352	662	591	625	336	161	369	451	887	931	643	577	283	592	797	1021	512	381	932	755	1046	712
Kansas City, MO (G-3)	581	510	564	486	414	819	313	518	565	436	453	187	164	421	352	843	860	564	480	250	438	753	950	363	311	777	711	1002	557
Kingsport, TN (H-9)	214	286	300	735	1019	972	925	491	682	996	717	1022	749	415	610	402	637	670	673	585	987	431	838	1198	651	1246	460	711	836
Lansing, MI (D-7)	414	364	323	369	654	394	586	723	317	630	351	671	627	562	344	347	163	304	307	486	622	177	284	796	389	722	120	304	470
Lebanon, OH (F-8)	126	140	99	463	747	662	655	525	410	724	445	740	537	359	340	260	364	397	401	368	715	192	553	886	338	990	175	466	563
Lexington, KY (G-8)		76	91	525	810	762	715	423	473	786	507	776	503	257	400	399	490	460	463	339	778	313	679	952	398	1036	301	592	626
Louisville, KY (G-7)	76		55	449	734	687	640	386	397	711	432	700	427	220	324	396	504	384	387	263	702	328	647	876	322	960	315	607	550
Madison, IN (G-7)	91	55		425	709	662	615	439	372	686	407	700	481	273	300	359	455	360	363	317	677	286	605	846	298	936	266	558	526
Madison, WI (D-5)	525	449	425		293	308	304	643	78	270	45	430	501	487	210	612	531	105	73	360	261	442	416	436	263	520	394	666	110
Mankato, MN (D-3)	810	734	709	293		468	116	819	360	80	342	285	552	722	431	897	816	387	358	551	87	727	613	156	502	424	678	951	249
Marquette, MI (B-6)	762	687	662	308	468		521	914	290	392	356	762	810	753	519	721	411	318	382	669	384	550	162	653	572	442	494	596	253
Mason City, IA (D-3)	715	640	615	304	116	521		703	370	138	235	256	452	606	315	829	748	397	265	435	140	659	645	223	387	479	610	883	259
Memphis, TN (I-5)	423	386	439	643	819	914	703		624	841	626	708	317	173	452	781	889	611	578	283	843	712	969	884	382	1154	700	991	744
Milwaukee, WI (D-6)	473	397	372	78	360	290	370	624		336	110	509	521	463	229	560	479	29	93	380	327	390	397	502	283	586	341	614	176
Minneapolis, MN (C-3)	786	711	686	270	80	392	138	841	336		318	379	574	748	453	874	793	363	334	573	9	703	537	270	524	344	655	927	191
Monroe, WI (E-5)	507	432	407	45	342	356	235	626	110	318		397	440	469	152	595	514	108	52	342	310	424	464	484	245	568	376	648	158
Omaha, NE (E-2)	776	700	700	430	285	762	256	708	509	379	397		354	611	400	914	833	507	423	439	381	744	923	182	425	720	695	968	500
Osage Beach, MO (G-4)	503	427	481	501	552	810	452	317	521	574	440	354		338	309	773	790	502	435	164	576	683	879	530	240	916	641	932	602
Paducah, KY (H-6)	257	220	273	487	722	753	606	173	463	748	469	611	338		309	614	722	450	421	174	739	546	808	787	239	997	533	825	588
Peoria, IL (F-5)	400	324	300	210	431	519	315	452	229	453	152	400	309	309		576	506	218	144	168	462	417	596	546	71	720	368	641	310
Pittsburgh, PA (E-10)	399	396	359	612	897	721	829	781	560	874	595	914	773	614	576		413	547	550	605	865	181	612	1039	574	1049	228	316	713
Port Austin, MI (C-8)	490	504	455	531	816	411	748	889	479	793	514	833	790	722	506	413		466	469	649	784	243	304	958	552	742	187	268	632
Racine, WI (D-6)	460	384	360	105	387	318	397	611	29	363	108	507	502	450	218	547	466		91	360	354	377	426	528	264	613	328	601	203
Rockford, IL (E-5)	463	387	363	73	358	382	265	578	93	334	52	423	435	421	144	550	469	91		294	325	379	489	499	197	583	331	603	173
St. Louis, MO (G-5)	339	263	317	360	551	669	435	283	380	573	342	439	164	174	168	605	649	360	294		612	514	738	616	98	871	473	763	461
St. Paul, MN (C-3)	778	702	677	261	87	384	140	843	327	9	310	381	576	739	462	865	784	354	325	612		695	528	271	516	339	646	919	182
Sandusky, OH (E-8)	313	328	286	442	727	550	659	712	390	703	424	744	683	546	417	181	243	377	379	514	695		441	869	462	879	58	345	543
Sault Ste. Marie, MI (B-7)	679	647	605	416	613	162	645	969	397	537	464	923	879	808	596	612	304	426	489	738	528	441		777	641	438	384	433	387
Sioux Falls, SD (D-2)	952	876	846	436	156	653	223	884	502	270	484	182	530	787	546	1039	958	528	499	616	271	869	777		602	611	820	1093	391
Springfield, IL (F-5)	398	322	298	263	502	572	387	382	283	524	245	425	240	239	71	574	552	264	197	98	516	462	641	602		774	414	687	364
Thunder Bay, ON (A-5)	1036	960	936	520	424	442	479	1154	586	344	568	720	916	997	720	1049	742	613	583	871	339	879	438	611	774		822	859	440
Toledo, OH (E-8)	301	315	266	394	678	494	610	700	341	655	376	695	641	533	368	228	187	328	331	473	646	58	384	820	414	822		289	494
Toronto, ON (C-9)	592	607	558	666	951	596	883	991	614	927	648	968	932	825	641	316	268	601	603	763	919	345	433	1093	687	859	289		767
Wisconsin Rapids, WI (D-5)	626	550	526	110	249	253	259	744	176	191	158	500	602	588	310	713	632	203	173	461	182	543	387	391	364	440	494	767	

Mileages in this chart are based upon the routes usually followed by motorists. Highway systems involved include interstate, U.S., and state highways.

ROAD CONSTRUCTION
AND ROAD CONDITIONS RESOURCES

Most of the hotlines and websites listed here offer information on both road construction and road conditions. For those that provide only one or the other, we've used an orange cone to indicate road construction information and a blue snowflake to indicate road conditions information. Those that provide both are marked with a green circle.

ARKANSAS
(800) 245-1672, (501) 569-2374
www.arkansashighways.com

ILLINOIS
(800) 452-4368, (312) 368-4636
www.gettingaroundillinois.com

INDIANA
(800) 261-7623
(317) 232-8298 *(12/1-3/31)*
www.in.gov/dot

IOWA
511, (800) 288-1047, www.511ia.org

KANSAS
511, (800) 585-7623, 511.ksdot.org

KENTUCKY
511, (866) 737-3767, www.511.ky.gov

MICHIGAN
www.michigan.gov/mdot/
(800) 381-8477
West and Southwest Michigan: (888) 305-7283
Metro Detroit: (800) 641-6368

MINNESOTA
511, (800) 542-0220, www.511mn.org

MISSOURI
(800) 222-6400, www.modot.mo.gov

NEBRASKA
511, (800) 906-9069, (402) 471-4533
www.nebraskatransportation.org/

NEW YORK
www.dot.state.ny.us
Thruway: (800) 847-8929, www.thruway.state.ny.us

NORTH DAKOTA
511, (866) 696-3511, www.dot.nd.gov/divisions/maintenance/511_nd.html

OHIO
(614) 644-7031, www.buckeyetraffic.org
Cincinnati/northern Kentucky area: 511, (513) 333-3333, www.artimis.org
Turnpike: (440) 234-2030, (888) 876-7453, www.ohioturnpike.org
In OH: (888) 264-7623

OKLAHOMA
(888) 425-2385, (405) 425-2385
www.okladot.state.ok.us

ONTARIO
www.mto.gov.on.ca
In ON: (800) 268-4686
In Toronto: (416) 235-4686

PENNSYLVANIA
www.dot.state.pa.us
In PA: (888) 783-6783
SmarTraveler, Camden/Philadelphia area: (215) 567-5678

SOUTH DAKOTA
511, (866) 697-3511
www.sddot.com/travinfo.asp

TENNESSEE
511, www.tn511.com

WEST VIRGINIA
(877) 982-7623, www.wvdot.com

WISCONSIN
(800) 762-3947, www.dot.state.wi.us

Get the info from the 511 hotline

The U.S. Federal Highway Administration has begun implementing a national system of highway and road conditions/construction information for travelers. Under the new plan, travelers can **dial 511 and get up-to-date information on roads and highways**. Implementation of 511 is the responsibility of state and local agencies. For more details, visit: www.fhwa.dot.gov/trafficinfo/511.htm

LODGING RESOURCES

AmericInn
(800) 396-5007
www.americinn.com

Baymont Inns & Suites
(877) 229-6668
www.baymontinn.com

Best Western
(800) 780-7234
www.bestwestern.com

Budget Host
(800) 283-4678
www.budgethost.com

Clarion Hotels
(877) 424-6423
www.clarioninn.com

Comfort Inns
(877) 424-6423
www.comfortinn.com

Comfort Suites
(877) 424-6423
www.comfortsuites.com

Courtyard by Marriott
(888) 236-2427
www.courtyard.com

Crowne Plaza Hotel & Resorts
(877) 227-6963
www.crowneplaza.com

Days Inn
(800) 329-7466
www.daysinn.com

Doubletree Hotels & Guest Suites
(800) 222-8733
www.doubletree.com

Drury Hotels
(800) 378-7946
www.druryhotels.com

Econo Lodge
(877) 424-6423
www.econolodge.com

Embassy Suites Hotels
(800) 362-2779
www.embassysuites.com

Fairfield Inn by Marriott
(800) 228-2800
www.fairfieldinn.com

Fairmont Hotels & Resorts
(800) 257-7544
www.fairmont.com

Hampton Inn
(800) 426-7866
www.hamptoninn.com

Hilton Hotels
(800) 445-8667
www.hilton.com

Holiday Inn Hotels & Resorts
(800) 465-4329
www.holidayinn.com

Homewood Suites
(800) 225-5466
www.homewood-suites.com

Hyatt Hotels & Resorts
(888) 591-1234
www.hyatt.com

InterContinental Hotels & Resorts
(888) 424-6835
www.intercontinental.com

Knights Inn
(800) 843-5644
www.knightsinn.com

La Quinta Inn & Suites
(800) 642-4271
www.lq.com

Loews Hotels
(866) 563-9792
www.loewshotels.com

MainStay Suites
(877) 424-6423
www.mainstaysuites.com

Marriott International
(888) 236-2427
www.marriott.com

Omni Hotels
(888) 444-6664
www.omnihotels.com

Park Inn
(888) 201-1801
www.parkinn.com

Preferred Hotels & Resorts
(800) 323-7500
www.preferredhotels.com

Quality Inns & Suites
(877) 424-6423
www.qualityinn.com

Radisson Hotels & Resorts
(888) 201-1718
www.radisson.com

Ramada Inn/Ramada Limited/ Ramada Plaza Hotels
(800) 272-6232
www.ramada.com

Renaissance Hotels & Resorts
(800) 468-3571
www.renaissancehotels.com

Sheraton Hotels & Resorts
(800) 325-3535
www.sheraton.com

Sleep Inn
(877) 424-6423
www.sleepinn.com

Super 8 Motel
(800) 800-8000
www.super8.com

Travelodge Hotels
(800) 578-7878
www.travelodge.com

Westin Hotels & Resorts
(800) 937-8461
www.westin.com

Wyndham Hotels & Resorts
(877) 999-3223
www.wyndham.com

NOTE: All toll-free reservation numbers are for the U.S. and Canada unless otherwise noted. These numbers were accurate at press time, but are subject to change. Find more listings or book a hotel online at go.randmcnally.com.